Cyber Security, Artificial Intelligence, Data Protection & the Law

Robert Walters • Marko Novak

Cyber Security, Artificial Intelligence, Data Protection & the Law

Springer

Robert Walters
Victoria University
Melbourne, VIC, Australia

Marko Novak
European Faculty of Law
The New University
Nova Gorica, Nova Gorica, Slovenia

ISBN 978-981-16-1664-8 ISBN 978-981-16-1665-5 (eBook)
https://doi.org/10.1007/978-981-16-1665-5

This Springer imprint is published by the registered company Springer Nature Singapore Pte Ltd.
The registered company address is: 152 Beach Road, #21-01/04 Gateway East, Singapore 189721, Singapore

Foreword by Leon Trakman and Bruno Zeller

This book discusses the interface of AI, cyber security and data protection. Increasingly they are becoming linked, yet, the legal frameworks that support them are separate and designed to achieve different things. They are often in tension. With the rapid rise of AI, the functions that support this technology are being widely adopted by the private and public sectors. The data protection laws have largely placed obligations on organisations to appoint or designate a point, person or position of responsibility to manage that data. However, when AI is being captured in the home and then used by an entity, the data protection laws are somehwat effectively useless. There is no one responsible for managing this data. For example, where an individual who attends a medical clinic or hospital for the first time, the person will provide their standard personal data, which is largely, and depending on the country, defined by the law. The medical clinic or hospital is likely to appoint, again depending on the legal requirements, a dedicated person to manage that data, such as a controller of processor.

For smart home AI appliances, there are no controllers or processors required. However, the entities that have developed that AI are likely to be able to gain access to personal data such as facial and voice recognition, movements, pictures, mood, iris and other types of data. Smart home appliances, personal robots, clothes, drones and toys are all finding their way onto the market. There have been concerns raised about their security and the potential to capture and use personal data as they are increasingly being connected to the Internet. Children's toys are also being made available on the market that have AI systems within them that could capture the personal data of kids, and be used at a later time by insinuating a bias against that person. This can also occur for people that have disabilities as well as racial and ethnic groups. If realised, the policy and regulatory settings are far from adequate to protect the most vulnerable in society. Thus, this book compares a number of countries' data protection laws and highlights how they are fragmented. It also highlights how the current principles, such as the definition of personal data and the concept of consent, amongst others, that have emerged in data protection law(s) are not compatible with AI or cyber security systems and the law. In AI systems, one of the challenges is determining the level of harm that might arise from its use, and the misuse of personal data. Furthermore, there is a need to better understand the impact or otherwise to privacy by AI systems, infrastructure and their platforms. AI in cybersecurity is set to provide greater protection of personal data by enabling an organisation to detect and monitor the collection and use of that data. Yet, the unknown is the extent to which the AI systems can be penetrated with ease by individuals and entities that have even higher sophisticated systems to monitor particular individuals, organisations and communities more broadly.

More importantly, due to the current legal and policy framework in relation to data protection, and because of its fragmentation around the world, AI systems developed in Australia that meet the Privacy Act 1988 may not meet the laws of Singapore, the European Union, the United States, China, Canada or other states. This is because the definition of personal data varies widely. Furthermore, the international legal principles that have been established by the Organisation for Economic Cooperation and Development do not lend themselves to AI technology. Thirdly, the regulation of AI is only just being considered and is far from settled. The challenges facing regulators and governments cannot be underestimated, if they fail to grapple with AI technology, cyber security technology and data protection as a collective, while maintaining a level of independence. This balance, along with ensuring innovation can thrive, the digital economy can grow, while protecting and securing personal data is going to be a formidable task. This book will highlight some of those challenges and the fragmentation in the law that, to date, has only begun to address some of the issues particularly in relation to personal data. More needs to be done to coordinate the regulatory response across the three different areas. This book highlights how some states have begun to align their data protection laws more closely with cyber security law, while others have adopted specific data protection laws. Finally, this book calls for more balance between the economic benefits of AI, with the need to protect the personal data from cyber intrusions, particularly to the most vulnerable in the community.

University New South Wales
Sydney, NSW, Australia

Leon Trakman

University Western Australia
Crawley, WA, Australia

Bruno Zeller

Preface

The world is coming to terms with artificial intelligence (AI), which now pervades the daily lives of everyone. Countries are developing, embracing and adopting AI at varying rates, some more rapidly than others. As people begin to adopt new technology in the home, otherwise known as smart home technology (robots, televisions, fridges, toys, etc.), access to our personal data – already at an unprecedented level – continues on an exponential curve. This book advocates for a stronger balance between the flow and use of personal data, and the protection of that data. Finding that balance is increasingly difficult, and some in the community may argue that we have lost our personal data. Apart from the social and economic benefits that AI will bring into the home, it will also have its downsides. There is a debate emerging as to the safety of personal data and privacy from these devices and systems. Arguably some of the most vulnerable groups from the use of this technology will be children, the disabled and the elderly, and the personal data that entities are able to capture, and subsequently use for financial gain, can create enormous imbalances in power and freedoms. For children, in particular, this technology has the potential to generate significant bias, and for the disabled, potentially extraordinary discrimination. In addition, we are seeing governments and private organisations also embrace the adoption of AI, for instance facial recognition, for national security and other purposes. Simon Chesterman makes the point that:

> benefits of facial recognition technology are that it offers a quick, non-invasive means of identifying people. Those are also the dangers. It is not too late to impose limits on how facial recognition is used. Unfortunately, it may also be too early. This use of biometrics for security – relying on the uniqueness of your face, fingerprint, or iris – offers the prospect of a world without passwords to remember or identity cards to show. Facial recognition in particular is fast, contactless, and able to identify multiple people at the same time. These benefits could smooth movement through passport control or keep a vigilant eye out for known criminals. Yet those same qualities could also enable mass surveillance on an unprecedented scale. Yet people in many countries are now acclimated to widespread use of surveillance cameras in public spaces. London remains at the forefront of Western democracies, with more than half a million cameras or one for every 15 persons. (The same study

> by Comparitech estimated that Singapore has about 86, cameras, or one for every 65 persons.) Even if we might bristle at stationary cameras, virtually every passer-by also has a high-definition camera in his or her pocket or purse. It is one thing to have your identity verified when unlocking your phone, entering the country, or voting in Parliament. It is quite another to be identified and logged every time you step onto the street, ride in a taxi, or enter a shop.[1]

The point made by Chesterman is very important when analysing AI, cyber security and personal data as a collective. Our personal data is and will be collected at unprecedented levels by AI systems in the future. However, AI systems are here to stay: they are going to provide significant economic and social benefits, although if not developed and used under a framework that ensures their responsible use, AI could pose a very great threat to humanity. AI will unquestionably become even more sophisticated and accurate as technology develops. This technology is also being used by people daily and found in mobile phones and other smart home devices. The AI systems that will find their way into the home are likely to process large quantities personal data, assist in decision making, predict people's movements and recognise voices. The question is, are people ready for even greater intrusion and use of their personal data from these devices? At the extreme end of AI is the potential for state actors, or entities acting on behalf of state actors, to collect personal data that enables them to undertake use the technology in a subversive way that undermines the social fabric and disrupts economic activity.

Currently, there is not enough information in relation to the law or technology to accurately assess the potential impact of AI. More work is needed to better understand the vulnerabilities of personal data by the most vulnerable cohort(s) in the community, while maintaining a balance of innovation and economic activity. What is apparent is the need for better regulation in this area of the law and cyber security systems to manage the onset of AI. We are heading into a period where governments and regulators will need to respond more rapidly to develop regulatory frameworks that address these issues. This monograph outlines many of the critical issues at hand, and sketches some of the ways forward – both in terms of the ongoing research and practical considerations and proposals for reform.

Dean and Head of School
Law University Tasmania
Australia

Michael Stuckey

[1] Chesterman, S, *Facing Up to Facial Surveillance*, Straight Time, Singapore, Dean, National University of Singapore Faculty of Law, December 2019, https://www.straitstimes.com/opinion/facing-up-to-facial-recognition-technology

Acknowledgement

This book draws upon the work undertaken by Robert Walters, Leon Trakman and Bruno Zeller, *Data Protection Law: A Comparative Analysis of European and Asia – Pacific Approaches*, Springer (2019).

This book has been prepared in acknowledgement and thanks to Prof. Dr. Leon Trakman, University New South Wales and Prof. Dr. Bruno Zeller, University Western Australia, who have allowed me to work with them both on national and international data protection, cyber security, trade and finance law, since 2016. I have been working with Prof. Zeller for a decade. Their collective guidance, mentoring and insight in addressing complex national and international legal-policy issues has allowed me to enhance and strengthen my practical and academic skills.

Thanks to Chris Brien, Senior Lecturer, Victoria University, Melbourne, Australia, for drafting two chapters on Laos and Vietnam. A special thanks goes out to Josh Sloan and his team from Statista for the use of important data highlighting the extent of internet use, and what this use means to data protection, cyber security and artificial intelligence. Thanks also to Jeanne Huang, Associate Professor Law, Sydney University, who reviewed the chapter on China's cyber security laws.

This book acknowledges the work undertaken by Prof. Dr. Graham Greenleaf and Prof. Dr. Simon Chesterman who have both written extensively in the area of data protection law, globally and regionally throughout Asia and Pacific. It also acknowledges the work of Abu Bakar Munir, Siti Hajar Mohd Yasin and Md. Ershadul Karim, who have also written about data protection laws throughout Asia. This book acknowledges the work undertaken by Colin Bennett, Canada.

Contents

About the Authors

Robert Walters Lecturer, Victoria University, Melbourne, Australia. Dr. Walters is also adjunct professor of law, European Faculty of Law, New University, Slovenia, Europe, and admitted to practice law in Australia. He is a member of ASEAN Law Association – Singapore, and part of the Asia Pacific Scholar (Privacy/Data Protection) Network. Dr Walters has chaired government appointed advisory committee and represented government departments to Government Law Reform Committees, in Australia. He also has a law enforcement/investigations background, and represented a government department as a prosecutor in the courts within Australia for more than 8 years. Dr. Walters also has a strong legal, policy and risk management background for more than a decade, ensuring market access as well as national and international trade – government and private sector. His legal and policy research interests include national and international trade and finance law. He also focuses on data protection, artificial intelligence and cybersecurity, along with immigration and citizenship (national identity and social coherence).

Marko Novak Associate Professor, New University, Nova Gorica, Slovenia. Dr. Novak is vice dean of the European Faculty of Law, New University, and professor of law in the Faculty of Management and Law, Ljubljana (MLC). In 2005, Dr. Novak first became an assistant professor and later associate professor of philosophy and theory of law and constitutional law at the European Faculty of Law and the Faculty of National and European Studies, teaching philosophy and theory of law, comparative law, legal history and fundamentals of law. Between 1996 and 2008, Dr. Novak was a legal adviser at the Constitutional Court of the Republic of Slovenia in the Analysis and International Consulting Service and assistant to the head of this service. He holds a number of appointments such as president of the Judicial Council of the Republic of Slovenia; member of the Council of the National Commission on Quality in Higher Education; committee member of the Republic of Slovenia for the Zois Award, Zois Award; and ambassador of science of the Republic of Slovenia and Puh's Award. He also is a court interpreter for English. Dr. Nova obtained his LL.M. from Georgetown University Law Center, USA.

Part I
Cyber Security & Artificial Intelligence

Chapter 1
Problem Definition, Structure and Methodology

Abstract Reconciling the differences between data protection, artificial intelligence (AI) and cyber security will be complex and needs to be finely balanced. More problematic is the balance between the free flow of personal data and the economic benefits this brings, with the need to protect that data. This book advocates for finding ways to better balance between these competing issues, particularly when smart home devices enter the market and are used within the home and office. Finding this balance is a formidable challenge and it may never be able to be achieved. This is because some in the community view our personal data as being lost to the large corporations that trade and use that data. In the contemporary world, this is becoming even more challenging, with many state actors going it alone, looking after their own sovereign needs. This Chapter discusses some of the challenges faced by state actors in relation to having to balance their sovereign needs while establishing data protection, AI and cyber security law that, is effective. The resulting effect has seen three competing forces emerge. First, is the rise in government surveillance of its citizens under the guise of national security. In other words, and what has emerged is that national security will come first and protecting people's privacy and protecting personal data will come second. Secondly, the economic benefits that arise from AI, trade in personal data and development of cyber security infrastructure and systems are on the one hand intertwined technologically, while on the other hand very seprate at law. Third, the evolving expectation that individual's personal data will be afforded a level of protection over the Internet varies form nation state to nation state. The challenges facing society are only beinging to be fully understood. That is, at the extreme end of AI, the lack of cyber security infrastructure and a robust legal framework, provides the potential for state actors, or, entities acting on behalf of state actors, to collect personal data that enables them to undertake subversive behaviour that undermines the social fabric and disrupts economic activity. In other words, there is a huge potential for these technologies to be used, in order to control populations, no matter where they are located in the world. This area is not well understood, and this book argues more is needed to better understand how states are to react to this behaviour. Contrary to this position is the evolving benefits from transnational flows of data. Yet, this is another area not well understood, and is outside the scope of this book.

R. Walters, M. Novak, *Cyber Security, Artificial Intelligence, Data Protection & the Law*, https://doi.org/10.1007/978-981-16-1665-5_1

This Chapter begins by discussing state sovereignty and public policy, because today, the laws pertaining to AI, personal data and cyber security are largely under developed and sovereign based. They are being developed and implemented by jurisdictions to meet their own sovereign needs. There is a lack of international agreement. It will also draw on the policy and laws of the European Union (EU), United States (US) and the nation states analysed in this book, to demonstrate some of the measures that have been adopted. It highlights how the EU have been successful not only in extending their sovereignty through data protection law across Europe but also to the rest of the world.

1.1 Introduction

The idea of state sovereignty is nothing new and can be traced to the Peace of Westphalia of 1648, which established the Westphalian system of considering states to have sovereignty over their respective territories and domestic affairs, in which other states should not interfere.[1] The principle of sovereignty, which is inseparable from International Law, is also associated with the principle of equality, which implies that each state is equal under International Law and therefore has no power over other states.[2] Sovereignty is one of the elements that constitute a state under International Law. Accordingly, for a state to exist, it must have a population, a territory, effective political power and sovereignty.[3]

More pervasively, what has also emerged from technology and sovereignty is the way in which states can assert their influence abroad with ease. What is being referred to as digital authoritarianism is the use of digital information technology by authoritarian regimes to survey, repress, and manipulate domestic and foreign populations. The resulting effect is how the power balance between democracies and autocracies, is being shaped and influenced.[4] It has been reported that countries have developed and exported distinct technology-driven playbooks for authoritarian rule. For instance, the use of digital tools for domestic censorship and surveillance has made it the supplier of choice for illiberal regimes looking to deploy their own surveillance systems, while other countries have developed lower-cost digital disinformation tools, which have proven effective in repressing potential opposition

[1] Franzese, P.W., (2009) *Sovereignty in Cyberspace: Can it exist?* Air Force Law Review 64, 1–42.

[2] Jensen, E.T., 2015. *Cyber Sovereignty: The Way Ahead.* Tex. Int. Law J. 50, 276–304.

[3] Daillier, P., Forteau, M., Pellet, A., Nguyen Quoc, D., 2009. *Droit international public: formation du droit, sujets, relations diplomatiques et consulaires, responsabilité, règlement des différends, maintien de la paix, espaces internationaux, relations économiques, environnement*, 8e édition. ed. L.G.D.J., Lextenso éditions, Paris.

[4] Polyakova, A., Meserole, C, *Exporting digital authoritarianism: The Russian and Chinese models*, https://www.brookings.edu/wp-content/uploads/2019/08/FP_20190827_digital_authoritarianism_polyakova_meserole.pdf

at home and undermining democracies abroad. Whether this is wrong or right, is for others to determine. It is a countries sovereign right to develop these tools, in whatever way they choose. This Chapter discusses some of the challenges faced by state actors in relation to having to balance their sovereign needs to the development of (1). data protection, (2). cyber security law and (3). AI, and the outcome of that approach. The resulting effect has seen three competing forces emerge. First, is the rise in government surveillance of its citizens under the guise of national security. Second, is the economic benefits that arise from AI, trade in personal data and development of cyber security frameworks. Third, is the call by some in the community to protect the privacy if individuals over the Internet, as a fundamental human right. Nonetheless, data protection, AI and cyber security law(s) are distinct from each other, and rightly so. They do different things, and address different issues. However, they are more interlinked than first realised. It would be far too complex for state actors to develop a single law that address all the issues related to these three areas of the law.

In a period of heightened geopolitical, human health and economic tension, state actors are asserting their sovereignty and sovereign needs in all areas of public policy, this also includes data protection, AI and cyber security. Max Weber highlights that the conceptualisation of state sovereignty is ordinarily expressed not through the instrumentality of language, but rather through consummatory nature of sovereign action.[5] The state as "a relationship of rule (*Herrschaft*) by human beings over human beings, and one that rests on the legitimate use of violence (that is, violence that is held to be legitimate)".[6] He goes onto describe three forms of legitimacy to exercise the monopoly of force. First, the authority of the eternal past of custom. Herbert Wulf further points out that it is the traditional power exercised by the patriarch, by the patrimonial prince or by elders. Secondly, Weber points to the authority based on the exceptional, personal gift of grace, or charisma. He continues by mentioning specifically the charismatic rule as exercised by religious leaders, the plebiscitarian ruler, the great demagogue and leader of a political party and, interestingly, the warlord. This exceptional personal charisma depends on the personal devotion to, and personal trust in the qualities of leadership of the individual. The third Weberian category of legitimacy are rationally devised rules, rule by virtue of 'legality', by virtue of belief in the validity of legal statute and the appropriate juridical 'competence'.[7] Thus, the normative postulation, based on the theory of the democratic state, is narrowing the perspective to a single type legitimacy of the monopoly of violence, namely that it should be based on the rule of law and democratic control.

---

[5] Trakman, L, *Aligning State Sovereignty with Transnational Public Policy,* Tulane Law Review Vol. 93:207 (2018).

[6] Wulf, H, *Challenging the Weberian Concept of the State: The Future of the Monopoly of Violence*, The Australian Centre for Peace and Conflict Studies Occasional Papers Series [Online] Number 9, (2007).

[7] Ibid.

Nevertheless, as highlighted by Wulf, modernization theory, especially in the Anglo-Saxon dominated development theory of the 1960s and 1970s predicted optimistically, but incorrectly, that once economic development was initiated it would naturally lead to a liberal market economy and stable polities resembling Western democracies. At a later stage, during the 1980s, the state was predominantly perceived as inefficient, bureaucratic and over-sized. Systematic liberalization and structural adjustment programmes – based on the so-called Washington Consensus – introduced conditionality into development policies. During this period, the state was criticized both for meddling too much in what should best be left to market actors as well as for the state's tendency to make war and trample the rights of individuals. The pendulum has now swung in favour of good governance: effective state institutions and a functional and legitimized state are promoted and assisted with aid by the international community. While the Washington Consensus of the 1980s threatened with more 'stick', the present policy offers more 'carrot'. However, in the area of data protection law, it has been the European Union who have largely been leading the way – from a human rights perspective. They have, in part, also been balancing those rights with the need to promote an environment of innovation. Since the establishment of their laws in the mid 1990s there has been a scramble by other states to implement similar laws.

Herbert Wulf further notes that the traditional characteristics of a state in the Westphalian system (territory, authority, and population) have been supplemented by a respect for human rights.[8] Thus, in part, the protection of personal data has a human rights dimension, along with an economic dimension as part of the new digital economy. This has been grounded in the neo-liberal project to trim down the state to its core functions. This neoliberal scheme of 'deregulation' aims at more efficiency, claiming that the private sector can perform many functions better than the state. This trend of trimming the role of the state to its core competencies has been dominant in Organization for Economic Development (OECD) member states but is not limited to this group of developed or highly-industrialized countries. The programmes of multilateral organizations like the World Trade Organization (and globalization in general) spill, not only, over into the non-OECD countries, but also, they are specifically aimed at including all countries into this design of a lean state. Thus, in the policy domain, the OECD has been instrumental in setting the policy principles for data protection, and to a lesser extent in the area of AI and cyber security.

In contrasting the current legislative and policy base and framework for cyber security, data protection and AI reinforces the sovereign. In other words, it is largely based on high level internationally agreed principles, however, there is a lack of transnational cooperation. The problem when understanding the current framework against well founded areas of international trade and finance, which have been successful in establishing common legal and policy mechanisms is that, states are generally going it alone. For instance, as highlighted by Professor Leon Trakman, there has been a slow decline to enforce foreign judgments that have annulled arbitration

[8] Ibid.

awards, pertaining to international trade.[9] Trakman proposes a way for domestic judges to apply transnational public policy to international commercial transactions, without displacing or circumventing domestic public policy. It applies this analysis to the "public policy exception" by which domestic judges decline to recognize and enforce international arbitration awards under the New York Convention.[10] Applying this analogy espoused by Trakman to cyber security, data protection, AI must be a consideration.

Leon Trakman promotes five conceptual ideas that transnational public policy is directed at counter-balancing domestic conceptions of public policy that are ill-conceived, incoherent in nature, unduly malleable in application, or vary unduly among domestic courts. The proposition is not the reliance on domestic conceptions of fundamental justice is unjustified, but transnational conceptions can help to remedy undue variations across jurisdictions and states. Secondly, he believes that transnational conceptions of public policy can avoid being sublimated by domestic interests that are unjust or discriminatory, such as by affirming price-fixing, de facto collusion, and other anticompetitive behaviour. Thirdly, domestic courts can advance transnational public policy in response to widely accepted commercial practices operating across national boundaries. Fourthly, just as "wholly" domestic interests can redress unfair domestic market practices, such as corporations not acting socially responsibly, transnational public policy can redress irresponsible market practices that undermine the economies of developing countries. Fifth, states that endorse transnational public policy can discourage their domestic courts from conflating that policy with lesser commercial or private interests that sublimate those shared policies.[11] Trakman further argues that these five arguments for recognising transnational public policy are, at best, imperfect responses to those who would dismiss transnational policy as sublimating state sovereignty. Thus, a number of states have signed and implemented the New York Convention to provide a consistent and coherent pathway to resolving cross broader commercial disputes. However, in the context of data protection, AI and cybersecurity, this is far from reality. To date, there is minimal consistency and coherency at the international level in these emerging areas of law.

However, this has not resolved the dichotomy that state signatories to the New York Convention are, and continue to be divided over the legitimacy of transnational public policy.[12] He highlights how in the support of its legitimacy in the enforcement of foreign judgments are laws in France, Singapore, Portugal, Italy, and Algeria. The Highest Arbitrazh Court of the Russian Federation has identified public policy with a pervasive natural law consisting of "universally recognized moral and ethical rules." The Quebec Court of Appeal has contended, *"erga omnes,"* that "public order" is so widely conceived internationally that it "does not require

[9] Trakman, L, *Aligning State Sovereignty with Transnational Public Policy,* Tulane Law Review Vol. 93:207 (2018).

[10] Ibid.

[11] Ibid.

[12] Ibid.

translation into the national system of law." In contrast, other courts resist transnational public policy, based on the pre-eminence of state sovereignty and by contending that "international" conceptions of public policy are unworkable. For example, the Supreme Court of India has explicitly rejected the concept of "international public policy" for the lack of a "workable definition" of it. Australian courts, on the other hand, have ruled that "[t]here is no express reference in the [New York] Convention to any concept of international or transnational public policy," and have adopted a narrow view focusing on the public policy of the enforcement state.[13] Therefore, if we look at how states have engaged the international rules and principles of transnational trade and finance, the adoption of internationally agreed legal and policy norms to ensure that the free flow of goods, services and finance continues, this is far from reality in AI, data protection and cybersecurity. This is on the backdrop of states beginning to look inwards, and traditional states that have promoted globalisation and regionalization trade and finance, are now looking at other trading alliances.

Moreover, the above could be problematic in the bourgeoning areas of law of data protection, AI and cyber security. This is because states have decoupled the technology from the law. Secondly, the law across these three areas are regulating different things. Data protection law to date, has largely be driven from the EU to protect privacy over the Internet, even though, there is significant economic trade of personal data that is making companies across the world extremely wealthy. Thirdly, to date, there is little known and knowledge of the regulation of AI and its impending activities. That is, the AI that will be used in machine learning and robotics, and appears in mainstream society. Fourthly, cyber security law has largely, focused on regulating the criminality of activities undertaken over the Internet, to protect citizens and entities from each other (national and international) and protecting the state (national security) from foreign state intrusions. Moreover, governments and states view technology differently, for different purposes. For instance, the resulting development of technology has been so fast that, it has not allowed government and regulators to develop a legal framework, which promotes the protection of, and free flow of personal data in a coherent manner. A further issue that has arisen from states exerting their sovereignty over these laws, is an inconsistent approach largely driven by policy ideology between Western democratic states and communist-authoritarian states.

In 2019, the G20 Meeting of the Leaders[14] declared that the:

---

[13] Ibid, Code De Procedure Civile [C.P.C.] arts. 1492, 1502 (Fr.); Décret 2011–48 du 13 janvier 2011, portant réforme de l'arbitrage [Decree 2011–48 of January 13, 2011, on the Reform of Arbitration] Journal Officiel De La Republque Francaise [J.O.], Jan. 14, (2011), 777. International Arbitration Act, Cap. 143A (2002) (Sing.). CÓDIGO DE PROCESSO CIVIL [C.P.C.] [Code of Civil Procedure] art. 1096(f) (Port.). [Code of Civil Procedure art. 839 (It.). Code of Civil Procedure art. 458 bis. 23(h) (Alg.). Postanovlenie Prezidiuma VAS RF ot 3 avgusta 2010 g. No. 8786/10 [Ruling of the Presidium of the Highest Arbitration Court of the Russian Federation of August 3, (2010).

[14] The Japanese Times, *Innovation: Digitalization, Data Free Flow with Trust*, 2019, https://www.japantimes.co.jp/news/2019/06/29/national/full-text-g20-osaka-leaders-declaration/#.

> Cross-border flow of data, information, ideas and knowledge generates higher productivity, greater innovation, and improved sustainable development, while raising challenges related to privacy, data protection, intellectual property rights, and security. By continuing to address these challenges, we can further facilitate data free flow and strengthen consumer and business trust. In this respect, it is necessary that legal frameworks, both domestic and international, should be respected. Such data free flow with trust will harness the opportunities of the digital economy. We will cooperate to encourage the interoperability of different frameworks, and we affirm the role of data for development. We also reaffirm the importance of interface between trade and digital economy, and note the ongoing discussion under the Joint Statement Initiative on electronic commerce, and reaffirm the importance of the Work Programme on electronic commerce at the WTO. To further promote innovation in the digital economy, we support the sharing of good practices on effective policy and regulatory approaches and frameworks that are innovative as well as agile, flexible, and adapted to the digital era, including through the use of regulatory sandboxes. The responsible development and use of Artificial Intelligence (AI) can be a driving force to help advance the SDGs and to realize a sustainable and inclusive society. To foster public trust and confidence in AI technologies and fully realize their potential, we commit to a human-centred approach to AI, and welcome the non-binding G20 AI Principles, drawn from the Organization for Economic Cooperation and Development (OECD) Recommendation on AI. Further, we recognize the growing importance of promoting security in the digital economy and of addressing security gaps and vulnerabilities. We affirm the importance of protection of intellectual property. Along with the rapid expansion of emerging technologies including the Internet of Things (IoT), the value of an ongoing discussion on security in the digital economy is growing. We, as G20 members, affirm the need to further work on these urgent challenges. We reaffirm the importance of bridging the digital divide and fostering the adoption of digitalization among micro, small and medium enterprises (MSMEs) and all individuals, particularly vulnerable groups and also encourage networking and experience-sharing among cities for the development of smart cities.[15]

Arguably, the G20 Leaders recognize and understand that the rise in AI, personal data and cyber security will provide many economic benefits. They are not only calling for the need and importance of bridging the digital divide and fostering the adoption of digitalization, but also calling for effective policy and regulatory approaches that are innovative, agile, flexible, and adapted to the digital era, including through the use of regulatory sandboxes. The G20 recognise the need for an ongoing commitment to draw from the OECD. Thus, the regulatory sandboxes have to be viewed broadly. They include not only allowing states to establish regulatory frameworks according to their sovereign needs, but also, the need to consider the internationally agreed policy and legal norms. At issue is the lack of jurisprudence in these three areas of law both internationally and domestically. Yet, and a further

---

XXGr4WVeKjQ. 10. Innovation is an important driver for economic growth, which can also contribute to advancing towards the SDGs and enhancing inclusiveness. We will work toward achieving an inclusive, sustainable, safe, trustworthy and innovative society through digitalization and promoting the application of emerging technologies. We share the notion of a human-centred future society, which is being promoted by Japan as Society 5.0. As digitalization is transforming every aspect of our economies and societies, we recognize the critical role played by effective use of data, as an enabler of economic growth, development and social well-being. We aim to promote international policy discussions to harness the full potential of data.

[15] Ibid.

issue that has emerged is a fragmented approach to defining and regulating personal data, AI and cyber security. This is largely because the users of the technology are regulated, while the developers are not – depending on the state regulating these activities. Take for example, the manufacture of food, the producer is just as accountable as the processor and the entire supply, to the end user. This is unlike any other sector and will not change any time soon. More pervasively, there appears to be a lack of international engagement, in examining these three areas as a collective. This is problematic. There needs to be more international engagement because, as AI continues to be part of the daily lives of all of us, it will come with significant benefits, however, it will bring significant challenges. Despite the role out of AI devices into the home and office being on a small scale, to date, this technology is likely to creep up on society, much like the social platforms that pervade society, and initially, having little regard to the impact these have to personal data and its security. In other words, the large entities developing AI are likely to employ a very strategic approach to the marketability of products, and have little regard to personal data or cyber intrusions as there will be a race to out-do and out-bid their competitors to get the products to market. The authors are of the view that there needs to be a better balance in regulating the security and use of personal data, while establishing an environment for innovation to thrive. To date, this is not occurring. Finally, a further challenge in reconciling the distinct features of these areas of the law is the balance government face in protecting personal data at the individual level with that of the broader public good. At this stage, the public policy approach has been driven through a mixture of both individual and sovereign needs. This book highlights how states such as China appear to have taken the sovereign approach. Whereas, other states such as South Korea have balanced the sovereign with the needs of the citizen. Thus, it is time that there is an international response to ensure these areas of the law, particularly data protection have a coherent level of protection no matter where a citizen resides in the world? The next section outlines the structure and methodology of this book.

1.2 Structure and Methodology

This book expands on the first book: *Data Protection Law: A Comparative Analysis of Asia-Pacific and European Approaches* authored by Dr. Robert Walters, Professor, Dr. Leon Trakman and Professor, Dr. Bruno Zeller. In the first book the data protection laws of Australia, India, Indonesia, Japan, Malaysia, Singapore, Thailand and European Union (EU) were compared. The first book demonstrated that, three distinct models and legal frameworks had emerged, from the EU to Singapore being at opposite ends of the spectrum, to Australia sitting somewhere in between. The countries of Malaysia and Japan also sit somewhere in between the EU and Singapore model. Indonesia have taken a sectorial approach to date, yet, they have been reviewing their legal framework which is expected to be established in 2020–2021. At the time of writing the first book Indonesia, India and Thailand had drafted data protection laws, but they had not been implemented. Yet, they had looked to the EU to develop their respective draft laws. In other words, the EU takes a hard-line human right(s) focus whereas, it was our view that Singapore took a business-friendly focus. On the other hand, they had looked to the EU to develop their respective draft laws. In other words, the EU has placed the protection of personal data as a fundamental right, whereas other states such as Singapore have taken a business friendly approach to the implementation of their data protection laws. In other words, the EU, for the most part is used as a benchmark. However, this book takes a neutral position, which has enabled the authors to identify additional models that have been developed in China and the United States (see final chapter). Therefore, throughout this book we will refer to the data protection laws of the EU, Singapore, amongst others, when discussion cyber security and AI law, policy and theory. These laws are also discussed and compared, briefly, when comparing the data protection laws – examined in this book.

Comparative legal research becomes the dominant theory when examining the differences between legislative and legal frameworks between the state's studies in this book. Therefore, the authors draw upon Peter de Cruz who makes the point that comparative law is primarily a method of study rather than a legal body of rules.[16] For de Cruz, there is no generally accepted framework for comparison, although most writers appear to assume that the comparative methods which should be employed are obvious. The basic concept, its aims, and its raison d'être, as well its methodology, have attracted somewhat disparaging critical comment. By comparing the legislation and legal principles in this book, it draws upon private international law. de Cruz argues that private international law is a discrete body of law which is also known as the conflict of laws, or the laws of conflicts, because it is a form of private law. It deals with situations, involving private individuals, in which there is a possible conflict of applicable laws.[17] de Cruz goes onto say that the function of private international law is to provide a solution as to which of several possible legal systems should be applied to a given case which has a foreign element. Therefore, it appears quite distinct from comparative law. The two in fact interlink, since they both deal with the analysis of the operation of specific rules in several legal systems. The difference is that private international law is much more selective than comparative law, to the extent that the 'choice of law rules' are very narrow. In practice, 'every legal system will decide a particular problem according to its own rules, and there is still a lack of international consensus on the question of which rules to apply across national frontiers'.[18]

More importantly, and the comparative legal research undertaken throughout this book predominantly examines the legislative frameworks of a number of states.

[16] De Cruz, P, (1999) *Comparative Law In A Changing World,* third Edit, Taylor & Francis Group, 10–30.

[17] Ibid.

[18] Ibid.

Thus, for de Cruz, legislative comparative law, refers to the process whereby foreign laws are invoked in order to draft new national laws.[19] This process was possibly resorted to even in ancient Rome, although this has never been definitively established. It apparently occurred in Germany in the middle of the nineteenth century and grew with the movement for codification and unification of Germany. One may therefore exclude older codes, such as the 1794 Prussian General Land Law, and the 1811 Austrian General Civil Code, which are predominantly based on natural law philosophies.[20] In France, the most influential code has been its Civil Code of 1804 which, at least to a certain extent, was an amalgamation of the customary Roman laws of Northern France, and the predominantly Germanic law of Southern France.[21] Therefore, de Cruz makes the point that for comparative legislative research to be successful, its function and purpose is to be based on the following concepts:

(a) comparative law as an academic discipline;
(b) comparative law as an aid to legislation and law reform;
(c) comparative law as a tool of construction;
(d) comparative law as a means of understanding legal rules; and
(e) comparative law as a contribution to the systematic unification and harmonisation of law.[22]

This book will compare the data protection frameworks of Canada, the United States, China (Hong Kong, Taiwan, Macau) South Korea, the Philippines, Lao and Vietnam and analyse their differences. This book will demonstrate the interconnectedness of data protection, cybersecurity and Artificial Intelligence, or the lack of it. AI, in the context of this book constitutes those devices that will be used in the home and office such as televisions, personal robots, fridge's, personal drones and children's toys, amongst others. Data protection constitutes the personal data that is regulated by the law, and is afforded a level of protection. Cyber security law constitutes how the personal data can be secured by the AI devices mentioned. In most states cyber security breaches are criminal offences. The importance of examining these three areas of law cannot be underestimated. As technology evolves and becomes more sophisticated, the security of personal data through AI devices, could become increasingly vulnerable. On the one side, AI devices are going to provide significant benefits to the community. These devices will be found in peoples places of residence and business. They will have the ability to capture, store and use personal data. Therefore, the security of that data has the potential to be compromised. This book will identify significant gaps in the currently legal framework to protect the most vulnerable in society. Thus, questions that will be attempted to be resolved from this book will be:

[19] Ibid.

[20] Ibid.

[21] Ibid.

[22] Ibid.

- Do the current day data protection laws adequately accommodate AI and cyber-security risks from this technology?
- Is the definition of personal data adequate for AI, particularly in relation to children and the most vulnerable in society?
- Is the concept of consent adequate in its current form?
- What other areas of data protection law may need to be reconsidered to protect personal data in AI devices?
- What needs to be done to protect the most vulnerable in the community such as children, people with disabilities, elderly and ethnic groups under the current regulatory framework?

This book will prompt more questions than it will resolve. It also demonstrates the need for additional comprehensive studies to be undertaken to reconcile the gaps in data protection law and technology with the onset of AI technology such as smart home appliances, personal robots and drones, along with toys. It draws upon the emerging theory in AI and cyber security, and will highlight how the theory, law and policy in all three areas is far from settled. Despite the advanced stage that cyber security technology and cyber security law have evolved, AI lags a long way behind. The book does not take the position of human rights to be protected at the cost of innovation. Rather it calls for a greater balance between protecting personal data and the development of AI technology.

Therefore, a further question will be – what is going to be the most effective and supported legal framework going forward over the coming decades. Will the human rights model prevail? More pervasively, as technology such as AI continues to increase, the intersection of AI data protection and cyber security will only be heightened. Firstly, states consider privacy very differently, particular over the Internet. Secondly, states are embracing AI technology at different rates, and, for different purposes across both the public and private sectors. Thirdly, states are viewing cyber security, and responding differently, both through technology and the law.

This book has been divided into 3 Parts. **Part I,** explores the concept of Cyber Security, Artificial Intelligence and Data Protection. **Part II**, builds on book Data Protection Law: A Comparative Analysis of Asia Pacific and European Approaches by Walters, Trakman and Zeller.[23] However, it diverges from that book, in that it highlights areas within the current day data protection laws that need further consideration and review, as AI devices are increasingly used by the public. In other words, this book from time to time will refer to that book that compared the EU data protection laws with states in the Asia Pacific. While it appears that most states when developing their data protection or privacy laws to protect personal data do so through the lens of the EU, this does not mean to say that the EU model is more superior than the other models discussed in this book or the previously mentioned book. **Part III**, concludes this book and compares the jurisdictions of China, Hong

[23] Walters, R., Trakman, L., Zeller, B, (2019) *Data Protection Law: A Comparative Analysis of Asia Pacific and European Approaches*, Springer.

Kong, Macau, Taiwan, South Korea, the Philippines, Laos and Vietnam along with Canada and the United States. It does not examine or compare the laws in Quebec province of Canada, and only addresses the current day national laws (public and private) of that state. The book while examining China, Hong Kong, Macau and Taiwan, it only compares some of the differences in their respective laws. The book does not determine a position of what could be viewed as the best laws within the region. By taking a neutral approach in comparing these laws, the book identifies the differences in the respective legal frameworks. There is no discussion of the geopolitical, economic or social tensions within and across the region, or, within and between China, Hong Kong, Macau and Taiwan. This book does not comment of the policy approach taken by the respective states compared towards China, Hong Kong, Macau or Taiwan. Any views on the comparative differences of the respective legal regimes compared are of the authors and are not to be viewed as a recommendation or otherwise from any government or nation state, in the world. The authors do not recommend any change, rather aggregate the recommendations across all nation states, calling for internationalisation of data protection law, and the law that governs AI and cyber security. This book concludes by providing a pathway forward that, will encourage and enable governments, regulators and the international community to further engage and undertake additional research in the examination of these three areas of law.

Due to the various laws discussed throughout the book there will be a need for references to be duplicated in full so as the reader can clearly identify the source of the information.

1.3 Limitation of this Research

There are limitations to this research. Firstly, making accurate comparisons where countries and cultures respect privacy, data protection, understand and have embraced AI and cyber security as a collective, poses significant challenges. Thus, the comparative discussion of the data protection law in Chap. 14 only focuses on the high priority areas related to AI. In other words, the relevant provisions of data protection law that could require further development from the use of AI devices in the home and business that could have significant impacts to children and the most vulnerable in the community. The book recognises that innovation is an inherent part of economic development, and it aims to promote and address this by ensuring there is a balanced discussion related to AI, data protection and cyber security. It is well understood that some countries have very little scholarly writing or jurisprudence in these areas of the law. Thus, the book will only discuss the laws as they currently stand.

Moreover, the development of AI and cyber security technology is being undertaken at such a rapid rate it is out of scope of this book to identify, in any depth the technology, systems, devices, platforms or infrastructure that supports them. Thus, the limited discussion takes into consideration the developments of AI and to a lesser extent, the developments in cyber security that will pervade our personal lives. A further limiting factor is the ability to report on how each country is implementing and enforcing its data protection, AI and cyber security laws. Therefore, this book does not consider or discuss the enforcement or implementation of the respective laws.

Data protection law has evolved and developed very differently from country to country. It has become very fluid and annually there are updates to the respective laws. No Chapter will be the same because the concepts and principles adopted by each jurisdiction vary, at least in title headings used. Each country has structured their respective laws significantly differently. It is beyond the scope of this book to compare the codes or practice, guidelines, standards and procedures that underpin these substantive law and statutes. Even though each country specific chapter discusses many of these concepts and principles, the structure of each chapter will vary according to the legislation that each jurisdiction has established. This, in itself poses challenges when comparing the laws of China, Hong Kong, Macau, Taiwan, South Korea, Philippines, Laos and Vietnam along with Canada and United States.

Data protection and cyber security has been viewed by some states as being highly political. This book does not comment on the political development, implementation, regional or internal political conflicts. The book only states, discuses, analyses, compares and describes the current day data protection laws, and to a lesser extent AI and cyber security law and policy.

This book advocates for more research to be undertaken in this area, and promotes the new digital economy, provided the most vulnerable in the community and their personal data has a higher level of protection.

1.4 Chapters

This Chapter highlights the problem definition, structure and methodology of the book. This Chapter identifies how states are increasingly faced with a formidable challenge having to balance their sovereign needs with the development of cyber security, AI and data protection law, and the outcome of that approach. The resulting effect has seen three competing forces emerge. First, is the rise in government surveillance of its citizens under the guise of national security. Second, is the economic benefits that arise from AI, trade in personal data and development of cyber security frameworks. Third, the evolving expectation that individual's personal data will be afforded a level of protection over the Internet.

Chapter 2 looks at cyber security. It highlights how over the past year there has been a significant rise in cyber security breaches and intrusions that have resulted in large quantities of aggregated personal data being illegally collected and used. Cyber security when coupled with AI and data protection is facing many obstacles. As technology develops and becomes even more sophisticated, the cyber security incursions are likely to become even more complex and harder to detect. This does not pose well for protecting personal data through AI devices. The concerns from cyber attacks cannot be underestimated and, today, they are having a profound impact not only to states, but also individuals in the community.

AI is beginning to pervade every aspect of our daily lives. **Chapter 3** discusses the current status of AI and highlights how there is a lack of international agreement and national law and policy. The rise of Smart Home devices such as personal robots, televisions, children's toys, fridges, amongst others can and will capture and store large quantities of personal data. There is currently a lack of legal harmonization and international agreement on what regulation of AI devices should look like. It is largely underdeveloped and is being left to nation states to go it alone.

The development and deployment of AI to the community is seeing people embrace the technology. **Chapter 4** discusses some of the issues related to data protection, from AI. It also highlights how technology cannot be decoupled from the law, and there will need to be a balance between innovation while protecting people's privacy by these AI devices and over the Internet. Data protection law while being a relatively new addition to the legal framework, is being challenged by states. There is a lack of international harmonization. States have gone it alone and largely developed these laws based on their local sovereign needs. This will pose challenges for the protection personal data as cyber-attacks continue to rise and AI becomes part of our daily lives.

South Korea is a technology hub throughout Asia. **Chapter 5,** examines the data protection laws of South Korea who have, in part, had to evolve quite rapidly, in order for the country to continue to participate in the emerging technology and data economy. Their laws can be best described as being a hybrid of the European Union model and Singapore model. They are viewed as some of the strictest laws throughout the Asia region. Since the introduction of the Personal Information Protection Act (the PIPA) in 2011, it has been amended no less than on 6 occasions. It reflects the importance of personal data to South Korea both economically and personally, so as there are appropriate levels of protection.

Chapter 6 explores the current day data protection laws of Hong Kong. Hong Kong has a fascinating history. On January 25, 1841, a British naval party landed and raised the British flag on the northern shore of Hong Kong, a small island located in the Pearl River Delta in southern China. The data protection laws of Hong Kong are significantly different to that of the other data laws examined in this book. Data protection in Hong Kong began in 1995, with the implementation of the Personal Data (Privacy) Ordinance that was enacted on 3 August 1995. The current day data protection laws of Hong Kong while reflecting the standard principles of the OECD and also, in part, those of the EU. Going forward the question will be how the laws of Hong Kong remain as they are, or, move ever closer to the recently established laws of China. This Chapter discusses the Definition of Personal Data, Public and Private, Transfer Matching and Transfer of Personal Data, Controller [Data User], Erasing Personal Data [Right to Be Forgotten], Data User Returns and Register of Data Users, Access and Correction of Personal Data, Consent and Direct Marketing, Privacy Commissioner, Enforcement and Security [Cyber].

Macau, similar to its neighbor Hong Kong has a long history. **Chapter 7** highlights how Macau in more recent times was occupied by the Portuguese, which heavily influenced their current day legal framework. Macau has adopted international law such as the International Covenant on Civil and Political Rights, International Covenant on Economic, Social and Cultural Rights 1966 (ICCPR), and international labour conventions. Chapter 6 further explores the 2005 Personal Data Protection Act. It will be argued that Macau, at least on paper has to some extent embraced the idea and need for the protection of privacy over the Internet. As Macau continue to integrate with China, in 2019, it marked its 20th anniversary of reunification. However, this reunification appears to have had little effect or impact on their current legal framework.

The Philippines is a member of ASEAN and they, like many other regional countries have a complex history. **Chapter 8** highlights how the Philippines have embraced the right to privacy and general rights. In other words, the modern-day Constitution of Philippines, was established in 1987, and provides for a Bill of Rights. This Chapter also highlights how is other important legislation whereby citizens' right to privacy is also protected. In other words, Civil Code (Republic Act No. 386), Revised Penal Code (Act No. 3185), Republic Act No. 8505, Rape Victim Assistance and Protection Act of 1998; Republic Act No. 9344, and Juvenile Justice and Welfare Act of 2006, goes some way to protecting a level or privacy. The Republic Act (RA) No. 10173 or also known as Data Privacy Act, came into effect in 2012. The 2012 Act created the National Privacy Commission, which is responsible for promoting, regulating, and monitoring data privacy compliance of both government agencies and private institutions. Importantly, the Philippines is a member of the APEC Cross Border Privacy Enforcement Arrangement, the government backstop enforcement network developed for the Cross-Border Privacy Rules. This Chapter examines the current data protection laws of the Philippines.

Chapter 9 discusses the legal framework of Taiwan. Privacy as a concept and right has gained traction in Taiwan. The right to privacy across the territory of Taiwan is alive. Taiwan has adopted the Personal Data Protection Act (PDPA) in 1995. Since then, the PDPA has only been amended twice, with the most recent changes in 2015. The PDPA generally follows the privacy principles approved by the Asia-Pacific Economic Corporation in 2004 and the former 1995 EU Data Protection Directive. This Chapter will highlight how the data protections laws of Taiwan do provide a solid framework for the protection of personal data over the Internet. However, it is questionable, along with the other jurisdictions discussed in this book, whether elements of the laws will be able to adequately accommodate AI and the cybersecurity issues that will evolve from the use of smart home appliances.

The cyber security laws of Lao make the direct connection between cybercrime and data protection. **Chapter 10** examines the current approach taken by Lao in relation to data protection. Lao is a member of ASEAN. The Lao People's Democratic Republic has enacted laws with cover provisions relating to the protection of personal information, Law Protection of Electronic Data (2017) and Law on Prevention and Combating Cyber Crime (2015). This highlights how the law, when compared with other states, goes someway to defining computer data as any data, messages, programs or database system, personal data, computerized traffic data in the form that can be processed and enable the operation of the computerized system. The reference to personal data has been reinforced and defined to include data related to or referred directly to the character or activity of individuals, legal entities or organizations in a direct or indirect way. Arguably this infers that the personal data become available through data base and computerized systems. Therefore, and in maintaining the same theme of other chapters, this chapter will confirm whether Lao legal framework is adequate to account for AI and cyber security incursion related to the misuse of personal data. It must be noted that there is not a lot of scholarly writing or jurisprudence available from Lao.

Chapter 11 looks at the country of Vietnam. Vietnam, located in South East Asia and a member of ASEAN has a complex history. This Chapter highlights how Vietnam had experienced colonization, war and conflict, and have been influenced by several different dynasties, empires and states. The current day Socialist Republic of Vietnam is the easternmost country on the Indochina Peninsula in Southeast Asia. With an estimated 90.5 million inhabitants as of 2014, it is the world's 14th-most-populous country, and the eighth-most-populous Asian country. This Chapter will examine the current approach taken by Vietnam to data protection and how these laws are evolving or otherwise, to consider the wider impacts from AI and cyber security.

China has emerged as an international leader in many areas of technology. **Chapter 12,** highlights how they have embraced technology to advance their sovereign needs. This chapter only analysis the current status of the data protection laws of China. This Chapter does not comment on the practical implementation of the laws by China. The cybersecurity laws that were recently implemented have evolved to not only serve the sovereign needs of the state, but also, provide a level of protection to its citizen's personal data over the Internet. Coupled with the 2019 implementation of new laws that establish tighter controls and protections for children, the Personal Information Security Specification have in our view embraced the key elements, principles and concepts that have been in place by the EU and other states for some time.

Chapter 13 looks at Canada, which is another country that has a remarkable story, with a rich and diverse history that dates back centuries. Canada is unique in that even though it is a Western democratic country it has adopted both the common and civil law. Privacy and data protection have been an evolving part of Canadian society. During the 1960s and 1970s, there was considerable debate regarding the extensive use of listening devices by private agencies. This Chapter only examines both the *Personal Information Protection and Electronic Documents Act*, S.C. 2000, and *Privacy Act 1985*. At the time of writing this book the Canadian government were undertaking a review of the *Privacy Act 1985*. This chapter does not consider the review and only discusses the laws in the current form. This Chapter does not deal with the indigenous community or information bank in any detail. The question for Canada, and their current review of the public sector Privacy Act may highlight whether the current laws can adequately respond to AI, particularly the smart home devices, along with AI more generally. It will briefly examine whether the current definition of personal data and the concept of consent is adequate in a time of heightened cybersecurity issues, and the onset of AI.

The right to privacy in the United States (US) can be traced to the late 1800s. However, and while the right to privacy has a long history in the US, it would not have been conceived that today the right has become one of the most important and contested rights. **Chapter 14,** discusses the laws of the US and how privacy has evolved. This is because it competes with many other policy areas of government such as national security and the economy. Due to the breadth and depth of the sectorial approach to data protection, this Chapter generally focuses solely on the laws of the Federal Trade Commission. The Chapter briefly highlights the other laws that consider personal data such as the Children's Online Privacy Protection Act and Health Insurance Portability and Accountability Act, amongst others. The Chapter further outlines what the year of 2020 will mean for some states, particularly the state of California in regards to their proposed new data protection law. With the impending implementation of the new state-based privacy law of California in 2020, it remains to be seen whether this will result in major changes at the federal level. There have been calls for more specific data protection laws at the federal level.

Chapter 15 compares the privacy and data protection laws of the countries discussed throughout this book, along with the Administrative Regions of Hong Kong and Macau. It also compares Taiwan's data protection laws with those of China's, to highlight the differences between the various regions under a single country. Due to the breadth and depth of data protection law, it will only compare the following concepts and principles of the Privacy and Data Protection Laws; its application, the Definition of Personal Data along with the concept of Consent. More importantly, this Chapter highlights how the pathway forward to reconcile the differences and gaps between AI, cyber security and data protection are formidable and require a lot more international cooperation. It argues that that there is a lack of international coordination and legal harmonisation in these three areas of the law, which will pose significant challenges to technology developers, governments and regulators. This is because AI technology and cyber security incursions know no international borders.

1.5 Conclusion

This Chapter has introduced cyber security, AI and data protections as a collective. It demonstrates that the world is facing a significant dichotomy as to whether to retain the current sovereign model of developing these laws, or, move to a regional or even an international model. In other words, with the challenges faced with the development of AI the threat of security breaches and the possibility that personal data will be significantly compromised, is real.

The book is not seeking to address any of the potential human rights issues that might arise from AI devices that will be used in every day. The book calls for a greater balance between technology and the law. It also calls for a greater balance-between understanding the economic benefits of the new digital economy that will see smart home devices pervade every area of sociaety, from the home to the office. The book promotes the idea of economic development and innovation, and the suggestions in Chap. 14 are not in any way provided to stifle future economic activity.

Cybersecurity, data protection and AI law and policy has been developed separately from each other. This response by states has served them well to date, however, this book challenging the current approach and seeks to highlight the interconnectedness of these three areas of the law. Moreover, AI technology continue to be strengthened and enhanced, it will be arguing that the most vulnerable in the community will be at risk of having their personal data compromised by AI systems. If and when realised, this will provide individuals, entities and governments with significant power and control over citizens.

Finally, there are a number of states data protection laws examined and compared in this book such as South Korea, China, Hong Kong, Macau, Taiwan, Philippine, Lao, Vietnam, Canada and United States.

References

Daillier, P., Forteau, M., Pellet, A., & Nguyen Quoc, D. (2009). *Droit international public: Formation du droit, sujets, relations diplomatiques et consulaires, responsabilité, règlement des différends, maintien de la paix, espaces internationaux, relations économiques, environnement* (8e édition. ed. L.G.D.J.). Paris: Lextenso éditions.

De Cruz, P, (1999). *Comparative law in a changing world* (3rd ed., pp. 10–30). Taylor & Francis Group.

Franzese, P. W. (2009). Sovereignty in cyberspace: Can it exist? *Air Force Law Review, 64*, 1–42.

Jensen, E. T. (2015). Cyber sovereignty: The way ahead. *Texas International Law Journal, 50*, 276–304.

Trakman, L. (2018). Aligning state sovereignty with transnational public policy. *Tulane Law Review, 93*, 207.

Walters, R., Trakman, L., & Zeller, B. (2019). *Data protection law: A comparative analysis of Asia Pacific and European approaches*. Singapore: Springer.

Wulf, H. (2007). *Challenging the Weberian concept of the state: The future of the monopoly of violence*, The Australian Centre for Peace and Conflict Studies Occasional Papers Series [Online] Number 9.

Chapter 2
Cyber Security

Abstract Cybersecurity has emerged as a global challenge and is becoming a tier one security threat for nation states. The modern-day cyber age will expose states to new challenges. Cyberspace and cyber attacks represent new ways of intruding on the sovereign prerogatives of states, and their citizens. It poses a threat to every area of society from government to the public and private sectors. Furthermore, it is undertaken by state actors, the private sector and individuals in the community. Cyber incursions are complex and difficult to detect. They are extremely subversive. These challenges are even enhanced by developing AI, which bring new tasks for cyber security specialists. It is the cyber attacks that pose the biggest challenge to states and their sovereignty, but also, and in our view, equally as pervasive is the challenge to personal data.

This Chapter highlights the interconnectedness of personal data, cyber security and AI. For instance, in 2018, there was an estimated 1.5 million Singaporean citizen's health personal data stolen following the system(s) being hacked.[1] The incident highlighted the vulnerability of Internet systems, platforms and infrastructure. The cyber-attack on SingHealth was a reminder for the state to push further in the area of cybersecurity collectively as a nation. Thus, it is argued that the public, government and regulators, do not fully understand the extent of the challenges and issues faced by individuals, public and private entities in relation to the cyber security and protection of personal data.

In addition to the above, this Chapter draws on Game Theory and Network Theory, and how these theories have largely focused on the technology response to cyber incursions. Yet, and even though there are technological developments, Graham Greenleaf believes that in the modern world it is hard to see how personal

[1] Singapore Cyber Landscape, Ministry of Communications and Information, 2018, https://www.csa.gov.sg/~/media/csa/documents/publications/csasingaporecyberlandscape2018.pdf?

R. Walters, M. Novak, *Cyber Security, Artificial Intelligence, Data Protection & the Law*, https://doi.org/10.1007/978-981-16-1665-5_2

data can be fully protected.[2] Greenleaf argues that whether data privacy laws can sufficiently protect privacy in a networked world is an open question, but they are the legal instrument most capable of so doing.

This Chapter demonstrates how the law and technology responses to cyber security are largely circular. They both regulate the behavior of individuals using the systems, platforms and infrastructure. In other words, the law relies not only on a behavior of the attacker but also on an operation of the defender. Technology on the other hand, is at the front end, to control the behavior of the person using the technology to capture and use data. While the law ensures that there is a level of deterrence and accountability placed on individuals and entities using technology and personal data. The challenges facing the protection of personal data from continued and more sophisticated cyber attacks will be a formidable challenge for both technology and the law.

2.1 Introduction

It is well understood that cybersecurity has emerged as a global challenge and is becoming a tier one security threat for sovereign states.[3] Put another way, the modern-day cyber age will expose sovereignty to new challenges.[4] These challenges are even enhanced by developing AI, which bring new tasks for cyber security specialists. Cyberspace and cyber attacks represent new ways of intruding on the sovereign prerogatives of states. It is the cyber attacks that pose the biggest challenge to states and their sovereignty, but also, and in our view, equally as pervasive is challenge to personal data. The number of cyber attacks that have resulted in the illegal collection (loss), storage and use of personal data and since 2010, and the list is growing. From Australia to Singapore, United States to United Kingdom, Europe to Indonesia, the cyber attacks have pervaded both the private and public sectors. Luke Irwin estimates that for the month of May 2019 alone, one cyber breach was so significant that 1,3 million people's records were compromised.[5] The offender was the First American Financial Corporation, which breached sixteen years' worth of insurance data. Irwin argues that the incident accounted for more than 60% of all records. In total, at least 1,389,463,242 records were compromised that, resulted in the annual running total to 7.28 billion (Table 2.1).[6]

---

[2] Graham Greenleaf, *Global data privacy in a networked world,* Chapter in Brown, I (ed) *Research Handbook on Governance of the Internet* Cheltenham: Edward Elgar, (2011), https://www.vatandoust.com.au/wp-content/uploads/2015/12/Global-Data-Privacy-in-a.pdf

[3] Hao Yeli, A, Three-Perspective Theory of Cyber Sovereignty, https://cco.ndu.edu/Portals/96/Documents/prism/prism_7-2/10-3-Perspective%20Theory.pdf

[4] Margulies, P, *Sovereignty and Cyber Attacks: Technology's Challenge to the Law of State*, Melbourne Law Review, Vol 14 (2013).

[5] Luke Orwin, *List of data breaches and cyber attacks in May 2019 – 1.39 billion records leaked,* https://www.itgovernance.co.uk/blog/list-of-data-breaches-and-cyber-attacks-in-may-2019-1-39-billion-records-leaked

[6] Ibid.

Table 2.1 Highlights the cyber attacks in May 2019

Cyber attacks	Ransomware	Personal data breaches
US energy companies report denial of service condition.	Hackers breach Philippines United Student Financial System for Tertiary Education	Popular US recruitment site ladders exposes users' data in security lapse 13 million+
Telangana power supplier website hit by a cyber attack	Hacker wipes Git repositories and asking for ransom	Seattle University laptop containing Social Security numbers lost 2000+
Rivalry between Bay Area lunch companies ends in cyber attack (200+)	New York newspaper firm faces attacks Ryuk	UK Government commits email privacy blunder 300
Hackers steal card data from 201 online campus stores in US and Canada	Connecticut school district thwarts ransomeware attack	Vulnerability in Tommy Hilfiger Japan database expose customers' data 1 million+
Austrian construction group hit by cyber attack	American Baptist Homes of Midwest hit by ransomeware	Louisiana's Madison Parish Hospital notifies patients of a security incident ,1400+
Airbnb customers say their accounts been hacked	Kentucky library closes due to ransomeware attack	Hong Kong government dental clinic loses patients' personal data 350+
Binance breached as hackers steal 38 million GBP in bitcoin	City of Baltimore hit by ransomeware attack	Man finds medical records from Cork University Hospital on city street
Michigan-based health clinic says an employee's account was compromised (1000)	Illinois-based Augustana College reports ransomeware attack	Cork university Hospital accuses man who found medical on city street of breaching data protection laws.
Student at NY-based school arrested, charged with hacking former superintendent's account	Southeastern Council on Alcoholism and Drug Dependence notifies patients of ransomeware attach 25,000+	Children's personal data found at dump in Yellwoknife Canada
NY-based Episcopal Health Service notifies patients of data breach	Oklahoma City Public Schools confirm ransomeware attack	Virginia hospital loses patient's personal data twice
US Virgin Islands-based FirstBank cancelling debit cards amid fears that accounts have been compromised (50)	Louisville Regional Airport Authority hit by ransomeware	Data at Canada's forth phone network exposed customer data 5 million
Affiliate of NBAs Indiana Pacers says it has fallen victim to as phishing scam		Database containing Indian personal records exposed 275,000,000+

(continued)

Table 2.1 (continued)

Cyber attacks	Ransomware	Personal data breaches
Oregon Health Authority sends speedy notification after phishing attack		School exam vendor exposes students' personal data 525,000
Paterson NY, public schools hit by cyber attack (more than 23,000)		Data breach at CT-based Greenwich school poses clear and present danger
Equitas Health says two employees' email accounts were compromised 500+		DVLA sends motorists' sensitive data to wrong address 2000
Hackers breach Uniqlo's online store, access customers details (460,000+)		Almost everyone in Panama has had their personal data exposed 3,427,396
Singapore Red Cross's website hacked, blood donors' details 4000		Oklahoma Dept of Securities notifies those affected by 2018 data breach 2 million +
Cancer Treatment Centers of America notifies patients of phishing attack		Data breach exposes passport info of Russian officials and citizens 360,000
Oregon Construction Contractors Board confirms data breach 8000+		Berger king online store for children exposes customer's data 37,000+
MnongDB databases deleted by Uninstaller attackers 12,000+		Unsecured survey database exposes respondents' personal details 8 million
Database containing Instagram influences contact details found more than 49 million		TeamViewer confirms undisclosed data breach of personal details.
Southerland City Council launches investigation after library users' personal data hacked (45)		Redtail CRM data breach might have exposed client info.
Graphic design firm Canva hit by data breach more than 139 million		
Hackers break into database of Dutch letting agent and steal identity card scans 200+		
Tampa-based Checkers Drive-In restaurants notifies guests about malware attack		

The statistics from this table highlight the extent of the subversive behavior that is being undertaken by individuals and entities that are obtaining access to millions of people's personal and other data for either economic or some other gain. With the approval of Luke Irwin to use the above data, the table further demonstrates the extent of where the data is illegally obtained from including small to medium sized businesses, educational institutions, government departments and organizations, and general consumer entities. It also demonstrates how it is not limited to a single sovereign state, these activities have taken place in Oceania, South East Asia, Europe and North America. What is not apparent is whether these intrusions are state actors or the private sector acting on behalf of state actors, or private individuals. Furthermore, it does not clarify how the breaches were undertaken and by what technology such as AI. Nonetheless, it is our view that there is a clear alignment of cyber security (attacks) and data protection. It will, as AI becomes more mainstream involve this technology where personal data will be vulnerable from misuse and cyber incursions. This, arguably, poses significant challenges to individuals, entities and state actors.

2.2 Interconnectedness of Cyber Security, Personal Data, and AI

On the backdrop of the above, the interconnectedness of personal data, cyber security and AI was recently highlighted from a technical perspective (not the law) in Singapore. In 2018, there was an estimated 1.5 million Singaporean citizen's health personal data stolen following the systems being hacked.[7] The incident highlighted the vulnerability of Internet systems, platforms and infrastructure. The cyber-attack on SingHealth was a reminder for the need to push further in our cybersecurity efforts collectively as a nation. On the international stage, Singapore remains firmly committed to the establishment of a rules- based international order in cyberspace; and condemns all malicious cyber activities, which threaten the safety and security of Singapore and Singaporeans.[8] This is one example, of what is happening around the world, however, many incidents of this type go unreported. Thus, the public, government and regulators never fully understand the extent of the challenges and issues faced by individuals, public and private entities in relation to the cyber security and protection of personal data. More pervasively, what the Singapore report highlights how AI is, and will likely have, an increased role to the adverse impact to personal data. In other words:

> machine learning and data- driven detection systems are being adopted in cybersecurity applications to cope with rapidly evolving cyber-attacks. However, threat actors are now leveraging adversarial Artificial Intelligence (AI) technologies to deceive these systems. One method of deception involves using Generative Adversarial Networks (GANs) to cre-

[7] Singapore Cyber Landscape, Ministry of Communications and Information, 2018, https://www.csa.gov.sg/~/media/csa/documents/publications/csasingaporecyberlandscape2018.pdf

[8] Ibid.

ate new variants from known malware that are able to bypass malware detectors. One way to counter this attack would be to include GAN samples during re-training, so that the malware detector is tuned to identify this class of mutated samples. To combat against new cyber- attacks, AI engines constantly train and update their models. This adaptive learning process, however, creates an opportunity for threat actors to poison data used to train the models and thus influence decision boundaries. One method of defending against this type of attack involves processing the training data to identify potential adversarial data manipulation first, before providing them to train the AI engines.[9]

Typically, the law has struggled to keep pace with technology.[10] Hao Yeli argues that there is and continues to be heated debate in international forums concerning the rules of cyberspace, and the systemic and revolutionary challenges to global governance in cyberspace. Cyber sovereignty has inevitably become the focus of great controversy. Yeli views cyber security as three dimensional. The first being what is referred to as the base level, secondly, the application level, and thirdly, the core level. The base level or otherwise referred to as the physical level constitutes the infrastructure that supports cyberspace (the Internet). The resulting effect has seen a select few organisations with the expertise to develop and control a standard global cyberspace and interconnectivity. The application level in the eyes of Yeli, includes the many internet platforms and internet carriers in the real world that have integrated such different sectors as technology, culture, economy, trade, and other aspects of daily life. For Yeli, sovereignty at this middle level is a balance between freedom and order, which allow the systems and platforms to be developed for local requirements. At this level, it assumes that people are able to conduct their daily lives under the constraints set and established by the states.

The final level, comprises state intervention and control through the law ensuring security, which is unchallengeable and includes the governing foundations and embodies the core interests of the country (the sovereign state). The resulting effect assumes a greater level of control over the conditions, religious, and cultural backgrounds, legitimate differences do exist between states. Diversity is the norm of human existence which cannot be formatted according to any single culture. Differences and diversity should be tolerated. What Yeli is saying, is that, one may not agree with a country's social system and ideology, but you should understand its national conditions, respect its existence, and tolerate its differences. This approach, in part, meets the 2019 G20 Leaders meeting declaration, where there was a call for states to respect each others cyber security and data laws. However, and while, in part, we agree with Yeli, there are issues with this approach. It espouses a continual international fragmented framework that, leaves it to states to develop their respective legal frameworks. If this continues to be realized, it poses greater challenges than resolutions, particularly in the area of transnational trade (over the Internet). The question arises how will this play out in the future? This is a complex question, however, with an estimated 3.2 billion people[11] now classed as netizens, and

[9] Ibid.

[10] Ibid.

[11] Ibid.

growing monthly, Yeli calls for an expansion of considerations of the perspectives of the international community and the citizen, because there is more than one voice that needs to be heard due to the continued openness and transnational nature of the Internet (cyber space).

2.3 Security

More recently in 2020, the British,[12] the Information Commissioner's Office (ICO) has fined Dixons Retail for poor security that led to a data breach and the theft of financial data of millions of customers. The ICO says it is impossible to know exactly how many people were compromised, but suspects roughly 14 million data subjects were compromised.[13] While some have had non-financial information stolen, such as names, addresses, phone numbers, others have had their credit card information taken. The ICO fined Dixons about $650,000. The investigation highlighted the lack of cyber security measures established by an entity to protect personal data.[14] This is an important point, because as AI and other technology is increasingly used, the judiciary is likely to take into consideration what measures and risk management steps were put in place by the entity to safe keep the personal data. The report goes onto to say that the ruling, focused squarely on how Dixons ran a poor security arrangement and failed to take adequate steps to protect personal data, including poor software patching practices, not having a local firewall, not segregating the network and failing to routinely test it for security issues.[15] The investigation found systemic failures in the way DSG Retail Limited safeguarded personal data and that these failures related to basic, commonplace security measures, showing a complete disregard for the customers whose personal information was stolen.[16]

Notwithstanding the above, following Edward Snowden's revelations on the US mass surveillance of the internet in June 2013, many states started to explore technical and legal ways to control data originating from and passing through their territories.[17] Primarily, attempts were focused on 'tying' data to a specific territory. Proposed technical solutions included: the construction of a submarine internet cable between Latin America and Europe, bypassing the US; building a regional

---

[12] Fadilpši, S, *Dixons hit with huge ICO fine over customer data failure*,

Company was fined in accordance to the data protection act from 1998, rather than GDPR. 2020–01-10 T12:30:08Z https://www.itproportal.com/news/dixons-hit-with-huge-ico-fine-over-customer-data-failure/

[13] Ibid.

[14] Ibid.

[15] Ibid.

[16] Ibid.

[17] Baezner, M., Robin, P, *Trend Analysis: Cyber Sovereignty and Data Sovereignty*, Center for Security Studies, Zürich, 2018 https://css.ethz.ch/content/dam/ethz/special-interest/gess/cis/center-for-securities-studies/pdfs/20180907_MB_TA_Cyber%20sovereignty_V2_rev.pdf

routing network; creating a national cloud computing service; and starting a national email service.[18] These technical solutions were shown to be both inefficient and ineffective in preventing foreign surveillance of data. Technical experts beleive that data would be better protected with encryption than by tying data to a specific territory. The authors go onto highlight the suggested technical and legal measures seem to miss the point of protecting data against foreign surveillance. In other words, to protect data originating in their territory (the sovereign state), states have, amongst other things developed a combination of data protection and cyber security laws.[19]

Lotrionte argues that cyberspace challenges not only the principles of International Law, but also the principle of state sovereignty, and relevant academic discussions revolve around the existence and recognition of state sovereignty in cyberspace.[20] He believes that state sovereignty exists in cyberspace due to the existence of physical infrastructures necessary for the existence of cyberspace, and sovereignty in cyberspace is therefore perceived as an extension of the territorial principle of sovereignty. Lotrionte further points out that despite the rise in national law for cyber security and data protection, this issue is further complicated by the problem of non-state actors committing malicious cyber- activities. These actors bring even greater uncertainty to the attribution process, as states may employ, finance or train such actors to attack another state. The question of non-state actors perpetrating malicious acts against another state is already a complex issue in International Law outside of cyberspace, as it raises problems regarding state responsibility for controlling or assisting non-state actors. In cyberspace, the problem is even more complicated, as both non-state actors and states are able to play on the attribution problem to avoid responsibility.[21]

However, some eighteen years earlier John Perry Barlow put forward a contrary position to the above arguing by governments of the industrial world, "you weary giants of flesh and steel, I come from Cyberspace, the new home of Mind. On behalf of the future, I ask you of the past to leave us alone. You are not welcome among us. You have no sovereignty where we gather."[22] Perry argued strongly that in the world of the Internet there is not government, nor is there likely to have one. Thus, for Perry, he declared the "global social space being built is to be naturally independent of the tyrannies you seek to impose on us. You have no moral right to rule us nor do you possess any methods of enforcement we have true reason to fear".[23] He points out how before the 1990s, the countries of China, Germany, France, Russia, Singapore, Italy and the United States, were all trying to ward off the virus of liberty by erecting guard posts at the frontiers of Cyberspace. At the time it was believed

---

[18] Ibid.

[19] Ibid.

[20] Lotrionte, C, *State Sovereignty and Self-Defense in Cyberspace: A Normative Framework for Balancing Legal Rights*. Emory Int. Law Rev. 26, (2013) 825–919.

[21] Ibid.

[22] Barlow, JP, *A Declaration of the Independence of Cyberspace*, Electronic Frontier Found. 1996, https://www.eff.org/cyberspace-independence

[23] Ibid.

that such measures may keep out the contagion for a small time, but they will not work in a world that will soon be blanketed in bit-bearing media.[24] Moving forward fourteen years, and as highlighted above, the international response to cyber security has been profound. It is now in the political domain, which has seen state actors assert their sovereign right to regulate cyber security at various levels such as national security (militarily, political elections, transnational crimes). On the other hand, and a further layer of complexity regarding cyber attacks that infringe on personal data are that, they are very different. The technical approach is also multilayered and often proceeds in stages over the short, medium and longer term. Largely, states have responded by criminalizing these offences. However, there appears to be a lack of international policy mechanisms, legal norms and instruments available to assist in regulating this transnational challenge, to get states on the same page.

Gina Fisk et al. are of the view that sharing cyber security data across organizational boundaries brings both privacy risks in the exposure of personal information and data, and organizational risk in disclosing internal information.[25] These risks occur as information leaks in network traffic or logs, and also in queries made across organizations. They are also complicated by the trade-offs in privacy preservation and utility present in anonymization to manage disclosure.[26] Yet, the legal framework has hardly kept pace with the developments of cybersecurity and data protection as a collective. This is evident with the extent to which the world is facing an increase in personal data breaches from cybersecurity intrusions. While many jurisdictions have gone some way to developing laws to protect personal data and account for cyber security intrusions, the law has, in part, been decoupled from reality. This has been reinforced by Fisk et al. who highlight that there are various laws around the world, such as the EU's Data Protection legal framework and US Health Insurance Portability and Accountability Act (HIPAA), which establish privacy requirements for an individual's data. US policies acknowledge this sensitivity for research in computer security. The National Science Foundation expects researchers to share data, but requires appropriate safeguards to protect the privacy of individuals.[27] While these policies constrain data sharing, there is also a need to share data. For example, in the US, the proposed Cyber Intelligence Sharing and Protection Act (CISPA) "directs the federal government to provide for the real-time sharing of actionable, situational cyber threat information between all designated federal cyber operations centers to enable integrated actions to protect, prevent, mitigate, respond to, and recover from cyber incidents".[28] Since data from cyber incidents often contains personal information from computers and smartphones/

---

[24] Ibid.

[25] Fisk, G., Ardi, C., Pickett, N., Heideman, J., Fisk, M., Papadopoulos, C, *Privacy Principles for Sharing Cyber Security Data,* 2015 https://www.isi.edu/~johnh/PAPERS/Fisk15a.pdf

[26] Ibid.

[27] Ibid.

[28] Ibid.

Iphones, systems for sharing cyber security information must consider privacy issues as they exchange and analysed information.[29] They go onto say that:

> Solving security research and operational security problems increasingly requires *sharing data across and within organizations*, but it must do so while considering the challenges of individual privacy. Research increasingly emphasizes open data that anyone can freely access, use, modify, and share for any purpose. Computer attackers often access systems from multiple organizations to hide their tracks; defenders must unravel these paths to understand attacker command and control systems. In both cases, information sharing is necessary to make progress, but carries significant privacy and security risks.[30]

In addition to the above, laws (such as wiretap laws) and ethical requirements constrain sharing, and even collection of such data may raise new risks of data theft as the and depth of laws that nation states including the EU have developed to respond to protecting personal data and cybersecurity attacks. However, cybersecurity has largely been taken up by criminal law, whereas, personal data has developed its own laws to protect a person's privacy over the Internet, and the trade and management of that data. This is an important distinction, because personal (identity) theft has largely been identified as a criminal act, along with the illegal intrusion of computer servers, infrastructure, systems and platforms. The authors take the position that the appropriate response to protecting privacy and personal data from cyber-attacks is through and via technology. Even so, the idea that technology can solely resolve these ongoing issues will not suffice. It must be coupled with an adequate legal and policy response.

Fisk et al., in part, have incorporated the following key policy principles of *Data Archive*[31]*; Anonymization*[32]*; Data Aging; and Controlled Disclosure* into their technology policy framework.[33] These principles can be found in data protection and privacy law. More specifically, the ability for data subjects to anonymize their personal data has been a recent addition. Data storage when coupled with data retention (the length of time data is to be stored) is an important component of data protection law. States have taken data storage a step further and require that certain personal data be stored within the state. For instance, Russia has data localization requirements whereby most, if not all their citizen's personal data must be stored on the

[29] Ibid.

[30] Ibid.

[31] Ibid, Organizations must also consider how their data is stored. Unlike end-to-end encryption, where the source and destination of data is explicitly known, and full- disk encryption, which is generally transparent to applications, a secure data archive must manage the challenges of long-term storage with multiple potential users of data. It must thus consider encryption of data-at-rest, but also key-rollover and aging (to be robust over the long term), and access control and access auditing.

[32] Ibid, anonymization is frequently used to sanitize data before release in such a way that any personal information or data is obfuscated or removed.

[33] Ibid, organizations must consider their risk tolerance in terms of long-term data storage. To meet our goals of both Least Disclosure and Forward Progress, tools for cyber security sharing must rate-limit queries and responses by assigning privacy allotments to each organization in order to mitigate the risk of privacy diffusion and secondary privacy damage, data query correlation.

territory of the state and not a third country. Furthermore, data-controlled disclosure, in part, can be found in those data protection laws that require a controller or processor to be appointed within an organisation who will be responsible for managing that data. Nonetheless, this approach while going someway to addressing some of the issues between data protection and cyber security, and its related infrastructure, further work is needed to reconcile the balance between having to balance the need to protect personal data-privacy over the Internet, the use and dissemination of data, organizational risk to respond to security events.

To resolve this ongoing dichotomy, as many scholars along with state actors have called for more international law to enable a governance concerning state responsibility in the cyber domain.[34] However, Peter Margulies argues that to address the kinetic attacks, international law defines state responsibility narrowly. A party asserting that a state is responsible for a kinetic attack must comply with the 'effective control' test adopted by the International Court of Justice in the Military and Paramilitary Activities in and against Nicaragua[35] decision or, at the very least, with the 'effective control' test adopted by the *International Criminal Tribunal for the Former Yugoslavia in Prosecutor v Tadić*.[36] Driven by concerns about the risks of escalation, the International Law Commission's ('ILC') Draft Article Responsibility of States for Internationally Wrongful Acts[37] hardened this narrow approach. Margulies notes how the US has called for 'the development of norms for state conduct in cyberspace does not require a reinvention of customary international law'. According to the US, '[l]ong-standing international norms guiding state behavior — in times of peace and conflict — also apply in cyberspace'. However, the US has also observed that the interpretation of international law must accommodate the 'unique attributes of networked technology'.[38] Accordingly, those special traits might require 'additional understandings' to 'supplement' traditional international norms. He argues that to avoid interference with sovereign prerogatives, international law has interpreted state responsibility narrowly in the domain of conventional or kinetic attacks. One vital aspect of sovereignty is the state's reliance on officials chosen according to the state's own rules. They have a significant influence of the future direction and response to cyber attacks both legally and practically.

---

[34] Margulies, P, *Sovereignty and Cyber Attacks: Technology's Challenge to the Law of State*, Melbourne Law Review, Vol 14 (2013).

[35] Nicaragua [1986] ICJRep14, 64.

[36] *International Criminal Tribunal for the Former Yugoslavia*, Appeals Chamber, Case No IT-94-1-A, (15 July 1999).

[37] Responsibility of States for Internationally Wrongful Acts 2001, DRAFT Articles - Text adopted by the International Law Commission at its fifty-third session, in 2001, and submitted to the General Assembly as a part of the Commission's report covering the work of that session (A/56/10). The report, which also contains commentaries on the draft articles, appears in the *Yearbook of the International Law Commission, 2001*, vol. II, Part Two, as corrected. http://legal.un.org/ilc/texts/instruments/english/commentaries/9_6_2001.pdf, http://legal.un.org/ilc/texts/instruments/english/draft_articles/9_6_2001.pdf

[38] Ibid.

To vindicate that reliance, international law holds that only decisions by officials can bind the state. Sovereign states therefore bear responsibility only for acts and omissions that a reasonable observer can trace to state officials. Margulies further highlights how Tallinn Manual on the International Law Applicable to Cyber Warfare ('Manual') tracks the ILC's analysis, appears to address some of the broader transnational issues pertaining to cyber attacks. He notes that the Manual is an exceptionally valuable effort to apply *lex lata* to the fluid cyber realm, caution may not serve international law in this context.[39] However, he believes that this Manual is too narrow and when coupled with the Draft Articles will be complex to provide any suitable level of controls, and there is likely to be opposition to shifting the burden of attribution back to the victim state and keep the standard at the overall control standard endorsed by the ICTY in Tadić. This is because the ICTY ruled that state officials may be accountable if they exercised 'overall control' over a group or entity. The test applied by the Tribunal was a broader standard hinging on 'overall control' by state officials. However, the Tribunal argues that the 'overall control' test is demanding,[40] and must be more than the 'mere financing and equipping of such forces'.[41] It requires 'coordinating or helping in the general planning of [the group's] military activity'.[42] While this reference by Margulies largely focuses on cyber attacks that would be placed in the national security and possibly warfare basket, it does not consider the broader international law that has been developed to enhance international trade, finance and investment rules.

However, Graham Greenleaf makes the point that in the modern world it is hard to see how personal data can be fully protected. He argues that whether data privacy laws can sufficiently protect privacy in a networked world is an open question, but they are the legal instrument most capable of so doing.[43] Other forms of legal protection (privacy torts, breach of confidence (both general principles and statutory rules), constitutional rights, surveillance limitation laws, consumer protection laws etc.) give intermittent protection in some countries (and sometimes very effectively in specific cases) but do not provide the thorough and evolving protection provided by sets of data privacy principles.[44] Arguably these areas of law are slowly evolving

[39] Ibid. Cyber reflects what I call 'attribution asymmetry': cyber threats from private groups assisted by states are both more difficult to trace than kinetic attacks for victims and easier to control for the state providing the assistance. Because of this asymmetry, the international law on state responsibility for kinetic attacks does not adequately address the issue of cyber attacks. A test of virtual control would be more effective, imposing responsibility on a state that has provided financial or other assistance to private groups. The virtual control test would deter states from using private groups to engineer plausible deniability. This heightened deterrence provides a more useful template for the development of international law in the cyber domain.

[40] Ibid.

[41] Ibid.

[42] Ibid.

[43] Greenleaf, G, *Global data privacy in a networked world,* Chapter in Brown, I (ed) *Research Handbook on Governance of the Internet* Cheltenham: Edward Elgar, (2011), https://www.vatandoust.com.au/wp-content/uploads/2015/12/Global-Data-Privacy-in-a.pdf

[44] Ibid.

and they are providing greater protection to personal data while strengthening cyber security incursions. Greenleaf in referring to the EU Commission in 2010 noted that:

> the world has seen dramatic technological change since the European Commission first proposed the Data Protection Directive in 1990. The Internet has moved out of the university lab into 56% of European homes and 95% of OECD businesses. Computer processing power has continued to follow Moore's Law, with transistor density doubling every 18-24 months – around one thousand-fold in the last two decades. Computer storage capacity and communications bandwidth have both been increasing even more quickly, doubling every 12 months and hence a thousand-fold each decade. These exponential increases have radically increased the ability of organisations to collect, store and process personal data. The physical environment is now saturated with sensors such as CCTV cameras and mobile phones, with biometric and electronic identifiers used to link data to individuals. In the digital world almost every communication and Web page access leaves behind detailed footprints. The Internet and mobile information appliances allow large quantities of personal data to be trivially moved between jurisdictions. Data mining tools attempt to find patterns in large collections of personal data, both to identify individuals "of interest" and to attempt to predict their interests and preferences. New multinational companies have sprung up around these technologies to service a global customer base, with smaller enterprises outsourcing employee and customer data processing to developing world companies. This is still relevant in 2020. More than a decade later and the world is continuing to see expediential rise in technology use that has resulted in vast more data being captured and used, along with more and more breaches of security systems that have been established to protect data and other personal and commercial arrangements.[45]

Central to the position taken by the EU, is how the technology has expanded rapidly from the simple desktop computer 30 years ago, to where people are connection 24 hours a day, 7 days a week through their Iphones that are laden with AI. This new technology is capturing enormous amounts of personal data, and the cyber intrusions are like no other period in the past. How the law and technology reconciles these challenges, is a long way off.

2.4 Cyber Security – Theory

Moreover, theories have emerged that underpin the law and practice of cyber security. It is out of scope of this book to examine off the theory related to cyber security. Thierry Balzacq and Myriam Dunn Cavelty apply the Actor-Network Theory (ANT) and its analytical toolbox. ANT is a heterogeneous conglomerate of ideas, with origins in Science and Technology Studies. They note that, it follows a rationalist tradition and focuses on 'dynamic relations between scientific and political sites', it rejects the dualism between the social (human) and the material (nonhuman) in the study of the social and it has close ties to the post-structuralism, but tends to be more empirical. ANT is gaining prominence in International Relations and security due to the new types of issues and research questions brought on by the 'material turn'– which signifies an interest in the importance of artefacts, natural forces, and

---

[45] Ibid.

material regimes in social practices and systems of power – as well as the 'practice turn'– which takes organised forms of doing and saying ('practices') as the smallest unit of analysis rather than actors or structures.[46]

On the other side, it has increasingly become evident that there is no single theory that can be used for cyber security because of the multilayered and multidimensional approach both technically and legally. The authors in referring to Nick Bingham who asserts the illusion that 'cyber-space as a singular exists at all'.[47] They further highlight how Stephen Graham suggests that 'cyberspace ... needs to be considered as fragmented, divided and contested multiplicity of heterogeneous infrastructures of actor-networks'.[48] The main task of cyber security experts in this view is to account for how and under what conditions 'cyber-threats' through different networks, and develop strategies to counter them effectively. Arguably this applies to the technical practitioner. For the law, it goes one step further to ensure that not only the systems and infrastructure are protected, but the information and data transmitted across these platforms have a level or protection.[49] Apart from the technological challenges, because it changes so rapidly, it is hardly surprising that the law has been challenged in how to deal with these issues. It hasn't been until nation states have seen the need to protect the political, economic and social fabric of society that has resulted in the law following the technology.

Moreover, one of the increasingly espoused theories in relation to cyber security that has emerged is Game Theory. Cuong Do[50] et al. undertook a survey to test this theory against privacy and cyber security, as a collective. To highlight how game theory is utilized in cyberspace security and privacy, the authors selected three main applications: cyber-physical security, communication security, and privacy. Through this work the authors attempted to present game models that could provide solutions to the dichotomy faced by privacy and cyber security. What the authors found was that, combining mainstream knowledge with new developments can provide a new direction of knowledge. For instance, combining network design with programming we now have software-defined networks. For security, integrating cyber space with physical space we have cyber-physical security, or combining security with

[46] Balzacq, T., Cavelty, M D, *A theory of actor-network for cyber-security*, European Journal of International Security, (2016), 1.

[47] Bingham, N,'*Objections: From technological determinism towards geographies of relations'*, Environment and Planning D: Society and Space, 14:6 (1996), p. 32, in Thierry Balzacq, Myriam Dunn Cavelty, *A theory of actor-network for cyber-security*, European Journal of International Security, (2016).

[48] Graham, S, *'The end of geography or the explosion of place? Conceptualizing space, place and information technology'*, Progress in Human Geography, 22:2 (1998), p. 178, in Thierry Balzacq, Myriam Dunn Cavelty, *A theory of actor-network for cyber-security*, European Journal of International Security, (2016).

[49] Ibid.

[50] Do, C., Tran, N., Hong, C., Kamhoua, C., Blasch, E., Kwait, K., Blasch, E., Ren, S., Pissinou, N., Iyengar, S, *Game Theory for Cyber Security and Privacy*, ACM Journal Name, Vol. NA, No. NA, Article NA, (2015).

economic elements creates cyber-insurance issues.[51] To solve security and privacy problems in a new domain, game theoretic approaches are the most suitable tools since they offer variety of sets of proven mathematic-methods for multi-players strategy-making and they also have a different form to capture the interaction of players in privacy and security issues.[52]

The essential elements of game theory is very evident in applying technology and policy to resolve the gap between cyber security and privacy. In applying a mathematical approach is arguably appropriate for technology. However, what is not evident is how game theory can be applied to resolve the legal gaps between the two issues. This is further reinforced by the authors who apply game theory to justify the benefits of a fully Open-Implementation cloud infrastructure, which means that the clouds implementation and configuration details can be inspected by both the legitimate and malicious cloud users.[53] The authors conclude that, even though Open-Implementation cloud may facilitate attacks, vulnerabilities or misconfiguration are easier to discover, which in turn reduces the total security threats and facilitate the clouds provable trustworthiness. They further highlight how Q-Learning as a means to react automatically to the adversarial behavior of a suspicious user in order to secure the system. The authors[54] compared variations of Q-Learning with a traditional stochastic game. Simulation results show the possibility of Naive Q-Learning as a promising approach when confronted with restricted information on opponents. It was demonstrated that the law is somewhat separated from the technology because it focuses on the behavior of individuals and entities.[55] That is, the law relies not only on a behavior of the attacker but also on an operation of the defender. In the physical system, the continuous physical system's state is governed by law. Thus, what has emerged is two separate forms of control that are circular. In other words, technology controls the behavior of individuals and entities, and the law has a similar outcome punishing the individual or entity that has committed the cyber security breach. Technology is in our view at the front end, to control the behavior of the person using the technology to capture and use data. While the law ensures that there is a level of deterrence and accountability placed on individuals and entities using technology and personal data.

---

[51] Ibid.

[52] Ibid.

[53] Kamhoua, C., Zhao, H., Rodriguez, M., Kwiat, K., 2016. *A Game-Theoretic Approach for Testing for Hardware Trojans*. IEEE Transactions on Multi-Scale Computing Systems, (2016), 200–209.

[54] Do, C., Tran, N., Hong, C., Kamhoua, C., Blasch, E., Kwait, K., Blasch, E., Ren, S., Pissinou, N., Iyengar, S, *Game Theory for Cyber Security and Privacy*, ACM Journal Name, Vol. NA, No. NA, Article NA, (2015).

[55] Ibid.

2.5 Conclusion

As technology grows and becomes more sophisticated, cyber security attacks are likely to increase and will also become even more complex. They are carried out by nation states, private sector organisations and entities, and individuals in the community. They [cyber attacks] are pervading all areas of government, commercial and social activity over the Internet. This Chapter has briefly highlighted the interconnectedness between cyber security, AI and data protection law, and to a lesser extent AI. Drawing on the Game Theory and Network Theory, it highlighted how these theories have largely focused on the technology response to cyber incursions, and not the law. Yet, some of the policy principles that have been developed by the technological response show how they have been accepted by the law, particularly in relation to data protection and privacy law.

Moreover, this Chapter further demonstrated how cyberspace itself needs to be considered as fragmented, divided and contested multiplicity of heterogeneous infrastructures of actor-networks. Arguably, the main task of cyber security experts is to account for how and under what conditions 'cyber-threats' through different networks, and develop strategies to counter them effectively. While this applies to the technical practitioner, it has been argued that the law is an extension of the practitioner. In other words, the law ensures that the systems and infrastructure are protected, but the information and data transmitted across these platforms has a level of protection. However, the law is challenged by this very notion. This is because the law lags behind the technology developments, and to date, there has been a lack of a coordinated approach to deal with the transnational cyber incursions that acquire personal data.

This Chapter also demonstrated how the law and technology responses to cyber security are largely circular. They both regulate the behavior of individuals using the systems, platforms and infrastructure. Put another way, the law relies not only on a behavior of the attacker but also on an the operation of the defender. Technology in our view is at the front end, which controls the behavior of the person using the technology to capture and use data. The law on the other hand, ensures that there is a level of deterrence and accountability placed on individuals and entities using technology and personal data. There is a lot of work for regulators and technology experts, to undertake to address the ongoing gaps that will emerged from AI technology alone to protect against cyber attacks and the loss of personal data. Arguably, AI will become even more mainstream, providing an ideal platform for cyber incursions to occur, making personal data vulnerable to misuse.

Today more than ever, cybersecurity is a transnational problem that must be resolved both nationally and internationally. The business community and individuals are faced with real risks of cyber intrusions that, will not only acquire large quantities of aggregated personal data, but also, the infrequency of these incursions is predicted to grow and expand. This will be particularly problematic as AI devices become even more mainstream. Thus, what this Chapter demonstrates is that the public and private sectors need to be vigilant and develop strong and robust policy settings to respond to cyber attacks. Moreover, there is a need for the private sector and broader community to better understand the complex regulatory frameworks that currently exist and will evolve in AI, cyber security and data protection. At the private sector level, this will be easier for large organisations, but will, be a formidable task for smaller and medium sized businesses. Understanding the legal obligations of a fragmented legal framework will be paramount. Therefore, it is argued that there is a greater role for international law to be developed to strengthen and support the already international principles.

References

Balzacq, T., & Cavelty, M. D. (2016). A theory of actor-network for cyber-security. *European Journal of International Security, 1*, 176–198.

Bingham, N. (1996). Objections: From technological determinism towards geographies of relations. *Environment and Planning D: Society and Space, 14*, 6, 32, in Thierry Balzacq, Myriam Dunn Cavelty, *A theory of actor-network for cyber-security*, European Journal of International Security, (2016).

Do, C., Tran, N., Hong, C., Kamhoua, C., Blasch, E., Kwait, K., Blasch, E., Ren, S., Pissinou, N., & Iyengar, S. (2015). Game theory for cyber security and privacy. *ACM Journal*, Vol. NA, No. NA, Article NA.

Graham, S. (1998). The end of geography or the explosion of place? Conceptualizing space, place and information technology. *Progress in Human Geography, 22*, 2, 178, in Thierry Balzacq, Myriam Dunn Cavelty, *A theory of actor-network for cyber-security*, European Journal of International Security, (2016).

Greenleaf, G. (2011). Global data privacy in a networked world. In I. Brown (Ed.), *Research handbook on governance of the Internet*. Cheltenham: Edward Elgar.

Kamhoua, C., Zhao, H., Rodriguez, M., & Kwiat, K. (2016). A game-theoretic approach for testing for hardware Trojans. *IEEE Transactions on Multi-Scale Computing Systems, 2*, 200–209.

Lotrionte, C. (2013). State sovereignty and self-defense in cyberspace: A normative framework for balancing legal rights. *Emory International Law Review, 26*, 825–919.

Margulies, P. (2013). *Sovereignty and cyber attacks: Technology's challenge to the Law of State. Melbourne Law Review, 14*, 496–519.

Chapter 3
Artificial Intelligence and Law

Abstract Artificial Intelligence (AI) is rapidly developing. It is predicted that over the coming decade people will find AI technology in the home, office, business and general community on a large scale. It will pervade nearly every aspect of our lives. The world is seeing the transformation of AI technology being used by governments and the broader community for security. Over the past decade people only have to travel to the major airports around the world and through the central business districts of major cities to find AI surveillance at work.

Today, AI can be found in many devices in our homes that we call "smart" because they operate in a more intelligent way, for example, smart phones, smart watches, robot vacuum cleaners and lawn mowers, self-driving cars, drones, etc. AI is very much used in robotics, technological industry, healthcare (in particular, medical diagnosing and surgery), transportation, military, video games, government and public administration, insurance, finance and economics, audit, advertising, art, amongst many others. Furthermore, it has been incrementally used in the area of law, such as predictive justice and the prediction of judicial decisions.

This Chapter will discuss some of the issues emerging in this area of law and technology. It will demonstrate how there is a lack of a single definition of AI. The Chapter demonstrates that there is a lack of international agreement on what AI constitutes. This Chapter does not examine the international agreements or laws as to whether there has been some agreement or proposal put forward by states to clearly define what is and is not military AI. It demonstrates is how there has been little discussion or debate regarding how AI will meet the cur- rent day controls and protection of data protection [laws].

Moreover, this Chapter highlights how the emerging area of AI is going to challenge individuals across the community, particularly vulnerable groups such as children, those with a disability and elderly along with racial and ethnic groups. These cohorts are only beginning to be captured by AI technology, whereby the use of their personal data is not fully understood. The potential ramifications for bias and discrimination based on sex, ethnicity, religion, amongst others could be enormous. As AI evolves a more comprehensive study will be needed to better understand whether the developers of the technology have been successful in building adequate safeguards into the systems and platforms to protect personal data from illegal collection and use. It will also require confirmation of whether current trade-consumer

R. Walters, M. Novak, *Cyber Security, Artificial Intelligence, Data Protection & the Law*, https://doi.org/10.1007/978-981-16-1665-5_3

practices law is adequate to regulate this at the point of sale of these devices, particularly in relation to protecting personal data.

3.1 Introduction

Artificial intelligence (AI) is no longer confided to imaginary landscapes of science fiction novels or fantasy movies in which robots take over humans, but has become our everyday reality. It is not locked in the labs and factories but very present around us increasingly affecting our practical lives. There are many devices already in our homes that we call "smart" because they operate including iPhone, smart watches, robot vacuum cleaners and lawn mowers, self-driving cars and drones. AI is very much used in robotics, healthcare (in particular, medical diagnosing and surgery), transportation, military, video games, government and public administration, insurance, finance and economics, audit, advertising, art, etc. Furthermore, it has been incrementally used in the area of law.

The notion of AI being a new phenomenon could not be further from the truth. According to Chris Smith et al., AI has been studied for decades and is still one of the most elusive subjects in Computer Science.[1] The term artificial intelligence was first coined by John McCarthy in 1956[2] when he held the first academic conference on the subject. But the journey to understand if machines can truly think began before that. The authors argue that this is partly due to how large and nebulous the subject is. In 1950, Alan Turing wrote a paper on the notion of machines being able to simulate human beings and the ability to do intelligent things, such as play Chess.[3] In this paper Turing proposed a method for evaluating whether machines can think, known as the Turing test. The test, or "Imitation Game" as it was called in the paper, was a simple test that could be used to prove that machines could think.[4] Nearly 80 years on and Themistoklis Tzimas asserts the potential emergence of a personhood—in the sense of autonomous intellect—of a different type and especially through the merging of AI and cyberspace.[5]

However, there is no internationally agreed definition of AI.[6] To date, there is no single definition of AI that has been accepted by all technology practitioners, or

[1] Smith, C., McGuire, B., Huang, T., Yang, G., *The History of Artificial Intelligence*, https://courses.cs.washington.edu/courses/csep590/06au/projects/history-ai.pdf

[2] Moor, J. *Artificial Intelligence Conference: The Next Fifty Years*, American Association for Artificial Intelligence (2006), 87–88.

[3] Ibid, Alan Turing, *Computing Machinery and Intelligence*. Mind 49, (1950), 433–460.

[4] Ibid, the turing test takes a simple pragmatic approach, assuming that a computer that is indistinguishable from an intelligent human actually has shown that machines can think.

[5] Tzimas, T, *Artificial Intelligence as Global Commons and the "International Law Supremacy" Principle*, Advances in Social Science, Education and Humanities Research, Vol 211 (2018).

[6] Walters, R., Coghlan, M, *Data Protection and Artificial Intelligence Law: Europe Australia Singapore - An Actual or Perceived Dichotomy,* American Journal of Science, Engineering and Technology 2019; 4(4): 55–65.

legal practitioners. Walters and Coghlan have identified that some define or otherwise categorize AI broadly as a computerized system exhibiting behavior thought of as requiring intelligence.[7] However, others define AI as a system, capable of rationally solving complex problems or taking appropriate action to achieve its goals in real-world circumstances. The authors trace the beginnings of an emerging definition to 1985, whereby Phillip Jackson, defined AI as the ability of machines to do things that people would say. The phrase sometimes refers to intelligent machines themselves.[8] Therefore, artificial intelligence attempts to emulate the mental steps of human beings. Such mental steps include understanding languages, responding to questions, identifying patterns, solving problems, and learning through experience.[9] Thus, the definition from 1985 falls short of what AI is today. Moreover, the Oxford English Dictionary arguably has taken a very broad approach to defining AI. In other words, artificial intelligence has been defined to mean "the field of study that deals with the capacity of a machine to simulate or surpass intelligent human behaviour".[10] While it is noted that at the international level there has been considerable work to gain agreement in relation to AI being used in, and by the military and motor vehicle automation, it is out of scope of this book to examine these reports of conventions.

Nevertheless, the US has made what appears to be an early move by developing a definition of AI. During the 115th Congress,[11] thirty-nine bills had been introduced that have the phrase "artificial intelligence" in the text. Four of these bills had been enacted into law. Nonetheless, section 238 of the John S. McCain National Defense Authorization Act for Fiscal Year 2019, directs the Department of Defense to undertake several activities regarding AI.[12] Subsection (b) requires the Secretary of Defense to appoint a coordinator who will oversee and direct the activities of the Department "relating to the development and demonstration of artificial intelligence and machine learning." Subsection (g) provides the following definition of AI: "(g) In this section, the term "artificial intelligence" includes:

(1) Any artificial system that performs tasks under varying and unpredictable circumstance without significant human oversight, or that can learn from experience and improve performance when exposed to data sets.
(2) An artificial system developed in computer software, physical hardware, or other context that solves tasks requiring human-like perception, cognition, planning, learning, communication, or physical action.
(3) An artificial system designed to think or act like a human, including cognitive architectures and neural networks.

---

[7] Ibid.

[8] Jackson, P, *Introduction To Artificial Intelligence* 1, Dover Publ'n, Inc., 2d ed. (1974), 192–338.

[9] World Intellectual Property Organization Technology Trends, Artificial Intelligence, https://www.wipo.int/edocs/pubdocs/en/wipo_pub_1055.pdf

[10] Oxford Dictionary 11th Edition 2008.

[11] Law library of Congress, Regulation of Artificial Intelligence in Selected Jurisdictions, January 2019, https://www.loc.gov/law/help/artificial-intelligence/regulation-artificial-intelligence.pdf

[12] Ibid, John S. McCain National Defense Authorization Act for Fiscal Year 2019, Pub. L. 115–232, § 238, 132 Stat. 1658 (2018), https://www.congress.gov/115/bills/hr5515/BILLS-115hr5515enr.pdf

(4) A set of techniques, including machine learning, that is designed to approximate a cognitive task.
(5) An artificial system designed to act rationally, including an intelligent software agent or embodied robot that achieves goals using perception, planning, reasoning, learning, communicating, decision making, and acting.[13]

However, subsection (f) instructs the Secretary of Defense to delineate a definition of the term artificial intelligence for use within the Department no later than one year after the law's enactment. While broad, but at the same time specific, the definition does direct the community generally on what AI constitutes, arguably as technology continues to evolve this definition is likely to change.

Rather than specifically define AI, at this early stage of development, states within the US and other countries have opted to define what an autonomous vehicle constitutes. In other words, states are starting to define AI in specific sectors of society. It is out of scope of this book to examine the different definitions. However, as an example, one only has to look at Singapore. Following an amendment to the Singapore Road Traffic Act in 2017, the legislation now includes a definition of automated vehicle technology. The definition states, 'automated vehicle technology, autonomous motor vehicle, and autonomous system, that an automated vehicle technology means any particular technology that (a) relates to the design, construction or use of autonomous motor vehicles; or (b) otherwise relates to advances in the design or construction of autonomous motor vehicles; autonomous motor vehicle means a motor vehicle equipped wholly or substantially with an autonomous system (also commonly known as a driverless vehicle), and includes a trailer drawn by such a motor vehicle; autonomous system, for a motor vehicle, means a system that enables the operation of the motor vehicle without the active physical control of, or monitoring by, a human operator'.[14]

In December 2018, a High-Level Expert Group on Artificial Intelligence (AI HLEG) from the European Commission, released draft AI Ethics Guidelines. Apart from setting out a framework for designing trustworthy AI, it proposed a broad definition of AI that states:

> Artificial intelligence (AI) refers to systems designed by humans that, given a complex goal, act in the physical or digital world by perceiving their environment, interpreting the collected structured or unstructured data, reasoning on the knowledge derived from this data and deciding the best action(s) to take (according to pre-defined parameters) to achieve the given goal. AI systems can also be designed to learn to adapt their behaviour by analysing how the environment is affected by their previous actions. As a scientific discipline, AI includes several approaches and techniques, such as machine learning (of which deep learning and reinforcement learning are specific examples), machine reasoning (which includes

---

[13] Ibid, FAA Reauthorization Act of 2018, Pub. L. 115–254, § 548, 132 Stat. 3186, https://www.congress.gov/115/billshr302/BILLS-115hr302enr.pdf/

[14] Road Traffic Act (Cap. 276) (Ordinance 26 of 1961, revised Dec. 31, 2004, version in force Aug. 31, 2018), https://sso.agc.gov.sg/Act/RTA1961?ValidDate=20180831&ViewType=Pdf&_=20181012232618. Max Ng & Amira Nabila Budiyano, *New Regulations to Address Automated Vehicle Technology*, LEXOLOGY (Apr. 10, 2017), https://www.lexology.com/library/detail.aspx?g=64a38d35-6b97-48a5-91ff-9a59817ac955, *archived at* https://perma.cc/E8HG-4536. Road Traffic Act (Cap. 276) s 2(1).

planning, scheduling, knowledge representation and reasoning, search, and optimization), and robotics (which includes control, perception, sensors and actuators, as well as the integration of all other techniques into cyber- physical systems).[15]

Most noteworthy, and unlike the definition of personal data, the term artificial intelligence has not gained a formal legal definition in the EU. As noted by Mihalis Kritikos:

> Defining the precise object of regulation in dynamic technological domains is a challenge in itself. Given that AI is still an open-ended notion that refers to a very wide range of products and applications, there is no transnational agreement on a commonly accepted working definition, neither at the technical nor the legal/policy level. As there is no legal and political consensus over what AI is, a plurality of definitions has emerged in Europe and worldwide that are either too inclusive or too sector- specific. This fragmented conceptual landscape may prevent the immediate development of a *lex robotica* and possibly undermine all efforts to create a common legal nomenclature, which is particularly instrumental for the drafting, adoption and effective implementation of binding legal norms. Alternatively, a broad and technology-neutral definition that is based on the fulfilment of a variety of structural criteria, including the level of autonomy and the function, may be a more plausible option.[16]

This poses significant challenges to not only AI, cyber security but also personal data. In our view a definition of AI is unlikely to be settled at the national or supranational level until the courts become involved. Nonetheless, Kritikos goes on to say that the problem of definitional ambiguity is closely associated with the issue of AI's legal classification and the categorization of its various applications. Should AI products and systems be approached under the umbrella of traditional legal categories, or are we simply experiencing the gradual creation of an entirely new domain of critical legal thinking that may trigger a shift from the traditional notion of code as law to a novel conceptualization of law as code.[17] Notwithstanding the above, the EU has yet to fully adopt a standard definition of AI into its legal framework and at the time of writing this book there had been no decisions by the Court of Justice of European Union or European Court of Human Rights that had attempted or actually defined AI. Thus, the fluid legal environment of AI is no doubt going to challenge legal practitioners and the judiciary. In the same way that the definition of personal data is fragmented, it appears that the definition of AI will head in the same direction. The problem is that jurisdictions and nation states will continue to have their own view on what AI constitutes and the level of regulation it requires. Thus, there is a need for an agreed level of legal harmonization in this area of the law. Apart from the regulatory challenges, a further complicating issue is the nature and speed of change in technology from health, law, finance, banking, agriculture and food production, amongst others.

---

[15] AI HLEG, *A Definition of AI: Main Capabilities and Scientific Disciplines* (2018), https://ec.europa.eu/newsroom/dae/document.cfm?doc_id=56341

[16] Kritikos, M, *European Parliamentary Research Service Scientific Foresight Unit* (STOA) PE 634.427—March 2019, https://www.europarl.europa.eu/at-your-service/files/be-heard/religious-and-non-confessional-dialogue/events/en-20190319-artificial-intelligence-ante-portas.pdf

[17] Ibid.

3.2 Artificial Intelligence and Law

3.2.1 Artificial Intelligence Facilitating Law

Similar to other areas of an individual's life and social interaction, it is expected that various AI tools will bring great benefits also in the area of law and legal procedures by reducing the costs of legal proceedings and enhancing their coherence at least. For instance, today there are automatic language translation devices and applications that can be downloaded onto an iPhone. AI algorithms can provide faster and easier data processing, prediction of legal decisions, and automation of legal decision-making. It could contribute to better information analysis, and also more precise and eventually just decision-making. Below there are examples of how AI has been used to facilitate law and legal business.

AI has begun to increase the possibilities across the legal profession and the law,[18] through the development of analytical tools.[19] One of the most identified projects has been the introduction of *Ravel Law*, which analyses judicial decisions and profiles judges on the basis of previous court decisions.[20] Such an analytical tool, was taken over by *Lexis Nexis*, which today deals with court and judge profiling. It also is able to anticipate a law firm's activities. These tools have developed to enable a judge's probable decisions to be predicted, with a level of accuracy. The tools follow rules, cases, precedents, specific language and arguments that the judge typically uses to arrive at their decision/judgment. Under this type of framework, it is also possible is to analyse arguments of other judges from other courts which influenced the decision-making and argumentation by the judge. Furthermore, a project of a British university has produced a programme to foresee decisions by the European Court of Human Rights with 75% reliability.[21]

Moreover, in the area of law there already exist decision-making or consulting tools such as *Lexis Answers* in the frame of *Lexis Answer Card,* where legal questions are asked in the natural language and (machine generated) replies are provided in return in the form of a best legal solution. On the basis of such technology the *Ross (Intelligence)* project was developed,[22] which was based on IBM Watson

[18] Williams, K., Facciola, J. M., McCann, P., Catanzaro, V. M., (2017), *The Legal Technology Guidebook.* Springer.

[19] Conrad, J.G., Branting, L., K., (2018) Introduction to the Special Issue on Legal Text Analytics. *Artificial Intelligence and Law,* 26, 99–102.

[20] O'Grady, J. P., (2018) *Dewey B Strategic—2017 Blogazine: Risk, Value, Strategy, Innovation, Knowledge and the Legal Profession.* Year of the Book Press.

[21] Aletras, N., Tsarapatsanis, D., Preoţiuc-Pietro, D. and Lampos, V., Predicting judicial decisions of the European Court of Human Rights: A natural language processing perspective. *PeerJ Computer Science*, (2016), 93.

[22] Riskin, G, *Ross Intelligence Update: How IBM Watson App Helps US Lawyers with Legal Research.* Law Firm Technology (2017).

technology.[23] It deals with trying to find the best possible answer on the basis of searching within natural language. In addition, the 2015 *Robot DoNotPay* project should be mentioned,[24] which was designed to generate appeals against incorrectly calculated parking fees.

To our knowledge not one of the above mentioned projects has proceeded to the area of decision-making itself by judges and courts. This in and of itself, continues to be a significant challenge concerning the ruling on legal matters. Thus, further research in this area is needed. The problem of AI in law is inseparably connected with legal argumentation. It is impossible to understand one without the other. One of the first attempts in that area was TAXMAN, a programme which had analysed computationally majority and minority opinions in a known legal case[25]. Since then, quite a few experts in AI and the law have dealt with legal argumentation either from a formal[26] or empirical aspect.[27] AI interests those legal argumentation experts who focus mostly on formal logical decision-making and justification in law.[28] Tax has been an area of relative ease to standardise the approach of what and how people pay tax no matter what country they reside. It is an area that by and large where similar laws apply, but the rates of tax differ.

AI is relevant for law especially with respect to deciding "clear" legal cases such as minor to major offences. Such kind of decision-making in law is similar to monotonic (technical) deciding that is close to automatism and is most appropriate for computer science to deal with. One needs to come close to formal logic or the so-called internal phase of legal inferring, as it is named in legal argumentation theory.[29] Therefore, legal theory calls such cases simple, easy or clear. In other words, typical cases include, deciding on the fulfilment of procedural requirements: whether an appeal was submitted in 15 days as required, a specific court has jurisdiction, or whether all available legal remedies have been exhausted. What is important for the use of AI is that cases have the least meanings possible. Automatic decisions (at least for some time) are not expected to be introduced in the so-called hard or unclear cases, in the framework of which legal norms have multiple meanings and whose interpretation is highly creative.

The foundation of legal decision-making is deductive inference based on the major premise (legal norm) and the minor premise (facts). The decision-maker must

---

[23] Ferrucci, D., Levas, A., Bagchi, S., Gondek, D., Mueller, E T, (2013) *Watson: Beyond Jeopardy*, Artificial Intelligence. 199: 93–105.

[24] Livni, E, *The world's first robot lawyer isn't a damn lawyer*. Quartz, 2017, https://qz.com/1028627/motion-to-dismiss-claims-the-worlds-first-robot-lawyer-is-a-damn-lawyer-by-a-damn-lawyer/

[25] McCarty, L. T, (1976) *Reflection on TAXMAN: an experiment in artificial intelligence and legal reasoning. Harvard Law Review*: 90: 837.

[26] Prakken, H., Sartor, G, (2015) *Law and logic: a review from an argumentative perspective*. Artificial Intelligence, vol. 227, 214–245.

[27] Bench-Capon, T, (2017) *Hypo'e legacy: introduction to the virtual special issue*. Artificial Intelligence and Law: 25:1–46.

[28] Feteris, E, (2017) *Fundamentals of Legal Argumentation*. Springer, 33–41.

[29] Alexy, R, (1989) *A Theory of Legal Argumentation*. Oxford University Press.

recognise that the facts of a legal case fall within a certain legal norm. Firstly, the more, the legal norm explicit, the greatest possibility for precise recognition of the facts. Secondly, the more is the language of the norm 'strict,' as it is sometimes termed in general legal theory, the greater possibilities for successful application of an automated system. Thirdly, legal cases that are grounded on numerical measurements (radar detection), which are the strictest dispositions in any legal system, promise successful results. However, legal decision-making such a numerical dimension will only be one type of a norm to be applied.

Central to this proposition is that, AI systems are routinely said to operate autonomously, exposing gaps in regulatory regimes that assume the centrality of human actors. Yet surprisingly, as noted by Simon Chesterman, little attention is given to precisely what is meant by "autonomy" and its relationship to those gaps. A key feature of modern AI is the ability to operate without human intervention. It is commonly said that such systems operate autonomously.

An example where a court has had to decide the extent of decision making undertaken is as recently as 2019 in Singapore. While this issue largely focused on software to make decisions regarding trades, it provides an example of where the courts, particularly, common law courts are likely to go where decision making has been autotomized. Arguably, this has direct and indirect impact to personal data. In *Quoine and B2C2*, used software programs that executed trades involving the cryptocurrencies Bitcoin and Ethereum, with prices set according to external market information. The case focused on seven trades that were made when a defect in Quoine's software saw it execute trades worth approximately $12m at 250 times the prevailing exchange rate.[30] Quoine claimed that this was a mistake and attempted to reverse the trades, reclaiming its losses. B2C2 argued that the reversal of the orders was a breach of contract, while Quoine argued that the contract was void or voidable, relying on the doctrine of unilateral mistake. At common law, a unilateral mistake can void a contract if the other party knows of the mistake.[31] If it cannot be proven that the other party actually knew about the mistake, but it can be shown that he or she should have, the contract may be voidable under equity. What became crucial in this case was the judge's finding that the computer programs in question were incapable of "knowing" anything:

> The algorithmic programmes in the present case are deterministic, they do and only do what they have been programmed to do. They have no mind of their own. They operate when called upon to do so in the pre-ordained manner. They do not know why they are doing something or what the external events are that cause them to operate in the way that they do. As a result, the question of knowledge rested with the original programmer of B2C2's software, who could not have known about Quoine's subsequent mistake.[32]

Moreover, the judge viewed the software as carrying out actions that could have been carried out by a human and that it was necessary to look at the intention and

---

[30] *B2C2 Ltd. v. Quoine Pte. Ltd.* [2019] SGHC(I) 3 (2019).

[31] Ibid.

[32] Ibid.

knowledge of the operator or controller of the machine to determine the intention and knowledge of the machine. In this case, the programmer, Mr. Tseung, believed that the computer would only force-close in circumstances that would have led to a margin call if everything was operating properly, hence there was no "mistake". The decision was upheld on appeal, with the majority emphasizing that the deterministic nature of the algorithms was central to its analysis.[33] Nonetheless, the regulatory response to such dates back to 1978, France adopted a law that prohibited administrative and private decisions based solely on automatic processing of data describing the "profile or personality" of an individual.

Though similar laws were adopted in Portugal and Spain, these remained outliers until the 1995 Data Protection Directive. That required EU member states to grant individuals the right not to be subject to decisions based solely on automated processing of data evaluating them in areas such as "performance at work, creditworthiness, reliability and conduct. Such processing was permissible only if it was part of a contractual relationship requested by the individual or if there were suitable measures to safeguard legitimate interests, such as arrangements allowing the individual "to put his [sic] point of view." An additional exception allowed for processing authorized by a law that also included measures to safeguard the individual's legitimate interests.[34]

Nonetheless, well before the above mention court decision, the 2016 General Data Protection Regulation (GDPR)[35] expanded both the possibilities for automated processing as well as the protections available. In addition to contractual arrangements, explicit consent can now be a basis for automated processing. Either basis, however, requires that safeguarding of interests goes beyond an opportunity to "put [one's] view" and includes the right to obtain "human intervention" to contest the decision.[36] However, the question arises does the current definition and accompanying regulatory controls advanced enough to protect personal data that is captured and used from smart home and other personal automated devices? It is out of scope to discuss the EU and its legal framework in this book. This is an area of further study. Yet, it is argued that there is additional work required for the

[33] *Quoine Pte. Ltd. v. B2C2 Ltd.*, [2020] SGCA(I) 2 (2020), at 97–128.

[34] Chesterman, S, (2019) *Artificial Intelligence and the Problem of Autonomy,* Notre Dame Journal on Emerging Technologies, 211–248.

[35] Regulation 2016/679 of the European Parliament and of the Council of 27 April 2016 on the Protection of Natural Persons with regard to the Processing of Personal Data and on the Free Movement of Such Data and Repealing Directive 95/46/EC (General Data Protection Act), 2016 O.J. (L 119) 1, 46. Recital 71 to the GDPR provides examples such as automatic refusal of an online credit application or e-recruiting practices without human intervention. Certain forms of sensitive personal data cannot be the basis for automated processing, unless it is necessary for reasons of "substantial public interest" or if the individual has given explicit consent. See also, id. at 38 (prohibiting the use of "personal data revealing racial or ethnic origin, political opinions, religious or philosophical beliefs, or trade union membership, and the processing of genetic data, biometric data for the purpose of uniquely identifying a natural person, data concerning health or data concerning a natural person's sex life or sexual orientation").

[36] Ibid.

jurisdictions compared in this book. What is crucial is that conditions are ensured for recognizing the text between legal norms (including applicable case law and commentaries) and the facts in the mentioned forms. What is crucial is that a sufficient level of flexibility or recognition of meaning is ensured. Today natural language techniques based on deep neural networks are capable of selecting relevant information from free texts very efficiently and thereby ensure that phase to become successful.

The above-mentioned projects predominantly focused on the work of attorneys and insurance companies. They were mostly successful in the United States, Canada, Western Europe, and the Netherlands. The most developed area of intersection between law and AI is definitely what is called predictive justice, by AI algorithms, on the basis of big data (in the form of all relevant case law) examined how certain courts or even specific judges would decide in essentially similar cases to those already decided by them. What is also a fast-developing area in the intersection between law and AI is "smart contracts" based on blockchain technology.

On the backdrop of the above, there have also been attempts by the judiciary to include this technology to help facilitate decision making within the court system. Thus, a robot judge in the US helped the courts to decide whether the suspect within a preliminary criminal procedure was to be detained or bailed.[37] However, the available information show that courts are still reluctant to use AI for judicial decision-making. For example, in Slovenia there is some use of ICT in the judiciary but still very far from AI. They mainly deal with the digitalization of the land register, e-files, e-notary public, IT as a management tool, and enforcement on the basis of a credible document (such as invoice) as a semi-automatic system. Similar systems have been developed in many other countries.

Accordingly, we think that there is a great potential for projects to develop new directions in the cross-section of AI and law. Development of AI will definitely lead to more quality legal decisions as application software take over in easy legal cases (with human supervision certainly), which is an opportunity for professionals to focus more on unclear cases.

3.2.2 Law to Regulate Artificial Intelligence

One of the functions of law is to prevent and resolve disputes. There could be a number of types of disputes with respect to AI that call for legal regulation of such. For example, there could be disputes over intellectual property rights concerning AI algorithms. On the one side, there could be disputes over who holds moral rights to their invention, and how material rights to invention are to be transferred to another person. Therefore, the dispute is likely to include contract, copy right, trade mark,

[37] Kleinberg, J., Lakkaraju, H., Leskovec, J., Ludwig, J., Mullainathan, S, (2018) *Human Decisions and Machine Predictions.* The Quarterly Journal of Economics 133: 237–293.

and intellectual property rights. How AI reconciles between these area is far from settled.

Moreover, a need for legal regulation occurs if there appear certain negative consequences from the utilization of AI to society or individuals. If AI is excellent at processing of big data in minutes or hours that would take a human weeks or months, the consequences of collecting and using the wrong data is real, particularly personal data. Thus, the question arises, does this potential new way of analyzing data pose any risks?

As it is the case with every major scientific invention or technical development in human history, such as, dynamite, nuclear power, new drugs, cloning, along with their important benefits, they also bring challenges, risks, and ethical dilemmas to society. Thus, in order to avoid social and individual risks, societies respond by regulating new inventions to prevent their detrimental consequences. Globally we have different legal responses to them, based on social agreements reached in specific societies, which are subject to cultural backgrounds. For example, the Safe City project, in which facial recognition technology is allegedly used for greater protection of city population enjoys a quite welcome in China, as they assume that it is good for them by being easier for state authorities to find perpetrators of crime. On contrary, when the project was launched in Belgrade, Serbia, many inhabitants have taken it as too intrusive on their fundamental rights. We can only speculate how fierce a resistance would come from local population in Western countries, in which individualism as a social value is even more integrated in people than it is in Serbia, if such a measure/project is introduced.

The burgeoning development and role of AI is multilayered and has been viewed as a threat along with providing a solution to many current day issues. It will be installed with the full knowledge of individual or be out of view to the unwitting eye. Ryan Goosen *et al.,* who in referring to the New York time report in May 2018, note that researchers in the US and China had successfully commanded artificial intelligence (AI) systems developed by Amazon, Apple, and Google to do things such as dial phones and open websites—without the knowledge of the AI systems' users.[38] The authors assert that it is a short step to more nefarious commands, such as unlocking doors and transferring money. In referring to the recent additions to the market for consumer use such as Alexa, Siri, and Google Assistant, they note that these products may be the most widely used AI programs in operation, they are hardly the only ones. However, they rightly point out that:

> It's not hard to imagine cyber-thieves targeting a financial institution's AI-controlled customer recognition software or a shady competitor attacking another company's AI pricing algorithm. In fact, more than 90% of cybersecurity professionals in the US and Japan expect attackers to use AI against the companies they work for, according to a survey by cybersecurity firm Webroot.[39]

---

[38] Goosen, R., Rontojannis, A., Deutscher, S., Rogg, J., Bohmayr, W., Mkrtchain, D, *Artificial Intelligence Is a Threat to Cybersecurity. It's Also a Solution*, 2018, https://www.bcg.com/publications/2018/artificial-intelligence-threat-cybersecurity-solution.aspx

[39] Ibid.

The resulting effect has seen individuals that have high levels of organizational responsibility for internal and external security, AI presents two types of risk that change the nature of their jobs.[40] The first is that criminals, bad state actors, unscrupulous competitors, and inside threats will manipulate their companies' fledgling AI programs. The second risk is that attackers will use AI in a variety of ways to exploit vulnerabilities in their victims' defences. Companies are in a cybersecurity arms race.[41] The authors go on to say how AI systems are generally empowered to make deductions and decisions in an automated way without day-to-day human involvement. They can be compromised, and that can go undetected for a long time. Second, the reasons that a machine-learning or AI program makes particular deductions and decisions are not always immediately clear to overseers. The underlying decision-making models and data are not necessarily transparent or quickly interpretable, even though there is significant effort currently underway to improve the transparency of such tools. This means that even if a violation is detected, its purpose can remain opaque. As more machine-learning or AI systems are connected to, or placed in control over, physical systems, the risk of serious consequences—including injury and death—from malevolent interference rises.[42]

Nonetheless, and even with the impending threats associated with the move towards more AI technology and systems, there is a silver lining that, could result in solutions and benefits. However, before exploring what some of the benefits might be, if the threats faced by AI impinge on cyber security and find their way into health, education and other government services such as defence and finance, then, personal data is and will be at risk. There are numerous examples over the past 2 years in Australia, US, EU, Singapore and many other countries where personal data has been breached or stolen from cyber security incursions. However, it has not been fully disclosed whether those incursions were as a result of the use of AI or general hacking and misuse. In some cases, government have reported such incidents when their systems have been hacked. On the backdrop of the above Goosen *et al.* assert that AI enhances existing detection and response capabilities but also enables new abilities in preventative defence. Companies can also streamline and improve the security operating model by reducing time-consuming and complex manual inspection and intervention processes and redirecting human efforts to supervisory and problem-solving tasks. They note that, in referring to AI cybersecurity firm Darktrace, it was highlighted how machine-learning technology identified 63,500 previously unknown threats in more than 5,000 networks. They also note that AI can reduce the workload for cybersecurity analysts by helping to prioritize the risk areas for attention and intelligently automating the manual tasks they typically perform (such as searching through log files for signs of compromises), thus redirecting human efforts toward higher-value activities.[43] AI can facilitate

[40] Ibid.

[41] Ibid.

[42] Ibid.

[43] Ibid.

intelligent responses to attacks, either outside or inside the perimeter, based on shared knowledge and learning.[44] Today we have technology to deploy semiautonomous, intelligent lures or "traps" that create a duplicate of the environment to be infiltrated to make attackers believe they are on the intended path and then use the deceit to identify the culprit.[45] Therefore, what does all this mean for personal data. Will AI systems and technology enhance and strengthen its protection? Or will it be made even more vulnerable to individuals and entities over the Internet?

Arguably, this is an area that is not fully settled. However, according to Remesh Tamachandran,[46] current day technology has come a long way with end-point security which has been is taken to the next level as AI, whereby it can quickly detect and block attacks while performing extensive behavioral analysis.[47] It can automatically block all kinds of suspicious actions before they get executed, and analyse unauthorized data transactions. He further points out how, AI-driven data privacy and protection can largely help enterprises to identify all sensitive data and track and control data movement within and outside the enterprise.[48] AI with ML will play a huge role in analysing and monitoring the risks involved for all sensitive data. AI-driven technology can help in the protection and monitoring of personal data to make sure that the organization is always in compliance with privacy standards.[49] Thus, technology has come a long way to reconcile the issues of protecting personal data online, however, it may never be settled that a single piece of technology, platform or system can 100% safeguard against illegal intrusions and the collection of personal data.[50] As technology advances these systems that purport to protect personal data, may in fact always be behind those individuals and entities that are highly sophisticated and can breach most if not all systems and platforms.

In December 2019, the Australian Human Right Commission (AHC) released a Discussion Paper in relation to Human Rights and Technology.[51] The AHC aim to identify any problematic gaps in the law, and propose targeted reform. For example, the use of facial recognition warrants a regulatory response that addresses legitimate community concern about people's privacy and other rights. Government should

---

[44] Ibid.

[45] Ibid.

[46] Tamachandran, R, *How Artificial Intelligence Is Countering Data Protection Challenges Facing Organizations: AI technology can help enterprises in endpoint security, data privacy and against phishing, malware and ransomware attacks.* https://www.entrepreneur.com/article/343267

[47] Ibid, Endpoint technology also monitors sandboxes and report any kind of suspicious activity in your app data. In the event of a security attack, AI combined with ML can help in quickly rolling back to the previously working and secure endpoint. Quickly analyse and isolate any suspicious endpoints and data processes.

[48] Ibid.

[49] Ibid.

[50] Ibid.

[51] Human rights Commission, Australia, Human Rights and Technology: Discussion Paper, December 2019, https://www.humanrights.gov.au/our-work/rights-and-freedoms/publications/human-rights-and-technology-discussion-paper-2019

lead the way. The Discussion Paper proposes strengthening the accountability protections for how it uses AI to make decisions. The paper highlights major concerns in relation to privacy. It points out that:

> The potential human rights impact is enormous and unprecedented. AI, for example, can have far-reaching and irreversible consequences for how we protect privacy, how we combat discrimination and how we deliver health care— to name only three areas.[52]

They go onto say that:

> The ease of collecting and using personal information through new technologies such as facial recognition can limit the right to privacy. Personal data can flow easily and quickly, across national and other borders. This can make privacy regulation and enforcement more difficult. It can be difficult to 'correct' or remove personal information once communicated. The ease of communicating and distorting personal information (e.g., through 'deep fakes') can lead to reputational damage and other harms.[53]

More problematic and where AI technology will become pervasive and used across society by governments and the private sector, they point out that the human rights engaged by facial recognition technology will differ depending on the context in which it is deployed. For instance, biometric data that is collected from an individual in one setting and for one purpose may be collected and merged with personal data from other surveillance mechanisms such as drone footage, satellite imagery and encrypted communications. This type of surveillance will affect the right to privacy, and may engage other rights such as the right to non-discrimination and the right to liberty. The AHC go on to highlight that from a human rights perspective personal information (data) is defined under data protection or privacy law when:

> Merged data of this kind may be used to draw inferences about an individual which are shared with third parties, without any meaningful consent from the affected individual. Sensitive personal information may be extracted or inferred from biometric identifiers, including in relation to the person's age, race, sex and health. This can be used to undertake 'profiling' activity, where intrusive action is undertaken by reference to people's age, race, sex or other characteristics. Examples of this kind of profiling, based on race, have emerged in other jurisdictions. This engages the right to non-discrimination or equality. Depending on the context in which the technology is deployed, it is also likely to engage other human rights as well. For example, if such technology is used for racial profiling in police identity and other checks, this could also limit rights such as equality before the law.[54]

Thus, the implications can be far reaching and not only impinge on people's privacy rights but broader rights such as association and free speech. However, this must be viewed in the context of how states view and apply human rights in general. For instance, countries such as Singapore and China view privacy (as a human right) over the Internet very differently to that of Australia and other countries. For Australia, and in the context of new and emerging technologies, the traditional lines

---

[52] Ibid.

[53] Ibid.

[54] Ibid.

between public and private accountability are becoming increasingly difficult to navigate. Private companies are developing new forms of technology that can have significant positive and negative human rights impacts. Companies outside the technology sector, and even governments, are integrating these new developments into their products and services.[55] Many of these new technologies rely on personal information, with large databases of personal information now held outside government, including a small number of unprecedentedly large holdings. The challenge of assigning accountability, liability and responsibility for human rights protection in this context was identified by several stakeholders. One answer to this challenge lies in the evolution of the international framework in business and human rights.[56] Again, this is the position Australia and other jurisdictions are considering where the answers lie in reconciling the gap between the use and application of this technology and the law. Yet, this is only one element, because the economic imperatives from the use of this technology, could outweigh any right(s) protections. It is out of scope of this book to examine what other states are doing in developing strategies to manage AI.

AI is increasingly being considered in government service delivery, including tools to detect children at risk of maltreatment in order to target protection interventions. This can engage the right to privacy, the right to work, the right to a family life and a number of children's rights, among others.[57] This is problematic because the same AI technology used in the home can capture and use children's personal data. Highlighting the problems for regulators and society in general the AHC detail a scenario that can easily play out in the health sector. They assert that the:

> potential for AI to improve health care, including through more accurate and speedy diagnosis, treatment and management of diseases, and in planning and resource allocation in the health sector. However, some stakeholders urged better regulatory oversight to promote ethical and accountable clinical practice in areas where AI research has been focused, such as radiology. There is also potential for human rights to be breached in this context. Many applications of AI will make use of health data in ways that may be unknown at the point of collection. Several stakeholders drew attention to how health data, including genetic data, can be used to discriminate unlawfully. Submissions also raised concerns about the My Health Record system and lack of safeguards against inappropriate access to sensitive personal information.[58]

More pervasively, it is this health data that is defined by many countries data protection and privacy laws, and constitutes general or sensitive personal data. In other words, when this data is classified or defined as sensitive data, it is afforded a higher level of control and protection. To reconcile these issues, amongst others the AHC believe that more needs to be done to protect this data through regulation, and be guided by Australia's obligations under international law to protect human

---

[55] Ibid.

[56] Ibid.

[57] Ibid.

[58] Ibid.

rights.[59] However, this is not going to work for other countries and jurisdictions, because of their economic and social policies. The law should be clear and enforceable. The broader regulatory framework should contain effective remedies and enforcement mechanisms. Australia's law-makers should fill any gaps necessary to achieve these regulatory aims.[60]

Co-regulation and self-regulation should support human rights, ethical decision making. The law cannot, and should not, address every social implication of new and emerging technologies. It can't. Good co and self-regulation—through professional codes, design guidelines and impact assessments—can promote the making of sound, human rights compliant decisions by all stakeholders.[61] Finally, under the Australian example, the AHC are of the view that the OECD AI Principles,[62] for example, state that "AI systems should be designed in a way that respects the rule of law, human rights, democratic values and diversity".[63] This has also been, in part, reinforced by DiploFoundation, who on behalf of the Ministry of Foreign Affairs, Finland make the point that when talking about the human rights implications of AI, we are in a lot of ways implicitly referring to the unprecedented need for data when it comes to building AI.[64] They go onto to say generally speaking, data in all its forms (big data, open data, personal data, sensitive data) is a critical juncture in understanding human rights with regard to AI.[65] Data can enable the exercise and enjoyment of human rights in new and exciting ways. At the same time, there are trails of data being left behind (e.g. location data, websites visited) which have functional and commercial value for AI models by reinforcing their learning potential.[66] More importantly they highlight how:

> The autonomy of AI, the quality of the training data it uses, and the opaque nature of the algorithms employed can lead to inadvertent interferences with human rights, most notably the prohibition of discrimination linked with the right to privacy, the right to employment, the right to liberty and security, the right to a fair trial, and the right to freedom of expression and information. There is concern that AI can result in unintended consequences for human rights and even has the propensity to harm. Therefore, the quality of data used by AI models is crucial. AI systems, trained on data which replicates existing racial and gender stereotypes, tend to amplify and perpetuate discriminatory practices which can interfere with the exercise and enjoyment of other human rights. Consider also the propensity to collect, aggregate, de-anonymise, and repurpose data (with a loss of the original context for its

[59] Ibid.

[60] Ibid.

[61] Ibid.

[62] Organization for Economic Cooperation and Development [OECD], The OECD Principles on AI (9 June 2019) https://www.oecd.org/going-digital/ai/principles/

[63] Human rights Commission, Australia, Human Rights and Technology: Discussion Paper, December 2019, https://www.humanrights.gov.au/our-work/rights-and-freedoms/publications/human-rights-and-technology-discussion-paper-2019

[64] Mapping the challenges and opportunities of artificial intelligence for the conductof diplomacy, DiploFoundation Ministry of Foreign Affairs Finland, https://www.diplomacy.edu/AI-diplo-report

[65] Ibid.

[66] Ibid.

collection) from an increasing array of data from different objects in the home and on the body (such as personal home assistants and fitness trackers), from which inferences can be drawn.[67]

There is a growing body of evidence that many in society could be impacted and their personal data compromised from the use of AI. At this stage more research and further studies are needed to fully understand what AI technology will be available and to whom, and used by. For instance, children and people with disabilities are likely to use different AI technology to that of healthy adults, particularly in the home. This is problematic, particularly for these two cohorts. The wider implications of this technology could result in segregation and discrimination (creating a bias and class across the community). The technology used wrongly for racial, religious and ethnic purposes, could have significant implications for multicultural societies. However, amongst all the problems and concerns, the economic and social benefits of AI are beginning to be seen, particularly in fighting crime and the medical sector. These benefits will only grow as the technology advances. It is in our view the smart technology that will be used in the home, raises possibly the highest level of concern. The AI technologies used in smart home appliances could be easily breached disclosing highly confidential information about children and the family that has, to date, been otherwise confidential, unless the family make it public. Moreover, some states will need to grapple with finding a balance between innovation, economic and social benefits, with a view to protecting rights, particularly personal data. Therefore, this book calls on states to find that balance. No matter what country is being discussed the challenges faced by governments and regulators will be formidable. To date, as has been the case with data protection laws, it is fragmented, although there are elements of these laws that are, in part, harmonized. This can be seen in the early stages of the development of law and AI.

3.2.3 Further Challenges for Law and Artificial Intelligence

Hildebrandt, Tzimas believes that AI might lead to the breach of the relationship between legal personhood—in the sense of rights and obligations—and sovereignty.[68] He goes onto say that what has been historically a fundamental part of sovereignty and thus of the national legal systems capacities, is territoriality. The latter comprehends as self- obvious the fact that every human being as well as any artificial entity which fulfils certain capacities exist in a certain part of a physical space which belongs to a state. Tzimas further points out the merging of AI and cyberspace on the contrary will potentially lead to entities which will have the capacities of intellect personhood, without any legal attachment to physical space and thus to

[67] Ibid.

[68] Hildebrandt, M, (2013) *"Extraterritorial Jurisdiction to Enforce in Cyberspace?* Bodin, Schmitt, Grotius in Cyberspace?" *Toronto Law Journal* 63: 196–224.

states. Therefore, entities possessing actual personhood will be out of reach of the legal authority of the state. This is why there is a need for regulation of potential legal personhood. To achieve this another legal system is likely to emerge. It is argued that it becomes the role of international law.[69] He is also of the view that, under an international framework a treaty would be a way to establish the policy and legal norms to regulate AI. Doing so would allow, as Tzimas puts it, to establish a legal characterization of the different levels of AI development, in the context of which the argument about legal commons or "*res communis*" is presented. However, the dichotomy with this position is, as Tzimas highlights, how governments and business sector see AI as innovative technology or as the sum of different technological advances; eventually as "res".[70] This is after all why development of AI technology until now is considered as the privilege of the private technological sector that has little—if any—public regulation.[71]

Central to this position is that, AI could emerge as new types of intellectual personhood and therefore they should be attributed a type of legal personhood. In other words, if they are both to be comprehended correctly and to avoid unfair treatment, towards humans as well.[72] In taking the extreme end of this proposition would be states asserting their sovereign right to develop AI within robots that are used in general policing and military to quell social unrest or used in war and conflict between states. More alarming, would be if states were to replace humans with robots and use them to take over other nations, and implement population controls on religious, ethnic and racial grounds. While it is acknowledged that this is a far-fetched scenario, AI in the wrong hands could have disastrous results for humanity in general. This possible scenario alone calls for immediate action and strong international regulation. It would need to be considered in light of the cyber security risks, and the use of personal data to identify individuals. For instance, a robot programmed by facial and voice recognition that is used for the above purposes.

Notwithstanding the above, a further challenge has arisen whereby AI will be used to allow state actors to exert their sovereign over their citizens with ease, and that of other states. Thomas Peter argues that AI technologies will enable high levels of social control.[73] He believes governments will be able selectively to censor topics and behaviours to allow information for economically productive activities to flow freely, while curbing political discussions. For instance, China's so-called Great Firewall provides an early demonstration of this kind of selective censorship. Selective censorship is not limited to China, it has emerged in Western countries with great haste following the Christchurch massacre where a gunman live streamed

[69] Ibid.

[70] Ibid.

[71] Ibid.

[72] Ibid.

[73] Peters, T, *How Artificial Intelligence Will Reshape the Global Order, The Coming Competition Between Digital Authoritarianism and Liberal Democracy*, https://webcache.googleusercontent.com/search?q=cache:P1-7JLptTAMJ:https://www.foreignaffairs.com/articles/world/2018-07-10/how-artificial-intelligence-will-reshape-global-order+&cd=2&hl=en&ct=clnk&gl=au

the shooting of 51 people.[74] Since then both the Australian and New Zealand governments have changed the law to impose harsher penalties on the companies that allow for live streaming and displaying of sensitive security and violent material through online applications such as the iPhone, which many do have AI technology. The disclosure of this material while not specifically providing personal data (in its raw sense), it did identify some people—in person. The security of this information once disclosed over the Internet could easily be obtained by the boarder public, even though it was taken down by internet providers. In response, at the 2019, G7 Leaders meeting in France, the Australian Prime Minister on behalf the New Zealand Prime Minister urged to push countries further on taking action against terrorist and violent extremist material on social media.[75] However, this form of social control is not new. It has been happening within and outside states since the humble radio and television were invented and made available on the market.

In a practical example, even the technology industry itself has advised that 'the growth of AI technologies in our homes have been increasing exponentially in the past few years, and with a large number of the United Kingdom workforce embracing the pandemic-imposed working-from-home culture, for many of us our homes and have become our office'.[76] Thus, the pandemic that has seen coronavirus cross international borders at a rapid rate. Moreover, Peter Wright and Max Harris summarise the following as a way, and 'the need for individuals to be aware of what simple devices can do, is collecting and using personal data'.[77] Arguably, this is only the beginning, and there will be further developments, as technology evolves and changes.

Know Your Devices
Smart speakers, such as Amazon Alexa and Google Home, are becoming mainstream in homes around the country. Many owners of smart speakers are by now aware that these devices are always "listening" for their "wake word"—which enables the device to listen to user queries and commands. The reality is that smart speakers are most likely not the only technology in your home which are "listening" for a "wake word"—mobile devices, tablets and computers also often have built-in virtual assistants, and it is becoming increasingly common for other devices (for example, TVs) to integrate virtual assistants too. You should become familiar with the smart tech in your home.

[74] Ibid.

[75] The Guardian, G7: Scott Morrison to push for action against online terrorist content, (2019) https://www.theguardian.com/australia-news/2019/aug/25/g7-scott-morrison-to-push-for-action-against-online-terrorist-content

[76] Peter Wright, Max Harris, *AI in the home, smart devices do's and don'ts*, Compare the Cloud, 2020, https://www.comparethecloud.net/articles/ai-in-the-home-smart-devices-dos-and-donts/

[77] Ibid.

Mute Voice-Input
A smart speaker may inadvertently start recording confidential conversations if it hears its wake command, and therefore ensuring that voice-input is muted can be effective in preventing this. However, in line with our recommendation above about getting to know your devices, remember it is not only smart speakers which may constantly be in "listening" mode. If you are having confidential conversations—analyse whether it would be best practice to mute voice-input on each of these devices.

Wear Headsets.
It might not always be practical for you to mute voice-input on all of your devices. Consider whether there are other ways to prevent data from being heard, and potentially recorded, by smart devices. For example, wearing a headset on your calls may result in only your voice being heard by your devices, thereby minimising the amount of data which would be recorded—it might even have the added benefit of clearer audio! Change Your "Wake Word" Some smart speakers allow you to change the "wake word." If you are finding that your device is constantly "waking" unintentionally, think about changing the wake word to something that is less likely to be used in every-day life.

Know Your Suppliers
Many, if not all, of the large tech companies producing smart speakers will use state-of-the-art technology to protect any data they collect—but even the best security systems can be vulnerable to rogue attacks. There are also a number of start-up companies which are developing exciting tech to be used in the home. Whatever company you are purchasing your smart tech from, you should ensure you know and trust them and understand their data policies. Tech companies should all have readily available privacy policies which will explain how your data will be used. Although these can be relatively lengthy documents, most should be written in a way which is easy-to-follow and if you are concerned by what data a company may store and how they may use your data, this can be a good place to start. If you are an employer, consider how you can assist your employees develop sensible working practices at home which will prevent the unintentional recording of data by third-parties.

Source: Peter Wright and Max Haaris[78]

A central response to the above, is whether the current regulatory framework and response is adequate to ensure individuals personal data is protected. Problematic too, is whether an organisation can, in part use the data captured to monitor employees (within and outside the workplace), and does the working from home

[78] Wright, P., Harris, M, *AI in the home, smart devices do's and don'ts*, Compare the Cloud, 2020, https://www.comparethecloud.net/articles/ai-in-the-home-smart-devices-dos-and-donts/

environment heighten the ability for state actors and individuals to easily intrude on organisations and illegally take highlight confidential information and data. Nevertheless, it is our view that there are areas of society where government intervention is warranted to control what people view over the Internet. AI and big data will allow predictive control of potential dissenters. More importantly, authoritarian regimes will have no compunction about combining such data with information from tax returns, medical records, criminal records, sexual-health clinics, bank statements, genetic screenings, physical information (such as location, biometrics, and CCTV monitoring using facial recognition software), and information gleaned from family and friends. AI is as good as the data it has access to. Using voice AI, Microsoft's AI translator is capable of translating Chinese into English with "accuracy comparable to that of a bilingual person".[79] The resulting effect is that these have numerous applications spanning across sectors, geographical boundaries, and cultural barriers.

Unfortunately, the quantity and quality of data available to government on every citizen will prove excellent for training AI systems. Countries should work to influence how states that are neither solidly democratic nor solidly authoritarian implement AI and big data systems. They should provide aid to develop states' physical and regulatory infrastructure and use the access provided by that aid to prevent governments from using joined-up data. They should promote international norms that respect individual privacy as well as state sovereignty. Additionally, they should demarcate the use of AI and metadata for legitimate national security purposes from its use in suppressing human rights.[80]

Fred Cate and Rachel Dockery affirm the interconnectedness between personal data (protection) and AI, resulting from the tensions that are emerging between technology and the law.[81] However, there is a subtle but important dichotomy and debate that has emerged, which recognizes that AI is a threat to the data protection, while on the other hand, it may offer a number of opportunities to bolster and provide additional protections to personal data. The authors note there is a need for data protection laws and practices that protect privacy effectively in an era of AI and the big data on which it often depends, but that also does not impose unnecessary roadblocks for the future development of these innovative technologies.[82]

---

[79] Del Bello, L, *AI Translates News Just as Well as a Human Would*, futurism.com (2018), https://futurism.com/ai-translator-microsoft/

[80] Ibid.

[81] Cate, F., Dockery, R, Artificial Intelligence and Data Protection: Observations on a Growing Conflict Cybersecurity Law Indiana University, https://ostromworkshop.indiana.edu/pdf/seriespapers/2019spr-colloq/cate-paper.pdf. The term "artificial intelligence" (AI) describes the broad goal of empowering "computer systems to perform tasks that normally require human intelligence, such as visual perception, speech recognition, decision-making, and translation between languages." English Oxford Living Dictionaries, Artificial Intelligence.

[82] AI can help companies limit or monitor who is looking at an individual's data and respond in real-time to prevent inappropriate use or theft of data. Companies are developing AI-based privacy tools, such as privacy bots, which remember privacy preferences and try to make them consistent

The broader challenges AI will pose to populations (economically, socially and environmentally) are formidable. It may introduce bias and new forms of discrimination, especially if the data used in AI development only represents partial segments of the population or reflects existing societal bias.[83] AI will challenge traditional notions of urban and residential planning, which have large spaces dedicated to parking lots and garages. More pervasively, AI technology may also raise important antitrust issues, particularly if the data necessary for its development is concentrated in the hands of a few entities.[84] Cate and Dockery highlight one of the most significant challenges to data protection and data protection law. They argue that:

> the more data are available, the harder it is to de-identify them effectively. Al only makes de- identification harder, in two ways. First, it facilitates the demand for more data, for example, from the sensors in cell phones, cars, and other devices. Second, it provides increasingly advanced computational capabilities to work with collected data. Facial features, gate, fingerprint, and other forms of biometric recognition technologies provide an apt example: they collect thousands of discrete, nearly meaningless data points and then combine them in a way to provide reliable identification of individuals.[85]

Moreover, as AI becomes increasingly mainstream, the pros and cons of this technology is also being realized. In other words, and on the one hand, these technologies are starting to improve our lives, from simplifying our shopping to enhancing our healthcare experiences. On the other hand, AI is slowly making its way in the family home.[86] Dewi *et al.* make the point that the modern residential home will be transformed in the future. They note that in referring to Statista, the market penetration of home appliance reached US $21.682 million in 2019,[87] with this set to expand enormously over the next decade. Statista believe in the North American market is a major revenue source for the industry as a whole, frequently amounting to over 100 billion dollars.[88]

Importantly, this sample size is quite small when across the world as this takes hold and people replace or upgrade their current house hold items with smart appliances, the economic growth will be significant. For instance, the Chinese Midea Group and Haier Electronics Group, the American companies General Electric and Whirlpool Corporation, the German Bosch and Siemens Group, the Swedish Electrolux, and the South Korean LG Electronics and Samsung Electronics are the

---

across various sites, and privacy policy scanners, which attempt to read and simplify privacy policies for users to more easily understand.

[83] Ibid.

[84] Ibid.

[85] Ibid.

[86] Dewi Rosadi, S., Walters, R., Pratama, B., Yuniarti, S, *Privacy in the Home—it is under threat from Artificial Intelligence?* (forthcoming)

[87] Arne Holst Statista, *US Home Appliance Industry - Statistics & Facts* https://www.statista.com/topics/2843/home-appliance-industry-in-the-us/

[88] Ibid.

leading household appliances manufacturers worldwide.[89] Thus as Dewi *et al.* highlight the protection of personal data will not be unique, it will intersect with AI, cyber security and data protection law, systems, platforms and infrastructure. Nonetheless, the position of the smart home appliance is at the end user whose position is different from the user of the software or social media services. It will generate further questions that remain unresolved. For instance, who has legal responsibility for a data breach? Legally, the person that controls the good is the party responsible for the goods he/she control.[90] In the context of the smart home appliances, currently there is little to no user awareness of the importance of securing his/her data on the smart home appliance he-she uses. Therefore, reconciling the privacy and data protection issues alone, where there has been a breach of the law or misuse of that data will likely be hard to detect.[91]

Moreover, their value to businesses also has become undeniable: nearly 80% of executives at companies that are deploying AI.[92] Although the widespread use of AI in business is still in its infancy and questions remain open about the pace of progress, as well as the possibility of achieving the holy grail of "general intelligence," the potential is enormous. McKinsey Global Institute research suggests that by 2030, AI could deliver additional global economic output of $13 trillion per year.[93] This will include, in part, home appliance that will be used by every-day people, and make their way into workplaces. However, they go onto highlight that even with the positive effects AI will have to society it will be welcomed by some, this new technology will not come without its criticisms. McKinsey note that some of the concerns and issues raised are quite serious. They assert that:

> AI generates consumer benefits and business value, it is also giving rise to a host of unwanted, and sometimes serious, consequences. And while we're focusing on AI in this article, these knock-on effects (and the ways to prevent or mitigate them) apply equally to all advanced analytics. The most visible ones, which include privacy violations, discrimination, accidents, and manipulation of political systems, are more than enough to prompt caution. More concerning still are the consequences not yet known or experienced. Disastrous repercussions—including the loss of human life, if an AI medical algorithm goes wrong, or the compromise of national security, if an adversary feeds disinformation to a military AI system—are possible, and so are significant challenges for organizations, from reputational damage and revenue losses to regulatory backlash, criminal investigation, and diminished public trust.[94]

---

89 Ibid.

90 Ibid.

91 Ibid.

92 Cheatham, B., Javanmardian, K., Samandri, H., *Confronting the risk of actual Artificial Intelligence*, McKinsey & Company 2019, https://www.mckinsey.com/business-functions/mckinsey-analytics/our-insights/confronting-the-risks-of-artificial-intelligence?cid=other-eml-ttn-mip-mck&hlkid=6b2be962aed847c9bf412ebcd03a151d&hctky=11472376&hdpid=82f208a8-85b8-46b3-95ae-c91e0ad0a0b6

93 Ibid.

94 Ibid.

Despite the challenges going forward, the current day data protection law is well ahead of any formal international or national regulation of AI that will use personal data. Therefore, it is our view, along with Cate and Dockery that entities developing AI will still need to comply with data protection laws. They rightly argue for a longer-term approach to resolve the interconnectedness between the AI and data protection. Another layer of complexity is the interconnectedness of these two with cyber security. It is argued that in the future, they will need to be viewed as a collective rather than in isolation. This is because the definition of personal data and AI are neither settled and fully explored by the courts. The definition of personal data is fragmented from country to country, and this alone will pose significant legal and policy issues facing AI and its development.

Thus, they are calling for a shift in the legal framework to enhance the data protection laws by introducing the concept of data stewardship, which would be a move away from the current and accepted concept of consent. Secondly, they propose the idea of a More Systemic and Well-Developed Use of Risk Management. This is not new to regulation, it has been used in food, environmental, primary industries and airline regulation, amongst others for many decades. The issues facing risk management will require a significant shift in thinking for the developer and user of technology. The industries mentioned are notably large entities, or private individuals working in specialized professions. The user of the Internet and AI is and will be the general community. Most of them will not fully understand complex risk management systems. Thus, the burden lies with entities to better educate, inform and raise awareness of risk management in AI and the Internet to retain the current levels and improve the protections around personal data. Thirdly, Cate and Dockery believe there need to be a greater focus on data uses and impacts, fourthly a framework of harms and lastly transparency and redress. In our view, the approach in 3 and 4 put forward by Cate and Dockery can largely be addressed by 2.

In reinforcing the above, data, and in particular big data, is crucial for the digital economy and for developing AI applications. Hence, access to data and the way it is governed becomes an important question for national AI strategies.[95] The authors highlight that one of the most pressing issues to be fully identified and understood is the impact to privacy, de-identification and security. They assert that the risks related to privacy, de-identification, and security are problematic and it is important to balance the need to instil trust and acceptance of data systems within the community with the need to empower citizens, governments, industries, and researchers.[96]

The benefits of having large amounts of commercial and personal data at hand, has many benefits for governments and industry. It can, in part, provide a significant advantage economically to states and the private sector. Yet, there remains the issue

---

[95] Mapping the challenges and opportunities of artificial intelligence for the conductof diplomacy, DiploFoundation Ministry of Foreign Affairs Finland, https://www.diplomacy.edu/AI-diplo-report

[96] Ibid.

of how personal data will be managed and regulated with continued competing challenges. The challenges are formidable as there are a number of competing issues that need to strike a balance between personal data and AI, along with security. Arguably, one of the most pressing issues is how sensitive personal data is managed by this new technology. The authors argue the need to balance the need to protect sensitive data and individuals' rights and the business opportunities for public service provision offered by that data. To achieve this, they assert that there is a need to ensure greater data interoperability that is mentioned as another factor in making AI work on a broad basis.[97] As this book highlights the challenges faced by the current day data protection laws are considerable, because they are different, fragmented and in some cases achieve different levels of protection.

Moreover, the report goes onto say that in response to the data needs of AI, calls for new means of sharing, governing, and producing data need to be developed. It emphasises that data is a common good and that economic actors need to be encouraged to share their data. The report makes another strong statement. It declares data an issue of sovereignty and argues: it is vital to maintain a firm stance on data transfer outside the European Union.[98] In referring to Germany, they have accumulated a 'specific data stock', which should be used to develop AI-based business models in Germany to make the country become a "new top export[er], whilst strictly observing data security and people's right to control their personal data".[99] Data sharing should be made easier to promote co-operation between business and research institutions and a national research data infrastructure should be built to enable centralised access for researchers. Yet, there is no mention of how this achieves the balance between economic activity and data security and protection.

However, as AI begins to take a hold, it is becoming increasingly apparent that this technology depends on the collection and processing of vast amounts of data which can potentially include personal and even sensitive data. Anonymization techniques—which have served as a wildcard, allowing companies to process anonymised personal data—could be more easily circumvented with the use of AI.[100] They note that only a very small amount of data is needed to uniquely identify an individual. In a study, it was found that 87% of the population in the United States could be uniquely identified based only on cross-referencing a 5-digit ZIP code, gender, and date of birth.[101] AI exponentially strengthens data processing capabilities. If anonymised personal data becomes part of a large data set, AI can de-anonymise this data based on inferences from cross-referencing information. This blurs the distinction between personal and non-personal data, which is a

[97] Ibid.

[98] Ibid.

[99] Ibid.

[100] Ibid.

[101] Ibid.

cornerstone of present legislation.[102] Therein lies the issue, whereby the current data protection laws are at odds with AI technology. Furthermore, it is not apparent, at this early stage whether the technology has advanced enough, whereby, AI developers have devised a way to secure and protect personal data. As the technology evolves, there is a good chance that this is likely to be realised. However, regulation and legislation will require a level of flexibility and adaptation so as it not only sets a minimum standard, it also needs to take into consideration future technology developments. This is complex to achieve, but not insurmountable.

Despite the ability to identify an individual through the personal data noted above, it can increasingly be used to identify and extrapolate trends and patterns of behaviour which can be used to influence opinions, choices, and decisions. This technology has significant ramifications for cybersecurity and data protection regimes. It has the ability to divide society. It also has the ability to create classes. Yet, it has the ability to bring communities together with greater connectivity. It also has significant economic advantages to individuals and entities, in the new digital economy. Thus, the importance for government and regulators to get this balance right, in a world of increasingly heightened anxiety, will be important.

The authors go onto use the EU law as an example of the current provisions of the General Data Protection Regulation (GDPR) in addressing the above. However, they highlight how the GDPR in terms of law and policy still falls short of closing the gap between AI, data protection and to a lesser extent cyber security. They go onto say that:

> the EU GDPR provisions that do take into consideration both AI and personal data, gaps still remain. It will be important to see how the application of the EU's GDPR will impact profiling practices, including with the use of AI, and on automated decision-making that impacts individuals. According to article 22 of the GDPR, '[t]he data subject shall have the right not to be subject to a decision based solely on automated processing, including profiling, which produces legal effects concerning him or her or similarly significantly affects him or her.' Moreover, according to article 29 Data Protection Working Party, 'to qualify as human intervention, the controller must ensure that any oversight of the decision is meaningful, rather than just a token gesture.' Importantly they note that Article 22 will not apply when the decision is (a) provided by the law, such as in the case of fraud prevention or money laundering checks; (b) necessary for the performance of or entering into a contract; or (3) based on the individual's prior consent. Nevertheless, even in these cases, the data controller needs to inform the data subject about the existence of automated decision-making, providing meaningful information about the logic involved, as well as the significance and the envisaged consequences of such processing for the data subject.[103]

They go further questioning whether the current concept of consent would address these issues:

> As regards the principle of consent, a GDPR-compliant privacy information notice cannot adopt the form of a blank cheque covering any type of machine learning or AI technology.

[102] Ibid.

[103] Ibid.

> The information notice to the data subject needs to explain the main elements considered in reaching the decision, the source of the information obtained and their relevance. In other words, these principles underscore the autonomy of and respect for the data subject by requiring, for example, explicit consent and clear proof of significant interference of the right.[104]

The current data protection laws largely provide for core principles such as consent, fairness, purpose limitation, and data minimisation that, remain important operational safeguards for the exercise and enjoyment of the right to privacy, but also need to be fine-tuned with regard to the introduction of AI technologies. An AI model which produces discriminatory results could fail the test of fairness. An AI model which is not conservative in the data it collects (because it has not made a lateral sweep of the amount and nature of the information needed) is not proportionate and could fail the test of data minimisation. An AI model which gathers or reuses personal data from various sources yet does not inform, explain, and/or obtain the consent of the data subject, could fail the purpose of the limitation principle.[105]

Moreover, it is well understood that [m]achines function on the basis of what humans tell them. If a system is fed with human biases (conscious or unconscious) the result will inevitably be biased. The lack of diversity and inclusion in the design of AI systems is therefore a key concern: instead of making our decisions more objective, they could reinforce discrimination and prejudices by giving them an appearance of objectivity.[106] There is increasing evidence that, ethnic minorities, people with disabilities and LGBTI persons particularly suffer from dis- crimination by biased algorithms.[107] At the same time, they are likely to engender risks *inter alia* to life, liberty, dignity, and work, many of which are not yet known nor fully understood. Apart from the human rights issues, if these biases are able to be realised in this technology, the issues faced by these groups in the community are problematic, and for society more broadly. In other words, these technologies have the potential to undermine national identity, and more importantly social cohesion. On the other side, the technology used appropriately can help to strengthen social cohesion and national identity. That is, provided the technology and legal framework is established to support innovation while ensuring that citizens personal information is secure.

Importantly, data protection is especially important for vulnerable groups whose ability and capacity to consent may be less developed and/or diminished. In referring to Rosa Kornfeld-Matte, the UN independent expert who stated that on the enjoyment of all human rights by older persons: "Older persons should also be able

[104] Ibid.

[105] Ibid.

[106] Ibid.

[107] Ibid.

to change their minds and opt out of technology at any time".[108] Unless there are viable alternatives, the older person does not, however, have a real choice. Consent is not merely an administrative requirement. It is an essential element to a rights-based and risk management approach. Therefore, the importance of the provision of simple and accurate information about the technology in order for them to be able to assess its implications.[109] AI has entered a digital landscape which lacks clear regulation and guidance from case law. It will quietly learn and increasingly assist people for good in their everyday lives. AI will drive us around, help us make choices, and complement the care for loved ones. In this regard, they will enable the effective exercise and enjoyment of human rights for many more people than ever before.[110]

Notwithstanding the above, the importance of this book cannot be underestimated. The need to know and understand the interconnectedness between AI and data protection is paramount. Moreover, the need to couple AI and data protection with cyber security is just as paramount, to ensure there is a whole of legislative and technology approach. It will take a multilayered approach to reconcile the challenges faced by AI, its technology to maintain a strong level of security and protect personal data. It will require regulators to be more adaptable than ever before, so as they can rapidly respond to continues technology change.

3.3 Conclusion

Technology over the internet knows no national boundaries. Therefore, the challenges facing the protection of personal data, at least, from a cybercrime and Internet perspective requires an international response. The sovereignty issues and challenges across these areas of the law are formidable. They will not be easily addressed in the short term, however, over the longer-term governments may be forced to develop and implement similar laws and strategies. This has largely occurred, with significant influence by the OECD, EU, and to a lesser extent APEC and ASEAN. Apart from identifying the sovereignty issues facing data protection, cyber security and AI, this Chapter has also highlighted that they are interconnected, albeit at a policy level, rather than regulatory. There is a need for further work to identify and close the gap between the three areas of law.

Even though cyber security and AI are evolving at an alarming rate, they are to varying levels directly or indirectly connected to personal data. This is because personal data can be compromised and misused through a cyber security intrusion or breach, and AI technology is and will be capturing personal data. It is our view this interconnectedness will be further accentuated as different technologies continue to

[108] Ibid.

[109] Ibid.

[110] Ibid.

be developed that enable even larger amounts of personal data to be collected and used.

The Internet and its supporting technology, including AI will pose significant challenges to government and the broader community. It challenges the very notion of the sovereign state and confers two distinct but related arguments: (1) intermediaries threaten state sovereignty; and (2) as a result of the world moving online, state power is in decline.[111] As large corporations are able to exploit arbitrage opportunities, they raise concerns about the "quasi-sovereign" power of intermediaries.[112] Unlike the development of technology through the industrial revolution, where largely governments had more time to react to change, the new Internet economy is moving so fast that governments and regulators cannot keep up. The ability for governments and regulators to meet the needs of the broader community and maintain elements of sovereignty over the Internet is diminishing. However, with the fragmented approach to the development of technology, states are also in a position to exert their sovereign power outside the law. This not only threatens the sovereignty of other states, but also large corporations. It enables other states to dictate, determine and shape the social and political discourse of citizens of other states. Furthermore, and because these large corporations have the flexibility and latitude that is not seen in other sectors or industries, it has been proven that they have unfettered power over customers. This is because only a handful of individuals and entities fully understand what has been occurring behind the computer screen. The level of sophistication involved in cyber intrusions, along with the gathering of personal data where the consumer is neither informed or understands what they have provided.

Moreover, one of the most pressing issues that is arising from the onset and use of AI technology is in the home and everyday life of individuals. Over the next decade the world is likely to see a significant shift in the devices used in the home, office and business. Smart Home appliances and devices (televisions, radios, fridges, amongst others), along with personal robots and drones all constitute forms of AI. These are not only going to provide significant benefits to individuals, but there is a lack of understanding as to their security and how they capture personal data. More work needs to be undertaken to better understand the potential cybersecurity risks posed to individuals in the home or office from these devices. This work also needs to extend to what personal data will be captured and potentially used by individuals and entities. The potential for vulnerable groups such as children, those with a disability and elderly to be captured by this technology is only beginning to be understood. The potential ramifications for bias and discrimination based on sex, ethnicity, religion, amongst others is enormous. As highlighted later in this book,

---

[111] Tamachandran, R, How Artificial Intelligence Is Countering Data Protection Challenges Facing Organizations. *AI technology can help enterprises in endpoint security, data privacy and against phishing, malware and ransomware attacks.* https://www.entrepreneur.com/article/343267

[112] Ibid.

the data protection, cyber security and AI laws will need to consider these issues. Furthermore, as AI evolves a more comprehensive study will be needed to better understand whether the developers of the technology have been successful in building adequate safeguards into the systems and platforms to protect personal data from illegal collection. Further work will also be required to confirm whether current trade-consumer practices law (in other countries this will be different) is adequate to regulate this at the point of sale of these devices.

Finally, this Chapter has highlighted how the definition of AI is far from agreed or settled at the national or even international level. While the Chapter did not examine the international agreements or laws as to whether, there has been some agreement or proposal put forward by states to clearly define what is and is not military AI. There are already calls for the legislation frameworks take into consideration the three areas as a collective. It has been demonstrated that to do so, governments and regulators have a significant challenge due to the need to balance innovation with the need to keep personal data secure and ensure its protection. The lack of any international framework only heightens this dilemma. Furthermore, and as this Chapter has also highlighted, there has been little discussion to the mainstream day to day appliances that will be adopted by individuals in the home that will have AI technology, as they will be connected to the Internet and subject to security breaches, and collect, store and use personal data.

References

Aletras, N., Tsarapatsanis, D., Preoţiuc-Pietro, D., & Lampos, V. (2016). Predicting judicial decisions of the European Court of Human Rights: A natural language processing perspective. *PeerJ Computer Science, 93*.

Alexy, R. (1989). *A theory of legal argumentation*. Oxford University Press.

Bench-Capon, T. (2017). *Hypo'e legacy: Introduction to the virtual special issue. Artificial Intelligence and Law, 25*, 1–46.

Conrad, J. G., & Branting, L. K. (2018). Introduction to the special issue on legal text analytics. *Artificial Intelligence and Law, 26*, 99–102.

Ferrucci, D., Levas, A., Bagchi, S., Gondek, D., & Mueller, E. T. (2013). *Watson: Beyond Jeopardy. Artificial Intelligence., 199*, 93–105.

Feteris, E. (2017). *Fundamentals of legal argumentation* (pp. 33–41). Springer.

Hildebrandt, M. (2013). Extraterritorial jurisdiction to enforce in cyberspace? Bodin, Schmitt, Grotius in cyberspace? *Toronto Law Journal, 63*, 196–224.

Jackson, P. (1974). *Introduction to artificial intelligence* (2nd Ed., Vol. 1, pp. 192–338). Dover Publication.

Kleinberg, J., Lakkaraju, H., Leskovec, J., Ludwig, J., & Mullainathan, S. (2018). *Human decisions and machine predictions. The Quarterly Journal of Economics, 133*, 237–293.

O'Grady, J. P. (2018). *Dewey B strategic—2017 Blogazine: Risk, value, strategy, innovation, knowledge and the legal profession.* Year of the Book Press.

Riskin, G. (2017). *Ross intelligence update: How IBM Watson app helps U.S. lawyers with legal research.* Law Firm Technology.

Tzimas, T. (2018). *Artificial intelligence as global commons and the "International law supremacy" principle* (Advances in Social Science, Education and Humanities Research, Vol. 211).

Walters, R., & Coghlan, M. (2019). Data protection and artificial intelligence law: Europe Australia Singapore—An actual or perceived dichotomy. *American Journal of Science, Engineering and Technology, 4*(4), 55–65.

Williams, K., Facciola, J. M., McCann, P., & Catanzaro, V. M. (2017). *The legal technology guidebook*. Springer.

Chapter 4
Data Protection

Abstract Data protection is a recent addition to national legal frameworks. Data protection has evolved as a tool of privacy over the Internet. Yet, privacy generally means different things to different people and nation states. The international community has in part developed high level agreed principles for protecting individual's personal data online. However, there is a lack of international law in this area. The current approach is fragmented, inconsistent and incoherent. While many states have looked to the EU model, other models have emerged. This book will highlight, what in our view, are the models that have been developed by states to address the protection of personal data over the Internet (see Chap. 15).

Data protection law has become complex and continues to evolve and change. How states respond in the future is the unknown. Some may take a stronger stance towards privacy, while others may open up their laws to ensure innovation and economic activity is not impeded. Yet, other states may take more of a surveillance approach towards social controlling their population. On the other hand, states may decide to take on all three policy areas. However, what is not clear, which will become evident in Part II of this book, is how states respond to AI, cyber security and personal data protection.[1] In other words, as AI develops the world will see an increased use in smart home devices, clothes, toys, personal robots and drones, which is becoming one of the most challenging areas to grapple with. These products and devices will be connected to the Internet, and with that, comes significant concerns over their security of personal data. Not only will the data be accessible by individuals and entities who have the potential to exploit the daily lives of individuals, whether in the home or at work on a grand scale. Used wrongly, the personal

[1] This chapter draws on the earlier work of Robert Walters, Leon Trakman, Bruno Zeller *Data Protection Law: A Comparative Analysis of Asia-Pacific and European Approaches*, Springer (2019).

R. Walters, M. Novak, *Cyber Security, Artificial Intelligence, Data Protection & the Law*, https://doi.org/10.1007/978-981-16-1665-5_4

data of people can be extracted and used for the wrong reasons by states and organizations. They have the potential to exploit the most vulnerable in the community such as children, elderly and disabled by creating biases.

This Chapter argues that even more problematic is that our everyday activities from the moment we are awake until we sleep and even while sleeping could be potentially monitored to varying degrees by these devices. The impact to individuals will be enormous and allow elements of both the public and private sector to gain even more control of individuals, groups and the broader community. The resulting effect from this transition in society and the economy, if fully realized, has the potential for less social cohesion based on ethnic, racial or religious grounds.

Moreover, this Chapter highlights how the interconnectedness of data protection and cyber security has begun to be acknowledged more broadly by governments. Yet, one of the challenges facing governments and regulators from Artificial Intelligence and Big Data, is how they can help unlock and share personal data within the legal and ethical frameworks, with a view to maximizing the benefits of data in a sustainable way, while minimizing the risks and harms to data subjects. To reconcile this gap will be challenging and will require both technology and the law to be cohesive. This is a long way from being achieved. Thus, the task for government and regulators is a formidable one and may never be settled in a similar way to other areas of long-standing commercial law such as intellectual property, contract or tort law. The balance is not only economic and social, it also will require states to consider security (national) policy drivers, so as they protect their citizens, business and area of national importance. This Chapter draws on the earlier work of Robert Walters, Leon Trakman and Bruno Zeller and their book Data Protection Law: A Comparative Analysis of Asia-Pacific and European Approaches, Springer, (2019).

4.1 Introduction

Simon Chesterman notes that the challenges to sovereignty lie in the fact that the traditional response to such developments would be through legislation.[2] Chesterman goes onto say that, such laws are generally jurisdiction-specific, their power and legitimacy tied to a territorially bounded state. In the case of global data flows, however, users in one country may store their data in a second country, accessing it using software run by a company in a third country and so on.[3] This leads to predictable co-ordination problems, but also market pressure. Establishing domestic standards for data protection that are too high may lead to multinational companies avoiding that jurisdiction; if standards are too low then users may not be confident in sharing their data. International regulation is possible, similar to the co-ordination of postal and telephone services, but key Internet functions continue to be performed

[2] Chesterman, S, *Data Protection Law in Singapore: Privacy and Sovereignty in an Interconnected World,* second edition; Singapore: Academy Publishing, (2018), 1–9.

[3] Ibid.

by a non-profit organisations and there is understandable wariness about transferring control of the Internet to a body like the United Nations.[4] For the time being, then, meaningful regulation with coercive powers therefore depends on states – but those regulations must be drafted with an eye on global as well as local concerns. This section highlights some of the mechanisms state actors including the EU have adopted to strengthen the sovereign control over the protection of personal data and privacy.

However, and whether viewed as a human right or a balance between economic activity and human rights, the acceptance of privacy is disparate amongst nation states. Most, if not all democratic states have embraced the idea that, human rights are to form an integral part of the legal framework. Although, the acceptance of human rights, and the right to privacy is fragmented. This, will inevitably allow for states to assert their sovereignty and sovereign power in developing their respective data protection laws. Take for example, Singapore, which unlike the EU, does not recognise a right to privacy. More pervasively, former Prime Minister Lee Kuan Yew's dismissal of the idea is often invoked in such discussions:

> I am often accused of interfering in the private lives of citizens … Had I not done that, we wouldn't be here today. And I say without the slightest remorse: that we wouldn't be here, we would not have made economic progress, if we had not intervened on very personal matters – who your neighbour is, how you live, the noise you make, how you spit, or what language you use.[5]

The EU on the other hand, has placed human rights, and the right to privacy over the Internet as a core policy value. Arguably, this level of recognition of privacy as a right not only competes with other economic and social policy areas, it reinforces the sovereign right of state actors to develop laws that suit their needs. It has become apparent that; some countries and jurisdictions are exerting their sovereign authority on other nation states. For instance, the EU have been leaders in developing data protection laws. Graham Greenleaf noted that in 2012 that, a total of eighty-nine countries, from almost all regions of the world, have now enacted data privacy laws covering most of their private sectors.[6] He goes onto say that the enactment of laws outside Europe is accelerating. In a few years, the majority of the world's data privacy laws will be found outside Europe. Greenleaf believe this geo-political change has implications. Firstly, by examining the most important differences between the two European privacy standards (the EU Directive and the Council of Europe Convention 108) and the two non- European standards (the OECD Guidelines and APEC Framework), it is possible to identify what can reasonably be characterised as 'European influences' on data privacy laws outside Europe.[7] This influence is increasing as states continue to develop and revise their respective data protection laws. States such as Indonesia and India, while not having implemented specific

---

[4] Ibid.

[5] In Quotes Le Kwan Yew, BBC, 2015, https://www.bbc.com/news/world-asia-31582842

[6] Greenleaf, G, *The influence of European data privacy standards outside Europe: Implications for globalisation of Convention 108,* University of Edinburgh School of Law Research Paper 2012/12.

[7] Ibid.

data protection laws, in their respective reviews and developments, they have looked to the EU.[8] Secondly, the Council of Europe data Protection Convention (Convention 108) and its Additional Protocol are examined from the perspective of the possibility and desirability of their becoming a global international agreement on data privacy.[9] It is argued that there are potential considerable advantages to both non-European and European states if Convention 108 (plus the Additional Protocol) were to become a global privacy agreement through accession of non-European states.

However, for such globalisation to occur, the Council of Europe had to settle and publicise appropriate policies on accession that are appropriate, transparent, and do not reduce European data privacy standards.[10] Thirdly, Greenleaf argues that Europe has no reason to retreat from its privacy standards developed over forty years. The rest of the world is moving its way, and it should not compromise fundamental standards for the sake of compromise with powerful outliers, particularly the United States of America (US) and China.[11] For Greenleaf, he believes that respect for their domestic prerogatives should not be confused with any need to reduce fundamental aspects of global data privacy standards. Arguably, the EU have been very strategic getting on the front foot and developing laws that, in part, require other nation states to buy into the EU sovereign approach towards current and future data protection law. This influence comes on the backdrop of states being able to develop similar laws to account for their respective needs. Moreover, and this is reflected by the fact that countries from the US to Australia to Singapore and the countries discussed in this book all view the notion of privacy over the Internet, slightly and in some cases very differently.

Neil Richards and Woodrow Hartzog[12] reinforce the above by arguing that data protection is also myopic because it ignores how industry's appetite for data is wrecking our environment, our democracy, our attention spans, and our emotional health. They go onto say that the European Union General Data Protection Regulation (GDPR) protects the personal data of Europeans, even when that data is processed in the United States. It was bound to affect how large American companies process the data of their European customers and employees. The reach of the GDPR have led many to global technology companies to comply with GDPR requirements firm-wide, a compliance effect that was also relatively easy to predict. Some effects of the GDPR were less obvious before the fact. The GDPR is the most

[8] Walters, R., Trakman, L., Zeller, B, *Data Protection Law: A Comparative Analysis of Asia-Pacific and European Approaches*, Springer (2019).

[9] Council of Europe, Council of Europe data Protection Convention (Convention 108), Convention for the protection of individuals with regard to the processing of personal data https://www.coe.int/en/web/data-protection/convention108-and-protocol

[10] Greenleaf, G, *The influence of European data privacy standards outside Europe: Implications for globalisation of Convention 108,* University of Edinburgh School of Law Research Paper 2012/12.

[11] Ibid.

[12] Richards, N., Hartzog, W, *Privacy's Constitutional Moment,* Washington University School of Law; Yale Information Society Project. Northeastern University School of Law (2019).

prominent example of the governing framework for collecting, storing, and using personal data, commonly referred to as "data protection."[13] Richards and Woodrow in referring to Margot Kaminski state that, data protection regimes that follow the GDPR typically follow a "binary governance" approach, which combines individual due process rights with a collaborative governance approach to follow and protect personal data to ensure it is always processed fairly.[14]

Data Protection regimes long predate the GDPR, but the GDPR has had the unexpected effect of turning European-style privacy protection into a global market norm, an example of what Anu Bradford has termed "the Brussels Effect" and what Paul Schwartz calls "global data privacy the EU way."[15] If you want to do business in the global data trade, regardless of where you are located, the GDPR sets the benchmark. Increasingly, this "Brussels effect" is also influencing the conceptual design of privacy laws around the globe, from Canada to Brazil, and from Japan to Switzerland. The extension of the "Brussels Effect", or another way of expressing the term is the European sovereign effect, has, and is, influencing the development of many other countries data protection laws from Indonesia, India, Australia, New Zealand and many others that Graham Greenleaf has noted. Thus, for the EU rather than dominate economically, which they cannot, they have been very successful, particularly in this area of the law to dominate the policy and legal setting.

However, it is still the sovereign right of states to develop their own legal frameworks. Moreover, the fragmented approach to these three areas of the law highlights that not everyone has bought into the EU narrative. Richards and Woodrow further argue that for the US they have yet to fully embrace the EU's data protection model. The patchwork approach taken by the US is more permissive, indeterminate, and based upon people's vulnerabilities in their commercial relationship with entities and individuals.[16] Furthermore, Richards and Woodrow in referring to William McGeveran draw upon these differences to distinguish between Europe's "data protection" and America's "consumer protection" frameworks for privacy.[17] Thus, what can be seen is several models emerging across the world that all consider elements of privacy over the Internet. However, some jurisdictions take a greater focus on the business and consumer needs rather while balancing the elements of privacy. This can also be seen in the EU, Singapore, Australian and US models.

In addition to the above, for Australia and the US and their respective federal systems of governance poses a further challenge as many states within these two countries have also implemented specific privacy or data protection laws. It is out of scope to analyse their differences, however, using the US as an example to highlight how countries are being jammed, in their regulatory approach. Richards and

[13] Ibid.

[14] Ibid, Kaminski, M, *Binary Governance: Lessons from the GDPR's Approach to Algorithmic Accountability*, 92 S. CAL. L. REV. (2019).

[15] Ibid, Schwartz, P, *Global Data Privacy: The E.U. Way*, 94 N.Y.U. L. Rev. (2019); Anu Bradford, *The Brussels Effect*, 107 Nw. U. L. Rev. 1 (2012).

[16] Ibid.

[17] Ibid, McGeveran, W, *Privacy and Data Protection Law*, Foundation Press; first Edit, (2016).

Woodrow point out how US American state legislatures have started to pass state-level data protection statutes, such as the California and Washington. For instance, the Californian Consumer Protection Act (see Chap. 14), which comes into effect in 2020 will have a national effect. This is an interesting point because they are home to Silicon Valley. On the other hand, Washington have also begun to consider their own mini-GDPR, and after years of opposition to regulation, big tech companies have also started to call for a baseline US, federal privacy law.[18] These calls are often paired with arguments for federal pre-emption to avoid multiple state data governance regimes, particularly from more aggressive state regulators. Even though advocates often claim that unification will help make US privacy laws adequate in the eyes of the EU, any omnibus bill that is likely to be passed seems destined to be a watered-down version of the GDPR, given the trans-Atlantic differences in rights, cultures, commitments, and regulatory appetites. Thus, a clear expression of the sovereign. Richards and Woodrow are of the view that today, more than ever, the US Congress now finds itself sandwiched between bottom-up momentum from the states, and top-down influence emerging from international norms and foreign law. At this critical juncture, the US Congress must now determine the trajectory of US privacy law. They believe that even if the US Congress does nothing, this convergence of privacy federalism and the Brussels Effect will define America's privacy identity.[19] The prevailing effect is likely to see the GDPR take a further hold and the EU continue to exert its sovereign over other countries in this area of the law. To say that is a bad thing is subjective. It requires a more in-depth analysis. However, it is our view that bringing states together and converging the systems to balance the needs of data protection rights could become more important than the economic activity generated from current and future technology.

Moreover, and the fluid nature states are imposing their sovereign views over data protection law, appears to change daily. In citing the US as an example in 2019, on 10 September of that year, a US Judge in California night ordered Facebook to face the brunt of a privacy class action lawsuit, chastising the social network for views about privacy he called "so wrong."[20] The Judge Vince Chhabria in San Francisco said users could try to hold Facebook liable under various federal and state laws for letting app developers and business partners harvest their personal data without their consent on a "widespread" basis. The Judge went onto reject Facebook's arguments that users suffered no "tangible" harm and had no legitimate privacy interest in information they shared with friends on social media.[21] The Court noted that Facebook's motion to dismiss is littered with assumptions about the degree to which social media users can reasonably expect their personal information

[18] Richards, N., Hartzog, W, *Privacy's Constitutional Moment,* Washington University School of Law; Yale Information Society Project. Northeastern University School of Law (2019).

[19] Ibid.

[20] Judge lets Facebook privacy lawsuit proceed, calls company's views 'so wrong' By Reuters September 10, 2019, https://nypost.com/2019/09/10/judge-lets-facebook-privacy-class-action-proceed-calls-companys-views-so-wrong/

[21] Ibid.

and communications to remain private. Judge Chhabria wrote: "Facebook's view is so wrong." However, a representative from Facebook stated the company considered protecting people's information and privacy "extremely important," but believed its practices were consistent with its disclosures and "do not support any legal claims."[22] The two plaintiffs Lesley Weaver and Derek Loeser, lawyers, argued that they were pleased with the decision, and "especially gratified that the Court is respecting Facebook users' right to privacy."[23] While not suggesting that the legal framework for privacy and data protection in the US will automatically adopt the EU model, as these issues arise in the courts, the outcome may in turn pressure governments and regulators to take a tougher regulatory approach to data protection.

Lingjie Kong makes the point that in the context of human society the need for greater controls over personal data is valid. Kong argues that personal data, as information relating to individuals, is a quite familiar object for each member of the information society.[24] Personal data is born with us, such as gender; some are given by others, such as, name; and most of them are created automatically in the course we interact with others.[25] Personal data is personal, because it can be used to identify us and it records who we are, where we go and what we do, from the very moment we were born to even after we leave this world. More importantly, Kong argues that record keeping on individuals is as old as civilization itself.[26]

Taking this one step further, Kong poses the following question as to why then, why does protection of personal data suddenly become a troublesome issue for western developed countries in 1950s? Kong argues that in the contemporary world, technology is a double-edged sword. While enhancing the wellbeing of the people, it may cause serious private and public problems. As a human made machine that transforms lives of human being, computer is of no exception. It was once heavily criticized as the magic hand that opened the 'Pandora Box' of the data protection problem.[27] Does it really have such great powers to bring us such a big headache? To some extent, it has to be admitted that computer does transform record keeping on individuals and personal data processing. It decreases the cost of data collection, storage, processing and transmission, and meanwhile increases the managerial utility and commercial value of both single and multiple pieces of personal data.

The appetite of public and private entities for more comprehensive, complete, accurate and detailed personal data increases as well. Following World War II, the world witnessed a sharp increase in population growth, gradual urbanization, expanding governmental functions of public administration and social welfare, enlargement of scale economy and booming of personalized advertising business.

---

[22] Ibid.

[23] Ibid.

[24] Kong, L, *Enacting China's Data Protection Act, International Journal of Law and Information Technology*, Volume 18, Issue 3, (2010), 197–226.

[25] Ibid.

[26] Ibid.

[27] Ibid.

These social, political, economic, along with the technical changes have pushed systematic record keeping into automatic data processing, and turned individuals into digital persons in the information society.[28]

Therefore, and as Kong rightly points out that when unchecked by law, personal data is randomly collected, stored, used and transferred, threatening and infringing privacy, personality and justified interests of individuals concerned. In other words, comprehensive development of the society demands more powerful and sophisticated record keeping and data processing tools. Innovative information technologies respond to and meet that demand.[29] Thus, for Kong, the rise of the data protection cannot be controlled by technology alone, but complex social, political and economic factors make data protection a complicated personal and social, political and economic, technical and international issue. This, in our view also includes a robust national and international legal framework. It also calls for greater integration with other laws such as AI and cybersecurity. Furthermore, in our view what Kong highlights correctly identifies that the law and policy, has evolved and changed significantly. Today, states continue to develop its legal framework to protect personal data, although they vary significantly from each other.

Data protection and privacy have converged primarily as a legal framework to protect people's personal data defined by the law and in some cases is now considered a fundamental right.[30] This convergence also includes finding a balance between economic development and innovation in the digital economy. Even though privacy and data protection are an evolving area of law and economic development, it has not matured as a measure of redressing economic and personal harm comparably to the protection of intellectual property, copyright, criminal procedure and international trade law. Data protection has also been characterized as a tool of 'privacy'.[31] In other words, data protection underpins privacy and constitutes the personal data used to identify a person. Data protection today is increasingly considered as the implementation of appropriate administrative, technical or physical measures that minimize the risk of or harm caused by unauthorized intentional or accidental disclosure.[32] These measures are embodied in the legal and policy frameworks by which nation states protect a person's privacy, including technological systems that collect, store and use data. Regulators are also increasingly recognising that the technological use of personal data represents the greatest threat to

---

[28] Ibid.

[29] Ibid.

[30] Walters, R., Trakman, L., Zeller, B, *Data Protection Law: A Comparative Analysis of Asia-Pacific and European Approaches*, Springer (2019) 5–15.

[31] De Hert p, Gutwirth S, (2006) *Privacy, Data Protection and Law Enforcement. Opacity of the Individual and Transparency of Power*, in Claes E, Duff A, Gutwirth S, *Privacy and the Criminal Law,* Antwerp-Oxford, Intersentia, 61–104, in Walters, R., Trakman, L., Zeller, B, *Data Protection Law: A Comparative Analysis of Asia-Pacific and European Approaches*, Springer (2019).

[32] International Organisation for Standardisation/IEC 2382–1-1993 and its successors.

individuals, accentuating their vulnerability and underscoring the need to protect their rights to privacy.[33]

On the backdrop of the above, there are a number of other regional and international programs that, in part, influence the sovereign development of the data protection law. This has largely evolved because of the fragmented approach of the legal framework. Beginning with the International Law Commission (ILC) has stated that the international binding and non-binding instruments, as well as the national legislation adopted by nation states, and judicial decisions reveal a number of core principles' of data protection.[34] Walters, Trakman and Zeller are of the view that data protection is an area 'in which state practice is not yet extensive or fully developed',[35] and the Statute of the ILC suggests that codification should take place in fields where there has already been extensive State practice, precedent and doctrine.[36] In addition, work in the area of data protection 'may nevertheless be able to identify emerging trends in legal opinion and practice which are likely to shape any international legal regime which would develop.[37] Therefore, a more coordinated approach is needed to collaborate on issues that are both in the national, commercial and private interest. Steps have been taken at the regional level to harmonize and develop a consistent framework for the management of data and protections.

In addition, Walters *etal* note that the co-regulatory and self-regulatory models to data protection have become synonymous across the world.[38] The authors highlight how that International Organization for Standardization (ISO) systems and standards are encouraged by some, but not all, national and EU data protection law, the GDPR, for organizations to adopt certified schemes. ISO 27001 provides oversight of three key areas 1) the security regime, 2) the people and 3) the processes and technology.[39] This scheme automatically requires organizations to undertake a comprehensive risk assessment of the potential impact to personal data, and in addition, cyber security. The authors also highlight how the International Organization of Securities Commissions has a policy role for the implementations of standards to prepare capital markets for a larger role in financing economic growth.[40] Committees have been formed for enforcement, data, asset management, bond market liquidity, market conduct, corporate governance, audit quality, long-term financing of small

[33] Kokott J, Sobotta C, (2013) The distinction between privacy and data protection in the jurisprudence of the CJEU and the ECtHR, *International Data Privacy Law*, Oxford University Press, vol 3, Issue 4, 22–228, in Walters, R., Trakman, L., Zeller, B, *Data Protection Law: A Comparative Analysis of Asia-Pacific and European Approaches*, Springer (2019).

[34] International Law Commission Report, Annex D, para. 11.

[35] Walters, R., Trakman, L., Zeller, B, *Data Protection Law: A Comparative Analysis of Asia-Pacific and European Approaches*, Springer (2019) 401–421.

[36] International Law Commission Report, Annex D, para. 11.

[37] Ibid.

[38] Walters, R., Trakman, L., Zeller, B, *Data Protection Law: A Comparative Analysis of Asia-Pacific and European Approaches*, Springer (2019) 401–421.

[39] Ibid.

[40] Ibid.

and mid-sized enterprises and infrastructure, and investor protection and education as a means to strengthen investor confidence and create the conditions for sustainable economic growth. This is particularly focused at the banking and finance sector. Over the past 5 years, the Committee on Payments and Market Infrastructures (CPMI) and International Organization of Securities Commissions (IOSCO) Harmonization Group has worked to develop guidance regarding the definition, format and usage of key OTC derivatives data elements reported to trade repositories (TRs), including the Unique Transaction Identifier (UTI), the Unique Product Identifier (UPI) and other critical data elements. Technical Guidance on the Unique Transaction Identifier (UTI) was published in February 2017 and Technical Guidance on the UPI will be published in Q3 2017.[41] A co-regulatory approach is needed for not only data protection but also AI and cybersecurity, particularly where the three area intersect.

4.2 Organisation for Economic Cooperation and Development

More importantly, these frameworks and institutions further highlight the internationalization of data protection law, which have, to varying levels, influenced the sovereignty of states when developing these laws. Nonetheless, and arguably since the influence from the OECD and EU, more work has been at the regional level, which is also influencing sovereign decisions in the area of data protection, and cyber security. The agreement and adoption of the OECD principles, can be summarized as quite remarkable. This is because there is only a total of 36 nation states that are formal members of this international organization.[42] In addition to the 36 members, there are key partners that include, Brazil, China, India, Indonesia, and South Africa. Of note is that the 36 members are predominantly Western democratic states, with the exception of Turkey. With the European Commission and most member states of the European Union actively participating in the work of the OECD on data protection, it is not difficult to assume that EU sovereignty has extended to formulating the original principles, now found in most, if not all data protection law across the world. This only further highlights the sovereign policy approach towards privacy, being the central pillar, with the economic activity from data being secondary. However, it must be noted that when the first OECD Guidelines were prepared in 1980, the thought of data trading was probably far from people's minds. The OECD Guidelines on the Protection of Privacy and Transborder Flows of Personal Data state that the development of automatic data processing, which enables vast quantities of data to be transmitted within seconds across national

[41] International Organization of Securities Commissions, Harmonization of critical OTC derivatives data elements (other than UTI and UPI) – third batch.

[42] Organisation for Economic Cooperation and Development, https://www.oecd.org/internet/ieconomy/oecdguidelinesontheprotectionofprivacyandtransborderflowsofpersonaldata.htm

frontiers, and indeed across continents, has made it necessary to consider privacy protection in relation to personal data. The OECD principles that have emerged as being critical to the overall regulation and protection of personal data include:

Collection Limitation – There should be limits to the collection of personal data and any such data should be obtained by lawful and fair means and, where appropriate, with the knowledge or consent of the data subject.

Data Quality – personal data should be relevant to the purposes for which they are to be used, and, to the extent necessary for those purposes, should be accurate, complete and kept up-to-date.

Purpose Specification – the purposes for which personal data are collected should be specified not later than at the time of data collection and the subsequent use limited to the fulfilment of those purposes or such others as are not incompatible with those purposes and as are specified on each occasion of change of purpose.

Use Limitation – personal data should not be disclosed, made available or otherwise used for purposes other than those specified in accordance with Paragraph 9 except: with the consent of the data subject; or by the authority of law.

Security Safeguards – personal data should be protected by reasonable security safeguards against such risks as loss or unauthorised access, destruction, use, modification or disclosure of data.

Openness – here should be a general policy of openness about developments, practices and policies with respect to personal data. Means should be readily available of establishing the existence and nature of personal data, and the main purposes of their use, as well as the identity and usual residence of the data controller.

Individual Participation – individuals should have the right to obtain from a data controller, or otherwise, confirmation of whether or not the data controller has data relating to them; b) to have communicated to them, data relating to them within a reasonable time; at a charge, if any, that is not excessive; in a reasonable manner; and in a form that is readily intelligible to them; c) to be given reasons if a request made under subparagraphs (a) and (b) is denied, and to be able to challenge such denial; and d) to challenge data relating to them and, if the challenge is successful to have the data erased, rectified, completed or amended.

Accountability – a data controller should be accountable for complying with measures which give effect to the principles stated above.[43]

The question arises that; while these principles have placed and served the beginnings of personal data regulation well – are they compatible with, or will they be relevant going forward as cyber security and AI systems will further integrate? Are they going to be relevant for AI used in the home? To date, their aim has gone some way to assisting in the regulation of the development of automatic data protecting that, as society and business evolve and continue to embrace technology is and has resulted in large quantities or personal data being transmitted across international borders daily. Thus, these principles, in part, have gone some way for governments, the business community and society to further consider the need for privacy protection. This book will answer these questions by comparing the countries data protections laws in Part III.

[43] Ibid.

4.3 Asia-Pacific Economic Cooperation

In addition to the above, similar principles have been accepted and adopted by other regional jurisdictions. The Asia-Pacific Economic Cooperation (APEC) is composed of 21 member economies that together represent approximately 55% of the world's GDP, 44% of world trade and 41% of the world's population.[44] APEC has developed several recent data protection initiatives. The three key initiatives include 1) the development of a set of common APEC Privacy Principles; 2) the development of a system for coordinating complaints that involve more than one APEC jurisdiction; and 3) the development of the Cross-Border Privacy Rules system (CBPRs).[45] The APEC CBPR system is an innovative self-regulatory mechanism for allowing the transfer of data between APEC members where a company has voluntarily joined the scheme. While in its infancy, self-regulation with government setting the minimum standards is more efficient for business and government collectively. The APEC privacy framework has set the course for member countries to cinder the following principles, as core elements to their respective legal frameworks.[46] However, as noted by Walters et al., APEC members are not obliged to implement domestically the APEC privacy Framework.[47] Thus, there continues to be inconsistencies in approach and adoption of data protection and privacy laws. More importantly, as APEC is a non-binding forum there is the opportunity for members to discuss current and future data protection issues freely. Of the countries studied in this book members of APEC include the US, China, the Philippines, South Korea, Canada and Vietnam.

María Vasquez Callo-Müller who has examined the commonalties between the EU GDPR and the APEC framework[48] noted that they only partially align with the GDPR and the OECD Guidelines as they include concepts such as the Privacy

[44] Asia-Pacific Economic Cooperation, https://www.apec.org/Groups/Committee-on-Trade-and-Investment/Electronic-Commerce-Steering-Group, in Robert Walters, Leon Trakman, Bruno Zeller, (2019) *Data Protection Law: A Comparative Analysis of Asia-Pacific and European Approaches*, Springer, 401–421.

[45] Ibid.

[46] Ibid. These include Preventing Harm, to prevent the misuse of information; Notice, ensuring that individuals are able to know what information is collected about them and for what purpose; Collection limitations, of personal information that is relevant to the purposes; Uses, should be used only to fulfill the purposes of collection; Choice, ensure that individuals are provided with choice in relation to the collection, use, transfer, and disclosure of their personal information; Integrity, to ensure personal information is accurate, complete, and kept up to date; Security, so as personal information is not used in a way to compromise the individual to who the data applies; Access and Correction, so as individuals have the ability to access and correct their personal information; and Accountability, to ensure organizations and individuals handling personal data are accountable.

[47] Walters, R., Trakman, L., Zeller, B, (2019) *Data Protection Law: A Comparative Analysis of Asia-Pacific and European Approaches*, Springer, 401–421.

[48] Callo-Müller, MV, *GDPR and CBPR: Reconciling Personal Data Protection and Trade*, APEC Policy Support Unit Policy Breif No. 23 October 2018.

Enforcement Authorities, privacy management programs, and promotion of technical measures to protect privacy. The GDPR on the other hand, includes principles and obligations that are not covered by the APEC Privacy Framework, the CBPR or the Privacy Recognition for Processes (PRP) system. The principle of "storage limitation" found in the GDPR does not appear to be reflected in the current APEC Privacy Framework.[49] As for the obligations, gaps are found with regard to mandatory data breach notifications, restrictions for automated processing and profiling, handling of special personal information, and onward transfers. The direct application of some those obligations to the processors is also an aspect that differs from the CBPR. Thus, there appears to be very little sovereign influence from the EU towards the APEC Framework. Callo-Müller believes the GDPR is a detailed regulation that works "top- down". It prescribes a series of obligations that should be met by companies and imposes hefty fines if those are not met. In contrast, the APEC – CBPR is a model of self-regulation. Furthermore, except for the intake questionnaire that an APEC member economy should fill up in order to submit its application to the Joint Oversight Panel, the CBPR is not prescriptive in the details and does not mandate how an economy should modify its data privacy laws.[50] Instead, the CBPR system works "bottom-up" towards a facilitated global data governance, which at the same time facilitates data sharing and reuse.[51] Analysing the APEC approach outside of the sovereign, Callo-Müller argues that the APEC-CBPR is a good example of promoting global interoperability of privacy regimes based on minimum standards. The authors are of the view that as more member economies and companies join the system, the APEC-CBPR could become an effective mechanism for privacy protection that works towards the avoidance of barriers to information flow, and ensures continuous trade and economic growth.

4.4 Asia Pacific Privacy Authorities

The Asia Pacific Privacy Authorities (APPA) promotes a partnership approach and exchange of ideas about privacy regulation, new technologies and the management of privacy enquiries and complaint.[52] Other topics discussed have been balancing privacy and security, cross-jurisdictional law enforcement in the Asia Pacific, cryptography, social media, international data transfer and the de-identification of data.[53]

---

[49] Ibid.

[50] Ibid.

[51] Ibid.

[52] Asia Pacific Privacy Authorities, http://www.appaforum.org/members

[53] Ibid. One of the gaps in the APEC policy framework has been addressing the cross-border transfer of data. Firstly, in 2014, the APEC and the European Union's Article 29 Working Party (on Data Protection) released Binding Corporate Rules (BCR). The BCRs govern international data transfers within companies or groups of companies. They reflect a code of conduct which defines the company policy on data transfers. Secondly, the APEC Cross Border Privacy Enforcement

While playing a minor role in the development of legislation, it provides a forum to discuss and resolve regional issues pertaining to privacy. In doing so the APPA have largely endorsed the APEC Privacy Framework and adopted the OECD Recommendation on Cross-border Co-operation in the Enforcement of Laws Protecting Privacy in 2007 and the commencement of the APEC Cooperation Arrangement for Cross-border Privacy Enforcement (CPEA) 2010, and the need for regional cooperative arrangements. Indirectly, there appears to be a continuum of sovereign influence even under the APPA, as minimal as it might be, but adopting the OECD framework to cross border cooperation would be influenced by elements of the EU and other states.

4.5 Association of South East Nations

Notwithstanding the above, the Association of South East Nations (ASEAN) being made up of countries from South East Asia,[54] have, at the regional level taken an EU approach. The countries examined in this book that are members of ASEAN include Vietnam, Lao and the Philippines. However, at the member state level this will vary. Firstly, the ASEAN Declaration on Human Rights sets the scene for the application of human rights across its member states. Article 21 states that every person has the right to be free from arbitrary interference with his or her privacy, family, home or correspondence including personal data, or from attacks upon that person's honour and reputation. Every person has the right to the protection of the law against such interference or attacks.[55] Walters, Trakman and Zeller argue that this is an important step in the recognition, understanding, management and protection of individual's personal data over the Internet. It serves to provide a level of privacy protection over the Internet. Although the Declaration does not require member states to fully

Arrangement (CPEA) established in 2015, underpins the Policy Framework to establish regional cooperation for enforcing Privacy Laws. APEC's Electronic Commerce Steering Group (ECSG) promotes the development and use of electronic commerce by supporting the creation of legal, regulatory and policy environments in the APEC region that are predictable, transparent and consistent. Since 2011, APEC has been undertaking a lot of work in the area of data protection and issues the Cross Border Privacy Rules System. The Rules system balance the flow of data across borders of member countries, and at the same time ensure effective protections are in place for private and personal information. In 2015, they established the Privacy Recognition for Processors (PRP) System, which assists controllers in complying with relevant privacy obligations, and helps controllers identify accountable processors. In the same year, APEC released the Privacy Framework that promotes electronic commerce throughout the Asia Pacific region.

[54] Brunei, Indonesia, Cambodia, Lao, Malaysia, Myanmar, Philippines, Singapore, Thailand, Vietnam.

[55] Association of South East Nations, Human Rights Declaration 2012, http://www.refworld.org/docid/50c9fea82.html

implement binding legal principles to protect personal data and privacy.[56] This is what sets ASEAN apart from the EU. The EU has been afforded a level of sovereignty by its member states, yet, ASEAN has none.[57] ASEAN have since its inception operate on a model on consensus.[58] It is our view that the Declaration enables ASEAN to guide member states to potentially adopt or move closer to EU model for data protection.[59] Furthermore, the ASEAN Economic Community (AEC) was established and marked an important milestone in ASEAN economic integration.[60] Its aim is to develop a coherent and comprehensive framework for personal data protection. This will require the development of Regional Data Protection and Privacy Principles (Rules System), and identify the responsibilities of businesses in personal data protection between 2016–2025.[61] It is also an objective to establish a common ASEAN consumer protection framework through higher levels of consumer protection legislation, improve enforcement and monitoring of consumer protection legislation and make available redress mechanisms including alternative dispute resolution mechanisms. In 2016, the ASEAN cybersecurity strategy was also announced, to ensure funds made available through the Cyber Capacity Programme (ACCP) launched by Singapore to support efforts to deepen cyber capacities across ASEAN. This is another example of how there is a multilayered approach being undertaken to the development and implementation of not only data protection but also, cyber security law. They are capturing elements of the sovereign states and amalgamating them into higher level principles, norms and standards that impart a top-down approach on states to adopt. Thus, what has also emerged is where states have or had already established privacy or data protection and cyber security laws, there is a convergence occurring from the bottom up. The resulting effect is a significant influence of state actors and the sovereignty of states, more or less, those that get in first, have the most influence in the development of these legal frameworks.

Even as these international and regional frameworks and programs have emerged to assist in the development, implementation and incorporation of standard principles within data protection laws, the sovereignty of state national laws have been further influenced with, and by, the Convention on Cybercrime 23.XI.2001 (CoC).[62] While the convention that has come out of the European Commission, there are a total of 64 countries that have ratified and acceded, with 3 signatories to the CoC. Apart from the member states of the European Union who has ratified the

[56] Walters, R., Trakman, L., Zeller, B, (2019) *Data Protection Law: A Comparative Analysis of Asia-Pacific and European Approaches*, Springer, 401–421.

[57] Ibid.

[58] Ibid.

[59] Ibid.

[60] ASEAN Economic Community, http://investasean.asean.org/index.php/page/view/asean-economic-community/view/670/newsid/755/about-aec.html

[61] ASEAN Economic Community 2025 Consolidated Strategic Action Plan, http://asean.org/storage/2017/02/Consolidated-Strategic-Action-Plan.pdf

[62] Convention on Cybercrime Budapest, 23.XI.2001 European Treaty Series – No. 185.

CoC, third countries such as Canada, Australia, Japan, the Philippines, the United States amongst others have either signed, acceded and ratified the CoC. The importance of the CoC, is another expression of the EU, and demonstrates the connectedness of personal data and cyber security. In other words, the CoC makes specific reference to right to the protection of personal data, as conferred, for example, by the 1981 Council of Europe Convention for the Protection of Individuals with regard to Automatic Processing of Personal Data. In addition, it makes criminal investigations and proceedings concerning criminal offences related to computer systems and data more effective and to enable the collection of evidence in electronic form of a criminal offence. Even though it does not define data or personal data, however, Article 1 defines computer data to be any representation of facts, information or concepts in a form suitable for processing in a computer system, including a program suitable to cause a computer system to perform a function. It goes onto define traffic data as any computer data relating to a communication by means of a computer system, generated by a computer system that formed a part in the chain of communication, indicating the communication's origin, destination, route, time, date, size, duration, or type of underlying service.

Arguably this could include forms of personal data. The interference of data generally can occur at different intervals, and Article 4 provides that each party is to adopt legislative and other measures as may be necessary to establish criminal offences under its domestic law, when committed intentionally, the damaging, deletion, deterioration, alteration or suppression of computer data without right. The resulting effect of Article 4, firstly guides nation states development of cybercrime laws. It aims to protect data generally, including personal data, and thirdly, while not taking away the sovereign right of nation states to regulate this area of the law, it does however, provide a platform for consistency across different states, by closing the gap in certain principles and concepts.

Based on the above, the nation state having a total sovereign right to develop data protection and to some degree cyber security law, has, in our view, been taken out of the hands of state actors. The regionalization of data protection and cyber security/crime principles have generally found their way into national laws, to varying degrees. However, there are exceptions, whereby some states have chosen not to embrace the internationally agreed principles, because they are largely based on Western thought. That being the case only highlights the difficulties that will be faced by regulators, lawyers, scholars and those other individuals implementing the laws, when having to understand the cross-border complexities.

4.6 Internet Use

The use of the Internet is growing annually. With that use, the extent of personal data that is being uploaded onto the various websites and platforms is enormous. There are a number of websites and platforms that, highlight the extent of internet use across the globe. Statista are of the view that reported in July 2019, across the world, the internet continues to transform how we connect with others, organize the flow of things, and share information. With its growing influence on individual consumers and large economies alike, it has become a crucial part of our day-to-day lives. As of 2017, it was estimated there were 3.8 billion internet users across the world.[63] This accounts for more than half of the global population, with China having the biggest online population at 829 million users, followed by India at 560 million and the United States at 293 million.[64] In terms of languages preferred, the English language represents 25.2% of global Internet users. Chinese ranked second with a 19.3% share, followed by Spanish at 7.9% (Table 4.1).[65]

The resulting effect from this Internet use is the expanded economic activity that, has now evolved in what is arguably the highest growth industry sector in decades. Statista, in 2019, estimated that the market value of the largest internet companies worldwide 2019 was enormous and only growing. They estimated that during in 2019 alone, e-commerce company Amazon's market value was 888 billion US dollars. Alphabet, the parent company Google, had a market value of 741 billion US dollars.[66] Moreover, the end of the 1990 in the United States saw the rise of a great number of internet companies, also called online companies or a variety of the name "dot com," where the ".com" domain is derived from the word commercial. Few companies have survived the burst of the dot com bubble and even fewer have managed to become internationally successful. A few notable exceptions are American

Table 4.1 Statista – Number of Internet users worldwide from 2009 to 2019, by Region

	Asia	Europe	North America	Latin America/ Caribbean	Africa	Middle East	Oceania/Australia
2009	764.4	425.8	259.6	186.9	86.2	58.3	21.1
2010	825.1	475.1	266.2	204.7	110.9	63.24	21.3
2011	1016.8	500.72	273.07	235.82	139.88	77.02	23.93
2012	1076.68	518.51	273.79	254.92	167.34	90	24.29
2013	1265.14	566.26	300.29	302.01	240.15	103.83	24.8
2015	1563.21	604.12	313.86	333.12	313.26	115.82	27.1
2016	1792.16	614.98	320.07	384.75	339.28	132.59	27.54
2017	1938.08	659.63	320.06	404.27	388.38	146.97	28.18
2018	2062.14	704.83	345.66	438.25	455.84	164.04	28.44
2019	2300.47	727.56	327.57	453.7	522.81	175.5	28.64

Source: Market Value of the largest internet companies worldwide 2019 (J Clement, Internet usage worldwide – Statistics & Facts, https://www.statista.com/topics/1145/internet-usage-worldwide/)

[63] Clement, J, Internet usage worldwide – Statistics & Facts, https://www.statista.com/topics/1145/internet-usage-worldwide/

[64] Ibid.

[65] Ibid.

[66] Ibid, Market Value of the largest internet companies worldwide 2019 https://www.statista.com/statistics/277483/market-value-of-the-largest-internet-companies-worldwide/ Statista provided approval for the use of these statistics.

companies such as Google, Amazon, eBay, and Alibaba, which have come to be some of the largest internet companies in the world.[67]

They go onto report that topping the ranking of largest internet companies worldwide is currently Alohabe, with a market capitalization of 741 billion US dollars as of June 2019. Due to a number of high profile acquisitions, Google has expanded its portfolio beyond search, to include the video content sharing site YouTube, the digital app platform Google Play Store, the webmail service Gmail and the web browser Google Chrome, to only name a few.[68] By March 2019, they note, it is also the most visited multi-platform website in the US, with almost 256 million US unique visitors during that month alone.[69] The largest internet companies in terms of their workforce are currently Amazon, Google and eBay. Without highlighting the potential anti-trust issues, it is important to understand that this new Internet or digital economy is creating new economic values. It is employing people for around the globe in areas of AI, cyber security and data protection-privacy experts that, only a decade ago were rarely conceived or thought of. Importantly, this area is likely to continue to grow, particularly as the legal frameworks that support them continue to be fragments. The three areas are fast becoming important economic drivers, and will pose enormous challenges to business and government to reconcile the gaps, not only in the law, but also socially. Moreover, the number of subscriptions taken out for mobiles phones have grown so fast that, it has arguably become the most efficient and effective way people access the Internet (Fig. 4.1).

The penetration of the Internet has been so pervasive that it is well understood, it will dominate our everyday lives, if it is not already doing so. Importantly, the statistics above highlight that there is considerable growth in the market to be had, and on a regional basis the Internet is having varying success. This is likely due to a number of different factors and issues such as economic, social, political, environmental and educational. As literacy rates continue to rise across the world, the resulting effect will likely see even more people utilizing the Internet.

Nonetheless, the various types of personal data that can and will be captured by AI (smart homes and personal devices) could be significant. Central to this, personal data that is protected under data protection laws can be further categorised as behavioural data or knowledge engineering, and that, under these devices is used for dataveillance. Firstly, dataveillance is where various forms of surveillance give rise to recording that data.[70] Roger Clarke and Graham Greenleaf argue that, this type of activity can include but not limited to, physical surveillance that records audio, image or video that can be associated with an individual. It can also constitute the communication between two or more individuals such as ephemeral messages (emails, sms, call data, IPSs logs). More pervasively, dataveillance logs and

[67] Ibid.

[68] Ibid.

[69] Ibid.

[70] Clarke, R., Greenleaf, G, *Dataveillance Regulation: A Research Framework*, Journal of Law and information Science, 25, 1 (2018).

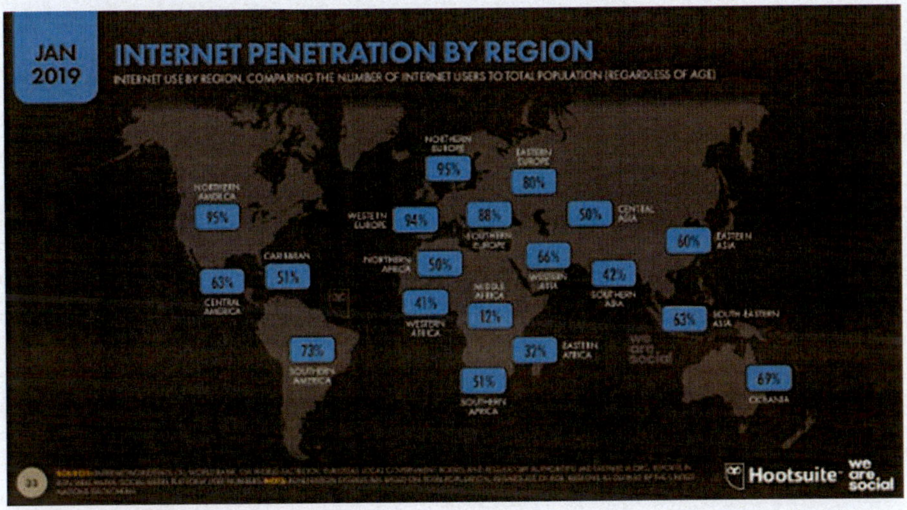

Fig. 4.1 Internet penetrations by region
Source: Simon Kemp (Kemp, S, Digital 2019, *Global Internet Use Accelerates,* https://wearesocial.com/sg/blog/2019/01/digital-2019-global-internet-use-accelerates) Citation and the use of the above is approved by Wraresocial in accordace woth their instructions - https://datareportal.com/citation

recordings, search terms used, webpages fetched, reading material downloads, biometrics that can measure heart rate, and identify a person.[71] What is not fully understood is the security around the smart home and personal devices, and how this dataveillance is used by state actors and non-state actors who capture and use this data. On the other side, and out another way, behavioural data[72] can detect and measure the behaviours of individuals.[73] It captures similar data to that described above by Clarke and Greenleaf. On the other side, personal data mining mechanisms and methods are employed patent is extended or adjust under to identify relevant information that otherwise would likely remain undiscovered.[74] Users supply personal data that can be analysed in conjunction with data associated with a plurality of other users to provide useful information that can improve business operations and/or quality of life. Personal data can be mined alone or in conjunction with third party data to identify correlations amongst the data and associated users. Applications

---

[71] Ibid.

[72] Alam, Mohammad Arif Ul; Roy, Nirmalya; Misra, Archan; and Taylor, Joseph. CACE: Exploiting behavioral interactions for improved activity recognition in multi-inhabitant smart homes. (2016). 2016 IEEE 36th International Conference on Distributed Computing Systems (ICDCS): Nara, Japan, June 27–30: Proceedings. 539–548. Research Collection School of Information Systems.

[73] Muhammad Habibur Rehman, Chee Sun Liew, Teh Ying Wah, Junaid Shuja and Babak Daghighi, Mining *Personal Data Using Smartphones and Wearable Devices: A Survey,* Faculty of Computer Science and Information Technology, 2015–15, 443–444.

[74] United States Patent, No. 7, 930, 197, B2. https://patentimages.storage.googleapis.com/ee/8f/2c/0bd80a64ef6a52/US7930197.pdf

or services interact with such data and present to its users in a myriad of manners, for instance as notification so opportunities.[75]

Viewed this way, data protection and privacy have converged primarily as a legal framework to protect people's personal data are defined by the law and as rights. This convergence also includes finding a balance between economic development, innovation and knowledge in the digital economy. Additionally, and central to this argument is the ability as Graham Greenleaf once put it, the idea of 'knowledge engineering'.[76] While Greenleaf argued that knowledge engineering constitutes both formal domain knowledge and the experience of domain experts have at various times been described as 'expert systems', 'knowledge-based systems' or just artificial intelligence ('AI').[77] Put another way, human reasoning is what is being modelled, whether based on causal models, heuristics based on experience, or interpretation of formalisms (standards, statutes). These traditional notions of expertise require that such 'expert systems' can give explanations for the conclusions they reach.[78] Greenleaf further argues that, there are varieties of successful development of such systems, including those that assist in the completion of tax returns, or determine entitlement to welfare benefits, and 'intelligent agent' software which roam through tax, audit, and accountancy data files looking for exceptions.[79] For example, document assembly systems generating complex documents through interactions with users are increasingly common, originally for use by lawyers but increasingly for lay use. In addition, online dispute resolution has numerous examples of systems successfully resolving very large numbers of disputes. Another major area of success has been 'predictive coding': using software to determine which documents should be disclosed in very large-scale litigation with more effectiveness than junior lawyers, and now with approval by United Kingdom courts. In medicine there are remarkable successes claimed, such as the pharmacy robot known as Epocrates that has issued more than a million prescriptions without error and automated the interaction of different drugs.[80] Expanding on these point, one can conclude similar knowledge engineering can be undertaken through smart home devices. This is because they are indirectly to the systems highlighted by Greenleaf, and, the data they capture will be generally personal data via dataveillance, which can determine behaviour and store vast quantities of knowledge data on an individual at home and in the workplace.

Even though privacy and data protection is an evolving area of law and economic development, it has not matured as a measure of redressing economic and personal harm comparably to the protection of intellectual property, copyright, criminal

[75] Ibid.

[76] Graham Greenleaf, *Thematic: Technology and the Professions,* UNSW Law Journal Volume 40(1) (2017), 310.

[77] Ibid.

[78] Ibid.

[79] Ibid.

[80] Ibid.

procedure and international trade law. It is argued that data protection is largely a tool of privacy.[81] Data protection has also been characterized as a tool of 'privacy'.[82] In other words, data protection underpins privacy and constitutes the personal data used to identify a person. Identifying a person by their personal data was historically achieved through state records, such as, a passport or birth certificate. Data protection today is increasingly considered as the implementation of appropriate administrative, technical or physical measures that minimize the risk of or harm caused by unauthorized intentional or accidental disclosure.[83] Therefore, in reconciling the gaps between the evolving area of AI law and data protection has to be a priority. The alternative is that regulators and governments will the market to determine the overall outcome, which for those jurisdictions that place human rights at the forefront of protecting personal data, will be significantly diluted.

For AI, cyber security and data protection this expansion poses ongoing vigilance and challenges to governments, private sector, community and regulators. While there will be considerable legal and policy issues to resolve, the economic benefits are likely to be significant. Thus, the balance between protection of personal data, cyber systems and innovation of AI all need careful consideration, not only as individual policy drivers, but also as a collective. The next section examines some of the issues and interrelationship between data protection and cyber security. It will also highlight the emerging concerns in AI.

4.7 Conclusion

Arguably, the interconnectedness of data protection and cyber security has begun. Stephen Kai-yi Wong, who is the Privacy Commissioner for Personal Data, Hong Kong, China, stated: "in this data-driven economy that keeps growing in parallel with the advent of big data and ICT developments – from which we benefit tremendously – it would not be in the interest of the community to have data locked up. One of the challenges in the face of Artificial Intelligence and Big Data, is how the governments and regulators can help unlock and share personal data within the legal and ethical frameworks, with a view to maximising the benefits of data in a sustainable way, minimising the risks and harms, creating healthy synergy with economic growth, and securing the innovative use of personal data".[84] Therefore, government

[81] Ibid.

[82] De Hert p, Gutwirth S, (2006) *Privacy, Data Protection and Law Enforcement. Opacity of the Individual and Transparency of Power*, in Claes E, Duff A, Gutwirth S, *Privacy and the Criminal Law,* Antwerp-Oxford, Intersentia, pp. 61–104, in Robert Walters, Leon Trakman, Bruno Zeller, (2019) *Data Protection Law: A Comparative Analysis of Asia-Pacific and European Approaches*, Springer.

[83] International Organisation for Standardisation/IEC 2382–1-1993 and its successors.

[84] Stephen Kai-yi Wong, *Grooving Privacy Evolution with Law Reform and Data Ethics*, 2019, https://www.pcpd.org.hk/english/news_events/media_statements/files/Paper_GroovingPrivacyEvolutionwithDataEthics_Feb2019.pdf

and regulators have a formidable task ahead to reconcile the gaps between data protection, AI and cyber security. It is likely never to be settled in the same way as traditional areas of law such as intellectual property, contract or tort law, because of the fluid nature of technology. The multilayered approach to policy and the law will not only be economic and social (health, education, environment, planetary health), it also will require states to consider national security, amongst others. Part I of this book has highlighted how data protection, AI and cyber security have evolved as separate policy and legal concepts. In the future, it is not inconceivable that these areas of the law as a collective converge, if jurisdictions take the position that personal data needs to be afforded greater levels of control and protection.

Internet use continues to rise across the world. That rise will provide even more personal data being made available over the Internet. Moreover, with the development of smart home technology, and as these devices connect to the Internet, even more personal data is likely to become available. It will enable organisations that collect this data to analyse and use this data to make significant profits. The development and increasing use of smart home, clothes, toys, personal robots and drones in our lives is becoming one of the most challenging areas to grapple with. These products and devices will be connected to the Internet, and with that, comes significant concerns over their security. Not only will they be accessible by individuals and entities who have the potential to exploit the daily lives of individuals, whether in the home or at work on a grand scale. Used wrongly, the personal data of people can be extracted and used for the wrong reasons by states and organizations. They have the potential to exploit the most vulnerable in the community such as children and disabled by creating biases. More problematic is that our everyday activities from the moment we are awake until we sleep and even while asleep could be potentially monitored to varying degrees by these devices. Thus, it will enable states and organizations to have even more control of individuals, groups and the broader community. If, fully realized, because the policy and legal frameworks are not adequate, also has the potential for even greater segregation based on ethnic, racial or religious grounds. It could have serious consequences for national security, national identity and social cohesion, along with personal data. As highlighted in Chaps. 1, 2, 3 and 4 this will pose significant challenges to government regulators.

Nonetheless, as reported in book 1 by Walters, Trakman and Zeller,[85] three data protection regulatory models have emerged. However, this book, and in our view additional models have also been identified such as the US, South Korea and China, which are vary from the EU, Singapore and Australia (see Chap. 15). It is no secret that the EU through the GDPR asserts is sovereign right to safeguard privacy, as it is a fundamental right under the European Convention on Human Rights 1950 and the European Charter of Fundamental Rights 2000. Yet, the Chinese model, not only asserts their sovereign needs, but is significantly different to the EU, US, Singapore, South Korea and Australia. China's Cybersecurity Law also identifies upholding

[85] Walters, R., Trakman, L., Zeller, B, (2019) *Data Protection Law: A Comparative Analysis of Asia-Pacific and European Approaches*, Springer.

individuals' privacy as an objective and specifies a series of protections and requirements for personal information.[86]

References

Chesterman, S. (2018). *Data protection law in Singapore: Privacy and sovereignty in an interconnected world* (2nd ed., pp. 1–9). Singapore: Academy Publishing.

De Hert, P., & Gutwirth, S. (2006). Privacy, data protection and law enforcement. Opacity of the individual and transparency of power. In E. Claes, A. Duff, & S. Gutwirth (Eds.), *Privacy and the Criminal Law* (pp. 61–104). Antwerp/Oxford: Intersentia.

Greenleaf, G. (2012). *The influence of European data privacy standards outside Europe: Implications for globalisation of Convention 108,* University of Edinburgh School of Law Research Paper 2012/12.

Kaminski, M. (2019). *Binary Governance: Lessons from the GDPR's Approach to Algorithmic Accountability*, 92 S. CAL. L. REV.

Kokott, J., & Sobotta, C. (2013). The distinction between privacy and data protection in the jurisprudence of the CJEU and the ECtHR. *International Data Privacy Law, 3*(4), 22–228, Oxford University Press.

Kong, L. (2010). Enacting China's Data Protection Act. *International Journal of Law and Information Technology, 18*(3), 197–226.

McGeveran, W. (2016). *Privacy and data protection law* (1st ed.). St. Paul: Foundation Press.

Richards, N., & Hartzog, W. (2019). *Privacy's constitutional moment.* Washington University School of Law; Yale Information Society Project. Northeastern University School of Law.

Schwartz, P. (forthcoming 2019). *Global Data Privacy: The E.U. Way*, 94 N.Y.U. L. Rev.; Anu Bradford, *The Brussels Effect*, 107 Nw. U. L. Rev. 1 (2012).

Walters, R., Trakman, L., & Zeller, B. (2019). *Data Protection Law: A comparative analysis of Asia-Pacific and European approaches.* Singapore: Springer.

[86] Grotto, A., Schallbruch, M, *The Great Anti-China Tech Alliance, The United States and Europe will regret letting Beijing win the race to govern digital technology.* https://foreignpolicy.com/2019/09/16/the-west-will-regret-letting-china-win-the-tech-race/ The authors identify four critical, mutually reinforcing factors that put China in a commanding position to influence the course of digital governance worldwide. The first factor is the size and attractiveness of its domestic market. The second factor is China's muscular, multifaceted industrial policy. Chinese authorities tap the leverage that comes from having an attractive market to impose a variety of market access conditions on foreign companies aimed at bolstering indigenous production and innovation. The third factor is China's ascendant innovation ecosystem, whose development over the past decade can be traced in significant part to the first two factors. The final factor is China's creative and empowered regulatory culture. China's regulatory apparatus has many flaws: corruption, vague rules, arbitrary enforcement, and so on. But Chinese regulators are also grappling with most of the same digital governance challenges as those in the United States, European nations, and other countries.

Part II
Data Protection Law – Asia

Chapter 5
South Korea

Abstract South Korea (This Chapter is from earlier work by Robert Walters, Data Protection law in South Korea, LexisNexis – Privacy Bulletin Vol 17 No 5:74–87 Sept 2020) has an amazing history being influenced by China, Japan, Russia and the West. Following WWII, they have developed and evolved into a highly sophisticated economy that has resulted in developing and using technology. Similar to other states they have had to grapple with how and to what impact the Internet has had to its citizens, particularly privacy and data protection. Today, the data protection laws of South Korea have, in part, had to evolve quite rapidly, in order for the country to continue to participate in the emerging technology and data economy. Their laws can be best described as being a hybrid of the European Union model and Singapore model.

Since the introduction of the Personal Information Protection Act (the PIPA) in 2011, it has been amended no less than on 6 occasions. It reflects the importance of personal data to South Korea both economically and personally, so as there are appropriate levels of protection. Consistent with the approach taken throughout the book, this Chapter refers to personal information and data protection interchangeably, as they are achieving a common goal. That is, to protect and provide a level of control to data subjects over their personal data over the Internet. South Korea place consent at the forefront of their laws, and also have placed considerable obligations on organizations when collecting and using personal data.

More importantly, what has emerged is the way South Korea has stepped away from many other states respective data protection laws, and inserted specific guarantee of rights. Nevertheless, and overall, the current day personal information protection laws are consistent with the worldwide trend that provides a level of control

R. Walters, M. Novak, *Cyber Security, Artificial Intelligence, Data Protection & the Law*, https://doi.org/10.1007/978-981-16-1665-5_5

and protection of personal data over the Internet. Korea's laws have arguably followed the institutional framework established by the OECD Privacy Guideline. Leading scholars from Korea are of the view that the general statutory structure of the data protection laws, shows many similarities to the EU's Data Protection Directive or the current day General Data Protection Regulation.[1] At the fundamental level, the laws replicate elements of the EU and the US model of data protection, particularly in relation to defining what personal data constitutes. However, and while elements of the laws do follow the EU model, Korea has exerted their sovereign needs, for example, whereby the concept of consent does not have an equivalent active role. That is, to protect and provide a level of control to data subjects over their personal data over the Internet.

Due to the breadth of the data protection laws of this state, this Chapter only discusses the following areas, Data Subject Rights, Definition of Personal Information [Data], Public and Private Application, Data Protection Principles, Consent Notification and Destruction Processing of Personal Information and Consent, Privacy Officer and Disclosure, Notification Impact Assessment Regulator [Commission], Damages, Data Localisation, Imposing a Penalty [Fine] and Cyber Security.

5.1 Introduction

South Korea and South Koreans are considered one of the leaders in technology throughout the Asia region. They are noted for its technology companies and ubiquitous high-speed Internet access.[2] Haksoo Ko, John Leitner, Eunsoo Kim and Jong-Gu Jung assert that South Korea also boasts a technology-literate general public, and many people carry brand-new smart phones with the latest functionalities. South Koreans are heavy users of social network services and various other Internet-based services. Along the way, the country has become an immensely information-intensive country.[3] This Chapter will identify the state in two ways, firstly South Korea or simply Korea.

South Korea is a peninsular country in the northeastern corner of the Asian continent. Its territory, which is now divided into North and South Korea, occupies 220,911 square kilometers, or 84,500 square miles.[4] Its history is complex, and the country is bounded to the north by two giant neighbors, China and Russia, and to the east and south it faces the islands of Japan across a 120-mile strait. Young Ick Lew argues the United States, another Pacific power, maintained significant

[1] Ko, H., Leitner, L., Kim, E., Jung, JG, (2016) *Structure and enforcement of data Privacy Law in South Korea*, Brussels Privacy Hub, Working Paper, Vol 2, No 7.

[2] Ibid.

[3] Ibid.

[4] Young Ick L, (2000) *Brief History of Korea, A Bird's-EyeView*, The Korea Society.

strategic and economic stakes in South Korea, and both North and South Korea remain a fulcrum of power politics among the great powers of the world. The Korean people belong to the Tungusic branch of the Mongoloid race.[5] Their polysyllabic, agglutinative language is a branch of the Altaic language family, which includes other tongues such as Turkish, Mongolian and Japanese. The Chinese culture has had a profound impact on Korea; Chinese elements found in today's Korean culture are a result of the Korean people's conscious and deliberate emulation of Chinese culture from mainly the second century BCE to 1895 CE.[6] Lew goes onto say that Korean's initial encounters with Europeans took place at the close of the sixteenth century. The first Westerner to set foot on Korean soil was Father Gregorio de Cespedes, a Spanish Jesuit priest who visited southern Korea as a chaplain in the train of Japanese soldiers during 1593–1595. The next Western visitors to Korea were 39 shipwrecked Dutch seamen, in 1628 and 36 in 1653.[7] One of the Dutchmen who was forcefully detained in Korea by the Chosŏn government was Hendrik Hamel.

Lew points out that he escaped from Korea in 1666 and eventually wrote *An Account of the Shipwreck of a Dutch Vessel on the Isle of Quelpart, together with the Description of the Kingdom of Corea.*[8] Throughout this period, Korean envoys who regularly visited Beijing came under the influence of Western science and Christianity early in the seventeenth century and shared their newly-acquired knowledge with Koreans at home. In 1905, in the wake of the Russo-Japanese War, the Japanese government unilaterally declared that Korea would henceforth be a Japanese protectorate.[9] In August 1910, this status was altered, and Korea became a formal colony of the Japanese empire. Nonetheless, as Lew highlights, Japan ruled Korea through the office of a Governor-General, who was usually a military man from the Japanese army or navy. During the first stage of the occupation (1910–1919), the Koreans were controlled by a draconian gendarmerie-police system, which deprived them of many basic civil freedoms. The stringent social controls finally produced a massive, nation-wide demonstration on 1 March 1919, referred to as the March First Movement.[10] Lew notes that following WWII and the defeat of the Japanese, this marked a significant period on the formation of the modern-day Korea. The Moscow Agreement between the United States and the Soviet Union, was finalized in December 1945. It was pivotal in that it clarified the procedure by which the Korean transition to autonomy would be conducted. Consequently, the Soviet Union influenced the development of North Korea and the South Korea was, and continues to be influenced by the West, particularly the United States.

Since WWII Korea has developed into a highly developed economy. Today, they are noted for their technology companies and ubiquitous high-speed Internet

[5] Ibid, p 6.
[6] Ibid, p 6.
[7] Ibid, p 18.
[8] Ibid, p 18.
[9] Ibid, p 23.
[10] Ibid, p 23.

access,[11] and are considered equal to Japan and Singapore in this area of the economy. The country also boasts a technology-literate general public, and many people carry brand-new smart phones with the latest functionalities. South Koreans are heavy users of social network services and various other Internet-based services. Along the way, the country has become an immensely information-intensive country.[12]

Similar to other countries throughout Asia, South Korea has had to grapple with various breaches of privacy law. The New York Times reported in 2015 that, South Koreans have had to deal with a series of affronts to their privacy recently, but one blow stings more than the rest: The country's three main telecommunication companies — KT, SK Telecom and LG Uplus — have been funnelling subscriber information to law enforcement agencies whenever a request is made, without demanding a warrant or informing affected customers.[13] They gave away names, addresses, resident registration numbers and other customer information pertaining to more than six million phone numbers in the first half of 2014 alone. All of that data now sits with law enforcement authorities, with no prospect of disposal. The collusion between telecom firms and the state is just another item in a long list of invasions of privacy by the government since President Park Geun-hye became a contender for high office more than four years ago. The issues became political, and threatened to derail the elections. That is, some commentators warned that Ms. Park's election might stoke authoritarianism because of her appeal among conservatives who honour her late father, the anti-Communist dictator Park Chung-hee, but no one predicted the Republic of surveillance that has taken shape under her watchful eyes.[14]

However, there were broader issues related to privacy in general from these internal actions by the government that, threatened to have a significant impact on the general privacy of their citizenry. Importantly, Articles 17 and 18 of South Korea's democratic Constitution prohibit the infringement of privacy and privacy of correspondence.[15] But conservatives have sought to minimize those guarantees by invoking Article 37 of the constitution, which allows for curtailing rights when necessary for national security, the maintenance of law and order or for public welfare.[16] The author notes that back in 2014 to 2016 there was considerable pressure and

[11] Organisation for Economic Cooperation and Development, broadband statistics http://www.oecd.org/sti/broadbandandtelecom/oecdbroadbandportal.htm For a journalistic account of South Korea's start-up culture, Amy Guttman, "How South Korea's $3 Billion Bet To Become A Regional Tech Start- up Hub Is Paying Off," Forbes (31 January 2016) http://www.forbes.com/sites/amyguttman/2016/01/31/why-south-koreas-3-billion-bet-to-become-a-regional-tech-startup-hub-is-paying-off/#4d24dc60a2f9

[12] *Supra note, 166.*

[13] Koo, S W (2015) South Korea's Invasion of Privacy New York Times https://www.nytimes.com/2015/04/03/opinion/south-koreas-invasion-of-privacy.html

[14] Ibid.

[15] Ibid.

[16] Constitution of the Republic of South Korea, Amended by July17, 1948 July 7, 1952 November 29, 1954 June 15, 1960 November 29, 1960 December 26, 1962 October 21, 1969 December 27, 1972 October 27, 1980 October 29, 1987.

condemnation from the international community over South Korea's direction. Freedom House now classifies South Korea's Internet and press freedoms as only "partly free" and has downgraded the country's political rights rating by a notch for 2014.[17] Amnesty International and Human Rights Watch have both called on the government to stop undermining freedom of expression, particularly in the arenas of politics and journalism.[18]

South Korea has opted for as slightly different name for their data protection laws, to that of other states. The Personal Information Protection Act (PIPA) was first introduced in 2011. Since then, it has been amended on 6 occasions.[19] However, as highlighted by Hanna Kim et al. South Korea developed separate laws to regulate the use of personal data in the public and private sectors. The *Act on Protection of Personal Information* of 1995, applied to public institutions while the *Act on Promotion of Information and Communications Network Utilization and Information Protection, Etc.* of 1999, applied to the private sector.[20] They go onto say that it:

> emphasizes the right to information privacy by specifying that the right to self-determination of the data subject includes a bundle of rights such as "the right to be informed of the processing of personal information;" "the right to agree or not to the processing of personal information and to the scope of consent;" "the right to request confirmation of personal information processing;" "the right to request access to personal information;" "the right to request the [processor] to suspend, correct, erase and destruct personal information;" and "the right to claim damages that result from personal information processing.[21]

Nonetheless, in recent times the Constitutional Court of the Republic of South Korea has decided on what constitutes data privacy. However, it must be noted that under the constitution of the state, there is no explicit right to data privacy or data protection, in the same way as the EU has established within the 2000 Charter of Fundamental Rights. The Constitutional Court, however, declared that data privacy rights are constitutional rights in case during 2005.[22] This case, commonly referred to as the *Fingerprint* case, raised a question about the constitutionality of requiring fingerprints from virtually all adult Korean citizens in the process of issuing national Resident Registration Cards and of utilizing the fingerprint information thus collected when the police conduct a criminal investigation. The Constitutional Court acknowledged that data privacy rights are not specifically set forth in South Korea's

---

[17] Ibid.

[18] Ibid.

[19] Personal Information Protection Act, established by Act No. 10465, March 29, 2011 Amended by Act No. 11690, Mar. 23, 2013 Amended by Act No. 11990, Aug. 6, 2013 Amended by Act No. 12504, Mar. 24, 2014 Amended by Act No. 12844, Nov. 19, 2014 Amended by Act No. 13423, Jul. 24, 2015 Amended by Act No. 14107, Mar. 29, 2016, Act No 14765 April 18 2017, Act No. 14839, Jul. 26, 2017, https://elaw.klri.re.kr/eng_mobile/ganadaDetail.do?hseq=46731&type=abc&key=PERSONAL%20INFORMATION%20PROTECTION%20ACT&param=P

[20] Kim, H., Kim, SY., Joly, Y (2018) *South Korea: in the midst of a privacy reform centred on data sharing Human Genetic,* 137(8): 627–635.

[21] Ibid.

[22] Constitutional Court of Korea, 99hunma513, 2004hunma190, 26 May 2005.

Constitution. The Constitutional Court, however, reasoned that data privacy rights should nonetheless be recognized as fundamental constitutional rights, which are derived from other rights that are explicitly stated, such as the right to private life (Article 17) and the right to dignity and to pursue happiness (Article 10). The Court further clarified that the "right to information self-determination" is the most crucial aspect when data privacy rights are concerned.[23] From this reasoning, the Court ruled that fingerprints are personal information and that an act of collecting and utilizing fingerprint information constitutes a restriction on the right to personal information self-determination.

However, and on the backdrop of the above, it must be noted that this case was decided upon before the implementation of the of the country's data protection laws. Even so, it highlighted the seriousness of personal data, by determining that it is a fundamental right. More recently, in 2015, the Constitutional Court reaffirmed its earlier position that data privacy rights are constitutional rights and that, as such, the right to information self-determination should be well-respected.[24] Furthermore, the Court ruled that South Korea's national Resident Registration Number system should provide a procedure allowing for possibilities of changing Resident Registration Numbers in the event that a legitimate need arises for such changes and should thereby guarantee Koreans the right to information and/or self-determination.[25]

What can be seen from these two Constitutional Court cases is how privacy and data protection is slowly evolving into the mainstream, and being treated as a constitutional right. Arguably, the Constitutional Court has set the policy and legal discourse in South Korea to ensure personal data is protected. In addition to the above, the PIPA is supported by the Personal Information Safeguard and Security Standard,[26] the Enforcement Rule of the Personal Protection Act,[27] and the enforcement Decree of the Personal information Act.[28] However, it must be noted that this chapter does not discuss or analyse how these supporting instruments have been implemented, or determine their effectiveness. More importantly, the PIPA places a number of obligations on the state to establish an additional level of controls on state and local governments to develop specific policies to prevent harmful consequences of beyond-purpose collection, abuse and misuse of personal information, indiscrete surveillance and pursuit.[29] The obligation further requires that state and

[23] Ibid.

[24] Constitutional Court of Korea, 2013hunba68, 23 December 2015.

[25] Ibid.

[26] Established by MOPAS Notification No. 2011–43, Sep. 30, 2011 Amended by MOI Notification No. 2014–7, December. 30, 2014.

[27] Established by MOPAS Ordinance No. 241, September. 29, 2011 Amended by MOPAS Ordinance No. 1, March. 23, 2013 Amended by MOI Ordinance No. 1, November. 19, 2014.

[28] Established by Decree No. 23169, September. 29, 2011 Amended by Decree No. 24425, March. 23, 2013 Amended by Decree No. 25531, August. 7, 2013 Amended by Decree No. 26776, December. 30, 2015. Amended by Decree No. 27370, July. 22, 2016.

[29] Article 5, Personal Information Protection Act, Amended by Act No. 14839, Jul. 26, 2017.

local governments shall work out policy measures, including the improvement of legislation, necessary to protect the rights of the data subject as stated in Article 4 (the rights of data subjects). The obligations on the state also extend to respecting, promoting and supporting self-regulating data protection activities of personal information controllers to improve irrational social practices relating to the processing of personal information.

Moreover, of the Asian nation states that have established specific and dedicated data protection laws, Korea's laws are considered one of, if not, the strictest.[30] Graham Greenleaf and Whon-il Park, while writing in 2012, and during a period when other states such as Singapore and Malaysia, amongst others had only begun to develop (China, India, Indonesia) specific data protection laws. The authors go onto say that the new South Korean law is, at least on paper, stronger in its requirements than any other Asian data privacy law. South Korea also has a good track-record of enforcement of its previous law, in relation to the private sector. Depending on how vigorously the new law is enforced in all sectors, future comparisons of effectiveness with laws in European countries, or other countries outside Europe, could see Korea rank favourably in the 'strongest privacy law' category. Businesses need to take very seriously its compliance requirements.[31]

Greenleaf and Park go onto make the point that South Korea is an OECD and APEC member, and a member of the Asia-Pacific Privacy Authorities (APPA). For Greenleaf and Park, Korea was considered an influential middle-ranking country, but its influence in data protection is less than it could be, partly because the strength and novelty of its data privacy laws are too little known. It is our view that Korea still maintains this status, however, since then the data protection laws have been amended and arguably introducing many more controls to protect individual's personal data over the Internet. Furthermore, Haksoo Ko, John Leitner, Eunsoo Kim and Jong-Gu Jung in 2016 argue that in relation to the structure and major provisions, the PIPA shows similarities to the approach taken in the EU, and both might generally be regarded as leading innovators in developing stringent personal data privacy standards.[32] However, once one begins to examine the relevant legal and regulatory structure in detail, differences can easily be noticed. The authors make the point that one of the most noteworthy differences is that, even after the enactment of the PIPA, other data privacy statutes continue to govern certain specific industries or specific types of information such as location information and credit information. In South Korea there are also multiple government agencies having a role in data privacy matters, each with differing mandates and enforcement authorities derived from different statutes.

---

[30] Greenleaf, G., Park, W, (2012) *Korea's new Act: Asia's toughest data privacy law* Privacy Laws & Business International Report, Issue 117, 1–6.

[31] Ibid.

[32] Ko, H., Leitner, J., Kim, E., Gu Jung, J, (2016)*Structured and Enforcement of Data Privacy Law in South Korea,* Brussels Privacy Hub, Vol 2, No 7.

5.2 Data Subject Rights

A distinctive feature of South Korea's data protection laws is the way data subjects have specific rights that have been established by the law. In other words, Article 4 provides that a data subject shall, in relation to the processing of his or her own personal information,[33] have certain rights. These include the right to:

(i) be informed of the processing of such personal information;
(ii) consent or not, and to elect the scope of consent, to the processing of such personal information;
(iii) confirm the processing of such personal information, and to demand access (including the issuance of certificate, hereinafter the same applies) to such personal information;
(iv) suspend processing of, and to make correction, deletion and destruction of such personal information; and
(v) appropriate redress for any damage arising out of the processing of such personal information in a prompt and fair procedure.[34]

While not specifically stated, the right to be erased/forgotten (RTBF) does exist in Korea. Apart from providing that a data subject can request that their personal data be deleted and destroyed, in 2016 guidance was issued by the government on the RTBF. On 29 April 2016, the Korean Government released the Korea Communication Commission, which provides that data subjects are able to request website administrators to remove personal information. The Guidelines on the Right to request access Restrictions on Personal Internet Postings, enables consumers to request data subjects to also remove data pertaining to them where the individual cannot delete that information themselves. It states that a data subject application for the removal of their personal information from a URL link can be requested for any reason. More importantly, following death of an individual, a family member can request on behalf of the deceased that their personal data be removed. The guidelines apply to all Korean and foreign entities providing Korean language services to South Koreans.[35]

Nonetheless, and in support of the above rights, Article 3 places considerable obligations on the controller to deliver on, and implement a process to ensure any processing of personal data is undertaken for a specific purpose. This is consistent with the OECD Guideline on data protection.[36] Article 3 goes further by specifying

---

[33] Article 4, Personal Information Protection Act, Amended by Act No. 14839, Jul. 26, 2017.

[34] Greenleaf, G., Park, W, (2012) *Korea's new Act: Asia's toughest data privacy law* Privacy Laws & Business International Report, Issue 117, 1–6, June 2012 Article 4.

[35] Lexology, South Korea Releases Guidance on Right to be Forgotten, https://www.lexology.com/library/detail.aspx?g=21be3837-0c43-4047-b8b5-9e863960b0b9

[36] Organisation for Economic Cooperation and Development, Guidelines on the Protection of Privacy and Transborder Flows of Personal Data, Purpose Specification Principle 9. The purposes for which personal data are collected should be specified not later than at the time of data collection

additional processes that must be undertaken by the controller when processing personal data, such as that data being accurate, complete and up to date, and manage the data safely. As part of taking steps to ensure that all data collected for processing is safe, the controller is also obliged to guarantee the data subject right of access to his/her personal information, and minimize the possibility to infringe upon the privacy of data subject. More importantly, there is an additional requirement to ensure that the data processed is done in a way to protect anonymity of the data subject, along with building trust of the data subject. Building trust strengthens the policy approach to providing certainty to the broader public, in an environment where data subjects have relatively little control over their personal data, when compared to the former paper-based systems of collecting and storing personal data. During this period, long before the internet, personal data was rarely traded as a distinctive commodity. It goes some way to providing and strengthening not only a data subjects control of their data over the Internet, but also, provides a level of guarantee that their broader statutory rights will be protected.

5.2.1 *Guarantee of Data Subject Rights*

A number of rights have been guaranteed under the personal information protection laws. Article 35 allows a data subject to demand access to his/her own personal data. However, and notwithstanding paragraph (1), when the data subject intends to request access to his/her own personal information from a public institution, the data subject may make a direct request for this data to the Minister of Interior. Upon any request the controller is responsible for managing the access request, and where justified the controller has the right to postpone the access. In addition, the controller may restrict access to that data where that access has been restricted by the law. It may also be restricted if that data is considered to cause damage to the life or body of others, or improper violation of properties and other benefits of others; or where the public institutions have grave difficulties in carrying out any of the following Items. Access to the data may also be restricted from the imposition, collection or repayment of taxes, or the evaluation of academic achievements or admission affairs at the schools established by the Elementary and Middle Education Act and the Higher Education Act, established by the Lifelong Education Act, and other higher educational institutions established by other laws.[37] Arguably, these rights have.

---

and the subsequent use limited to the fulfilment of those purposes or such others as are not incompatible with those purposes and as are specified on each occasion of change of purpose.

[37] Article 35, Personal Information Protection Act, Amended by Act No. 14839, Jul. 26, 2017. Testing and qualification examination regarding academic competence, technical capability and employment.

5.2.2 *Correction and Deletion of Personal Data*

The ability for a data subject to get their personal data either corrected or deleted from an Internet website or platform is fast becoming one of the most important rights afforded to data subjects. Having the ability to delete one's data has many similarities to the EU's conception of the right to be erased (right to be forgotten). Article 36 provides that a data subject, who have access to his/her own personal information in accordance with Article 35, may seek correction or deletion of their personal data to the personal information controller. However, this can only be achieved provided that deletion is not allowed where the personal data shall be collected under other laws and regulations.[38] In fulfilling this requirement, the controller must undertake to allow for the correction or deletion without any delay and take the necessary action to correct or delete the data.

The Korean Constitutional Court in 2010,[39] had to decide on the constitutionality of the temporary measures subject to Article 44-2 of the Network Act. In this case, the so-called takedown system under Article 44-2 of the Act on Promotion of Information and Communications Network Utilization and Data Protection, (Network Act) is at issue. Thus, when a user demands the deletion of the information made public via the information and communications network by claiming it has violated the privacy or legitimate rights of the claimant, what should the Internet service provider do? A further question arising was whether the publisher of the information in violation of privacy or likely to cause defamation would resist to take down his/her posting by insisting that it belongs to the freedom of expression. Article 44-2 (Request for Deletion of Information) of the Network Act No. 9119 on June 13, 2008, provides that:

- A provider of information and communications services shall, upon receiving a request for deletion or rebuttal of the information under paragraph delete the information, take a temporary measure, or any other necessary measure, and shall notify the applicant and the publisher of the information immediately. In such cases, the provider of information and communications services shall make it known to users that it has taken necessary measures by posting a public notice on the relevant open message board or in any other way.

[38] Article 36 (3) Personal Information Protection Act, Amended by Act No. 14839, Jul. 26, 2017. The personal information controller shall take measures not to recover or revive the personal information in case of deletion pursuant to paragraph (2). (4) When the demand of data subjects is applicable to the proviso of paragraph (1), the personal information controller shall, without delay, notify the relevant data subjects of its content. (5) While investigating the personal information in question pursuant to paragraph (2), the personal information controller may, if necessary, demand to the relevant data subjects the evidence necessary to confirm the correction and deletion of the personal information. (6) Necessary matters in relation to the demand of correction and deletion, notification method and procedure, etc. pursuant to paragraphs (1), (2) and (4) shall be provided by the Presidential Decree.

[39] Constitutional Court - Decision 2010Hun-Ma88, decided May 31, 2012 Regarding the constitutionality of the temporary measures subject to Article 44-2 of the Network Act.

- A provider of information and communications services may, if it is difficult to judge whether information violates any right or it is anticipated that there will probably be a dispute between interested parties, take a measure to block access to the information temporarily (hereinafter referred to as "temporary measures"), irrespective of a request for deletion of the information under paragraph (1). In such cases, the period of time for the temporary measure shall not exceed 30 days.[40]

The Court concluded that the provisions of the Network Act at issue do not amount to excess prohibition nor infringe upon the freedom of expression under Article 21 of the Constitution. This is because the public interest protected by taking down unlawful information prevails even though the same provisions have the danger of abating lawful information by requiring ISP to take some actions on all take-down requests. In coming to this position, the Court noted that:

> The above provisions at issue in this case have been inserted to let the Internet service provider take temporary measures up to 30 days subject to applicant's request to delete the information concerned and publisher's vindication of such infringement on privacy or reputation of other persons. Its legislative purpose is to prevent temporarily unlawful information from being distributed and diffused and its policy means seem to be appropriate. Privacy is too fragile to be made public, reputation could be violated when information leading to other person's defamation is placed to be recognized by many and unspecified persons. Consequently, texts, photography, videos and other information related with other's privacy and reputation used to spread quickly in the cyberspace, and cannot be sufficiently explained through arguments and debates. And it is ex post facto useless and repairable to compensate the victims suffering character destruction with damages and criminal punishment. The most efficient way is to block the diffusion of unlawful information temporarily.[41]

The Court further highlighted the importance of privacy over the Internet being a fragile concept. They believe that a person's privacy can be infringed with ease over the Internet. Thus, the use of texts, photographs, videos and other systems, platforms and information used in the wrong way can have serious reputational issues of other peoples' data protection. The Court went further arguing that the:

> requirements for temporary measures call for ISP's review in a reasonable manner of the vindication of victims; short-period of take-down up to 30 days; ISP's fair and self-regulatory settlement of disputes between the publisher and the victim after the take-down period, lest the freedom of expression of the publisher should be restricted in a narrow and necessary way.[42]

More noteworthy, the Court was of the view that Article 21(4) of the Constitution, the public interest protected by an ex-ante prevention of unlawful information from spreading indiscreetly to damage other person's character and rights irreparably[43]

---

[40] Ibid.

[41] Ibid.

[42] Ibid.

[43] Ibid.

seems to be bigger than the loss of private interest suffered by the publisher of such information. Nonetheless, apart from ability for individuals to delete their personal information, citizens of South Korea have the ability to seek a suspension of their personal data.

5.2.3 *Suspension of Personal Information*

In addition to the provision regarding the creation and deletion of personal information, Korea has gone one step further by allowing a data subject to demand that their personal data, one being processed by a controller, be suspended. However, Article 37 goes onto specifically provide that the suspension of any processing of personal data can only be undertaken of and to that data, which is contained within the personal files pertaining to the data subject. Nonetheless, any suspension will not apply where it is specified by the law, or there is the potential of danger or damage to a person.[44] Suspension of personal data is a further control mechanism that, places the data subject in a position of greater control over the use of their data.

5.2.4 *Method of Exercising One's Rights*

The exercise of the above-mentioned rights can be delegated to attorney or legal representative for minor under the age 14. The controller again is responsible for meeting the demands of the data subject. The controller can demand a fee and postage in order to meet any demands of the data subject.[45] The age limit varies from country to country and this is an area in our view that needs to be reconciled at the international level.

[44] Article 37, 3. Personal Information Protection Act, Amended by Act No. 14839, Jul. 26, 2017Where the public institution cannot carry out its work as prescribed by other laws without processing the personal information in question; or 4. Where the data subject fails to express explicitly termination of the contract even though it is difficult to perform the contract such as provision of service as agreed upon with the said data subject without processing the personal information in question. (3) When rejecting the demand pursuant to the proviso of paragraph (2), the personal information controller shall, without delay, notify the data subjects of the reason. (4) The personal information controller shall, without delay, take necessary measures including destruction of the relevant personal information when suspending the processing of personal information as demanded by data subjects. (5) Necessary matters in relation to the method and procedure of the demand or rejection of suspension of processing, notification, etc. pursuant to paragraphs (1) through (3) shall be provided by the Presidential Decree.

[45] Ibid, Article 38.

5.3 Definition of Personal Information [Data]

Article 2 defines personal data to mean any information which relates to a living natural person who can be identified or identifiable from those data including name, resident registration number and image, etc. (including the information that does not, on its own, permit direct identification of a specific individual, but that does identify specific individual when it is easily combined with other information). This broad definition could mean anything and everything that can identify a person. It provides a strong basis for Koreans to argue that anywhere, or, anything that captures any personal data would fall within this meaning. However, and while the courts are yet to determine what personal data falls within the above meaning, the current definition could pose challenges to individuals because of the lack of clarity. On the other hand, having such a broad definition does provide Korea with room to move when new technology enters the market and also captures personal data. In addition to the definition of personal data, Article 2 (3) and (4) defines a data subject to mean the natural person who is identifiable by the information processed hereby to become the subject of such information. Personal information file means a set or sets of personal information arranged or organized in a systematic manner based on a certain rule for easy access to the personal information.[46]

Despite this definition, Korea has not defined sensitive personal data. However, Korea deal with personal data quite differently. In accordance with Article 23, they have described sensitive data to constitute a person's ideology, belief, admission/exit to and from trade unions or political parties, political mindset, health, sexual life, and other personal information which is likely doing harm to privacy of data subjects. The flexibility in this approach is twofold. Firstly, the Presidential Decree which prescribes other elements of data that would be considered sensitive, allows sensitive data outside of Article 23 to be prescribed quite narrowly. Secondly, it does allow Korea to prescribe other areas of personal data to be sensitive, when it is required to do so. It is out of scope of this chapter to examine the frequency and application of change to the Presidential Decree.

5.4 Public and Private Application

The laws of Korea are silent on whether the laws apply to both the public and private sectors. However, Article 14 requires that the government is to establish policy measures so as to enhance the data protection standard in the international environment. Furthermore, the government shall work out relevant policy measures so that the rights of data subjects may not be infringed upon owing to cross border transfer of personal information.[47]

---

[46] Ibid, Article 2.

[47] Ibid, Article 14.

5.5 Data Protection Principles

Article 3 sets out the Personal Information Protection Principles that are import to South Korea. The core principles require that the controller is to make the personal information processing purposes explicit and specified, and shall collect minimum personal information lawfully and fairly to the extent necessary for such purposes. The controller shall process personal information compatibly to the extent necessary to attain the personal information processing purposes, and shall not use beyond such purposes.[48] This is consistent with other national and EU data protection laws. Additionally, the controller is required to ensure the personal information accurate, complete and up to date to the extent necessary to attain the personal information processing purposes; and manage personal information in a safe way according to the personal information processing methods, types, etc. in consideration of the possibility that the data subject rights are infringed upon and the degree of such risks.

Notwithstanding the above, the controller shall make public its privacy policy and other personal information processing matters, and shall guarantee the data subject rights including the right to access to his/her personal information.[49] Arguably this provides for greater transparency. More importantly the controller has a responsibility to minimize the possibility to infringe upon the privacy of data subject, and to process personal information in anonymity, if possible. They are required to develop a trust of data subjects by observing and carrying out such duties and responsibilities as stated in this Act.

5.6 Processing of Personal Information and Consent

The processing of personal information in the Korean context is the responsibility of the information controller. The personal information controller may collect personal information in any of the following cases, and use it within the scope of the collection purposes:

- Where the consent is obtained from data subjects;
- Where special provisions exist in laws or it is unavoidable so as to observe legal obligations;
- Where it is unavoidable so that the public institution may carry out such work under its jurisdiction as prescribed by laws and regulations;
- Where it is unavoidably necessary so as to execute and perform a contract with data subjects;
- Where it deems necessary explicitly for the protection, from impending danger, of life, body or economic profits of the data subject or a third party in case that

[48] Ibid, Article 3.

[49] Ibid.

the data subject or his/her legal representative is not in a position to express intention, or prior consent cannot be obtained owing to unknown addresses; or

- Where it is necessary to attain the justifiable interest of personal information controller, which is explicitly superior to that of data subjects. In this case, it is allowed only when substantial relation exists with the justifiable interest of personal information controller and it does not go beyond the reasonable scope.[50]

However, a further obligation imposed on the controller is to inform data subjects of when they obtain the consent to process their personal data that, they (data subject) is to be informed of the purpose of collection and use of personal information, (2) particulars of personal information to be collected; (3) the period when personal information is retained and used; and (4) the fact which data subjects are entitled to deny consent, and disadvantage affected resultantly from the denial of consent.[51]

Notwithstanding the above, Article 16 limits the collection of personal information by the information controller for the purposes outlined in Article 15. These limitations include, but not limited to consent being obtained from the data subject, and includes where the consent is obtained from data subjects. It also pertains to where special provisions exist in laws or it is unavoidable so as to observe legal obligations or if it is unavoidable so that the public institution may carry out such work under its jurisdiction as prescribed by laws and regulations. This is a major exemption and would require further clarification of what laws and where this might apply. The exemption goes further to include situations where it is unavoidably so as to execute and perform a contract with data subjects.[52]

Nevertheless, the protection of personal data must be undertaken where a data subject is in immediate threat or impending danger, of life, body or economic profits of the data subject or a third party in case that the data subject or his/her legal representative is not in a position to express intention, or prior consent cannot be obtained owing to unknown addresses. This also extends to where it is necessary to attain the justifiable interest of personal information controller, which is explicitly superior to that of data subjects. In this case, it is allowed only when substantial relation exists with the justifiable interest of personal information controller and it does not go beyond the reasonable scope.[53] The data subject is to be informed of the purpose of collection and use of personal information, and particulars of personal information to be collected. In addition, they must be informed of the period when personal information is retained and used. This accords with the notion of overall purposive principle provided by the OECD principles. Yet in order to meet the requirements of Article 15, the controller needs to prove of the minimum personal information is collected shall be borne by the personal information controller. Furthermore, the controller shall collect the personal information by informing the

[50] Article 15, Personal Information Protection Act, Amended by Act No. 14839, Jul. 26, 2017.

[51] Ibid.

[52] Ibid.

[53] Ibid.

data subject of the fact concretely that he/she may deny the consent to the collection of other personal information than the minimum information necessary in case of collecting the personal information by the consent of the data subject. However, the controller cannot deny the provision of goods or services to the data subjects on ground that they would not consent to the collection of personal information exceeding minimum requirement. Further clarification is needed as to how this would operate. On the one hand, the law is seeking to provide a level of control to the data subject over their personal data, through the concept of consent. On the other hand, where the data subject does not consent to the collection of their personal data, that consent appears to be negated where there are the provision of goods and services involved.

While the controller has a high level of responsibility for protecting the collection and use of personal data, they, may provide that data to a third party only where they have obtained consent from the data subject.[54] In addition, Article 17 requires that the controller only provides the personal data for the purposes outlined in Article 15. However, this provision could be problematic. This is because the level of consent beyond the third party, for example, beyond the second point of dissemination is not clear within the law. Further, this is an evolving issue across most, if not all data protection laws. In other words, the law has yet to fully grasp and reconcile the point where consent begins and concludes beyond the first level of consent obtained. Apart from general level of consent being obtained, the controller is required to reinforce and inform the data subject of the purpose for the use of the data, the exact particulars of personal data required; the period for which the data will be retained, and that the data subject can deny consent. It would need to be read in conjunction with the definition of personal data. As stated in this chapter, the definition of personal information is very broad, and therefore, the controller will need to be very specific on what data they are going to use.

On the backdrop of the above, Article 18 places a number of obligations on the personal information controller when using personal information beyond the scope of Article 15, and is not to provide it to a third party beyond the scope stated in Article 17(1) and (3). However, where any of the following subparagraphs applies, the personal information controller may use personal information for other purpose than the intended one, or provide it to a third party, unless it likely infringes upon unfairly the interest of data subjects or a third party; provided, however, that subparagraphs 5 through 9 are applicable only to the public institutions.[55] In other words, additional consent may be required from the data subject, where it is deemed to be necessary to protect that data should it fall into the wrong hands and pose a threat or danger to the data subject's life (economic profits of the data subject or a third party) in case that the data subject or his/her legal representative is not in a position to express intention. Consent will also be required where:

---

[54] Ibid, Article 7.

[55] Ibid, Article 18.

- personal information is provided in a manner keeping individuals unidentifiable necessarily for the purposes of statistics and academic research;
- it is impossible to carry out the work under its jurisdiction as stated in other laws unless personal information controller uses personal information for other purpose than the intended one, or provides it to a third party, and it is subject to the deliberation and resolution of the Commission;
- it is necessary to provide personal information to a foreign government or international organization so as to perform a treaty or other international convention;
- it is necessary for the investigation of crimes, indictment and prosecution;
- it is necessary for the court to proceed the case; or
- it is necessary for punishment, and enforcement of care and custody.[56]

However, there are specific controls for public institutions holding and using personal information. In other words, 'Article 18 (4) requires that when, the public institution uses personal information for other purpose than the intended one, or provides it to a third party under subparagraphs 2 through 6, 8 and 9, the public institution shall post the legal grounds for such use or provision, purpose and scope, and other necessary matters on the Official Gazette or its Website as prescribed by the Ordinance of the Ministry of Interior. In addition, Article 18(5) imposes an obligation on a controller when providing data to a third party, the controller shall request the recipient of personal information to restrict the purpose and method of use and other necessary matters, or to prepare any safeguards to ensure the safety of that data'.[57] In this case, the person who is requested shall take necessary measures to ensure the safety of personal information. However, this does not stop the individual or entity from passing on that data to another party.

More importantly, and what can be considered a stand-out for the data protection laws of Korea, is the use limitation provision placed on the recipient. Article 19 requires that the individual receiving (the recipient) the data from a controller is not to use personal information for other purpose than the intended one, or shall not provide it to a third party except the case applicable to any of the following subparagraphs. Additionally, the use of that data can be undertaken where additional consent is obtained from data subject, or there are special provisions that exist in other laws, such as criminal law. However, this still does not resolve the dichotomy that, once the data has been passed onto the third party, that party can hand it onto a

[56] Ibid. (3) The personal information controller shall inform data subjects of the followings when it obtains the consent under subparagraph 1 of paragraph (2). The same shall apply when any of the followings is modified: 1. The recipient of personal information; 2. The purpose of use of personal information (in case of provision of personal information, it means the purpose of use of the recipient); 3. Particulars of personal information to be used or provided; 4. The period when personal information is retained and used (in case of provision of personal information, it means the period for retention and use by the recipient); and 5. The fact which data subjects are entitled to deny consent, and disadvantage affected resultantly from the denial of consent.

[57] Ibid, Article 18(4)-(5).

fourth or fifth party without consent. Andrew Neville[58] believes that the Korean guidelines are on par with the principles of the right to be forgotten in the EU context. This is an important point because most countries throughout Asia have, in part, adopted elements of the European approach. Furthermore, to date, have gone it alone and have not fully embraced the idea of the right to be forgotten.

5.6.1 Limitation to Processing

Placing limitations on the processing of personal data provides another layer of control to and for data subjects to control their data over the Internet. Article 23 achieves this by limiting the processing of sensitive personal data. As highlighted above sensitive data in the Korean context constitutes ideology, belief, admission/exit to and from trade unions or political parties, political mindset, health, sexual life, and other personal information which is likely doing harm to privacy of data subjects, as prescribed by the Presidential Decree.[59] Nevertheless, and on the backdrop of the above, limitations on the processing of personal data exist where consent from the data subject has not been obtained. In addition to this, the processing of data is limited where the laws or regulation require a permit, specifically for sensitive personal data. Having a permit arrangement (system) for managing sensitive personal data is arguably an innovative feature of the Korean data laws. The approach does not exist in any other laws examined in this book, or that of the other book on data protection law mentioned previously.

Despite this approach, the controller of sensitive personal data is to ensure the highest possible safety procedures are in place to ensure that this data cannot be lost, stolen, leaked, forged, altered or damaged. Arguably, during a period where cybercrime continues to grow, the potential for the personal data to be lost, stolen, leaked, forged, altered or damaged is on the increase. Rather, the question is how effective will this provision be in practice? As a deterrence, it will likely achieve a level of further control over that data.

5.6.2 Limitation to Processing [Unique Identifier]

Article 24 provides that the controller should not process the identifier assigned so as to identify an individual in accordance with laws and regulations, as prescribed by the Presidential Decree. That is the controller has an obligation not to process personal data without consent and ensure steps are taken to safety mechanism are

[58] Andrew Neville, *Is it a Human Right to be Forgotten? Conceptualizing the World View*, 15 Santa Clara J. Int'l L. 157 (2017), 158–168.

[59] Article 23, Personal Information Protection Act, Amended by Act No. 14839, Jul. 26, 2017.

established including encryption, as prescribed by the Presidential Decree, so that the Unique Identifiers may not be lost, stolen, leaked, forged, altered or damaged.[60] The Minister of Interior shall inspect periodically as prescribed by the Presidential Decree whether the personal information controller falling into such criteria as prescribed by the Presidential Decree in consideration of the type and size of personal information, number of employees, sales volume, etc. has taken the measures necessary to ensure the safety subject to paragraph (3). The Minister of Interior may authorize a specialized institution stated by the Presidential Decree to conduct inspection subject to paragraph (4). This section affords a degree of flexibility to the relevant minister for the management of sensitive personal data.

5.6.3 Limitation on Visual Data Processing Devices

A notable difference in the laws of South Korea is that they place limitations on the use of certain devices. This is because in other states laws largely place provisions such as this into their cyber security or criminal laws. Nevertheless, they control over visual data processing devices is an area that requires careful, but, strong regulation because the extent of devices available on the market and how easily they can be used, poses many challenges to the protection of personal data and information. Thus, in accordance with Article 25, no one shall install and operate visual data processing devices at open places. However, there are exceptions to this rule. They include cases where the laws and regulations allow it in a concrete manner; the prevention and investigation of crimes; the safety of facilities and prevention of fire; regulatory control of traffic; and where it is necessary for the collection, analysis and provision of traffic information.[61] The laws go onto place significant controls over these devices so as no one shall install and operate visual data processing devices so as to look into the places which likely threat individual privacy noticeably, such as a bathroom open to the public, toilet, sweating room and dressing room; provided, however, that the same shall not apply to the facilities, which detain or protect persons pursuant to laws and regulations, such as a penitentiary, mental health centre stated by the Presidential Decree.

The head of public institutions who intends to install and operate visual data processing devices is to gather opinions of relevant specialists and interested persons through such formalities as public hearings, information sessions, that are stated by the Presidential Decree.[62] Furthermore, the person who intends to install and operate visual data processing devices is to take necessary measures including posting on a signboard containing the items the purpose of installation and location; (2). the range of V/D operation and duration; and (3). the name of V/D manager in

[60] Article 24, Personal Information Protection Act, Amended by Act No. 14839, Jul. 26, 2017.

[61] Article 25, Personal Information Protection Act, Amended by Act No. 14107, Mar. 29, 2016.

[62] Ibid.

charge and contact number; and any other matters as prescribed by the Presidential Decree.[63]

The importance of regulating the use of certain devices cannot be underestimated. From the simple mobile phone to more sophisticated subversive surveillance equipment can track and trace, and release individual's personal data. Thus, a V/D operator is not to handle arbitrarily visual data processing devices for other purposes than the initial one, nor direct the said devices toward different spots, nor use sound recording functions. They are also required to take measures to ensure the personal information is not lost, stolen, leaked, forged, altered or damaged. There obligations on the operator also extend to requiring them to also establish a policy so as the equipment is managed and used appropriately, to minimize the misuse of the data.

5.6.4 Processing Limitation [Consignment of Work]

A further obligation of the controller is the management of the personal data when consigning processing obligations to a third party.[64] The obligation extends to prevent the processing of personal data for any other purpose than that has been described. In addition, the controller has an obligation to ensure that there are appropriate safeguards for the data and comply with any safety prescriptions prescribed by the Presidential Decree. The controller is required to ensure that a third party disclose what data has been consigned and who carries out the consigned processing of personal information so that data subjects may recognize it at any time with ease. In addition to the controller is required to when having consigned the data to or as part of any goods or service, or soliciting of sales, notify the data subjects of the work. Apart from the above, the consignor has a role to educate the consignee to ensure that the data is not be lost, stolen, leaked, forged, altered or damaged owing to the consignment of work. In reinforcing the principle of only processing personal data for a specific purpose, the consignees is not to use the data beyond the scope of work consigned to them.[65]

[63] Ibid, the same shall not apply to the military facilities subject to Article 2 ii of the Military Base and Military Facilities Protection Act, important national facilities subject to Article 2 xiii of the United Defense Act and other facilities as prescribed by the Presidential Decree.

[64] Ibid, Article 26.

[65] Article 26, (6) With respect to the compensation of damages arising out of processing personal information consigned to the consignee in violation of this Act, the consignee shall be deemed as an employee of the personal information controller. (7) Articles 15 through 25, 27 through 31, 33 through 38 and 59 shall apply mutatis mutandis to the consignee.

5.6.5 *Limitation to Transfer Business Transfer*

In addition to the above limitations on the processing, use and consignment of personal data.[66] Korea has also chosen to strengthen controls of the systems and processes when transferring personal data to others. As part of this process the data subject must be informed that their data will be transferred and to which company or entity. They are to be provided the address, telephone number and other contact points of the recipient of the data. The method and procedure to withdraw the consent is where the data subject would not want the transfer of his/her personal information.[67] Upon receiving the personal information, the transferee shall without delay notify data subjects of the fact of such transfer. The transferee may, in case of receiving personal information owing to business transfer, merger use, or provide to a third party, the personal information only for the initial purpose prior to transfer. In this case, the business transferee shall be deemed as the personal information controller.

5.6.6 *Processor Oversight [Supervision]*

A further procedural step by the controller is to ensure they provide adequate supervision of the individual processing personal data. Article 28 requires that while processing data, 'the controller is to conduct an appropriate level supervision of the processing'.[68] Where required the controller is to provide adequate level of training to the handler and processor of the information. This standard arguably provides a minimum requirement that can and should be enhanced through organizational policies, procedures and guidelines. It reinforces and promotes the co-regulatory model that has become a pivotal part of the overall legal framework for personal data throughout the world.

5.7 Notification and Destruction

Notification is also considered an important concept afforded to data protection law. Arguably, the concept relates to organizations, or specific individuals within an organization to notify the data subject of the use of their personal data. In the Korean context, Article 20 requires that the controller notify the data subject of the source of collected personal data, its purpose for the collection and processing, along with providing the data subject with the option to suspend the processing of that data.

[66] Article 27, Personal Information Protection Act, Amended by Act No. 14839, Jul. 26, 2017.

[67] Ibid.

[68] Article 28, Personal Information Protection Act, Amended by Act No. 14839, Jul. 26, 2017.

This is a unique option afforded by Korean law, because the exemption places another layer of control in the hands of the data subject. Nonetheless, the controller will need to consider the type and size of personal information, number of employees, sales volume, etc. processes, personal information collected from other sources than data subject pursuant to Article 17(1); the personal information controller shall notify such data subject of everything stated in each subparagraph of paragraph (1); provided, however, that the same shall not apply if the information collected by the personal information controller does not contain a contact number, etc. where such data subject can be reached.[69] Upon the data subject being contacted they are to be provided information in relation to the time and method of that contact. However, this does not apply where or when personal information, which is the object to demand notification, is included in the personal information files applicable to any of the subparagraphs of Article 32(2); or where such notification likely causes harm to the life or body of other person, or unfairly damages the properties and other profits of other person. However, this only pertains to a controller that is prescribed by a Presidential Decree. Article 32(2) provides that the Minister of Interior may certify whether the data processing and other data protection related action of the personal information controller abides by this Act.[70]

The destruction of personal data like many other areas of the law is very important. There has been considerable debate about the length of time an organization should be afforded to retain personal data. The personal information controller is responsible for destroying the personal data of a data subject. The requirement(s) in accordance with Article 21 is that the personal data is to be destroyed without delay. The method of destruction is not specified; however, a number of methods have

---

[69] Article 20, Personal Information Protection Act, Amended by Act No. 14839, Jul. 26, 2017.

[70] Ibid, Article 32, (2) The certification pursuant to paragraph (1) shall be effective for 3 years. (3) The Minister of Interior may withdraw the certification pursuant to paragraph (1) as prescribed by the Presidential Decree if any of the following subparagraphs falls on the case; provided, however, that it shall be cancelled in case of subparagraph 1. 1. Personal information protection has been certified by fraud or other unjust means; 2. Ex post facto management under paragraph (4) has been denied or obstructed; 3. The certification criteria under paragraph (8) have not been satisfied; or 4. Personal information protection related statutes are breached in a serious manner. (4) The Minister of Interior shall conduct ex post facto management more than once a year to maintain the effectiveness of the certification of personal information protection. (5) The Minister of Interior may authorize a specialized institution stated by the Presidential Decree to conduct certification subject to paragraph (1), withdrawal of such certification subject to paragraph (3), ex post facto management subject to paragraph (4), management of the certification examiners subject to paragraph (7). (6) Any person who has obtained the certification subject to paragraph (1) may display or publicize the certification as prescribed by the Presidential Decree. (7) The qualification, criteria of disqualification, etc. of the certification examiners who conduct the certification examination subject to paragraph (1) shall be stated by the Presidential Decree taking account of specialty, career and other necessary things. (8) Other necessary matters for the certification criteria, method, procedure, etc. subject to paragraph (1), including whether the personal information management system, guarantee of data subject's rights and secured safeguards are based on this Act, shall be stated by the Presidential Decree.

been highlighted under the Presidential Decree.[71] At the time of writing this book the Presidential Decree was not made available in English. However, the controller is required to take measures to block recovery or revival of personal data, and is obliged to preserve, rather than destroy by storing that data. The standard of preservation, destruction or storage of data is not specified, and largely left to the controller and organization.

5.8 Consent

It is well understood that the concept of consent has become one of the most important concepts that makes up the legal framework for data protection. However, what are people consenting to? The notion of consent is coupled with the definition of personal information/data. Despite, Article 22 providing for the method by which consent can be obtained, the concept of consent has been dealt with in other areas of the law (within this chapter).

When the personal information controller obtains the consent from the data subjects with respect to personal information processing under this Act, the personal information controller shall notify the data subjects of the fact by separating the matters requiring consent and helping the data subjects to recognize it explicitly, and obtain their consent thereof, respectively. Upon obtaining consent,[72] the controller is to segregate the personal information which needs the data subjects' consent to processing, from the personal information which needs no consent in executing a contract with data subjects. This is an important stage of the process, and provides a level of guarantee to data subjects that only certain elements or components of their personal data will be processed in accordance with the level of consent provided. Nonetheless, in this case, the burden of proof that no consent is required in processing the personal information shall be borne by the personal information controller. The level of responsibility placed on the controller is high. They will need to have in place specific processes and system, to ensure they meet the required threshold for segregating that personal information that has been provided consent for processing, and that which has not.

Nonetheless, when dealing with children and minors the laws require a different level of consent. There are major differences from country to country in this area of

[71] Article 21, Personal Information Protection Act, Amended by Act No. 14839, Jul. 26, 2017.

[72] Ibid, Article 22, When the personal information controller obtains the consent from the data subjects with respect to personal information processing in accordance with Articles 15(1) i, 17(1) i, 23(1) i and 24(1) i. The personal information controller shall, when it intends to obtain the data subjects' consent to personal information processing so as to promote goods and services or solicit purchase hereof, notify the data subjects of the fact by helping the data subjects to recognize it explicitly, and obtain their consent thereof. (4) The personal information controller shall not deny the provision of goods or services to the data subjects on ground that the data subjects would not consent to the matter eligible for selective consent pursuant to paragraph (2), or would not consent pursuant to paragraph (3) and Article 18(2) i.

the law. The controller is required to obtain consent for the processing of personal information of minors of age below 14, however, this is to be undertaken through their legal representatives. In this case, the minimum personal information necessary to obtain the consent from legal representatives may be collected directly from such minors without the consent of their legal representatives.

As a result, companies obtaining personal data (location) are now required to ask the children aged under 14 whether their parents or legal guardian give consent. Parental consent can be given via payment information, authentication through smartphones or through text.[73] However, a written agreement will be then sent to the parents or legal guardians by the companies to confirm the consent. Any company found violating the law and collecting data from children before consent will be fined of up to 3% of their revenue and face administrative punishments.[74] They argue that, for Koreans, and particularly protecting the most vulnerable group of people online, is a matter of ethics, and an obligation of the state. While consent plays a crucial role regarding permissibility of collecting and processing personal information, a data subject is given certain control rights over the personal information even after granting consent.[75] The authors argue that, first, a data subject has a right to access the personal information collected. Second, a data subject can make a request to correct the data if the information that the processor holds is incorrect. Third, a data subject can make a request to stop further processing of his or her data. Fourth, upon receiving these requests, processor is obliged to comply.[76]

In 2012, the High Court of Seoul Decision 2011Na75166, 2012, was faced with resolving the question of whether consent, which H Telecom obtained from its customers without discriminating the collection and use of personal information from activation of services, was legal? Six years earlier in 2006, the H Telecom[77] entrusted its marketing business to Telemarketer Y to manage its customers. This resulting in Y obtaining large quantities of personal data. In September of the same year, H Telecom issued the partnership card associated with S Bank to its customer-applicants. For this purpose, H Telecom entrust its customer relations to Y, and inserted, in its card users' terms and conditions, the statement that H Telecom will use customers' personal information in promoting the partnership card. H Telecom posted the said statement on its website, but failed to obtain a separate consent from its customers.[78] However, between July and September of 2006, H Telecom provided Y with the personal information of an estimated 515,000 customer names,

[73] South Korea revises child data protection laws, https://gdpr.report/news/2019/06/24/south-korea-revises-child-data-protection-laws

[74] Ibid.

[75] Other matters than those provided from paragraphs (1) through (5), necessary to secure a detailed method to obtain the consent from data subjects and the minimum information pursuant to paragraph, shall be stated by the Presidential Decree in consideration of collection media of personal information.

[76] Ibid.

[77] Soul High Court south Korea, Decision 2011Na75166, 2012.

[78] Ibid.

service type, telephone number, the first six-digit first sequence (birth date) and the first-digit second sequence (gender) of the resident registration number, address, inquiry of tariffs, amongst others. The resulting effect allowed Y to access the central information system, which in turn saw Y solicit H Telecom's customers to apply for a member's card via telephone. The Court held that:

> consent which H Telecom obtained afterwards from its customers in relation to the collection and use of personal information could not cure the illegality caused by its provision of personal information without appropriate consent.[79]

The Court went further also ruling the mere posting the amended provisions of card users' terms and conditions would not constitute an effective consent to the entrusted processing of personal information by pointing out entrusting the processing of personal information is quite different from the provision of personal information to a third party. The broader issue highlighted by the Court was the fact that:

> H Telecom actually violated customers' right to self-determination of personal information by providing their personal information to an entrusted party without an appropriate consent.[80]

The Court ruled that, H Telecom was responsible for damages – 200 thousand won to the customers without consent on the collection and use of personal information and 100 thousand won to the customers without consent on the entrusting the processing of data to a third party, respectively.[81]

On the backdrop of the above, the defendant appealed to the Supreme Court, however, the appeal was dismissed. The case highlights the ongoing challenges faced by data subjects once they have provided consent to an entity, and that entity is subcontracted and uses that personal data for any type of gain.

5.9 Privacy Officer and Disclosure

There are a number of similarities between the Korean laws and that of the EU. The requirement to establish a Privacy Officer is something different to the EU model. However, this responsibility is different from that of a controller or processor. The Privacy Officer (PO) is responsible for the processing of personal data.[82] They are appointed by the controller. This has similarities to the controller and processors that are established by the EU under the GDPR.

In addition to the above, the controller has a responsibility for establishing technical, managerial and physical measures as internal management plan and preservation of log-on records, to ensure that personal information is not be lost, stolen,

---

79 Ibid.

80 Ibid.

81 Ibid.

82 Article 31, Personal Information Protection Act, Amended by Act No. 14839, Jul. 26, 2017.

leaked, forged, altered or damaged. Article 30 requires that the 'controller establish relevant privacy policy, for the management of personal data files'.[83] The policy and procedure process provide the basis for the management of personal data (collection, storage, use and disclosure). They also form part of the co-regulatory model. Furthermore, Article 32 places obligations on the Minister for Interior, who being the head of a public institution and holding files that contain personal data.[84] Therefore, the Minister of Interior is required to develop a register to manage the registration and public disclosure of the personal information files retained by the National Assembly, the Court, the Constitutional Court and the National Election Commission (including their affiliated entities) shall be provided by the respective rules of the National Assembly, the Court, the Constitutional Court and the National Election Commission.

While not specifically highlighting the issues surrounding the disclosure of personal data from the Minister from Interior, the Seoul Court has dealt with disclosure issues pertaining to personal data. In 2016, the Seoul Central District Court[85] was required to determine whether Google's forced disclosure of status quo of its provision of personal information and service details of domestic users to a third party. Google Inc., a US (defendants) corporation, provides about 60 Internet-based services including Google Search, YouTube, and Gmail worldwide. Co-defendant Google Korea, Ltd. (hereinafter referred to as "Google Korea") is engaged in sales

---

[83] The purpose of personal information procession; 2. The period for processing and retention of the personal information; 3. Provision of the personal information to a third party (if applicable); 4. Consignment of personal information processing (if applicable); 5. The rights and obligations of data subjects and their legal representatives, and how to exercise the rights; 6. The name of the privacy officer subject to Article 31 or the name of department in charge of personal information protection affairs and related complaints, telephone numbers and other contact points. 7. Installation, operation and denial of automatic data collection devices including the Internet log-on file, etc., if any; and 8. Other matters in relation to personal information processing as stated in the Presidential Decree.

[84] Article 32, The title of the personal information files; 2. The grounds and purposes for the operation of the personal information files; 3. Particulars of personal information which are recorded in the personal information files; 4. The method of processing personal information; 5. The period of retaining personal information; 6. The recipient of personal information in case it is provided routinely or repetitively; and 7. Other matters as prescribed by the Presidential Decree. (2) paragraph (1) shall not apply to the personal information files applicable to any of the following subparagraphs: 1. The personal information files which record the national security, diplomatic secrets and other matters relating to grave national interests; 2. The personal information files which record the investigation of crimes, indictment and prosecution, punishment, and enforcement of care and custody, corrective order, protective order, security observation order and immigration; 3. The personal information files which record the examination of law violating activities pursuant to the Law of Punishment on Tax Criminals and the Customs Act; 4. The personal information files which are used exclusively for internal job performance of the public institution; or 5. The personal information files which are classified as secret pursuant to other laws and regulations. (3) The Minister of Interior may, if necessary, review the registration and its content of the personal information files stated in paragraph (1), and advise the relevant head of the public institutions to improve such files.

[85] Seoul Central District Court Decision 2014GaHap38116 decided October 16, 2015.

and marketing of online advertisement products, services, direct marketing (DM) products and services in Korea. Plaintiffs are Google service users who became members by generating Google account or using corporate mail service provided by Google Inc. Two years earlier in February, 2014, the Plaintiffs requested Defendants to respond to whether Defendants had provided information about Plaintiffs and to provide details of such information. However, Google Korea did not give any answer to Plaintiffs. Google Inc. sent Plaintiffs emails dated February 22, 2014 to the effect that (1) Google Korea is not in a position to respond to the information disclosure request because it is not the supplier of Gmail service; and (2) Google Korea provides the information of users to government agencies only when required by laws. Google Inc. lawyers examined all the individual requests and most of cases of such requests have been rejected because of improper procedure or too broad questions.[86] The Court noted that for the privacy protection of users, Google Inc. shall not make any statement whether a certain user is subjected to the said request of information. Unless otherwise prohibited by law or court orders, Google Inc. used to inform the users of the particulars required to provide by law.[87]

Nonetheless, in response, the Plaintiffs requested again that the Defendants provide a detailed answer about whether what kind of information of Plaintiffs has been provided to a third party. However, the defendants did not give any response. As a result, the Court ruled that:

> Google Korea cannot be the principal providing Google services nor become the service provider jointly with Google Inc. because such company is subcontracted for improving the performance or handling personal information for and on behalf of Google Inc. Therefore, Google service users have no right to request Google Korea to disclose the status quo of personal information provided to a third party pursuant to Article 30(2) of the Network Act.[88]

However, the Court went onto conclude that it is reasonable to consider that the principal providing location information service and location-based service related to Google products is Google Korea because the end user agreement for those services clearly states that those services provided for Google products are provided by Google Korea. The Court further ruled that:

> In this regard, the complaint filed by the Plaintiffs against Google Korea is grounded on Article 30(2) of the Network Act, while any disclosure of detailed location information shall be subject to Article 24(4) of the Act on Protection and Use of Location Information. The end user agreement for location information service and location-based service is not mentioned in the complaint of Plaintiffs.[89]

Thus, based on the above, the Court concluded that the Plaintiffs' suits are unlawful and accordingly shall be dismissed because of wrongfully targeted defendant as well as incorrectly invoked statutory grounds.

---

[86] Ibid.

[87] Ibid.

[88] Ibid.

[89] Ibid.

5.10 Regulator [Commission]

Article 7 establishes the Personal Information Protection Commission. It is established under the Presidential Office to have oversight over, deliberate and resolve the matters regarding data protection across Korea. The Commission independently conduct the functions belonging to its authority and consist of no more than 15 Commissioners, including one Chairperson and one Standing Commissioner, who shall be a public official in political service. Importantly, the Commissioners are appointed or commissioned by the President. A total of five Commissioners shall be appointed or commissioned from among the candidates elected by the National Assembly, and other five Commissioners from among the candidates designated by the Chief Justice of the Supreme Court:

1. Persons recommended by privacy-related civic organizations or consumer groups;
2. Persons recommended by the trade associations composed of personal information controllers; and.
3. Other persons who have ample academic knowledge and experiences related with personal information.[90]

Commissioners can only be appointed for a three year and their term of appointment can only be extended once.[91] Meetings of the Commission is to be convened by the Chairperson when the Chairperson deems it necessary or more than one quarter of Commissioners demand it.

5.11 Impact Assessment

A common feature of most, if not all data protection laws around the world that exists, except for a small few, is the requirement for an Impact Assessment to be undertaken.[92] They have become another important part of the multilayered framework surrounding data protection by providing a further level of control. Article 33 requires that a public institution is to conduct an assessment where there has a been a breach in relation to personal data. Any Impact Assessment is to identify the number of personal information being processed; the personal information is provided

[90] Article 7, Personal Information Protection Act, Amended by Act No. 14839, Jul. 26, 2017.

[91] Ibid, Article 7 (5), (7) The resolution of the meeting of the Commission shall be made by the affirmative votes of the majority of present Commissioners if more than half of the Commissioners are present at the meeting. (8) A secretariat shall be established within the Commission to support the administration of the Commission. (9) Other matters than those provided from paragraphs (1) through (8), necessary to the organization and operation of the Commission, shall be stated by the Presidential Decree.

[92] Ibid, Article 33.

to a third party; the probability to violate the rights of data subjects and the degree of such risk.[93]

Moreover, there is the ability for a Privacy Impact Assessment to be conducted by the National Assembly, the Court, the Constitutional Court and the National Election Commission. In this situation, the impact assessment is largely governed by the rules of these institutions. At the time of writing this book, those rules were not available in English. The rules will need to be consulted by data subjects and legal practitioners to better understand how they are to be applied. Finally, the controller has an obligation to undertake an impact assessment even where there is the potential for personal data to be violated.

5.12 Notification

The protection from the misuse of personal information is a fundamental part of these laws. Thus,

Article 34, requires that the controller is to notify a data subject of the personal data that was leaked. In addition, the data subject is to be notified of how the data was leaked, and the probable damaged suffered by the data subject from the leak. They are also to be informed of the remedial steps that will be taken to address the leak, and provide assistance and a contact point within the organisation[94] so as the data subject can report any likely personal damage.

In 2014, Changwon District Court[95] in dealing with personal data being leaked, is one of the first cases involving the connection between cyber security and data

[93] (3) The Minister of Interior may provide its opinion subject to the deliberation and resolution of the Commission upon receiving the PIA result as stated in paragraph (1). (4) The head of the public institution shall register the personal information files in accordance with Article 32(1), for which the Privacy Impact Assessment has been conducted pursuant to paragraph (1), with the PIA result attached thereto. (5) The Minister of Interior shall work out necessary measures, such as fostering relevant specialists, and developing and disseminating PIA criteria, so as to activate the Privacy Impact Assessment. (6) Necessary matters in relation to the Privacy Impact Assessment, such as the designation criteria and designation revocation of the PIA institution, assessment criteria, method and procedure, etc. pursuant to paragraph (1) shall be provided by the Presidential Decree.

[94] Ibid, Article 34, (2) The personal information controller shall prepare countermeasures to minimize the damage in case of personal information leakage, and take necessary measures. (3) In case where a large scale of data breach above the level specified by the Presidential Decree takes place, the personal information controller shall, without delay, report the notification stated in paragraph (1) and the result of measures stated in paragraph (2) to the Minister of Interior and such specific institution as stated in the Presidential Decree. In this case, the Minister of Interior and such specific institution as stated in the Presidential Decree may provide technical assistance for the prevention and recovery of further damage, etc. (4) Necessary matters in relation to the time, method and procedure of the data breach notification pursuant to paragraph (1) shall be provided by the Presidential Decree.

[95] Changwon District Court Decisions 2014GoDan64·2014GoDan602 (consolidated), 2014GoDan602 (consolidated), 2014GoDan947 (consolidated), 2014GoDan948 (consolidated), 2014GoDan1097 (consolidated) decided June 20, 2014.

protection. The Court was responsible for determining whether a personal data leakage committed by persons entrusted to develop and install computer and communications systems, would be liable. The Court noted that the defendant employed by a credit information company was developing and installing a credit card fraud detection system for Bank E. In the course of the said work, defendant used the customer information which had been processed, stored and transmitted in the server of Bank E from May 2012 to December 2012.[96] While working at the office of G card business department located in Seoul in October 2012, Defendant inserted his USB to the PC for business use, stored the information including name, resident registration number, mobile phone number, credit card number, credit limit and the amount of card use of about 25 million card users of Bank E at his own discretion, and got out of that office. After then, Defendant connected his PC, which contained the stolen information of card users of Bank E to the PC of his friend, thus storing such information in his friend's PC.[97] The Court ruled that:

> In view of the danger and harm caused by the leakage of personal information, it is necessary to sentence serious punishment against such person as entrusted to do the security job, who can fully foresee that such information will be spreading fast and extensively regardless of his intention, and will be used continuously for unlawful purposes thereafter. Thus, the responsibility of Defendant shall not be relieved even though Defendant demanded a promise to prevent further leakage from the person to whom the information was handed over.[98]

While specifically pertaining to Article 34, and the leakage of personal information, the case highlighted how in South Korea that the Court will consider the interconnectedness of cyber security and data protection. More importantly, where it can be determined that there has been a level of harm or danger incurred by data subjects from the cyber leakage, the courts are of the view that a severe penalty should be imposed regardless of the intention of the person who caused the leak.

A year earlier, the District Court[99] found a Police Officer guilty of breaching the personal data protection laws as a result of the disclosure or leakage of personal information. The Police Officer disclosed a four-digit telephone number which was decided as leakage of personal information. The facts of this case saw a policeman assaulted a gambling place upon receiving the report of a victim. The gambler was arrested by the policeman, and then was released. Later at the request of the gambler, the policeman informed him of the four-digit number of the victim-reporter's smartphone. The policeman was accused of the leakage of personal information without the consent of data subject.[100] Therefore the Court was required to determine whether the four-digit number of a smartphone was personal information that,

---

[96] Ibid.

[97] Ibid.

[98] Ibid.

[99] Daejeon District Court Nonsan Branch Decision 2013GoDan17 decided August 9, 2013.

[100] Ibid.

could be used to identify the data subject. Even though the Court never went into the extent of the definition of personal information, the Court noted that:

> everybody is using a smartphone at any time, any place, even the four-digit number of a smartphone is the personal information enough to identify the data subject. In this case, the four-digit number of the reporter's smartphone is the personal information which represents the information about a living person, or would identify the reporter when it was easily combined with other information.[101]

The Court concluded that the four-digit number of the reporter's smartphone is his personal information to be protected in accordance with the Personal Information Protection Act. Therefore, the policeman was guilty. The case not only highlights the nature and circumstance where personal information can be leaked or illegally disclosed with ease. It also informs the community that, government officials are not immune from the proper and appropriate management and control of citizens, personal data, is today, becoming an important societal issue.

5.13 Data Localisation

Data localization is increasingly being established within national laws. It refers to domestic laws or regulations that force localization of data, limiting the storage, movement and processing of data to specific jurisdictions, or limiting companies that can operate with countries' data.[102] In practice it restricts the transfer of data to a third country, restricting the server location to be located within national borders. In the case of Korea, the PIPA, South Korea has two more major laws that regulate strictly on spatial and location information–the Act on the Protection Location Information and the 1961 Korean Land Survey Act. South Korean data localization regulations on data not only are meant to protect the privacy and security of citizens, but also put strict limitations on geographical data for national security reasons. Article 15(1) of the Act on the Protection of Location Information states that, no one shall collect, use, or provide the location information regarding an individual or mobile object without the consent of the individual or the owner of the mobile object. It regulates the collection of location information without consent from the owner of that location. No other country has the same legal strictness around on location information nor have separate law regulating the collection of such information.[103]

Article 17(3) of PIPA states that, when a personal information manager provides a third person at any overseas location with personal information, he/she shall notify

[101] Ibid.

[102] Hill, JF, (2014) *The Growth of Data Localization Post-Snowden: Analysis and Recommendations for US Policymakers and Business Leaders*, Cyber Governance, 3.

[103] Yoon, J, (2018) *South Korean Data Localization: Shaped by Conflict, Data Localization Laws & the International Movement of Information* University of Washington.

a subject of information of the matters referred to in each subparagraph of paragraph (2) and obtain the consent thereto, and shall not enter into a contract concerning the transborder transfer of personal information stipulating any details contravening this Act. Julia Yoon argues that the Korea government has used data localization requirements to protect local e-commerce and online payment operators and these restrictions do place some burdens on organizations that intend to send data across borders. She goes further asserting that the purpose of the policies is to mainly protect user's data from possible malicious act, but some data security experts argue that storing data within the country is ineffective against foreign surveillance and creates a "honeypot" for criminals to practice data breaches and abuse.[104]

5.14 Imposing a Penalty [Fine] – Damages

The fines and penalties attached to individuals and entities for breaching these laws vary amongst the countries and jurisdictions studied. Similar to other jurisdictions, the imposing of a fine is not necessarily left with the courts, but rather the Ministry of Interior (MoI). The MoI can impose and collect penalty surcharges not exceeding 500 million won where a controller has caused the loss, theft, leak, forgery, alteration or damage of specific personal identifying data, being resident registration numbers. However, this penalty will not apply where the controller can demonstrate that they have taken the necessary steps and established relevant measures to ensure the safety of that data. Thus, the loss of this personal data from an illegal intrusion (cyber hack). More importantly, the MoI has the ability to impose a further charge for any unpaid penalty. The additional sum totals 6/100 per annum of the unpaid penalty surcharge that is determined by the Presidential Decree.[105]

Notwithstanding the above, Article 39 allows the courts to impose a penalty for damage that has been suffered by a data subject from the misuse of their personal data. A damage to a data subject constitutes the loss, theft, leak, forgery, alteration or damage of personal information, caused by wrongful intent or gross negligence of the controller. Thus, the court may fix the damages within the scope not exceeding three times of such damage; provided, however, that it shall not apply to the said personal information controller who has proved non-existence of its wrongful intent or gross negligence. The court can 'in fixing the damages take into account the intent or expectation of likelihood of losses; (2). the amount of loss caused by violations; and (3). economic benefit caused by violations and gained by the controller'.[106] Further to this, the court in fixing damages impose a levy subject to violations for

---

[104] Ibid. Note there are other laws that need to also be considered, which is out of scope of this chapter, notably the Land Survey Act, Network Act 1961, Use and Protection of Credit Information Act (Credit Information Act) 1995.

[105] Ibid.

[106] Ibid.

the duration and velocity of violations, along with the wealth of the controller. Finally, the efforts to retrieve the affected personal information exerted by the personal information controller after the loss, theft and leak of personal information; and the efforts to remedy the damage suffered by a data subject exerted by the controller.[107] However, it is arguable whether these penalties are adequate, due to the extensive profits that are being made by the large organisation, who are essentially controlling the worlds data.

5.15 Cyber Security

One of the most formidable threats to personal data is not so much the misuse of that data, but resides in the state's ability to respond to cyber security incursions. This has been reinforced by the Korean National Cyber Security Strategy (the Strategy).[108] The Strategy highlights how cybercrime damage to businesses and people continues to grow with the increasing use of advanced technology and sophistication of cyber-attacks, such as stealing and encrypting personal information. The involvement of state actors and terrorist groups is also creating greater and more serious cybercrime damage, increasing the number of incidents that threaten national security.[109] It goes onto say that political, economic, and military disputes among states are escalating to conflicts in cyberspace. In some cases, cyber-attacks are conducted prior to or after physical attacks. By recognising cyber capabilities as asymmetric powers with potential to significantly impact national security, states have long fostered cybersecurity experts and expanded cybersecurity organizations. In addition, governments have invested substantial budget in developing state-of-the-art cyber technologies based on artificial intelligence (AI) and big data analytics, as well as strengthening capabilities to collect cyber intelligence, disturb Internet networks, and disrupt major facilities.[110] The national strategy highlights the need for the development of advanced systems and platforms in the area of cryptographic and confidential information security systems so the government's confidential information is protected

---

[107] Ibid, Article 39. Article 39-2 (Claim for Statutory Damages) (1) Notwithstanding Article 39(1), the data subject, who suffers damage out of loss, theft, leak, forgery, alteration or damage of personal information, caused by wrongful intent or negligence of the personal information controller, may claim a considerable amount of damages to the extent not exceeding three million won. In this case, the said personal information controller may not be released from the responsibility for damages if it fails to prove non-existence of its wrongful intent or negligence. (2) In case of the claims subject to paragraph (1), the court may fix the reasonable amount of damages to the extent stated by paragraph (1) taking account of whole arguments in the proceedings and the examination of evidence. (3) The data subject who has claimed damages pursuant to Article 39 may change such claim to the claim subject to paragraph (1) until the closing of fact-finding proceedings.

[108] Korean *National Cyber Security Strategy*, Publication 12-1025000-000003-01, https://www.krcert.or.kr › filedownload

[109] Ibid.

[110] Ibid.

against data leaks or damage. This includes, and not limited to the protection of commercial and national security data, but, also personal data of its citizens.

On the backdrop of the above, Korea has adopted a multilayered and sectorial regulatory approach to cybersecurity. They have been grouped into the public and private sectors, along with the financial and critical Infrastructure sectors. Apart from the PIPA, the cyber security laws include, the Act on the Promotion of IT Network Use and Information Protection (the Network Act). The Network Act principally promotes cybersecurity in terms of protecting personal information and enhancing data security in the context of IT networks.[111] It also prohibits any unauthorised access to a network system by means of a transfer or distribution of a program that may damage, destroy, alter or corrupt the network system, or its data or programs. In addition to the above, the Electronic Financial Transactions Act (EFTA), prohibits electronic intrusion into the network systems of financial companies, and data protection is mandated for financial companies in accordance with the Regulation on Supervision of Electronic Financial Transactions (the RSEFT).[112]

Finally, other legislation that supports the cyber security regulatory framework includes; the Credit Information Use and Protection Act (the Credit Information Act) regulates entities that collect, use, investigate, manage or provide credit information (called 'credit information companies'), and requires that such entities employ technological, physical and administrative security measures in order to protect credit information computer systems.[113] The Act on the Protection and Use of Location Information (the Location Information Act) specifically targets the protection of 'location information' and 'personal location information', which allows a certain individual to be located on its own or in combination with other information. Moreover, the Protection of Information and Communications Infrastructure Act (PICIA) is more engaged with the protection of information and communications infrastructure against 'electronic intrusion', which is defined as an act of attacking information and communications infrastructure by hacking, computer viruses, logic bombs, email bombs, denial of service, high-power electromagnetic waves and other means.

5.16 Conclusion

South Korea has, along with many other countries across Asia, established a comprehensive legal framework to protect personal data. The data protection laws of South Korea are very different to that of its regional counterparts and those of Canada, Hong Kong, Macau, the US and China. Underpinning the data protection

[111] Cyber Security Korea, https://webcache.googleusercontent.com/search?q=cache:V6Umd6gA-rYJ:https://gettingthedealthrough.com/area/72/jurisdiction/35/cybersecurity-korea/+&cd=2&hl=en&ct=clnk&gl=au

[112] Ibid.

[113] Ibid.

laws, cyber security law also plays an important role by minimizing the illegal collection, hacking and incursions of systems and platforms supporting personal data. It is our view that amongst all of the data protection laws examined by the authors across the East Asia, Korea's laws have emerged as arguably the strictest. The strict nature of the South Korean laws is also reflected in a recent decision by the European Commission[114] to open dialogue and discussions about meeting the adequacy requirements under the EU GDPR.

With the recent introduction of an age limit of 14 for minors for the application of consent, was a significant step forward. However, the age limited across various countries differs greatly. This is an area that call for greater consistency in the law, as it is the minors that are the most vulnerable. Moreover, it is argued that the current definition of personal data may not be adequate enough to take into consideration current and future developments in AI. In its current form it is unlikely to protect children and other vulnerable groups in Korean society that will be exposed to smart homes, clothes, toys and personal robots. Furthermore, even though the data localization laws are viewed as favouring Koreans, they are considered quite strict. They regulate the collection of location information without consent from the owner of that location. No other country has the same legal strictness around on location information nor have separate law regulating the collection of such information. Both the public and private sectors are subject to these laws and must ensure that personal data rights of data subjects are protected according to the provisions of the Act. While this places a heavy burden on entities and organizations, it highlights the position that Korea views that personal data must be managed in a way that does not advantage a particular sector.

More importantly, the interface between data protection, AI and cyber security is unclear within these laws. While they are evident, to some degree with cyber security, they are lacking in relation to AI. The most pressing issue will be whether the current definition of personal data is adequate to capture AI. Furthermore, as highlighted in other country chapters, how will consent operate when AI captures personal data? This is far from being resolved. These are only two issues that become evident, and there are issued that will also need to be considered such as notification requirements, storage and retention of personal data within AI systems. While technology may be able to address some of these issues, the data protection laws may need to be amended to ensure AI technology does not create an environment for large scale extraction of personal data.

South Korean data protection laws have been described as being some of the strictest data protection laws throughout Asia.[115] However, they go onto note the enforcement of the Korean laws to establish a complex administrative and enforcement structure which involves five parties, and includes the (1). Data Protection Commission (DPC), (2). Korea Internet & Security Agency and its Personal Data

---

[114] European Commission, Adequacy Decisions, https://ec.europa.eu/info/law/law-topic/data-protection/international-dimension-data-protection/adequacy-decisions_en

[115] Greenleaf, G., Park, W, (2012) *Korea's new Act: Asia's toughest data privacy law* Privacy Laws & Business International Report, Issue 117, 1–6.

Protection Centre (PDPC); (3). The Personal Information Dispute Mediation Committees; (4). The Ministry of Public Administration and Security; and (5). The Korea Communications Commission. Greenleaf and Park believe Korea has developed a system unique in the Asia-Pacific of two independent bodies, one for complaint resolution, serviced by a government agency (PPDC) and the other (DPC) for 'policy matters' (with its own internal secretariat). What is lacking when compared to other countries is a robust framework that promotes co-regulation and self-regulation, and how the current framework will allow for the respective laws to converge, so as to manage data protection in AI.

References

Greenleaf, G., & Park, W. (2012). Korea's new act: Asia's toughest data privacy law. *Privacy Laws & Business International Report, Issue, 117*, 1–6.

Hill, J. F. (2014). The growth of data localization post-Snowden: Analysis and recommendations for U.S. policymakers and business leaders. *Cyber Governance* 3.

Kim, H., Kim, S. Y., & Joly, Y. (2018). South Korea: In the midst of a privacy reform centred on data sharing. *Human Genetic, 137*(8), 627–635.

Ko, H., Leitner, L., Kim, E., & Jung, J. G. (2016). *Structure and enforcement of data Privacy Law in South Korea, Brussels Privacy Hub*, Working Paper, Vol 2, No 7.

Yoon, J. (2018). South Korean data localization: Shaped by conflict, data localization. In *Laws & the International Movement of Information*. University of Washington.

Young Ick, L. (2000). *Brief history of Korea, A Bird's-EyeView*. The Korea Society.

Chapter 6
Hong Kong

Abstract Hong Kong has a fascinating history. On January 25, 1841, a British naval party landed and raised the British flag on the northern shore of Hong Kong, a small island located in the Pearl River Delta in southern China. The next day, the commander of the British expeditionary force took formal possession of the island in the name of the British Crown (Carroll, JM, (2007) *A Concise History of Hong Kong* Rowman & Littlefield Publishers, 1.). Except for three and a half years during World War II when Hong Kong was part of the short-lived Japanese Empire, the British occupation would last until midnight on July 1, 1997, whereby Hong Kong became a Special Administrative Region of the People's Republic of China.

The data protection laws of Hong Kong are significantly different to that of the other data laws examined in this book. Data protection in Hong Kong began in 1995, with the implementation of the Personal Data (Privacy) Ordinance. It was the first comprehensive data protection law in the region with reference to the OECD Privacy Guidelines 1980 and the draft EU Data Protection Directive 1995. Arguably, the implementation of data protection law was necessary in order to discharge Hong Kong's obligations for human rights and retain their status as an international trading centre. Thus, for Hong Kong one of their key objectives is to retain their international business status as a financial and services hub. Interestingly, the first laws came into effect 2 years before the handover of the territory from the former rule of the United Kingdom back to China.

This Chapter begins by highlighting how Hong Kong was ruled by the British before being handed back to the China in 1997. This former British rule had a profound influence on the legal framework of Hong Kong. The current day data protection laws of Hong Kong reflect the framework set out by the OECD and the EU. However, the data protection laws of Hong Kong do significantly differ from other states in the Asia region. Going forward the question will be whether the data protection laws of Hong Kong remain as they are, or, move closer to the recently established laws of China. This Chapter discusses Definition of Personal Data, Public and Private, Transfer Matching and Transfer of Personal Data, Controller

R. Walters, M. Novak, *Cyber Security, Artificial Intelligence, Data Protection & the Law*, https://doi.org/10.1007/978-981-16-1665-5_6

[Data User], Erasing Personal Data [Right to Be Forgotten], Data User Returns and Register of Data Users, Access and Correction of Personal Data, Consent and Direct Marketing, Privacy Commissioner, Enforcement and Security [Cyber].

6.1 Introduction

On January 25, 1841, a British naval party landed and raised the British flag on the northern shore of Hong Kong, a small island located in the Pearl River Delta in southern China.[1] According to John Carroll, on 26 January 1841, the commander of the British expeditionary force took formal possession of the island in the name of the British Crown. Except for three and a half years during World War II when Hong Kong was part of the short-lived Japanese Empire, the British occupation would last until midnight on July 1, 1997, whereupon Hong Kong became a Special Administrative Region of the People's Republic of China.

The official languages use throughout Hong Kong are English and Chinese, with English being widely used in business and education. Most residents speak Cantonese, followed by English, Mandarin and other Chinese regional dialects, as well as other Asian languages. The laws discussed in this chapter were those in force as at December 2019. It does not account for any changes to the Basic Law [Constitution] during 2020–2021. The culture and religion of Hong Kong is best represented by a mixture of Atheism, Taoism, Buddhism, Christianity that, all co-exist in general harmony. Focusing on trade, tourism, banking and finance, Hong Kong is one of the wealthiest economies in the world. Thus, within the territory the right of privacy at common law has been defined as "an outcome of a person's wish to withhold from others certain knowledge as to his past and present experience and action and his intentions for the future."[2] Although the right of privacy is not legally enforceable at common law, English judges have acknowledged its importance on occasion. In one case, Lord Denning stated that "while freedom of expression is a fundamental human right, so also is the right of privacy."[3] In another case, Lord Scarman described the right to privacy as "fundamental".[4] Nearly a decade later, Lord Keith pointed out that "the right to personal privacy is clearly one which the law [of confidence] should ... seek to protect".[5]

---

[1] Ibid.

[2] Jourard, SM (1966) *Some Psychological Aspects of Privacy,* Law and Contemporary Problems, 307–318.

[3] *Schering Chemicals v Falkman* [1982] QB 1 at 21.

[4] *Morris v Beardmore* [1981] AC 446, 464. He described the right as "fundamental" because of the importance attached by the common law to the privacy of the home and the fact that the right enjoys the protection of the European Convention on Human Rights.

[5] *AG v Guardian Newspapers Ltd* (No 2) [1990] 1 AC 109, 255.

John Carroll makes the point that the name Hong Kong means Fragrant Harbor in Chinese, and refers to Hong Kong Island, which was ceded by the Qing dynasty to Great Britain in 1842 under the Treaty of Nanking.[6] Located about 80 miles southeast of the city of Canton (known today as Guangzhou), this tiny island is only 11 miles from east to west and 2 to 5 miles from north to south. The name "Hong Kong," however, is generally used to cover a larger area with three main parts: Hong Kong Island; Kowloon Peninsula, consisting of 8 square miles and ceded to Britain in 1860 under the Convention of Peking; and the New Territories, an area of 365 square miles leased to Britain for ninety-nine years in 1898 that includes approximately 230 outlying islands.[7] Although Hong Kong has no natural resources to speak of, its harbor, deep and sheltered by steep granite hills, is one of the best in the world. With a population of around seven million and very little good land for building, Hong Kong is one of the most densely populated places on earth.

Hong Kong by adopting the common law has approached the notion of privacy in a similar way to that of Australia and United Kingdom. According to the Basic Law of Hong Kong, it has been part of the territory of China since ancient times; it was occupied by Britain after the Opium War in 1840.[8] On 19 December 1984, the Chinese and British Governments signed the Joint Declaration on the Question of Hong Kong, affirming that the Government of the People's Republic of China will resume the exercise of sovereignty over Hong Kong with effect from 1 July 1997, thus fulfilling the long-cherished common aspiration of the Chinese people for the recovery of Hong Kong.[9]

Hong Kong, while embracing the general idea of privacy has developed its own data protection laws for the territory. Hong Kong has a very different history to other regional countries in East Asia. Today, it is a special administrative unit of China.[10] The Hong Kong constitution, otherwise known as the Basic Law[11] has retained the common law, rules of equity, ordinances, subordinate legislation and customary law, except for any that contravene this Law, and subject to any amendment by the legislature of the Hong Kong Special Administrative Region.[12] More importantly, under the Basic Law a number of rights and freedoms have been

[6] Carroll, J (2007) *A Concise History of Hong Kong* Rowman & Littlefield Publishers, 1.

[7] Ibid.

[8] The Basic Law of the Hong Kong Special Administrative Region of the People's Republic of China. Adopted at the Third Session of the Seventh National People's Congress on 4 April 1990 Promulgated by Order No. 26 of the President of the People's Republic of China on 4 April 1990 Effective as of 1 July 1997.

[9] Ibid.

[10] Sino-British Joint Declaration-Elaboration by the Government of the People's Republic of China of its Basic Policies Regarding Hong Kong, Archived from the original on 29 November 2005.

[11] The Basic Law of the Hong Kong Special Administrative Region of the People's Republic of China. Adopted at the Third Session of the Seventh National People's Congress on 4 April 1990 Promulgated by Order No. 26 of the President of the People's Republic of China on 4 April 1990 Effective as of 1 July 1997.

[12] Ibid, Article 8.

protected. These include, but not limited to equality before the law; permanent residents' right to vote and to stand for election in accordance with law; freedom of speech, of the press and of publication; freedom of association, of assembly, of procession and of demonstration; freedom to form and join trade unions, and to strike; and the right from arbitrary or unlawful arrest, detention and imprisonment. In addition, the general right from torture and unlawful deprivation of the life and arbitrary or unlawful search of, or intrusion into resident's home or other premises. In other words, Article 29 provides that the homes and other premises of Hong Kong residents shall be inviolable. Arbitrary or unlawful search of, or intrusion into, a resident's home or other premises shall be prohibited. Article 30, on the other hand, provides the freedom and privacy of communication of Hong Kong residents shall be protected by law.[13] No department or individual may, on any grounds, infringe upon the freedom and privacy of communication of residents except that the relevant authorities may inspect communication in accordance with legal procedures to meet the needs of public security or of investigation into criminal offences. This limited form of privacy right has arguably been a fundamental pillar of Hong Kong society.[14] In addition to the above, Chapter III, of the Basic law provides for Fundamental Rights and Duties of the Residents, these include the freedom of movement within Hong Kong, of emigration to other countries or regions, and freedom to enter or leave Hong Kong; freedom of conscience; freedom of religious belief and to preach and to conduct and participate in religious activities in public. Many of the rights and freedoms expressed by the Basic law are consistent with the European Union, United Kingdom, United States, Singapore, Australia and regional neighbours. Furthermore, Chapter III provides for the freedom of choice of occupation; freedom to engage academic research, literary and artistic creation, and other cultural activities; the right to confidential legal advice, access to the courts, choices of lawyers for timely protection of their lawful rights and interests or for representation in the courts, and to judicial remedies.[15] The right to institute legal proceedings in the courts against the acts of the executive authorities and their personnel along with the right to social welfare in accordance with law is a further expression of the safeguards Hong Kong citizens enjoy in the territory. The citizens also have the right and freedom of marriage and the right to raise a family freely.

Nonetheless, and more importantly, the Basic Law in accordance with Annex 2, section 3(2) of the Personal Data (Privacy) Ordinance (Cap. 486, Laws of Hong Kong [Data Privacy]) were the first comprehensive data protection law in the region when it was enacted in 1995 with reference to the OECD Privacy Guidelines 1980. Moreover, they clearly reference elements of the former EU Data Protection

[13] Ibid, Article 30, The freedom and privacy of communication of Hong Kong residents shall be protected by law. No department or individual may, on any grounds, infringe upon the freedom and privacy of communication of residents except that the relevant authorities may inspect communication in accordance with legal procedures to meet the needs of public security or of investigation into criminal offences.

[14] Ibid.

[15] Ibid.

Directive 95/46/EC. It is out of scope of this book to compare the differences between the former EU Directive on Data Protection 95/46/EC with the Data Privacy laws. In the early 1990s, it was identified that, an increasing number of jurisdictions had enacted data protection laws commensurable to the OECD Privacy Guidelines 1980, and the lack of information privacy regime in Hong Kong was hindering the flow of data to the city because the legislation of these jurisdictions often prohibited the flow of data to another jurisdiction[16] which did not provide for adequate data protection.[17] In the circumstances, it was considered necessary to give internationally agreed data protection standards statutory force in Hong Kong in order to discharge Hong Kong's obligation in human rights protection and retain Hong Kong's status as an international trading centre.[18]

Of importance is that Article 39 expressly states that the provisions of the International Covenant on Civil and Political Rights (ICCPR), the International Covenant on Economic, Social and Cultural Rights (ICESCR), and international labour conventions as applied to Hong Kong shall remain in force in Hong Kong to the extent that they shall not contravene the provisions of the rights protected by the Basic Law. These two important treaties, apart from providing a level of rights to the citizens of the territory, go some way to protecting people's privacy. However, there is no mention as to whether this extend to the right to privacy over the Internet. Art. 17(1) ("Right to Privacy"), provides that no one shall be subjected to arbitrary or unlawful interference with his privacy, family, home or correspondence, nor to unlawful attacks on his honour and reputation.[19] Luke Marsh argues that following the Handover, these instruments were referenced in Article 39 of the Hong Kong Basic Law—China's constitutional blueprint for the HKSAR—to ensure continuity in human rights protection following Hong Kong's return to China on 1 July 1997.[20]

Notwithstanding the above, and although these rights are explicitly vested in Hong Kong residents, non-residents in Hong Kong may also enjoy these rights and freedoms in accordance with law by Article 41. In addition, Article 87 protects and preserves the rights previously enjoyed by parties to any criminal or civil proceedings, especially the right to fair trial by the courts without delay and the presumption of innocence until convicted by the courts. Article 105 protects the rights of

---

[16] Kai-yi Wong, S Barrister, *Privacy Commissioner for Personal Data, Hong Kong, China Grooving Privacy Evolution with Law Reform and Data Ethics,* 2019, https://www.pcpd.org.hk/english/news_events/media_statements/files/Paper_GroovingPrivacyEvolutionwithDataEthics_Feb2019.pdf

[17] Ibid, The Law Reform Commission of Hong Kong, "Reform of the Law Relating to the Protection of Personal Data" (August 1994), paragraph 17.9: https://www.hkreform.gov.hk/en/docs/rdata-e.pdf

[18] Ibid, The Law Reform Commission of Hong Kong, "Reform of the Law Relating to the Protection of Personal Data" (August 1994), paragraph 5.2: https://www.hkreform.gov.hk/en/docs/rdata-e.pdf

[19] Marsh, L (2016), *The Strategic Use of Human Rights Treaties in Hong Kong's Cage-Home Crisis: No Way Out?* Asian Journal of Law and Society, 3, 159–188.

[20] Ibid.

property and the right to compensation for lawful deprivation of property of individuals and legal persons.

Moreover, the Bill of Rights Ordinance (Cap. 383) (Bill of Rights) 1991,[21] is the local adaptation of the provisions of the ICCPR as applied in Hong Kong. The Bill of Rights has largely been recognised by the courts as one of the constitutional documents alongside the Basic Law. However, the fact that the Bill of Rights was enacted in the form of an Ordinance (as a local primary legislation) means that the Legislature can amend or repeal the Bill of Rights by an ordinary enactment through ordinary legislative procedure, subject to judicial review. Furthermore, if any part of the Bill of Rights is held unconstitutional (i.e. any part contravenes the Basic Law), the courts are bound to strike down that part. However, following the transfer of sovereignty, specific provisions of the Bill of Rights ceased to have effect, these include, sections 2(3) (duty to have regard to purpose of Ordinance in interpretation), 3(1) (duty to construe pre-existing legislation consistently with the Ordinance), 3(2) (pre-existing legislation that cannot be construed consistently is repealed) and 4 (all future to be construed so as to be consistent with the ICCPR as applied to Hong Kong). However, due to the entrenchment of the ICCPR as applied in Hong Kong in Article 39 of the Basic Law, the significance of the Bill of Rights Ordinance, which was modelled after the ICCPR, has been reinstated.[22]

The Personal Data (Privacy) Ordinance (PDPO) Cap 486 (the Ordinance), establishes Hong Kong's data protection and privacy legal framework, which came into effect in 1996. Its core provisions are encapsulated in the six data protection principles which include:

- Purpose and manner of collection;
- Retention of data for a period no longer that is necessary;
- Use of personal data;
- Security of the data;
- Information to be generally available; and
- Access to personal data.[23]

The importance of the principles underpinning the general legislation cannot be underestimated. In other words, the Hong Kong Administrative Appeals Board (AAB) became involved in determining the level information that can identify a person, and whether divulging that information would amount to a breach of the law. Moreover, the Personal Data (Privacy) Ordinance (Cap. 486) has been underpinned by 6 Data Protection Principles, which include:

1. Collection;
2. Accuracy and Retention

[21] Chapter 383 Hong Kong Bill of Rights Ordinance 1991, 21 July 2011.

[22] Young, S, (2004). "*Restricting Basic Law Rights in Hong Kong*". Hong Kong Law Journal. 34 (1): 110.

[23] Data Protection Principles in the Personal Data (Privacy) Ordinance—*from the Privacy Commissioner's perspective (2 Edition)* (2010) Office of the Privacy Commissioner for Personal Data Hong Kong. Schedule 1. https://www.elegislation.gov.hk/hk/cap486!en-zh-Hant-HK.pdf?FROMCAPINDEX=Y

3. Use;
4. Security;
5. Openness; and
6. Access and correction. [24]

DPP1—Data Collection Principle Personal data must be collected in a lawful and fair way, for a purpose directly related to a function /activity of the data user. Data subjects must be notified of the purpose and the classes of persons to whom the data may be transferred. Data collected should be necessary but not excessive.[25] DPP2—Accuracy & Retention Principle: provides practicable steps shall be taken to ensure personal data is accurate and not kept longer than is necessary to fulfil the purpose for which it is used. DPP3—Data Use Principle Personal data must be used for the purpose for which the data is collected or for a directly related purpose, unless voluntary and explicit consent with a new purpose is obtained from the data subject.[26] DPP4—Data Security Principle: A data user needs to take practicable steps to safeguard personal data from unauthorised or accidental access, processing, erasure, loss or use. DPP5—Openness Principle:[27] a data user must take practicable steps to make personal data policies and practices known to the public regarding the types of personal data it holds and how the data is used. DPP6—Data Access & Correction Principle: a data subject must be given access to his/her personal data and allowed to make corrections if it is inaccurate.[28]

When coupled with the principles set out in Schedule 1 of the Ordinance, the principles largely meet the privacy principles under the OECD Guidelines. Therefore, Hong Kong has continued to bring the data protection laws in line with the international standards. However, as this Chapter will demonstrate how Hong Kong, have unique provisions to meet their sovereign needs.

In *Apple Daily v Privacy Commissioner*,[29] the AAB overturned a ruling by the Privacy Commissioner that the publisher of Apple Daily had breached DPP 4 (security of data) by publishing the name of the street to which victims of an attack had moved out of fear of a further assault by their assailant. The basis for the Commissioner's decision was that the publication of the address in Apple Daily had put the individuals concerned at risk because their assailant might learn of their new location from the article and attack them again. The Commissioner concluded that this was a breach of DPP 4 because DPP 4 provides for a requirement to take all practicable steps to ensure that personal data are protected against unauthorised or accidental access having particular regard to the harm that could result from such access. The Privacy Commissioner ruled that Apple Daily had failed to meet this

[24] Data Protection Privacy Principles, https://www.pcpd.org.hk/english/data_privacy_law/ordinance_at_a_Glance/ordinance.html

[25] Ibid.

[26] Ibid.

[27] Ibid.

[28] Ibid.

[29] Administrative Appeal No 5 of 1999, unreported decision of the Administrative Appeals Board dated 30.11.99, discussed in Wacks, R, *"Privacy and Process"* (1999) 29 HKLJ 176.

requirement by publishing the street name in the article.[30] Despite the AAB handing down the decision and not the courts, it is consistent with the definition of data and personal data under the current day laws of Hong Kong. The definition of data and more importantly personal data is very broad and can, by its interpretation mean any information that, can identify an individual.

On the backdrop of the above, the courts of Hong Kong have begun to consider personal data. Where personal data are collected from the individual who is the subject of the data (as may occur, for example, where a journalist records information given by an individual about himself during an interview), the provisions of Data Protection Principle[31] (DPP 1(3)) requires that all practicable steps shall be taken to inform the individual concerned of certain matters.[32] In particular, the individual must be explicitly informed of the purpose for which the data are to be used. The Court of Appeal in *Eastweek Publisher Ltd v Privacy Commissioner*[33] highlighted the limitation of the application of the various requirements of DPP 1 relating to individuals whose identities are known to the collecting party or data of individuals the collecting party intends to identify (see below). Accordingly, where a person whose identity is unknown and whom the photographer or film-maker does not intend to identify, the photographing or filming of the individual is not subject to the provisions of DPP 1, even though the subsequent use of the photograph or film may result in the individual being recognised and identified by his acquaintances.

In 2018, one of the largest ever data breaches occurred in Hong Kong, which saw an estimated 9.4 million people's personal data illegally obtained from Cathay Pacific.[34] At the time of writing this book, there was a review underway into the data protection laws of Hong Kong. Work was underway to bring the laws in line with the implementation of the EU GDPR. This is an area of vigilance, to determine whether Hong Kong take on the principles and concepts of data protection from the EU, or diverge closer to mainland China's framework. To date, there are four key areas of focus that will form part of this review: 1). data breach notifications, 2). non-compliance penalties, 3). data processors, and 4). the international transfer of personal data.[35] If realized, the expected reforms will bring Hong Kong's laws closer to the EU GDPR. However, further detail on the proposed reforms appears to some time away.

---

[30] Ibid.

[31] Data Protection Principles in the Personal Data (Privacy) Ordinance—*from the Privacy Commissioner's perspective (2 Edition)* (2010) Office of the Privacy Commissioner for Personal Data Hong Kong.

[32] Berthold, M,. Wacks, R, (2003) *Hong Kong Data Privacy Law—Territorial Regulation in a Borderless World* (Sweet Maxwell Asia, 2 edn).

[33] [2000] 1 HKC 692.

[34] Healey, R, *Changes to Hong Kong's Data Privacy Law: What They May Mean For Your Business*, Relentless Partnerships, 2019, https://relentlessdataprivacy.com/changes-to-hong-kongs-data-privacy-law-what-they-may-mean-for-your-business/

[35] Ibid.

A year earlier, the High Court in Hong Kong[36] heard an appeal from Judge K W Wong who transferred the present action (DCCJ No. 2736/2016) from the District Court to the Court of First Instance of the High Court so the case was able to be dealt with together with another action in the Court of First Instance (HCA 168/2016) brought by the same plaintiff against the same defendant. The case began in 1999, which involved a bank carrying on a business in Hong Kong. In 1999, the bank advanced money to the plaintiff and one Madam Lee on the security of a landed property. They defaulted. The defendant then exercised its mortgagee power. After the sale of their security, there was still a shortfall of slightly less than $1.8 million as at 2008. The defendant and the plaintiff entered into a written compromise dated 19 January 2009 whereby the plaintiff agreed to pay a total sum of $500,000.[37]

At issue, was whether the District Court has exclusive jurisdiction to hear claims brought under section 66(1) of the PDPO and, second, if not, whether the Judge had properly exercised his discretion to transfer the District Court action to the Court of First Instance.[38] The plaintiff claimed that the defendant had failed and/or refused to update the plaintiff's credit information provided to a consumer credit reporting company, namely, TransUnion Limited despite repeated requests and demands.[39] The total loss quantified by him amounts to about $5.4 million.[40] Subsequently, there was a claim for damages against the defendant for breach of Principle 2 of the Personal Data (Privacy) Ordinance, Cap. 486 ('PDPO'). In considering section s.66(1) PDPO, the Court noted that:

> the Judge had properly exercised his discretion in ordering the transfer. If not for the transfer, there will be two proceedings in different Courts between the same parties and based on the same facts and substantially the same law. The defendant had not applied to strike out either of these proceedings on the basis of abuse before or when the plaintiff applied for transfer.[41]

Subsequently the appeal was dismissed. Nevertheless, the Court lay ground work for future jurisprudence to strike the correct balance between Hong Kong's business needs, while providing a level of protection to personal data.

The Global Privacy Enforcement Network (GPEN) was established in 2010. The GPEN Committee comprises 5 members from the Office of the Privacy Commissioner of Canada; the Israeli Law, Information and Technology Authority; United Kingdom Information Commissioner's Office; United States Federal Trade Commission; and Office of the Privacy Commissioner for Personal Data, Hong Kong, China.[42] It aims

---

[36] *Lee Kwok Tung Albert v Chiyu Banking Corporation Limited*, [2018] HKCA 123.

[37] Ibid. All payments under the said compromise were duly paid. A written release dated 6 January 2011 was signed by the defendant, discharging the plaintiff (but not Madam Lee) from all liabilities under the original loan agreement.

[38] Ibid.

[39] Ibid.

[40] Ibid.

[41] Ibid.

[42] Global Privacy Enforcement Network (GPEN), https://www.privacyenforcement.net/system/files/Annual%20Report%20for%202015_0.pdf. The informal network has grown by the end of

to foster cross-border cooperation among privacy authorities in an increasingly global market in which commerce and consumer activity relies. Its members seek to work together to strengthen personal privacy protections in this global context. The network also works towards improving the international enforcement cooperation by promoting better dialogue among relevant networks of privacy enforcement authorities. It also, goes some way, to enhancing dialogue with enforcement authorities from other sectors in the second instance, to maximize opportunities for the privacy enforcement community's development.

6.2 Definition of Personal Data

The definition of personal data in the Hong Kong context can be seen in both the meaning of data and personal data. That is, in section 2 has defined data (資料) to mean any representation of information (including an expression of opinion) in any document, and includes a personal identifier.[43] This section goes onto define personal data (個人資料) as any data relating directly or indirectly to a living individual; from which it is practicable for the identity of the individual to be directly or indirectly ascertained; and in a form in which access to or processing of the data is practicable. In addition to the terms data and personal data, personal identifier can also be considered as part of the overall definition of personal data.[44] That is, personal identifier (個人身分標識符) means an identifier that is assigned to an individual by a data user for the purpose of the operations of the user; and that uniquely identifies that individual in relation to the data user, but does not include an individual's name used to identify that individual. Arguably, when combined, the definition of personal data that, data can identify anyone and by anything.[45]

Notwithstanding the above and despite the legislative definition of data and personal data, it has not come without some debate. In the early implementation of the data protection laws, the Principles have been an important part of the overall framework underpinning the laws. This has been reinforced by the decision of *Kam Sea Hang Osmaan v Privacy Commissioner*[46] whereby, the Administrative Appeals Board was asked to consider a case in which an individual alleged that a magazine had published fabrications about him. The Appeals Board found, however, that a lie or fabrication about an individual fall outside the definition of personal data and, hence, that the provisions of the PD(P)O, including the provisions of DPP 2, did not apply at all in the case before it, stating that:

2015 to comprise 59 privacy enforcement authorities in 43 jurisdictions around the world, and the number of privacy enforcement professionals with GPEN website user accounts has increased since 2014 by 50% to 293 (user totals, as of March 1, 2016).

[43] Section, Hong Kong Bill of Rights Ordinance 1991, 21 July 2011.

[44] Ibid.

[45] Ibid.

[46] Administrative Appeal No 29 of 2001, unreported decision of the Administrative Appeals Board dated 28.2.02.

> The wordings of the definition [of personal data in section 2(1) of the PD(P)O] are clear enough to exclude any fabrication or lies told about a person by another person. ... A lie or fabrication always remains a lie or fabrication and can never convert into 'personal data'.[47]

The 2004 Law Reform Commission of Hong Kong Report on Civil Liability for Invasion of Privacy,[48] noted from the above decision that the definition of personal data in section 2(1) of the PD(P)O for the contention that it excludes lies or fabrications. Centrally, the Board's view would mean that the requirements of DPP 2, and the PD(P)O generally, apply where personal data are inaccurate as a result of inadvertence but not where the inaccuracy is deliberate.[49] There was difficulty in finding a justification for such a distinction in the Ordinance. It is also at odds with our Report on Reform of the Law Relating to Personal Data (on which the PD(P)O was based) that all data relating to an individual that facilitate directly or indirectly the identification of the individual to whom they relate should be regulated by law "whether true or not".

On the face of this definition it could be argued that AI capturing personal data is likely to be included. In other words, the reference to personal identifier would be captured by any system that can collect and use personal data, including AI. However, this is untested and further work is required to better understand how and under what circumstances will AI collect and use personal data.

6.3 Public and Private

The laws of Hong Kong apply to both the public and private sectors.[50] However, there are exemptions for complying with the Ordinance for domestic and recreational purposes, along with certain employment and personal related data and relevant process. National security is now an important part of the policy discourse in relation to data protection, as highlighted in Chap. 1. Therefore, further exemptions apply from access and use limitation requirements for data which are likely to prejudice security, defence and international relations; crime prevention or detection; assessment or collection of any tax or duty; news activities; health; legal proceeding; due diligence exercise; archiving; handling life-threatening emergency situation.[51]

---

[47] Ibid.

[48] The 2004 Law Reform Commission of Hong Kong Report on Civil Liability for Invasion of Privacy, https://www.hkreform.gov.hk/en/docs/rprivacy-e.pdf

[49] Ibid.

[50] Section 3, Data Protection Principles in the Personal Data (Privacy) Ordinance—*from the Privacy Commissioner's perspective (2 Edition)* (2010).

[51] Part 8, The Personal Data (Privacy) Ordinance (PDPO) Cap 486.

6.4 Matching and Transfer of Personal Data

Section 30 is supported by the concept of consent. It provides that a matching procedure not to be carried out except with consent of data subject. Nevertheless, the matching procedure[52] constitutes four criteria, that include a comparison of two sets of personal data, each of which is collected for different purposes, each comparison involves the personal data of 10 or more data subjects. Thirdly, a comparison is not carried out by manual means but by a computer program designed and applied for performing the comparison process. Fourth, the end result of the comparison may be used, whether immediately or at any subsequent time, for the purpose of taking adverse action against any of the data subjects concerned.[53] Thus, and as noted by the Matching Procedure, section 30 of the Ordinance provides that a matching procedure cannot be undertaken unless all the individuals who are the subjects of the data to be matched have voluntarily given express consent to the matching procedure being carried out. In addition to the above, the Privacy Commissioner for Personal Data ("the Commissioner") has given consent under section 32 of the Ordinance for the matching procedure to be carried out. Furthermore, the matching procedure belongs to a class of matching procedures which the Commissioner has specified by notice in the Government Gazette as a class of such procedures that may be carried out. Finally, the matching procedure is required or permitted by Schedule 4 to the Ordinance.[54] The Matching Procedure Example in the table below:[55]

---

[52] Section 2, The Personal Data (Privacy) Ordinance (PDPO) Cap 486, matching procedure means any procedure whereby personal data collected for 1 or more purposes in respect of 10 or more data subjects is compared (except by manual means) with personal data collected for any other purpose in respect of those data subjects where the comparison—(Amended 18 of 2012 s. 3) (a) is (whether in whole or in part) for the purpose of producing or verifying data that; or (b) produces or verifies data in respect of which it is reasonable to believe that it is practicable that the data, may be used (whether immediately or at any subsequent time) for the purpose of taking adverse action against any of those data subjects.

[53] Matching Procedure, Office of the Privacy Commissioner for Personal Data, https://www.pcpd.org.hk/english/resources_centre/publications/files/InfoLeaflet_MatchProc_ENG_web.pdf

[54] Ibid. However, note that the Commissioner has not specified any class of matching procedures as a class of such procedures that may be carried out under condition (c); neither have any provisions of an Ordinance requiring or permitting a matching procedure been specified in Schedule 4 to the Ordinance under condition (d). Accordingly, if someone wishes to carry out a matching procedure in compliance with section 30, they must meet either condition (a) or (b). That is to say, they must either obtain the express and voluntary consent of the individuals who are the subjects of the data to be matched or seek the consent of the Commissioner to carry out the matching procedure concerned.

[55] Ibid.

Data user A is responsible for making payments to several thousand individuals who meet certain eligibility criteria. Data user A collects and uses the personal data of individuals applying for such payments for the purpose of determining whether they are eligible for the payments and arranging that the money be paid to those who are. One of the eligibility criteria is that the applicant should not own property. To check whether the applicant meet this criterion, data user A compares the personal data collected with that contained in a register of property owners maintained by data user B. The register contains personal data collected by data user B for purposes related to land and property ownership matters. The comparison of the first set of personal data held by data user A with the set of personal data held by data user B will confirm whether or not the applicant concerned owns property. As the number of applicants involved is large, data user A uses a computer program to compare the personal data it holds with the personal data held by data user B to ascertain "hits" of individuals matched in both databases to indicate that they own property. Any applicant identified as owning property by this automated comparison will have his or her application for payment declined or, in the case of a recipient currently receiving payment, payment will be discontinued.

In addition to the above, section 31 sets out the process for making a matching request. This is a procedural step that requires the data user to obtain the specified form.[56] Section 31 goes onto require where 2 or more data users may each make a matching procedure request in respect of the same matching procedure,[57] then any of those data users may make such a request on behalf of all those data users. A data user who, in a matching procedure request, supplies any information which is false or misleading in a material particular for the purpose of obtaining the Commissioner's consent to the carrying out of the matching procedure to which the request relates, commits an offence and is liable on conviction to a fine at level 3 and to imprisonment for 6 months.[58] In determining the request for a matching procedure, the Commissioner in accordance with section 32 must make a decision within 45 days of receipt of the request. The Commissioner will need to seek the consent of the individual requesting the matching procedure. A data subject that is not satisfied with the administration of the conditions set out in the matching request may appeal to the Administrative Appeals Board.

[56] Matching Procedure Request Form (OPS002), www.pcpd.org.hk/english/publications/les/ops002.pdf

[57] Section 31 (3), The Personal Data (Privacy) Ordinance (PDPO) Cap 486, Without prejudice to the generality of subsection (2), it is hereby declared that a matching procedure request may be made in relation to 2 or more matching procedures, or a series of matching procedures, and the other provisions of this Ordinance (including section 32) shall be construed accordingly.

[58] Ibid.

6.5 Transfer

It is well understood that the transfer of personal data outside of the Hong Kong territory is a daily occurrence whether legal or illegal. Nonetheless, section 33 prohibits the transfer of personal data outside the territory under specific circumstances. It is noteworthy that, section 33 does not apply to personal data other than personal data collected, held, processed or used within Hong Kong. This also extends to where the personal data is controlled by the data user, whose principal place of business is within the territory of Hong Kong. More importantly, at the time of writing this book Hong Kong had not given effect to this provision. Thus, the transfer of personal data cannot be undertaken to a place (country) outside of Hong Kong unless *(a).* the place is specified for the purposes of this section in a notice under subsection (3); *(b).* the user has reasonable grounds for believing that there is in force in that place any law which is substantially similar to, or serves the same purposes as, this Ordinance; *(c).* the data subject has consented in writing to the transfer. Furthermore, the transfer outside of Hong Kong can take place where the user has reasonable grounds for believing that the transfer is for the avoidance or mitigation of an adverse action against the data subject; or it is not practicable to obtain the consent in writing of the data subject to that transfer; and if it was practicable to obtain such consent, the data subject would give it.[59]

In addition to the above, the data can be transferred outside of the territory of Hong Kong where the data user has, and can demonstrate they will ensure that the data will not, in that place, be collected, held, processed or used in any manner which, if that place were Hong Kong, would be a contravention of a requirement under this Ordinance. Hong Kong has followed most other jurisdictions in this regard and seek to ensure that any personal data of its citizens transferred outside the territory is being received in another jurisdiction that, the laws meet the same level of controls to protect that data. Similar to the EU's process for the recognition of other jurisdiction data protection laws provide similar level of protection, the Commissioner can publish in the Government Gazette notifying the broader public of any law that is similar to the Ordinance. Hong Kong have not commenced discussions with the EU in relation to the obtaining adequacy under the EU GDPR.[60] At the time of writing there appears to be no gazette issued by the government providing a list of countries that would have similar level of control over personal data.

Moreover, section 33 is further underpinned by DPP3. Therefore, the transfer of personal data to a place outside Hong Kong would require the data subject's prescribed consent under DPP3 if it is for a new purpose unless such transfer falls within the exemptions under Part VIII of the Ordinance. Data users who, without

[59] Ibid, section 33. Office of the Privacy Commissioner for Personal Data, Guidance on Personal Data Protection in Cross-border Data Transfer, https://www.pcpd.org.hk/english/resources_centre/publications/files/GN_crossborder_e.pdf

[60] European Commission, Adequacy Decisions, https://ec.europa.eu/info/law/law-topic/data-protection/international-dimension-data-protection/adequacy-decisions_en

reasonable excuse, contravene section 33 commit an offence under section 64A of the Ordinance, which carries a fine of up to HK$10,000. The Commissioner may also issue enforcement notices to data users who have contravened section 33 or DPP.[61] Contravention of an enforcement notice issued by the Commissioner is an offence which carries a fine and imprisonment. Finally, the storage of personal data in cloud needs to be undertaken with care, and could also constitute data being transferred outside of the territory of Hong Kong. This is because the server storing the personal data is likely to be located outside of Hong Kong and in another state. However, section 33 had not yet been implemented at the time of writing this book.

Mark Parsons believes that should section 33 were brought into force as currently drafted, it would not expressly contemplate sectorial adequacy, but instead invites the PCPD to consider if a "place" has a law substantially similar.[62] If section 33 were brought into force as currently drafted, it would support data users making their own assessment of whether or not there are reasonable grounds for believing that there is in force in the place of transfer a law which is substantially similar to or serves the same purpose as the PDPO. In the International Transfer Guidance, however, the PCPD articulated an expectation that the self-assessment would be carried out only in respect of transfer jurisdictions not already assessed and rejected by the PCPD if section 33 were administered as contemplated in the guidance.[63] The law itself does not list the substantive standards for establishing comparable data protection standards. In the International Transfer Guidance, the PCPD has suggested various factors for data users' consideration when conducting the assessment of the comparable standard.[64]

6.5.1 *Repeated Collections*

Section 35 requires that a data user provided they have complied with DPP1 in relation to the collection of personal data, and collects that data on more than one occasion is not required to comply provided that data has been collected within a 12 month period. The collection, but not the repeat collection of personal data and information had been raised to the courts in *Eastweek*.[65] The Court in this case

---

[61] Office of the Privacy Commissioner for Personal Data, Guidance on Personal Data Protection in Cross-border Data Transfer, https://www.pcpd.org.hk/english/resources_centre/publications/files/GN_crossborder_e.pdf

[62] Parsons, M, *Regulation of Cross-Border Transfers Of Personal Data in Asia* Jurisdictional Report Hong Kong SAR (The People's Republic of China), Asian Business Law Institute, Singapore, https://cis-india.org/internet-governance/files/dp-compendium

[63] Ibid.

[64] Ibid.

[65] *Eastweek Publisher Ltd v the Privacy Commissioner of Personal Data* [2000] CACV 331/1999, in Raymond Wacks *"What has data protection to do with privacy?"* [2000] PrivLawPRpr 11; (2000) 6(9) Privacy Law and Policy Reporter 143.

argued that the taking of photographs did not constitute an act of data collection. The Court stated that:

> the essence of the required act of personal data collection [is] that the data user must thereby be compiling information about *an identified person* or about a person whom the data user intends or seeks to identify. The data collected must be an item of personal information attaching to the identified subject ... This is missing in the present case. What is crucial here is the complainant's anonymity and the irrelevance of her identity so far as the photographer, the reporter and the plaintiff were concerned. Indeed, they remained completely indifferent to and ignorant of her identity right up to and after publication of the offending issue of the magazine. She would have remained anonymous if she had not lodged a complaint and made her identity known. In my view, to take her photograph in such circumstances did not constitute an act of personal data collection relating to the complainant.[66]

The Court relied on the application of DPP 1 to the facts of the case that would unduly inhibit press freedom, since a newspaper may wish to publish photographs of unidentified persons to illustrate social phenomenon(s), for example, teenagers consuming alcohol or smoking. Furthermore, the Court noted that there were other provisions of the Ordinance, such as, access rights and the use limitation requirement in DPP 3. point to the necessity for a data subject whose identity is known or sought to be known by the data user as an important item of information. In other words, the right of access, for example, makes sense only if the data user holds the data collected in relation to each identified data subject. This was of course not the case here. Moreover, in balancing the protection of personal data with other rights, freedoms and responsibilities, the Court went onto say that:

> the Ordinance protects only personal data; it is not intended to create a general right of privacy against all forms of intrusion into the private domain.[67]

Raymond Wacks believed that the Court stressed that it was not deciding that taking someone's photograph could never be an act of personal data collection. It depended on the circumstances and the events that have taken place. Therefore, where someone's photograph is taken with a view to its inclusion as part of a dossier being compiled about him as an identified subject, the act of photography would clearly be an act of personal data collection.[68] For example, the portfolio of photographs of particular actors, entertainers or fashion models maintained by a theatrical impresario or fashion modelling agency would clearly constitute personal data collected in relation to the individuals in question. Similarly, law enforcement agencies are likely to have databases including photographs of wanted persons whose identities may or may not be known. If unknown, their identities would be considered important and sought-after items of information. Such photographs clearly would constitute part of the personal data collected in relation to such wanted persons.[69]

---

[66] Ibid, at 10–11.

[67] Ibid.

[68] Ibid.

[69] Ibid.

Wacks highlights how none of the three judges doubted either that a photograph could constitute ‘personal data’ (an issue upon which the trial judge had expressed uncertainty) or that the press or other media organizations fell beyond the scope of the Ordinance.[70] He goes onto say that on the contrary, it is clear that they are caught by its provisions if and to the extent that they engage in the collection of personal data. While the case began more than 20 years ago, it highlights the earlier considerations and debate around the challenges that collection of personal data will pose by various sectors of the community. The balancing of the protection of personal data versus other rights, responsibilities, economic and social needs are going to be formidable, if, and where people choose to challenge, not only the law but individuals and entities in the community on the capture, use and storage of personal data. This will also be problematic with repeat collections from AI systems in the home that, will be able to expose personal data and information of individuals from repeated collections. Over time, for example, in a period of a decade an organisation or entity could build up an entire profile of a person, which could be harmful to that person. The adverse effects of having such a profile may impact on educational and employment opportunities.

6.6 Erasing Personal Data [Right to Be Forgotten]

While there is no formal right to be forgotten recognized within Hong Kong law, data subjects do have the ability for their personal data to be erased. Section 26, provides that a data subject can request that their personal data be erased when and where that data is no longer required. However, the requirement of erasure of personal data, in our view is not settled. This is because section 26 allows the data user to only take all practicable steps to erase personal data held by the data user where the data is no longer required. This does not apply where the personal data is prohibited under any law or it is in the public interest (including historical interest) for the data not to be erased. This, in and of itself provides a high level of flexibility for when and where the personal data might be erased.[71] Thus, this is subtly different to the concept of the right to be forgotten. Put simply, and on the backdrop of section 26, the formal right to be forgotten does not exist in the same way as it does in the EU.

Across Hong Kong, the Office of the Privacy Commissioner for Personal Data, imposes an obligation on a data user to erase personal data as more specifically spelt out in Data Protection Principle (DPP) 2(2) in Schedule 1 of the PDPO and section

[70] Wacks, R, *"Privacy and Process"* (1999) 29 HKLJ 176.

[71] For the avoidance of doubt, it is hereby declared that a data user must take all practicable steps to erase personal data in accordance with subsection (1) notwithstanding that any other data user controls (whether in whole or in part) the processing of the data; the first-mentioned data user shall not be liable in an action for damages at the suit of the second-mentioned data user in respect of any such erasure.

26.[72] In addition to the above, the Privacy Commissioner has issued the *Guidance on Personal Data Erasure and Anonymisation* to provide practical advice to data users as to when personal data should be erased, as well as how personal data may be permanently erased by means of digital deletion and/or physical destruction.

Apart from section 26, the Data Protection Principle (DPP) 2(2) in Schedule 1 supports section 26 in the administration of erasing personal information. Thus, DPP 2 provides that to the Ordinance requires data users to take all practicable steps to ensure that personal data is not kept longer than is necessary for the fulfilment of the purpose (including any directly related purpose) for which the data is or is to be used.[73] Furthermore, DPP2(3) provides that if a data user engages a data processor, whether within or outside Hong Kong, to process personal data on the data user's behalf, the data user must adopt contractual or other means to prevent any personal data transferred to the data processor from being kept longer than is necessary for processing of the data.[74] On the other hand, Kong Jojo Y.C. Mo highlights how, as seen in the 'Do No Evil' application,[75] a data user has to comply with DPP 3, which states that unless the prescribed consent of the data subject is obtained, personal data cannot be used for a new purpose.[76] Mo further points out that, to fulfil the compliance requirements of DPP 3 will only apply to voluntarily or mandatorily obtained personal data. Mo believes that while the right to be forgotten has not considered in the Hong Kong decisions, the outcome of both the 'Do No Evil' and *Webb*[77] decisions resulted in a closer step to a right to delete since the use of publicly available data is considered use for a new purpose and a breach of DPP 3 if prescribed consent is not obtained.[78] Thus, the right to delete makes little difference when the data user will be prohibited from using personal data for that new purpose upon the issuance of an enforcement notice. Finally, DPP4(1) requires a data user to take all practicable steps to ensure that personal data held by it is protected against unauthorised or accidental access, processing, erasure, loss or use, including the consideration of: (a) the kind of data and the harm that could result if any of those incidents should occur; (b) the physical location where the data is stored; (c) any security measures incorporated (whether by automated means or otherwise) into any equipment in which the data is stored; (d) any measures taken for ensuring the

---

[72] Section 26, The Personal Data (Privacy) Ordinance (PDPO) Cap 486.

[73] Office of the Privacy Commissioner for Personal Data, Hong Kong, *Guidance on Personal Data Erasure and Anonymisation*, https://www.pcpd.org.hk/english/publications/files/erasure_e.pdf

[74] Ibid.

[75] Office of the Privacy Commissioner for Personal Data Hong Kong, Report No. R13-9744, 13 August 2013 https://www.pcpd.org.hk/english/publications/les/R13_9744_e.pdf, in Kong Jojo Y.C. Mo Privacy and Publicly Available Information: An Analysis of the Common Law and Statutory Protection in Hong, *Statute Law Review*, 2019, Vol. 40, No. 2, 188–205.

[76] KongJojo Y.C. Mo (2019), *Privacy and Publicly Available Information: An Analysis of the Common Law and Statutory Protection in Hong, Statute Law Review*, Vol. 40, No. 2, 188–205.

[77] Ibid, *Webb* v. *Privacy Commissioner for Personal Data* Administrative Appeal No. 54/2014, 27 October 2015.

[78] Ibid.

integrity, prudence and competence of persons having access to the data; and (e) any measures taken for ensuring the secure transmission of the data.

Mo argues that section 26 the PDPO provides for a limited right to delete which states that a data user must take all practicable steps to erase personal data where such data are no longer required for the purpose when it was used unless such erasure is against the law or it is in the public interest for the data not to be erased. Mo further states that the data user must take all practicable steps to erase the personal data notwithstanding that there are other data users who control the processing of the data.[79] For Mo, there is a limited right to be forgotten.

6.6.1 Log Book

An important feature of the laws of Hong Kong is the requirement for the data user to keep a log book. Section 27 requires a data user to keep and maintain a log book. It must be kept in both the English and Chinese language, and the records must be retained for no less than a 4 year period from when the records were first entered. More importantly, the specific requirements to be recorded are where the data user refuse to comply with a data access request in accordance with section 20 and 21.[80] This unique reporting and recording feature goes someway to strengthening the overall controls to data subjects. Having access to a log book, is a significant step forward providing the framework for effective auditing of data records.

6.7 Controller [Data User]

The data user, or otherwise referred to as the controller in other jurisdictions has substantial responsibility for the management of personal data. The laws of Hong Kong, unlike other states does not set out specific roles and responsibilities of the data user. Rather, Hong Kong has highlighted the role and obligations of the data user throughout their data protection laws. For instance, section 2 provides that a

---

[79] KongJojo Y.C. Mo (2019) Privacy and Publicly Available Information: An Analysis of the Common Law and Statutory Protection in Hong, *Statute Law Review*, Vol. 40, No. 2, 190–204.

[80] Section 20–21,The Personal Data (Privacy) Ordinance (PDPO) Cap 486, A data user shall in accordance with subsection (3) enter in the log book—(a) where pursuant to section 20 the data user refuses to comply with a data access request, particulars of the reasons for the refusal; (b) where pursuant to section 21(2) the data user does not comply with section 21(1), particulars of the prejudice that would be caused to the interest protected by the exemption concerned under Part 8 if the existence or non-existence of the personal data to which the data access request concerned relates was disclosed; (Amended 18 of 2012 s. 2) (c) where pursuant to section 24 the data user refuses to comply with section 23(1) in relation to a data correction request, particulars of the reasons for the refusal; (d) any other particulars required by regulations made under section 70 to be entered in the log book.

person who either alone or jointly controls the collection, holding, processing or use of the personal data. Thus, and more importantly, the Commissioner is required to specify a class of data users. However, in doing so, the Commissioner must consult anybody or other individuals. This is a broad consultative process that, enables the Commissioner to consult widely across society.

More pervasively, there is obligation or legal requirement like other jurisdictions around the world for the data user to appoint, for example, a data protection officer or data processor. While out of scope of this book, the Hong Kong government have been working to improve the internal structural framework of organizations managing and handling personal data. For instance, in February 2014, the PCPD issued a best practice guide to advocate the development of a privacy management program and encourage data users to appoint or designate a responsible person to oversee the data users' compliance with the Ordinance.[81] The Best Practice Guide goes onto say that:

> Organisations are advised to appoint someone to oversee the development, implementation and maintenance of the organisation's personal data protection programmes and practices. Policies and processes are needed, and training of employees is required. Contracts (or other means) are required when organisations transfer personal data to data processors for processing, to ensure that the data is protected in a manner that is comparable to how the organisation would protect it. Organisations should have systems in place to respond to data access and correction requests from individuals for their personal data, and to respond to complaints from employees and customers about infringement of personal data privacy.[82]

If, and where there is a lack of take up, Hong Kong could consider codifying this requirement. Nevertheless, data user's role extends to the collection, use and transfer of personal data for purpose(s) that the data subject has been informed of. That is, and unless there is a limited exemption set out in the Ordinance applies.

6.8 Data User Returns and Register of Data Users

Part IV of the Ordinance: Data User Returns and Register of Data Users provides for the basis of the Data User Return Scheme (DURs).[83] The background of what was behind the reasoning to introduce DURs came about as a result of an increasing number of public enquiries and complaints received by the Office of the Privacy Commissioner for Personal Data. Thus, between 2010 and 2011, the PCPD received and estimated 18,000 enquiries and 1179 complaints from the public in relation to the use of personal information.[84] During the same period there was a

[81] Office of the Privacy Commissioner for Personal Data, A Best Practice Guide, https://www.pcpd.org.hk/pmp/files/PMP_guide_e.pdf

[82] Ibid.

[83] Personal Data (Privacy) Ordinance Data User Return Scheme Consultation Document, https://www.pcpd.org.hk/english/enforcement/consultations/files/durs_eng.pdf

[84] Ibid.

series of major data breaches that obtained the attention from local media, resulting on pressure being applied to government and the regulator to improve the processes and practices surrounding the collection, storage and use of personal data. Thus, today, the Commissioner may specify a class of data users and require them to submit to him data user returns containing "prescribed information" which includes, among other things, the kinds of personal data they control and the purposes for which the personal data are collected, held, processed or used.[85] The Commissioner shall use the Returns to maintain a register of data users containing particulars of the prescribed information supplied by Data Users. The Register shall be made available for inspection by the public. The Ordinance also provides that Data Users shall submit their Returns accompanied by a fee to be prescribed by the Commissioner.[86]

Therefore, section 14, regulates the application and use of DURs. However, the class of data users, which are required to use DRUs will be specified by the Commissioner and published in the government Gazette. However, DURs do not apply to a data user unless that class of data user is specified in the Government Gazette. To improve the accountability of data users, they are also required to submit a return[87] to the Commissioner. In addition to the above, section 14A, requires the verification of the accuracy of information in a data user return. However, there are exemptions to this verification requirement. Thus, a person whom has been issued a notice does have the option to refuse to provide a document or record and respond to any question, where they are exempted[88] under any other Ordinance. Effectively, the interpretation of this requirement extends to any other legislative instrument (Ordinance) that, provides any such exemption. Section 15, 16 and 17 allow for the Commissioner to establish a register that can support the DRU process. More specifically, section 15, provides that a register be established of data users. As part of the registry process, the Commissioner must keep and maintain a register of data users who have submitted data user returns, using information in those returns and in any change notices. Operationally, the register is to be in the form of a database; and contain, in respect of each data user who has submitted a data user return, such particulars of the information supplied in that return and any change notice as the Commissioner thinks fit.

---

[85] Ibid.

[86] Ibid.

[87] Ibid, a data user shall submit to the Commissioner a return (a) in the specified form; (b) containing the prescribed information required by the return in relation to the data user; (c) in the case of (i) a data user which belongs to the class of data users concerned on the day on which the notice under subsection (1) specifying that class commences, not earlier than 3 months before, and not later than, each anniversary of that day.

[88] Ibid, If, having regard to any document, record, information or thing, or any response to any question, provided under subsection (1), the Commissioner has reasonable grounds to believe that any information in a data user return or change notice is inaccurate, the Commissioner may, by written notice, require the data user to correct the information in the data user return or change notice.

The DURs are viewed as a positive addition to the Ordinance. That is, data users are expected to ensure that Returns are completed correctly. In the process, corporate awareness on personal data privacy protection will be raised.[89] It has raised the awareness and importance of individuals and entities who collect, store and use personal data, to do so in accordance with the law, and that it is an important component of the economy. The requirement of the data user to provide and disclose full details within the DURs, provides greater creditability, accountability and transparency of the data user.

6.9 Access and Correction of Personal Data

Providing access and correction of one's personal data has become another important feature of data protection law.[90] Thus, section 18 enables individuals to obtain access to their personal data. An individual, or, a personal who has the authority to do so, such as a legal practitioner, can on behalf of the data subject make a request for access to that personal data. Importantly, section 18 (1)(b) ensures that where a data user holds personal data that, data is to be supplied by the data user with a copy of the data.[91] However, the above must be understood in accordance with section 55. That is, section 55 provides for the process of a relevant process, and DPP6 along with section 18 (1)(b) is exempted (i.e. no need to comply with a data access request) until completion of a relevant process in determining suitability, eligibility or qualification of the data subject for employment or appointment to office. Nonetheless, this only applies to a process where an appeal may be made against a determination.

The correction of personal data ensures that the principle of accuracy is maintained. Section 22 provides that where a copy of personal data has been supplied by a data user in compliance with a data access request; and the individual, or a relevant person on behalf of the individual, who is the data subject considers that the data is inaccurate, then that individual or relevant person, as the case may be, may

[89] Personal Data (Privacy) Ordinance Data User Return Scheme Consultation Document, https://www.pcpd.org.hk/english/enforcement/consultations/files/durs_eng.pdf. An annual submission of the Returns ensures that Data Users are continuously reminded of their obligations and therefore enables them to review and maintain high standards in personal data privacy protection throughout the organization. Data Users may optionally provide more information than that prescribed by the Commissioner regarding the measures they have taken to protect the personal data held by them. By showing their commitment to the protection of customer data in this manner, their market competitiveness may be enhanced.

[90] Data Protection Principles in the Personal Data (Privacy) Ordinance—*from the Privacy Commissioner's perspective (2 Edition)* (2010) https://www.elegislation.gov.hk/hk/cap486!en-zh-Hant-HK.pdf?FROMCAPINDEX=Y

[91] Ibid, (2) A data access request under both paragraphs of subsection (1) shall be treated as being a single request, and the provisions of this Ordinance shall be construed accordingly.

make a request that the data user make the necessary correction to the data.[92] However, if a data user, subsequent to the receipt of a data correction request but before complying with the request[93] or refusing to comply with the request,[94] discloses to a third party the personal data to which the request relates, then the user shall take all practicable steps to advise the third party that the data is the subject of a data correction request still under consideration by the user (or words to the like effect). A person who, in a data correction request, supplies any information which is false or misleading in a material particular for the purpose of having the personal data corrected as indicated in the request, commits an offence and is liable on conviction to a fine at level 3 and to imprisonment for 6 months. DDP 6 underpins the access to personal data, whereby data subjects have the right of access to and correction of their personal data held by data users.[95] Data users are required to comply with such request within 40 days after receiving the request. That is, where a customer may make a request to an insurance institution to be informed whether it holds his personal data contained in, for example, an insurance application, medical report, risk assessment or claim form, and be supplied with a copy of such data within 40 days or 12 month period.[96] Where the correction cannot be made within the expiration period the data subject requesting the correction must be informed that the correction will not meet this requirement.

Notwithstanding the above, there may be circumstances where a data user can refuse to comply with data correction request where the identity of the person is to be verified. However, this does not apply where the individual requesting the correction is the same person as the individual who has made the request. Refusal to carry out this request can be undertaken where the request is not in writing and in either the Chinese or English language. In addition, the request is not required where the data user is not satisfied that the personal data to which the request relates is inaccurate, or where the data user is not supplied with such information as the data user may reasonably require to ascertain in what way the personal data to which the

---

[92] Section 22, 23, 24 and 25, The Personal Data (Privacy) Ordinance (PDPO) Cap 486. A data user who does not hold the personal data but controls the processing of that data in such a way as to prohibit the data user who does hold the data from complying (whether in whole or in part) with section 23(1) in relation to a data correction request which relates to the data, shall be deemed to be a data user to whom such a request may be made, and the provisions of this Ordinance (including subsection (1)) shall be construed accordingly.

[93] Ibid, in accordance with section 23.

[94] Ibid, in accordance with section 25.

[95] Ibid, section 23, Guidance on the Proper Handling of Customers' Personal Data for the Insurance Industry, Office of the Privacy Commissioner for Personal Data, https://www.pcpd.org.hk/english/publications/files/GN_insurance_e.pdf

[96] Ibid. (3) A data user is not required to comply with subsection (1)(c) in any case where the disclosure concerned of the personal data to the third party consists of the third party's inspection of a register or other like document—(a) in which the data is entered or otherwise recorded; and (b) which is available for inspection by the public, but this subsection shall not apply if the third party has been supplied with a copy, certified by or under the authority of the data user to be correct, of the data.

request relates is inaccurate. Moreover, the data user is not required to comply with section 23(1), 'to correct an individual's personal data, where the data user is not satisfied that the correction which is the subject of the request is accurate; or the processing of the personal data to which the request relates prohibits the first-mentioned data user from complying section 23(1)'.[97] However, data users need to act with care and not use these provisions as an excuse not to undertake the correction. In other words, the data user cannot apply the above so as to not comply with section 23(1). Nevertheless, and on the backdrop of the right by the data user to refuse to undertake a correction, the data user is to notify of the refusal. This must be undertaken no later than 40 days[98] following receipt of the request and it must inform the individual of the reasons of the refusal.

6.10 Consent and Direct Marketing

6.10.1 Consent

The expression and application of consent within Hong Kong law is quite different to that of the other countries analysed. Section 30 requires that data matching cannot be undertaken without the consent of the data subject. More specifically, section 30 states that a data user shall not carry out, whether in whole or in part, a matching procedure unless and until each individual who is a data subject of the personal data the subject of that procedure has given his prescribed consent to the procedure being carried out. In addition to the above, data matching cannot be undertaken unless and until the Commissioner has consented under the procedure[99] being carried out unless the procedure belongs to a class of matching procedures specified in a notice and is carried out in accordance with the conditions, if any, specified in the notice. However, the requirement may be subject to the Provisions of Ordinance under

[97] Ibid, section 23(1).

[98] Ibid, (2) Without prejudice to the generality of subsection (1), where (a) the personal data to which a data correction request relates is an expression of opinion; and (b) the data user concerned is not satisfied that the opinion is inaccurate, then the data user shall, (i) make a note, whether annexed to that data or elsewhere, (A) of the matters in respect of which the opinion is considered by the requestor to be inaccurate; and (B) in such a way that that data cannot be used by a person (including the data user and a third party) without the note being drawn to the attention of.

[99] Section 32, The Personal Data (Privacy) Ordinance (PDPO) Cap 486. The Commissioner shall determine a matching procedure request (a) not later than 45 days after receiving the request; and (b) by taking into account the prescribed matters applicable to the request and where he is satisfied as to those matters, serving a notice in writing on the requestor stating that he consents to the carrying out of the matching procedure to which the request relates subject to the conditions, if any, specified in the notice where he is not so satisfied, serving a notice in writing on the requestor stating that he refuses to consent to the carrying out of the matching procedure to which the request relates; and such of those matters in respect of which he is not so satisfied and the reasons why he is not so satisfied.

which Matching Procedures are Required or Permitted.[100] This is something individuals and entities will need to confirm.

The transfer of personal data outside of Hong Kong can be undertaken provided the data subject has provided consent for doing so. However, this is limited where it is practicable to do so. Thus, there is an implied level exception to this consent. Consent is not required where it is not practicable to obtain that consent. This broad approach to consent for the transfer of data outside the territory obviously meets the sovereign needs of the one state two systems across the territory. Furthermore, consent for such a transfer of data can be undertaken if it was practicable to obtain such consent, and the data subject would provide it. Thus, if, and when the data subject failed, or, refused to provide consent any such transfer of data could not be achieved.

The level of consent is largely controlled through procedure, rather than providing the power to the data subject. Consent, while not clear as to when it commences and conclude can be summarized as allowing a data subject to control their personal data. It can also be found in Use of Personal Data in Direct Marketing Division, and in accordance with section 35C. In *Eastweek Publisher v Privacy Commissioner for Personal Data*,[101] the plaintiff's photographer took a photograph of the complainant in a public street. The photograph was later used to illustrate an article about women's fashion in Hong Kong, in which the complainant's dress sense was criticised. After a hearing as part of his investigation into the complaint, the Privacy Commissioner found inter alia that:

> the photograph had been taken using a long-range lens without the complainant's knowledge or consent, and that after it appeared in the magazine concerned, the complainant's colleagues and others made fun of her and made her too embarrassed to wear the same clothing (which was new) again. [102]

As a result of his investigation into the complaint, the Privacy Commissioner concluded that there had been a breach of the requirement of DPP 1 to collect personal data by means that are fair in the circumstances of the case (i.e. that the taking of the photograph had been a collection of personal data by means that were unfair in the circumstances of the case). The Court of First Instance upheld the Privacy Commissioner's finding on an application for judicial review. However, a majority of the Court of Appeal held otherwise.[103]

---

[100] Ibid, schedule 4.

[101] [2000] 1 HKC 692.

[102] *Eastweek Publisher Ltd v Privacy Commissioner for Personal Data*, HCAL 98 of 1998 (Unreported judgment of Keith JA, sitting as an additional judge of the Court of First Instance) (24.9.99).

[103] [2000] 1 HKC 692; Godfrey VP and Ribeiro JA (as he then was) in the majority, Wong JA dissenting.

6.10.2 Direct Marketing

Direct marketing is a unique and specific feature of the Hong Kong data laws. Throughout Hong Kong, direct marketing is common practice and involves collection and use of personal data by an organization for direct marketing itself and in some cases, the provision of such data by the organization to another person for use in direct marketing.[104] Firstly, it must be noted that the Ordinance does not regulate direct marketing—the activity. Direct marketing has been defined to include the offering, or advertising of the availability, of goods, facilities or services; or the solicitation of donations or contributions for charitable, cultural, philanthropic, recreational, political or other purposes.[105] The Privacy Commissioner will take into account such factors as to whether the data subject is, in fact, free to choose between giving and withholding consent without fear of any adverse consequence, and whether the consent is bundled consent (where the data subject has no real choice not to give consent). However, David Swain is of the view that, even if such consent is kept separate, if a data subject arguably has no real choice as to whether or not to give consent to use his personal data for direct marketing purposes (e.g. if it is a condition to enter into a competition to consent to receiving marketing emails), this would mean that, in this author's view, it would be unlikely that the Privacy Commissioner would find that such consent had been "voluntarily" given. This is because, in the case of the present example, consent must be given by the data subject to enter the competition.[106] Section 35B states that this Division does not apply in relation to the offering, or advertising of the availability, of social services run, subvented or subsidized by the Social Welfare Department. It does not also apply to health care services provided by the Hospital Authority or Department of Health; or any other social or health care services which, if not provided, would be likely to cause serious harm to the physical or mental health of the individual to whom the services are intended to be provided; or any other individual.[107]

Nonetheless, section 35C requires the data user to take specific action before that data is used in direct marketing, this includes, informing the data subject that their data is intended to be used, and ensure that they have obtained consent for that use. Failure by the data user who uses a data subject's personal data in direct marketing without taking each of the actions specified in subsection (2) is liable on

[104] Office Of Privacy Commissioner, New Guidance on Direct Marketing, https://www.pcpd.org.hk/english/publications/files/GN_DM_e.pdf. According to the Guidance Note, an example of such "bundled consent" is where a data subject is provided with only one place to sign/accept the form, thus giving the data subject the choice between: (a) giving up the application; or (b) giving his "bundled consent" by agreeing to the terms and conditions of the service as well as the use of his personal data for direct marketing purposes (even if, in fact, he finds such use objectionable).

[105] Section 35A(1), The Personal Data (Privacy) Ordinance (PDPO) Cap 486.

[106] David Swain, Direct Marketing in Hong Kong: A Summary of Key Privacy Issues, 2016, https://www.cpomagazine.com/data-privacy/direct-marketing-hong-kong-summary-key-privacy-issues/

[107] Section 35B, The Personal Data (Privacy) Ordinance (PDPO) Cap 486.

conviction[108] to a fine of $500,000 and to imprisonment for 3 years. However, under section 35D, there are exemptions that will apply where a data subject had been explicitly informed by a data user in an easily understandable and, if informed in writing, easily readable manner of the intended use or use of the data subject's personal data in direct marketing in relation to a class of marketing subjects. Additionally, an exemption applies where the data user had used any of the data; the data subject had not required the data user to cease to so use any of the data; and the data user had not, in relation to the use, contravened any provision of the Ordinance at the time of the use. Thus, section 35C does not apply in relation to the intended use,[109] on or after the commencement date, of the data subject's personal data. Such is the focus on personal data in direct marketing, Hong Kong has also ensured that a data subject's consent has been obtained before any the data is used.[110] Furthermore, section 35F requires the data user to notify the data subject when their personal data is going to be used in direct marketing for the first time. Furthermore, the data user must inform the data subject of when their personal data will no longer be used in direct marketing. This applies regardless of whether the personal data is collected from the data subject by the data user. Failure to comply, the data user who does not comply with this section could be liable to conviction or a fine of $500,000 and to term of imprisonment for 3 years.

Nonetheless, at any time a data subject has the right to request that the data user cease to continue to use their personal data at any time—in direct marketing.[111] Failure to comply with this request, the data user commits an offence and is liable on conviction to a fine of $500,000 and to imprisonment for 3 years. On 26 January 2017, the Court of First Instance was required to make a decision on the interpretation and function of section 35G of Personal Data (Privacy) Ordinance (Cap. 486). In the case of *HKSAR v Hong Kong Broadband Network Limited*,[112] a telecommunications service provider (the data user) (X) approached its then customer (the data subject) by telephone to offer an extended service at a discounted price. The facts of this case also included the data subject having been a customer of X for 2 years

[108] Ibid, section 35C.

[109] Ibid, section 35C, If—(a) a data subject's personal data is provided to a data user by a person other than the data subject (*third person*); and the third person has by notice in writing to the data user, stated that sections 35J and 35K have been complied with in relation to the provision of data; and specified the class of marketing subjects in relation to which the data may be used in direct marketing by the data user, as consented to by the data subject.

[110] Ibid, section 35E. A data user who has complied with section 35C must not use the data subject's personal data in direct marketing unless—(a) the data user has received the data subject's consent to the intended use of personal data, as described in the information provided by the data user under section 35C(2)(b), either generally or selectively; (b) if the consent is given orally, the data user has, within 14 days from receiving the consent, sent a written confirmation to the data subject, confirming—(i) the date of receipt of the consent; (ii) the permitted kind of personal data; and (iii) the permitted class of marketing subjects; and (c) the use is consistent with the data subject's consent.

[111] Ibid, section 35G.

[112] *HKSAR v Hong Kong Broadband Network Limited*, HCMA 624/2015.

between December 2011 until the contract expiring in December 2013. The data subject had previously demanded that the data user cease using their personal data in direct marketing, this was never honoured. In fact, the data user left a voice message to the data subject informing them that his contract would expire soon and that any renewal would be at a discounted price. The Court noted that the voice message read:

> Hello Mr. Chan … your contract is about to expire … there will be an increase in price in June and we do not wish you to pay a higher price … therefore I would like to let you know that if you are happy with our 1000M services, we can give you a promotional offer this month so that you will not be affected by the increase in price. Please return a call to me when you receive this voice message … .[113]

The Court believed that the data user had contravened section 35G because they had not fulfilled the procedural requirements when requested by a data subject to cease using their personal data in direct marketing. Subsequently the Court held:

> on the true construction of the legislative intent of the PDPO and having regard to the regulatory nature of s. 35G, it is not necessary for the Prosecution to prove mens-rea in respect of s. 35G, particularly in view of the wording used and the statutory defence provided in the same section.[114]

The Court went onto say that direct marketing refers to the offering or advertising of the availability of goods, facilities or services. Thus, it was held that the:

> first part of the voice message which reminded the data subject of his expiring contract was merely an opening remark for A to offer other services. The voice message went beyond a simple reminder, and since "offering" and "advertising" must not be narrowly interpreted, the voice message constituted a "new purpose" and direct marketing.[115]

The resulting effect saw the court fine the defendant HK$30,000. Finally, section 35H requires that prescribed consent for using personal data in direct marketing conforms with data protection principle 3. Despite section 2(3), where a data user requires, under data protection principle 3, the prescribed consent of a data subject for using any personal data of the data subject in direct marketing, the data user is to be taken to have obtained the consent provided the data user has met the conditions set out in sections 35C, 35E or 35G. Section 35 does not apply where the data user provides, otherwise than for gain, personal data of a data subject to another person for use by that other person in offering, or advertising the availability. The critical issue, which is not apparent is what is meant by 'for gain'. It is our view that this would constitute any material, monetary or other type of gain. Nevertheless, it does not apply to social services run or subsidized by the Social Welfare Department or a health care services provided by the Hospital Authority or Department of Health. It will not apply where there is any other social or health care services

---

[113] Ibid.

[114] Ibid.

[115] Ibid.

which, if not provided, would be likely to cause serious harm to the physical or mental health of the individual(s).

In addition to the above, a data user will need to take certain action before providing personal data for direct marketing.[116] Section 35K goes on to require that a data use must not provide personal data for use in direct marketing without data subject's consent, and section 351 allows a data subject to request the data user to cease any further action or use of their data in direct marketing. Despite section 2(3), where a data user requires, under data protection principle 3, the prescribed consent of a data subject for providing any personal data of the data subject to another person for use in direct marketing, the data user is to be taken to have obtained the consent if the data user has not contravened section 35J, 35K or 35L. Section 35M ensures that there is a level of prescribed consent provided for the use of personal data in direct marketing. Where the data user has not complied with section 35J, K, or L they may be liable on conviction to a fine of $1,000,000 and to imprisonment for 5 years, or, if the data is provided otherwise than for gain, the data user can obtain a fine of $500,000 and to imprisonment for 3 years.[117]

6.11 Privacy Commissioner

Section 5 provides the power for the establishment of the Hong Kong Privacy Commissioner (PC). The Commissioner shall be a corporation sole with perpetual succession. The Commissioner is appointed for a period of 5 years, but for not more than 1 further period of 5 years. The office of the PC is considered a responsible position that restricts the individual from holding any other office, without the appropriate approval.[118] Section 8 sets out the functions of the Commissioner. They include *(a)* monitoring and supervising compliance of the Ordinance; *(b)* promoting and assisting bodies representing data users to prepare, codes of practice and data protection principles; *(c)* promote awareness and compliance; and *(d)* examine any proposed legislation for future data protection legislative reform. The broad powers of the PC enable the Commissioner to undertake inspections of any personal data systems used by data users which are departments of the Government or statutory corporations.

Notwithstanding the above, the authority also extends to enable the Commissioner to undertake research into, and monitor developments in, the processing of data and information technology to ensure the privacy of individuals their personal data is protected. However, this does not exclude the possibility for individuals and entities to undertake illegal activates that will result in breaching cyber security protocols and mechanism, gaining access to personal data. For the size of Hong Kong the PC also has a role to liaise and consult with individuals outside of the Hong Kong

[116] Ibid, section 35J, 35K, 35L, 35M.

[117] Ibid.

[118] Ibid, section 17A–18.

territory.[119] To ensure the operation of the PC is effective, section 9 provides the power to appoint staff. Thus, the administrative powers are quite broad and enable the office to appoint staff, determine the level of remuneration and any pension contributions for those staff. In addition to these powers the PC in accordance with section 9, is bale to delegate certain functions. On the other hand, the Commission cannot delegate any functions or powers under—(a) subsection (1); (b) any provisions of any regulations made under this Ordinance which are specified in the regulations as provisions which shall not be subject to subsection (1); (c) any provisions of Schedule 2 which are specified in that Schedule as provisions which shall not be subject to subsection (1). A further examination of the regulations will need to be undertaken to confirm what specific functions can be delegated.

6.11.1 Codes of Practice

Even more important is the role the commissioner has in promoting a co-regulatory approach to data protection. In other words, section 12 provides approval for the Commissioner to approve Codes of Practice.[120] The Commissioner also has the power to revise the whole or any part of any code of practice. This enables the code to be updated according to any legislative changes. Furthermore, the Commissioner may at any time withdraw the approval of any code of practice by notice in the Gazette. Yet, section 13 reinforces the importance of the function of codes of practice in controlling the use of personal data. However, there is an exemption to complying with any code of practice. That is, where there is a failure on the part of any data user to observe any provision of an [approved] code of practice shall not of itself render the data user liable to any civil or criminal proceedings but where in any proceedings under the Ordinance[121] a data user is alleged to have contravened a requirement under this Ordinance.

[119] Ibid, (g) liaise and co-operate with any person in any place outside Hong Kong—(i) performing in that place any functions which, in the opinion of the Commissioner, are similar (whether in whole or in part) to any of the Commissioner's functions under this Ordinance; and (ii) in respect of matters of mutual interest concerning the privacy of individuals in relation to personal data; and (h) perform such other functions as are imposed on him under this Ordinance or any other enactment.

[120] Ibid, Part 3 Codes of Practice 12. Approval of codes of practice by Commissioner (1) Subject to subsections (8) and (9), for the purpose of providing practical guidance in respect of any requirements under this Ordinance imposed on data users, the Commissioner may—(a) approve and issue such codes of practice (whether prepared by him or not) as in his opinion are suitable for that purpose; and (b) approve such codes of practice issued or proposed to be issued otherwise than by him as in his opinion are suitable for that purpose. (2) Where a code of practice is approved under subsection (1), the Commissioner shall, by notice in the Gazette—(a) identify the code concerned and specify the date on which its approval is to take effect; and (b) specify for which of the requirements under this Ordinance the code is so approved.

[121] Ibid, (2) Any provision of a code of practice which appears to a specified body to be relevant to a requirement under this Ordinance alleged to have been contravened shall be admissible in evi-

6.11.2 *Advisory Committee*

The Personal Data (Privacy) Advisory Committee (PDPAC)[122] plays a pivotal role in advising the Commissioner on matters relevant to the privacy of individuals in relation to personal data. It currently comprises 9 members from both the public and private sectors.[123] While writing this book, in its most recent meeting in April 2019, the Advisory Committee highlighted the initial views of the Privacy Commissioner for Personal Data (PCPD) on the review of the PDPO to Members; particularly on (i) the threshold for mandatory data breach notification; (ii) the proposed time period for notifying the PCPD; (iii) the proposed timing for notifying the affected persons; (iv) the possible exemptions for notifying affected persons; (v) self-regulation on data retention periods with statutory requirements for specifying maximum retention period; (vi) conferment of sanctioning power on PCPD; and (vii) direct regulation on data processors.[124]

Apart from above, the Chairman of the Advisory Committee opined that if the PCPD was conferred with the sanctioning power, clear standards and criteria for levying fines as well as a reasonable level of fines should be formulated and the factors to be taken into account when exercising sanctioning power should be devised. However, the PCPD would not blindly follow the requirement of the EU GDPR. Local circumstances would have to be emphasized. Some of the factors included the number of the affected individuals, the nature of personal data being leaked, amongst others. This would enable Hong Kong to be the regional data hub for the Mainland China under "One Country, Two Systems" and the "Belt and Road Initiative".[125]

The transparency of these meetings has become an integral component of the overall process to improve the data protection laws. They appear to meet quarterly, and by making the information publicly available, allows citizens from any country, the business community, regulators and governments from around the world to better understand and follow the developments of data protection law in Hong Kong. The point about not specifically following the EU GDPR is recognition of the local sovereign needs Hong Kong need to consider, in a region that, has growing

---

dence in the proceedings under this Ordinance concerned and if it is proved that there was at any material time a failure to observe any provision of the code which appears to that body to be relevant to any matter which it is necessary to prove in order to establish a contravention of such requirement, that matter shall be taken as proved in the absence of evidence that such requirement was in respect.

[122] Ibid, Section 11.

[123] Personal Data (Privacy) Advisory Committee, Privacy commissioner for Personal Data, https://www.pcpd.org.hk/english/about_pcpd/committees/pdac/personal_data_advisory_committee.html

[124] PD(P)AC Paper No. 08/19 Minutes of the 56th Meeting of the Personal Data (Privacy) Advisory Committeeheld at 12/F, Sunlight Tower, 248 Queen's Road East, Wan Chai, Hong Kong at 10:00 a.m. on 2 April 2019, https://www.pcpd.org.hk/english/about_pcpd/committees/pdac/files/minutes_56_PDPAC_Meeting.pdf

[125] Ibid.

geopolitical and economic tensions. They consider themselves as being a regional data hub that, will highlight how personal data and its governance under the One Country-Two Systems and the Belt and Road Initiative.

6.11.3 *Standing Committee*

The multilayered governance process for the governance of data protection is also supported by a Standing Committee on Technological Developments (SCTD), in Hong Kong. The approach taken by Hong Kong is similar to many other countries. Arguably this committee is likely to play an even greater role in the future, as different technologies are developed and released onto the market that, capture and use personal data. The SCTD[126] was established to advise the Commissioner on matters relevant to the effect that developments in the processing of data and computer technology have on the privacy of individuals in relation to personal data. The committee comprises of individuals from academia and the Privacy Commissioner. In the most recent meeting of September 2019,[127] the committee had been charged with advising the PCPD on the draft information leaflet on "*Addressing the privacy risks of artificial intelligence, profiling, automated decision-making and re-identification" (SCTD Paper No. 05/19)*. That confirms the rising concerns of the interconnectedness between the application and use of AI, and what that will mean for personal data collection, storage and use.

6.12 Enforcement

In accordance with section 35G (3) of the Ordinance, a service provider who receives a request for cessation of using the customer's personal data in direct marketing must, without charge to the data subject, comply with the request.[128] Thus, the approach taken by Hong Kong is the use of enforcement notices. Section 47 allows the Commissioner to issue an enforcement notice, following an investigation to a data user, so as to meet the conditions set out in the notice. Breaching an

---

[126] Standing Committee on Technological Developments, Privacy commissioner for Personal Data, https://www.pcpd.org.hk/english/about_pcpd/committees/sctd/standing_committee_on_technological_developments.html

[127] The Twenty-eighth Meeting of the Standing Committee on Technological Developments Date : 5 September 2019 (Thursday)Time : 10:00 a.m.Venue : Conference Room, PCPD Office, 12/F, Sunlight Tower, 248 Queen's Road East, Wan Chai, https://www.pcpd.org.hk/english/about_pcpd/committees/sctd/files/sctd_28th_agenda.pdf

[128] The Personal Data (Privacy) Ordinance (PDPO) Cap 486, section 35, Data subject may require data user to cease to use personal data in direct marketing.

enforcement notice is an offence in accordance with section 50,[129] which can result in either civil or criminal proceedings. Furthermore, section 66 allows an individual to seek compensation from the misuse of their personal data, directly from the data user. Failure to abide to the enforcement notice is a criminal offense, punishable by a fine of up to HK$50,000 and imprisonment for up to two years, as well as a daily penalty of HK$1000 if the offense continues after conviction.

Despite the possible fines attached to not complying with an enforcement notice, it is noteworthy that the intention behind the six data protection principles is the creation of a new culture in effecting the handling of personal data during their whole life cycle from their collection to their destruction.[130] Importantly the DPPs do not regulate the conduct of the data users in detail. In most cases, contraventions of the principles do not constitute criminal offences. It is when a data user fails to comply with the terms of an enforcement notice issued by the Commissioner after a finding of a contravention that he becomes liable to be punished under the Ordinance.[131] The enforcement notice to the offending data user is normally issued after an investigation and when certain conditions are met. However, a contravention of a data protection principle can form the basis of a civil suit against the data user whether or not an enforcement notice has been issued.[132]

More importantly, large fines can be incurred by individuals and entities that, for example, have breached the provision related to direct marketing or, disclosing personal data of a data subject. The fine can be up to HK$1 million and imprisonment of up to five years, where such disclosure is made with certain intent, or where the disclosure causes psychological harm to the data subject. Even though there is a cap on the extent of fine imposed where psychological harm, it is arguable that the Hong Kong law may accept a tort in data protection law. A tort in data protection law has not been fully accepted in other common law countries. The challenge will be how the Hong Kong judiciary measure psychological harm. This is an area of further research.

---

[129] Ibid, section 50. Enforcement notices (1) If, following the completion of an investigation, the Commissioner is of the opinion that the relevant data user is contravening or has contravened a requirement under this Ordinance, the Commissioner may serve on the data user a notice in writing, directing the data user to remedy and, if appropriate, prevent any recurrence of the contravention.

[130] Data Protection Principles in the Personal Data (Privacy) Ordinance—*from the Privacy Commissioner's perspective* (2Edition) 2010, https://www.pcpd.org.hk/english/publications/files/Perspective_2nd.pdf

[131] Ibid.

[132] Ibid.

6.12.1 International Enforcement

Section 46 of the PDPO empowers the PCPD to disclose matters to an authority outside of Hong Kong, either for the purposes of performing its functions or exercising its powers under the PDPO or for the purpose of enabling or assisting that foreign authority.[133] In the administration of this provision, the PCPD must ensure that the co-operating authority has undertaken to be bound by the PCPD's secrecy requirements. Any disclosure to support a foreign authority may only be made if the PCPD is of the opinion that the foreign jurisdiction in question has a law in force that is substantially similar to or serves the same purpose as the PDPO.[134] In addition section 47(10) attaches specific conditions, whereby the Commissioner can only disclose the personal data of a data subject is to avoid or mitigate an adverse action against the data subject; (ii) it is not practicable to obtain the consent in writing of the data subject; and if it was practicable to obtain such consent, the data subject would give it. Thus, consent continues to play an important role, providing a level of control to the data subject over their personal data in international use of personal data. Failure to comply with this provision, the individual is liable on conviction to a fine at level 3 and to imprisonment for 6 months.

6.13 Security [Cyber]

In asserting their sovereignty over the territory, section 57 enables Hong Kong to protect security, defence and international relations are exempt from the provisions of data protection principle 6 and section 18(1)(b).[135] Furthermore, the exemptions also extend to personal data from the provisions of DPP3, for the use of the data for any of the purposes concerning security, defence or international relations. In the continuing geopolitical and economic tensions throughout the region and across the world, states are wanting to hold their important strategic security institutions such as defence, amongst others closer to the state. This is another area that continues to be challenged, because of the rise in cyber security intrusions across international borders, and is likely to also extend to the use of AI. Yet, and even though Hong Kong has established legislation to protect personal data, they have not to date

[133] Sections 46(7), (8), (9), (10), The Personal Data (Privacy) Ordinance (PDPO) Cap 486.

[134] Ibid, in fulfilling the requirements set out in section 46(10), at (d) it requires that the personal data to which the matters relate is exempt from the provisions of data protection principle 3 because of an exemption under Part 8; or (e) the Commissioner has taken all reasonable precautions and exercised all due diligence to ensure that the personal data to which the matters relate will not, in that place, be collected, held, processed or used in any manner which, if that place were Hong Kong, would be a contravention of a requirement under this Ordinance.

[135] Ibid, section 18 provides for data access request (1) An individual, or a relevant person on behalf of an individual, may make a request (b) if the data user holds such data, to be supplied by the data user with a copy of such data.

introduced specific cyber security laws. It has largely remained sectorial approach. Thus, as cyber security, AI and data protection become ever more intertwined, Hong Kong may need to consider similar cybersecurity and cybercrime specific laws.

6.14 Conclusion

The data protection laws of Hong Kong do differ in structure, composition and content. The data protection framework is relatively mature, when compared to other countries in the region. The laws have been established to deal with different issues such as direct marketing, matching procedures, access amongst others. The data protection laws of Hong Kong have a considerable history dating back to when the first EU Directive on Data Protection was established. They have evolved since 1995 to be laws that largely balance the ongoing business and financial hub that Hong Kong has become, while providing a level of protection to individual's personal data.

Even though Hong Kong understand the potential impacts from AI and cyber security breaches to personal data, they have, in part, continued to express their own territorial-sovereign needs. In other words, the difference between the laws of Hong Kong to those of Macau and China is, in our view, derived from their historical connections to the UK. Hong Kong have embraced the common law, whereas Macau is largely based on the civil law. Yet, unlike other states Hong Kong has not extended its laws to establish specific data localization provisions. Hong Kong, unlike many other states including the EU have not implemented any privacy certification schemes. Even though the laws promote the need for codes of practice to be approved by the Commissioner, they do not promote the need for international accepted standards such as the ISO (International Organization for Standardization), amongst others that have been recognized across the world. However, this does not mean that through codes of practice approved by the Commissioner ISO may be used in practice. Furthermore, in 2013, the PCPD coordinated with the GPEN (Global Privacy Enforcement Network) Sweep a study into the privacy transparency of mobile apps. The study involved 60 of the most popular apps developed by Hong Kong entities and found that their privacy policies were generally inadequate.[136] The broader privacy issues surrounding mobiles apps also transcend cyber security and AI.

Another notable absence from the Hong Kong framework is the requirement for the data user to appoint a data protection officer or processor. There have been calls for organisations to establish such arrangements internally, however, these are voluntary. The question is whether Hong Kong should consider codifying this requirement? Choosing to do so would bring their legal framework in line with other jurisdictions around the world, and would improve certainty, transparency and trust

[136] Global Results from the first GPEN Internet Privacy Sweep, Office of the Privacy Commissioner for Personal Data 2013 https://www.pcpd.org.hk/english/news_events/media_statements/press_20130814.html

in the regulation and management of not only personal data, but also cyber security breaches.

Moreover, and possibly a more important gap in the Hong Kong legal framework is the requirement for data impact assessments to be undertaken. In 2018, the PCPD published a "New Ethical Accountability framework",[137] which under the framework, there have been calls urging businesses operating located in Hong Kong to undertake privacy impact assessments, referred to as "Ethical Data Impact Assessments". Yet, a unique feature that has been established by Hong Kong is the need for a Log Book to be maintained. This, risk management approach further strengthens the accountability of personal data records. Importantly they are to be retained for 4 years, thus providing authorities with sufficient time to conduct any necessary investigations. They are also to be maintained in English and Chinese language.

The current definition is similar to other states whereby it is a catch all meaning of personal data. It picks up the point that people can be identified by what is termed as a personal identifier. Arguably, this would also mean the identifying information that can be obtained through, and by AI systems. However, it is unclear whether the definition would be flexible enough to protect personal data in AI. Thus, it is recommended that Hong Kong review this definition, to ensure AI will be included. Furthermore, more needs to be done to protect the youth of Hong Kong, and thus, a review of the current definition would also confirm or otherwise whether they are going to be protected from smart home appliance, toys and personal robots. How will a person be able to request that their data be deleted permanently? Apart from this more work is required to better understand what other areas of the law such as consent, retention and storage requirements, amongst others will be adequate to regulate and protect personal data through AI.

Apart from the above, Hong Kong, in part, further reinforces the point that the interconnectedness between personal data, cyber security and AI is going to challenge the law. The possibilities of billions of people connected by mobile devices, with unprecedented processing power, storage capacity, and access to knowledge are unlimited. These possibilities will be multiplied by emerging technology breakthroughs in fields such as artificial intelligence, robotics, the Internet of Things, autonomous vehicles, 3-D printing, nanotechnology, biotechnology, materials science, energy storage, and quantum computing.[138] More importantly, they note that since data and analytics technologies generate great return on investment, companies increasingly see the goal to be the transformation of data into information and information into insight. Artificial intelligence and machine learning assist in transforming data. However, current privacy and data protection legislation are ill-equipped to keep up with, let alone anticipate, technological changes such as advanced data-processing activities.[139]

---

[137] Privacy Commissioner for Personal Data Hong Kong, Ethical Accountability Framework for Hong Kong, China A Report prepared for the Office of the Privacy Commissioner for Personal Data Analysis and Model Assessment Framework, https://www.pcpd.org.hk/misc/files/Ethical_Accountability_Framework.pdf

[138] Ibid.

[139] Ibid.

The importance of data protection to Hong Kong goes beyond protecting its citizen's privacy over the Internet. In a similar way to Singapore, Hong Kong has for decades prided itself on being a central regional business hub. In 2002, the PCPD has signed a memorandum of understanding (MOU) for Cooperative Research on Personal Data Protection with the Korea Information Security Agency.[140] The MOU was established to help facilitate cooperation in the area of research in regards to personal data. However, the MOU is non-binding but acts as an expression of both parties' genuine interest to explore opportunities for future co-operation. To date, this is the only bilateral agreement established by Hong Kong with another state. On 31 May 2019, the Data Protection Authorities of Singapore and Hong Kong signed a MoU intended to strengthen cooperation in data protection in the two jurisdictions.[141] The MOU goes a long way to help facilitate joint research projects, and cross-share experiences and information on potential and ongoing breaches between the Singapore's Personal Data Protection Commission and Hong Kong's Privacy Commissioner for Personal Data. In addition, the cooperation will also help Hong Kong and Singapore to strengthen cooperation between them and provide a reliable framework for promoting data sharing against the background of an evolving digital economy.

References

Carroll, J. M. (2007). *A concise history of Hong Kong* (p. 1). Rowman & Littlefield Publishers.

Jourard, S. M. (1966). Some psychological aspects of privacy. *Law and Contemporary Problems*, 307–318.

KongJojo, Y. C. M. (2019). Privacy and publicly available information: An analysis of the common law and statutory protection in Hong. *Statute Law Review, 40*(2), 188–205.

Marsh, L. (2016). The strategic use of human rights treaties in Hong Kong's cage-home crisis: No way out? *Asian Journal of Law and Society, 3*, 159–188.

Wacks, R. (1999). Privacy and process. *Hong Kong Law Journal, 29*, 176.

Young, S. (2004). Restricting basic law rights in Hong Kong. *Hong Kong Law Journal, 34*(1), 110.

140 Hong Kong SAR and Korea signed MOU to foster Personal Data Privacy Protection, Privacy Commissioner for Personal Data, https://www.pcpd.org.hk/english/news_events/media_statements/press_20021129.html

141 Personal Data Protection Commission Singapore, HK and SG Sign Memorandum Of Understanding to Strengthen Cooperation in Personal Data Protection, https://www.pdpc.gov.sg/news/press-room/2019/05/hk-and-sg-sign-mou-to-strengthen-cooperation-in-personal-data-protection. In the last 18 months, companies based in Singapore and Hong Kong have suffered significant data breaches. In early 2018, a Singaporean health conglomerate was fined following a data breach that impacted 1.5 million individuals, and only a few months later a Hong Kong-based airline disclosed a breach affecting the data of 9.4 million users. As both Singapore and Hong Kong are members of international data privacy organisations such as the Asia Pacific Privacy Authorities ("APPA") and the Global Privacy Enforcement Network ("GPEN"), the PDPC and PCPD have a working history of collaboration in global personal data.

Chapter 7
Macau

Abstract Macau similar to its neighbor Hong Kong has a long history. Macau in more recent times was occupied by the Portuguese, which heavily influenced their current day legal framework. Today, they have largely retained their legal framework inherited by the Portuguese. Macau's legal framework is based on the civil law tradition of continental European legal systems. It has also been influenced by Chinese law, Italian law, and some aspects of the common law.

Macau has adopted international law such as the International Covenant on Civil and Political Rights, International Covenant on Economic, Social and Cultural Rights 1966 (ICCPR),[1] and international labour conventions. Importantly, Article 17 of the ICCPR provides for the right to a level of privacy. However, it is argued that the concept of privacy in Macau, like in many other countries across the world has been influenced by regional neighbors, international law, and past rulers. The current day data protection laws of Macau vary greatly to that of Hong Kong. Nonetheless, Article 79 of the 1999 Civil Code, provides protection of personal data by an entity in charge of monitoring the collection, storing and use of that data. Article 79 prescribes the duty of, when collecting personal data for computer processing, to do it in strict obedience to the purposes of the collection and to inform the persons concerned about such purposes. Furthermore, the right of every person to know about any data on himself or herself stored in any computer databases and the purposes of the collection, as well as the right to demand the rectification or update of such data, except for what is regulated about the secrecy of criminal procedures.

[1] Portugal April 1993, Macau, https://treaties.un.org/Pages/ViewDetails.aspx?src=TREATY&mtdsg_no=IV-3&chapter=4&clang=_en#EndDec

R. Walters, M. Novak, *Cyber Security, Artificial Intelligence, Data Protection & the Law*, https://doi.org/10.1007/978-981-16-1665-5_7

The Administrative Region of Macau, developed and implemented its own Personal Data Protection Act that, came into effect in 2005. In other words, the Act 8/2005 Personal Data Protection Act, pursuant to subparagraph (1) of Article 71 of the Basic Law of the Macau Special Administrative Region, and to implement the fundamental regime established by Articles 30, 32, and 43 of the said Basic Law. This Chapter asserts that Macau's current day data protection laws comprise of 45 Articles. Article 1, highlights how the act establishes the legal regime on the processing and protection of personal data. Importantly, the processing of personal data shall be carried out transparently and in strict respect for privacy and for other fundamental rights, freedoms and guarantees set out in the Basic Law of the Macau Special Administrative Region. Arguably, Macau, at least on paper has to some extent embraced the idea and need for the protection of privacy over the Internet. As Macau continues to integrate with China, in 2019, it marked its 20th anniversary of reunification.

7.1 Introduction

The Macau Special Administrative Region (SAR) of the People's Republic of China (PRC) is one of the smallest but also one of most economically successful regions of China, with industries including entertainment and gambling, textiles and household goods manufacture. Portugal administered Macau from the sixteenth century until the transfer of sovereignty to the PRC in December 1999.[2] During its 450 year history as a Portuguese settlement, Macau transformed itself from a fishing village to a modern city. It has a rich and diverse history. Although the Portuguese had been coming to, and living in, Macau since as early as 1553, it was only in 1845 that the monarchy in Portugal claimed its sovereignty over the settlement.[3] When the Portuguese arrived in the region known today as Southeast Asia, Tomé Pires, later appointed ambassador to China, identified Malacca and the surrounding region as the principal source of Venetian goods that had once been transported along the Silk Road through the Middle East to Europe.[4] Roy Eric Xavier believes that as the chief advisor to Afonso de Albuquerque, Captain-General and the chief architect of Portugal's Asian empire, Pires had been in Malacca before its fall in 1511.

At this time in history there was a wide variety of exotic goods, a conspicuous display of wealth, and a high volume of trade conducted by Muslims, Egyptians, Bengalis, Siamese, Goans, Cambodians, Turks and merchants from many other

[2] Greenleaf, G., Macao's EU-influenced *Personal Data Protection Act* in (2008) 96 *Privacy Laws & Business International Newsletter*, 21–22.

[3] Wank-Nolasco Lamas, R, (1999) *History of Macau: A student's manual.* Macau: Institute of Tourism Education.

[4] Xavier, R.E, *Luso-Asians and the Origins of Macau's Cultural Development,* University of California, Berkeley Journal of the Royal Asiatic Society-Hong Kong, Vol. 57, HKU Press (2017).

nations.[5] Xavier is of the view that China at the time had little appetite for commerce, which left the door open to the Portuguese occupation of Malacca in 1512, and trade settlements in the lands that make up modern- day Indonesia, Thailand, Burma, Malaysia and Vietnam. In the intervening years (1512–1553) before the Middle Kingdom could decide how to deal with Europeans, each new port was quickly incorporated into the economic orbit of Goa, a city on the western coast of India whose influence now extended from the Middle East to Asia. C.R. Boxer observed that Ormuz (in the Persian Gulf) at one end of the Indian Ocean and Malacca at the other were the two great Asia entry ports for the collection and distribution of luxury goods, including the Indonesian spices that eventually reached Europe via the Levant.[6] He notes that as Goa became the administrative hub of this vast network of ports, the regions of Portuguese Asia became noted for the immense wealth produced for the crown, as well as corruption, religious persecution, slavery, and the pacification of indigenous people under its control.

A distinguishing feature of the Portuguese presence was its pursuit of two principal objectives. The first was the trading of spices, precious stones, and other goods, and the second was religious conversion of indigenous populations, policies that closely tied the Portuguese Crown and the Roman Catholic Church. Thus, the influence of Christianity began to take hold and up until the territory was handed back to China in 1991, it played a vital role in the development of its legal framework. Thus, today, the legal system of Macau is based on Portuguese law, and the civil law tradition of continental European legal systems. It is in stark contrast to Hong Kong who adopted the British common law. However, Chinese law, Italian law, and some aspects of common law, have also been influential.[7] In 2019 Macau, celebrated its 20th anniversary of its return back to China. The Special Administrative Region, which measures 12 square miles (31 sq km),[8] yet it has still been able to carve out its own economy and data protection laws.

The Basic Law of the Macau Special Administrative Region of the People's Republic of China was adopted at the First Session of the Eighth National People's Congress on March 31, 1993. It came into effect by Order No.3 of the President of the People's Republic of China on March 31, 1993. It came into effect on 20 December 1999, and Chapter III provides for Fundamental Rights and Duties of the Residents. Apart from noting the divergent citizens (Chinese and Portuguese) that have occupied the territory, all citizens have been afforded equality before the law and shall be free from discrimination.[9] More importantly, Article 30 provides that the human dignity of Macau residents shall be inviolable. Humiliation, slander and false accusation against residents in any form shall be prohibited, and they are able

[5] Ibid.

[6] Ibid.

[7] Ibid.

[8] Williams, S, *Macau: China's other 'one country, two systems' region,* 2019, https://www.bbc.com/news/world-asia-china-50832919

[9] The Basic Law of the Macao Special Administrative Region of the People's Republic of China 1999, Article 24–25.

to enjoy the right to personal reputation and the privacy of their private and family life.[10] Article 31 goes onto provide that the homes and other premises of Macau residents shall be inviolable, along with arbitrary or unlawful search of, or intrusion into, a resident's home or other premises shall be prohibited. Of note is how Article 32 provides for the freedom and privacy of communication of Macau residents shall be protected by law. No department or individual may, on any grounds, infringe upon the freedom and privacy of communication of residents except that the relevant authorities may inspect communication in accordance with the provisions of the law to meet the needs of public security or of investigation into criminal offences. The protection of an individual's privacy through communication while not specifically referring to personal data and the protection of that data, indirectly personal data forms part of online communication.

Additionally, Article 40 states the provisions of International Covenant on Civil and Political Rights, International Covenant on Economic, Social and Cultural Rights 1966 (ICCPR), and international labour conventions as applied to Macau shall remain in force and shall be implemented through the laws of the Macao Special Administrative Region. The ICCPR, in accordance with Article 17, provides that one shall be subjected to arbitrary or unlawful interference with his privacy, family, home or correspondence, nor to unlawful attacks on his honour and reputation. The acceptance of the right to privacy and the protections afforded to individuals from it, goes some way to ensuring the local laws provide a level of protection to personal data.

More specifically, the Article 79 of the 1999 Civil Code, provides protection of personal data by an entity in charge of monitoring the collection, storing and use of that data. Article 79 prescribes the duty of, when collecting personal data for computer processing, to do it in strict obedience to the purposes of the collection and to inform the persons concerned about such purposes. Furthermore, the right of every person to know about any data on himself or herself stored in any computer databases and the purposes of the collection, as well as the right to demand the rectification or update of such data, except for what is regulated about the secrecy of criminal procedures. More importantly, Article 79(3) states that the creation of an authority in charge of monitoring the collection, storing and use of computerised personal data, authorising the access to a third person's personal data contained in any computerised database and authorising the interconnection of computerised databases. Thus in summary, the protection of personality includes the deceased, integrity of the body and mind, honour, intimacy of private life, confidential correspondence, notes by relatives and other confidential documents, non-confidential correspondence, secrecy of personal history, personal data, portrait, accuracy in personal information, and name and other personal identifier.[11] Furthermore, Article 5 of the Publication Law also provides the right to access the source of information shall

[10] Ibid, Article 30.

[11] The Law Reform Commission of Hong Kong Report, Civil Liability for Invasion of Privacy, https://www.hkreform.gov.hk/en/docs/rprivacy-e.pdf

cease if it involves the protection of any facts or documents about the intimacy of private and family life.[12]

Apart from placing the protection of privacy and personal data as a right within the Macau legal framework, they have taken that one step further by criminalizing the certain protection under the Criminal Code 1995. In accordance with Article 186 an individual can incur a punishment with possible imprisonment of up to 2 years or fine up to 240 days for various acts of interference in another's private life, such as, the interception, recording, use, transmission or disclosure of a private telecommunication. The same level of penalty also applies where there is the taking, recording, use or disclosure of another's picture or intimate places or objects, eavesdropping, or, the disclosure of facts related with another's private life or health condition. Personal information in relation to health data is considered to require a higher level of control and protection. Moreover, Article 187 provides for a term of imprisonment of up to 2 years or fine up to 240 days "whoever creates, keeps or uses a computerised base of data on political or philosophical ideology, religion, race or private life of individuals which allows the identification of the data concerning each individual".[13] Arguably this also includes personal data. This is a unique feature of Macau's laws, which had not only created a tort, but also criminalized the misuse of personal data. A distinguishing feature is criminal penalties reflected within the data protection laws, and the interconnectedness with cyber security.

Moreover, Graham Greenleaf believes that, Macau's personal data protection laws have been influenced by both the EU and its nearest neighbor Hong Kong. He is of the view that the laws are very similar to Portugal's legislation, and therefore, it is closer to the EU privacy Directive of 1995 than any other data protection legislation in Asia.[14]

7.2 Application and Scope

The Act 8/2005 Personal Data Protection Act (the Act), pursuant to subparagraph (1) of Article 71 of the Basic Law of the Macao Special Administrative Region, and to implement the fundamental regime established by Articles 30, 32, and 43 of the said Basic Law, the Legislative Assembly hereby decrees that the following shall be enforced as law. Of all the countries, including the EU laws that have been examined in this book, and the first book, Macau's data protection laws are by and large the most succinct, comprising of only 45 Articles. Article 1 highlights how the act establishes the legal regime on the processing and protection of personal data. Furthermore, the processing of personal data shall be carried out transparently and

---

[12] Ibid.

[13] Ibid, Article 87.

[14] Greenleaf, G, *Macau's EU-influenced Personal Data Protection Act* [2008] ALRS 9; (2008) 96 Privacy Laws & Business International Newsletter.

in strict respect for privacy and for other fundamental rights, freedoms and guarantees set out in the Basic Law of the Macao Special Administrative Region, the instruments of international law and the legislation in force.[15]

The Act applies to both the public and private sectors. The data protection laws apply to the processing of personal data whether manually or by an automated system or platform.[16] The laws also apply to video surveillance and other forms of capture, processing and dissemination of sound and images allowing persons to be identified. However, this is on the basis that the controller is domiciled or based in the Macao Special Administrative Region (the MSAR). Alternatively, computer or data communication network access provider is established on the MSAR territory, the laws will also apply. In other words, where the communication network access provider is established in Australia, Singapore or the United States the laws do not apply, unless there is a specific bilateral or some other state agreement in place. However, it does not apply to the processing of personal data carried out by a natural person in the course of a purely personal or household activity. An exception to this, is where there is systematic communication and dissemination.

7.3 Defining Personal Data

Article 4 defines personal data to mean, any information of any type, irrespective of the type of medium involved, including sound and image, relating to an identified or identifiable natural person ("data subject"); an identifiable person is one who can be identified, directly or indirectly, in particular by reference to an indication number or to one or more factors specific to his physical, physiological, mental, economic, cultural or social identity. Despite the lack of a definition of sensitive personal data, Article 7 provides some guidance of what constitutes this type of data. Sensitive personal data includes data that discloses the philosophical or political beliefs, political association or trade-union membership, religion, privacy and racial or ethnic origin, health or sex life, including genetic data. This type of data has a high threshold of control afforded to it, as there are prohibitions in place for its processing.[17] The current definition may however be tested in the future with more sophisticated technology coming onto the market such as AI.

The issue of publishing sensitive personal data on social networking sites has recently been considered by the Macau Office for Personal Data Protection (OPDP).

---

[15] Act 8/2005 Personal Data Protection Act, Article 2 General Principle.

[16] Ibid, Article 3. This Act shall apply to the processing of personal data regarding public safety without prejudice to special rules in instruments of international law and inter-regional agreements to which the MSAR is bound and specific laws pertinent to public safety and other related regulations.

[17] Ibid, Article 7.

In case complaint 0217/2017/IP[18] whereby, an individual or entity (X) had published on a social networking site containing a female's (Y) photos, and descriptions of her private life, but without her consent. The matter transcended two fundamental principles of data protection law. That is, the definition of personal data and the application and use of the concept of consent. However, the OPDP largely focused on whether consent was provided for the publishing of the personal data. The OPDP noted that:

> According to Article 4(1)(1) and 3(1) of the PDPA (*Personal Data Protection Act*/Law 8/2005), the data processing of the current case is subject to the same Law. During the investigations, X confessed that he did publish the said post, because of his grudge against B's cheating on her spouse. A took it on Y for her infidelity, and thus published the online post, which contained the information of the latter's family life and personal, casual relationships. According to Article 7(1) of the PDPA, the information was sensitive data in nature, whose processing must be underpinned by any of the legitimate processing conditions laid down in the same Article. X admitted that, prior to publishing the said sensitive data, he had not obtained X's consent, which was contrary to the situation where "the data subject has given his explicit consent for such processing", laid down in Article 7(2)(3) of the PDPA. The current case also was not a situation where any of the legitimate processing conditions of the same Article applies. Based on the above, X's publishing, due to his indignation at Y's infidelity, of the said sensitive data on the social networking site violated Article 7.[19]

Subsequently, Y was fined MOP$10000 according to Article 33(2) of the PDPA. The OPDP did not discuss the definition of personal data, particularly sensitive personal data. It reinforces the point that the concept of consent when coupled with the definition of personal data cannot be separated. They reinforce each other, and play a major role in providing a level of protection to data subjects, for their personal data.

7.4 Data Subject – Rights

The Personal Data Protection Act provides a number of rights to data subjects including the right to information, right to access personal information and the right to object. Additionally, a data subject also has the right not to be subject to automated individual decisions. Beginning with Article 10 and the right to information. Firstly, the controller is responsible for providing a data subject with the following information when requested;

- 'the identity of the controller and of his representative;
- the purposes of the processing;
- the recipients or categories of recipients;

[18] Complain Case Note No, 0217/2017/IP Title, Publishing someone's sensitive data on social networking sites. Office of Personal Data Protection.

[19] Ibid.

- whether replies to the questions are obligatory or voluntary, as well as the possible consequences of failure to reply;
- the existence and conditions of the right of access and the right to rectify, provided they are necessary, taking account of the specific circumstances of collection of the data in order to guarantee the data subject that they will be processed fairly'.[20]

In addition, the personal data is collected on open networks the data subject shall be informed, except where he is already aware of it, that personal data relating to him may be circulated on the network without security measures and may be at risk of being seen and used by unauthorised third parties. However, the obligation to provide information may be waived by (1). a legal provision; (2). on the grounds of security and criminal prevention or investigation; or (3). in particular for processing for statistical purposes or for the purposes of historical or scientific research, when the provision of such information proves impossible or would involve a disproportionate effort or if recording or disclosure is expressly laid down by law or administrative regulations, in which case notification to the public authority is required.[21] Finally, subject to paragraph 3 of Article 11, the obligation to provide information under this Article shall not apply to the processing of data carried out solely for journalistic purposes or the purpose of artistic or literary expression.

Data subjects are afforded the right to access their personal data online. They are afforded access to the following information such as whether their personal data has been processed, the purpose for that data being processed, and the specific information and/or data that was processed. That is, where an entity has processed health data, the data subject has the right to know what exact health data was processed. Furthermore, the data subject is entitled to know what institution received their personal data, where the controller obtained that data and why the data was processed by a computer. Despite these requirements, any communication between the data subject and entity is to be undertaken in an intelligible form of the data undergoing processing and of any available information as to their source.

7.4.1 Right to Erasure

Even though there does not appear to be a comprehensive right to erasure (right to be forgotten) in the same way as in the EU, a data subject can request in accordance with Article 11(4) for their personal data to be rectified, deleted or blocked, including

[20] Act 8/2005 Personal Data Protection Act, Article 10. 2. The documents supporting the collection of personal data shall contain the information set down in the preceding paragraph. 3. If the data are not collected from the data subject and except where he already has it, the controller or his representative must provide the data subject with the information set down in paragraph 1 at the time of undertaking the recording of data or, if a disclosure to third parties is envisaged, no later than the time the data are first disclosed.

[21] Ibid.

any incomplete or inaccurate data. Specifically, the rectification, erasure or blocking of data can be undertaken where the processing does not comply with the provisions of the Act. This particularly applies to data that is incomplete or inaccurate. However, where it can be proved that to undertake the rectification, erasure or blocking of personal data that, it is impossible to achieve or disproportionately cumbersome, the entity would not be required to undertake this step. Nonetheless, further exemption applies where the processing of personal data relates to security and criminal prevention or investigation, the right of access shall be exercised through the competent authority in that case.

In cases provided for in paragraph 6 of the preceding Article, the right of access shall be exercised through the public authority, while securing the applicable provisions, in particular those guaranteeing freedom of expression and information, freedom of the press and the professional independence and secrecy of journalists.[22] In the cases provided for in paragraph 2 and paragraph 3, if communication of the data to the data subject might prejudice security, criminal prevention or investigation and freedom of expression and information or the freedom of the press, the competent authority in that case or the public authority shall only inform the data subject of those measures taken which are unlikely to adversely affect the values under the scope of protection of this paragraph.[23]

Moreover, and on the backdrop of the above, the right of access to information relating to health data, including genetic data is allowed. This is important, as this data is considered the most sensitive personal data. This builds in a higher level of control, and another procedural step over personal health data. It appears to relate to any health data, no matter the age of that data. If the data is not used for taking measures or decisions regarding any particular individual, the law may restrict the right of access where there is clearly no risk of breaching the fundamental rights, freedoms and guarantees of the data subject. This is particularly case in relation to the right to privacy, and when the data IS used solely for purposes of scientific research or kept in personal form for a period which does not exceed the period necessary for the sole purpose of creating statistics.[24]

Apart from the right to access one's personal data and information, the right to object provides another layer of control to data subject over their personal data. Thus, Article 12 enables a data subject to object to the processing of their personal data.[25] A data subject has the right to object to the processing of their personal data at any time. Although, once objected to that processing, the entity in control of the processing of that data, must cease any further data processing. However, this would not apply where other laws exist that enable the continuing processing of personal

[22] Act 8/2005 Personal Data Protection Act, Article 11.

[23] Ibid.

[24] Act 8/2005 Personal Data Protection Act, Article 11(6).

[25] Ibid. Article 12 Right to object. Save where otherwise provided by law, the data subject has the right to object at any time on compelling legitimate grounds relating to his particular situation to the processing of data relating to him, and where there is a justified objection the processing instigated by the controller may no longer involve those data.

data. In addition, this will not apply where there are legitimate or significant reasons for doing so. For example, continued processing of personal data may be required on grounds of national security.

A data subject also has the right to object, on request and free of charge, to the processing of personal data relating to him which the controller anticipates being processed for the purposes of direct marketing or any other form of commercial research, or to be informed before personal data are disclosed for the first time to third parties for the purposes of direct marketing or for use on behalf of third parties, and to be expressly offered the right to object free of charge to such disclosure or uses. In a 2008 matter of 0003/2008/IP[26] that related to direct marketing, it was highlighted how a Resident (G) claimed that he was Company A's client, and Company A made phone calls to him in an attempt to sell its goods or services. G demanded that Company A cease the practice, however it continued. The OPDP noted that:

> In accordance with the provisions in articles 4.1.(1) and 3.1 of the Personal Data Protection Act, the data processing involved in this case is within the scope of regulation by the said Act. After investigation, GPDP confirmed that fact in Resident X's complaint. In GPDP's opinion, X had demanded that Company A stop the practice of calling him for direct marketing, as exercising his right of objection, but Company A continued to use X's telephone number for direct marketing purpose. This could be a violation of Article 12.2 of the Personal Data Protection Act.[27]

In summary, the OPDP ruled that Company A's behavior could be not in compliance with Article 12.2 of the said Act. However, and although it did not constitute an administrative offence in 2008, there was room for improvement. They were not penalized by a fine or other compliance measure.

On the backdrop of the above Article 13 provides a data subject with the right not to be subject to automated individual decisions. This is an important feature of the Macau laws. Every person shall have the right not to be subject to a decision which produces legal effects concerning him or significantly affects him and which is based solely on automated processing of data intended to evaluate certain personal aspects relating to him, in particular his performance at work, creditworthiness, reliability or conduct. That is, decision making by profiling algorithms and algorithms and automated decision-making are a growing reality in the actual data-driven society.[28] Policy-makers, scholars and commentators are more and more concerned with

---

[26] Complaints Case Note No: 0003/2008/IP, Direct marketing behavior without respect to clients' right of objection, Office of Personal Data Protection.

[27] Ibid.

[28] Pasquale, F, *The Black Box Society: The Secret Algorithms That Control Money and Information*, Cambridge-London, 2015. Virginia Eubanks, *Automating Inequality – How High Tech Tools Profile, Police, and Punish the Poor*, St. Martin Press, New York, 2018. Joshua A. Kroll, Joanna Huey, Solon Barocas, Edward W. Felten, Joel R. Reidenberg, David G. Robinson, and others, 'Accountable Algorithms' (2016), *University of Pennsylvania Law Review*, Giovanni Comandé, *Regulating algorithms regulation? First ethico-legal principles, problems and opportunities of algorithms*, in Tania Cerquitelli, Daniele Quercia, Frank Pasquale (eds) "Towards glass-box data mining for Big and Small Data", Springler International, (2017), 169–207.

the risks of black box society in several fields: finance, insurance, housing, police investigations, e-commerce, work life, amongst others.[29] Nonetheless, Article 13 goes onto say that without prejudice to compliance with the other provisions of this Act, a person may be subject to automation decision where that decision is taken in the course of the entering into or performance of a contract. However, this is provided that, the request for the entering into or the performance of the contract has been satisfied, or that there are suitable measures to safeguard his legitimate interests, such as allowing the individual to put his point of view. Further, a decision by automation could apply where that decision is authorised by a legal provision which shall lay down measures to safeguard the data subject's legitimate interests.

The right not to be subject to automated individual decisions has many similarities to Article 22 of the EU GDPR.[30] The interpretation of the automated decision-making regulation in the GDPR has triggered a vivid debate in the legal doctrine.[31] Gianclaudio Malgieri argues that several scholars have interpreted this set of provisions as a new right to algorithm explanation. On the other hand, Malgieri highlights that, other scholars have preferred a contextual interpretation of Articles 13–15 and 22, suggesting that the scope of those provisions is not so limited and that they actually can provide individuals with more transparency and accountability. Article 29 Working Party (WP29) has confirmed this last viewpoint in its guidelines on profiling and automated decision-making. WP29 has confirmed that the scope of Article 22 should be interpreted extensively: decisions based "solely on automated means" must include any decision in which the human intervention is not meaningful.[32] Also the "legal effects or similarly significant effects" should be considered in a wide sense: even online marketing or price discrimination, at some conditions, could be considered significant effects relevant under Article 22.[33] Malgieri argues that another relevant issue is which suitable measures should be taken in order to enable the automated decision making in particular cases. Indeed, since Article 22(2) allows an automated decision making under wide and general

[29] Malgieri, G, *Automated decision-making in the EU Member States: The Right to explanation and other "suitable safeguards" in the national legislations*, Computer Law & Security Review 35 (2019) 105327. Michael Veale, Lilian Edwards, Clarity, surprises, and further questions in the Article 29 Working Party draft guidance on automated decision-making and profiling, Computer Law & Security Review 34 (2018) 398–404.

[30] Article 22 GDPR, Automated individual decision-making, including profiling. Regulation (EU) 2016/679 Of The European Parliament and of the Council of 27 April 2016 on the protection of natural persons with regard to the processing of personal data and on the free movement of such data, and repealing Directive 95/46/EC, Official Journal of the European Union L 119/1.

[31] Malgieri, G, *Automated decision-making in the EU Member States: The Right to explanation and other "suitable safeguards" in the national legislations*, Computer Law & Security Review 35 (2019) 105327. Article 29 Working Party, 'Guidelines on Automated individual decision-making and Profiling for the purposes of Regulation 2016/679', WP251rev.01, adopted on 3 October 2017, as last Revised and adopted on 6 February 2018; Lilian Edwards and Michael Veale, 'Slave to the Algorithm?', (2017), 21–22.

[32] Ibid.

[33] Ibid.

conditions (contract, explicit consent, EU or Member State law), the real challenge is to understand which safeguards (ex post explanation, ex ante information, right to contest) could protect and empower more the data subjects in those wide cases.[34]

While Article 13 of Macau's laws reflects that of the EU GDPR, however, Article 13 has not been fully explored or challenged yet within Macau. Arguably, the provision goes some way to address the future issues surrounding the use of profiling and automated decision-making, which have, to date emerged in the banking and finance, healthcare, taxation, insurance, marketing and advertising sectors,[35] amongst others. How, and whether individuals will adopt and use this right remains to be seen. It is our view that it may be a generational issue, and as the younger generation become accustomed to adopting and using this technology, and as human interaction may be phased out, the provision may not be of any importance. On the other hand, the older generation that are suited to human interaction could adopt and apply this provision in the near future.

Finally, in accordance with Article 14, individuals have the right to compensation, who has suffered damage, from the unlawful processing operation or of any other act incompatible with legal provisions or regulations in the area of personal data protection is entitled to receive compensation from the controller for the damage suffered.[36] On the other side, it must be noted that a controller may be exempted from this liability, in whole or in part, if they prove that they were not responsible for the event giving rise to the damage. Where a processor is involved, the provisions of the Article 492 Civil Code in Article 492 will apply. Thus, this enables individuals to pursue a claim through the courts.

[34] Ibid.

[35] Guidelines on Automated individual decision-making and Profiling for the purposes of Regulation 2016/679, European Commission, Justice and Consumers, https://ec.europa.eu/newsroom/article29/item-detail.cfm?item_id=612053. Advances in technology and the capabilities of big data analytics, artificial intelligence and machine learning have made it easier to create profiles and make automated decisions with the potential to significantly impact individuals' rights and freedoms. The wide spread availability of personal data on the internet and from Internet of Things (IoT)devices, and the ability to find correlations and create links, can allow aspects of an individual's personality or behaviour, interests and habits to be determined, analysed and predicted. Profiling and automated decision-making can be useful for individuals and organisations, delivering benefits such as: increased efficiencies; and resource savings. They have many commercial applications, for example, they can be used to better segment markets and tailor services and products to align with individual needs. Medicine, education, healthcare and transportation can also all benefit from these processes.

[36] Article 14.

7.5 Processing, Access and Quality of Personal Data

The quality of data upon processing provides a level of safety and certainty to data subjects that their data will be managed in a way to ensure it is accurate. Thus, all personal data must be processed lawfully and with respect for the principle of good faith and the general principle laid down in Article 2. Article 2 introduces a general principle for processing personal data. It states that the processing of personal data ("processing") as any operation or set of operations which is performed upon personal data, whether or not by automatic means, such as collection, recording, organisation, storage, adaptation or alteration, retrieval, consultation, use, disclosure by transmission, dissemination or otherwise making available, alignment or combination, blocking, erasure or destruction.[37]

Moreover, the processing of personal data must be also undertaken in accordance with Articles 5, 6, and 7. In accordance with Article 5, Macau have looked to the OECD data protection principles, which require personal data under the data quality principle to be relevant for the purpose it is to be used, and it is to be accurate and kept up to date. In meeting this internationally agreed principle, Macau require that personal data must be processed lawfully and with respect for the principle of good faith and the general principle laid down in Article 2. Importantly, the personal data being processed also meets the OECD purpose specification principle, which requires that personal data is to be collected for specified, explicit, legitimate purposes and for purposes directly related to the activity of the controller and not further processed in a way incompatible with those purposes. It has to also be adequate, relevant and not excessive in relation to the purposes for which they are collected and/or further processed. The accuracy of personal data collected, used and processed cannot be underestimated, and Article 5(4) requires that the personal data is to be accurate and, where necessary, kept up to date; adequate measures must be taken to ensure that data which are inaccurate or incomplete, having regard to the purposes for which they were collected or for which they are further processed, are erased or rectified. It must also be kept in a form which permits identification of their subjects for no longer than is necessary for the purposes for which they were collected or for which they are further processed. However, the storing of personal data can be undertaken by only a public authority at the request of the controller and on the grounds of a legitimate interest.

Nonetheless, the processing of personal data under Article 5, also has to be considered in light of Article 6, which sets out criteria for making personal data legitimate. That is, the criteria for making data processing legitimate personal data may be processed only if the data subject has unambiguously given his consent for that processing. Secondly, where there is a requirement for a contract to be performed. Thirdly, to ensure the controller meets their compliance obligations. Fourth, in order to protect the vital interests of the data subject if the latter is physically or legally incapable of giving his consent. Fifth, for the performance of a

[37] Act 8/2005 Personal Data Protection Act, Article 2.

task carried out in the public interest or in the exercise of official authority vested in the controller or in a third party to whom the data are disclosed. Sixth, for pursuing the legitimate interests of the controller or the third party to whom the data are disclosed, except where such interests should be overridden by the interests for fundamental rights, freedoms and guarantees of the data subject.

In a recent case No: 0084/2016/IP[38] regarding the prohibition of the rights of access to personal data, the OPDP had to decide on the administration of Articles 4, 6, 11, 33 and 36 of the PDPA. The case arose as a result of an unsolicited marketing text messages sent by Company A to the Complainant. According to the latter, he never provided his personal data to the former and therefore he tried to call, and also sent text messages to, Company A, which, however, never responded. The Complainant believed that this was a violation of the PDPA (Personal Data Protection Act) and therefore asked the GPDP (Gabinete para a Protecção de Dados Pessoais) to investigate.[39] Initially, at issue was how and whether the processing of the personal data was undertaken according to Article 4(1). The GPDP noted that the:

> numbers of the text messages were registered by Company A. B is the sole administrator and shareholder of this Company. B denied that he had provided a list of numbers for Company A's staff to send out messages, and it was the Company's staff who generated the numbers for their telemarketing. However, the messages were sent out according to Company A's order, in addition to the equipment used was provided by the Company. This revealed that Company A has the right to decision over the processing purposes and processing methods, and it should be regarded as the data controller of the processing of the case.[40]

The terms of the lawfulness requirements of data processing, a data controller must at least rely on one of the conditions laid down in Article 6 of the PDPA. Before sending out unsolicited text of marketing purpose, a commercial entity should have obtained the explicit consent from the data subjects, as a sign of respect and safeguards to their rights. Unlawful personal data processing is constituted otherwise. Given that Company A failed to demonstrate that it had obtained the consent from the Complainant before sending him marketing text messages, this might violate Article 6 of the PD.

Notwithstanding the above, the right of access, laid down in Article 11 of the PDPA, specifies that the data controller is obliged to allow his data subject(s) to exercise such a right. The Court noted the Complainant had on several occasions called, or sent messages to, Company A, trying to find out how it obtained his personal data, but this Company was beyond reach.[41] B alleged that it might have missed the calls or text messages, but failed to provide proof demonstrating possible connection problems. Since the messages were sent out by Company A and normally

[38] Complaint Case Note No: 0084/2016/IP, Prohibition of the right of access, Office of Personal Data Protection.

[39] Ibid.

[40] Ibid.

[41] Ibid.

a message recipient would directly reply to, or call the numbers shown on, the message, in order to reach the sender.[42] As long as foreseeing the high likelihood of precluded direct contacts, Company A should have specifically noted other means of contact in the message. The declaration of B was apparently unwarranted. The GDPD highlighted that the central issue was how Company A in its processing of personal data had not obtained the Complainant's consent and did not satisfy his lawful rights. Consequently, both Articles 6 and 11 of the PDPA were violated, and it was decided to impose a fine of MOP$8000 according to Articles 33 and 36. In addition, a penalty of MOP$4000 was imposed for violation of Article 11.[43] Importantly, the GDPD highlighted the importance for the need for the controller to obtain consent from the data subject. It reinforced that the concept of consent, has, developed into one of the most important principles within a data protection legal framework. However, under the current laws of Macao the concept of consent has not been specifically detailed. Article 4(9) defines the data subject's consent shall mean any freely given specific and informed indication of his wishes by which the data subject signifies his agreement to personal data relating to him being processed.[44]

7.6 Controller and Processor

The specific roles and responsibilities of the controller and processor, however, Article 2 defines a controller to be the natural or legal person, public entity, agency or any other body which alone or jointly with others determines the purposes and means of the processing of personal data. On the other hand, the processor is defined to be a natural or legal person, public entity, agency or any other body which processes personal data on behalf of the controller. The specific reference of a controller and processor has many similarities to the EU data protection framework. However, and understandably Macau being such a small Special Administrative Region of the People's Republic of China, would not require an extensive multilayered approach for controllers, joint controllers and processors.

Nevertheless, the roles and responsibilities afforded to controllers under the Macau laws are varied throughout the Act. Thus, this section only highlights briefly some of the more important responsibilities of the controller. Importantly they play a vital role in administering the rights of data subjects access[45] to personal data, security or processing[46] the data, ensuring there are security[47] measures in place to protect data and upon the collection of personal data treat that data with a high level

[42] Ibid.

[43] Ibid.

[44] Act 8/2005 Personal Data Protection Act, Article 4.

[45] Act 8/2005 Personal Data Protection Act, Article 10.

[46] Ibid, Article 15.

[47] Ibid, Article 16.

of secrecy.[48] Additionally the controller is responsible for notifying a public authority in writing within 8 days following initial processing of personal data or set out any related purposes.[49]

Despite the important role of the controller in handling and managing personal data, a processor may be appointed to assist the controller in administering the Act and managing personal data. Therefore, in accordance with Article 17 one of the most recognized functions of the processor is the processing of personal data. Centrally, any person acting under the authority of the controller or the processor, including the processor himself, who has access to personal data must not process them except on instructions from the controller, unless he is required to do so by law.

7.6.1 *Notification*

The case for controllers to be formally recognised in the law cannot be underestimated. At a minimum, it allows for an individual or entity to have single point of contact. Coupled with the principle of notification, the appointment of a controller is another demonstration that Macau have adopted the OECD data protection principles, particularly in relation to accountability. The automatic processing of personal data requires the controller or their representative to notify the public authority in writing within 8 days following the commencement of the data processing.[50] Generally, where the processing could adversely impact on the rights and freedoms of the data subject the above applies. However, consideration of the level of impact to a data subjects rights and freedoms may result in an exemption from notification.[51] This would apply where an assessment has been undertaken that, would prove there is little to know privacy impact to the individual.

In a further expression of implementing the OECD data protection principles Article 21(3) requires that any authorisation shall be published in the Official Gazette of the MSAR and must specify the purposes of the processing, the data or category of data to be processed, the category or categories of data subjects, the recipients or categories of recipients to whom the data may be disclosed and the length of time the data are to be stored. On the other hand, the processing of personal data where the sole purpose is to keep a register, which, in part, will provide information to the public and is open to consultation, the data subject does not have to be notified of the processing.

More importantly, Macau maintains a higher threshold for the management (processing) of sensitive personal data in accordance with Article 7. Thus, the general (non-automatic) processing of sensitive personal data is subject to notification. In addition to the above, the management and processing of sensitive

48 Ibid, Article 18.

49 Ibid, Article 23.

50 Ibid, Article 21.

51 Ibid, Article 21(2).

personal data is to be checked.[52] Article 22(2) goes onto require that the checking of personal data is to be undertaken when it relates to credit and solvency of data subjects. The procedural step of checking goes hand in hand with the requirement to ensure the personal data is accurate before being processed.

Article 9, provides that the combination of personal data that is to be managed separately. Combination of data is a form of processing which consists of the possibility of correlating data in a filing system with data in a filing system or systems kept by another or other controllers or kept by the same controller for other purposes.[53] Therefore, combination of personal data not provided for in a legal provision or a provision of a regulation is subject to the authorisation of the public authority, requested by the controller or jointly by the corresponding controllers and applies to only those data subjects related to credit and solvency subjects in accordance with Article 22(2). The combination of personal data must (1). be necessary for pursuing the legal or statutory purposes and legitimate interests of the controller; (2). not involve discrimination or a reduction in the fundamental rights and freedoms of the data subjects; (3). be covered by adequate security measures; and (4). take account of the type of data to be combined.

7.7 Transnational Transfer of Personal Data

Macau, similar to Hong Kong does not have a large territory. It is inevitable that personal data is transferred outside of Macau. Article 19 establishes a number of principles that require any personal data being transferred to a third country must have an adequate level of protection. This principle is not new and further confirms that, Macau has adopted elements of the EU legal framework to provide protection for personal data. The EU have established a similar principle under the GDPR. However, any adequacy of the level of protection provided by another state is to be assessed in the context of what and how then data transfer will be undertaken. That is, consideration needs to be undertaken in relation to the purpose and duration of the proposed processing operation or operations, the place of origin and place of final destination, the rules of law, both general and sectorial, in force in the destination in question, and the professional rules and security measures which are complied with in the destination state. In addition to these considerations, it is up to the public authority to decide whether a legal system ensures an adequate level of protection referred to in the preceding paragraph.[54] This provides a lot of flexibility for a public authority, and there appears little oversight from the regulator to ensure similar levels of controls are in place at the destination state. Nonetheless, in the

[52] Ibid, Article 22, (3) the combination of personal data provided for in Article 9; (4) the use of personal data for purposes not giving rise to their collection. 2. The processing referred to in the preceding paragraph may be authorised by legal provisions or provisions of a regulation of an organic nature, in which case it does not require the authorisation of the public authority.

[53] Ibid, Article 2.

[54] Ibid, Article 19.

context of Macau, a lot of data would be entering China and other regional states, which, in part, would not have similar level of controls over personal data. Thus, a level of discretion is required, which is expanded upon by Article 20.

Notwithstanding the above, any transfer of personal data to a destination state where the legal system does not ensure there is an adequate level of protection of the data. In order to achieve this transfer, it can be done on the condition that the public authority is notified, and that the data subject has given his consent unambiguously. On the other hand, the following must be achieved, before that transfer can be undertaken. This includes the requirement to meet any contractual (performance) obligations between the data subject and controller (and that include meeting any pre-contractual measures). It will also be important to confirm whether the transfer of personal data meets the public interest test, that is, the defence of a legal claim. Furthermore, a transfer can take place where that transfer of data is in the 'vital' interest of the data subject, and if it is made from a register which according to laws or administrative regulations is intended to provide information to the public and which is open to consultation either by the public in general or by any person who can demonstrate legitimate interest, provided the conditions laid down in law for consultation are fulfilled in the case.[55]

Apart from the above conditions being met, the transfer of personal data can be undertaken where there is not adequate level of protection, provided the controller adduces adequate safeguards that, ensure the data is protected according to the rights of the individual citizen. This can be achieved through appropriate contractual clauses. However, the transfer of personal data which is necessary for the protection of defence, public security, for the prevention, investigation and prosecution of criminal offences and for the protection of public health, shall be governed by special legal provisions or by the instruments of international law and regional agreements to which the MSAR is a party.

In an earlier case involving the transfer of personal data to servers located outside of the territory of Macau, the OPDP[56] noted that the Complainant had signed up for an activity organized by Organization A. Yet, they later found out that the server of its online application system was located outside the Macao SAR. In addition, the Complainant also suspected that the applicants' data was transferred outside the Macao SAR without their prior consent. The investigations reveal that Organization A intended to arrange a visit to somewhere in the Mainland China, and therefore it collected from the applicants their identity document details, ways of contact and the information which could help it to select participants. In addition to submitting a printed application form, applicants could also visit the organization's website to apply online. The OPDP noted that:

> According to Article 4(1)(1) and 3(1) of the PDPA, collection of the applicants' personal data by Organization A, through its website, was an automatic processing of personal data that is subject to the regulations of the same Law.[57]

[55] Ibid, Article 20(1).

[56] Complaints Case Note No: 0158/2014/IP Personal data transfer to foreign servers, Office of Personal Data Protection.

[57] Ibid.

The OPDP in its investigation contacted, by writing, Organization A, to obtain further information, in addition to calling their attention that: if it had established any foreign websites or had used any information equipment, for personal data processing, located in a location outside the Macao SAR, and if it was true that the data subjects had never given their consent to its data transfer or its data processing did not comply with Article 19 and 20 of the PDPA. If so, the following three measures had to be introduced. Firstly, Organization A should stop collecting personal data through the said website or by the said equipment. Secondly, they are required to permanently delete the personal data that was transferred to a location outside the Macao SAR, but data backups should be undertaken before the deletion and backups should be stored in databases or equipment located inside the Macao SAR. Thirdly, it should inform the data subjects that were affected by the transfer of data. The following day, Organization A informed the GPDP that the personal data earlier transferred outside the Macao SAR were deleted and would inform the data subjects being affected accordingly.[58]

The OPDP went onto to say that any transfer of personal data to a location out of the Macao SAR, Article 19 and 20 must be complied with. Consequently, it would be revealed that the server of the said online application system was in fact located in Hong Kong SAR. Therefore, its transfer would only be legitimate as long as Article 20 was fulfilled.[59] Thus, the OPDP ruled that:

> In the first place, Organization A has never applied for any transfer authorization from the GPDP according to Article 20(2) of the PDPA. Nor the current situation fulfilled Article 20(3) of the same Law (which means personal data transfer is aimed at measures for safeguarding public safety, prevention of crime, criminal investigations and preventing criminal acts and protection of public health. Such objectives shall be governed by specific legal provisions or by the instruments of international law and regional agreements to which the MSAR is a party). In this regard, Organization A's transfer of data did not fulfil the requirements of paragraph (2) and (3) of Article 20 of the PDPA. Moreover, with regard to the mandatory notification of overseas data transfer to the GPDP, as laid down by Article 20(1) of the PDPA, obviously the purpose of Organization A's transfer of applicants' personal data was other than those for the "establishment, exercise of defence of legal claims", as given in Article 20(1)(3). In the same token, the purposes as governed by subparagraph (4) (transfer is necessary in order to protect the vital interests of the data subject) and subparagraph (5) (transfer is made from a register which according to laws or administrative regulations) of Article 20(1) were incompatible with the transfer purpose of Organization A.[60]

The OPDP went further to ensure relevant principles of the Act had been met, namely whether consent had been provided by the data subject, and transfer met the requirements to meet any contractual arrangements, along with determining, if any public interest applied. Thus, the OPDP argued that:

> Whether the transfer was proceeded after having obtained explicit consent from the data subjects: applicants were applying online for participation voluntarily, specifying that the applicants' personal data was collected with their consent. However, it is dubious whether their consent included their agreement to transferring their personal data to a location

[58] Ibid.

[59] Ibid.

[60] Ibid.

> outside the Macao SAR, and this should be considered alongside whether they had been informed of the transfer. The online application system was found with a locally registered domain (of Macao SAR), with which the applicants could hardly find out where the server was actually located. The application details and its online application system also failed to include the information specifying whether the data would be transferred overseas or not, to say nothing of whether or not the applicants gave their consent for the transfer, as they had never been informed of the possible overseas data transfer when submitting their personal data. These explicated that said data transfer was proceeded without the data subjects' consent.[61]

In relation to whether the transfer formed part of the performance of a contract, the OPDP ruled that:

> Whether the transfer was necessary for the performance of contract: the information available failed to justify that the data transfer was necessary for performing a contract concluded between Organization A and the applicants, or the transfer was necessary for the interests of the applicants. These proved that the transfer did not comply with subparagraph (1) and (2) of Article 20(1) of the PDPA.[62]

In addition to the above the OPDP had to determine whether there was a level of public interest involved, in the reasoning for the transfer of that personal data. The OPDP ruled that:

> Whether the transfer was necessary for a vital public interest: Organization A is not a public entity nor has it been declared as "collective persons with public administrative interest (*pessoa colectiva de utilidade pública administrativa*)". Generally, activities that Organization A organized were not for safeguarding public interests, and the same applies to its activities even when they were publicly funded. The previously mentioned justified that the said data transfer failed to comply with the requirements of "public interests" as laid down in Article 20(1)(3) of the PDPA. Based on the above, the transfer of data by Organization A failed to fulfil the conditions of data transfer, as laid down in Article 19 and 20 of the PDPA, and therefore it constituted an administrative offense.[63]

Subsequently, the OPDP imposed to Organization A – a penalty of MOP$12,000 in accordance to Article 33(2) of the PDPA. The case highlighted the fundamental requirements that need to be addressed before any personal data can be transferred outside of the Macau territory, even where that data is only going over the border to neighbouring China or Hong Kong.

Later, in 2018, the OPDP was required to determine whether Article 20 had been complied with, in relation to the transfer of employee personal data to the parent company in Hong Kong.[64] The case was a result of a complaint by an employee against a company who allegedly transferred the employee's personal data without notifying from the Office for Personal Data Protection, to its parent company in Hong Kong. The OPDP in its analysis noted that:

---

61 Ibid.

62 Ibid.

63 Ibid.

64 Complaints Case Note No: 0035/2018/IP, Transfer of employee personal data to the parent company in Hong Kong, Office of Personal Data Protection.

> Company A is a Macao branch office, as it revealed, of its parent company in Hong Kong. For salary, insurance and taxation, Company A has to transfer the personal data of its employees to the human resources department of the Hong Kong parent company. All the involved employees, prior to undertaking their posts, have signed a consent form for the transfer of their data to the Hong Kong parent company. The GPDP examined the consent form and sample employment contract provided by Company A. In spite of the explicit consent, given by its employees in the said written documents, for the data transfer to the Hong Kong parent company, Company A, being a data controller, under Article 20(1) of the PDPA, is obliged to notify such transfer of data outside the Macao SAR to the GPDP before the transfer takes place. Notification to the GPDP is mandatory, notwithstanding Company A's transfer based on data subjects' consent. Company A's failure to notify the GPDP of the transfer of data thus violated Article 20(1) of the PDPA. On the other hand, Company A's employee consent form was once amended, as the GPDP found out; therefore the GPDP reminded Company A to ask the existing employees, who once signed the old consent form, to also sign the new version, to ascertain unambiguous information are imparted to employees and the lawfulness of such data transfer.[65]

Thus, Company A's lack of notification to the GPDP and its transfer of employee personal data outside the Macao SAR violated Article 20 of the PDPA. The resulting effect of this breach saw the company being fined MOP$8000 for its violation, according to Article 33(2). The case highlighted the importance and need for individuals and entities transferring personal data outside of Macau to ensure they meet the requirements of Article 20. When transferring personal data outside of Macau, one of the most important procedural steps to be completed is informing the OPDP. Macau has arguably placed considerable control measures on personal data being transferred outside the territory.

7.8 Codes of Conduct

Macau, rather the require Codes of Practice to be established under the Act, the approach adopted has been to develop Codes of Conduct. The forms of Codes are very different in practice. Generally, a Code of Conduct directs activity voluntarily, whereas Codes of Conduct can be underpinned by legislation and have penalties attached for non-compliance. Article 26 requires the establishment of Codes of Conduct, whereby a public authority shall encourage the drawing up of codes of conduct intended to contribute to the proper implementation of the provisions in this Act. The importance of this approach is similar to other co-regulatory models that use Codes of Practice. The difference in approach will be how they are developed and the content of them. Further, Article 27 allows professional associations and other bodies to develop codes of conduct. That is, Article 27 promotes the idea that professional associations and other bodies representing other categories of controllers, after having drawn up draft codes of conduct may submit them to the public authority for registration if they so wish. However, if the public authority considers the draft as in accordance with the laws and regulations in force in the area of

[65] Ibid.

personal data protection, a registration shall be made. Moreover, the registration of the codes of conduct has the effect of a mere declaration of its lawfulness and does not have the nature of a provision of law or regulation.

For instance, the Banking sector has had a Code of Conduct in place since 2009.[66] The code notes that the ethical conduct on business is a factor of utmost importance for the development and growth of corporations, and particularly to financial institutions, bringing unaccountable benefits, such as attracting and retaining the customer loyalty, as well as the satisfaction of expectations of all stakeholders(1) (internal or external parties), the reputational differentiation and consolidation, and efficiency gains in the working processes or, through a prudent risk management. Moreover, the importance and the dimension of Banco Nacional Ultramarino, S.A. within the Special Administrative Region of Macau, together with the purpose of disclosure to all stakeholders and to the public in general, of all ethical principles that govern its actions, constitute additional reasons for adopting a Code of Conduct, an ever-evolving document intended to be always present and followed in the daily activity of the Bank, by its employees. Of note Article 19 deals with Personal Data Protection, which requires the Bank to respect all the laws and guidelines of the competent authorities regarding the protection of personal data, namely in what concern to the existence and alteration of costumer's files, rights of consultation and correction of personal data inserted on them.[67] While not a lot of detail, it does reflect self-regulation within the organizations, and it is our view that there is likely to be additional internal policies, procedures and guidelines the support the implementation of Article 19.

7.9 Regulator

The Officer for Personal Data Protection[68] is the public authority established under Chief Executive Instruction 83/2007 of the Macao Special Administrative Region, operating independently under the supervision of the Chief Executive. Being the public authority referred to in Article 79(3) of the *Civil Code* and Law 8/2005 (the *Personal Data Protection Act,* or PDPA), the GPDP exercises the legal competence invested in it in supervising and coordinating the public implementation of and

---

[66] Banco Nacional Ultramarino, S.A. The version that is now adopted by the Bank is an updating of the Code of Conduct that was previously approved by BNU, which was published and entered into force on 15.05.2009 (OS 09/09), https://www.bnu.com.mo/en/our-bank/code-of-conduct/Pages/code-of-conduct.aspx. The management of business ethics is an essential tool in decision making process in an entrepreneurial environment, since the vast majority of these decisions have explicitly or implicitly, an ethical content. It is therefore necessary the existence of instruments that institutionalize in a formal manner this management of ethics, assuming hereby particular importance the Code of Conduct.

[67] Ibid.

[68] Officer for Personal Data Protection, https://www.gpdp.gov.mo

compliance with the PDPA, and devising professional secrecy regulations as well as supervising their implementation.[69] However as noted by Graham Greenleaf, the formation of a data protection authority was first discussed by legal officials as far back as 1998, possibly influenced by developments in the Portuguese legislation at that time. Its subsequent history is documented in a book published by Macao's Legislative Assembly (in Portuguese and Chinese).[70] The president of Legislative Assembly ordered a study by its legal experts, which concluded that privacy and data privacy are protected in the legal system of Macao and that a specific data protection Act should be formulated. In 2005 eight legislators proposed legislation which was almost a copy of Portugal's law, though they claimed that they also used Hong Kong's ordinance as a reference. Greenleaf points out that the main difference is in the formation of supervising public authority, because it is considered that this function is legally reserved to the government, according to the Basic Law of Macao (its 'mini-Constitution').[71] The proposal was endorsed by the Legislative Assembly in June 2005 and sent to a Standing Committee for further study. Greenleaf highlights further that following consultation with the government and the public (including submissions and opinions from both), press discussion, and visits to the Hong Kong Commissioner's office, the Committee presented a legal opinion in November 2005 on the proposal, including proposed amendments. The Law was passed by the Assembly in August 2005 and came into force in February 2006.[72]

7.10 Crimes [Cyber Security]

An important feature of Macau's laws is the inclusion of breaches of data protection to crime. Arguably, and in part, these inclusion address breaches to personal data that would otherwise fall within the realm of cyber security. Article 37 states that an individual or entity who does not meet their obligations under the data protection laws – may be subject to criminal proceedings. Thus, any person who intentionally omits notification or the application for authorisation referred to in Article 21 and Article 22, will be in breach of the laws. Further any person who provides false information in the notification or in applications for authorisation for the processing of personal data or makes alterations in the latter which are not permitted by the legalisation instrument will also be in criminal breach of the law. The other criminal offences that apply will be where a person misappropriates or uses personal data in a form incompatible with the purpose of the collection or with the legalisation instrument, and promotes or carries out an illegal combination of personal data. A

[69] Ibid.

[70] Graham Greenleaf, Macao's EU-influenced *Personal Data Protection Act* 96 *Privacy Laws & Business International Newsletter,* (2008), 21–22.

[71] Ibid.

[72] Ibid.

crime will have been undertaken where a person fails to comply with the obligations provided for in this Act or in other data protection legislation after the time limit fixed by the public authority for complying with them has expired.[73] Thus, based on the above requirements, a person who breaches the laws will be liable to up to 1 year's imprisonment or a fine of up to 120 days. However, the penalty shall be increased to double in the case of the personal data referred to in Article 7 and Article 8. Under Article 38,[74] any person who without due authorisation and by any means accesses personal data prohibited to him shall be liable to up to 1 year's imprisonment or a fine of up to 120 days, if a more severe punishment is not to be enforced due to a specific law.

Moreover, criminal offences also extend to the destruction of personal data, qualified non-compliance and violation of secrecy. That is, in accordance with Article 39, any person who without due authorisation erases, destroys, damages, deletes or changes personal data, making them unusable or affecting their capacity for use, shall be liable to up to 2 years' imprisonment or a fine of up to 240 days,[75] if a more severe punishment is not to be enforced due to a specific law. Further, any person who after being notified to do so does not interrupt, cease or block the processing of personal data shall be subject to a penalty corresponding to the crime of qualified non-compliance.[76] Article 41 becomes important to preserve secrecy and confidentiality in the management of personal data. Therefore, any person bound by professional secrecy according to the law who without just cause and without due consent reveals or discloses personal data, totally or in part, shall be liable to up to 2 years' imprisonment or a fine of up to 240 days,[77] if a more severe punishment is not to be enforced due to a specific law.

In addition to the above, in 2018, the Legislative Assembly of Macau approved the Cybersecurity Law.[78] The Cybersecurity Law were implemented in 2019, and

---

[73] Act 8/2005 Personal Data Protection Act, Article 38.

[74] Ibid. The penalty shall be increased to double the maxima when access: (1) is achieved by means of violating technical security rules; (2) allows the offender or third parties to obtain knowledge of the personal data. (3) provides the offender or third parties with a benefit or material advantage. In the case of paragraph 1 criminal proceedings are dependent upon a complaint.

[75] Ibid, Article 39, 2. The penalty shall be increased to double the maxima if the damage caused is particularly serious. 3. If the offender acts with negligence as referred to in the preceding two numbers the penalty in both cases shall be up to 1 year's imprisonment or a fine of up to 120 days.

[76] Ibid, Article 40, 2. The same penalty shall apply to any person who after being notified: (1) without just cause refuses to provide his cooperation specifically required by the public authority; (2) does not erase or totally or partially destroy the personal data; (3) does not destroy the personal data after the period for keeping them provided for in Article 5 has elapsed.

[77] Ibid, Article 41. 2. The penalty shall be increased by half the maxima if the offender: (1) is a civil servant or equivalent, according to penal law; (2) acts with the intention of obtaining a material advantage or other unlawful gain; (3) adversely affects the reputation, honour and esteem or the privacy of another person. 3. A person guilty of negligence shall be liable to up to 6 months' imprisonment or a fine of up to 120 days. 4. Other than the cases provided for in paragraph 2, criminal proceedings are dependent upon a complaint.

[78] The Cybersecurity Law No. 13/2019.

largely apply to public sector's networks and data systems, as well as to the private entities that operate critical infrastructures in Macao. This includes, but not limited to transportation, telecommunication, banking and insurance, medical affairs, electricity and water supply. These entities all collect personal data from consumers and customers, and therefore, these laws do in part, go some way to underpinning the protection of data protection. This has been reinforced by Deloitte who argue that the Macau laws, aim to protect information networks, computer systems and data of critical infrastructure operators.[79] Moreover, Deloitte note that the Cybersecurity Laws promote and encourage companies to undertake a risk assesses. Risk assessments are important tools for entities to protect the collection and use of personal data.

7.11 Conclusion

The Macao Special Administrative Region (SAR) of the People's Republic of China (PRC) is one of the smallest but also one of most economically successful regions of China. Portugal administered Macao from the sixteenth century until the transfer of sovereignty to the PRC in December 1999.[80] During its 450 year history as a Portuguese settlement, Macau transformed itself from a fishing village to a modern city. It has a rich and diverse history, along with-it neighbour Hong Kong.

The Personal Data Protection Act established in 2005 applies to both the public and private sectors. Macau data protection laws differ from China and Hong Kong. They have been based largely on both the EU and Hong Kong legal frameworks. The data protection laws apply to the processing of personal data whether manually or by an automated system or platform. However, the laws also apply to video surveillance and other forms of capture, processing and dissemination of sound and images allowing persons to be identified. Yet, this is on the basis that the controller is domiciled or based in the Macao Special Administrative Region.

The definition of personal data while consistent with other states, in that, it is a broad definition, and its most important elements are identifying individuals directly or indirectly. However, and while the definition addresses the more sensitive elements of personal data, such as philosophical or political beliefs, political association or trade-union membership, religion, privacy and racial or ethnic origin, health or sex life, genetic data, it is questionable whether it will capture all data that can be captured by AI. The consistent message that has emerged so far in each of the chapter discussion is how and whether the current definition is adequate for children that will be subject to smart home appliances, toys and personal robots. Therefore, it is

[79] Macau Cybersecurity Law, *General Introduction and Impact Analysis* https://www2.deloitte.com/content/dam/Deloitte/cn/Documents/risk/deloitte-cn-risk-macau-cybersecurity-law-en-190802.pdf

[80] Graham Greenleaf, Macao's EU-influenced *Personal Data Protection Act* 96 *Privacy Laws & Business International Newsletter*, (2008), 21–22.

unclear whether the laws in their entirety will adequately address the issues of protecting personal data in Smart Home AI technology.

Macau has, in part, adopted a co-regulatory approach to data protection through the requirement for codes of practice. Moreover, there is no formal requirement for a controller or processor to be appointed. This is, in part, a significant gap and Hong Kong could consider applying more accountability on organisations. Yet, the data processors do have a level of responsibility such as the requirement to establish and implement policies, procedures and any other measures that will minimise the risk to the accidental or unlawful destruction, loss or disclosure.

Finally, they have begun to criminalize offence for certain breaches of the Act. However, and unlike other states there is not requirement for an individual or entity to notify the regulator when there has been an incursion or a breach of the laws. This, in our view, is a significant gap in the law and Hong Kong should consider reviewing this concept, so as to ensure not only greater accountability within the framework, but also it will go some way to strengthening the Regulators oversight of the laws, and more broadly the governance of personal data across the Region. Doing so, will also prepare the Regulator to also manage cybersecurity breaches, along with handling and responding to personal data misuse in AI technology.

References

Eubanks, V. (2018). *Automating inequality – How high tech tools profile, police, and punish the poor*. New York: St. Martin Press.

Greenleaf, G. (2008). Macao's EU-influenced personal data protection act. *Privacy Laws & Business International Newsletter*, 96, 21–22.

Kroll, J. A., Huey, J., Barocas, S., Felten, E. W., Reidenberg, J. R., Robinson, D. G., & others. (2017). 'Accountable algorithms' (2016), University of Pennsylvania Law Review, Giovanni Comandé, regulating algorithms regulation? First ethico-legal principles, problems and opportunities of algorithms. In T. Cerquitelli, D. Quercia, & F. Pasquale (Eds.), *Towards glass-box data mining for big and small data* (pp. 169–207). Cham: Springer.

Pasquale, F. (2015). *The black box society: The secret algorithms that control money and information*. Cambridge/London: Harvard University Press.

Wank-Nolasco Lamas, R. (1999). *History of Macau: A student's manual*. Macau: Institute of Tourism Education.

Xavier, R. E. (2017). *Luso-Asians and the origins of Macau's cultural development*. University of California, Berkeley Journal of the Royal Asiatic Society-Hong Kong, Vol. 57, HKU Press.

Chapter 8
The Philippines

Abstract The Philippines have a long and diverse history. The state is a member of the ASEAN community and located in a region of the world that is diverse culturally. They have been heavily influenced by the United States, and is an archipelago compromising of 7100 islands. It has a land area of 300,000 square kilometres, 92% of which is found on the 11 largest islands. The country can be grouped geographically into the three major islands groups: Luzon, Visayas, and Mindanao. Philippines culture is the result of traditions of the pre-Hispanic villages and regions and a variety of foreign influences including Islam, Catholicism, and Spanish, American, Chinese and Japanese rule. The Philippine legal system can be best described as a blend of customary usage, Roman (civil law) and Anglo-American (common law) systems. Although, in some Southern parts, Islamic law is observed.

The modern-day Constitution, was established in 1987, and provides for a Bill of Rights. Section 3 and 7 are of importance as they go some way to ensuring a level of privacy and data protection of its citizens. Section 3 states that the privacy of communication and correspondence shall be inviolable except upon lawful order of the court, or when public safety or order requires otherwise as prescribed by law. In addition, section 7 provides the right of the people to information on matters of public concern shall be recognized. In addition, there is other important legislation whereby citizens' right to privacy is also protected. This includes the Civil Code (Republic Act No. 386), Revised Penal Code (Act No. 3185), Republic Act No. 8505, Rape Victim Assistance and Protection Act of 1998; Republic Act No. 9344, and Juvenile Justice and Welfare Act of 2006. They have criminalized privacy in certain circumstances, whereby, there is a need to protect the most vulnerable in the community, such as children and disability.

Nonetheless, the Republic Act (RA) No. 10173 or also known as Data Privacy Act, came into effect in 2012. The 2012 Act created the National Privacy Commission, which is responsible for promoting, regulating, and monitoring data privacy compliance of both government agencies and private institutions. Some commentators are of the view that the Philippines data protection laws are based on the EU's framework. Importantly, the Philippines is a member of the APEC Cross Border Privacy Enforcement Arrangement, the government backstop enforcement network developed for the Cross-Border Privacy Rules.

R. Walters, M. Novak, *Cyber Security, Artificial Intelligence, Data Protection & the Law*, https://doi.org/10.1007/978-981-16-1665-5_8

This Chapter examines the current data protection laws of the Philippines, particularly in relation to the onset of AI. For instance, compared to other countries discussed in this book the law treats both kinds of personal information (general and sensitive) differently. Personal information may be processed, provided that the requirements of the Data Privacy Act are complied with. Yet, the processing of sensitive personal information is generally restricted.

8.1 Introduction

South East Asian countries have a rich and complex history that spans centuries of migration and colonization. The Philippines is no different. The Philippines were discovered in 1521 by Portuguese explorer Ferdinand Magellan and colonized by Spain from 1565 to 1898.[1] Following the end of the Spanish-American War, which was followed by the signing of the Treaty of Paris on 10 December 1898, paved the way for the cession of the Philippines to the United States (US).[2] Upon the establishment of American sovereignty, the political laws of the Philippines were totally abrogated and Spanish laws that, were inconsistent with the US Constitution and American principles were superseded. The government operated under different organic laws, namely, President MacKinley's Instructions to the Second Philippine Commission on 07 April 1900; the Spooner Amendment of 1901; the Philippine Bill of 1902; the Jones Law of 1916 and the Tydings-MacDuffie Law of 1934. Pursuant to the Tydings- MacDuffie Law, a Commonwealth government was to be established for a transitional period of 10 years before independence could be granted.[3] Thus, by 1935 the Philippines had a constitution.

On July 4, 1946, the United States formally recognized Philippine independence which was declared by Filipino revolutionaries from Spain. The Philippine archipelago is composed of about 7100 islands and lies strategically within the arc of nations that sweeps southeastward from mainland Asia to Australia. It has a total land area of 300,000 km^2, 92% of which is found on the 11 largest islands.[4] The country can be grouped geographically into three major islands groups: Luzon, Visayas, and Mindanao. Accounting for 47% of the total land area, Luzon is the largest island group and is situated in the north. Mindanao, the second largest group is located in the south and occupies 34% of the total land area, while the Visayas is a group of smaller islands between Luzon and Mindanao comprising the remaining 19% of land area.

[1] DH Program, United States Agency for International Development https://dhsprogram.com/pubs/pdf/fr01/01chapter01.pdf

[2] ASEAN Law Association http://www.aseanlawassociation.org/papers/phil_chp1.pdf

[3] Ibid.

[4] DH Program, United States Agency for International Development https://dhsprogram.com/pubs/pdf/fr01/01chapter01.pdf

Philippine culture is the result of traditions of the pre-Hispanic villages and regions and a variety of foreign influences (Islam, Catholicism, and Spanish, American, Chinese and Japanese rule).[5] According to Aberto Vargas, Philippine society is diverse, especially considering its distribution over some 1000 inhabited islands. Muslims and upland tribal peoples remain somehow distinct, but approximately 90% of the society by 1990 were united by a common cultural and religious background. Vargas notes that among the lowland Christian Filipinos, language was the main point of internal differentiation, but the majority interacted and intermarried regularly across linguistic lines. However, and because of political centralization, urbanization, and extensive internal migration, linguistic barriers were eroding, and government emphasis on Tagalog and English (at the expense of local dialects) also reduced these divisions.[6] In 1941 Japan launched an attack on the Philippines only ten hours after the attack on Pearl Harbor. Japanese occupation of the Philippines during World War II brought the issue of elite collaboration with foreign powers into sharp relief.[7] Tensions between landlords and tenants exacerbated during this period. The Huk rebellion lasted from 1946 to 1954 due to land distribution inequalities.[8]

Notwithstanding the above, the Philippine legal system is aptly described as a blend of customary usage, and Roman (civil law) and Anglo-American (common law) systems.[9] The civil law operates in areas such as family relations, property, succession, contract and criminal law while statutes and principles of common law origin are evident in such areas as constitutional law, procedure, corporation law, negotiable instruments, taxation, insurance, labour relations, banking and currency.[10] In some Southern parts, Islamic law is observed. Nonetheless, the modern day Constitution, was established in 1987, and provides for a Bill of Rights.[11] Section 3 and 7 are of importance as they respectively go some way to ensuring a level of privacy and data protection rights of its citizens. Section 3 states that the privacy of communication and correspondence shall be inviolable except upon lawful order of the court, or when public safety or order requires otherwise as prescribed by law. In addition, section 7 provides the right of the people to information on matters of public concern shall be recognized. Access to official records, and to documents, and papers pertaining to official acts, transactions, or decisions, as well as to government research data used as basis for policy development, shall be afforded the citizen, subject to such limitations as may be provided by law. It also provides that

[5] Vargas, A, *The Philippine Country Brief: Property Rights and Land Markets*, https://nelson.wisc.edu/ltc/docs/philippinesbrief.pdf

[6] Ibid.

[7] Ibid.

[8] Ibid.

[9] ASEAN Law Association http://www.aseanlawassociation.org/papers/phil_chp1.pdf

[10] Ibid.

[11] The Constitution of the Republic of the Philippines 1987, https://www.officialgazette.gov.ph/constitutions/1987-constitution/

basis for the development and implementation of their current data protection laws, because personal data would fall within the provisions of both sections 3 and 7.

Carl Abelardo[12] et al. highlights other important legislation in the Philippines that also provide a level of protection of privacy. A person's general right to privacy is affirmed in the Civil Code (Republic Act No. 386). It provides that every person shall respect the dignity, personality, privacy and peace of mind of another. The Civil Code likewise makes any person who abuses the rights of another liable for damages.[13] Furthermore, criminal offences for privacy have been established under the Revised Penal Code (Act No. 3185), Republic Act No. 8505, Rape Victim Assistance and Protection Act of 1998; Republic Act No. 9344, and Juvenile Justice and Welfare Act of 2006. Arguably, criminalizing privacy is relevant in certain circumstances, whereby, there is a need to protect the most vulnerable in the community, such as children and disability.

Thus, on the backdrop of establish a strong level or protection for the general right to privacy in the Philippines, the Data Privacy Act is the principal laws regulating personal data protection. in 2012 the Data Privacy Act 10173 of the Philippines came into effect. The Data Privacy Act (the Act) reinforces the national policy approach to the protection of personal data. Section 2 states that it is the policy of the State to protect the fundamental human right of privacy, of communication while ensuring free flow of information to promote innovation and growth. The State recognizes the vital role of information and communications technology in nation-building and its inherent obligation to ensure that personal information in information and communications systems in the government and in the private sector are secured and protected. Broadly speaking, the Act applies to individuals and any legal entity that collects, stores and processes personal information. As this Chapter highlights, the Act has extraterritorial reach, particularly in relation to businesses and equipment used to process personal information in the Philippines. However, the law does not apply to the processing of personal information in the Philippines that was lawfully collected from residents of foreign jurisdictions – an exception helpful for Philippines companies that offer cloud services. The Philippines, have arguably declared that privacy is a fundamental right to be afforded to all of its citizens. They also recognise that there needs to be a balance between privacy and innovation, and the need to allow for the economic development of new technology to create new economic activity.

[12] Abelardo T, C., Ivy D. A., Alvin B. P, (2016) *Marcelo Health Information Privacy in the Philippines: Trends and Challenges in Policy and Practice* Acta Medica Philippina Vol. 50 No. 4.

[13] Ibid.

8.2 Rights

The *Data Privacy Act of 2012* (DPA)[14] provides a number of rights to data subjects. The approach taken by the Philippines has been to ensure that the data subject is fully informed of the what personal information is to be processed, and the entry of that information into a processing system by the relevant controller.[15] In addition, the data subject is to be informed of the purpose for processing the personal data, along with the scope and method of the processing. While there is a requirement for the data subject to be notified of the above, there are exemptions to this rule. Thus, a notification would not apply where there is a subpoena or when the collection and processing generally including for the performance of a contract or a service is to be met. Based on this exemption, it may also apply where there is an employer-employee relationship, between the collector and data subject, or when the information is being collected and processed as a result of legal obligation. The exemption further extends to where the right to access ones' personal information is also based on the contents of that information, the source, name and addresses of the recipient(s), and the manner the data was processed and the reasons for such a disclosure. Nonetheless, where the personal information is processed by automated systems, the data will or likely to be made as the sole basis for any decision significantly affecting or will affect the data subject. Reasonable access to personal information by the data subject also extends to the date their personal information was last accessed and modified, along with the designation name or identity and address of the personal information controller.

The large quantities of this data being collected, stored and used can, at times, result in errors of its recording. Therefore, to ensure the accuracy of personal information is of the highest standard, a data subject has the right to dispute any inaccuracy or error of their personal data. All data subjects, upon detection of their personal data being inaccurate can request of the controller to correct that information. The request for the correction must not be vexatious. Furthermore, where the personal information has been corrected, the controller is to ensure the data subject has access to the new and retracted personal information. This is based on whether the[16] third parties who have previously received the personal information be informed of its inaccuracy and its rectification upon reasonable request of the data subject. In addition, this is also based on the suspension, withdrawal or order the blocking, removal or destruction of personal information from the controller's filing

---

[14] Republic Act No. 10173 An Act Protecting Individual Personal Information in Information and Communications Systems in The Government and The Private Sector, Creating For this Purpose a National Privacy Commission, and for Other Purposes.

[15] Ibid, section 16. (5) Methods utilized for automated access, if the same is allowed by the data subject, and the extent to which such access is authorized; (6) The identity and contact details of the personal information controller or its representative; (7) The period for which the information will be stored; and (8) The existence of their rights, i.e., to access, correction, as well as the right to lodge a complaint before the Commission.

[16] Ibid, section 16.

system upon discovering that the personal information is incomplete, outdated, false, unlawfully obtained, used for unauthorized purposes or is no longer necessary for the purposes for which they were collected. In situations such as this, the controller is to notify third parties who have previously received the personal information, and furthermore, they are indemnified for any damages due to such inaccurate, incomplete, outdated, false, unlawfully obtained or unauthorized use of personal information.

The additional rights that have been provided by the DPA include the transmissibility of rights of the data subject and data portability. On the one side, the transmissibility of personal information allows the data subject to obtain the personal information of another data subject where they are an heir or an assignee at any time following the death of the data subject.[17] On the other side, the right to transmissibility also applies when the data subject is incapacitated or incapable of exercising this right. In other words, where a data subject may have a disability or be psychologically incapable of handling their personal information, another individual can do so on their behalf. Another important control measure that has found its way into some jurisdictions data protection and privacy laws, is the ability to allow the data subject to export their personal information to another controller. The right itself, places additional systems control measures on controllers and organisation because they need to ensure that their systems, applications and infrastructure that collect and store the personal information also have the function that enables that information to be transmitted and ported.[18] Firstly, in accordance with section 18 allows a data subject, where their information has been processed by electronic system, are able to obtain from the controller a copy of that information Secondly, it further allows places an obligation on the Commission where they may outline the specific format along with the technical standards, modalities and procedure for this portability to take place. While it is not a mandatory obligation, it allows the commission to be involved and ensure there is a general consistent approach taken to the portability of personal information. However, under section 19, data portability will not apply where the personal information is used for scientific and statistical research. Yet, this is based on the fact that the personal information is held under strict confidential terms, and only used for that purpose. Data portability will not apply where that personal information has been collected for an investigation into any criminal, administrative or tax liabilities of the data subject. The investigation of a data subject where their personal data is used for a criminal, tax or administrative investigation could extend to cybercrime. One of the most important rights that has emerged from the development and implementation of data protection and privacy law over the Internet has been the right to be forgotten. For instance, some jurisdictions, such as the EU, have embraced this right, while other states have not.

---

[17] Ibid, section 17.

[18] van Schaijck, M, *Data Portability,* Deloitte, https://www2.deloitte.com/ch/en/pages/risk/articles/gdpr-data-portability.html

8.2.1 *Right to Be Forgotten and Deletion*

The right to be forgotten (RTBF), in the Philippines, can be best described as a piece of the jigsaw puzzle that, is still being developed. It is far from settled. At issue is that under the DPA there is no provision that specifically enable for the erasure or deletion of personal information. Rather, section 3 defines processing to include any operation or any set of operations performed upon personal information including, but not limited to, the collection, recording, organization, storage, updating or modification, retrieval, consultation, use, consolidation, blocking, erasure or destruction of data. Sections 16 and 20 are the only sections that refer to the destruction of personal information.

In one of the strongest indications that the Philippines are moving closer to fully embracing this right began in *Vivares v. St. Theresa's College.*[19] In this case, the court had to decide on the extent to which privacy rights would apply to personal information and data on the Internet. The Court ruled that there:

> could be no expectation of privacy as regards photos posted on social media networks under a "Friends Only" setting, because the public at large may still view the photos.[20]

In the decision, the Court went further making the following statement that "internet consumers ought to be aware that, by entering or uploading any kind of data or information online, they are automatically and inevitably making it permanently available online, the perpetuation of which is outside the ambit of their control."[21] The Court adopted a narrow approach towards the right of privacy online and highlighted the need for individual, even minors, to demonstrate that they have taken steps to protect their personal data online. In citing the tools that were made available by Facebook that, in part, provide a level of privacy protection, the Court also placed a heavy burden on data subjects to demonstrate how and what measures they took to also protect their personal information. Nonetheless, the Court went onto provide direction on the notion of what privacy over the Internet would constitute in the Philippines. The Court noted that the concept of privacy has, through time, greatly evolved, with technological advancements. In referring to the former Philippines Chief Justice Reynato S. Puno's speech, on privacy, the Court highlighted how:

> the Common Right to Privacy, where he explained the three strands of the right to privacy, viz: (1) locational or situational privacy; (2) informational privacy; and (3) decisional privacy. Of the three, what is relevant to the case at bar is the right to informational privacy—usually defined as the right of individuals to control information about themselves.[22]

---

[19] *Rhonda Aves. Vivares and SPS. Margarita and David Suzara, Petitioners, vs. ST. Theresa's College, Mylene Rheza T. Escudero, and John Does*, Respondents. G.R. No. 202666, 2014.

[20] Ibid.

[21] Ibid.

[22] Ibid.

More pervasively, the Court highlighted the challenges facing the protection of personal information over the Internet. The Court stated that:

> with the availability of numerous avenues for information gathering and data sharing nowadays, not to mention each system's inherent vulnerability to attacks and intrusions, there is more reason that every individual's right to control said flow of information should be protected and that each individual should have at least a reasonable expectation of privacy in cyberspace.[23]

While not specifically referring to the right for data subject to request that their personal data be deleted or erased, the court made the point that data subject should have the right to control the flow and have an expectation that their privacy will be protected over the Internet. Having control over the flow of personal data would also constitute the ability for a data subject to have their data deleted. This control would also extend to other areas of securing personal data within the cyber world, including AI. Nevertheless, in meeting these challenges it is incumbent that courts identify way to provide remedies for and to individuals that have their personal information misused. The court in looking to the South African High Court case of *H v. W*,[24] recognized that "[t]he law has to take into account the changing realities not only technologically but also socially or else it will lose credibility in the eyes of the people. It is imperative that the courts respond appropriately to changing times, acting cautiously and with wisdom."[25] Consistent with this, the Court, by developing what may be viewed as the Philippine model of the writ of habeas data, in effect, recognized that, generally speaking, having an expectation of informational privacy is not necessarily incompatible with engaging in cyberspace activities, including those that occur in OSNs.[26] This recognition and understanding by both the Philippines and South African courts is also applicable to every other nation state and supra national polity, which will at some stage, likely to be faced with similar challenges. It provided an incite not only to the development of the right to be forgotten but to better understand what the judiciary considers to be responsible reaction and activity to minors protecting their data. Even though the above case provided a narrow view of privacy over the Internet, the DPA goes further by a data subject to seek the suspension, blocking, removal or destruction of their personal information by a controller and the controller's filing system. Arguably the RTBF requires further consideration in the Philippines.

---

[23] Ibid.

[24] Ibid, *H v. W.*, Case No. 12/10142, January 30, 2013, High Court, Johannesburg, Republic of South Africa.

[25] Ibid.

[26] Ibid.

8.3 Definition Personal Information

Personal information means any information whether recorded in a material form or not, from which the identity of an individual is apparent or can be reasonably and directly ascertained by the entity holding the information, or when put together with other information would directly and certainly identify an individual.[27] This catch all definition goes a long way to capturing the many different permutations that, will challenge the definition. More importantly, the recognition and provision of sensitive personal information has a distinctive meaning that includes, a data subjects race, ethnic origin, marital status, age, colour, and religious, philosophical or political affiliations. It also includes health, education, genetic or the sexual life of a person, along with any proceeding for any offense committed or alleged, or, the sentence of any court. Sensitive information has been extended to also include other identifiable information that, such as, social security numbers, previous or current health records, licenses or its denials, suspension or revocation, and tax returns.

There has been concern in the Philippines in relation to their personal health data. As highlighted above, privacy is also protected by the Civil Code (Republic Act No. 386) and the Revised Penal Code (Act No. 3185).[28] This becomes particularly important for health information. In other countries personal health information has been provided a higher level of protection than general personal data.[29] As highlighted later in this chapter, the current definition of personal data in the Philippines is a catch all definition. It does not separate general personal data from that of sensitive personal data. The authors go onto say that where a physician may be held liable for failing to observe the general mandate of the law that every person, in the performance of his duties, act with justice, give everyone his due, and observe honesty and good faith.[30] Since a physician has an acknowledged duty to maintain patient confidentiality, any injury that a patient may incur as a direct result of the violation of this duty will make the physician liable for damages. By criminalizing some offences through the Penal Code, the right to privacy has placed a higher level of protection on confidential information such as health records or abuse. They assert that the offences within the Penal Code protecting the secrets of any person may find application in cases of government physicians who have custody of patient records.[31] Finally, Abelardo *et al.* argue that individual who are subject to conflict and sexual offences, their privacy is protected by the Republic Act No. 8505, Rape Victim Assistance and Protection Act of 1998; Republic Act No. 9344, Juvenile Justice and Welfare Act of 2006.

---

[27] Data Privacy Act 2012, 10173 section 3.

[28] Carl Abelardo T. Antonio, Ivy D. Patdu· Alvin B. *Marcelo Health Information Privacy in the Philippines: Trends and Challenges in Policy and Practice* Acta Medica Philippina Vol. 50 No. 4 2016.

[29] Ibid.

[30] Ibid.

[31] Ibid.

The nature of confidentiality in health data and information was on display more than a decade ago, when a Yuotube video surfaced in relation to an individual's medical procedure. The issue arose in 2008, when:

> at the Vicente Sotto Memorial Medical Center (VSMMC) for extraction of a foreign body lodged in his rectum. He was allegedly asleep at the time of the operation, and was not made aware that the procedure was going to be filmed, nor was he informed post facto that the medical staff took a footage of his operation. He claimed that he only learned of the existence of the YouTube video when it was brought to his attention by their barangay captain, who saw the video on YouTube. As a response to the public outrage generated by the incident, various investigating bodies were formed – the hospital, Department of Health (DOH), National Bureau of Investigation (NBI), House of Representatives – to determine the culpability of those involved in the operation, as well as to identify the person who first uploaded the video. Without denying any liability, the hospital and relatives of medical personnel involved were quick to point out that the public should focus on the successful outcome of the operation; that those involved were, in fact, first rate health professionals and calling for a revocation of their licenses was an excessive punishment; and that the incident was an isolated case of mischief. While some nurses and doctors were initially placed on a three-month preventive suspension, the case filed with the Professional Regulation Commission was eventually dismissed on the basis of a technicality. The identity of the person who first uploaded the video on YouTube was never discovered, and the incident, which died a natural death, became a mere footnote in the annals of Philippine medical history.[32]

Apart from the embarrassing case, this incident would have had wider ramifications for the data subject and impacted on other areas of their rights such as discrimination due to their sexual orientation. What the case demonstrates is the confidential nature of this information that, people have for years been able to hold sacred, to them and the people they want to inform. The potential impact of this data being readily available could see it being used against data subjects for employability, socially and economically. The authors note that some states such as the US and Canada have gone some way to address these issues through a national health policy, Pan-Canadian Health Information Privacy and Confidentiality Framework and the United States' Health Insurance Portability and Accountability Act (HIPAA). At the time of writing this book the Philippines had implemented the Health Privacy Code that, implements the Joint Administrative Order No 2016-0002,[33] Privacy Guidelines for the Implementation of the Philippine Health Information Exchange. Nonetheless, this would need to be reviewed in light of the developments of AI and security threats to personal data in the health sector.

[32] Ibid.

[33] Health Privacy Code Specifying the Joint A.O. No. 2016-0002, Privacy Guidelines for the Implementation of the Philippine Health Information Exchange.

8.4 Application

The DPA was as Ching *et al.* puts it created to establish the National Privacy Commission (NPC) to promote, regulate, and monitor data privacy compliance of both government agencies and private institutions benchmarked with international standards set for data protection [34] Put another way, Presbitero and Ching argue that the DPA defines the rights of Filipino citizens to data privacy and created the National Privacy Commission to monitor compliance, by both public agencies and private organizations.[35] Nonetheless and more specifically the DPA in accordance with section 22 applies to the heads of agencies who are in control of personal information. That is, sensitive personal information maintained by the government, or any of its agencies is to be secured, as recommended by the Commission. Further, the head of each government agency shall be responsible for complying with the security requirements, and the Commission is responsible for monitoring its compliance. By raising the level of controls over sensitive personal data, the Philippines in accordance with section 23 ensures that both on-site and off-site access to personal information is tightly regulated. In other words, no employee of a government can have access to sensitive personal information on government property or through any online facility. That is however, unless the employee has received a security clearance from the head official of that agency. In relation to the off-site governance of sensitive personal information, an agency is not to transport or access the personal information from a location that is not government property,[36] and that has been approved by the head official of that agency. This is an important feature of the Philippines law. It is like no other, in that, the state is regulating an area to minimize the cyber risk of sensitive personal information being illegally obtained or compromised by accessing off-site. By ensuring that sensitive personal information is afforded the highest level of protection, Article 24 requires that government contractors and its employees to register their personal information system with the Commission. Thus, it is important that any contract between a government agency and the contract, reflect this requirement and ensure their system used to collect, store and use sensitive personal information be registered. However, where that system only deals with less than 1000 individuals, this does not apply.

[34] Ching MRD., Fabito, BS., and Celis, NJ, (2018) *Data Privacy Act of 2012: A Case Study Approach to Philippine Government Agencies Compliance,* ICEEG '18.

[35] Presbitero, J., Renee, D., M, C (2018) *Assessing compliance of Philippine state universities to the data privacy act of 2012: the case of Caraga State University* ICEEG '18.

[36] Data Privacy Act 2012, However, and note there are at (2) limited to One thousand (1,000) Records – If a request is approved, the head of the agency shall limit the access to not more than one thousand (1,000) records at a time; and (3) Encryption – Any technology used to store, transport or access sensitive personal information for purposes of off-site access approved under this subsection shall be secured by the use of the most secure encryption standard recognized by the Commission. The requirements of this subsection shall be implemented not later than six (6) months after the date of the enactment of this Act.

8.5 Controller

The Philippines has adopted a similar approach to the formal appointment of a controller, in a similar way to that of the EU. Importantly, the DPA make a distinction between (a) the personal information controller – the organization which controls the processing of personal data, or instructs another to process personal data on its behalf, and (b) the personal information processor – an organization to whom the personal information controller outsources or instructs the processing of personal data.[37] Typically, the data controller should put in place safeguards to ensure that the processing of personal data complies with the data protection obligations. For instance, the data controller will need to ensure that safeguards are in place to ensure that the personal data is processed lawfully, the confidentiality of personal data is protected, and to prevent its use for unauthorized purposes.[38] Thus, in accordance with section 20, the security of personal data is the responsibility of a controller. In other words, the controller is to undertake a risk management approach to the overall management of personal information, including identifying any foreseeable vulnerabilities to ensure the appropriate steps are taken to prevent, correct and mitigate any action so as to safe guard the collection, use and processing of personal data. It promotes an ongoing monitoring process to be established and continuous improvement to also ensure third parties processing personal information on its behalf shall implement the security measures required by this provision. In protecting the overall management of personal information, the controller is also responsible for notifying[39] the Commission, along with affected data subjects when their sensitive personal information or other information has been used without the correct authority. Apart from the above, the controller has further obligations when processing personal information.

---

[37] AmazonWeb Services – Using AWS in the Context of Philippines Privacy Considerations May 2018, https://d1.awsstatic.com/whitepapers/compliance/Using_AWS_in_the_context_of_Philippines_Privacy_Considerations.pdf

[38] Ibid.

[39] Data Privacy Act 2012, section 20, The notification shall at least describe the nature of the breach, the sensitive personal information possibly involved, and the measures taken by the entity to address the breach. Notification may be delayed only to the extent necessary to determine the scope of the breach, to prevent further disclosures, or to restore reasonable integrity to the information and communications system. (1) In evaluating if notification is unwarranted, the Commission may take into account compliance by the personal information controller with this section and existence of good faith in the acquisition of personal information. (2) The Commission may exempt a personal information controller from notification where, in its reasonable judgment, such notification would not be in the public interest or in the interests of the affected data subjects. (3) The Commission may authorize postponement of notification where it may hinder the progress of a criminal investigation related to a serious breach.

8.6 Processing and Consent

In addition to the above, the controller has further responsibilities for the correct and accurate processing of personal information. It has become apparent over the past 5 years that the collection of personal information has been undertaken on a grand scale by the likes of Facebook, Google, amongst others. The collection of that data has resulted in its processing, equally on a large scale. However, it is out of scope of this chapter to analyse the statistics pertaining to the processing of personal information of the citizens of the Philippines. That said, Pitogo[40] is of the view that the DPA apart from being established to provide a level of protection for personal information, upon establishing the Commission, it led the way to provide controls over the processing of this data. He goes onto say that the national Data Privacy Accountability and Compliance Framework established five critical pillars:

1. Appoint a Data Privacy Officer (DPO);
2. Conduct a Privacy Impact Assessment (PIA);
3. Develop a Privacy Management Program and Privacy Manual (PMP/PM);
4. Implement Privacy and Data Protection Measures (PDPM); and
5. Develop Breach Reporting Procedures (BRP).[41]

As highlighted in this chapter, the appointment of a DPO ensures there is a dedicated individual who within an organisation, who is responsible for compliance the controller and processor, which in turn are accountable for the processing of personal information. According to section 11, the processing of personal data can only be undertaken for a legitimate purpose, fairly and lawfully, accurate, relevant, and where that data is inaccurate it is to be corrected. Additionally, it can only be retained for a period that enables it to be processed, and kept in a form that, permits identification of the data subject.[42] However, where that information has been collected for historical, statistical or scientific purposes, it can be retained for longer periods.

Nevertheless, the processing of personal information is only permitted when data subject has provided their consent, and it is related to the performance of a contract.[43] It is also permitted when it is necessary for compliance with a legal obligation that a controller is required to meet and that, the processing is in the interests of the data subject including life, health, national emergency, public order and safety. Moreover, the processing of personal information can be undertaken in the interests of the personal information controller or third party, however, this will not apply where the fundamental rights and freedoms of the data subject are to be protected according to the Constitution. Thus, it is asserted that the Philippines consider that the protection of privacy of the individual's personal information is a fundamental right. That said, it places the Philippines closer to the EU rights-based framework.

---

[40] Vincente Pitogo, *National Government Agency's Compliance on Data Privacy Act of 2012 a Case Study* 2019 *J. Phys.: Conf. Ser.* 1201 012021.

[41] Ibid.

[42] Data Privacy Act 2012, section 11.

[43] Data Privacy Act 2012, section 12.

More importantly, sensitive personal information has been specifically dealt with separately whereby, the processing of this information can only be undertaken when the data has provided their consent. On the other hand, the processing of privileged information can only be undertaken when all parties to the exchange have consented. Privileged information is any and all forms of data which under the Rules of Court and other pertinent laws constitute privileged communication.[44] This is yet another feature of the Philippines law that does not appear in the respective laws that form part of this book. Although, section 15 goes onto to require an extension of privilege communication whereby controllers may invoke this principle in order to process privileged information.[45] On the one side, an exemption applies where any evidence gather is inadmissible. Nonetheless, consent only extends where another law or regulation does not require that consent. Consent is not required where the processing of that data is required to protection the life and health of the community, and the data subject is not legally or physically express their consent.[46] It is also not required where the processing is necessary to achieve the lawful and non-commercial objectives of a public organization and their association. On the other side, this is on the basis that the processing is confined to members of the relevant organisation, and that the sensitive personal information is not transferred to third party.[47] Thus, where the personal information is transferred to a third party, the data subject would need to provide consent before the information is processed. Although where a subcontractor is involved in that processing, the controller is responsible for ensuring the appropriate safeguards are in place so as that personal information is secure and confidential.[48]

More pervasively, the concept of consent varies significantly from other states. While the general concept requires a data subject to provide their consent, particularly for the processing of sensitive information, the concept as a legal principle the Philippines does not extend to how consent is to be obtained. In other words, it is open as to whether consent is to be provided orally or in writing, and how far consent continues to follow the personal information. The question is whether once a data subject has provided consent for the first collection, does this provide consent for that entity to sell that personal data? This is unclear.

[44] Ibid, section 2.

[45] Ibid, section 15.

[46] Ibid, section 2(c).

[47] Ibid, (e) The processing is necessary for purposes of medical treatment, is carried out by a medical practitioner or a medical treatment institution, and an adequate level of protection of personal information is ensured; or (f) The processing concerns such personal information as is necessary for the protection of lawful rights and interests of natural or legal persons in court proceedings, or the establishment, exercise or defence of legal claims, or when provided to government or public authority.

[48] Ibid, section 14.

8.7 Transferring Personal Information

Apart from the definition of personal information and the concept of consent, the principle of accountability has also emerged as an important policy principle that, ensures the personal information controller conducts themselves in accordance with the law. Thus, section 21 requires that the controller has sole responsibility for the transfer of personal information nationally and transnationally.[49] The level of responsibility can be delegated to another individual or group of individuals within the organisation. They are also held to the same level of accountability to that of the controller, when in the control of personal information being transferred to a third country or another location within the state. The transfer of personal information outside of the country of origin to where it was first collected is increasingly becoming more common. Therefore, the question arises whether the Philippines laws have extraterritorial reach? Put simply, yes it does.

8.7.1 Extraterritorial Reach

The extraterritorial reach of the DPA extends to any act, practice or processing of personal information about a citizen or a resident of the Philippines. This reach also applies to an entity that has a direct link with the Philippines, particularly where that entity is processing personal information in the Philippines or even if the processing is outside the state. This is on the basis that as long as the personal information is about a Philippine citizen or resident where there a contract has been established with the Philippines. In addition, section 6 applies where the entity is unincorporated in the state, however the central management and control (branch, agency, office or subsidiary in the Philippines and the parent or affiliate) is located in the state.[50] This also applies where the entity carries on a business anywhere within the states and that the personal information is collected in the state. Arguably, this is a further expression of sovereignty by the Philippines by ensuring there is a level of protection of their citizens and residents personal data when processed inside or outside of the state.

8.8 Commission

The National Privacy Commission (NPC) has been established under section 7 of the DPA. It is the country's privacy watchdog that is an independent body mandated to administer and implement the DPA, and to monitor and ensure compliance of the

[49] Ibid, section 21.

[50] Ibid, section 6.

country with international standards set for data protection.[51] Apart from their regulatory and enforcement function they are charged with upholding the right to privacy and data protection while ensuring the free flow of information, committed to excellence, driven by a workforce that is highly competent, future-oriented, and ethical, towards a competitive, knowledge-based, and innovative nation.[52] The NPC today are considered the national authority on data privacy and protection, providing knowledge, know-how, and relevant technology. They establish a regulatory environment that ensures accountability in the processing of personal data and promotes global standards for data privacy and protection. At the same time, they aim to build a national culture of privacy, through people empowerment, that enables and upholds the right to privacy and supports free flow of information.[53]

In addition to the above, the NPC plays a vital role to ensure all personal information controllers comply with the DPA when administering the collection, storage, use and dissemination of personal data. On behalf of the business and general community the NPC also has established a complaints process whereby they are able to investigate, facilitate or enable settlement of complaints through the use of alternative dispute resolution, adjudicate, award indemnity on matters affecting any personal information, prepare reports on disposition of complaints and resolution of any investigation it initiates, and, in cases it deems appropriate, publicize any such report. Importantly, the NPC promotes the dispute resolution rather than settling matters through the judiciary. Although settling breaches of the DPA via the judiciary is still an option. In any case, when resolving issues related to personal data, the Commission will, in most situations be required to collect and access that information. Doing so, may require them to issue cease and desist orders, impose a temporary or permanent ban on the processing of personal information, particularly where that information or data is detrimental to national security and public interest. These immediate processes steps are an important regulatory tool to not only protect personal data but also protect the state. In addition, the NPC can compel any entity, government agency or instrumentality to abide by its orders or take action on a matter affecting data privacy.

Apart from being able to monitor compliance of government agencies to ensure the standards for data privacy are being met, the NPC, also has a coordinating[54] role across government. The confidentiality bar for the Commission has been set quite high and they are to ensure that at all times any personal data and information is

---

[51] The National Privacy Commission, https://www.privacy.gov.ph/about-us/#comms

[52] Ibid, Data Privacy Act 2012, section 7.

[53] Ibid.

[54] Ibid, (f) Coordinate with other government agencies and the private sector on efforts to formulate and implement plans and policies to strengthen the protection of personal information in the country; (g) Publish on a regular basis a guide to all laws relating to data protection; (h) Publish a compilation of agency system of records and notices, including index and other finding aids; (i) Recommend to the Department of Justice (DOJ) the prosecution and imposition of penalties specified in Sections 25 to 29 of this Act.

managed confidentially. Structurally, the NPC is attached to the Department of Information and Communications Technology (DICT) and shall be headed by a Privacy Commissioner, who also act as Chairman of the Commission. The Privacy Commissioner shall be assisted by two (2) Deputy Privacy Commissioners, one to be responsible for Data Processing Systems and one to be responsible for Policies and Planning. The Privacy Commissioner and the two (2) Deputy Privacy Commissioners shall be appointed by the President of the Philippines for a term of three (3) years, and may be reappointed for another term of three (3) years. Vacancies in the Commission shall be filled in the same manner in which the original appointment was made.[55]

8.9 Data Impact Assessments

In 2017, the NPC issued guidelines[56] whereby, sections 4, 5, and 6 of the Circular 2016-01 requires government agencies to conduct a Privacy Impact Assessment (PIA). The pia must be undertaken for each program, process, or measure within the agency that involves personal data. At the same time, Section 6 of NPC Circular 2016-03 recommends the conduct of a PIA as part of any organization's security incident management policy.[57] This is an important risk management approach that, in part, provides another layer of control over the governance of personal data. They define Privacy Impact Assessment as a process undertaken and used to evaluate and manage impacts on privacy of a particular program, project, process, measure, system or technology product of a PIC or PIP program, project, process, measure, system or technology product of a PIC or PIP. It takes into account the nature of the personal data to be protected, the personal data flow, the risks to privacy and security posed by the processing, current data privacy best practices, the cost of security implementation, and, where applicable, the size of the organization, its resources, and the complexity of its operations.[58] They attempt to set a minimum standard, however, there is no prescribed standard or format for a PIA. As such, Guidelines allow the controller and processor to determine the structure and form of the PIA that it will use. It is not precluded from utilizing any existing methodology, provided the latter is acceptable based on the following criteria it provides a systematic description of the personal data flow and processing activities of the controller or processor. This includes the purpose of processing, including, where applicable, the legitimate interest pursued by the controller or processor; data inventory identifying the types of personal data held by the controller or processor. The Guidelines

[55] Ibid, section 9, see also, National Privacy Commission, https://www.privacy.gov.ph/about-us/#comms

[56] Republic of Philippines, National Privacy Commission, Guidelines on Privacy Impact Assessments, NPC Advisory No. 2017-03.

[57] Ibid.

[58] Ibid.

promote the use of ISO/IEC 29134, which provide standards for the conduct of the PIA. The promotion of the use if ISO cannot be underestimated. ISO is an internationally recognised risk management system that allows individuals and entities to assess the risk to their business systems. ISO has been successfully used by various industry sectors. It provides another layer of control and protection over personal data. Importantly, the Philippines have looked to the EU for guidance and states that they take into consideration Art 29 Data Protection Working Party Guidelines on Data Protection Impact Assessment (DPIA) and determining whether processing is "likely to result in a high risk" for the purposes of Regulation 2016/679, which is the EU GDPR.

By utilizing an international standard also reinforces the earlier point made in this book that, while the state has the sovereign responsibility for developing their respective data privacy laws, the national standards and principles are derived from internationally agreed, and, predominantly Western influence. Nevertheless, the DPA, as a risk management tool provides a better understanding of the risks associated with 1). sources of personal data and procedures for collection; 2). the functional description of personal data processing, including a list of all information repositories holding personal data and their location, and types of media used for storage; 3). transfers of personal data to another agency, company, or organization, including transfers outside the country, if any; 4). storage and disposal method of personal data; 5) accountable and responsible persons involved in the processing of personal data; and 6). existing organizational, physical and technical security measures. As part of the risk management system, three import risk factors are to be considered, these include:

- *identification.* Risks include natural dangers such as accidental loss or destruction, and human dangers such as unlawful access, fraudulent misuse, unlawful destruction, alteration and contamination.
- *evaluation based on impact and likelihood.* The severity or extent of the impact of a breach or privacy violation on the rights and freedoms of data subjects must be determined. The probability of the risk happening and the sources of such risk should also be taken into consideration; and
- *measures.* Based on an assessment of risks, measures should be proposed on how to address and manage the said risks.[59]

In supporting the above risk management approach, the Guidelines also play a major role in promoting the co-regulatory and self-regulatory approach. They also require controllers and organizations to consider and implement planning, conduct, document and review measures, which are consistent with ISO's internationally agreed structure. However, and on the backdrop of the above, unlike other jurisdictions, the Philippines may consider revising the DPA to make these a formal regulatory requirement.

[59] Ibid.

8.10 Enforcement

The enforcement of the DPA is one for the final steps to ensure overall protection of personal information and data in the Philippines. Penalties for breach have been distinguished in accordance with section 25, and include:

- ***Unauthorized Processing of Personal Information and Sensitive Personal Information*** – could result in imprisonment ranging from one (1) year to three (3) years and a fine of not less than Five hundred thousand pesos (Php500,000.00) but not more than Two million pesos (Php2,000,000.00) shall be imposed on persons who process personal information without the consent of the data subject, or without being authorized under this Act or any existing law. The unauthorized processing of personal sensitive information shall be penalized up to three (3) years to six (6) years and a fine of not less than Five hundred thousand pesos (Php500,000.00) but not more than Four million pesos (Php4,000,000.00) can be imposed on persons who process personal information without the consent of the data subject, or without being authorized.[60]
- ***Accessing Personal Information and Sensitive Personal Information Due to Negligence.*** – an individual could be imprisoned from one (1) year to three (3) years and a fine of not less than Five hundred thousand pesos (Php500,000.00) but not more than Two million pesos (Php2,000,000.00). However, there are additional penalties for accessing sensitive personal information. That is, accessing sensitive personal information due to negligence can be imprisoned for three (3) years to six (6) years and a fine of not less than Five hundred thousand pesos (Php500,000.00) but not more than Four million pesos (Php4,000,000.00).[61]
- ***Improper Disposal of Personal Information and Sensitive Personal Information,*** can result in an individual being imprisoned from six (6) months to two (2) years and a fine of not less than One hundred thousand pesos (Php100,000.00) but not more than Five hundred thousand pesos (Php500,000.00) shall be imposed on persons who knowingly or negligently dispose, discard or abandon the personal information of an individual in an area accessible to the public or has otherwise placed the personal information of an individual in its container for trash collection.[62]
- ***Processing of Personal Information and Sensitive Personal Information for Unauthorized Purposes,*** could be imprisoned from one (1) year and six (6) months to five (5) years and a fine of not less than Five hundred thousand pesos (Php500,000.00) but not more than One million pesos (Php1,000,000.00) shall be imposed on persons processing personal information for purposes not authorized by the data subject, or otherwise authorized under this Act or under existing laws".[63]

---

[60] Data Privacy Act 2012, section 25.

[61] Ibid.

[62] Ibid, section 27. b) The improper disposal of sensitive personal information shall be penalized by imprisonment ranging from one (1) year to three (3) years and a fine of not less than One hundred thousand pesos (Php100,000.00) but not more than One million pesos (Php1,000,000.00) shall be imposed on persons who knowingly or negligently dispose, discard or abandon the personal information of an individual in an area accessible to the public or has otherwise placed the personal information of an individual in its container for trash collection.

[63] Ibid, section 28. The processing of sensitive personal information for unauthorized purposes shall be penalized by imprisonment ranging from two (2) years to seven (7) years and a fine of not less than Five hundred thousand pesos (Php500,000.00) but not more than Two million pesos (Php2,000,000.00) shall be imposed on persons processing sensitive personal information for pur-

The above arguably establishes a tort for personal data protection. It will be up to the judiciary to determine whether and what the harm is or was, and how to measure it. Nevertheless, the breakup of penalties under the DPA also apply to the:

- ***Unauthorized Access or Intentional Breach,*** could result in a one (1) year to three (3) years and a fine of not less than Five hundred thousand pesos (Php500,000.00) but not more than Two million pesos (Php2,000,000.00) shall be imposed on persons who knowingly and unlawfully, or violating data confidentiality and security data systems, breaks in any way into any system where personal and sensitive personal information is stored.[64] Arguably there is a criminal element to this penalty provision, and more importantly it cuts across cyber security by imposing a penalty whereby systems have been breached or compromised; and
- ***Concealment of Security Breaches Involving Sensitive Personal Information,*** could result in a penalty of imprisonment of one (1) year and six (6) months to five (5) years and a fine of not less than Five hundred thousand pesos (Php500,000.00) but not more than One million pesos (Php1,000,000.00) shall be imposed on persons who, after having knowledge of a security breach and of the obligation to notify the Commission pursuant to Section 20(f), intentionally or by omission conceals the fact of such security breach".[65]

In addition to the above, there are penalties for Malicious Disclosure; Unauthorized Disclosure; and Combination or Series of Acts.[66] Section 34 provides some guidance on the extent of liability where an employee of an entity is liable from negligence. If the offender is a public official or employee and lie or she is found guilty of acts penalized under sections 27 and 28 of this Act, and in addition to the penalties. Finally, for large scale offences, in accordance with section 35, any maximum penalty is based on when the personal information of at least one hundred (100) persons is harmed, affected or involved. A public officer who commits a breach can be penalized by disqualification from office under section 36. On the other hand, section 37 allows for restitution for any aggrieved party in accordance with the Civil Code.

8.11 Cyber Security

The interconnectedness between personal data and cyber security has not gone unnoticed in the Philippines. In 2018, the Philippines Commission on Human Rights released a report into the inputs to Human Rights and the Right to Privacy in the Digital Age.[67] The report notes the reliance on data-driven analytics,

---

poses not authorized by the data subject, or otherwise authorized under this Act or under existing laws.

[64] Ibid, section 29.

[65] Ibid.

[66] Ibid, sections 31, 32, 33.

[67] Commission on Human Rights of the Philippines, Inputs to Human Rights Council Adopted Resolution 34/7 On The Right to Privacy in the Digital Age, https://www.ohchr.org/Documents/Issues/DigitalAge/ReportPrivacyinDigitalAge/CHR_Philippines.pdf

innovations, and decisions has a huge impact to the right to privacy of individuals. Undoubtedly, big data has its rewards but it also poses risks.[68] As discussed throughout the book, the interconnectedness of AI and personal data is evident in various data sets including big data. This has been reinforced by Kibria *et al.* who highlight how the variety of data sources, analytics requires more effort than traditional optimization, but it also provides a unified and converged platform for multiple targets of optimization.[69] They point out how more recently the network data analytics has been introduced to deliver slice and traffic steering and splitting related analytics automatically. Consequently, the European telecommunications standards institute has created the industry specification group called experimental network intelligence that defines a cognitive network management architecture based on artificial intelligence techniques and context-aware policies. The experimental network intelligence model helps the network operators in automating the network configuration and monitoring process. This is because of the systematic exploitation of big data that, include personal data, which dramatically helps in making the system smart, intelligent, and facilitates efficient as well as cost-effective operation and optimization. They envision data-driven next-generation wireless networks, where the network operators employ advanced data analytics, machine learning, and artificial intelligence. Thus, the future implication to personal data protection will be challenging. Subsequently, in the context of the Philippines they have been working towards establishing a Big Data Center that will develop a range of standards to use software and tools for analytics on massive amounts of data being generated from the use of the Internet and other technology. The Center will create another layer of protection to the existing protective measures against data breaches that violates the right to privacy in the Data Privacy Act.[70] However, the extent of the protective measures proposed were yet to be fully studied and analysed at the time of writing this book.

In the same year as the release of the Data Privacy laws, the *Cybercrime Prevention Act of 2012*[71] (CPA) came into effect. While referring to or defining personal data, the term data is captured within the definition of computer data, which refers to any representation of facts, information, or concepts in a form suitable for processing in a computer system including a program suitable to cause a computer system to perform a function and includes electronic documents and/or electronic data messages whether stored in local computer systems or online.[72] The reference

[68] Ibid.

[69] Golam Kibria, M., Nguyen, K., Villardi, P., Zhao, O., Ishizu, K., Kojima, F, *Big Data Analytics, Machine Learning, and Artificial Intelligence in Next-Generation Wireless Networks,* in *IEEE Access*, vol. 6, (2018) 32328–32338.

[70] Commission on Human Rights of the Philippines, Inputs to Human Rights Council Adopted Resolution 34/7 On The Right to Privacy in the Digital Age.

[71] Republic Act No 10175, An Act Defining Cyber Crime Providing for the Prevention, Investigation, Suppression and the Imposition of Penalties Therefore and for other Purposes. https://lawphil.net/statutes/repacts/ra2012/ra_10175_2012.html

[72] Ibid, section 3.

to data, in our view would also include the personal data that has been defined within the DPA. Moreover, there are a number of offences that capture data. These include the breach of confidentiality, integrity and availability of computer data and systems, from illegal access, interception, interference, and system interference. Arguably, the DPA and the CPA while serving and addressing two distinctive areas, they are interrelated because large quantities of data is likely to include personal data.

The Philippines have been impacted from the implementation of the cyber laws vary, but include key sectors that capture and use personal information. These include, but not limited to health, transportation, energy, water, emergency services, banking and finance, business process outsourcing, telecommunications, media and the government sectors.

More recently, there was a hacking of the Commission on Elections (Comelec) website, led to a data leak of millions of voter registration records in what can be considered the biggest leak of personal data in Philippine history.[73] The incident was a demonstration of how personal information while under a protective national legal framework, can be penetrated, with ease. However, a lawyer who used to work at the poll body said the nature of the leaked data should be determined first before ascertaining liability. It had been highlighted how the data controller of the personal information of registered voters, is liable under Republic Act 10173 section 26, on Accessing Personal Information Due to Negligence. RA 10173 – the Data Privacy Act. The Comelec's negligence lies in its "failure to 'implement reasonable and appropriate measures to protect personal information against...unlawful access' under RA 10173, Section 20".[74] In conclusion, the incident demonstrated how an individual could bring a case against an entity under both the cybercrime and data privacy law. Thus, in this situation, a criminal case may also be filed against the said poll officials, invoking Section 6 of the Cybercrime Prevention Act in relation to the Data Privacy Act.[75]

8.12 Conclusion

The Philippines have a long and diverse history. They are a member of the ASEAN community and located in a region of the world that is diverse culturally and legally. They have been influenced by the US. This chapter has demonstrated that the Philippines have taken data protection seriously. They have also, in part, understood the need to develop specific data laws that reflect the challenges faced from cybersecurity. With the implementation of the Cybercrime Prevention Act in 2012 it has gone some way to reconciling the gap between the two areas of the law. In a recent

[73] Buezza, M, *Is Comelec liable for website data leak?* 2016, https://www.rappler.com/newsbreak/in-depth/127465-comelec-hackers-liability-website-hacking-data-leak

[74] Ibid.

[75] Ibid.

criminal matter, both the Cybercrime Prevention Act in relation to the Data Privacy Act were invoked. This is arguably a step in the right direction. While other states are likely to have similar laws and responses with criminal laws, such as theft of identity from personal data, it is our view that viewing and addressing these issues in isolation are likely to become even more complex when AI is embraced.

The definition of personal data (information), constitutes any information whether recorded in a material form or not, from which the identity of an individual is apparent or can be reasonably and directly ascertained by the entity holding the information, or when put together with other information would directly and certainly identify an individual. Furthermore, sensitive personal information includes, a data subjects race, ethnic origin, marital status, age, colour, and religious, philosophical or political affiliations. Sensitive data also includes health, education, genetic or the sexual life of a person, along with any proceeding for any offense committed or alleged, or, the sentence of any court. Sensitive data has been extended to also include other identifiable information that, has been issued by government, such as, social security numbers, previous or current health records, licenses or its denials, suspension or revocation, and tax returns. The definition is broad, and arguably quite limited. While a more comprehensive definition can be problematic because it is difficult to account or describe every piece of personal information, it is our view that the current definition should be reviewed. It is argued that in its current form, it will not address the issues that arise from personal data being capture from AI. More problematic, further work is needed to address whether this definition will protect children and other vulnerable people in the community, within AI systems.

This Chapter has asserted that the right to be forgotten, while not recognised with the statute, or specifically stated by the court, it could form part of the future legal framework. As highlighted above, the Court recognised the need for data subjects to be able to control the flow of personal data. Arguably, the flow of personal data would also extend to the ability for the data subject to delete or erase their personal data so as it can no longer flow across the Internet. This control would also extend to other areas of securing personal data within the cyber world, including AI.

Consent in AI will be problematic. While it is acknowledged that technology may evolve that can manage consent, the current regulatory frameworks of many, if not all, jurisdictions laws do not adequately address consent in AI, particularly for children and other vulnerable individuals. As highlighted above, consent has largely been limited to the processing of personal data. For the processing of sensitive data, specific consent if required prior to any processing and goes further to require that all parties consent. However, consent is not required in certain circumstance where the processing is provided by an existing law such as protecting health, amongst other national security and commercial matters. Yet, any transfer of sensitive personal information to third parties can only be undertaken with the consent form the data subject. Therefore, in our view this is another challenge for the Philippines in AI systems that will be mainstream in the future. Finally, and in addition to the definition of personal data, the concept of consent should be looked at, to confirm whether it addresses children and others in the community. Apart from these two key principles, the Philippines will also need to address whether the remaining provisions of the Data Protection Act to ensure they capture those elements of AI technology that will store, repeat collect, retain, delete, use and collect personal data.

References

Abelardo, T. C., Ivy, D. A., & Alvin, B. P. (2016). Marcelo Health Information Privacy in the Philippines: Trends and challenges in policy and practice. *Acta Medica Philippina, 50*(4).

Ching, M. R. D., Fabito, B. S.., & Celis, N. J. (2018). *Data privacy act of 2012: A case study approach to Philippine Government Agencies Compliance*. ICEEG '18.

Golam Kibria, M., Nguyen, K., Villardi, P., Zhao, O., Ishizu, K., & Kojima, F. (2018). Big data analytics, machine learning, and artificial intelligence in next-generation wireless networks. *IEEE Access, 6*, 32328–32338.

Presbitero, J., Renee D., & Ching, M. (2018). *Assessing compliance of Philippine state universities to the data privacy act of 2012: The case of Caraga State University*. ICEEG '18.

Chapter 9
Taiwan

Abstract This Chapter expands on the other states data protection laws within the Asia region. Taiwan, similar to many other nation states throughout the Asian region have a long and complex history that dates back centuries. Privacy as a concept and right has gained traction in Taiwan. It must be noted that this Chapter does not in any way discuss the current political tensions between mainland China and Taiwan. It only examines the current day data protection laws of Taiwan.

They were a prefecture of Imperial China's Fujian province from the late seventeenth century and formally became a province beginning in 1884. China ceded the island to Japan after losing the Sino-Japanese War of 1894–95. During World War II, the government of the Republic of China, led by Generalissimo Chiang Kai-shek and dominated by his Nationalist Party, declared the return of Taiwan to China as one of its aims. What followed, Franklin Roosevelt readily agreed because he wanted China's help in preserving post-war peace. The Cairo Conference of late 1943 ratified this decision, in the process denying the people of Taiwan a say in their future. Taiwan returned to Chinese jurisdiction soon after the United States dropped nuclear bombs on Hiroshima and Nagasaki in 1945. They have also been ruled and influenced by both the Dutch and Portuguese at various times. Thus their current day legal framework has been influenced by civil and common law traditions.

The right to privacy across the territory of Taiwan is alive. Taiwan has adopted the title of Personal Data Protection Act in 1995 (PDPA). Since then, the PAPDA has only been amended twice, with the most recent changes in 2015. The PDPA generally follows the privacy principles approved by the Asia-Pacific Economic Corporation (APEC) in 200426 and the EU legal framework. The PDPA not only regulates private entities but also imposes rules for data collection, use, and disclosure by the public sector. The PDPA was designed to provide an overarching protection of personal data with an extensive scope but has faced a number of problems regarding its implementation due to incorrect perception of the law. Taiwan have, similar to other states, been grappling to balance the need for national security while protecting personal data. In other words, where a country is threatened by terrorism plans to establish a national biometric database, where all citizens will be required to submit their facial and other physical identifiers for national security or prevention of crime, it is much more difficult to justify a privacy breach. It will not be easy to strike a balance between these prominent interests.

R. Walters, M. Novak, *Cyber Security, Artificial Intelligence, Data Protection & the Law*, https://doi.org/10.1007/978-981-16-1665-5_9

This Chapter highlights how the data protections laws of Taiwan do provide a solid framework for the protection of personal data over the Internet. However, it is questionable, along with the other jurisdictions discussed in this book, whether elements of the laws will be able to adequately accommodate AI and the cybersecurity issues that will evolve. This is particularly relevant to the definition of personal data and the concept of consent when applied to smart home technology, toys, and robots amongst others. Nevertheless, they have begun to converge some of the criminality associated with personal data within the provisions of the current day laws, such as stolen personal data and other offences.

9.1 Introduction

The development of the data protection law in Taiwan has taken on a different approach to mainland China. This Chapter does not comment on the geopolitical tensions between mainland China and Taiwan. The role of this Chapter is to provide the reader with knowledge and incite into the history of privacy in Taiwan, and discuss the current day data protection laws that apply across the territory. Similar to its regional neighbours Taiwan has a long and what could be described as a complex history. They were a prefecture of Imperial China's Fujian province from the late seventeenth century and formally became a province beginning in 1884.[1] Richard Bush and Ryan Hass make the point that China ceded the island to Japan after losing the Sino-Japanese War of 1894–95. They go onto say how during World War II, the government of the Republic of China (ROC), led by Generalissimo Chiang Kai-shek and dominated by his Nationalist Party (Kuomintang, KMT), declared the return of Taiwan to China as one of its war aims. What followed, Franklin Roosevelt readily agreed because he wanted China's help in preserving post-war peace.[2] The Cairo Conference of late 1943 ratified this decision, in the process denying the people of Taiwan a say in their future. Bush and Hass assert that Taiwan returned to Chinese jurisdiction soon after the United States dropped nuclear bombs on Hiroshima and Nagasaki in 1945. In their view, the US directed the Chiang Kai-shek's ROC government to accept the Japanese surrender on Taiwan and take control of the island. The authors highlight how this was cautiously welcomed by the populace, the new authorities soon subjected the Taiwanese to predatory, corrupt, and arbitrary rule.[3]

As WWII conclude, the ROC Constitution was adopted on December 25, 1946, by the National Assembly convened in Nanking. It would be promulgated by the

[1] Bush, R., Hass, R *Taiwan's democracy and the China challenge: Taiwan's democratic progress over the last 20 years is remarkable, but the looming presence of China could threaten the future of the island's democracy*, 2018, https://www.brookings.edu/wp-content/uploads/2018/12/FP_20190226_taiwan_bush_hass.pdf

[2] Ibid.

[3] Ibid.

National Government on January 1, 1947, and put into effect on December 25 of the same year. In addition to the preamble, the Constitution comprises 175 Articles in 14 chapters.[4] They note that Taiwan has a semi-presidential system of governance, similar to that of France, which contains elements of both a presidential and parliamentary system. The president and vice president are elected by a simple majority popular vote to 4-year terms, and are eligible to run for a second 4-year term upon completion of their first term. The president serves as head of state, and in that capacity, appoints a premier to serve as head of government. Moreover, Taiwan's government is comprised of five branches of government. The constitution divides government into the Executive Yuan, the Legislative Yuan, the Judicial Yuan, the Control Yuan, and the Examination Yuan. The Executive Yuan serves as the cabinet. Cabinet ministers are appointed by the president on recommendation of the premier.[5] Chapter II, Article 7 of the ROC[6] sets out the rights and duties of is citizens. Article 7 provides that all citizens of the Republic of China, irrespective of sex, religion, ethnic origin, class, or party affiliation, shall be equal before the law. More importantly, Article 12 provides citizens with the right to freedom of privacy of correspondence. The constitutional privacy right is limited to correspondence and it is not clear what that actually means in practice. Could it include correspondence over the Internet? In addition to the right to privacy, Taiwan has adopted a number of important international treaties that support the right to privacy. The International Covenant on Civil and Political Rights 1966, whereby Article 17[7] provides that no one shall be subjected to arbitrary or unlawful interference with his privacy, family, home or correspondence, nor to unlawful attacks on his honour reputation.

Shin-Yi Peng highlights how in 1992, the Council of Grand Justices expressed its opinion on privacy for the very first time in Taiwanese judicial review history in 1992 in its Interpretation of Council of Grand Justices No. 293 on Disputes Concerning Debtors' Rights.[8] In this interpretation, the Grand Justices pointed out the privacy right of bank customers and the banks' obligation to keep the credit record confidential. On the one hand, it is regrettable that the interpretation only vaguely suggested that the "privacy" right should be protected, without declaring or confirming that right to privacy is a freedom and right under Article 22 of the R.O.C. Constitution, and therefore, the restriction of the right to privacy is only

[4] Ibid.

[5] Ibid.

[6] Taiwan Constitution, 1946, 2013 version, https://constitutii.files.wordpress.com/2013/01/taiwan-constitution.pdf, and https://law.moj.gov.tw/ENG/LawClass/LawAll.aspx?pcode=A0000001

[7] International Covenant on Civil and Political Rights, G.A. res. 2200A (XXI), 21 U.N. GAOR Supp. (No. 16) at 52, U.N. Doc. A/6316 (1966), 999 U.N.T.S. 171, entered into force Mar. 23, 1976. According to the Ministry of Law, the ICCPR came into effect in 2009. https://law.moj.gov.tw/ENG/LawClass/LawAll.aspx?pcode=Y0000041. Instrument of Ratification to the International Covenant on Civil and political Rights, https://law.moj.gov.tw/ENG/LawClass/LawAll.aspx?pcode=Y0000050

[8] Pemng, SY, (2003) *Privacy and the Construction of Legal Meaning in Taiwan*, The International Lawyer, Vol 37, No 4.

allowed under conditions set forth in Article 23. In the dissenting opinions, three Grand Justices expressed their regrets that the interpretation did not directly pronounce that the right to privacy is a constitutional right under Article 22.[9] Peng also makes the point that by the early 2000's a number of other laws such as the Telecommunications Act, Communications Protection and Surveillance Act, and the Computer-Processed Personal Data Protection Act provided a model of how existing Taiwanese laws cope, or fail to cope, with the need to balance government interests with personal privacy. On the other hand, it is out of scope of this chapter to examine how these laws protect or restrict privacy. The Taiwan Constitutional Court has gone some way to solidifying the right to privacy across the territory. Chang highlights how the Constitutional Court ruled that the right to privacy, though not clearly enumerated under the Constitution, is an indispensable fundamental right protected under Article 22 of the Constitution because it is necessary to preserve human dignity, individuality, and the wholeness of personality development, as well as to safeguard the freedom of private living space from interference and the freedom of self-control of personal information.[10] Some years later, the Constitutional Court interpreted the concept of privacy to expressly recognize the right to information privacy:

> As far as the right to information privacy is concerned, which regards the self-control of personal information, it is intended to guarantee that the people have the right to decide whether or not to disclose their personal information, and, if so, to what extent, at what time, in what manner and to what people such information will be disclosed. It is also designed to guarantee that the people have the right to know and control how their personal information will be used, as well as the right to correct any inaccurate entries contained in their information.[11]

However, prior to the Constitutional Court ruling, cases began appearing in the courts to address privacy matters relating to personal information. One of the first case involving online activity was in 2001. In *Privacy v Property Rights: The United Semiconductor E-mail Surveillance Dispute* Taiwan's United Semiconductor Co. fired about ten employees and put 200 other employees under surveillance. Peng notes that the issue began with an e-mail sent by the CEO of the corporation, entitled A Letter to all the Employees, with explanations of the company's outstanding accomplishments and future goals. Some of the employees, after receiving the letter, forwarded it to their friends who were not employees of United Semiconductor Co. The IT/MIS department of the corporation traced out the forwards through its e-mail

[9] Ibid.

[10] Chen-Hung Chang, Eyes on the Road Program in Taiwan - Information Privacy Issues under the Taiwan Personal Data Protection Act, 31 J. Marshall J. Info. Tech. & Privacy L. 145 (2015). J.Y. Interp. No. 585, at reasoning 17 (2004) (Taiwan), *translated in* http://www.judicial.gov.tw/constitutionalcourt/EN/p03_01.asp?expno=585(the quoted language is a translation from Taiwanese to English by the author).

[11] Ibid, J.Y. Interp. No. 603, at holding 1 (2005) (Taiwan), *translated in* http://www.judicial.gov.tw/constitutionalcourt/EN/p03_01.asp?expno=603(the quoted language is a translation from Taiwanese to English by the author).

surveillance on its IP servers. Based on the records of employees' online messages and activities, ten employees were terminated for transmitting what the company deemed confidential.[12] Peng goes onto say that:

> in terms of how the tort of invasion of privacy should be applied to cases of e-mail monitoring, the primary question that needs to be answered is whether the employee has a reasonable expectation of privacy in employer-provided computers and e-mail services. How to balance the personal dignity of employees with the proprietary interests of employers is the central issue.[13]

The struggle that had emerged in the early 2000s of how to find a balance between competing needs of society, individuals, and entities is a formidable task. In more recent times, with the advent of technology and the internet, the practice of human rights has taken on increasing complexity whether in Taiwan, China, Hong Kong or Macau. This is because, human rights are viewed and practiced differently. They come with economic and social implication and directly compete with other areas of the law. Reconciling the competing policy principles can be played out anywhere in society from the boardroom, classroom, office, sporting field, public, private and nongovernment sectors.

Notwithstanding the above, a year later in 2002, Peng further details how the case of *Privacy v Freedom of Press: The "Scoop Week"* began to balance the need for people to know information, with the right to privacy. Peng highlights how, a widely circulated videotape featuring a female Taiwanese politician, Ms. Chu Mei-Fang, stirred a debate on the island about where to draw a line between protection of privacy and freedom of press.[14] The original forty-seven minute video footage of Chu's sexual intercourse with a married man was filmed by a hidden camera installed at her home by Chu's friend, Kuo Yu-ling, and Chu's estranged boyfriend. Kuo Yu-ling and Tsai Jen-chien installed pin-hole cameras in Chu's apartment and bugged her phones. Eavesdropping devices and surveillance cameras were found in Chu's car and office, too.[15] They would be distributed to adult shops across Taiwan, and Scoop Weekly managed to obtain a copy. Scoop Week attached a copy of the VCD to the January 2002 issue. Since the news article transcript and the video present different legal issues, e.g. spreading of obscenity, this paper focuses on the transcript of the magazine, rather than the attachment.[16] The charges laid following a two-month investigation, included violation of privacy, defamation, and violation of decency. Prosecutors sought a twenty-six month sentence for Scoop Magazine founder Shen Yeh and separate jail terms for his daughter who runs the Chinese-language weekly and acts as her father's aide.[17] In addition, prosecutors called for Tsai to be jailed for one year and Kuo for four years. Scoop Week magazine,

[12] Ibid.

[13] Ibid.

[14] Ibid.

[15] Ibid.

[16] Ibid.

[17] Ibid.

however, defended itself arguing that the magazine is protected by "freedom of press" and that the people have the right to know.

Although the government's actions have been supported by some academics who say Taiwan's unbridled tabloid press has ventured far beyond the limits of privacy in the search for the sensational, the court is struggling in interpreting the statutory language of "with the knowledge of the illegal recording," and must carefully draw the line between the constitutional rights of free press and the criminal offense of illegal speech.[18] From this case Peng makes the point that in the early stages of the judiciary recognizing the right to privacy; offences against privacy challenge the need to balance freedom of speech and privacy interests. However, this is nothing new, states from all over the world are having to increasingly find a balance between conflicting rights such as free speech and privacy. This challenge will not be reconciled any time soon. In fact, it is our view that as AI systems and platforms are developed these amongst other rights will be further challenged and the right balance may be difficult to obtain. Thus, as with many privacy cases that have emerged over the last 50 years, no matter what country, it is likely courts will make decisions on a case by case basis.

Nonetheless, what has emerged, as highlighted by Tsung-Fu Chen, is how Taiwan along with China and Japan have been influenced by western legal thought. Raising this is an important point because, it is well understood that many countries around the world, particularly across Asia have looked to the west to develop their privacy and data protection laws. Chen argues that western civil codes have been transplanted in Japan, Taiwan and China.[19] Chen asserts that it has been primarily undertaken to accommodate for social and economic changes that occurred following the shift towards market economies. Secondly, Chen notes that the reception of legal theories of western law played an important role in the westernization of East Asian legal systems. Chen further argues that following East Asian countries carrying out market economic reforms resulted in social change, their legal systems were revised to embody the western concept of equality and individualism.[20] Additionally, the traditional culture appears to be eroding following the implementation of western-style civil codes. East Asian civil codes are actually reinforcing these personal rights which are used to support economic development.[21] What Chen is saying is that, such has the influence of western legal transplantation had to these states,

[18] Ibid.

[19] Chen, TF, (2011) *Transplant of Civil Code in Japan, Taiwan, and China: With the Focus of Legal Evolution,* Taiwan University Law Review [Vol. 6: 1].

[20] Ibid.

[21] Ibid. Chen notes that, In Taiwan, a civil code was first introduced following the Japanese colonial occupation in 1895 (rather than following the Nationalist rule beginning in 1945). Since Taiwan's first Civil Code experience started in 1895, Taiwan was able to receive western civil law earlier than Mainland China. Following the return of Taiwan to the Nationalist Government of China in 1945 and subsequent democratization in the 1980s, Taiwan has enacted many special civil laws to deal with legal issues that emerged as a result of immense social and economic changes.

amongst others in the region that they have accepted notions of privacy and data protection, to varying degrees. This is evident in the current day legal frameworks of Taiwan, China and Japan. On the other hand, they do vary.

On the backdrop of the above, arguably, the Civil Code has also had a significant role in protecting elements of people's rights. Generally, the evolution of the Civil Code has not been smooth sailing. Chen asserts that the Taiwanese Civil Code has been governing Taiwan for over six decades, and during this time, Taiwanese society has changed dramatically from agricultural to an industrial society and underwent political transition from authoritarianism towards democratic rule. It should be noted that, Taiwan's economy continued to expand consistently even under the authoritative rule, and private market economy prospered in the past decades. Following the democratization in the 1980s, the Taiwanese rights consciousness emerged with citizen's eager to claim their rights. This is a radical departure from the traditional Taiwanese society that emphasized self-sacrifice and fulfilment of one's own duties. In response to these social changes, a large number of special civil laws were enacted significantly revising the Civil Code. Chen further notes that in relation to rights:

> The first was the expansion of the right to personality. Taiwanese Civil Code received the protection of the right to personality both from German and Swiss laws. Prior to 1999, the right to personality under protection of the civil code was limited to the rights to lives, body, health, freedom, and reputation. The scope of protection was expanded to the right to privacy, the right to sexual autonomy, and "other personal interests seriously infringed upon" after the revision of the Civil Code. The expansion of protection to the right to privacy was significant, since traditional Chinese society did not recognize such right due to the prevalence of big closely knitted families.[22]

Thus, the current day Civil Code provides for the right to privacy. The Civil Code 2019[23] (Code) has undertaken reform over a long period of time and it is out of scope of this Chapter to provide an account of the reform process where privacy was finally inserted. Nonetheless, the most important provisions of the Code include Articles 18, 184 and 195. Beginning with Article 18, provides for when one's personality is infringed, the individual may apply to the court for removing. Further it allows the individual to apply for prevent, when their personality. In the preceding paragraph, an action for damages for emotional distress may be brought only it is otherwise provided by the act. Moreover, Taiwan provide for a level of legislative tort. Article 184, states that a person who, intentionally or negligently, has wrongfully damaged the rights of another is bound to compensate him for any injury arising therefrom. The same rule shall be applied when the injury is done intentionally in a manner against the rules of morals. It goes on to say that a person, who violates a statutory provision enacted for the protection of others and therefore prejudice to others, is bound to compensate for the injury, except no negligence in his/her act can be proved. Arguably, this could apply to where an individual's right to privacy over

---

[22] Ibid.

[23] Civil Code 2019 version, Ministry of Justice, https://law.moj.gov.tw/ENG/LawClass/LawAll.aspx?pcode=B0000001

the Internet has been breached. The challenge in the modern world is measuring the harm or injury to the person from a breach or misuse of their personal data over the Internet. In the context of Taiwan, it is out of scope of this Chapter to explore this any further. While the reference to privacy does not exist in Articles 18, 184 or any other Article with the Code, Article 195 does provide for the right. In other words, Article 195 states that:

> If a person has wrongfully damaged to the body, health, reputation, liberty, credit, *privacy* or chastity of another, or to another's personality in a severe way, the injured person may claim a reasonable compensation in money even if such injury is not a purely pecuniary loss. If it was reputation that has been damaged, the injured person may also claim the taking of proper measures for the rehabilitation of his reputation. The claim of the preceding paragraph shall not be transferred or inherited, except a claim for compensation in money has been promised by contract or has been commenced. The provisions of the preceding two paragraphs shall be mutatis mutandis applied when a person has wrongfully damaged to another's status based on the relationship to their father, mother, sons, daughters, or spouse in a severe way.[24]

Based on the above, privacy can be applied broadly and would include elements of privacy over the Internet. Moreover, it confirms that an individual would be able to apply a level of tort to a claim of breach of privacy over the Internet. Noteworthy too, this would be for the judiciary to decide, and as highlighted, measuring the harm incurred would be challenging and complex because it is an area that is far from settled. What has emerged in Taiwan is the acceptance of privacy and the adoption of western principles and thought into their legal framework. The next section discusses the current day data protection laws of Taiwan. What is not evident, to date, is how the judiciary will deal with breaches of personal information – to protect the privacy rights of citizens.

9.2 Data Protection Law

Taiwan has adopted the title of Personal Data Protection Act (PDPA)[25] which was originally promulgated in 1995. Since then, the PAPDA has only been amended twice, with the most recent changes in 2015. Chang argues that the PDPA generally follows the privacy principles approved by the Asia-Pacific Economic Corporation (APEC) in 2004 and the EU legal framework.[26] Chang goes onto highlight that the PDPA not only regulates private entities but also imposes rules for data collection, use, and disclosure by the public sector. More importantly, it appears that the

[24] Ibid, Article 195.

[25] Personal Data Protection Act 1995, Promulgated by Presidential Decree Ref. No. ROC-President-(I)-Yi-5960 dated August 11, 1995. Amended on May 26, 2010. Amended on December 30, 2015, Ministry of Justice 2019, https://law.moj.gov.tw/ENG/LawClass/LawHistory.aspx?pcode=I0050021

[26] Chang, CH, *Eyes on the Road Program in Taiwan - Information Privacy Issues under the Taiwan Personal Data Protection Act*, 31 J. Marshall J. Info. Tech. & Privacy L. 145 (2015).

requirements surrounding the management of consent when it comes to non-sensitive data were wound back. That is, the amendments removed the requirement that government agencies or private sector entities to obtain written consent to collect, process or use non-sensitive personal data. In addition, the amendments require that "special personal data" be collected, processed or used with the written consent of the data subject. Special personal data is equivalent to sensitive personal data that has been defined as such by other countries. It includes information such as medical records, information on medical treatment, genetic information, sexual background, health examination information and criminal records.[27]

The PDPA was designed to provide an overarching protection of personal data with an extensive scope but has faced a number of problems regarding its implementation due to incorrect perception of the law.[28] Chang highlights how it has not been all smooth sailing for the PDPA. In other words, concerns have been raised by some in the community that the rules are not strict enough for certain data, while others complain that the same level of strictness will discourage innovation in technology development.[29] Chang goes onto assert that the complexity is compounded because not all data is created equal. The value of data varies depending on the nature and the context of application, thus calling for different levels of privacy protection. Similarly, personal data is used for various reasons. For instance, the same health data may be applied for multiple purposes, ranging from generating commercial profits to supporting academic research.[30] For Chang, Taiwan have, similar to other states, been grappling to balance the need for national security while protecting personal data. In other words, Chang states that a country threatened by terrorism plans to establish a national biometric database, where all citizens will be required to submit their facial and other physical identifiers for national security or prevention of crime, it is much more difficult to justify a privacy breach. It will not be easy to strike a balance between these prominent interests.[31] In addition to the above, the Enforcement Rules of the Personal Data Protection Act (Enforcement Rules)[32] while being enacted in accordance with Article 55 of the PDPA, underpin the implementation of the principal Act.

---

[27] Ibid.

[28] Ibid.

[29] Ibid.

[30] Ibid.

[31] Ibid.

[32] Enforcement Rules of the Personal Data Protection Act, promulgated by the Ministry of Justice on May 1, 1996 Per Ruling Ref. No. (85) Law-10,259, Amended on Sep 26, 2012, Amended on March 2, 2016. The joint announcement was made on January 10, 2019 by the Ministry of Justice Order faluzi No. 10803500010 and the National Development Council fa-fa-zi No. 1080080004A. The relevant matters set out in Article 33 pertaining to "The Ministry of Justice" shall be handled by "The National Development Council" as governing body.

9.3 Definition of Personal Data

Taiwan define personal data similarly to many other states. They have embraced a broad definition that includes a natural person's name, date of birth, ID Card number, passport number, features, fingerprints, marital status, family information, education background, occupation, medical records, healthcare data, genetic data, data concerning a person's sex life, records of physical examination, criminal records, contact information, financial conditions, data concerning a person's social activities and any other information that may be used to directly or indirectly identify a natural person.[33] The all-encompassing definition does not separate sensitive personal data from general data. Moreover, the Enforcement Rules Article 4 clarifies what and how personal data is defined, and is also attributable to other laws. For instance, Article 4 specifies how personal data pertaining to a person's "medical records", as referred to under Subparagraph 1, Paragraph 1, Article 2 of the PDPA, shall mean the data specified in the subparagraphs of Paragraph 2, Article 67 of the Medical Care Act. In relation to healthcare, personal data, shall mean medical histories and any other data pertaining to check-ups or treatments implemented by physicians or other medical professionals for the purpose of treating, correcting or preventing diseases, harms or disabilities of human body or for other legitimate medical reasons, or shall mean other data produced from the prescription, medication, operation or disposition based on the findings of the above-mentioned check-ups.[34]

Moreover, personal data that would include genetics, means the information on a heredity unit, consisting of one segment of deoxyribonucleic acid (DNA) of human body, for controlling the specific functions thereof. The sex life of an individual is considered sacrament, and personal data that discloses this information and data constitutes the personal data on sexual orientation or sexual habits.[35] Personal data that highlights the data that comes from a physical examination can only be the data produced by medical examinations conducted not for the purpose of diagnosing or treating a specific disease. Thus, this limitation obviously protects public health policy, particularly where there might be a pandemic. And, criminal records data, means records of deferred prosecutions, ex officio non-indictments, or a final guilty verdict rendered by a court and its enforcement. On the one side, the Enforcement Rules does not define or provide any further guidance on what constitute sensitive personal data. On the face of this definition by the PDPA, it appears that most if not all data that can be personal, which could be collected by AI is covered. Importantly, the reference to features could include facial, voice and body recognition. On the other side, as AI systems become increasingly complex and part of the home, it is questionable whether this definition will capture all the personal data these systems might. This will be particularly important for children.

---

[33] Personal Data Protection Act 1995, Article 2.

[34] Enforcement Rules of the Personal Data Protection Act 1996, Article 4.

[35] Personal Data Protection Act 1995, Article 2.

9.4 Rights of Data Subjects

Article 3 of the PDPA provides data subjects with rights that may be exercisable and cannot be waived or limited unless by contractual arrangements. Data a subject's rights include the right to:

- make an inquiry of and to review their personal data;
- request a copy of their personal data;
- supplement or correct their personal data;
- demand the cessation of the collection, processing or use of their personal data; and
- erase their personal data.[36]

One of the most important rights provided to data subject is the right to erase their personal data. Arguably, this reinforces the proposition below that the right to be forgotten exists in Taiwan.

9.4.1 Right to Be Forgotten

The PDPA in accordance with Article 3 provides individuals with the right to request that an entity, store or organisation delete his or her personal information from its database or system.[37] Furthermore, Article 20 also provides that an individual who requests their unwillingness to receive any marketing material, the entity must cease to send that individual any marketing material using their personal information.[38] Failure to follow the requirements of these two articles in particular the entity will be liable, and it arguably highlights how the right to deletion underpins the notion of the right to be forgotten. In October 2014, the Court awarded civil damages of NT$26,000 in accordance with the Taiwan Civil Code and the PDPA, because an entity failed to delete the personal information of an individual, who had requested it be deleted.[39]

9.5 Public and Private – Applicable

The PDPA applies to government and non-government organisations. Article 4, states that, whoever is commissioned by a government agency or non-government agency to collect, process or use personal data shall be deemed to be acting on

---

[36] Personal Data Protection Act 1995, Article 3.

[37] Ibid.

[38] Ibid, Article 20.

[39] Chang, H., Tsai, C, *Taiwan-first court case based on the right to be forgotten*, Baker McKenzie, https://www.lexology.com/library/detail.aspx?g=644356dc-6da9-4fc8-ad3e-1deb18f48848

behalf of the commissioning agency to the extent that the PDPA applies.[40] This is consistent with most states' laws.

9.6 Collection and Processing

The collection, processing and use of personal data shall be carried out in a way that respects the data subject's rights and interest, in an honest and good-faith manner, shall not exceed the necessary scope of specific purposes, and shall have legitimate and reasonable connections with the purposes of collection.[41] Furthermore, data pertaining to a natural person's medical records, healthcare, genetics, sex life, physical examination and criminal records shall not be collected, processed or used unless on any of the following bases:

- where it is expressly required by law;
- where it is within the necessary scope for a government agency to perform its statutory duties or for a non-government agency to fulfill its statutory obligation, provided that proper security and maintenance measures are adopted prior or subsequent to such collection, processing or use of personal data;
- where the personal data has been disclosed to the public by the data subject or has been made public lawfully;
- where it is necessary for statistics gathering or academic research by a government agency or an academic institution for the purpose of healthcare, public health, or crime prevention, provided that such data, as processed by the data provider or as disclosed by the data collector, may not lead to the identification of a specific data subject;
- where it is necessary to assist a government agency in performing its statutory duties or a non-government agency in fulfilling its statutory obligations, provided that proper security and maintenance measures are adopted prior or subsequent to such collection, processing, or use of personal data; or
- where the data subject has consented to the collection, processing and use of his/her personal data in writing, except where the collection, processing or use exceeds the necessary scope of the specific purpose, or where the collection, processing or use based solely on the consent of the data subject is otherwise prohibited by law, or where such consent is not given by the data subject out of his/her free will.[42]

Importantly, the concept of consent begins to emerge in Article 6 for the collection, processing and use of personal data. Additionally, other internationally agreed concepts and principles also emerge ensuring the collection, processing and use of data is undertaken for a specific purpose and it is secure.

---

[40] Personal Data Protection Act 1995, Article 3.

[41] Personal Data Protection Act 1995, Article 5. Article 7 and 8 of the Enforcement Rules of the Personal Data Protection Act supports Article 5.

[42] Personal Data Protection Act 1995, Article 6, Articles 8 and 9 shall apply mutatis mutandis to the collection, processing, or use of personal data in accordance with the preceding paragraph; Paragraphs 1, 2 and 4 of Article 7 shall apply mutatis mutandis to the consent required under Subparagraph 6 of the preceding paragraph.

9.6.1 Government Agency

Taiwan have taken that position that the collection, processing, use, by government and nongovernment agencies have unique and specific requirements. For government agencies,[43] Article 15 places obligations on government agencies to collect, use and process personal data for a specific performance where it is within the necessary scope to perform its statutory duties; where consent has been given by the data subject; or where the rights and interests of the data subject will not be infringed upon. More generally, this is subject to the requirements and except for the personal data specified under Paragraph 1, Article 6. Furthermore, Article 16 and in addition to the previous article whereby except for the personal data specified under paragraph 1, Article 6, a government agency shall 'use' personal data only for the specific purpose of collection. However, the use of personal data can be used where it is required by the law, for national security and in the public interest, to prevent harm to life, body, freedom, or property of the data subject.[44]

Significant too, the personal data can also be used to prevent harm to the rights of others or for statistics gathering or academic research that is in the public interest. It goes on to also ensure that personal data can be used by a government agency where it is in the interest of the data subject or where consent has been provided by the data subject. Also a pertinent observation is that while not specifically stating how that consent would be valid, Article 7 would apply. In addition to Articles 15 and 16, Article 17 allows a government agency to publicize certain data and information such as the names of the personal data files; the name and contact information of the agency that is in possession of the personal data files; the legal basis and purpose of keeping the personal data files; and the category of the personal data.[45] A safeguard that has been built into the legal framework and ensure there is a line of continuity and responsibility within a government organization, requires that in accordance with Article 18, an individual is assigned to implement security and maintenance measures to prevent the personal data from being stolen, altered, damaged, destroyed or disclosed.[46] Arguably, this has all the hallmarks of appointing a controller or processor. That said, the legislative requirement that this individual has an obligation to ensure that appropriate security and maintenance measures are in place to protect the personal data has two functions. Firstly, it is argued that there is a level of cybersecurity built into the system, and it does not limit this function to any specific platform, system or infrastructure. Secondly, it can be asserted that it would or could ensure the security of personal data that is collected and used by AI systems within a government agency.

---

[43] Personal Data Protection Act 1995, Chapter II Data Collection, Processing and Use by a Government Agency.

[44] Personal Data Protection Act 1995, Article 16.

[45] Ibid, Article 17.

[46] Ibid, Article 18.

9.6.2 Non-government Agency

In addition to the above, Taiwan has specific requirements for the collection, use and processing of personal data by non-government agencies.[47] While similar to government agencies, there are specific requirements for collection and processing versus the use of personal data. Thus, Article 19 allows for the collection and processing of personal data by non-government entities where it is expressly required by the law. The difference in requirement between non-government and government is that with the private sector it is likely that personal data issues will find their way into contracts. Therefore, Article 19 goes onto to describe how personal data can be used where there is a contractual or quasi-contractual relationship between the non-government agency and the data subject, and proper security measures have been adopted to ensure the security of the personal data; and where the personal data has been disclosed to the public by the data subject or has been made public lawfully.[48] The collection and processing of personal data by non-government organizations can also be undertaken where it is necessary for statistics gathering or academic research, to further the public interest. This public interest could include but not limited to health, education or national security. However, consent must be obtained from the data subject.

The collection and processing of personal data can also be undertaken in circumstances where the personal data is obtained from publicly available sources unless the data subject has an overriding interest in prohibiting the processing or use of such personal data; or where the rights and interests of the data subject will not be infringed upon. More importantly, a data collector or processor within a non-government agency, upon the request of the data subject, is to erase or cease processing or use of the personal data. This procedural step must be undertaken as soon

[47] Ibid, Chapter III Data Collection, Processing and Use by a Non-government Agency. Article 20 of the Enforcement Rules of the Personal Data Protection Act 1996 Article 19, Except for the personal data specified under Paragraph 1, Article 6, the collection or processing of personal data by a non-government agency shall be for specific purposes and on one of the following bases. Article 26 A "contractual or quasi-contractual relationship", as referred to under Subparagraph 2, Paragraph 1, Article 19 of the PDPA, is not limited to the relationship formed after the amendment to the PDPA has taken into effect. Article 27 A "contractual relationship", shall include the contractual relationship between a non-government agency and a data subject, and also the relationship where a non-government agency and a data subject are either contacting, negotiating or communicating with, receiving delivery from or making delivery to a necessary third party for the purpose of performing the contract between the non-government agency and the data subject. A "quasi-contractual relationship", as referred to under Subparagraph 2, Paragraph 1, Article 19 of the PDPA, shall mean any of the following: 1. any relationships involving the contact and negotiation between a non-government agency and a data subject before the execution of a contract for the purpose of preparing for or negotiating the terms of such contract or transaction; or 2. any relationships involving the communication between a non-government agency and a data subject upon the extinguishment of a contract due to the invalidation, rescission, cancellation or termination thereof or upon the complete performance of a contract, for the purpose of exercising their rights, performing their obligations, or ensuring the integrity of the personal data.

[48] Ibid.

as the agency becomes aware of such a request or been notified by the data subject. This requirement has similarities to the right to erasure (forgotten) under EU law. It provides a level of certainty to data subjects that they have control over their personal data, by allowing them to request that their data be erased.

Article 20 describes how non-government organizations can use personal data.[49] Thus the use of personal data by these agencies can only be undertaken where it is expressed by the law, it is in the public interest or to prevent harm on life, body, freedom, or property of the data subject. It also applies to prevent a material harm on the rights and interests of others or, for statistical purposes undertaken by an academic research or government agency. This data can be also used provided that the data subject has provided consent. Note, that consent and the way in which consent is to be applied would be in accordance with Article 7. Nonetheless, the use of this data can be used in the interest of the data subject and their rights. Thus, there is broader consideration of other rights, although not specifically specified that will be considered prior to the data being used. Finally, when a non-government agency uses personal data for marketing purpose pursuant to the preceding paragraph, upon the data subject's objection to such use, the agency shall cease using the data subject's personal data for marketing.[50] A non-government agency, when using the data subject's personal data for marketing purpose for the first time, shall provide the data subject of the ways that he/she can object to such use, and the agency shall pay for the fees therefrom.[51]

9.6.3 *Cross-Border Transfer of Personal Data*

The growth in the cross-border transfer of personal data is growing annually. Most, if not all states that have specific data protection laws have recognized the need for specific provisions to manage cross border transfer of data. Article 21 requires that where personal data will be transferred outside of Taiwan, and is carried out by a non-government agency, the central government authority in charge of the industry concerned may impose restrictions on such a transfer. Any limitation of cross border transfer only applies to where that data is a major national interest or where an international treaty or agreement applies. Importantly, where the country receiving the personal data lacks proper regulations on protection of personal data and the data subjects' rights and interests may consequently be harmed any transfer of data may be limited or not proceed. Indirectly, Taiwan is ensuring there is a level of protection equivalence in data protection when data is being transfer to third countries. Many other states have established the same procedure. However, it is out of scope of this

---

[49] Ibid, Article 20, Except for the personal data specified in Paragraph 1, Article 6, a non-government agency shall use personal data only within the necessary scope of the specific purpose of collection; the use of personal data for another purpose.

[50] Ibid.

[51] Ibid.

chapter to provide that comparative analysis. This limitation also extends to where the cross-border transfer of the personal data to a third country (territory) is carried out to circumvent the PDPA.[52]

Notwithstanding the above, the central government of Taiwan play an important role in having a level of oversight in relation to the cross-border transfer of personal data. Thus, Article 22 requires that the central government authorities in charge of the industries or the municipality/city/county governments concerned may, when they deem necessary or suspect any possible violation of the PDPA, inspect compliance with the security control measures, the guidelines on disposing personal data upon business termination, and the restrictions on cross-border transfers, or conduct any other routine inspections by having their staff enter non-government agencies' premises upon presentation of their official identification documents and order relevant personnel at the non-government agencies to provide necessary explanations, cooperate on adopting relevant measures, or provide supporting documents.[53]

The above regulatory power of inspection allows the designated government agency who has been designated with the power to undertaken enforcement of the PDPA to ensure that security controls have been established to protect personal data. This, in part, reaches across the cyber security and AI lines, because personal data is supported by these technologies. To ensure the enforcement functions are effective additional power has been provided for the authorities to retain or make duplications of the personal data or the files thereof that can be confiscated or be admitted as evidence. The owner, holder or keeper of such data or files that shall be confiscated or copied shall submit them to the authorities upon request. If the non-government agency refuses to submit or deliver the requested data or files or rejects the confiscation or duplication thereof without any legitimate reason, a compulsory enforcement that will do the least harm to the rights and interests of the non-government agency may be applied.[54] However, the process for managing any confiscated or duplicate files are to be sealed or tagged.[55] This is a procedural and operational

[52] Ibid, Article 21.

[53] Ibid, Article 22.

[54] Ibid. Additionally, When the central government authorities in charge of the industries concerned or the municipality/city/county governments concerned conduct the inspections described in Paragraph 1, professionals in the field of information technology, telecommunications or law may accompany the inspectors during the inspections.

Non-government agencies and their personnel may not evade such inspections, obstruct the investigators from accessing the premises or data, or refuse to comply with the inspections or decisions referred to in Paragraphs 1 and all personnel who take part in the inspections shall keep in confidence all the personal data that they become aware of due to the inspections.

[55] Personal Data Protection Act 1995, Article 23, The confiscated files or duplicates referred to in Paragraph 2 of the preceding article shall be sealed or tagged and properly handled; if it is unfeasible to move or take possession of such files, the authority shall assign personnel to guard such files or order the owner of such files or an appropriate person to take possession of the files. If it is no longer necessary to keep the confiscated files or the duplicates, or the authority has decided not to impose any penalties or confiscate any files, the confiscated files and duplicates shall be returned except for the files or duplicates that shall be confiscated or kept for the investigation of other cases.

process to ensure the continuity of information is maintained and any evidence cannot be contaminated. For non-government agencies, Article 24 requires that any interested persons of those confiscated files or duplicates may raise an objection with the central government authority in charge of the industry concerned or the municipality, city, county government concerned against the acts of demand, compulsory enforcement, detention, or duplication mentioned. However, where an objection has been received, the central government authority in charge of the industry concerned or the municipality, city, county government concerned shall immediately cease or rectify such acts if the objection is considered reasonable; otherwise, it may continue such acts.[56]

9.7 Consent

Consent comes in different forms. Be aware that as highlighted above there are specific requirement for consent for government and non-government agencies when collecting, processing and using personal data. The challenge and a problem in the future is the collection, processing and use of personal data where AI technology automatically captures that data, and there is no human intervention such as smart home appliances. This, arguably, apply for not only that states discussed in this book, but, more broadly other states and jurisdictions that have specific data protection laws.

Nonetheless, Article 7 effectively describes how consent can be and will apply according to other provisions with the PDPA. Consent comes in the form of actual, express or presumed-implied consent. In other words, consent, referred to in subparagraph 2, paragraph 1 of Article 15 and subparagraph 5, paragraph 1 of Article 19, means a declaration of agreement given by a data subject after he/she has been informed by the data collector of the information required under the PDPA. Arguably the declaration of consent is a form of express consent. What is not clear is whether the consent by declaration is to be provided orally or in writing, and which one is required. Furthermore, consent in subparagraph 7, paragraph 1, Article 16 and subparagraph 6, paragraph 1, Article 20, means a separate declaration of agreement given by a data subject after he/she has been informed by the data collector of any of the purposes other than that originally specified, the scope of other use, and the impact of giving or not giving consent on the rights and interests of the data subject. Moreover, an implied level of consent has been presumed to have been provided by the data subject in accordance with subparagraph 2, paragraph 1, Article 15 and subparagraph 5, paragraph 1, Article 19 if the data subject does not indicate his/her objection and affirmatively provides his/her personal data after the government or non-government agency has informed the data subject of the relevant information

[56] Personal Data Protection Act 1995, Article 24.

specified in Paragraph 1, Article 8 of the PDPA. Arguably, this applies to both government and non-government agencies. Finally, the collector of the personal data within these agencies has the burden of proof that the data subject has provided consent.[57]

9.7.1 Inform

Key to the operation of the PDPA is the requirement of agencies, public and private inform the data subject of certain points of collection, processing and use of that data. Therefore, in accordance with Article 8, both a government or non-government agency shall expressly inform the data subject of the following information when collecting their personal data in accordance with Article 15 or 19 of the PDPA.[58] This includes informing the data subject of the name of the government or non-government agency, along with the purpose of the collection of the personal data, and the categories of data collected. Additionally, the data subject is to be informed of the time period, territory, recipients, and methods of data use, their rights[59] under Article 3. However, there are exceptions to the obligation to inform the data subject and applies to circumstances where notification may be waived in accordance with the law; the collection of personal data is necessary for the government agency to perform its statutory duties or the non-government agency to fulfil its statutory obligation. The exemption to inform also extends to circumstances where giving notice will prevent the government agency from performing its statutory duties; giving notice will harm public interests; the data subject has already known the content of the notification; or the collection of personal data is for non-profit purposes and clearly has no adverse effect on the data subject.

The need to inform the data subject of the processing or use of their personal data under Articles 15 or 19 is required under Article 9. However, this obligation to inform is not required under any of the circumstances provided in paragraph 2 of Article 8. There is not requirement to inform where the personal data has been disclosed to the public by the data subject or has been made public lawfully, or, it is unable to inform the data subject or his/her statutory representative. Likewise, the data subject does not need to be informed where the data is used for statistical purposes by an academic institution for research, or, where the personal data is collected by mass communication enterprises for the purpose of news reporting for the benefit of public interests.[60] Nonetheless, the requirement to inform the data subject

[57] Personal Data Protection Act 1995, Article 7.

[58] Ibid, Article 8.

[59] The data subject's rights and interests that will be affected if he/she elects not to provide his/her personal data.

[60] Personal Data Protection Act 1995, Article 9.

must be undertaken at the time of the first use of the personal data towards the data subject.

9.7.2 *Replying to a Data Subject*

The data subject has a further right by being able to request the government or non-government agency to reply for the personal data that has been collected. These agencies are also required to provide the data subject with a copy of that information. Yet, similar to the requirement to inform (above in Article 9) there are exemptions. Thus, the agency will not be obliged to reply to the data subjects request on national security diplomatic or military grounds. In addition, there is no requirement to reply where a government agency may be prevented from performing its statutory duties; or the material interests of the data collectors or any third parties may be adversely affected.[61] However, under Article 13, where a data subject has requested information from these agencies in accordance with Article 10, that agency (whether government or non-government) has the choice to accept or reject any request. Even so, there is a time limit for such a request to be accepted or rejected, and must be done within 15 days from receipt of the request.[62] A further 15-day extension can apply provided the data subject is notified of that extension.

9.8 Accuracy

Maintaining the accuracy of personal data has become another important feature of the legal framework. The principles of accuracy can also be found within international and regional guidelines. Both government or non-government agencies are required to take steps to ensure all personal data they handle is accurate, and where necessary, correct or supplement such data on its own initiative or upon the request of data subjects.[63] However, where there is a dispute between the parties, the

---

[61] Ibid, Article 10.

[62] Personal Data Protection Act 1995, Article 13, Where a request is made by a data subject to a government or non-government agency pursuant to Article 11, the agency shall determine whether to accept or reject such request within thirty days; such deadline may be extended by up to thirty days if necessary, and the data subject shall be notified in writing of the reason for the extension.

[63] Ibid, Article 11. Article 20 of the Enforcement Rules of the Personal Data Protection Act 1996 The circumstances "where the specific purpose no longer exists" referred to under Paragraph 3, Article 11 of the PDPA shall mean any of the following circumstances: 1. the government agency has been dissolved or reorganized without another agency to take over its tasks; 2. the non-government agency has ceased its business or been dissolved without another agency to take over its business, or the non-government agency has changed the scope of its business, thereby causing the purpose for which the personal data were collected to be no longer applicable; 3. the specific purpose has been reached, and there is therefore no longer necessary to continue the processing and

relevant agency government or non-government agency can on its own initiative or upon the request of the data subject, cease processing or using the personal data. That is, and unless the processing or use is either necessary for the performance of an official or business duty, or has been agreed to by the data subject in writing, and the dispute has been recorded.[64] Further, if any failure to correct or supplement any personal data is attributable to a government or non-government agency, the government or non-government agency shall notify the persons who have been provided with such personal data after the correction or supplement is made.[65] The risk of not maintaining accuracy of data can have significant consequences for both the organization or the individuals. For example, the data subject's data has been collected and portrays them as someone else who has been flagged as a national security target. That person could find themselves being the target by foreign governments, for no reason other than the inaccurate recording, use and storage of their data.

9.8.1 *Stolen Data*

As highlighted in Chap. 1, the vulnerability of personal data today has been on the increase over the past twelve months. The number of cybersecurity breaches and the illegal collection of personal data has also excelled significantly. Thus, in accordance with Article 12, any personal data stolen, disclosed, altered, or otherwise infringed upon due to a violation of the PDPA by a government or non-government agency, the data subject shall be notified via appropriate means after the relevant facts have been clarified.[66] The potential to steel personal data could be a lot easier

use of personal data; or 4. other circumstances where the specific purpose evidently can no longer be reached or no longer exists.

[64] Ibid. When the specific purpose of data collection no longer exists, or upon expiration of the relevant time period, the government or non-government agency shall, on its own initiative or upon the request of the data subject, erase or cease processing or using the personal data, unless the processing or use is either necessary for the performance of an official or business duty, or has been agreed to by the data subject in writing. A government or non-government agency shall, on its own initiative or upon the request of the data subject, erase the personal data collected or cease collecting, processing or using the personal data in the event where the collection, processing or use of the personal data is in breach of the Act.

[65] Ibid.

[66] Personal Data Protection Act 1995, Article 12. Article 22 of the Enforcement Rules of the Personal Data Protection Act 1996, A notification given via "appropriate means", as referred to under Article 12 of the PDPA, shall mean a notification that is given in a prompt manner via verbal words, in writing, over the phone, via text messages, email, fax, electronic documents or other means that can effectively make the information known or available to the data subjects. However, if such notification entails disproportionate costs, a government or non-government agency may, taking into consideration the technical feasibility and privacy protection of the data subjects, notify the data subjects through the Internet, the media or other proper and public means. A notification given under Article 12 of the PDPA shall include the facts pertaining to the data breach and the response measures already adopted to address such breach of personal data.

as AI becomes mainstream. The ease at with AI systems might be hacked is unknown and their security systems have not been fully settled. Thus, government and regulators will need to consider the theft of personal data with in their legal frameworks. In some countries this has already been addressed where the theft of personal data has been used to create false identities. However, there is likely to be many other areas where the theft of personal data can be used for other state or private purposes.

9.9 Regulator

To date, Taiwan has not established Commission, Commissioner or a separate dedicated Regulatory authority. The Ministry of Justice has a major role in administrating and updating the PDPA and Enforcement Rules. Additionally, other ministries such as Health and Education have their own responsibilities. This could pose a problem for Taiwan in the future. While it is their choice, other states have clearly seen the need for such regulatory mechanism to be established. The benefit of doing so provides a single dedicated authority with the expertise to deal with the very and increasing fluid nature of the issues that are arising from technology, cyber security and protecting personal data.

9.9.1 Penalties

The enforcement of general privacy can be enforced in two ways with Taiwan. Chapter 28 of the Criminal Code,[67] entitled Offences Against Privacy. Secondly damages can be obtained under the PDPA. Firstly, though it is worthwhile understanding the criminal offences afforded to privacy matters. Criminal offences for privacy can be found from Article 315 to 319. Article 315 provides that a person who without reason opens or conceals a sealed letter or other sealed document belonging to another shall be sentenced to short-term imprisonment or a fine of not more than three thousand yuan. A person who without reason looks into the contents of a sealed letter by other means than opening shall be subject to same punishment. These penalties would have very little to do with privacy over the Internet, and it is not clear whether a letter include an email?

An individual can be imprisoned for up to three years where they have used instruments or equipment without reason to peep at or eavesdrop on other's non-public activities, speeches, talks, or the private part of the body. This also applies where a person has used audio recording, photographic, visual-taping, or electromagnetic means without reason to record other's non-public activities, speeches,

[67] Criminal Code, 1928, version 2019, Ministry of Justice, https://law.moj.gov.tw/ENG/LawClass/LawAll.aspx?pcode=C0000001

talks, or the private bodily part.[68] The technology devices to detect and record this information is being developed and on the market. It is also being purchased by consumers that exhibit AI technology. More importantly, Article 316 medical doctor, pharmacist, druggist, midwife, mental therapist, clergyman, lawyer, defender, notary public, accountant, one of their business assistants, or one who has previously engaged in such occupation who without reason discloses the secrets of another which he knows or possesses because of his occupation shall be sentenced to imprisonment for not more than one year, short-term imprisonment, or a fine of not more than fifty thousand yuan. This is an important point because the personal data in the hands of medical staff, is in many countries considered the most sensitive data that a person holds. Thus, this provision covers not only health and medical information, but also financial and legal data that in our view should be sacrament to any one person.

Article 317 goes onto say that a person who is required by law, order, or contract to preserve the commercial or industrial secrets of another which he knows or possesses because of his occupation and who discloses such secrets without reason shall be sentenced to imprisonment for not more than one year, short-term imprisonment, or a fine of not more than one thousand yuan.[69] Moreover, Article 318-1, in part deals with technology and the Internet. That is, any person without reason discloses the secrets of another which he knows or possesses through the use of a computer or other relating equipment shall be sentenced to imprisonment of not more than two years, short-term imprisonment, or a fine not more than five thousand yuan. While not referencing the PDPA, it balances offences of cybersecurity and in part, data protection, at least the systems and infrastructure that support the collection and use of personal data. Finally, a person who commits, by using a computer or relating equipment, offenses specified in Articles 316 to 318 shall be sentenced to punishment by increasing it up to one half.[70]

[68] Ibid, Article 315-1 Article 315-2 A person who for purpose of gain provides a locality or an instrument to facilitate another to engage in an act specified in the preceding article shall be sentenced to imprisonment for less than five years and short-term imprisonment; in lieu thereof, or in addition thereto, a fine of not more than five hundred thousand dollars may be imposed. A person who for purpose of dissemination, broadcast, or sale has the act specified in the preceding paragraph shall be subject to the same punishment. An offense of manufacturing, distributing, broadcasting or selling the recorded materials specified in the two preceding paragraphs or item 2 of the preceding article shall be punished in accordance with the provisions of paragraph 1. An attempt to commit an offense specified in the three preceding paragraphs is punishable. Article 315-3 The contents of the recording specified in the preceding two articles and the articles on which the recording is made and the recording articles shall be confiscated whether or not they belong to the offender.

[69] Ibid, Article 317. Article 318 A public official or one who has previously been a public official who discloses without reason commercial or industrial secrets of another that he knows or possesses because of his official position shall be sentenced to imprisonment for not more than two years, short-term imprisonment, or a fine of not more than two thousand yuan.

[70] Ibid, Article 318-1-2. Article 319 Prosecution for an offense specified in Articles 315, 315-1, and 316 through 318-2 may be instituted only upon complaint.

9.9.2 Damages and Class Action

Data subjects have the ability to claim damages and institute a class action for damages where there have been breaches of the PDPA. Arguably there is the beginnings of a statutory Tort where a data subject has incurred an injury caused by any unlawful collection, processing or use of personal data, or other infringement on the rights of data subjects due to such government agency's violation of the PDPA, unless such injury was caused by any natural disaster, emergency or other force majeure event.[71] Specifically though damages will only be awarded where the data subject has had their reputation. Apart from seeking monetary compensation, the data subject can request appropriate corrective measures be taken by the organization responsible to restore their reputation. However, the monetary compensation is limited to an amount NT$500 but no more than NT$20,000 per incident, per person based on the severity of the damage. In the event there are multiple data subjects that are seeking compensation under Article 28, the total amount that can be awarded is NT$200 million. However, if the interests involved in the incident exceed NT$200 million, the compensation shall be up to the value of such interests.

Moreover, for non-government agencies damages under Article 29 extend to any injury caused by any unlawful collection, processing or use of personal data, or other infringement on the rights of data subjects due to such non-government agency's violation of the PDPA, unless the non-government agency can prove that such injury is not caused by its wilful act or negligence.[72]

However, based on the above, there are exception and any claim must be lodged within 2 years of becoming aware of the damage.[73] This again is fluid, although, it would be up to the judiciary or regulator to determine when the person became aware of such damage. Nonetheless, and as expected, incorporated entity or charity that breach the PDPA and where it is proved that data subjects have incurred an injury from that breach, the entity or charity will be liable. However, damages will only be imposed where the total registered assets of an incorporated foundation shall be NT$10 million or more, or the total number of members of an incorporated charity shall be 100 or more; and the protection of personal data shall be set forth as

[71] Personal Data Protection Act 1995, Article 28. If the total amount of damages for the injuries attributable to the same incident exceeds the amount referred to in the preceding paragraph, the compensation payable to each victim shall not be limited to the lower end of damages, i.e. NT$500, per incident as set forth in Paragraph 3 of this Article. The right of claim referred to in Paragraph 2 above may not be transferred or inherited. However, this does not apply to the circumstances where monetary compensation has been agreed upon in a contract or a claim therefor has been filed with the court.

[72] Personal Data Protection Act 1995, Article 29. Paragraphs 2 to 6 of the preceding article apply to the damage claims raised in accordance with the preceding paragraph.

[73] Personal Data Protection Act 1995, Article 30. Article 31 With regard to matters pertaining to damages, aside from the provisions of the PDPA, the State Compensation Law may be applied to a government agency and the Civil Code may be applied to a non-government agency.

one of its purposes in its charter. Additionally, it shall have been established for more than three years following its receipt of the approval.[74]

Finally, the governance arrangements for how law suits are to be filed and where the hearing will take place is governed under Article 33. It requires that any lawsuit filed with the court for damages against a government agency in accordance with the PDPA shall be subject to the exclusive jurisdiction of the district court where the agency is located.[75] The lawsuit against a non-government agency is subject to the exclusive jurisdiction of the district court where its main office, principal place of business or domicile is located. If the non-government agency referred to in the preceding paragraph is a natural person and has no place of domicile in the Republic of China, or the address thereof is unknown, such natural person's place of residence in the Republic of China shall be deemed to be the place of domicile.[76] If the natural person has no place of residence in the Republic of China or the address thereof is unknown, data subjects last known domicile in the Republic of China shall be deemed to be the place of domicile. If the natural person has no last known domicile, the district court where the central government is located shall have exclusive jurisdiction.[77]

Article 34 provides that where the rights of multiple data subjects have been infringed upon due to the same incident, the incorporated foundation or incorporated charity may file a lawsuit with the court in its own name after obtaining a written delegation of litigation rights of at least 20 data subjects. Thus, for this element to be successful a minimum of 20 people need to file. The data subject may withdraw their delegation in writing before the conclusion of the oral argument and the data subjects are to notify the court.[78] The court may issue a public notice, either upon receiving a petition therefor or on its own initiative, informing other data subjects that suffer damages due to the same incident that they may delegate their litigation rights to the incorporated foundation or charity.[79] In conclusion, an incorporated foundation or charity that brings a case to the court in accordance with paragraph 1, if the claim value of the case exceeds NT$600,000, the court fee attributable to the excess portion of the claim value shall be waived.[80]

---

[74] Personal Data Protection Act 1995, Article 32.

[75] Personal Data Protection Act 1995, Article 33. If the non-government agency referred to in Paragraph 1 is a legal person or a group and has no main office, principal place of business, or the addresses thereof are both unknown, the district court where the central government is located shall have exclusive jurisdiction.

[76] Ibid.

[77] Ibid.

[78] Personal Data Protection Act 1995, Article 34.

[79] Ibid. The incorporated foundation or the incorporated charity may expand demand for the relief sought before the conclusion of the oral argument. If other data subjects that suffer damages due to the same incident chose not to delegate their litigation rights pursuant to the preceding paragraph, they may still bring the case to the court within the timeframe specified in the public notice for the court to combine the cases.

[80] Ibid.

9.9.3 *Cyber Security*

Since the late 1990s the criminal laws of Taiwan, were strengthened to enhance their response to cybersecurity. Today, the Criminal Law to deal with cybercrime deals with computer files have been classified as movable property, stealing, copying, or downloading computer files onto a computer or other medium without the owners' permission are regarded as criminal acts. Articles 358 and 359 of the Criminal Code to deal with hackers who gain unauthorized access to proprietary computer systems. Article 358 stipulates that anyone who uses any other person's password without previous permission and/or otherwise gains unauthorized access to proprietary computer systems shall be sentenced to a prison term not more than 3 years and fined not more than NT$100,000. According to Article 359, any person who tries to steal, erase or otherwise change information stored on discs of any person, and whose said act results in serious damage to the latter, shall be sentenced to a prison term of not more than 5 years and fined not more than NT$200,000 (US$1 = NT$35). Thus, there is much to do in Taiwan to address the gaps and shortfall to addressing the interrelationship between data protection, AI and cybersecurity.

9.10 Conclusion

Taiwan, its people and territory have a complex history and storey to tell the world. The current framework is very different to that of China, Hong Kong and Macau. This Chapter has demonstrated that the right to privacy is considered a valuable right in Taiwan. That is, Chapter II, Article 7 of the ROC sets out the rights and duties of is citizens. Article 7 provides that all citizens of the Republic of China, irrespective of sex, religion, ethnic origin, class, or party affiliation, shall be equal before the law. Article 12 further provides citizens with the right to freedom of privacy of correspondence.

However, the constitutional privacy right is limited to correspondence and it is not clear what that actually means in practice. As highlighted above, does this right extend to correspondence over the Internet? This needs to be clarified. The courts have ruled on privacy in Taiwan, although limited. The Civil Code has also had a role in protecting elements of people's rights. However, the evolution of the Civil Code has not been smooth sailing. The Taiwanese Civil Code has been governing Taiwan for over six decades, and during this time, Taiwanese society has changed dramatically from agricultural to an industrial society and underwent political transition from authoritarianism towards democratic rule. It should be noted that, Taiwan's economy continued to expand consistently even under the authoritative rule, and private market economy prospered in the past decades.

The Civil Code 2019 has undertaken reform over a long period of time. Article 18 provides for when one's personality is infringed, the individual may apply to the court for removing. Furthermore, it allows the individual to apply for prevent, when their personality. In the preceding paragraph, an action for damages for emotional distress may be brought only it is otherwise provided by the act. Article 195 states that if a person has wrongfully damaged to the body, health, reputation, liberty, credit, *privacy* or chastity of another, or to another's personality in a severe way, the injured person may claim a reasonable compensation in money even if such injury is not a purely pecuniary loss. If it was reputation that has been damaged, the injured person may also claim the taking of proper measures for the rehabilitation of his reputation. The provisions of the preceding two paragraphs shall be *mutatis mutandis* applied when a person has wrongfully damaged to another's status based on the relationship to their father, mother, sons, daughters, or spouse in a severe way. Thus, privacy can be applied broadly and would include elements of privacy over the Internet. It confirms that an individual would be able to apply a level of tort to a claim of breach of privacy over the Internet.

The Personal Data Protection Act dates back to the 1995, at a time when the EU legislation was a Directive and not a current day Regulation. The PDPA provides an overarching protection of personal data with an extensive scope but has faced a number of problems regarding its implementation due to incorrect perception of the law. Taiwan have been grappling to balance the need for national security while protecting personal data. Along with other jurisdictions around the world, it will not be easy to strike a balance between these prominent interests.

Taiwan has embraced a broad definition that constitutes a person's name, date of birth, ID Card number, passport number, features, fingerprints, marital status, family information, education background, occupation, medical records, healthcare data, genetic data, data concerning a person's sex life, records of physical examination, criminal records, contact information, financial conditions, data concerning a person's social activities and any other information that may be used to directly or indirectly identify a natural person. Rather healthcare personal data, constitutes any other data pertaining to checkups or treatments implemented by physicians or other medical professionals for the purpose of treating, correcting or preventing diseases, harms or disabilities of human body or for other legitimate medical reasons, or shall mean other data produced from the prescription, medication, operation or disposition based on the findings of the above-mentioned checkups.

Moreover, personal data that would include genetics, means the information on a heredity unit, consisting of one segment of DNA of human body, for controlling the specific functions thereof. The sex life of an individual is considered sacrament, and personal data that discloses this information and data constitutes the personal data on sexual orientation or sexual habits. It has been argued that on the face of this definition, it appears that most if not all data that can be personal, which could be collected by AI is covered. However, as AI systems become increasingly complex and part of the home, it is questionable whether this definition will capture all the personal data these systems might. This will be particularly important for children. It is our view that to fully cover off on AI, it is advisable that Taiwan consider inserting the term Artificial Intelligence into the definition, or the definition of personal data into the PDPA.

The concept of consent in Taiwan has been coupled with the need for the data subject to be informed. As highlighted in other chapters the concept of concept is also going to challenge the regulatory framework along with AI technology. Consent comes in the form of actual, express or presumed-implied consent. Furthermore, a requirement of agencies, both public and private inform the data subject of certain points of collection, processing and use of that data. This includes informing the data subject of the name of the government or non-government agency, along with the purpose of the collection of the personal data, and the categories of data collected. Additionally, the data subject is to be informed of the time period, territory, recipients, and methods of data use, their rights. However, there are exceptions to the obligation to inform the data subject and apply to circumstances where notification may be waived in accordance with the law; the collection of personal data is necessary for the government agency to perform its statutory duties or the non-government agency to fulfil its statutory obligation. The right to inform goes some way to addressing the potential issues in AI. The issue with the current provision(s), it is limited to the above, and begs the question how do data subjects be informed through AI.

Finally, the criminalisation of data offences related to personal data is also present in Taiwan. Additionally, the criminalisation of computer files has been classified as movable property, stealing, copying, or downloading computer files onto a computer or other medium without the owners' permission are regarded as criminal acts. Thus, the beginnings of cybersecurity and data protection have converged. However, what this Chapter did not examine was the extent of laws surrounding the protection of networks, systems and infrastructure that support the use of personal data and AI.

References

Chang, C. H. (2015). *Eyes on the road program in Taiwan – Information privacy issues under the Taiwan personal data protection act*, 31 J. Marshall J. Info. Tech. & Privacy L. 145.

Chen, T. F. (2011). Transplant of civil code in Japan, Taiwan, and China: With the focus of legal evolution. *Taiwan University Law Review, 6*(1), 389.

Pemng, S. Y. (2003). Privacy and the construction of legal meaning in Taiwan. *The International Lawyer, 37*(4), 1037.

Chapter 10
Lao

Abstract Formerly known as Laos, the Lao People's Democratic Republic (Lao PDR) is a small developing country in South East Asia. Over the past decade, Lao has established a number of laws to strengthen their response to cyber security intrusions and to a lesser extent the protection of personal data. That is, the Government of the Lao PDR has enacted a slew of technology and data related laws including: (a) the Law on Electronic Transactions (No. 02/NA, 7 December 2012); (b) Law on Prevention and Combating of Cyber Crime (No. 61/NA, 15 July 2015); (c) Law on Information and Communication Technology (No. 02/NA, 7 November 2016); and (d) Law on the Protection of Electronic Data (No. 25/NA, 12 May 2017). Furthermore, the Ministry of Post and Telecommunications has also implemented the Instruction on Computer Security (No. 3623/MPT, 11 December 2017), under Law on Prevention and Combating of Cyber Crime.

Lao finds itself in a region of the world where the growth in digital technology is growing at one of the fastest rates. Southeast Asia is the world's fastest growing Internet region with nearly four million new users coming online every month over the coming years (Ibid). This translates into a user base of 480 million. There are over 700 million active mobile connections in Southeast Asia. (Ibid) Online spending is expected to reach US$ 200 billion by 2025. This means that there will be a flourishing digital economy if every one of the 480 million users are secure and cross- border transactions are not hijacked by hackers (Ibid).

However, these laws are silent with respect to artificial intelligence and given the nature of how laws are issued it is likely that in due course new laws will be introduced to cover this activity. Assessing how these laws operate has been problematic given the lack of publicly available information.

Noteworthy too, is the emerging area of specific data protection law in the state of Lao. That is, it appears there is little to no appetite for dedicated data protection laws. The current legal framework is further limited as they do not fully accept and account for the OECD or ASEAN data protection principles outlined in Chap. 3. This, could in itself be problematic as the region becomes increasingly digitised.

R. Walters, M. Novak, *Cyber Security, Artificial Intelligence, Data Protection & the Law*, https://doi.org/10.1007/978-981-16-1665-5_10

Furthermore, the laws in Lao are structured differently form the other states that have been examined in this book.

10.1 Introduction

The Lao People's Democratic Republic (Lao PDR) is a landlocked country in South East Asia which occupies approximately 235,000 square kilometres. With a population of just over 7 million people it borders China, Vietnam, Thailand, Cambodia and Myanmar (formerly known as Burma). Beginning in the 14th century the country was ruled by the Lao monarchy for more than three hundred years.[1] In the 1700s the country was occupied by Siam (now Thailand) and in the late 1800s French colonial government was installed. It was during this time that French economic and strategic interests largely shaped what are now the current borders of Laos.[2] Michel Lorrillard believes that history of Lao is somewhat confusing and not so clear as first thought. He states that Lao history of the 60-odd years between 1887 and 1953 is in fact the history of the gestation of this new geographical and political entity, caused by the brutal irruption of colonial power into the region.[3] This power then replaced imprecise and fluid traditional 'boundaries' with a clear and fixed demarcation that was formalized by cartography. The treaties that France signed, beginning in 1893 with Siam, Great Britain and China, were designed not to return to the Lao the territories of their former kingdoms, but rather to legitimize French claims over a vast space that they considered strategic.[4] The borders of Laos have never matched those of the unified Lan Xang (mid fourteenth to late seventeenth centuries), which was a realm of uncertain geography, and whose power was probably more political and economic than territorial.[5]

Nonetheless, in 1945 independence was declared but this unfortunately resulted in several years of internal instability. It was not until after the Indo-China Wars that the Lao People's Democratic Republic was established in 1975.[6] Since that time there has been economic reform.[7] Fifty years on and Lao joined ASEAN in 1997, whereby, it is apparent that this association has encouraged the creation of significant laws with

---

[1] Evans, G, *A Short History of Laos: The Land in Between*, Allen and Unwin (2002). see also Church, P, *A Short History of South East Asia* 2017 John Wiley and Sons 74–87.

[2] Ibid xiii–xiv.

[3] Lorrillard, M, *Lao history revisited Paradoxes and problems in current research. South East Asia Research, IP Publishing*, (2006) 387–401.

[4] Ibid.

[5] Ibid.

[6] See 'Laos: The Transformation of Periphery Socialism' in A Croissant, Lorenz, P, *Comparative Politics of South East Asia: An Introduction to Governments and Political regimes* (2018) Springer 113–141.

[7] S Kim *Transition to E-Governance in Laos*, A Dissertation Presented to the Faculty of the Graduate School of Cornell University in partial fulfillment of the Requirements for the degree of Master of Public Administration May 2018.

respect to cybersecurity and changes in technology.[8] Restrictions on foreign investment were relaxed during the 1980s and this led to the development of infrastructure but significant numbers of people are still impoverished.[9] Lao PDR is not part of APEC but is a member of the WTO (World Trade Organisation).[10] Nevertheless, in September 2016, a Master Plan on ASEAN Connectivity 2025 (MPAC 2025) was developed to address this digital technology aspect of the 2025 vision focusing on five strategic areas: sustainable infrastructure, digital innovation, seamless logistics, regulatory excellence and people mobility. This is particularly important to ASEAN member states. It provides a clear platform for states to expand and integrate technology across the public and private sphere. For instance, Malaysia established the world's first Digital Free Trade Zone in 2017. On the other side, its neighbour, Thailand has developed a multi- year blueprint to develop digital capabilities in all sectors of the economy. Indonesia is focusing its attention on helping its SMEs digitise their operations. Singapore has a Smart City initiative and Vietnam has been busy investing in digital infrastructure. These initiatives, while fragmented are likely to converge as states develop their specific data protection laws.[11]

More importantly, Lao finds itself in a region of the world where the growth in digital technology is growing at one of the fastest rates. That is, it is well understood that there are opportunities abound for Southeast Asia in digital technology. To put it in context, Southeast Asia is the world's fastest growing Internet region with nearly four million new users coming online every month over the coming years.[12] This translates into a user base of 480 million by 2020. There are over 700 million active mobile connections in Southeast Asia. Online spending is expected to reach US$ 200 billion by 2025. This means that there will be a flourishing digital economy if every one of the 480 million users.[13]

On the backdrop of the above, the current constitution was promulgated in 1991 and was subsequently amended in 2003 and 2015. It comprises of 14 Chapters with a total of 119 Articles.[14] In Chapter IV Fundamental Rights and Obligations of Citizens are documented in Articles 34–51 of the Constitution. Amongst many rights, individuals have been afforded the right to the freedom of speech, assembly and religion but there is no right of privacy. Article 44 specifies "[t]he right of Lao

---

[8] Ibid.

[9] Alston, P, *Lao PDR's Economic Strategy Entrenches Poverty* Special Rapporteur, Human Rights, Office of the High Commissioner, United Nations 28 March 2019 https://www.ohchr.org/EN/NewsEvents/Pages/DisplayNews.aspx?NewsID=24416&LangID=E

[10] Asia Pacific Economic Cooperation, https://www.apec.org/About-Us/About-APEC/Member-Economies.aspx. World Trade Organisation https://www.wto.org/english/thewto_e/countries_e/lao_e.htm

[11] Gan, TT, Cyber Risk Leader, Deloitte Southeast Asia, Data and privacy protection in ASEAN – what does it mean for businesses in the region? 2028 https://www2.deloitte.com/content/dam/Deloitte/sg/Documents/risk/sea-risk-data-privacy-in-asean.pdf

[12] Ibid.

[13] Ibid.

[14] *Constitution of the Lao People's Democratic Republic* (Revised 2015) No 63/NA Vientiane 8 December 2015 https://www.policinglaw.info/assets/downloads/2015_Constitution_of_Laos_(English_translation).pdf

citizens by their lives, bodies, dignities and shelters are inviolable. Lao citizens cannot be arrested or searched without warrant order from the Public Prosecutor or the people's courts, unless otherwise enforced by the laws."[15] This is the closest the Constitution comes to in protecting privacy.

Lao PDR signed the International Covenant on Civil and Political Rights in 2000 and ratified the convention in 2009 but it has yet to sign the optional protocol which would give jurisdiction to the UN Human Rights Committee to hear complaints.[16] In 2012, the Decree and Law on Electronic Transactions was issued by the National Assembly of the Ministry of Science and Technology.[17] This defined electronic documents for use in contracts and evidence before a court.[18] It established how electronic data should be stored so that the identification of the originator and addressee together with the time and date would be preserved.[19] In addition digital signatures and the activities of certification authorities were also included.[20] Responsibilities of intermediaries are outlined and the Ministry of Posts and Telecommunications was identified as being the responsible authority for developing regulations and procedures.[21]

In 2014, the Decree and Law on Internet Information Management was issued by the National Assembly with the Ministry of Posts and Telecommunication being the responsible agency.[22] This is the first time the Internet is recognised in law. The Decree includes references to social media and requires users to correctly identify their names and current address when disseminating information.[23] Website Managers are required to prevent any content as defined in Article 10 from being disseminated. This includes material concerning bribery, terrorism, pornography, false information and the distribution of user's personal information although the latter is not defined.[24] The Ministry has responsibility in coordinating related parties including the monitoring and inspection of information on the Internet.[25] Any violation of the Decree may

[15] Ibid, Article 44.

[16] United Nations, Human Rights, Office of the High Commissioner, Status of Ratification Interactive Dashboard https://indicators.ohchr.org

[17] Decree and Law on Electronic Transaction No. 20/NA, dated 7 December 2012, Ministry of Science and Technology, Issuing Date: 2012-12-07. See Part 1 General Provisions, Article 3 Definitions.

[18] Ibid Part II Contracts, Data Messages and Electronic Documents. Chapter 1 Electronic Contracts. See also Chapter 3 Electronic Documents, Articles 13–15.

[19] Ibid See Chapter 3 Electronic Documents, Articles 16–18.

[20] Ibid Chapter 1 Types of Electronic Signatures, Articles 19–22, Chapter 2 General Requirements of Electronic Signatures, Articles 23–25, Chapter 3 Specific Requirements for Secure Digital Signatures, Articles 26–30.

[21] Ibid Part V Intermediary, Articles 33–35.

[22] Decree on Internet Information Management No. 327/GOV, dated 16 September 2014, Ministry of Posts and Telecommunications, Issuing Date: 2014-09-16.

[23] Decree on Internet Information Management above n 15, Section II Dissemination of Information on the Internet, Article 8 Creating a Personal Account on Social Media.

[24] Decree on Internet Information Management above n 15, Section V Restrictions, Articles 10 and 17. See also Article 15.

[25] Decree on Internet Information Management above n 15, Section V Restrictions, Article 23.

result in a violator being 'warned, educated, penalised, fined and subject to civil or criminal charges'.[26] Therefore, this chapter will only discuss the law on Resistance and Prevention of Cybercrime, and the Law on Electronic Data Protection.

10.2 Prevention of Cybercrime

The Law on Resistance and Prevention of Cybercrime was issued in 2015.[27] This is a very extensive Decree by comparison to earlier laws and contains more than 60 Articles. Cybercrime is defined as the 'wrongful act in the computer system that causes loss'.[28] Activities include disclosure of safeguard measures, unauthorised access, censoring of data, theft, dissemination of pornography, forgery and destruction.[29] The Ministry of Post and Telecommunications has responsibility for cybercrime resistance and prevention activities which include training courses, knowledge sharing on cyber safety, developing data protection activities, emergency safeguarding and the collection of statistics.[30]

10.3 Definition of Personal Data

Personal data is defined as 'data related to or referred directly to the character or activity of individuals, legal entities or organisations in a direct or indirect way'.[31] In addition, they have defined the term "User Data", to mean any data sending to the user, such as postal address, electronic address, geographical address, Internet code number, telephone number or others that being used in the computerized system. This is important because, it expand on the definition of personal data by providing the general personal identifiers that generally identify a person. Thus, it is argued that both terms would likely need to be read concurrently to understand how personal data is defined across the Lao state.

[26] Decree on Internet Information Management above n 15, Section VIII Final Provisions, Article 27. See also Section VII Implementation Measures, Article 26.

[27] Law on Resistance and Prevention of Cybercrime No 61/NA dated 15 July 2015, Responsible Agency: Ministry of Posts and Telecommunications, Issuing Date: 2015-07-15. See also Guidelines on the Implementation of the Law on Counter and Prevention of Cybercrime No 2543/MPT, dated 24 September 2018, Responsible Agency: Ministry of Posts and Telecommunications, Issuing Date: 2019-04-08.

[28] Ibid Part 1 General Provisions, Article 2 Cybercrime Resistance and Prevention.

[29] Ibid Article 8 Cybercrime-Prone Behaviour.

[30] Ibid Chapter 1 Cybercrime Resistance and Prevention Activities Article 19. See also Article 24.

[31] Ibid Part 1 General Provisions, Article 3 Definition of Terms.

Notwithstanding the above, viruses, malicious code and phishing are also defined.[32] That is, a virus has been defined to mean a special program being created which can be expanded, cause damages and destroy the computerized system, computer network and computer data. Additionally, malicious code refers to a set of computer command created in order to destroy the computerized system or to steal the computer data. Yet, phishing refers to any newly created website that is similar to the former one in order to deceive data from the users. While not specifically referring to personal data or data that can identify a person, the respective definition does mention data generally. Thus, it is argued that data generally would also include personal data. However, without any clear authority to clarify this position, further clarification is needed for the regulator or the courts to confirm this position.

In 2017, the Ministry of Post and Telecommunications has issued the Instruction on Computer Security (No. 3623/MPT) under Law on Prevention and Combating of Cyber Crime. While, at the time of writing this book there was no an English version of the Instruction, the brief information available highlights it establishes a minimum to be adhered to by businesses on: (i) setting up and protecting networks; (ii) managing and using networks; (iii) maintaining security standards; (iv) coordination and cooperation with the Computer Emergency Prevention and Solution Center in case of emergencies; and (v) monitoring of cyber threats.[33] Kirsty Newby notes that with respect to electronic data, under the Law on the Protection of Electronic Data, data managers (which includes individuals, businesses or legal entities which manage electronic data) need to consider what authorizations and processes are required to be followed for: (i) data collection; (ii) maintenance of electronic data; (iii) utilization and dissemination of electronic data; (iv) domestic or international transmission and transfers of electronic data; and (v) deleting electronic data. What is not apparent, is whether the Instruction goes some way to defining personal data or providing for the concept of consent.[34]

10.4 Regulator

The Centre for Deterring and Solving Computer Emergencies is established 'as a secretariat for the Ministry of Post and Telecommunications'.[35] Amongst many duties the Centre is to study and propose regulations to the Ministry, coordinate with other relevant sectors and to deal with foreign countries with respect to

[32] Ibid. Article 3 Definition of Terms (11) Virus, (12) Malicious Code and (13) Phishing.

[33] Newby, K, *Lao PDR Legal Alert: New Data and IT Security Standards applicable to Companies: Are You Compliant?* https://www.dfdl.com/resources/legal-and-tax-updates/lao-pdr-legal-alert-new-data-and-it-security-standards-applicable-to-companies-are-you-compliant/

[34] Ibid.

[35] Ibid Chapter 3 The Centre for Deterring and Solving Computer Emergencies.

cybercrime resistance and prevention.[36] International cooperation includes the provision of technical assistance.[37] Requests from foreign countries for mutual legal assistance are also catered for if sufficient detail of the necessity for assistance is established, a summary of the data involved is produced and legal reference involving the accused person is provided.[38] Such requests are also confidential.[39] Extensive prohibitions are detailed for service providers and officials.[40] They include abuse of power and social unrest.[41] The process of investigation and interrogation is also outlined.[42] Ultimately the Ministry of Post and Telecommunications is responsible although duties are also shared at the city and district/municipality levels.[43] Responsibilities are also conferred on other sectors of Government.[44] Power to conduct inspections is shared between the Ministry and other government organs including the National Assembly, the State Audit Authority and the Anti-Corruption Authority.[45] Rewards are available for parties 'who show outstanding performance in implementation of this law' although no details are provided.[46] Measures against violators are the same as documented above.[47] They include being warned, educated, penalised and fined. Penal measures include imprisonment together with a fine being imposed on the following basis:[48]

[36] Ibid Article 31.

[37] Ibid, Part IV International Cooperation in Cybercrime Resistance and Prevention, Articles 33–34.

[38] Ibid Articles 35–16.

[39] Ibid Article 38.

[40] Law on Resistance and Prevention of Cybercrime, Article 39–41.

[41] Law on Resistance and Prevention of Cybercrime, Articles 41(4)–(5) and 39(2).

[42] Law on Resistance and Prevention of Cybercrime, Part VI Investigation-Interrogation of Computerised System Cases.

[43] Law on Resistance and Prevention of Cybercrime, Part VII Management and Inspection, Chapter 1 Management, Article 48–51.

[44] Law on Resistance and Prevention of Cybercrime, Article 52.

[45] Law on Resistance and Prevention of Cybercrime, Part VII Management and Inspection, Chapter 2 Inspection, Articles 53–55.

[46] Law on Resistance and Prevention of Cybercrime, Part VIII Rewards for Persons with Outstanding Performance and Measures against Violators, Article 56.

[47] Law on Resistance and Prevention of Cybercrime, Articles 57–59. See also the Decree on Internet Information Management, Section VIII Final Provisions, Article 27.

[48] Law on Resistance and Prevention of Cybercrime, Part VIII Rewards for Persons with Outstanding Performance and Measures against Violators, Article 62 Penal Measures.

10.4.1 Criminal Offences and Penalties

Criminal offence	Imprisonment	+ Fine (Kips)
(1) Revelation of Computer Access	1–12 months	1–4 million
(2) Unauthorised Access	3–12 months	2–5 million
(3) Censor Content	3–12 months	3–10 million
(4) Data Theft	3–36 months	4–20 million
(5) Damage from Social Media	5–36 months	4–20 million
(6) Pornography Published	12–60 months	5–30 million
(7) Interference with Computer	12–60 months	5–30 million
(8) False Data	12–60 months	12–60 million
(9) Destroy Data	36–60 months	5–30 million
(10) Operate Cybercrime Business	36–60 months	10–50 million

Law on Resistance and Prevention of Cybercrime No 61/NA dated 15 July 2015, Responsible Agency: Ministry of Posts and Telecommunications, Issuing Date: 2015-07-15, Article 62 Penal Provisions.

A civil fine may also be imposed in accordance with Article 60. There are three types of offences. The first is the provision of incorrect computer data to government authorities which incurs a penalty of 1.5–2 million kips. The second offence is the failure to provide computer data within a set period of time and the penalty is 2.5–3 million kips. The third offence is the deletion of 'data in a computer system or computer data of other persons without authorisation' and the fine is 4–5 million kips.[49]

10.5 Electronic Data Protection

In 2017 the Law on Electronic Data Protection was issued.[50] Several new terms are introduced. They include 'Data Owner' which is the individual or organisation that owns the data, 'Official Data' is data relating to government activities, 'Electronic Data Administration Authorities' are Ministries, service providers and banks, and the 'Computer Emergency Interception and Resolution Centre' is part of the Ministry of Posts and telecommunication.[51]

[49] Law on Resistance and Prevention of Cybercrime, Article 9.

[50] Law on Electronic Data Protection 25/NA, Date 12 May 2017, Responsible Agency Ministry of Posts and Telecommunications, Issuing Date: 2017-11-15.

[51] Ibid, Article 3 Definitions, (10) Data Owner, (11) Official Data, (14) Electronic Data Administration Authorities and (18) Computer Emergency Interception and Resolution Centre.

A distinction is made between general and specific data.[52] The former is data of individuals or organisations that may be accessed or distributed and the only requirement is that the source must be indicated.[53] The latter is data that may only be used or disclosed with the consent of the data owner and it can include both official and personal material.[54] When data is collected the nature and purpose must be disclosed to the data owner.[55] There is also a need for the Data Administration Authority to use or disclose personal data only after approval has been granted by the Data Owner.[56] The same applies for the sending or transferring of data with the requirement that the receiver is able to securely store the material.[57] This also applies to when data is sent outside the country. A Data Owner is in control of their data. They can make a request to Data Administration to update or edit the material or to stop transferring the data.[58] The Data Administration must respond. There is also an obligation upon the Data administration authority to delete data when the particular purpose has been fulfilled.[59] Official data must also be ranked according to the following scale; namely, Level 1 where data disclosure or destruction causes damage. Level 2 serious damage occurs or Level 3 it damages national security.[60]

Data Owners have the right to delete their data and the obligation to ensure the data is correct.[61] Arguably they are considered to be equivalent to data controllers and processors that are established by law in other states. The Data Administrative Authority also has rights with respect to interception, inspection and suspension of services where data adversely affects society.[62] Obligations include securing the data and coordinating with the Ministry.[63] Disputes may be settled by the parties themselves, before the Administrative Authority, by the Economic Dispute Settlement Organisation or before the People's Courts.[64] The Ministry of Post and Telecommunications is the responsible agency although obligations are imposed on provincial, district, municipality and city levels of government.[65] Like the Law on Resistance and Prevention of Cybercrime in 2015 rewards are available for outstanding conduct together with measures for violators that include warnings,

[52] Ibid, Chapter 2 Types of Electronic Data, Article 8.

[53] Ibid, Article 9 General Data.

[54] Ibid, Article 10 Specific Data.

[55] Ibid, Chapter 3 Electronic Data Protection Tasks, Article 12 Data Collection.

[56] Ibid, Article 16 Using and Disclosing Data.

[57] Ibid, Article 17 Sending or Transferring of Electronic Data.

[58] Ibid, Article 19 Updating or Editing of Electronic Data.

[59] Ibid, Article 20 Deleting of Electronic Data.

[60] Ibid, Chapter 4 The Measures on Securing of Electronic Data, Articles 21–23.

[61] Ibid, Article 5 Rights and Obligations of the Data Owner, Articles 27–28.

[62] Ibid, Chapter 6 Rights and Obligations of the Data Administration Authority, Article 29 rights of the Data Administration Authority.

[63] Ibid, Article 30 Obligations of Data Administration Authority.

[64] Ibid, Chapter 8 Dispute Settlement, Articles 34–39.

[65] Law on Electronic Data Protection above n 42, Chapter 9 The Administration of Electronic Data Protection, Articles 40–44.

education, civil and criminal sanctions.[66] Activities which are not criminal will result in 15 million kip fines being imposed.[67]

10.6 Consent

Interestingly, neither of the laws discussed above provide for the concept of consent. While this is for Lao to decide the concept of consent for the collection and use of personal data should be reflected in the legal framework, not doing anything, places the law out of step with regional countries.

On the backdrop of the above, the Instruction on Computer Safety[68] (Instruction) supports the implementation of Article 24 of the Law on the Prevention and Defence of Cybercrime that relating to the specific measures on governing computer safety in order for the creation, prevention, management, surveillance and monitor on computer safety are united throughout the country. While there is no definition of personal data, it does provide a level of data protection. In other words, section 6 requires that computer restoration be undertaken to prevent any damage to the systems and infrastructure. Indirectly this requirement does go some way to ensuring a level of protection to personal data. More importantly, there is a requirement that the storage of data is safe, in particular, the names, date and time on the coming in-out of people at data centre shall be recorded.[69] It is argued that this data would constitute personal data, although limited. A further protection mechanism for data also includes the requirement to undertake a risk assessment, for the detection of computer networks, operators, and impact assessment of the potential damages to an organisation. The impact assessment has similarities to the impact assessments required under data protection laws of other states. However, Lao do not go into detail of what the impact assessment would examine.

---

[66] Law on Electronic Data Protection above n 42, Chapter 11 Policies toward Persons with Outstanding Achievements and Measures Against Violators, Articles 48–54. See also Law on Resistance and Prevention of Cybercrime above n 20, Part VIII Rewards for Persons with Outstanding Performance and Measures against Violators.

[67] Law on Electronic Data Protection above n 42, Chapter 11 Policies toward Persons with Outstanding Achievements and Measures Against Violators, Articles 48–54. See also Article 31 General Prohibition, Article 32 Prohibition for the Data Owner and Article 33 Prohibition for the Data Administration Authority.

[68] Pursuant to Law No. 61/NA, dated 15th July 2015 on the Prevention and Defence of Cybercrime. Pursuant to Prime Ministerial Decree No. 22/PM, dated 16th January 2017 on the Organizational Structure and Activity of the Ministry of Posts and Telecommunications.

[69] Ibid.

10.7 Conclusion

The laws of Lao are comprehensive with respect to cybersecurity but there is no reference to artificial intelligence. However, to date, it has been a fragmented approach towards data protection. The respective laws are limited and quite broad. Yet, and on the other hand, they serve the Lao state well as they develop their legal framework and digital economy. Given the nature of issuing laws in Lao one would expect direct reference to be made rather than it being a matter of construction based upon interpretation. The existing laws place emphasis upon the control of data rather than notions of privacy. Arguably they are focused, to date, in regulating and protecting cyber incursions, rather than specifically protecting personal data. There are, however, limited protection in relation to data protection.

The current legal framework is limited in adopting the principles espoused by the OECD and ASEAN such as transparency, accountability, consent and more importantly defining personal data or personal information. Not specifically providing for consent and defining personal data will pose significant challenges for the adoption of AI. It has the potential to leave and expose the most vulnerable of Lao society to individuals and entities within the state but also in third countries to easily gain access to the personal data of its citizens (particularly – children). More pervasively, and unlike other laws examined in this book, the laws are neither specific or descriptive on whether they provide for special protection for children, by setting an age limit. While it is understood that it is likely an age limit may exist in other laws of the state, third countries are specifically implementing laws that provide for specific protections to children to a certain age.

Assessing how these laws operate is also problematic due to the lack of publicly available information. Reliance has been placed upon English translations available from the Lao Services Portal which is managed by the Department of Foreign Trade Policy in the Ministry of Industry and Commerce.[70] There is no doubt that the Lao People's Democratic Republic regards data protection important and that key developments have occurred especially with regard to cybercrime.

The Ministry of Science and Technology initially took responsibility but within two years the Ministry of Post and Telecommunications assumed control. This shift in the responsible agency might be considered a minor administrative concern but it represents a change in attitude with how digital technology is viewed. Digital technology is not so much a technical development but a form of communication like posting a letter and using a telephone. The technology itself largely becomes invisible and the focus is on content flowing through the pipes or wires. The influence of neighbouring nation states will also continue to shape activities. In 2016 the ASEAN Telecommunications and Information Technology Ministers adopted a Framework

[70] Lao Services Portal, Department of Foreign Trade Policy in the Ministry of Industry and Commerce on behalf of all Government Agencies http://www.laoservicesportal.gov.la

which was an expression of intention on Personal Data Protection and this has largely been implemented in the 2017 Law on Electronic Data Protection.[71]

At the state level there are signs that Lao has taken an integrated approach towards cyber security and data protection. However, it is our view that they have a way to go and would benefit from working with ASEAN states to implement that regional programs. In another words, from a cyber risk perspective, the importance of data security and privacy cannot be further emphasised in, the face of such staggering numbers and potential socio- economic impact. An ASEAN Framework on Personal Data Protection was adopted in November 2016, establishing a set of principles to guide the implementation of measures at both national and regional levels to promote and strengthen personal data protection in the region.[72] Unfortunately, there has been little to no commentary from legal experts or scholars on Lao's data protection framework. Even though, Lao appear to have little appetite for establishing specific data protection laws, this may impede their economic digital integration with other ASEAN member states. It will further limit their ability to influence the future direction of data protection, and impede their ability to benefit from the trade in personal data, and the benefits this economic activity would bring to the state.

References

Church, P. (2017). *A short history of South East Asia* (pp. 74–87). Wiley.

Evans, G. (2002). *A short history of Laos: The land in between.* Allen and Unwin.

Lorenz, P. (2018). *Comparative politics of South East Asia: An introduction to governments and political regimes* (pp. 113–141). Springer.

Lorrillard, M. (2006). *Lao history revisited paradoxes and problems in current research. South East Asia research* (pp. 387–401). IP Publishing.

[71] Framework on Personal Data Protection, ASEAN Telecommunications and Information Technology Ministers Meeting (TELMIN) 25 November 2016 https://asean.org/storage/2012/05/10-ASEAN-Framework-on-PDP.pdf

[72] Gan, TT, Cyber Risk Leader, Deloitte Southeast Asia, Data and privacy protection in ASEAN – what does it mean for businesses in the region? https://www2.deloitte.com/content/dam/Deloitte/sg/Documents/risk/sea-risk-data-privacy-in-asean.pdf

Chapter 11
Vietnam

Abstract Vietnam, located in South East Asia and a member of ASEAN has a complex history. Vietnam is the easternmost country on the Indochina Peninsula of South East Asia. With an estimated 90.5 million inhabitants, it is the world's 14th-most- populous country, and the eighth-most-populous Asian country (Yılmaz, O, *History of Vietnam and Socialist Republic of Vietnam* ed. https://www.academia.edu/22247531/History_of_Vietnam_and_Socialist_Republic_of_Vietnam-Ed._Oğuzhan_Yılmaz). The name Vietnam translates as "Southern Viet" (synonymous with the much older term Nam Viet); it was first officially adopted in 1802 by Emperor Gia Long. The name was formally adopted again in 1945 with the founding of the Democratic Republic of Vietnam under Ho Chi Minh.

There is no specific constitutional recognition of a right to privacy in Vietnam. They have, to date, taken a sectorial approach to personal data regulation. More importantly, there is no specific data protection laws. Over a relatively short period of time, a series of laws have been issued which regulate personal data. Commencing in 2005 the Law of E-Transactions asserted that data messages could be used to form contracts and they could also be used as evidence before the court. In addition, the use of digital certificates and signatures was established. The Civil Code, Law No. 33/2005/QH11 has also established rights for the citizens of Vietnam. Two years later, the 2007 Information Technology Law was enacted and identified prohibited acts and specified that data could only be acquired with consent and that it had to be securely stored. Furthermore, the law recognized the need for children's privacy to be protected. Disabled people were also to be provided with a favourable environment online.

R. Walters, M. Novak, *Cyber Security, Artificial Intelligence, Data Protection & the Law*, https://doi.org/10.1007/978-981-16-1665-5_11

Three years later, the 2010 Law on protection of Consumer Rights extended information handling principles that had been previously introduced. In 2016 the Law on Network Information Security significantly expanded state controls on information. This included use of cryptography. Conducting business in network information security required a government license and company's core staff had to be Vietnamese citizens permanently residing in Vietnam. These efforts were further strengthened by the 2018 Law on Cybersecurity. This law came into effect on 1 January 2019, and identifies various threats and attacks. Most controversially it requires service providers to monitor the flow of information and to prevent certain prohibited materials from being distributed. Service providers, both foreign and domestic are also required to authenticate the identity of their users. Records must also be kept in Vietnam of user activities. This data is also to be provided to Government agencies upon request. There are no presently existing laws with respect to artificial intelligence. Given the pace within which laws have been issued recently, regulations regarding the use of artificial intelligence may be expected. Thus, this Chapter highlights that, yet another country has adopted a sectorial approach to protecting personal data.

11.1 Introduction

Like its neighbours and countries throughout the region Vietnam has experienced colonization, war and conflict, and has been influenced by several different dynasties, empires and states. The current day Socialist Republic of Vietnam is the eastern most country on the Indochina Peninsula in Southeast Asia. With an estimated 90.5 million inhabitants as of 2014, it is the world's 14th-most- populous country, and the eighth-most-populous Asian country.[1] The name Vietnam translates as "Southern Viet" (synonymous with the much older term Nam Viet); it was first officially adopted in 1802 by Emperor Gia Long, and was adopted again in 1945 with the founding of the Democratic Republic of Vietnam under Ho Chi Minh. The country is bordered by China to the north, Laos to the northwest, Cambodia to the southwest, and Malaysia across the South China Sea to the south- east. Its capital city has been Hanoi since the reunification of North and South Vietnam in 1975.[2]

Vietnam was part of Imperial China for over a millennium, from 111 BC to AD 939. The Vietnamese became independent in 939, following the Vietnamese victory in the Battle of Bạch Đằng River.[3] However, successive Vietnamese royal dynasties flourished as the nation expanded geographically and politically into Southeast Asia, until the Indochina Peninsula was colonized by the French in the

[1] Yılmaz O, *History of Vietnam and Socialist Republic of Vietnam* ed. https://www.academia.edu/22247531/History_of_Vietnam_and_Socialist_Republic_of_Vietnam-Ed._Oğuzhan_Yılmaz

[2] Ibid.

[3] Ibid.

mid-nineteenth century.[4] Following Japanese occupation in the 1940s, the Vietnamese fought French rule in the First Indochina War, eventually expelling the French in 1954. What followed resulted in Vietnam being divided politically into two rival states, North and South Vietnam. Conflict between the two sides intensified, with heavy intervention from the United States, in what is known as the Vietnam War. The war ended with a North Vietnamese victory in 1975.

Throughout their long history, the Vietnamese have been exposed to many different religious influences.[5] The result is a mosaic of many of the world's great faiths. Although some Vietnamese practice more than one religion at a time, most consider themselves Buddhists (55 percent).[6] Buddhists believe in reincarnation and karmic destiny (if a man is good in this life, he/she will be rewarded with a better life after he/she is reincarnated). Taoism and Confucianism are also widely practiced. Vietnamese is the main language, spoken by 85 percent of the population with minor regional accents.[7] Other than the official Vietnamese language, Chinese, French, English, Khmer, and tribal languages are used. Khmer is spoken by the Cambodian minority in the south and Chinese is used by two million ethnic Chinese. English is widely spoken among the emerging middle class and the political and economic elite. French language use is diminishing, despite popularity among the elderly. The majority of media is in Vietnamese, although some stations and publications can be found in English and French. Most business will involve English speaking Vietnamese.[8]

Despite their complex beginnings, Vietnam has emerged as a strong developing nation, who is a member of ASEAN. The current legal system of Vietnam is based on the ideologies of the former Soviet Union. The Soviet legal system is based on the civil law system together with modifications from Leninist ideology. Vietnam relied deeply on the support of Soviet Union during the war and after reunification in 1975. The resulting effect was that the 1980 Constitution was drafted based on the constitution of Soviet Union as a significant example for reference.

The current day Constitution of Vietnam 2013 Preamble states that "beginning in 1930, under the leadership of the Communist Party of Vietnam, formed and trained by President Ho Chi Minh, our People waged a protracted revolutionary struggle full of hardships and sacrifices for independence, freedom of the nation and happiness of the People. In the wake of the triumph of the August Revolution, on 2 September 1945, President Ho Chi Minh announced the Declaration of Independence, declaring the birth of the Democratic Republic of Vietnam which is now the Socialist Republic of Vietnam. With the will and the power of the entire nation as well as with the assistance of friends across the world, our People have gained great victories in

[4] Ibid.

[5] United States Department of Defense Intelligence Production Program (DoDIPP), Vietnam Country Handbook, https://info.publicintelligence.net/MCIA-VietnamHandbook.pdf

[6] Ibid.

[7] Ibid.

[8] Ibid.

national liberation wars, unified the country, defended the Fatherland and fulfilled international duties, attained great achievements of historical significance in the cause of restructuring, leading the nation to socialism. Institutionalising the Platform of national construction during the transitional period towards socialism, inheriting the 1946 Constitution, 1959 Constitution, 1980 Constitution, and 1992 Constitution, the Vietnamese People frame, implement, and protect this Constitution for the objectives of prosperous people and a powerful nation, democracy, justice and civilisation."[9]

The current day constitution reinforces the notion that Vietnam has retained their socialist past. Article 2 refers to the Socialist Republic of Vietnam being a socialist rule of law State of the People, by the People and for the People. Additionally, it highlights how the people are the masters of the Socialist Republic of Vietnam; all state powers belong to the people whose foundation is the alliance between the working class, the peasantry and the intelligentsia. Of importance is how Article 21 provides for the right to privacy, for the citizens of Vietnam, and this right is to be protected. Article 21 states that everyone is entitled to the inviolability of personal privacy, personal secrecy and familial secrecy and has the right to protect his or her honour and prestige.[10] Information regarding personal privacy, personal secrecy and familial secrecy is safely protected by the law.[11] However, it stops short of providing that privacy is a fundamental right. Yet, Article 20 does go some way to achieving this by providing that everyone shall enjoy the inviolability of the individual and the legal protection of his or her life, health, honour and dignity and is protected against torture, violence, coercion, corporal punishment or any form of treatment harming his or her body and health and offence against honour and dignity. The reference to dignity, could arguably be viewed in the same way as the EU and other states that, protection peoples' personal data and privacy over the Internet relates to protecting the dignity of individuals. Furthermore, Article 102 requires the People's Court the protect people's justice, human rights, citizen's rights, socialist regime, interests of the State and legal rights and interests of organisations and individuals. Thus, at the constitutional level the right to privacy over the Internet has been, in part, protected. Nevertheless, in practice this may differ, and therefore, understanding their data protection framework of Vietnam will enable individuals and entities to navigate this complex environment.

---

[9] Vietnam Constitution adopted 28 November 2013 http://constitutionnet.org/sites/default/files/tranlation_of_vietnams_new_constitution_enuk_2.pdf

[10] See Article 38 Right to private life, personal secrets and family secrets, Civil Code No 33/2005/QH11, 24 November 2015. This Code came into force 1 January 2017. See also Criminal Code No 100/2015/QH13 27 November 2015. The law came into force 1 July 2016.

[11] See Article 34 Right to protection of honour, dignity and prestige, Civil Code No 33/2005/QH11, 24 November 2015. This Code came into force 1 January 2017. See also Criminal Code No 100/2015/QH13 27 November 2015. The law came into force 1 July 2016. The laws of Vietnam can be accessed through legal Normative Documents, Portal, http://vbpl.vn/TW/Pages/vbpqen-toanvan.aspx?ItemID=4773&Keyword=Law%2067/2006/QH11

In support of the constitution, the Civil Code[12] provides for the right to private life. Article 38 states that the private life, personal secrets and family secrets of a person are inviolable and protected by law. Furthermore, Article 38(2) goes onto say that the collection, preservation, use and publication of information about the private life of an individual must have the consent of that person; the collection, preservation, use and publication of information about the secrets of family must have the consent of all family's members, unless otherwise prescribed by law. The principles espoused here are consistent with the protection of personal data over the Internet, without making reference to the Internet. Arguably, in the modern world where technology pervades the everyday lives of individuals, protecting the collection, preservation, use and publication of information, and the consent of the family to publicise information. While broad, it could be argued that this would include personal data such as name, place of residence, sex, amongst others of individuals. Moreover, Article 38(3) arguably provides another layer of protection for personal data. It states that the safety of mails, telephones, telegrams, other forms of electronic information of an individual shall be ensured and kept confidential. This would include personal information collected via electronic form over the Internet. However, Article 38(4) provides that parties to a contract may not disclose information about each other's private life, personal secrets or family secrets that they know during the establishment and performance of the contract, unless otherwise agreed. What this provision does not do, is protect the personal data of individuals that are not party to the contract.

Notwithstanding the Constitutional and Civil Code protection of privacy, the current day data protection laws can be best described as being fragmented. Personal data protection is regulated across the 2005 E-Transactions Law, the 2007 Information Technology Law, the 2010 Law on Protection of Consumer Rights, the 2016 Law on Network Information Security and the 2018 Law on Cybersecurity.[13] Generally, under Vietnamese law on personal data, protection applies to Vietnamese agencies, organisations and individuals, and foreign organisations and individuals directly involved in or related to cyber information security activities in Vietnam. Importantly, the law has extraterritorial reach in that it applies to data users outside of Vietnam. Due to the structure and fragmented approach taken by Vietnam, this chapter will discuss each of the laws. However, Patrick Sharbaugh and Phan Thi Le Trang are of the opinion that the concepts of personal information protection and

[12] Socialist Republic of Vietnam, Civil Code, http://itpc.hochiminhcity.gov.vn/investors/how_to_invest/law/Law_91_2015_QH13/view

[13] Law on E-Transactions No 51–2005-QH11, 29 November 2005. This law came into effect 1 March 2006.Law on Information Technology 67/2006/QH11, 29 June 2006. This law came into effect 1 January 2007.Law on Protection of Consumer Rights No 59/2010/QH12, 17 November 2010. This law came into effect 1 July 2011. Law on Network Information Security No 86/2015/QH13, 19 November 2015. This law came into effect 1 July 2016. Law on Cybersecurity No 24/2018/QH14, 12 June 2018. This law came into effect 1 January 2019.

data privacy are still new to Vietnam.[14] They go onto say that the current legal framework lacks many of the most fundamental regulations on the protection of such information. To date, Vietnam has no comprehensive privacy legislation and existing regulations are obscure and widely ignored. This chapter will confirm the position of Sharbaugh and Trang. Moreover, Graham Greenleaf, makes the poin that Vietnam enacted a consumer law covering most aspects of private sector privacy protection in 2010, following e-commerce laws in 2005 and 2006, further strengthened by a 2013 regulation.[15] This chapter will examine the E-Transaction Law and the 2007–2008 Law on Information Technology.

11.2 E-Transaction Law

The 2005 E-Transaction Law (ETL) of Vietnam established protocols for both business and government in the use of networked information systems.[16] The ETL comprises of 54 Articles that regulate e-transactions in operations of State bodies; and in the civil, business and other sectors as provided by the laws. Article 1 goes onto say that the Law shall not apply to grants of certificates of land use rights, house ownership rights and other immovable properties, writings related to inheritance, marriage certification, divorce decision, birth declaration, death declaration, land and other immovable assets; bills of exchange and other valuable papers.[17] Due to the scope of the ETL, the discussion in this section will be limited to defining data, application, principles and prohibited activities.

11.2.1 Defining Data

The ETL does not specifically define personal data. What ETL does is define *An e-certificate, Data, A data message and electronic data interchange.* Article 4 defines *an e-certificate* to mean a data message issued by an e-signature certification service organization in order to verify certified organizations, individuals being the persons who sign e-signatures. Furthermore, data constitutes information in the form of symbol, writing, number, image, sound or other similar formats. While a

[14] Sharbaugh, P., Le Trang., PT, *What's Mine Is Yours: An Exploratory Study of Online Personal Privacy in the Socialist Republic of Vietnam*, https://s3.amazonaws.com/academia.edu.documents/30725679/sharbaughcpaper.pdf?response-content-disposition=inline%3B%20filename%3DWhat_s_Mine_Is_Yours_An_Exploratory_Stud

[15] Graham Greenleaf, *Data Privacy Laws in Asia—Context and History*, Oxford University Press (2014), 11.

[16] Law on E-Transactions No 51-2005-QH11, 29 November 2005. This law came into effect 1 March 2006.

[17] Ibid, Article 1.

data message is information created, transferred, received and stored by electronic means. Electronic data interchange constitutes the transfer of information from one computer to another computer by electronic means in accordance with agreed standards on information structure. Importantly, there is no reference to a specific type of data that is defined. It could be argued that the reference to data, includes both general and personal data. However, when looking closely at what data means, a limited set of personal data would fall within a symbol, writing, number, image, sound or other similar formats. This would need further clarification as to the extent to which personal data could constitute any of the above. Yet, a data message, is information created, transferred, received and stored by electronic means, which could contain personal data. The current definition is broad and could be quite problematic for the protecting of personal data that is transacted across AI platforms. On the other hand, the respective definitions do go some way to providing a level of protection to personal data that is being transacted.

11.2.2 Application

The application of the ETL appears to capture both the public and private sectors. Article 2 states that the law shall apply to bodies, organizations, individuals selecting to transact through e-means. Additionally, Article 3 goes onto state that in case there is a difference between the provisions of the Law on E-transactions and provisions of other laws concerning one and the same matter on e-transactions, the Law on E- transactions shall apply.[18]

11.2.3 Principles

Article 5 sets out the core principles of the ETL. It provides that e-transactions will undertake:

- To voluntarily select to use electronic means to carry out transactions;
- To self agree on selection of type of technology to carry out e-transactions;
- No technology shall be considered as a sole [technology] in e-transactions;
- To ensure equality and security in e-transactions;
- To protect lawful rights and interests of organizations, agencies, individuals, interests of public interests;
- E-transactions of the State bodies shall comply with principles stipulated in Article 40 of this Law.[19] Article 40 establishes specific principles for conducting e-transactions in state agencies.[20]

---

[18] Ibid, Articles 2–3.

[19] Ibid, Article 5.

[20] Ibid.

The above principles arguably focus on protecting data through transactions. The protection of right of individuals could include the protection of personal data. However, even this is unclear. The principles in their current form do not encompass the principles of data protection such as accuracy, transparency, accountability, amongst others that have been established by the OECD.

11.2.4 Prohibited Activities

The ETL has specified a number of specific prohibited activities related to e-transactions. Firstly, Article 9 requires that individuals should prevent the selection of the use of e-transactions. However, it is not clear as to what this means. Secondly, there should be no illegal prevention or blockage of transmission of, access to and receive data messages. Thirdly, there is to be no illegal alteration, deletion, falsification, reproduction, disclosure, display and relocation of part of or the whole data messages. Fourth, one of the most important prohibitions is the creation and dissemination of software programs that trouble, change, destroy the operating system or other activities to destroy the technology infrastructure on e-transactions. However, this prohibition is largely focused on the infrastructure and not the protection of personal data. Fifth, individuals or entities are not to create data messages in order to carrying out illegal activities. In addition, there should be no fraudulent, wrongly identification, appropriation or illegal use of e-signatures of others. E-signatures are a form of personal data, as it is usually the name of a person. However, some personal signatures are hard to decipher and may not necessarily be the full name of the person. There is little here that would account for specific protection of personal data. Article 9(3) does go some way to protecting personal data that forms part of a data message.

11.2.5 Data Message

A key feature of the ETL is validating data messages. That is, Article 10 outlines that the forms showing data messages are to be shown in the form of exchanges of electronic data, electronic documents, e-mails, telegram, telegraphy, faxes and other similar forms. Article 11 recognises the validity of that message whereby, information in data message cannot be denied [its] validity for the sole reason that such information is shown in the form of data messages. Furthermore, Article 12 provides that where the law requires information to be in writing, a data message shall be considered as meeting this condition if information containing in the data message is accessible and usable for reference when necessary.[21] Data messages shall

[21] Ibid, Articles, 10, 11, 12.

have validity as an original copy when the contents of the data message are ensured being intact since its first origination in the form of a complete data message. Additionally, the content of a data message is considered intact when such contents remain unchanged except changes in its appearance, which arise in the process of sending, storage or display of the data message. The contents of the data message are accessible and usable in its entirety for reference when necessary.[22]

A data message will be valid for evidentiary purposes. The validity as evidence of a data message shall be determined based on the reliability of the manner in which the data message was generated, stored or communicated; the manner to ensure and maintain the integrity of the data message; the manner in which its originator was identified, and on other relevant factors.[23] Finally, Article 15 provides that in case where the laws require records, files or information to be stored, such records, files or information can be stored in the form of data messages when the information in the data message is accessible for reference when needed. Additionally, the data message is to be retained in the format in which it was generated, sent or received, or in a format which can be demonstrated to represent accurately the contents of the data message. The information is to be retained in a way to enable the identification of the origin and destination of a data message and the date and time when it was sent or received. Contents, time limit of storage of data message shall be carried out in accordance with the law on storage.[24]

It is out of scope of this chapter to examine any further provisions of the ETL. It is important to note that the ETL is silent on a specific definition of personal data. It does not provide for consent for the use of data messages, and is limited in its controls if and when AI devices are used to transmit data and data messages. This, however, does not preclude from other national laws having the ability to control this area of technology and personal data. Therefore, a further examination of broader national laws of Vietnam is needed to ensure there are no gaps.

11.3 2007 Law on Information Technology

The 2007 Law on Information Technology (LIT) is focused primarily upon promoting the use of IT across all sectors of the economy.[25] The LIT is somewhat limited when compared to the ETL. It is out of scope to compare the LIT with the ETL. This section will only provide an overview of the LIT, and determine whether the concept of consent and a definition of personal data exists. It will also confirm or otherwise of whether the LIT applies to both public and private sectors.

---

[22] Ibid, Article 13.

[23] Ibid, Article 14.

[24] Ibid, Article 15.

[25] Law on Information Technology 67/2006/QH11, 29 June 2006. This law came into effect 1 January 2007.

Under Article 7 the Ministry of Post and telematics is ultimately responsible for the management of information technology. Prohibited acts in Article 12 include obstructing lawful activities, storing or using digital information opposing the State, encouraging violence against the State, revealing state secrets and distorting the honour, dignity or prestige of citizens.

In accordance with Article 21, the collection, processing and use of personal information is identified. Organisations and individuals when collecting information must disclose the purpose for which it is to be used and take necessary steps to securely store the information. Under Article 22 the storage and transmission of personal information to third parties must not occur unless with consent or as required by law.[26] Websites that are created using the country code domain name for Vietnam must inform the Ministry of Posts and Telematics of their contact details under Article 23. In particular protection is provided for children and a favourable environment shall be created for disabled people.[27] That is, Article 29, provides that children have the right to be protected; to access information; to participate in social, entertainment and recreational activities; to keep their personal secrets confidential, and other rights when they participate in cyberspace.[28] Yet, it stops short of mentioning personal data and information. The meaning of personal secrets would need clarification, as to the extent of its meaning and whether it would also include personal data. Nonetheless, in reinforcing the Vietnamese approach to cyber security, Article 19 highlights that preventing cyber attacks is a high priority. The focus is largely in the infrastructure and systems so as informatics programs which cause harm to a telecom network, the Internet, a computer network, information system, information processing and control system, database or e-facility are protected.

Article 19 goes onto say that and individual is not to hinder, disorder, paralyse, interrupt or stop the operation of, and/or illegally preventing the transmission of data by a telecom network.[29] However, and while there is a greater focus on protecting the infrastructure, Article 19 provides a level of protection to data. Article 19

---

[26] Ibid, Article 22.

[27] See also: Article 29 Child Protection in Cyberspace, Law on Cybersecurity No 24/2018/QH14, 12 June 2018. This law came into effect 1 January 2019.

[28] Ibid, Information system administrators and cyberspace service providers are responsible to control information on [their] information systems or on services provided by them, in order not to cause harm to or mistreatment of children or infringing children's rights; and to block the sharing of and to delete information the contents of which may cause harm to or mistreat children or infringe their rights; and [are responsible to] promptly notify and co-ordinate with the CTF under the Ministry of Public Security for resolution. 2. Agencies, organizations and individuals participating in activities in cyberspace are responsible to coordinate with competent State administrative agencies to guarantee children's rights in cyberspace, and prevent [block] network information with contents causing harm to children, in accordance with this Law and the law on children. 3. Agencies, organizations, parents, teachers, child carers and other relevant individuals are responsible to guarantee children's rights and to protect children in accordance with the law on children when they [the former] participate in cyberspace. 4.Cybersecurity Task Forces and functional agencies are responsible to take measures to preclude, discover, prevent and strictly deal with the use of cyberspace to cause harm to or intrude on children or to infringe their rights.

[29] Ibid, Article 19.

goes further to define data by the law as both personal data and general commercial data. Nevertheless, what has emerged in the Vietnamese framework is a higher level of protection being placed on the infrastructure so as to ensure children do not become targets. This approach, while different to many other states, who protect children's personal data more specifically, is a step in the right direction.

11.3.1 Definition of Personal Data

The LIT does not specifically define personal data, personal information, data or any other phrase that has the word data within.

11.3.2 Consent

Consent has become an important concept to the management and governance of personal data. However, the LIT is limited and does not provide for a data subject to consent for the collection and use of their personal data. Article 8 provides the rights for organisations and individuals engaged in information technology and its development. Essentially individuals and organisation that are engaged in information technology are able to seek, exchange and use information in the network environment, except information with contents specified in Clause 2, Article 12 of this Law. Individuals and entities are also able to request the restoration of their information or the restoration of the ability to access their sources of information when the contents of such information do not breach the provisions of Clause 2, Article 12 of this Law.[30] Additional rights are afforded where the restoration of information or the restoration of the ability to access such sources of information is rejected. More important, an individual and organisation has the right to distribute contact addresses available in the network environment after obtaining the *consent* of owners of such addresses. Importantly, the address of individuals would constitute personal data that in other states has a level of protection.

Notwithstanding the above, Article 21 allows for the collection, processing and use of personal information in the network environment. Article 21, is one of the closest provisions within the LIT that resembles the elements of data protection laws that, have emerged in other states, discussed in this book. In other words, under this article, unless otherwise provided for by law, organizations and individuals that collect, process and use personal information of other people in the network environment must obtain the consent of those people. Additionally, organizations and individuals that collect, process and use personal information of other people have to inform those people of the form, scope, place and purpose of collecting,

[30] Law on Information Technology 67/2006/QH11, Article 8.

processing and using their personal information. It also requires the use of that personal data for proper purposes and store it only for a given period of time set by law or as agreed upon by the two parties. The LIT, arguably incorporates elements of the OECD principles for the governance of personal data. Importantly Article 21, obliges an organization and individual(s) may collect, process and use personal information of other people without their consent only when signing, modifying or performing contracts on the use of information, products or services in the network environment. Consent is not required when calculating charges for use of information, products or services in the network environment. Finally, consent is not required when performing other obligations provided for by law.[31] It is outside of scope of this chapter to highlight the other obligations.

The storage and supply of personal information in a network can be undertaken provided that the data subject requests of the organisations to store their personal information in the network environment to inspect, correct or cancel such information. However, the personal information stored cannot be forwarded to a third party without the consent of the data subject.[32] The fundamental elements of consent for the collection and use of personal data in Vietnam has begun. However, they differ significantly from other states compared in this book.

11.3.3 Children

Vietnam have, along with other states recognised that children are important, and have afforded them specific protections. Article 73, places obligations on the state society and schools to protect children against negative impacts of information in the network environment; and prevent and combat information technology applications with violence-inciting or obscene contents. However, Article 73 also places obligations on the family to share the responsibility for the protection of children. It requires families to prevent children from accessing harmful information.[33] What information that means in the context of Vietnam needs to be confirmed. State agencies also need to take the following measures to prevent children from accessing harmful information by ensuring building, and disseminating the use of, content filter; and create tools to prevent children from accessing information harmful to them.[34] It is questionable as to whether these laws will apply to AI technology. If so,

[31] Ibid, Article 12.

[32] Ibid, Article 22.

[33] Ibid, Article 73.

[34] Ibid, Article 23, Guiding the establishment and management of websites exclusively for children with a view to promoting the establishment of websites with information contents suitable and not harmful to children; raising the capability to manage information contents in the network environment, which are suitable and not harmful to children. Service providers shall take measures to prevent children from accessing harmful information in the network environment. Information technology products and services with contents harmful to children must bear warning signs.

children will have a level of protection by the state. However, if these laws are not broad enough, the children of Vietnam will be as vulnerable as those of other states. More importantly, other vulnerable groups such as those with a disability or an ethnic, religious group could be exposed, if these laws are not reviewed. Nonetheless, it must be noted that other laws of Vietnam may fill this gap. It is out of scope of this chapter to explore any other laws.

11.4 Law on Protection of Consumer Rights [LPCR]

The LPCR regulates the rights and obligations of consumers, the liability of organizations or individuals trading goods and/or services to consumers, the liability of social organizations in protecting the interests of consumers; resolving disputes between consumers and organizations or individuals trading goods and/or services, the liability of the State on the protection of consumers' interests.[35]

Personal data or data general is not defined. Furthermore, personal information or consumer information is not defined. However, Article 6 takes the position of providing a level of protection of consumer information. In other words, consumers' information (personal data) is to be kept safe and confidential when they participate in transactions, use of goods or services, except where competent state agencies required the information. This presumably includes both in person and online. Although, further clarification would be needed to confirm this position. Where the collection, use and transfer of consumer information, the organizations or individuals trading goods and/or services shall:

a) notify clearly and openly the consumer of the purpose of the collection and use of consumer information before such activities being done;
b) use information in conformity with the purpose informed to consumers, and with the consent by the consumers;
c) ensure safety, accuracy, completeness during collection, use and transfer of consumer information;
d) update or adjust by themselves or help consumers to update and adjust as the information is found to be incorrect;
e) only transfer consumer information to third parties upon the consent of consumers, except where otherwise provided by law.[36]

Based on the above, this protection of consumer information (data) is not mandatory. The use of the term provides a level of ambiguity and does not oblige the organisation or individual to ensure they meet the requirements of Article 6(2). Thus, to enhance consumer confidence, Vietnam should review this provision and make it mandatory, so as the personal information of data subjects has a higher level of protection.

---

[35] Law on Protection of Consumer Rights No 59/2010/QH12, Article 1, 17 November 2010. This law came into effect 1 July 2011.

[36] Ibid, Article 6.

Moreover, consumers do have a level of rights. Article 8 goes some way to ensuring that consumers are protected (life, health, property, and other legitimate rights and interests) when being involved in transactions, use of goods and/or services provided by organizations or individuals trading goods and/or services. Consumers will also be protected by ensuring that they are provided accurate and complete information about organizations or individuals trading goods or services; contents of transaction of goods and/or services; the source and origin of goods; being provided with invoices and vouchers and documents relating to the transactions and other necessary information about goods and/or services that consumers purchase and/or use.[37] They will be able to select goods or services, organizations or individuals trading goods and/or services according to their actual needs and conditions; decide to participate or not participate in the transaction and agreed contents when joining transaction with organizations or individuals trading goods and/or services. Additionally, the consumer will be entitled to offer suggestions to organizations or individuals trading goods and/or services on price, quality of product or service, service style, trading methods and other content concerning transactions between consumers and organizations or individuals trading goods and/or services. They can also participate in formulating and implementing policies and legislation on protection of the interests of consumers.[38] While the rights espoused are broad, they do not clearly specify that there are substantial rights afforded to the protection of personal data. However, it could be argued that protecting the life, health, property, and other legitimate rights and interests of the consumer, this would capture most, if not, all the personal data that can be collected and used by various government and non - government entities. What is needed, is clarification of how and the full reach of Article 8. More importantly, and something that is uniquely specified by Article 8, is the ability for consumers to be involved in the development of organizational policies and government legislation. This is arguably, an avenue for consumers to ensure there are adequate protections within the laws that, pertain to personal data.

Moreover, Article 16 requires the protection of consumer information.[39] A trader must inform customers about the purpose for which their information is being collected, that the information will be stored securely, that the information may be updated or corrected by the customer and that the information will not be transmitted to third parties without consent unless required by law. This approach is consistent with the information handling requirements of Article 21 in the 2007 Law on

---

[37] Ibid, Article 8.

[38] Ibid, Article 8(5). 6. Being entitled to rrequire compensation if the provided goods or services do not match technical standards or norms, quality, quantity, features, usage, pricing or other contents that organizations or individuals trading goods and/or services already announced, posted, advertised or pledged. 7. Being entitled to complaint, denounce and take a lawsuit or propose social organization to take a lawsuit in order to protect their rights under the provisions of this Law and other provisions of law involved. 8. Getting Advice, support and guidance on the knowledge for consumption of goods and/or services.

[39] Ibid, Article 16.

Information Technology.[40] Thus, and while these laws are not compared with other states examined in this book, there are similarities emerging between Vietnam and the US. This is another area for further research.

11.5 Law on Network Information Security [LNIS]

The 2016 Law on Network Information Security introduces new terms regarding network information security, national important information system, information security incident and risk management.[41] Emphasis is upon personal information which is information associated with the identity of a particular person and civil cryptography as a means to maintain confidence or authentication which does not include state secrets.[42] One of the principles of networked information security is the handling of information 'without infringement upon the private and secret life of individuals, family secrets of individuals and private information of organisations'.[43]

Article 6 acknowledges International Cooperation regarding network security. Ultimate responsibility is imposed upon the Ministry of Information and Communications for network security with the Ministry of Defence and the Ministry of Public Security also have roles.[44] Articles 16–20 concern protection of Personal Information and these provisions are consistent with previous principles indicated above.[45]

[40] Article 21 Collection, Processing and Use of Personal Information in Law on Information Technology 67/2006/QH11, 29 June 2006. This law came into effect 1 January 2007.

[41] Law on Network Information Security No 86/2015/QH13, 19 November 2015. This law came into effect 1 July 2016.

[42] Ibid, Article 3 Definitions, clauses 15, 16 and 18.

[43] Ibid, Article 4 Principles of Network Information Security, Clause 3.

[44] Ibid, Article 11 Prevention, Detention, Blocking and Treatment of Malware. See also Article 12 Assurance of Telecommunications resources, Clause 3.

[45] Ibid, Chapter II Assurance of Network Information Security, Section 2 Protection of Personal Information, Article 16 Principles of Personal Information Protection in Network, Article 17 Collection and Use of Personal Information, Article 18 Updating, Change and Deletion of Personal Information Article 19 Protection of Personal Information Security in Network and, Article 20 Obligations of Sate Administration Agencies in Network Personal Information Protection. See also Article 16, Law on Protection of Consumer Rights No 59/2010/QH12, 17 November 2010. This law came into effect 1 July 2011 and Article 21 Collection, Processing and Use of Personal Information in Law on Information Technology 67/2006/QH11, 29 June 2006. This law came into effect 1 January 2007.

11.6 Consent

The LNIS provides for a limited form of consent. Article 17 becomes important because the collection and use of personal information can only be undertaken after obtaining the consent of its owners regarding the scope and purpose of collection and use of such information.[46] This article has incorporated some of the OECD principles to effectively govern the use of personal data. Article 17 goes onto state that the use of personal information is to be undertaken for the purpose for which it was obtained.[47] The dissemination of personal information to a third party cannot be undertaken without the consent of the owner (data subject). In addition to the above requirements, any data that has been collected by state agencies must ensure that its storage is secure, and a data subject can request an outline of what data has been collected and stored.[48]

Underpinning the concept of consent, Article 3 defines personal information as information associated with the identification of a specific person. This broad definition could arguably mean any information that has been, and can be, collected and used over the Internet.[49] While not specifically referring to children, it would also include all personal information of children. It could also be argued that the definition is broad to the extent that is also enables any personal information that is collected and used by AI. In other words, any AI device that captures personal information that can identify a person, could fall under this definition. This is arguably another area of clarification for Vietnam. Additionally, supporting the definition of personal information is how Vietnam have defined the owner of personal information. That is, Article 3 defines the owner of personal data to be a person identified based in such information. Furthermore, the processing of personal information means the performance of one or some operations of collecting, editing, utilizing, storing, providing, sharing or spreading personal information in cyberspace for commercial purpose. Arguably, this would include AI devices. For Vietnam, the interconnectedness between AI, cyber security and personal data, while limited, it has emerged. It has also been underpinned by the need for the state to ensure social order and national security are protected. Thus, information is to be classified according to the following security levels (Table 11.1).

According to the security level the Government will stipulate details regarding procedures.[50] Another new requirement is the prevention of network use for the purpose of terrorism but more significantly a whole chapter concerns Civil

---

46 Article 17, Law on Network Information Security No 86/2015/QH13.

47 Ibid.

48 Ibid.

49 Ibid, Article 3.

50 Article 21, Classification in Security of Information Systems, Section 3 Information System Protection, Clause 3 in Law on Network Information Security No 86/2015/QH13, 19 November 2015. This law came into effect 1 July 2016.

Table 11.1 highlights how information is classified

Level	Classification
1	When an information system is Sabotaged, will damage organisations, individuals, not public benefits, social order and safety, national defence or security
2	When an information system is Sabotaged, will severely damage organisations, individuals, not public benefits, social order and safety, national defence or security
3	When an information system is Sabotaged, will severely damage production, public benefits, social order or damage safety, national defence or security
4	When an information system is Sabotaged, will extremely public benefits, social order or damage safety, severely damage national defence or security
5	When an information system is Sabotaged, will extremely damage national defence or security

[a]Article 21 Classification in Security of Information Systems, Section 3 Information System Protection, Law on Network Information Security No 86/2015/QH13, 19 November 2015. This law came into effect 1 July 2016

Cryptography.[51] Companies involved with civil encryption products must be licensed regarding 'information that is out of state secret domain'.[52] Applications are to be submitted to the Government Cipher Committee.[53] Article 34 regulates the import and export of civil cryptography products. Chapter V concerns Standards and Norms on Network Information Security and Network Information Security Business is contained within Chapter VI. Conducting business in network information security requires a license.[54] It is a requirement that the 'company's legal representatives, and the managerial, operational and technical staff being Vietnamese citizens permanently residing in Vietnam'.[55] The same applies if the business provides services without involving cryptography.[56]

The LNIS, while limited in relation to personal data, it does provide a level of protection of personal data. It also takes the position of protecting that data in the context of national security, with a greater emphasis on protecting and securing the infrastructure that supports the collection of personal data. Nonetheless, the LNIS also generally applies to the processing of personal data inside and outside of the

[51] Chapter II Assurance of Network Information Security, Section 3 Information System Protection, Article 29 Prevention of Network Use for the Purpose of Terrorism. Chapter III Civil Cryptography Articles 30-36.

[52] Article 31 Trading in Civil Encryption Products, Clause 1.

[53] Article 32 Sequence, Procedures to get Business Licenses for Trading in Civil Cryptographic Products and Services. See also Article 33 Amendment. Reissue, Suspension and Withdrawal of Business Licenses for Trading in Cryptographic Products and Services.

[54] Chapter VI Network Information Security Business, Section 1 Grant of License for Business in Network Information, Security Products and Services, Articles 40–46.

[55] Article 42 Conditions for Granting Business License for Trading in Network Information Security Products and Services, Clause 2(c). See also Article 26 Guarantees relating to Information Security, Clause 3 in Law on Cybersecurity No 24/2018/QH14, 12 June 2018. This law came into effect 1 January 2019. Foreign and domestic service providers must store data about user activity in Vietnam.

[56] Ibid, Clause 3(a).

state. More importantly, in protecting children, the law is not specific in stating an age limit.

11.7 2018 Law on Cybersecurity [LoC]

The 2018 Law on Cybersecurity comprises of 43 Articles and came into force on 1 January 2019.[57] Lin Biu highlights that that Vietnam's National Assembly has passed its new *Law on Cybersecurity*. The Law on Cybersecurity becomes effective 1 January 2019, and will monitor cyberspace activities with the ultimate goal of maintaining Vietnam's national security and 'social order'. While not being the first legal instrument for regulating the handling of cyber data and information, the law is unprecedented in its far-reaching coverage and the extensive powers it gives to the state.[58] The author that the law takes a particular focus in relation to government control of IT systems. They are of the view that under the new law, the CTF (Cyber Task Force) can inspect any IT system (i) on the ground of Cybersecurity Law breaches that harm national security or cause serious damages to social order and security, or (ii) upon request of the system owner.[59] This approach is clearly centred around the government maintaining control over its citizens. To what extent that control means, is a decision for the state. However, it must be noted that Vietnam is governed by a socialist government. It also allows the government to protect its sovereign national interests. The LNIS has many similarities to that of China's Cyber laws. Yet, it is out of scope to fully compare both laws. In addition, the right to an inspection, as the author assert, contemplates extensive powers for the authority to block, limit, suspend or terminate operation of an IT system.[60] However, as Bui argues, it is unclear if IT systems located overseas are also subject to the law in the way foreign service providers to Vietnam are, although it is doubtful the authority can enforce against them from a practical point of view.[61]

Cybersecurity is defined as 'the assurance that activities in cyberspace will not cause harm to national security, social order and safety, or the lawful rights and interests of agencies, organisations and individuals'.[62] The term 'Cyberspace protection' means 'the prevention, detection, avoidance of and dealing with acts which infringe cybersecurity'.[63] A distinction is made between cyberspace and national cyberspace. The former 'means the connected network of computers where people

[57] Law on Cybersecurity No 24/2018/QH14, 12 June 2018. This law came into effect 1 January 2019.

[58] Nguyen, B., K. *Nguyen 'Client Update: Vietnam issues a stringent new cybersecurity law'*, Allens, Linklaters, 22 June 2018 https://www.allens.com.au/mobile/page.aspx?page=/pubs/priv/cupriv22jun18.htm

[59] Ibid.

[60] Ibid.

[61] Ibid.

[62] Ibid, Article 2 Definitions, Clause 1 Cybersecurity.

[63] Ibid, Article 2 Definitions, Clause 2 Cybersecurity protection.

perform social acts without being limited by time or space'.[64] The latter encompasses 'cyberspace established, managed and controlled by the Government'.[65] A further distinction is made with respect to 'core service systems comprising of the national information flow and navigation system, the national domain name resolution system (DNS), the national authentication system (PKI/CA), service supply systems for internet connection and access of service providers on telecom networks, the internet and other added value services in cyberspace'.[66] Cybercrime means using cyberspace to commit a crime as defined in the Criminal Code.[67] Cyberattack is to destroy or interrupt a computer/network.[68] Cyberterrorism and Cyberespionage consist of the traditional definitions but are achieved through the use of cyberspace.[69]
A further distinction is made with respect to the following terms:

> *Cybersecurity threat* means a situation occurring which presents indications of a threat to infringe national security, and or to cause serious harm to social order and safety and/or to the lawful rights and interests of agencies, organizations and individuals.[70]
>
> *Cybersecurity incident* means any unusual occurrence in cyberspace which infringes upon national security, social order and safety and/or the lawful rights and interests of organizations and individuals.[71]
>
> *Dangerous cybersecurity situation* means an occurrence in cyberspace when there is an act which seriously infringes national security causes particularly serious harm to social order and safety and/or to the lawful rights and interests of agencies, organizations and individuals.[72]

Article 7 provides for international cooperation with respect to cybersecurity. Responsibility is shared amongst the Ministry of Public Security, the Ministry of National Defence and the Ministry of Foreign Affairs within the scope of their activity.[73]

Conduct which is strictly prohibited is documented in Article 8 and includes the following; namely,

(1) (a) conduct to breach social order which includes the following; namely, posting prohibited information, gambling online, breach of intellectual property rights, falsifying website information and fraud, (b) distorting history, (c) pro-

---

[64] Ibid, Article 2 Definitions, Clause 3 Cyberspace.

[65] Ibid, Article 2 Definitions, Clause 4 National Cyberspace.

[66] Ibid, Article 2 Definitions, Clause 5(b) Core service systems.

[67] Law on Cybersecurity No 24/2018/QH14, 12 June 2018. This law came into effect 1 January 2019, Chapter One General Provisions, Article 2 Definitions, Clause 7 Cybercrime. See also Criminal Code No 100/2015/QH13, 27 November 2015. The law came into force 1 July 2016.

[68] Law on Cybersecurity No 24/2018/QH14, 12 June 2018. This law came into effect 1 January 2019, Chapter One General Provisions, Article 2 Definitions, Clause 8 Cyberattack.

[69] Ibid, Article 2 Definitions, Clause 9 Cyberterrorism and Clause 10 Cyberespionage.

[70] Ibid, Article 2 Definitions, Clause 12 Cybersecurity threat.

[71] Ibid, Article 2 Definitions, Clause 13 Cybersecurity incident.

[72] Ibid, Article 2 Definitions, Clause 14 Dangerous cybersecurity situation.

[73] Ibid, Article 7 International Cooperation on Cybersecurity Clauses 3 and 4.

viding false information, (d) prostitution, human trafficking and the publication lewd information, (e) inciting crime,
(2) conducting a cyberattack, cyberterrorism, cyberespionage or cybercrime,
(3) producing tools to achieve the same,
(4) opposing the Cybersecurity Task Force,
(5) misusing cybersecurity protective services and
(6) other conduct in breach of this law.[74]

Article 9 details consequences for breach of the cybersecurity law and includes being disciplined, penalty for an administrative offence, criminal prosecution and the payment of compensation.[75] Moreover, Article 10 identifies information systems which are critical for national security to include all aspects of the state including military, energy, finance, medical and culture. The Prime Minister has discretion to include other systems to the list.[76] The Cybersecurity Task Force as part of the Ministry of Public Security is to plan, assess, evaluate and report for the upgrading of such information systems.[77] There are two exceptions; namely, military systems which are managed by the Cybersecurity Task Force in the Ministry of National Defence and the Government Cipher Committee.[78]

Inspections or audits of information systems that are critical for national security must also be undertaken. The administrator of such systems must provide written reports to the Cybersecurity Task Force prior to October each year.[79] One-off inspections may also occur after the Cybersecurity Task Force provides 12 h written notice with respect to a cybersecurity incident and at least 72 h written notice when a request is made by a state agency.[80] Within 30 days of such an inspection the Cybersecurity Task Force shall inform the system administrator of the findings.[81] The Cybersecurity Task Force manages the cybersecurity of information systems critical for national security.[82] Responsibility for the prevention of and combatting

[74] Ibid, Article 8 Conduct which is strictly prohibited.

[75] Law on Cybersecurity No 24/2018/QH14, 12 June 2018. This law came into effect 1 January 2019, Chapter One General Provisions, Article 9 Dealing with breaches of the law on cybersecurity.

[76] Ibid, Chap. 2 Protection of Cybersecurity of Information Systems Critical for National Security, Article 10 Information Systems critical for national security, Clause 3.

[77] Article 11 Evaluation of cybersecurity of information systems critical for national security. Article 12 Assessment of cybersecurity of information systems critical for national security.

[78] Ibid, Article 11 Evaluation of cybersecurity of information systems critical for national security, Clause 4(a)-(c) and Article 12 Assessment of cybersecurity conditions of information systems critical for national security.

[79] Article 13 Inspections of cybersecurity of information systems critical for national security, Clause 4.

[80] Ibid, Clause 5(a).

[81] Article 13 Inspections of cybersecurity of information systems critical for national security, Clause 5(b).

[82] Article 14 Supervision of cybersecurity of information systems critical for national security. See also Article 15 Responding to and remedying any cybersecurity incident on an information system critical for national security.

cyberespionage is placed upon System administrator although the Cybersecurity Task Force within the Ministry of Public Security has ultimate responsibility.[83]

The Cybersecurity Task Force also has responsibility for coordinating for the prevention and combat of cyberattacks and relevant organisations.[84] Again, the distinction made above with respect to the Ministry of Defence and the Government Cipher Committee is maintained. The prevention and combatting of Cyberterrorism is divested to state authorities although the Cybersecurity Task Force must be informed.[85] Once again the distinction made above with respect to the Ministry of Public Security and the Government Cipher Committee is maintained. It also reinforces the focus of this law towards protecting state interests, rather than incorporating the interests of individual citizens or the private sector.

On the other side, dangerous cybersecurity situations involve causing unrest, attacking critical information systems, large scale attacks, serious infringement of national sovereignty including 'very serious loss' to agencies, organisations and individuals.[86] Again the Cybersecurity Task Force has coordination responsibilities.[87] Measures in dealing with a dangerous cybersecurity situation include sending a notice, collecting information and ceasing network provision.[88] After the Cybersecurity Task Force has been notified then the Prime Minister shall make a decision about an appropriate response via the Ministry of Public Security.[89] The same applies for the Ministry of National Defence and the Government Cipher Committee.

An organized activity conducted by the Cybersecurity Task Force to protect social order is referred to as 'fighting to protect cybersecurity'.[90] This includes monitoring the situation, restricting the use of cyberspace together with proactively attacking targets in cyberspace.[91] Cybersecurity protective measures are distributed on state and local levels.[92] Article 24 permits inspection of information systems not considered critical for national security on the following basis where there is a

[83] Article 17 Prevention of and combatting cyberspace; and protection of information systems classified secret, work secrets, business secrets, personal secrets, family secrets and private life in cyberspace. See also Article 18 Prevention of and combatting use of cyberspace, information technology and electronic media in order to breach the law on national security, social order and safety.

[84] Article 19 Prevention of and combatting cyberattacks.

[85] Article 20 Prevention of and combatting cyberterrorism.

[86] Article 21 Prevention of and dealing with dangerous cybersecurity situations.

[87] Ibid, Clause 2.

[88] Article 21 Prevention of and dealing with dangerous cybersecurity situations, Clause 3.

[89] Ibid Clause 4 (b).

[90] Article 22 Fighting to protect cybersecurity.

[91] Ibid.

[92] Article 23 Implementation of cybersecurity protective activities in state agencies and political organisations at the central and local levels.

breach of cybersecurity or upon the request of a system administrator.[93] Without a doubt the most controversial aspect of the Cybersecurity law is Article 26 Guarantees relating to information security in cyberspace.[94] Heavy responsibilities are imposed upon system administrators of websites. They are not to permit matters identified in Article 16 being disseminated.[95] This includes propaganda against the states and inciting public disorder. Furthermore service providers (foreign and domestic) must authenticate the identity of users and provide that information upon request to the Cybersecurity Task Force.[96] In addition, service providers must terminate services to any user who is in breach of Article 16 upon request of the Cybersecurity Task Force or any other agency part of the Ministry of Information and Communications.[97] A further requirement is that service providers both domestic and foreign must store user information in Vietnam for a period time as specified by the Government.[98]

One of the most important provisions, in the context of this book is Article 29. That is, in accordance with Article 29 Children are afforded a level of protection with respect to their private information. System administrators and service providers must protect them from harmful information.[99] Even so, Article 29 is extended further by providing children with the right to be protected; to access information; to participate in social, entertainment and recreational activities; to keep their personal secrets confidential, and other rights when they participate in cyberspace. Apart from providing a level of protection towards children accessing the internet, the provisions do not specifically deal with personal data and information. At best, it requires that children's personal secrets be kept confidential. How broad the concept of personal secrets extends to is not fully understood. The question is whether that whether personal data and information of children could be included. If not, the LoC, while ensuring a level of protection for children, does not extend to personal data. Further clarification is needed to confirm or otherwise, whether Article 29 would include data. The remainder of Article 29 largely requires that information system administrators and cyberspace service providers be responsible for the control of information on the systems or on services under their control. They must ensure that they minimise, and where possible there is no harm caused to children.[100]

---

93 Article 24 Inspection of cybersecurity systems of agencies not on the list of information systems critical for national security.

94 Article 26 Guarantees relating to information security in cyberspace, Clause 1.

95 Article 16 Prevention of and dealing with information in cyberspace with contents being propaganda against the Socialist Republic of Vietnam; information contents which incite riots, disrupt security or cause public disorder, which cause embarrassment or are slanderous; or which violate economic management.

96 Article 26 Guarantees relating to information security in cyberspace, Clause 2.

97 Article 26 Guarantees relating to information security in cyberspace, Clause 2 (c).

98 Article 26 Guarantees relating to information security in cyberspace, Clauses 3 and 4.

99 Article 29 Child Protection in Cyberspace, Clause 1. See also Article 73, Law on Information Technology No 51–2005-QH11, 29 November 2005.

100 Ibid. Agencies, organizations and individuals participating in activities in cyberspace are responsible to co- ordinate with competent State administrative agencies to guarantee children's

In Chap. 6 the Responsibilities of Agencies, Organisations and individuals is outlined. In particular the Ministry of Public Security and the Ministry of National Defence are liable before the Government for the sphere of their activities.[101] The same applies for the Ministry of Information and Communication, and the Government Cipher Department.[102] Other Ministries together with branches and provincial people's committees also have jurisdiction according to the scope of their powers.[103] Chapter 6 reinforces the objectives of the LoC, whereby, national security is clearly the principal focus, protecting the sovereignty interests of the state.

Service Providers have additional responsibilities which include issuing warnings, formulating quick plans to respond to cybersecurity matters, reporting to the Cybersecurity Task Force and applying technical solutions/measures to prevent further loss or damage to data breaches.[104] The law came into force on 1 January 2019. Within 12 months administrators for service providers which are involved with 'information system critical for national security' are responsible for satisfaction of the law and the Cybersecurity Task Force shall assess compliance.[105] The requirement under Chap. 7 need to meet the requirements of Article 12. In other words, there is a form of Risk Assessment required to be undertaken to ensure that, cybersecurity conditions requires reviewing whether an information system satisfies cybersecurity conditions prior to its being commissioned for operation and use.[106] Furthermore, an extension of this, is the requirement to ensure that the relevant Ministry certifies[107] the security systems established by the organisations. This has

rights in cyberspace, and prevent [block] network information with contents causing harm to children, in accordance with this Law and the law on children. Agencies, organizations, parents, teachers, child carers and other relevant individuals are responsible to guarantee children's rights and to protect children in accordance with the law on children when they [the former] participate in cyberspace. Cybersecurity Task Forces and functional agencies are responsible to take measures to preclude, discover, prevent and strictly deal with the use of cyberspace to cause harm to or intrude on children or to infringe their rights.

[101] Article 36 Responsibilities of the Ministry of Public Security, Article 37 Responsibilities of the Ministry of National Defence.

[102] Article 38 Responsibilities of the Ministry of Information and Communications, Article 39 Responsibilities of the Government Cipher.

[103] Article 40 Responsibilities of Ministries, branches and provincial people's committees.

[104] Article 41 Responsibilities of service providers in cyberspace.

[105] Chapter 7 Implementing Provisions, Article 43 Effectiveness, Clauses 2–3.

[106] Article 12, Information systems critical for national security must satisfy the following conditions regarding: (a) Regulations, procedures and plans on ensuring cybersecurity; personnel operating and administering the system; (b) Ensuring cybersecurity of equipment, hardware and software being system components; (c) Technical measures for supervising and protecting cybersecurity; protective measures for the automatic control and monitoring system, and for the internet of things, complex virtual reality system, cloud computing, large data system, fast data system and artificial intelligence system; (d) Measures ensuring physical security comprising special isolation, data leakage prevention, prevention of information collection, and access control.

[107] Ibid, Authority to assess cybersecurity conditions of an information system critical for national security is regulated as follows: The CTF under the Ministry of Public Security shall assess and certify satisfaction of cybersecurity conditions of information systems critical for national security,

many similarities to Impact Assessments required under data protection law. However, Vietnam are not assessing the risk to data, but rather, assessing the risk of cyber intrusions by the private sector, individuals or other state actors. Thus, this accords with the focus of these laws to take a national security approach. Despite the national security approach, the laws are likely to have an indirect benefit to personal data, by ensuring that the systems and infrastructure are safe and secure from intrusions. In reality, this is most likely hard to achieve due to the extent of technology being advanced by individuals and entities to develop new ways of undertaking cyber attacks.

11.8 Additional Law that Governs the Use of Personal Data

In addition to the above, the data protection rules can also be found in the following sectoral laws. It is out of scope of this book to examine these laws, and is an area of further research:

- The Law on CinematographicNo.62/2006/QH11(June29,2006). This law sets out rights and obligations for those involved in activities involving the film, cinematography, and television industry; and
- The Law on Telecommunications No. 41/2009/QH12 (Nov. 23, 2009). This law regulates telecommunications activities and the rights and obligations of those working in the telecommunication industry; and
- The Law on Credit Institution No. 47/2010/QH12 (June 16, 2010). This law governs the establishment and operations of credit institutions in Vietnam; and
- The Law on Postage No. 49/2010/QH12 (June 17, 2010). This law governs the administration of the postal service;
- The Law on Publication No. 19/2012/QH13 (Nov. 20, 2012). This law sets out the rights and obligations of individuals and organisations in the publishing industry; and
- The Press Law No. 103/2016/QH13 (Apr. 5, 2016). This law governs the press, including citizens' rights to freedom of press and freedom of speech in the press and the rights and obligations of agencies, organisations, and individuals involved in the media industry; and
- The Ordinance on Protection of State Secrets No. 30/2000/ PL-UBTVQH10 (December 28, 2000). This ordinance sets out the basics involving state secrets and specifies the different levels of State Secrets. This Ordinance will be replaced on July 1, 2020 by the Law on Protection of State Secrets No. 29/2018/QH14 (November 15, 2018). [108]

except in the cases prescribed in sub-clauses (b) and (c) below; (b) The CTF under the Ministry of National Defence shall assess and certify satisfaction of cybersecurity conditions of military information systems; (c) The Government Cipher Committee shall assess and certify satisfaction of cybersecurity conditions of cipher information systems under such Committee. Information systems critical for national security shall be commissioned for operation and use after they have been certified as satisfying cybersecurity conditions. The Government shall provide detailed regulations for implementation of clause 2 above.

[108] Data Protection in Vietnam: Overview, https://www.amchamvietnam.com/wp-content/uploads/2019/05/Data-Protection-in-Vietnam-Overview-April-2019.pdf

The above approach makes for a complex legal regime for data protection in Vietnam. They could consider consolidating these laws, to ensure the state is well placed to participate in the new digital economy.

11.9 Conclusion

The Vietnam experience provides insights with respect to data protection and changing technologies. Vietnam's framework has many similarities to its neighbour China, although they do vary significantly. It is our view that international trade was a catalyst no doubt in the issuing of the 2005 Law on E Transactions. This law was complemented by the 2007 Information Technology Law. Despite the latter being relatively brief, important provisions were made for protecting children and assisting disabled people online. Information principles were extended in the 2010 Law on Protection of Consumer Rights. A shift occurred in 2016 Law on network Security with respect to the Government exercising greater control of digital information. This is evidenced by risk management becoming a substantive concern, the requirement for cryptography services to be licensed and the same was applied to businesses conducting information security services. These measures were further enhanced by the 2018 Law on Cybersecurity and the requirement that all service providers (Domestic and Foreign) store the data of users in Vietnam.

Overall the framework for cybersecurity and data protection in Vietnam can be best described as being fragmented. However, over the past decade it has evolved, and continues to evolve and consider various elements of data protection. It is does consider and implement some of the internationally agreed principles for data protection such as definition of personal data and providing data subjects with a level control over their data through consent. However, as discussed above this is limited to certain laws such as LNIS. Problematic too, is the definition of personal data across the various laws. Where defined, it does differ and the variables could pose challenges in the future, particularly where AI devices are being used, whether by the private or public sector. Additionally, where defined, it could be argued that personal data will be identified through such devices. At issue is that the above laws examine in this Chapter make reference to AI.

The sectorial approach taken by Vietnam towards data protection makes it difficult, and is a departure from other ASEAN countries, who have adopted specific data laws. In June – July 2019 Vietnam announced the establishment of a three Decrees on the Management, connection and Sharing of Digital Data, Electronic Identification and Authentication and personal data protection. Yen Vu notes that the Decree for Personal data Protection is likely to consider and provide for greater controls over personal data.[109] Vu believes that the new regulations will, amongst

[109] Vu, Y,Vietnam: *Three New Important Regulations on Data protection in the Making,* 2019, https://www.rouse.com/magazine/news/vietnam-three-new-important-regulations-on-data-protection-in-the-making/

other things, define protections for personal data, determine ownership and include principles of personal data protection. This is an area to watch, to determine whether Vietnam following a similar path to other ASEAN countries and implement the OECD principles. Doing so, will go some way to strengthening the framework of controls over personal data, while enabling AI to thrive. It is also proposed that the Decree will also establish clear responsibilities for individual and entities handling personal data, specify rights and obligations for citizens of their personal data, and the processing of that data.[110] If realised, citizens of Vietnam are likely to be afforded greater set of rights and controls over their personal data. It provides an opportunity for Vietnam to include AI into the framework and to also ensure children and other vulnerable groups in the community are also protected from AI technology. Finally, it will place Vietnam as a state in a position to better participate in the ASEAN wide digital economy.

References

Greenleaf, G. (2014). *Data privacy laws in Asia—Context and history* (Vol. 11). Oxford University Press.

Nguyen, B., & Nguyen, K. (2018). *Client Update: Vietnam issues a stringent new cybersecurity law*, Allens Linklaters, 22 June 2018. https://www.allens.com.au/mobile/page.aspx?page=/pubs/priv/cupriv22jun18.htm

Sharbaugh, P., & Le Trang, P. T. *What's mine is yours: An exploratory study of online personal privacy in the socialist Republic of Vietnam*. https://s3.amazonaws.com/academia.edu.documents/30725679/sharbaughcpaper.pdf?response-content-disposition=inline%3B%20filename%3DWhat_s_Mine_Is_Yours_An_Exploratory_Stud

Vu, Y. (2019). *Vietnam: Three new important regulations on data protection in the making*. https://www.rouse.com/magazine/news/vietnam-three-new-important-regulations-on-data-protection-in-the-making/

Yılmaz, O. *History of Vietnam and socialist Republic of Vietnam* ed. https://www.academia.edu/22247531/History_of_Vietnam_and_Socialist_Republic_of_Vietnam-Ed._Oğuzhan_Yılmaz

[110] Ibid.

Chapter 12
China

Abstract China (This chapter comes from earlier publication, Robert Walters, Current status of China's cybersecurity-data protection laws, Privacy Law Bulletin 17(4):60–64 (5 pages) 04 Aug 2020. They have embraced technology to advance their sovereign needs. China and its people have a remarkable story emerging from third world status to arguably first world status in a very short period of time, when compared to many western countries. They have lifted more than 1 billion people out of poverty in less than 50 years. Thus, the resulting effect has seen the development of quite different laws for the protection and management of personal data.

The cybersecurity laws that were recently implemented have evolved to not only serve the sovereign needs of the states, but also, provide a level of protection to its citizen's personal data over the Internet. Coupled with the 2019 implementation of new laws that establish tighter controls and protections for children, and the Personal Information Security Specification have in our view embraced the key elements, principles and concepts that have been in place by the EU and other states for some time. It would be incorrect to think that China do not consider privacy as a broader concept or right that requires protection. On the contrary, four stages of privacy have emerged in China that include, protection by analogy,[1] personality interest protection,[2] protection by tort law,[3] and a separate human right, whereby privacy is protected under Article 110 of the General Provisions of the Civil Law 2017.

[1] The 1980s, privacy was protected under the General Principles of the Civil Law by deeming it as part of the right to protection of a person's reputation.

[2] Starting from the early 1990s, privacy was recognised as a personality interest. An individual whose privacy has been infringed was granted a right to seek compensation for psychological damages under Article 1 of the Interpretation of the Supreme People's Court on Issues Regarding the Ascertainment of Liability for Compensation for Psychological Damages in Civil Torts. However, privacy was not yet recognised as a separate human right.

[3] Privacy right was expressly recognised as one of the protected interests under the Law of Tort enacted in 2009. An individual may take civil action for infringement of privacy right under the Law of Tort. For the first time, the concept of privacy right has been acknowledged under the civil law in the mainland of China.

R. Walters, M. Novak, *Cyber Security, Artificial Intelligence, Data Protection & the Law*, https://doi.org/10.1007/978-981-16-1665-5_12

Through the current legal framework, the Chinese government has sought to make Chinese companies more accountable stewards of data given rising public concerns over fraud and misappropriation of personal information by private sector and criminal actors. This will become even more important to China as it further embraces the use of AI and technology, big data and smart cities.[4] This Chapter is limited in its discussion to only Children, Industry, Regulation, Security Impact Assessments Agency, Organization & Controller – Responsibilities, Consent, Protections, Definition Personal Data and Principles of Personal Information Security. It must be noted that there is very little jurisprudence and scholarly articles available in relation to privacy or data protection matters in China. Thus, this Chapter will largely discuss and describe the current day laws that exist in the state.

12.1 Introduction

China has an amazing history and can be traced to the Shang Dynasty at around 1600 BC. The Shang state had its centre in northern Honan, north of the Yellow river.[5] Modern day China can be found in socialism and communism. Wolfram Eberhard believes that communism had no real prospects for China, as a dictatorship of the proletariat seemed to be relevant only in a highly industrialized and not in an agrarian society. Thus, in its beginning the "Movement of May Fourth" of 1919 had Western ideological traits but was not communistic.[6] This changed with the success of communism in Russia and with the theoretical writings of Lenin. Here it was shown that communist theories could be applied to a country similar to China in its level of development. Eberhard highlights how from 1919, some of the leaders of the Movement turned towards communism: The National University of Peking became the first centre of this movement, and Ch'en Tu-hsiu, then dean of the College of Letters, from 1920 on became one of its leaders. Hu Shih did not move to the left with this group; he remained a liberal. Wolfram Eberhard in referring to Lu Hsün (1881–1936), makes the point that while following Hu Shih in the "Literary Revolution," identified politically with Ch'en. Thus, the nucleus of the Communist Party, which was officially created as late as 1921, was a student organization including some professors in Peking.[7]

---

[4] Sacks, S, China's Emerging Data Privacy System and GDPR, 2018, https://www.csis.org/analysis/chinas-emerging-data-privacy-system-and-gdpr. So far, China's data protection regime consists of the Cybersecurity Law, a handful of accompanying measures, and at least 10 draft standards that deal with both data flows and protection of personal information. In addition, the government is working on a new law focused specifically on personal information protection.

[5] Eberhard, W, (2004) *A History of China* Gutenburg Ebook A History of China, http://library.umac.mo/ebooks/b30863582.pdf

[6] Ibid.

[7] Ibid.

Moving forward to more recent times, it was in 1949, post WWII, the People's Republic of China (PRC) was founded by the Chinese Communist Party (CCP).[8] For almost three decades after the PRC's establishment, there was a perception that a formal legal system for many areas of national life was unnecessary since the economy was centrally controlled and conflicts could thus be resolved through mediation or administrative means without reference to legal rights and obligations. Following Deng Xiaoping taking over the Chinese leadership, the Cultural Revolution, had pushed China's economy to the edge of collapse.[9] At the 1978 Third Plenary Session of the Eleventh Central Committee of the National People's Congress (the Eleventh NPC) was held in Beijing, Chinese leaders stated that the law must be used to establish stability and order for economic development.[10] As Deng Xiaoping put it; there is a lot of legislative work to do, and we do not have enough trained people. Therefore, legal provisions will inevitably be rough to start with, and then be gradually improved upon. Some laws and statutes can be tried out in particular localities and later enacted nationally after experience has been evaluated and improvements have been made. In terms of revision and supplemented, we should not wait for a complete set of equipment. In short, it is better to have some laws than none, and better to have them sooner than later.[11] Ever since, and even today, as China's economy changes they continue to witness massive and rapid enactment of various laws and regulation.[12] There is no better example than with data protection and privacy law in China. They, like other nation states have had to grapple with the expansion of technology, and what this means to the country and their people. China, have also had to balance the ongoing need to expand their economy and employment opportunities for their people, with the application and use of technology. These challenges are formidable and have challenged their regulators and law makers, to find a pathway forward.

Nevertheless, Jingjing Liu argues the modern Chinese law in its current form, structure, and methodologies exhibits many western characteristics, though it is generally modelled on the European Continental civil law tradition in its legislative techniques.[13] Liu asserts that here has also been development in the public law areas and significant implications for protecting human rights (written into the 2004 Constitutional Amendment) since China's entry into the World Trade Organization (WTO), which imposes requirements on transparency and accessibility of law, reasonable administration of law, and impartiality, independence, and effectiveness of judicial review. Thus, whether by accident, design or external influences the Chinese legal system has, in part, had to come into line with the rest of the world, but, it

[8] Liu, J, *Overview of the Chinese Legal System*, https://elr.info/sites/default/files/chinaupdate1.1.pdf

[9] Chen JF (1999) *Chinese law: towards an understanding of Chinese law, its nature, and development*, Kluwer, The Hague.

[10] Ibid.

[11] Ibid.

[12] Ibid.

[13] Eberhard, W, (2004) *A History of China* Gutenburg Ebook A History of China, http://library.umac.mo/ebooks/b30863582.pdf

retains its own grounded principles and concepts. Today, the hierarchy of China's laws and regulations can be summarized as having a constitution, laws that cover both the National People's Congress and Standing Committee of the National People's Congress, along with administrative regulations by State Council and local People's Congress. In addition, there are governing rules for local governments and ministries.[14]

Nevertheless, and according to Li-ming Wang[15] the concept of privacy is virtually non-existent in China's traditional culture. It has much to do with the lifestyles and social habits in China's thousand years of agricultural society, in which people lived closely together and were interdependent on one another. He is of the view that the concept of privacy has slowly emerged in the mainland of China as it underwent the economic reform and urbanization in the late twentieth century, with its people calling for greater privacy protection.[16] For Wang there have been four stages of development of privacy, (1) protection by analogy,[17] (2) personality interest protection,[18] (3) protection by tort law,[19] and (4) a separate human right, whereby privacy is protected under Article 110 of the General Provisions of the Civil Law that was enacted in 2017. Put another way, privacy and the extension of this being data protection in China comes with its own characteristics. In other words, as Wang highlights, the concept of privacy differs to that in the West, in three ways. Wang argues that, firstly, privacy is a basic human right protected under the constitutional law in many western countries with emphasis on regulation of the government. In mainland China, privacy protection is mainly a civil right. Secondly, he highlights the differences in culture have led to variation in the scope and extent of privacy right protection. In western society, privacy largely protect one's autonomy. In China, the purpose of privacy is to develop a harmonious society through coordinating the relationship between individuals and the community. Thirdly, privacy as a right is embodied under different mechanisms. He argues that under western society, privacy is protected through regulating people's conduct and behaviour by established rules. In China, traditionally, privacy has been protected by self-restraint

---

[14] Ibid.

[15] Wang, L,M *Privacy Protection in China: Paths, Characteristics and Issues,* The International Conference of Data Protection and Privacy Commissioners (ICDPPC) 2017, https://www.privacy-conference2017.org/eng/files/programme_booklet.pdf

[16] Ibid.

[17] Ibid, in the 1980s, privacy was protected under the General Principles of the Civil Law by deeming it as part of the right to protection of a person's reputation.

[18] Ibid, starting from the early 1990s, privacy was recognised as a personality interest. An individual whose privacy has been infringed was granted a right to seek compensation for psychological damages under Article 1 of the Interpretation of the Supreme People's Court on Issues Regarding the Ascertainment of Liability for Compensation for Psychological Damages in Civil Torts. However, privacy was not yet recognised as a separate human right.

[19] Ibid, privacy right was expressly recognised as one of the protected interests under the Law of Tort enacted in 2009. An individual may take civil action for infringement of privacy right under the Law of Tort. For the first time, the concept of privacy right has been acknowledged under the civil law in the mainland of China.

and mutual respect of individuals. The different thoughts between the East and West sometimes clash. No position is wrong, and it is the sovereign right of countries to choose what and how they view, apply and ultimately regulate the concept of privacy and personal data. Nonetheless, Wang also expressed his view that more attention should be given to privacy when handling personal data. When collecting and using personal data, one should always seek to protect individual's right to control his own personal data, and bear the responsibility of protecting personal data privacy, in order to uphold individuals' dignity and maintain individuals' self-determination and self-recognition.[20]

However, Hao Wang highlights that the view in China is that only a natural person has the right to privacy and can enjoy privacy protection.[21] Wang in referring to Liang Huixin and Liao Xinzhong state that people's perception is the origin of privacy, therefore only natural persons are able to enjoy privacy.[22] They believe that the confidential information of enterprise legal persons and other social organizations are trade secrets, and there is no connection between these confidential information and people's feelings.[23] Furthermore, in referring to Wang Lizhong and Yang Junxing also emphasize the existence of the right to privacy is based on the emotions of natural persons.[24] They believe that enterprise legal persons or other organizations cannot enjoy the right to privacy on the basis of they do not have feelings or emotions, and the parallel right is that relating to trade secrets, which is a property right.[25] Therefore, at present, enterprise legal persons cannot enjoy privacy protection in China. Wang goes on to highlight that in the case of *Luo Ling v Wu*,[26] the court pointed out that Luo did not invade Sun's (defendant's inamorata) right to privacy. That is because Luo took photos in her own house, she thus was not an intruder at that time. She has right to enter her own house anytime. More importantly, she used these photos as the evidence only in the divorce litigation. In China, if the photographs of the adultery are taken by the innocent party in a third party's premise or the public area such as park or cinema, it will be deemed as that the parties of the adultery have abandoned their rights to privacy. Moreover, Article 70(3) of the Several Provisions of the Supreme People's Court on Evidence in Civil Procedure (2002) clearly states that the doubtless audiovisual materials obtained by legal means with other evidence to support or certified copies of these audiovisual materials should be deemed as effective evidence by the Chinese people' court, if the other party objected to the following evidence provided by a party without the

[20] Ibid.

[21] Wang, H, *Protecting Privacy in China: A Research on China's Privacy Standards and the Possibility of Establishing the Right to Privacy and the Information Privacy Protection Legislation in Modern China*, Springer (2011).

[22] Ibid.

[23] Ibid.

[24] Ibid.

[25] Ibid.

[26] Ibid.

evidence to the contrary that can sufficiently refute.[27] Therefore, the photos or records of the adultery that are taken in other places rather than innocent party's own premise have also been accepted by the Chinese court as effective evidence. He is of the view that based on the foregoing analysis, it is clear that if the individual does not disclose the photos of adultery to the public, "Zhuojian" in both innocent party's own house and public areas has been permitted in China. In fact, there is no conflict between the right to privacy and "Zhuojian." What has been protected by the law is the legal right of the involvers rather than the action carried out by them. People involved in bigamy or cohabits with a married person can claim their right to privacy to defend any third party, but they cannot use right to privacy as the excuse of their immoral act or to prohibit their spouse's right to know. "Zhuojian," as the most frequently used way to confirm the disloyal act of spouse, cannot be tread as an action trespassing individual's right to privacy.[28] Thus for Wang the concept of privacy and the legal development and the existence of law in China started with the introduction and domination of a Chinese-style Marxist ideology. This is an important point, when comparing the laws of China with other countries in this book. This is because, and as noted by Wang, there is a fundamental difference between the principle of Chinese socialist law, and the principle of law in states governed by the Rule of Law, in their respective attitudes toward individual rights. In Western legal systems, the agencies of the State are required to observe the laws in order to respect individual freedom.[29] By contrast, under the Chinese legal system, the individual is required not only to adhere to the law, but he or she must also collaborate actively in the implementation of law. As a result, Wang argues that all these features of Chinese society and law have determined or partly determined that there is no adequate protection for privacy in China.[30]

The point to note is that, which is no different to any other nation state, is the fact that the recording keeping on citizens can be traced to ancient China. Particularly, since China undertook the opening up and reform policy at the end of 1970s, science and technology has been promoted as the core driving force of economic growth and social development.[31] Lingjie Kong highlights how over the past three decades there have been significant changes within China in relation to technology and the management-governance of personal data. Beginning in the 1990s, a series of national informatization projects were launched by the central government, building information infrastructures, expanding application of information techniques in numerous sectors and areas, such as foreign trade, finance, education, taxation, agriculture, library, sanitation and heath.[32] Later, in 2006, the National Informatization Development Strategy

[27] Ibid.

[28] Ibid.

[29] Ibid.

[30] Ibid.

[31] Kong, L, *Enacting China's Data Protection Act*, International Journal of Law and Information Technology, Vol 18, Issue 3, (2010), 197–226.

[32] Ibid.

of China (2006–2020) was released. It highlights the importance of data and personal information to the economy and the need to ensure there is a framework exists that protects information but also, helps facilitate economic activity.[33] Thus, across China there is the recognition that personal data warrants a level of protection.

The National Informatization Development Strategy of China was released in 2013, it was reported that public prosecutors in Shanghai warned of a sharp increase in the theft of personal information online, with criminals stealing and selling data for various criminal purposes, ranging from telecom fraud to racketeering.[34] Wenting makes the point that between 2012 and 2013 there was a rise in this theft. He notes that there was only one such case involving eight suspects during the first half of 2012, but the same period in 2013 has seen 30 cases involving 57 suspects.[35] "More than half of the suspects committed the crime by taking advantage of their positions, and their motive is to promote products or obtain money by the transaction", Gu Xiaomin, director of the public prosecution division of the Shanghai People's Procuratorate, said at a news conference.[36] Wenting asserts that many cases involve employees in online shopping companies passing on the financial data obtained from their customers. Most of the suspects are under 30 years of age and have a good educational background, at least a college degree, with some holding PhDs. Most of the stolen information was passed to sales people wishing to promote products. Some of those sales people even sold the information, publishing it online.[37]

More pervasively, an individual paid around 4000 yuan ($652) for personal information and then resold it to a dozen people across the country, making a profit of more than 40,000 yuan. The lack of social integrity is highlighted by one case, in which Shanghai police detained four suspects on suspicion of illegally purchasing the family details of at least 400 students online and then obtaining money from their parents by disguising themselves as surgeons and teachers and claiming the children required urgent medical treatment. Concern over the security of personal data is not restricted to online shopping, however.[38] As result there have been concerns over data security across the country. Since then, China has made significant developments in their legal framework to enhance the protection of personal data. Thus, it is argued that the challenge for the international community is to properly understand how and what these differences mean between countries and jurisdictions. This is because, the laws themselves will be directed by this thought and the courts when having to decide in cross border issues. Conversely, cross border enforcement may be difficult to achieve when one state places less importance on the need to protect personal data and privacy. However, there are signs that China is

---

[33] Ibid.

[34] Wenting, Z, *Online personal data thefts on the rise in Shanghai*, https://www.chinadaily.com.cn/china/2013-07/31/content_16854401.htm

[35] Ibid.

[36] Ibid.

[37] Ibid.

[38] Ibid.

slowly moving towards the West. In the past 2 years there have been two important instruments issued by the government. Firstly, in March 2018, the TC260 issued a national standard, the Personal Information Security Specification (PISS), which covers the collection, storage, use, sharing, transfer, and disclosure of personal information.[39] Wei Sheng is of the view that, the Personal Information Security Specification[40] is similar to the EU GDPR.

However, and on the other hand, the 2019 Cybersecurity Law summarizes fundamental principles of personal information, the TC260 Personal Information Security Specification provides detailed guidance for compliance in information processing. Thus, the approach achieved by China has many similarities to that of the West in regulatory frameworks, however, this does not extend in relation to data protection and privacy. That is, across many industries such as primary industries and airline industry, whereby the law (legislation) set by government establishes the minimum standards, while similar instruments to that of the Chinese Specification is a tool that assists in facilitating self-regulation. Put another way, codes of practice that are used frequently by Western nations and the business community also achieve the same. Sheng argues that the standard was followed by strengthened regulations on businesses' in the collection and use of personal information. Arguably, and in our view, the complex legal framework of China, has many similarities with the legal framework of the EU. Although, the EU differs slightly with developing treaties, conventions, regulations, directives and opinions. The member states are obliged to implement EU law, but, retain their national laws and have the ability to establish national state, provisional and local government regulations.

Nevertheless, Article 40 of the 2004 Constitution provides for the freedom and privacy of correspondence of citizens of the People's Republic of China are protected by law. No organization or individual may, on any ground, infringe upon the freedom and privacy of citizens' correspondence except in cases where, to meet the needs of state security or of investigation into criminal offenses, public security organs are permitted to censor correspondence in accordance with procedures prescribed by law. The Constitution of the People's Republic of China provides for the "personal dignity" and "residences" of citizens are inviolable and that citizens' "freedom and privacy of correspondence" are protected by law.[41] The General Principles of Civil Law further provides that: all citizens and legal persons are entitled to the right to reputation. The personal dignity of citizens is protected by law. The use of "insults, defamatory statements and other means to damage the reputation of citizens and legal persons is prohibited."[42]

[39] Wei Sheng, One year after GDPR, China strengthens personal data regulations, welcoming dedicated law, In with Chinese Characteristics, (2019), https://technode.com/2019/06/19/china-data-protections-law/

[40] Personal Information Security Specification, English version, https://www.newamerica.org/cybersecurity-initiative/digichina/blog/translation-chinas-personal-information-security-specification/ Chinese version, https://www.tc260.org.cn/upload/2018-01-24/1516799764389090333.pdf

[41] Articles 38–40.

[42] Article 101.

In the opinion of the Supreme People's Court, a person who uses such means as giving publicity to the private facts of another in writing or in spoken words, or publicly subjecting the personality of another to ridicule by the fabrication of facts, or using insults or defamatory statements to damage the reputation of another, should be liable for infringement of the right to reputation if his conduct has caused special damage.[43] The Supreme People's Court further advises that a person who publishes the private facts of an individual, or gives publicity to the same in writing or in spoken words, without the permission of that individual so that his reputation has been damaged may be tried for infringement of the right to reputation.[44] However, this notion and protection of privacy, in the context of modern day technology and the Internet, in practice, means something quite different than that of the West and other Asian states. Arguably, China in asserting their sovereign rights, have established quite a different framework for protecting personal data over the Internet. This Chapter explores China's current day Cyber Security laws, and contracts them against the states discussed in this book, along with those jurisdictions and the different models identifies in book one.

China's relatively new Cybersecurity Law of the People's Republic of China,[45] provides the basis for data protection. The Cybersecurity Law of the People's Republic of China, as adopted at the 24th Session of the Standing Committee of the Twelfth National People's Congress of the People's Republic of China on November 7, 2016, is hereby issued and shall come into force on June 1, 2017. Thus, this Chapter will discuss the Cyber Law, and will be supported by the PISS and the grounding principles of collection, storage and use of personal data. In a further sign that China is expanding their regulatory framework occurred in October 2019. On 1 October 2019, China's Provisions on Cyber Protection of Children's Information (CPCPCI) came into effect.[46] This is a significant step forward, as it is our view that children are the most vulnerable cohort in the community that, are using the Internet. The vulnerabilities they are exposed to are formidable and challenging not matter what states they reside. Children of today have access to information (whether positive or negative) more than any time in the past 50 years. One of the most important elements of this new provision is that it finally sets and defines minors to be under 14 years old. Thus, those children under the age of 14 years are afforded a higher level of protection than people 15 years and older. The CPCPCI has limited

[43] Supreme People's Court's Tentative Opinion on the Enforcement of the PRC General Principles of Civil Law, 26 January 1988, para 140.

[44] Supreme People's Court's Answers to Questions about the Trial of Reputation Cases, 7 August 1993, Question 7.

[45] Cybersecurity Law of the People's Republic of China, Order No. 53 of the President, http://en.pkulaw.cn/display.aspx?cgid=4dce14765f4265f1bdfb&lib=law

[46] Xia, S *China's New Child Privacy Protection Rules*, (2019), https://www.chinalawblog.com/2019/09/chinas-new-child-privacy-protection-rules.html Huton Andrews Kurth LLP, China Issues Provisions on Cyber Protection of Children's Personal Information, https://www.lexology.com/library/detail.aspx?g=625d3bb3-ec70-4626-b37d-ae0b9092c307&utm_source=lexology+daily+newsfeed&utm_medium=html+email+-+body+-+general+section&utm_campaign=australian+ihl+subscriber+daily+feed&utm_content=lexology+daily+newsfeed+2019-10-09&utm_term

jurisdictional effect and only applies to the personal information of this cohort, within the territory of China. In other words, there is not extra territorial effect, and it does not affect the collection, storage, use, transfer and disclosure of personal information outside of the Chinese territory.

The implementation of the CPCPCI, obliges network operators to establish personal information protection rules, designate a person responsible for protecting children's personal information, and obtain parental consent for collecting using, transferring or disclosing children's personal information. Additionally, it aims to safeguard children's personal information by encryption and ensure that the personal information of children is not collected that is relevant to that network operator. This, in itself, has similarities to the purposive principle and approach to the collection, storage, use and disclosure of personal information espoused by the OECD and other states. In other words, the personal information of children can only be collected and used by a network operator, for the specific purpose of that operator. The obligations imposed on network operators also extend to limiting their employees access to the personal information of children under 14 years of age. More importantly, the parental controls over the use of their children's personal information have also been strengthened to include the requirement for network operators to obtain parental consent. That is, network operators must inform the parents of the information they will be collecting, its use, purpose, method and scope of collection, storage, use, transmission and disclosure of children's personal information.[47] However, and where a network operator engages a third party to process children's personal information that, network operator must conduct a security assessment of the third party and sign an agreement with the third party in addition to obtaining parental consent to utilize the third part. The agreement between the network operator and its third-party processor must specify relevant details of the processing, such as each party's responsibilities, the duration of the relationship and what is to be processed and the purpose of the processing. In extending the purposive principle, any agreement between the network operator and its third-party processor must specify relevant details of the processing, such as each party's responsibilities, the duration of the relationship and what is to be processed and the purpose of the processing.[48] This process has similarities with the risk assessment obligations found in the data protection laws of other states. The notable difference is however, that other states generally require such an assessment for all personal data transferred to a third country.

Moreover, Article 1 of the Cybersecurity Law provides that this Law is developed for the purposes of guaranteeing cybersecurity, safeguarding cyberspace sovereignty, national security and public interest, protecting the lawful rights and

[47] Ibid, additionally, parental consent is needed for the network operator where and for how long data will be stored. How the data will be handled upon expiration of the retention period. The measures that will be undertaken to safeguard children's personal information. The consequence of not giving parental consent. How to lodge a complaint. How to modify or delete children's personal information. Other matters of which the parents should be aware.

[48] Ibid.

interests of citizens, legal persons and other organizations, and promoting the sound development of economic and social information.[49] It appears that the protection of personal data is secondary to the protection of networks, systems and platforms in the state. China, to date, have taken a minimalist role in relation to consent, when compared, for example with the EU. Article 22 provides that network products and services shall comply with the compulsory requirements of relevant national standards. Providers of network products and services shall not install malware.[50] When a provider discovers any risk such as security defect and vulnerability of its network products or services, it shall immediately take remedial measures, inform users in a timely manner, and report it to the competent department in accordance with relevant provisions.[51] Providers of network products and services shall continuously provide security maintenance for their products and services, and shall not terminate the provision of security maintenance within the stipulated period or the period agreed upon by the parties.[52] Nonetheless, the framework for personal information and data has been evolving rapidly in China, and in part, they continue to resemble elements of other countries in the region and internationally. That is, the principles established for the protection of the personal information go some way to replicate those that have been formulated by the OECD.

12.2 Principles of Personal Information Security

Rather than the Cyber Law highlight the general principles of personal information protection, this has been left to the ISTPISS.[53] The ISTPISS places considerable obligations on personal information controllers to implement the principles. Generally, the principles are similar to those of the OECD on data protection. The ISTPISS requires that the management of personal information be undertaken that is commensurable of powers and responsibilities that, minimize the damage to the lawful rights and interests of the personal information subject. The processing of personal information is to be undertaken and justified, necessary and for specific purposes. Furthermore, the principles of consent appear to be at the forefront of the ISTPISS, to ensure that data subjects provide a level of express consent for the purpose, method, scope and rules pertaining to the processing of that personal information. In addition to consent, the ISTPISS requires that the processing of personal information is only undertaken to minimize the extent of personal information to be processed. In other words, any processing of personal information is to be

[49] Cybersecurity Law of the People's Republic of China, Order No. 53 of the President, http://en.pkulaw.cn/display.aspx?cgid=4dce14765f4265f1bdfb&lib=law

[50] Ibid.

[51] Ibid.

[52] Ibid.

[53] Ibid.

undertaken that, pertains to the actual personal information to be processed and no more. The ISTPISS espouses the notion that, openness and transparency are important features of the overall framework requiring that any processing be undertaken in an open, intelligible and reasonable manner.

Arguably, this is consistent not only with the OECD principles on data protection, but also, many other states' data protection and privacy laws. The importance of promoting and practicing the idea of openness and transparency has mutual benefits to the state and its citizens, because it provides for a level of certainty and trust in the law. Finally, the ISTPISS promotes the idea of security and participation. These two principles go as far as to ensure data subjects have confidence in the system to ensure their personal information is secure, and allows them to participate by having access to their personal information for correction, deletion, withdrawal of consent and to close an account. In part these principles go hand in hand with Article 3[54] of the Cyber Law that, requires cybersecurity and informatization development, abides by the principles of active use, scientific development, management in accordance with law, and ensuring security.

The Cybersecurity Law arguably take a greater focus on securing the infrastructure through formulating and continuously improving cybersecurity strategies, policies and procedures for key sectors.[55] Article 5[56] reinforces this point whereby the state is required to monitor and prevent cybersecurity risks and threats arising both within and without the mainland territory of the People's Republic of China. Article 6 is an important expression of the sovereign needs of the state, and reinforces the current governance arrangements of the state. It enables the state to promote and advocate the notion of cyber security more broadly in a sincere, honest, healthy and civilized way to require the conduct of individuals is undertaken according to the core socialist values of the state.[57] To protect the states, Article 7 enables the international exchange and cooperation in areas of cyberspace governance, research and development of network technologies, formulation of standards, and follow up enforcement of cybercrime and illegality. Article 7 goes on to promote an environment of peaceful, secure, open, and cooperative cyberspace, by establishing a multilateral, democratic, and transparent Internet governance system.

---

[54] Cybersecurity Law of the People's Republic of China, Order No. 53 of the President. Article 3, goes onto state, the State advances the construction of network infrastructure and interconnectivity, encourages the innovation and application of network technology, supports the cultivation of qualified cybersecurity personnel, establishes a complete system to safeguard cybersecurity, and raises capacity to protect cybersecurity.

[55] Ibid, Article 4.

[56] Ibid, Article 5, The State protects critical information infrastructure against attacks, intrusions, interference, and destruction; the State punishes unlawful and criminal cyber activities in accordance with the law, preserving the security and order of cyberspace.

[57] Ibid, Article 6.

Notwithstanding the above, traditional obligations have been afforded to network operators and individuals and entities that construct these networks. In other words, Article 9 requires that, network operators carrying out business and service activities to not only comply with the law, but also, abide by commercial ethics, be honest and credible, perform obligations to protect cybersecurity, accept supervision from the government and public, and bear social responsibility.[58] This level of obligations while largely expressing additional principles for network operators to follow, more broadly, across society, it ensures individuals and entities behaviors are consistent with the state's values and norms. This is a positive attribution of China's model, in our view, because it imparts broader social policy principles and concepts that impart a higher level of compliance and cooperation in the complex area of cyber security. In the other hand, Article 10 places a level of responsibility on those individuals and entities constructing and operating these networks to ensure they are developed according to national standards. They are required to adopt technical measures to safeguard cybersecurity while ensuring operational stability, and as efficiently as possible respond to cybersecurity incidents. This would arguably also include breaches of personal information, both adults and children. Moreover, when constructing these networks, entities are required to consider ways in which to prevent cybercrimes and preserve the integrity, secrecy, and usability of online data.

12.3 Definition Personal Data

The Cybersecurity Law[59] of China largely set the framework for the protection of its cyberspace sovereignty and national security. The laws are structurally very different to other countries throughout Asia and the world. It extents to regulating the construction, operation, maintenance, and use of networks, as well as to cybersecurity supervision and management within the mainland territory of the People's Republic of China.[60] The China's Cybersecurity Law of the People's Republic of China[61] does not define personal data or personal information or sensitive personal data. The only reference to personal information can be found in Article 22. It states that where network products and services have the function of collecting users' information, their providers shall explicitly notify their users and obtain their consent. If any user's personal information is involved, the provider shall also comply

[58] Ibid, Article 9.

[59] Translation: Cybersecurity Law of the People's Republic of China (June 1, 2017) https://www.newamerica.org/cybersecurity-initiative/digichina/blog/translation-cybersecurity-law-peoples-republic-china/

[60] Cybersecurity Law of the People's Republic of China, Order No. 53 of the President, http://en.pkulaw.cn/display.aspx?cgid=4dce14765f4265f1bdfb&lib=law. Article 2.

[61] Ibid.

with this law and the provisions of relevant laws and administrative regulations on the protection of personal information.[62]

However, such a definition can be found in the Information Security Technology-Personal Information Security Specification (ISTPISS),[63] for both personal informant and sensitive personal information. Firstly, personal information constitutes all information whether recorded by electronic or other means. It also means that that information can be used alone or combined with other information and can identify a natural person. Personal information also extends to that information that reflects the activities of the natural person. A person being able to be identified from their activities is a unique feature of the framework, and is something that is not explicitly stated in third countries laws. Nonetheless, personal information generally is consistent with other states, including the EU, names, date of birth, identity card numbers, biometrics, addresses, telecommunication contact methods, communication records and content, account passwords, property, credit, location data, accommodation, health, physiological and transaction information. Yet, China have taken a slightly different approach to other states in regards to defining sensitive personal data. Sensitive personal information includes that once leaked, illegally provides or abused can threaten the personal property and property security of the individual. It also extends to that information that can cause personal reputational, physical or mental health damage, or, discriminate against the individual. Similar to general personal information, sensitive information includes identity card numbers, biometrics, addresses, telecommunication contact methods, communication records and content, account passwords, property, credit, location data, accommodation, health, physiological and transaction information. It also includes all personal information pertaining to children under the age of 14,[64] which, as stated above has been afforded extra protection in 2019.

---

[62] Ibid, Article 22.

[63] TC260 Chinese, (English version) Information Security Technology-Personal Information Security Specification, https://www.newamerica.org/cybersecurity-initiative/digichina/blog/translation-chinas-personal-information-security-specification/ Chinese Version, https://www.tc260.org.cn/upload/2018-01-24/1516799764389090333.pdf

[64] Ibid, section 3.1, 3.2. SXia, S,*China's New Child Privacy Protection Rules*, (2019), https://www.chinalawblog.com/2019/09/chinas-new-child-privacy-protection-rules.html Huton Andrews Kurth LLP, China Issues Provisions on Cyber Protection of Children's Personal Information, https://www.lexology.com/library/detail.aspx?g=625d3bb3-ec70-4626-b37d-ae0b9092c307&utm_source=lexology+daily+newsfeed&utm_medium=html+email+-+body+-+general+section&utm_campaign=australian+ihl+subscriber+daily+feed&utm_content=lexology+daily+newsfeed+2019-10-09&utm_term

12.4 Protections

Citizens' rights in the new cyber world are nothing short of complex, no matter what state is being discussed and analyzed. This is because they will vary from state to state, and as stated in Chap. 1, each state, depending on what lens is used to analyze these laws have different sovereign needs. In the case of China, Article 12 of the Cyber Law ensures that the rights of their citizens' are protected, by ensuring that organization operating networks are securer to protect individual's personal information. Furthermore, in accordance with Article 9, individuals and entities are required to comply with not only the general law, but also, the constitution, to observe public order, and respect social morality. Individuals and entities must not endanger cybersecurity, and must not use the Internet to engage in activities endangering national security, national honor, interests, incite subversion of national sovereignty, overturn the socialist system, incite separatism, break national unity, advocate terrorism or extremism. They are also not allowed to advocate ethnic hatred and ethnic discrimination, disseminate violent, obscene, or sexual information, create or disseminate false information to disrupt the economic or social order. Importantly no individual or entity is to endanger information that infringes on the reputation, privacy, intellectual property or other lawful rights and interests of others, and other such acts.[65] This is a broad provision and clarity would be needed to fully unpack the extensive legal requirements, when compared to other provisions within the laws. Furthermore, it reaffirms the position taken by China to assert their sovereign right to develop these laws for their own internal needs.

While there is no formal recognition of the Right to Be Forgotten, yet the ISTPISS extends the rights of citizens to seek that their personal information is managed to rectify and correct an error or that information is incomplete, the controller is to modify the information.[66] Moreover, Article 7.6 allows a data subject to request of a controller that their personal information be deleted. Although, the ability for personal information to be deleted can only be achieved when a controller has violated the laws in relation to the collection of that information, or the agreement for the collection of that information has been violated. This also extends to any agreement for the transfer of the personal information to third parties and disclosure of that information. Any transfer to a third party is to cease as soon as possible upon a request by a data subject is received for the deletion of their personal data. The disclosure of personal information is to also cease as soon as the data subject has requested that it be deleted.

[65] Cybersecurity Law of the People's Republic of China, Order No. 53 of the President, Article 12.

[66] Chinese, (English version) Information Security Technology-Personal Information Security Specification, https://www.newamerica.org/cybersecurity-initiative/digichina/blog/translation-chinas-personal-information-security-specification/ Chinese Version, https://www.tc260.org.cn/upload/2018-01-24/1516799764389090333.pdf, Article 7.5.

12.5 Consent

Where network products and services have the function of collecting users' information, their providers shall explicitly notify their users and obtain their *consent*. If any user's personal information is involved, the "provider shall also comply with this Law and the provisions of relevant laws and administrative regulations on the protection of personal information".[67] A notable difference is the term consent is only used once. Consent is neither defined of described in terms of how and what it might constitute. Arguably, the fluid nature of the term has been developed to meet China's sovereign needs, with such a large population, when compared with many other countries in the world. Nevertheless, it is argued that at a minimum consent is required where a network or other service which collects information (personal or otherwise), the data subject must be notified, and they must provide a level of consent. Even so, the answer might lie in the ISTPISS.

The ISTPISS describes how the concept of consent operates in relation to personal information. In other words, prior to the collection of personal information authorized consent is to be obtained by the controller.[68] While it is not clear as to what authorized consent means, it applies to the purpose, manner, frequency of collection along with the storage location and period to which the information will be stored (the controller's data security capabilities, information related to sharing, transfer and public disclosure). On the other hand, when personal information is collected indirectly there is a requirement on the provider of that information to inform the recipient of the information source and ensure its legitimacy has been confirmed. Again, the processor of the personal information that has been collected indirectly is to understand the authorized consent, including, the purpose, sharing, transfer and public disclosure. However, where an organization needs to process the personal information for its own business needs, which are beyond the scope of the initial authorized consent, the organization will need to obtain explicit consent from the data subject.

Nevertheless, there are exceptions to the above, and the controller responsible for handling personal data is not required to obtain authorized consent for the collection and use of that information when it directly relates to national security, national defence, public safety, public health and interest.[69] It also applies to criminal investigations, prosecution, trial and a judgement of enforcement. Further exemptions apply when there is a need for safeguarding major lawful rights and interests pertaining to property of the data subject or other persons, and moreover, when it is

---

[67] Ibid.

[68] Cybersecurity Law of the People's Republic of China, Order No. 53, Article 5.3–5.4. Note further exemption also apply where the controller who is acting as a news agency to make legal news reports, or as an academic research institute to conduct statistical or academic research that is in the public interest, which has also de-identified the personal information before providing to these institutions (academic research), or specified by any other law.

[69] Ibid.

difficult to obtain the consent from the data subject. The exemptions also extend to when the data subject voluntarily allowed the collection of their personal information to the general public. This would likely arise when individuals upload their personal information to apps and websites that are generally available to the broader public. When the personal information has been made public for example, through news reports and open government information, authorized consent is also not required. It also pertains to when it is necessary to sign and perform a contract that has been agreed and approved with a data subject, and, to maintain the safe, stable operation of products and services.

On the backdrop of the above exemption (s), the requirement for a controller to obtain explicit consent for the collection of sensitive personal data extends to when a data subject has provided the information freely, it is specific, clear and unequivocal.[70] Additionally, there are further requirements whereby a controller collects personal sensitive information. Thus, prior to the collection of this information whether voluntarily or automatically, the controller is to inform the data subject of the core function of the provided products or services and the sensitive information that will be collected. The controller is also required to disclose the impacts which may occur of the data subject refuses to provide it or refuses to provide consent. However, there are different requirements for consent, for children who are 14 years old or younger. Controllers are encouraged to provide choice to the data subject, whereby, they are to allow the subject to choose whether the provisions or automatic collection of sensitive data should be allowed. In practice, it would be interesting to better understand how this operates. Nonetheless, where the products or services provide additional functions and sensitive personal information is collected, the data subject would need to be fully informed as to why that information is being collected. Importantly, where the data subject rejects the collection of that sensitive data, effectively the function of collection is to cease.[71] Yet, any request to cease the collection of data should not impede the business operations of the organization. For instance, this would be important information for a hospital, yet, a local garage that services one's car, might not require sensitive personal information to be collected and used.

12.6 Agency, Organisation & Controller – Responsibilities

In a similar manner to other states, the Cyber Law imposes obligations of specific agencies to ensure measures are established to protect individuals, business and the state from cyberattacks. This is a clear demonstration that cyber security and data protection are close, and continuing to move closer together. Thus, Article 8 imposes

---

[70] Cybersecurity Law of the People's Republic of China, Order No. 53, Article 5.5.

[71] Ibid.

responsibilities[72] to the State Council department for telecommunications to ensure the public security, and other relevant organs, are responsible for cybersecurity protection, supervision, and management efforts within the scope of their responsibilities, in accordance with the provisions of this Law and relevant laws and administrative regulations.

In addition to the above, and apart from managing cyber security related to data and information in general, the ISTPISS,[73] adds an additional layer of responsibility on organizations. That is, within an organization or department there are to be personal information controllers appoint to manage the governance and security of personal information. Article 10 of the ISTPISS, requires a personal information controller to assume fully responsibility for the security of personal information. They are also required to appoint a person who will be responsible for the protection of that information, where appropriate. That is, where the organization is large enough and requires more than one person to manage and protect the governance arrangements surrounding personal information, another person can be appointed to assist. Thus, accordingly, the organization is required to ensure the in-house personal information officer and the department in-charge of that personal information security, does so in a way that ensures the main business with more than 200 employees and establishes a multilayered approach. This requirement resembles the multilayered approach to that of the EU, whereby there is a requirement for the appointment of a controller and/or processor. Nonetheless, where an organization processes more than 500,000 people's personal information or expects to exceed this number as part of the processing requirements within a 12 month period, the entity is to appoint both a controller and processor. Apart from overseeing the security of this information/data, the minimum protections extend to, but not limited to, coordinating personal information security work. They are also required to formulate, issue and implement regular updates to internal privacy policies and relevant procedures. This is a further extension of the self and co-regulatory model that exists around the world for data protection, amongst many other industries such as primary industries, motor vehicle and airline sectors. As part of this co-regulatory approach, they are also encouraged to undertake impact assessments, training, examine before a product is launched the extent of security for personal information, and implement audits.

The security of cyber networks is important to the states, and Article 14 provides that any individual or entity has the right to report conduct endangering cybersecurity to cybersecurity and informatization, telecommunications and public security. Additionally, departments receiving these reports shall promptly process them in accordance with law; where matters do not fall within the responsibilities of that department, they shall promptly transfer them to the department empowered to

[72] Ibid, Article 8, cybersecurity protection, supervision, and management duties for relevant departments in people's governments at the county level or above will be determined by relevant national regulations.

[73] Ibid.

handle them. However, there is no specific timeframe that has been reported for this process to be undertaken.

Nevertheless, Article 13 enable the state to undertake research and development of network products and services conducive to the healthy upbringing of minors. Thus, and as stated earlier with the recent implementation of the 2019 child protections, the state recognises the need for greater protection and controls to be in place for children. In other words, individuals and entities will be punished from the use of networks that engage in activities endangering the psychological and physical well-being of minors. Minors are those children that are 14 years old and younger.

12.6.1 Security Impact Assessments

It is well understood that impact assessments have assisted in strengthening the overall understanding of security issues related to personal data collection, use and disclosure. They are a tool that enhances an organizations ability to detect and improve their internal system and process to safeguard personal information. Nonetheless, Article 10.2 obliges a controller to undertake an impact assessment at least annually. An impact assessment is required to evaluate the processing activities of personal information of the organisation. It also requires that the collection of any personal information comply with principles of consent, specification and minimization. The impact assessment must determine whether the processing of that information could endanger the personal and property safety, infringe the individual's reputation and mental health or lead to discriminatory treatment. In addition to these requirements, the impact assessment is to also determine the effectiveness of the overall security measures, and identify the data subject from anonymized or de-identified data sets, and any other possible negative impacts to the data subject from the transfer or disclosure of that data. Finally, the controller and/or processor is required to prepared an evaluation report, outlining the impact and measures taken to protect the personal information from any illegal collection and use. Arguably, this complements the overall framework and acts as a continuous improvement process.

12.6.2 Industry Regulation

The emergence of the technological industry has resulted in government not only being left behind in terms of policy formulation and regulation, and China is no exception along with the rest of the world. Nonetheless, to assist in combating the ongoing and wide-ranging cyber security issues, there has been a string push towards self-regulations. China, similar to other states, in accordance with Article 11, promotes this concept of industry establishing standards to self-regulate itself. Article 11 states that relevant Internet industry organizations, according to their

Articles of Association, shall strengthen industry self-discipline, formulate cybersecurity norms of behavior, guide their members in strengthening cybersecurity protection according to the law, raise the level of cybersecurity protection, and stimulate the healthy development of the industry.

12.7 Children

2019 marked, in our view a significant turning point in China's approach to protecting personal data over the Internet. They established a very important legal initiative to provide further protection for children online. While, in large part, the new controls do resemble the developments of the EU, China subtly digress from the European equivalent.

On August 22, 2019, the Cyberspace Administration of China (CAC) released a new data privacy regulation related to children, the Provisions on Cyber Protection of Personal Information of Children (儿童个人信息网络保护规定) (PCPPIC).[74] The regulation came into effect on October 1, 2019, and applies within the People's Republic of China (PRC). The PCPPIC's purpose is to protect the security of children's personal information and promoting the healthy growth of children in the PRC. However, the PCPPIC is limited to minors under the age of 14, but leaves a regulatory gap for minors aged 14 or above.[75] In particular, this could also give rise to issues such as what rights minors will have in relation to their personal information which has already been collected when they reach the age of 14 and whether they should be treated as adults under data protection laws at that time. Furthermore, 29 Articles, set requirements for the collection, storage, use, transfer, and disclosure of the personal information of children within PRC territory.[76]

Moreover, in our view one of the most important inclusion China has introduced is the expansion on the concept of consent for children 14 years old and younger. That is, the new laws require data controllers to treat the personal information (data) of children as sensitive information. They must obtain express consent from the child's guardian for the processing of personal information.[77] The special protection measures applicable to sensitive personal information under the Security Standards will also apply to children's personal information.[78] The law further provides that these required measures including separate consent for each function of a service or

---

[74] Ip, K., Lau, N., Gong, J., *China: China's First Regulation On Children's Online Privacy*, Herbert Smith Freehills, September 2019, https://sites-herbertsmithfreehills.vuturevx.com/95/20753/september-2019/china-s-first-regulation-on-children-s-online-privacy.asp?sid=56d3bb39-faab-43a3-967a-6cbeb683e586&utm_source=Mondaq&utm_medium=syndication&utm_campaign=inter-article-link

[75] Ibid.

[76] Ibid.

[77] Ibid.

[78] Ibid.

product, encryption of data for storage and transmission, request-based internal access authorisation, prior notification and express consent before data sharing or transferring.[79] The privacy policy attached to the Security Standards also includes a section on processing of children's personal information.[80]

Thus, there are six key areas where consent will be required from a guardian, these include the purpose, (1) scope, method, and term of collection, storage, use, transfer, and disclosure of information. Additionally, (2) for the storage location and treatment of information after the agreed term expires. (3) Security measures to keep information protected, and (4) consequences of parents' or guardians who refuse to provide consent along with (5) and a platform where parents or guardians to report violations or file complaints with the network operator in regards to mishandling children's personal information. (6) Consent will be viewed as necessary when methods for the revision and deletion of children's personal information, or, a substantial change by network operators are required to re-obtain parental or guardian consent.[81]

Karen Ip et al., further highlight that network operators are required to have a higher level of understanding and operational consideration when dealing with children's personal information. The authors go onto say that network operators are required to set up specific rules for protecting children's personal information and to enter into an agreement with third party users. Network operators should take measures to ensure the security of information via encryption or other reasonable methods.[82] Under a principle of minimal authorization, network operators are required to establish strict access permissions for personnel responsible for handling children's personal information. When network operators engage third-party vendors, they are required to conduct a security assessment of the transferee prior to any transfers of personal information.[83] Furthermore, where any child's personal information is divulged, damaged, or lost, network operators should provide notice to the parent or guardian and immediately take remedial measures.[84]

In May 2018, the EU introduced a data privacy regulation related to children under Article 8 of the GDPR. However, one of the fundamental differences is the age limitations. In the EU, the GDPR has an age limit of 16,[85] whereas, China has 14. However, in accordance with Article 8 of the GDPR, member states of the EU can regulate to the age of 13 years. While not viewed as a huge issue, an observation for consideration is how children develop and vary rates, particularly between these

[79] Ibid.

[80] Ibid.

[81] Ibid.

[82] Ibid.

[83] Ibid.

[84] Ibid.

[85] General Data Protection Regulation 2016/679 Article 8.

age groups. Put another way, at the ages between 10 to 16 the development patterns of children vary significantly in any one year.

Another area of different is the concept of how the respective laws apply to children whether they are located within or outside each of the jurisdictions. For children of the EU, the GDPR focuses on the geographic location of children and applies only to companies processing and holding personal information of data subjects residing within the EU, regardless of the company location. In other words, the children who are citizens of a member state of the EU have protection in third countries. However, for the children of China, the PCPPIC applies to children within the territory of the PRC and is silent as to whether it has any extraterritorial effect.[86] Moreover, where there has been a breach of the respective laws towards children, the laws vary greatly. That is, the PCPPIC does not expressly provide any maximum penalties. Whereas, the GDPR imposes administrative fines for breaching the regulations.[87]

The data protection and cyber security landscape within China, like no other country is continuing to evolve, adapt and change to local societal and sovereign needs. In part, these small changes could be perceived as China considering elements of harmonization in this area of the law with other states and the EU. What stands out, is their willingness, which is no different to anywhere in the world that has either implemented specific data protection laws, or in the process of doing so, to take a wider view of societal needs and protect, future generations of Chinese children, albeit to the age of 14. This poses well for China, and this is another area of the law in which they will need to be vigilant as AI pervades the family home where personal data and information of children could be readily accessed for the wrong reasons, in the future.

12.8 Emergency Response

A unique feature of the Chinese model that underpins the state base model, is the requirement for the state to establish cybersecurity monitoring, early warning, and information communication system.[88] The State cybersecurity and departments shall do overall coordination of relevant departments to strengthen collection, analysis, and reporting efforts for cybersecurity information, and follow regulations for the unified release of cybersecurity monitoring and early warning information. The burden placed on state departments is high, and there is a clear determination to

[86] Karen Ip, Nanda Lau, James Gong, *China: China's First Regulation On Children's Online Privacy*, Herbert Smith Freehills, September 2019, https://sites-herbertsmithfreehills.vuturevx.com/95/20753/september-2019/china-s-first-regulation-on-children-s-online-privacy.asp?sid=56d3bb39-faab-43a3-967a-6cbeb683e586&utm_source=Mondaq&utm_medium=syndication&utm_campaign=inter-article-link

[87] Ibid.

[88] Cybersecurity Law of the People's Republic of China, Order No. 53, Article 51.

ensure that critical information infrastructure is secure that, house built in early warning systems[89] to detect and deter possible intrusions. The remainder of this Chapter of the Cyber laws largely directs departments on how they are to coordinate, respond, plan, scope, and assess the risk[90] of actual and potential breaches. To combat any intrusions into the systems Article 55 requires that the emergency response plan is to be immediately implemented that, focusses on evaluating and assessing the full cybersecurity incident.

12.9 Breaching the Law

China have adopted a multilayered approach to enforcement actions, and hold not only departments responsible, but also, individuals employed within these departments. This has similarities to the controller and processor responsibilities und the EU framework. Yet, for the protection of personal information-data, the enforcement focus is largely on the systems, infrastructure and platforms being subject to security infringements.

12.9.1 Network Operators

The enforcement actions taken across China for the breach of these laws, places heavy burden on not only departments, but also individual managers and network operators. There are considerable obligations placed on network operators to ensure that the laws are complied with. The enforcement outcome can result in a fine, corrections order or warning. China believes that providing the opportunity to resolve the breach or non-compliance can be remedied by ensuring the individual or entity makes the necessary corrections. This is reflected by Article 59 that states where network operators do not perform cybersecurity protection duties provided for in Articles 21 and 25, the competent departments will order corrections and give warnings; where corrections are refused or it leads to harm to cybersecurity or other such consequences.[91]

However, where these obligations have not been fulfilled a fine of between RMB 10,000 and 100,000 can be imposed and the directly responsible management personnel can be fined between RMB 5000 and 50,000.[92] Network operators have further obligation to ensure they do not breach Article 24. Should this occur, the

[89] Cybersecurity Law of the People's Republic of China, Order No. 53, Article 52.

[90] Cybersecurity Law of the People's Republic of China, Order No. 53, Articles 53 and 54.

[91] Cybersecurity Law of the People's Republic of China, Order No. 53, Articles 21–25.

[92] Ibid, Article 59. Unauthorized ending of the provision of security maintenance for their products or services.

network operator in failing to require users to provide real identity information or providing relevant services to users who do not provide that information, and are ordered to make corrections by the relevant competent department, and do not undertake the correction may face a fine of between RMB 50,000 and 500,000, and the person directly in charge may be fined between RMB 10,000 and 100,000.[93] Moreover, Article 64, requires network operators along with network product or service providers to ensure that personal information is protected, according to Articles 22–3, 41–43, and where this requirement has been infringed fines can be imposed of up to RMB 1,000,000, and a fine of between RMB 10,000 and 100,000 shall be given to persons who are directly in charge and other directly responsible personnel.[94] For serious breaches the department can order a temporary suspension of operations, and the closing down of websites, along with cancellation of any relevant operations permits, or cancellation of business licenses. Network operators failing to stop the transmission of information under Article 47, can face fines of between RMB 100,000 and 500,000 and persons who are directly in charge and other directly responsible personnel are fined between RMB 10,000 and 100,000.[95] Finally network operators who do not following the requirements of relevant departments to adopt disposition measures such as stopping dissemination or deleting information for which laws or administrative regulations prohibit publication or dissemination; refuse or obstruct departments in their lawful supervision and inspection; or refuse to provide technical support and assistance to public security organs and state security organs, could incur fines. The level of fine currently stands at RMB 50,000 and 500,000 shall be imposed, and directly responsible management personnel and other directly responsible personnel are to be fined between RMB 10,000 and 100,000.[96]

12.9.2 Information Infrastructure Operators

Nonetheless, the fines that can be imposed for information infrastructure operators slightly vary to that of network operators. For example, Article 59 allows fines of up to RMB 100,000 and 1,000,000, to be imposed on department where it is found to be in breach of Article Articles 33, 34, 36, and 38. In addition the responsible management personnel can also be fined RMB 10,000 to 100,000. The remaining enforcement actions that can be imposed focus on specific provisions within the laws. For instance, in accordance with Article 60, where Article 22 paragraphs 1 or

---

[93] Ibid, Article 61.

[94] Ibid, Article 64.

[95] Ibid, Article 68. Where electronic information service providers and application software download service providers do not perform their security management duties provided for in Paragraph 2 of Article 48 of this Law, punishment shall be in accordance with the provisions of the preceding paragraph.

[96] Ibid, Article 69.

2 or Article 48 paragraph 1 has been breached, the relevant departments have the ability to issue a corrections order, provide a warning. However, where the corrections order has not been implemented a fine of RMB 50,000 and 500,000 can be imposed or persons directly involved can incur a fine of between RMB 10,000 and 100,000. This applies to where malicious programs have been installed, or there was a failure to take the necessary actions to address the security flaws and did not inform users or report the issues to the relevant department. Additional obligations for information infrastructure operators include the requirements for using network products and services. Thus under Article 65, where critical information infrastructure operators violate Article 35 of this Law by using network products or services that have not had security inspections or did not pass security inspections, the relevant competent department shall order the usage to stop and levy a fine in the amount of 1–10 times the purchase price; the persons who are directly in charge and other directly responsible personnel shall be fined between RMB 10,000 and 100,000.[97] Information infrastructure operators in accordance with Article 66 will occur fines for breaching Article 37 of this Law by storing network data outside the mainland territory, or provide network data to those outside of the mainland territory. The fines that can be imposed include RMB 50,000 and 500,000, or, suspension of operations or business for corrective measures, closing down of websites, revoking – cancellation of any relevant permits or licenses. Persons who are directly in charge and other directly responsible personnel shall be fined between RMB 10,000 and 100,000.

12.9.3 General

General enforcement action can result in fines, the closing of website, amongst other things being imposed. Thus, in accordance with Article 62 where Article 26 has been breached in relation to cybersecurity certifications, testing, or risk assessments, or publishing cybersecurity information such as system vulnerabilities, computer viruses, cyber attacks, or network incursions, corrections. The resulting breach can see a fine imposed of between RMB 10,000 and 100,000 to a department and for the responsible person a fine of between RMB 5000 and 50,000. A common theme in the fines, corrections orders and other enforcement actions that can be imposed have a dual effect.[98] Enforcement actions can be imposed on departments and the individual responsible for managing the system or infrastructure. This places a high level of responsibility on these people to ensure they follow the law. Further where individuals or departments have been involved in harming cybersecurity infrastructure or providing software to undertake such a harm, Article 63 provides that fines can be imposed of between RMB 50,000 and 500,000; and where

[97] Ibid, Article 65.

[98] Ibid, Article 62.

circumstances are serious, shall impose between 5 and 15 days detention, and may levy a fine of between 100,000 and 1,000,000 RMB.[99]

The illegal selling or providing of personal information will be met with swift enforcement action and the individuals and entities involved could be fined of a fine of between 1 and 10 times the amount of unlawful gains, and where there are no unlawful gains, levy a fine of up to RMB 1,000,000.[100] Further criminal offences apply where a person establishes a website or communications group used for the commission of illegal or criminal activities, or the network is used to publish information related to the commission of illegal or criminal activities, even though a crime has not been committed.[101] Breaching Article 69 can result in 5 days detention or fine between RMB 10,000 and 15,000, and where circumstances are serious, they may impose between 5 and 15 days detention, and may give a fine of between 50,000 and 500,000 RMB. They may also close websites and communications groups used for illegal or criminal activities. However, there is not clarification on what might constitute serious or what criminal activities would be subject to this provision.

12.10 End of 2019

The conclusion of 2019 was an important period in the further development and implementation of data protection legal framework throughout China. As discussed earlier in this Chapter there was a concerted effort to provide children with greater protections. In addition, according to Michael Tan and Heather Jian, China[102] has undertaken steps to update the controls over APP related incidents. On 28 November 2019, China provided further guidance on the implementation of the Measure on Identifying Misconducts of APPs in Collection and Use of Personal Information in Violation of Laws and Regulations (Guo Xim Ban Mi Zi [2019] No. 910). In regards

[99] Ibid, Article 63. Where units have engaged in the conduct of the preceding paragraph, public security organizations shall confiscate unlawful gains and levy a fine of between RMB 100,000 and 1,000,000, and the directly responsible persons in charge and other directly responsible personnel shall be fined in accordance with the preceding paragraph. Where Article 27 of this Law is violated, persons who receive public security administrative sanctions must not engage in cybersecurity management or key network operations positions for 5 years; those receiving criminal punishments will be subject to a lifetime ban on engaging in work in cybersecurity management and key network operations positions.

[100] Ibid, Article 64.

[101] Ibid, Article 69. Where units have engaged in conduct covered by the preceding paragraph, a fine of between RMB 100,000 and 500,000 shall be levied by public security organizations, and the principal responsible managers and other directly responsible personnel shall be fined in accordance with the preceding paragraph.

[102] Tan, M., Jiang, H., Wessing, T, *New Guidelines for APP Privacy Behaviour*, https://www.lexology.com/library/detail.aspx?g=e0c55fd3-7347-48db-b0ce-2ca285ae1426&utm_source=Lexology+Daily+Newsfeed&utm_medium=HTML+email+-+Body+-+General+section&utm_campaign=Australian+IHL+subscriber+daily+feed&utm_content=Lexology+Daily+Newsfeed+2020-01-10&utm_term=

to consent will be deemed to be missing where an APP the collection of personal data has been undertaken without actual consent, and following that the data subject declined the pop-ups that seek consent or opt-out instead of opting in. This also applies to where there has been changes in configurations and updates by APPs, and pushing information based on profiling.[103] Thus any absence of these will be deemed that consent has not been obtained.

In addition, any APP or APP transmission of data to a third party is subject to a valid consent where anonymization has a role absence of which may frustrate any consent.[104] For the right to be forgotten the measures require that APPs are to provide adequate means for an individual to de-register or delete their personal information, and this is to be done within 15 days of the request.[105] These measures or guidelines while adding a further layer of complexity to the legal framework, they go some way to detailing what and how APPs should provide functions to protect individual's personal data.

12.11 Proposed 2020 Law Reform

In 2020, it has been reported that China will embark on implementing more specific data protection laws. It is proposed that China will implement two separate laws (1) The Personal Data Protection Law and a (2)[106] Qiheng Chen[107] believes that the draft adopted a contractual approach to transferring data from domestic network operators to foreign data receivers. This approach draws from the European Union General Data Protection Regulation's (GDPR's) binding corporate rules that allow multinational companies to transfer data internationally between their subsidiaries. Both the Chinese and EU regulations emphasized the need for an adequate level of data protection in destination countries and mandated regulatory approval prior to transfer. Yet, there is a difference. Binding corporate rules are more lightweight, an internal code of conduct without obligation to report the current year's outbound transfers.[108] Another development is a provision to allow the termination of

[103] Ibid.

[104] Ibid.

[105] Ibid.

[106] Theil, S., Bigg, C., Tam, K, DLA Piper Data Protection https://blogs.dlapiper.com/privacymatters/china-privacy-security-and-content-regulation-to-increase-in-2020/

[107] Chen, Q, *China's New Data Protection Scheme: China has released a draft regulation fleshing out its cybersecurity law,* https://thediplomat.com/2019/07/chinas-new-data-protection-scheme/ See also, A look at China's draft of Personal Information Protection Law, https://iapp.org/news/a/a-look-at-chinas-draft-of-personal-data-protection-law/ China unveiled its draft of the Personal Information Protection Law for public consultation Oct. 21, 2020. Taking a closer look at the draft PIPL, it is easy to see many provisions in it are inspired by the EU General Data Protection Regulation.

[108] Ibid.

cross-border data transfers if the contract cannot be implemented due to changes to the legal environment of the country where the recipient is located. This clause, together with restrictions on onward data transfer to third parties, can be interpreted as a response to extraterritorial data laws such as the US CLOUD Act.[109] The draft cemented the separate treatment of personal information and important data. The latter refers to information that, if leaked, may infringe on national security. It proposes to have extra-territorial reach that, will require all processing to be done on the territory. It will also require all data to be stored on the territory under the data localisation proposal. The proposed definition, whole not available at the time of writing, has reportedly been prepared whereby it will be similar to the EU definition under the GDPR.[110] Further, the International Association of Privacy Professionals notes that the proposal will provide for a level of consent, and allow a data subject a copy of personal data, right to correction, right to object processing, right to withdrawing consent and right to deletion.

Chen goes onto say that the old data localization guidelines (April 2017) treated both types of data under one umbrella. The new draft focused solely on the outbound transfer of personal information, which hinted at a forthcoming twin draft for important data.[111] This separation stands in line with the National People's Congress' legislative plan, where a personal information protection law and a data security law are in the pipeline. In addition, Chen notes that consent is likely to be diluted. Currently, no outbound transfer would be allowed without consent by the personal information subject. The proposal is likely to result in consent being needed only for the onward transfer of sensitive personal information – a small subset of PI – to third parties.[112] However, these new proposals require further vigilance until China release the final versions that will be implemented. Yet, China appear to be watching other states very closely as to what principles and concepts can apply to their laws, which will serve their policy needs. They are, in part, increasingly adopting some of the important provisions from the EU GDPR to provide a balance between the protection of personal data and its economic activity. Arguably China, at this stage, see a greater importance in the economic and social value to the state for regulating data, rather than viewing data protection as a right to and for its citizens. As the regulatory landscape continues to evolve and change in China, individuals and entities are going to have to be vigilant to any law reform, as it may or may not enhance or hinder their personal and business activities. At the time of concluding this book, the above had not been implemented.

---

[109] Ibid.

[110] A look at China's draft of Personal Information Protection Law, https://iapp.org/news/a/a-look-at-chinas-draft-of-personal-data-protection-law/

[111] Ibid.

[112] Ibid.

12.12 Conclusion

The concept of privacy over the Internet and privacy generally in China is complex. The historical development of China has had a significant impact on the way the state addresses privacy through the law. This is because they view the rule of law quite differently to that of Western democratic states. Nonetheless, China has begun to embrace the idea that a level of privacy over the internet is needed.

China's Cybersecurity laws have a pivotal role in protecting their citizens' personal data over the internet. China, has a distinctive model when compared to other states and the EU. Of the current data protection laws compared in this book and the previous book, China's model highlights, in depth the interconnectedness of data protection and cybersecurity. They, have to date, taken a greater focus on establishing strong laws around protecting the systems, platforms and infrastructure. Even though there are signs that China is developing similar law or elements of the law to that of other nations including the EU, they have by and large, developed a model that other states could also consider building into their respective legal frameworks. Their legislation and regulations are structured very differently to that of the other states discussed in this book. However, this does not mean that they have not or have diverged significantly from the legal framework that has emerged internationally in the last decade to protect personal data. Arguably, the current day legal framework has Chinese characteristics that, serve the country well and delivers on their own internal sovereign needs.

It must be kept in mind that, China has a population that far exceeds the US, EU, Australia, Korea and the other states discussed in this book. Thus, they have valid reasons for adopting the approach towards data protection that, they have to date. Nonetheless, in our view, and while not explicitly stated by commentators in China, there appears to be a move towards adopting a similar approach to the rest of the world, and particularly the EU model. This was reinforced by Samm Sacks who believes China approach is better understood as a kind of policy guideline or regulation, and that government authorities are likely to refer to the specification when conducting various reviews and approvals.[113] Sacks goes onto highlight an important and positive point when it comes to China. He is of the view China's Personal Information Security Specification includes guidance on user consent, data protection, data access, the obligation of disclosure, and the evaluation of data security, but overall it is more permissive. Sacks makes the point, the GDPR has provided six lawful bases that allow data controllers to process personal data, such as user consent, legal obligation, and vital interests, but the specification only lists four circumstances where data controllers are not allowed to process personal data.

Nonetheless, China's recent addition to the legislative framework in relation to tighter controls and protections for children 14 years old and younger, is another example where they have taken a similar approach to the EU and other states. It is

---

[113] Sacks, S, China's Emerging Data Privacy System and GDPR, Center for Strategic and international Studies, 2018, https://www.csis.org/analysis/chinas-emerging-data-privacy-system-and-gdpr

moving ever closer to the EU framework. Arguably, the framework established by China also represents any other legal frameworks for industry sectors, whether that be food and agriculture production to environmental protection. In other words, the cybersecurity laws establish the minimum standard, and the Personal Information Security Specification[114] build on those minimum standards providing more direction of the responsibilities and obligations afforded to individuals and entities to protect personal data.

Moreover, China has sought to integrate cybersecurity with data protection. Doing so, demonstrates the argument that this book makes that increasingly cybersecurity and data protection have been intertwined and cannot be decoupled. This position has been reinforced by Article 1 and 2 of the laws that ensure cybersecurity; safeguard cyberspace sovereignty and national security, and social and public interests; protect the lawful rights and interests of citizens, legal persons, and other organizations; and promote the healthy development of the information of the economy and society. This is also supported by Chap. 2 and 3 of the laws. Further, the law applies to the construction, operation, maintenance, and use of networks, as well as to cybersecurity supervision and management.

One of the challenges for China is to reflect on whether these laws and the steps taken in 2019 to strengthen controls over children's personal data, will extend to AI systems within the home. This along with the number of criminal offences recorded across China throughout 2019 is high. Between January and October, the country's Internet Cleanup 2019 led to the investigation of almost 46,000 cases of internet crimes, the arrest of nearly 66,000 suspects and the breakup of criminal gangs, many of which were involved with fintech and big data companies that used personal data obtained illicitly to enable predatory lending and shady debt collection.[115] With the increase in use of APPs the violations could increase, and when coupled with AI systems the criminal activity and threat to privacy and personal data will only be heightened. Thus, a more comprehensive study will be required to determine how children and the broader community will be impacted.

Despite the current direction by China, it has been reported that they are moving towards implementing dedicated data protection laws, sometime in 2020–2021. Although, what is evident, China has placed the economic activity and social behaviour of data use ahead of protecting the data as a fundamental right. Finally, it will be interesting to watch how China react to the onset and implementation of AI, and whether they take a similar approach to data protection, or take a different route that could see further protections afforded to children and other vulnerable groups in the community.

---

[114] Information Security Technology – Personal information security specification, https://www.tc260.org.cn/upload/2018-01-24/1516799764389090333.pdf – Chinese version.

[115] Yin, D, *China Internet Regulators Define Privacy Violations for Apps, Data Companies,* December 2019, https://www.caixinglobal.com/2019-12-31/china-internet-regulators-define-privacy-violations-for-apps-data-companies-101499601.html

References

Chen, J. F. (1999). *Chinese law: Towards an understanding of Chinese law, its nature, and development*. The Hague: Kluwer.

Eberhard, W. (2004). *A history of China*. Gutenburg ebook a history of China. Project Gutenberg. http://library.umac.mo/ebooks/b30863582.pdf

Ip, K., Lau, N., & Gong, J. (2019, September). *China: China's first regulation on children's online privacy*. Herbert Smith Freehills. https://sites-herbertsmithfreehills.vuturevx.com/95/20753/september-2019/china-s-first-regulation-on-children-s-online-privacy.asp?sid=56d3bb39-faab-43a3-967a-6cbeb683e586&utm_source=Mondaq&utm_medium=syndication&utm_campaign=inter-article-link

Kong, L. (2010). Enacting China's data protection act. *International Journal of Law and Information Technology, 18*(3), 197–226.

Liu, J. (2013) *Overview of the Chinese legal system*. Hogan Lovells. https://elr.info/sites/default/files/chinaupdate1.1.pdf

Wang, H. (2011). *Protecting privacy in China: A research on China's privacy standards and the possibility of establishing the right to privacy and the information privacy protection legislation in modern China*. Springer.

Wang, L. M. (2017). *Privacy protection in China: Paths, characteristics and issues*. The International Conference of Data Protection and Privacy Commissioners (ICDPPC). https://www.privacyconference2017.org/eng/files/programme_booklet.pdf

Part III
Data Protection Law – North America

Chapter 13
Canada

Abstract Canada, another country that has a remarkable story, with a rich and diverse history that dates back centuries. Canada is unique in that even though it a Western democratic country it has adopted both the common and civil law. Privacy and data protection have been an evolving part of Canadian society. During the 1960s and 1970s, there was considerable debate regarding the extensive use of listening devices by private agencies. A common example often cited is how car salesmen would bug cars to determine how much customers would pay for them, to dance studios that eavesdropped on customers' conversations to determine the most effective sales pitch. During the 1950s and 1960s, the police employed electronic listening devices when investigating criminal activity, however, there was limited success. Canada has embraced the concept of the right to privacy, along with the need to protect its citizens' personal data and information over the Internet. This Chapter explores the current data protection laws of Canada. It does not examine the equivalent laws in Quebec.

This Chapter only examines both the *Personal Information Protection and Electronic Documents Act*, S.C. 2000 (PIPEDA), and *Privacy Act 1985* (PA). At the time of writing this book the Canadian government were undertaking a review of the Privacy Act 1985. This Chapter does not consider the review and only discusses the laws in the current form. It is acknowledged that any reform could have a significant impact to the structure and provisions of the current law. Despite the reform program currently underway, the data protection and privacy laws of Canada are different to that of many other jurisdictions, including those discussed in this book. The PIPEDA regulates the private sector, while the PA is only applicable to the public sector.

Due to the comparative analysis of two separate laws, the footnotes in this Chapter will be duplicated so as the relevant law and section is clearly identified. However, due to the differing structure and framework of the respective laws, this Chapter will only discuss the definition of personal information, the concept of consent, the regulator, codes of practice, notification, transnational data use, penalties, tort and cyber security. This Chapter does not deal with the indigenous community or information bank in any detail. The question for Canada, and their

R. Walters, M. Novak, *Cyber Security, Artificial Intelligence, Data Protection & the Law*, https://doi.org/10.1007/978-981-16-1665-5_13

review of the public sector Privacy Act is whether the laws adequately respond to AI, and the devices that will use AI. It will briefly examine whether the current definition of personal data and the concept of consent is adequate in a time of heightened cybersecurity incursions.

13.1 Introduction

The occupation of the Canadian territory dates back 14,000 years ago. Canadians have lived on the land which is now Canada for thousands of years. Few traces remain of the earliest inhabitants, but it is known that they eventually settled from coast to coast and were the ancestors of modern Indigenous people. By late 16th century, the population of Canada is thought to have reached 350,000 to 500,000. Its Indigenous communities were organized and governed in many different ways.[1] During the 17th century, both France and Great Britain established permanent settlements in Canada. As a result, a conflict arose with the Indigenous peoples between 1756–1763.[2] Following the internal conflict, the United States emerged as a powerful new rival. The Royal Proclamation of 1763 is a key document in Canadian history. Among other things, it declared that Indigenous peoples had the right to all lands that had not already been sold or given to the Crown.[3] More importantly, this became the basis of Canadian treaty law. In the same year, the Proclamation was also mentioned in the *Canadian Charter of Rights and Freedoms*. The Charter saw the beginning of the guarantee and protection of many rights or freedoms. This, also went some way to the establishment of Canada as an independent state. It was not until 1867 that the *British North America Act*[4] was established. The significance of this legislation, created what is now understood to be the current day Canada. More importantly, it was also the country's first Constitution, laying out many of the rules and traditions that still govern Canada today.[5] It provided for the Legislature in accordance with sections 92 and 94 to make laws in relation to property and civil rights, amongst others. The legislative instrument never went further than this, and does not make any reference to the right to privacy. However, it must be noted that the right to privacy during the 1800s was not widely understood as something important enough to protect.

As Canada moved into the 1900s, they gained more autonomy. In 1926, following a meeting of Commonwealth leaders, the Balfour Report provided the pathway for the United Kingdom and its Dominions, which included Canada to be

[1] Foundations, A History of Canada and Its Parliament, Parliament of Canada, https://lop.parl.ca/staticfiles/Learn/Documents/ParliamentaryPrimer/LOP_TimelineBroch_EN.pdf

[2] Ibid.

[3] Ibid.

[4] *British North America Act*, http://www.legislation.gov.uk/ukpga/1867/3/pdfs/ukpga_18670003_en.pdf

[5] Foundations, A History of Canada and Its Parliament, Parliament of Canada, https://lop.parl.ca/staticfiles/Learn/Documents/ParliamentaryPrimer/LOP_TimelineBroch_EN.pdf

autonomous and equal.[6] Late in 1931, The statute of Westminster was established and this was significant because it officially provided Canada, the right to full independence from the United Kingdom. During the late 1800s and 1900s, there were a number of Dominions of the United Kingdom that, would gain more independence, including Australia. Post WWII, similar to other former colonies of the United Kingdom marked a period of legislative development that would advance the rights, obligations and protections of its citizens. In 1960 the Canadian Bill of Rights[7] had been established.

Privacy and data protection have been an evolving part of Canadian society. During the 1960s and 1970s, there was considerable debate regarding the extensive use of listening devices by private agencies.[8] For instance, car salesmen would bug cars to determine how much customers would pay for them, to dance studios that eavesdropped on customers' conversations to determine the most effective sales pitch. The police employed electronic listening devices (though by the late 1960s, their use had secured only six or seven convictions). Throughout British Columbia, a public inquiry was instituted after a private investigator was caught bugging the Pulp and Paper Workers of Canada. The media were able to obtain evidence that the police had used wiretaps against two Ontario magistrates for nearly 2 months without authorization.[9] More pervasively, there was no legislative or other regulatory restraint on the private or public use of listening devices, and it largely went unfettered. In 1969, John Turner, the Federal Minister for Justice highlighted the dangers of electronic eavesdropping in a speech before the Canadian Bar Association stating at:

> A remote-controlled amplifier and microphone, no larger than the head of a pin, can capture a conversation of people and transmit it by wire for twenty-five miles. A parabolic microphone without wires or radio transmitter can catch the conversation of two people in a boat in mid-lake, and record it on shore. The switching of a single wire can convert any telephone in Canada into a live microphone conducting sounds, even when the telephone is in its cradle. Cameras the size of a cigarette can photograph a room two blocks away by moonlight. Infra-red light techniques permit a room to be watched and photographed from an adjoining room through apparently opaque walls. Radio pills substituted for the subject's aspirins and lodged in his stomach can transform him into a living electronic beacon. The investigator's dream – making his subject a walking transmitter, and enabling the investigator to hear everything the subject says to anybody else, or even what he mutters to himself – can be realized by the wiring of a person's clothing. We are told that there are transmitters

---

6 Ibid.

7 Bill of Rights 1960 Canada, https://laws-lois.justice.gc.ca/pdf/c-12.3.pdf

8 Canada's Human Rights History, https://historyofrights.ca/encyclopaedia/main-events/privacy/. Beck, S., *Canadian Bar Review* (1968), Flinn, A., Jones, H., eds. *Freedom of Information: Open Access, Empty Archives?* London: Routledge, 2009. Robert Hayward, "Federal Access and Privacy Legislation and the Public Archives of Canada." *Archivaria* 18, 1 (1984): 47–58. Robert Hazell, Ben Worthy. "Assessing the Performance of Freedom of Information." *Government Information Quarterly* 27, 4 (2011): 352–359. Larsen, M., Walby, K, eds. *Brokering Access: Power, Politics and Freedom of Information Process in Canada.* Vancouer: UBC Press, (2012).

9 Ibid.

> so small they can be mounted as a tooth in a dental bridge … The Orwellian society of 1984 may be here already.[10]

While not specifically mentioning privacy, the former Minister was clearly highlighting the intrusive nature from the use of this equipment. More importantly the reference to the Orwellian society in 1984, pictured Eric Blair, who, at the time was writing under a pseudonym George Orwell, published a novel. The novel tells the story of Winston Smith, a hapless middle-aged bureaucrat who lives in Oceania, where he is governed by constant surveillance. Even though there are no laws, there is a police force, the "Thought Police," and the constant reminders, on posters, that "Big Brother Is Watching You."[11] The society portrayed in "1984" is one in which social control is exercised through disinformation and surveillance. Under the concept of the Orwellian society, there is a steady rise of "reality TV," beginning in the '60s with "Candid Camera," "An American Family," "Real People," "Cops" and "The Real World," television has also contributed to the acceptance of a kind of video surveillance.[12] The reality today, across the world is that this fictional novel was not far off the mark. In the contemporary world we see that, modern day technology and the ability for surveillance to be undertaken not only by governments, but also, the private sector pervades society. It has resulted in large scale intrusion and misuse of personal data. The resulting affect has also seen the debate broaden to better understand the level of intrusion to people's privacy, and the impact from cyber intrusions and cybercrime.

In 1982, the Canadian Charter of Rights and Freedoms was established. However, there is no mention of privacy or data protection. Furthermore, and interestingly the Canadian constitution does not mention privacy once.[13] In same year, personal information emerged in *Canada (Privacy Commissioner) v Blood Tribe Department of Health*,[14] whereby the Privacy Commissioner argued that:

> this case is about calling the private sector to account for its claims of privilege over documents containing personal information of others. Whether their claims turn out to be completely right, honestly equivocal, overly broad, inadvertently wrong, or intentionally misleading, they must be independently verified in order to give proper meaning to the fundamental right of access to one's personal information.[15]

The Commissioner was required to resolve a conflict between, on the one hand, the Privacy Commissioner's statutory power to have access to personal information. Interestingly the Act defined both personal information and personal health

---

[10] Ibid.

[11] The Conversation, *What Orwell's '1984' tells us about today's world, 70 years after it was published,* http://theconversation.com/what-orwells-1984-tells-us-about-todays-world-70-years-after-it-was-published-116940

[12] Ibid.

[13] Canada's Constitution of 1867 with Amendments through 2011 https://www.constituteproject.org/constitution/Canada_2011.pdf?lang=en

[14] [2008] 2 S.C.R. 574, 2008 SCC 44.

[15] Ibid, [15].

information separately. This is a consistent approach to other modern day states who place personal health information as requiring a higher level of control and protection.[16]

There are four key statutes that support and govern the collection, use, disclosure and management of personal information throughout Canada. These include the:

(i) Federal *Personal Information Protection and Electronic Documents Act*, S.C. 2000;
(ii) Alberta's *Personal Information Protection Act*, S.A. 2003, ("PIPA Alberta");
(iii) British Columbia's *Personal Information Protection Act*, S.B.C. 2003, ("PIPA BC"); and
(iv) Québec's *An Act Respecting the Protection of Personal Information in the Private Sector*, R.S.Q., ("Québec Privacy Act").

This Chapter only examines both the *Personal Information Protection and Electronic Documents Act*, S.C. 2000 (PIPEDA),[17] and *Privacy Act 1985* (PA). Both the PIPEDA and PA regulate the management and use of personal information. However, they have separate roles. The PIPEDA only regulates personal information/data pertaining to the private sector, while the PA regulates its use within and across the public sector. The PIPEDA defines a commercial activity as any particular transaction, act, or conduct, or any regular course of conduct that is of a commercial character, including the selling, bartering or leasing of donor, membership or other fundraising lists.[18] Yet, and while not defining a public activity, section 3 of the PA defines government institution to mean any department or ministry of state of the Government of Canada, or anybody or office and any parent Crown corporation, and any wholly owned subsidiary of such a corporation, within the meaning of section 83 of the *Financial Administration Act*.[19]

This Chapter will, in part, compare the differences between the two laws. This will provide a comparison of the differences afforded to the public and private

[16] Personal Information Protection and Electronic Documents Act 2000, section 5. *personal health information* - with respect to an individual, whether living or deceased, means (a) information concerning the physical or mental health of the individual; (b) information concerning any health service provided to the individual; (c) information concerning the donation by the individual of any body part or any bodily substance of the individual or information derived from the testing or examination of a body part or bodily substance of the individual; (d) information that is collected in the course of providing health services to the individual; or (e) information that is collected incidentally to the provision of health services to the individual. *Personal information* - means information about an identifiable individual.

[17] Osler, Hoskin and Harcourt, *International comparative Legal Guide, Data Protection 2018*, https://www.osler.com/osler/media/Osler/reports/privacy-data/Data-Protection-Laws-in-Canada-2018.pdf

[18] Personal Information Protection and Electronic Documents Act, S.C. 2000, section 2. For example, sectors include but not limited to airports, aircraft and airlines; banks and authorized foreign banks; inter-provincial or international transportation companies; telecommunications companies; offshore drilling operations; and radio and television broadcasters.

[19] Privacy Act 1985, section 3.

sectors. Both Acts have incorporated the internationally agreed and accepted data protection principles of the OECD, such as accountability, purpose, consent, limited collection, disclosure and retention, accuracy, openness, safe guards and access.[20] The privacy standards in Canada were developed in 1995–96 by the Canadian Standards Association (CSA) Model Code for the Protection of Personal Information. These standards address the way organizations collect, use, disclose, and protect personal information.[21] George Yee highlights how it also defines the right of individuals to have access to personal information about themselves, and, if necessary, to have the information corrected. More importantly, Yee confirms that the standards are largely based on the former EU Privacy Directive(95/46/EC), and the Code of Fair Information Practices defined in 1973 by the United States (US) Department of Health, Education and Welfare. Thus, the fundamentals of privacy over the Internet in Canada have, in part, taken elements from both the EU and US. Colin Bennett and Robyn Bailey believe that all privacy protection laws, therefore, are based on the transparent communication of the purposes for which personal data will be processed.[22] This transparency establishes a relationship of *trust* that personal data will not be re-used, re-purposed and disclosed to other organizations, which arguably the Canadian laws aim to achieve.[23] This principle is at the heart of the theory of information privacy and reinforces powerful social norms. It also governs both the processing of personal data.

More recently, Colin Bennett, Christopher Parsons and Andrew Molnar highlight that Canada has played a pivotal role in the overall development of privacy law – worldwide.[24] The authors note that the former Privacy Commissioner of Canada Jennifer Stodart has played a significant role internationally, for her leadership in this area of the law. They highlight that in 2011, how Canadian regulators were able to enforce successfully the privacy laws against Google and Facebook. However, Canadian privacy laws, as highlighted by Bennett, Parsons and Molnar has not come without pressure from the international community. Even though the current legal framework is serving the country well, it remains to be seen whether Canada will retain the current dualist approach of having separate laws for the public and private sectors.

[20] Personal Information Protection and Electronic Documents Act, S.C. 2000, Schedule 1 Principles Set Out in the National Standard of Canada Entitled Model Code for the Protection of Personal Information, CAN/CSA-Q830–96. Principle 1 Accountability, Principle 2 Identifying, Purposes, Principle 3 Consent, Principle 4 Limiting Collection, Principle 5 Limiting Use, Disclosure, and Retention, Principle 6 Accuracy, Principle 7 Safeguards, Principle 8 Openness, Principle 9 Individual Access, Principle 10 Challenging Compliance.

[21] George Yee, *Privacy Protection for E-Services* IGI Global, 2006. 1–304. Web. (2019), 3–6.

[22] Bennett, C., Bailey, R. *Privacy Protection in the Era of Big Data: Regulatory Challenges and Social Assessments* in Bart vander Sloot, Dennis Broeders, Erik Schrijvers, Exploring the Boundaries of big Data, Amsterdam University Press, (2015), pp. 205–227.

[23] Ibid.

[24] Bennett, C., Parsons, C., Molnar, A, *Real and Substantial Connections: Enforcing Canadian Privacy law against American Social Networking Companies*, Journal of Law, information and science, Vol 23, No.1 (2014).

Bennett et al. reinforce the above, stating that in 2009, the OPC announced that Facebook had violated various provisions of PIPEDA. Facebook initially resisted the question of jurisdiction – and, at the time, lacked physical offices in Canada – but finally cooperated (without prejudice) in the investigation and made changes as a result of the OPC's investigation report and subsequent audits. They go onto say that since 2009 the company has opened Canadian offices and, in 2011, the OPC opened another investigation addressing online tracking linked to "Like buttons" and "social plug-ins."[25] The issue highlighted the extraterritorial effect of the PIPEDA, and the ongoing challenges facing not only Canada, but also, other states that are having to govern large and profitable multinational organizations, located in different states. As technology develops, and AI is potentially concentrated to a few, this issue is likely to continue unabated. How states will respond will be even more challenging, when there continues to be a lack of consistency in the law.

13.2 Definition – Personal Information

The definition of personal information differs greatly between the PIPEDA and PA. The PIPEDA defines personal information to mean information about an identifiable individual. This all-encompassing definition arguably means what it states that all and any information that can identify a data subject, is considered personal information.[26] Based on this definition elements of artificial intelligence such as biometric information such as facial and body mapping would come within this definition, along with the traditional identifying information such as name, address and date of birth. In support of the definition of personal information, the PIPEDA goes onto identify personal health information. The PIPEDA states that personal health information constitutes whether the individual is living or deceased, and includes information concerning the physical or mental health of the individual; any health service provided to the individual; and the donation by the individual of any body part or any bodily substance of the individual or information derived from the testing or examination of a body part or bodily substance of the individual.[27] Additionally, personal health information also constitutes information that is collected in the course of providing health services to the individual; or is collected incidentally to the provision of health services to the individual.

On the other hand, the PA has what can be regarded as one of the most comprehensive definition of personal information. Section 3 defines personal information means information about an identifiable individual that is recorded in any form including race, national or ethnic origin, colour, religion, age or marital status of the

[25] Colin Bennett, Christopher Parsons, Andrew Molnar, *Real and Substantial Connections: Enforcing Canadian Privacy law against American Social Networking Companies*, Journal of Law, information and science, Vol 23, No.1 (2014).

[26] Personal Information Protection and Electronic Documents Act, S.C. 2000, section 2.

[27] Ibid.

individual. It also includes any information relating to the education or the medical, criminal or employment history of the individual, financial transactions, identifying number, symbol or other particular assigned to the individual, address, fingerprints or blood type of the individual.[28] The PA has included health data and information into this definition. Apart from general identifiable information, personal information goes onto mean the personal opinions or views of the individual except where they are about another individual or about a proposal for a grant, an award or a prize to be made to another individual by a government institution or a part of a government institution specified in the regulations. It also includes correspondence sent to a government institution by the individual that is implicitly or explicitly of a private or confidential nature, and replies to such correspondence that would reveal the contents of the original correspondence. The expanded list is arguably very prescriptive and the definition in the PIPEDA captures all of the personal information of the PA. The question is whether it is time for Canada to consider amending the PA to reflect the defining of personal information of the PIPEDA? At issue is whether this definition in the PA will be effective enough when AI becomes mainstream.

Notwithstanding the above, the definition of personal information under the PA goes onto include, the views or opinions of another individual about the individual.[29] Furthermore, personal information constitutes that information about an individual who is or was performing services under contract for a government institution, including the terms of the contract, the name of the individual and the opinions or views of the individual given in the course of the performance of those services. Finally, it also includes that personal information relating to any discretionary benefit of a financial nature, including the granting of a licence or permit, conferred on an individual, including the name of the individual and the exact nature of the benefit, and information about an individual who has been dead for more than twenty years.[30]

---

[28] Ibid, section 3.

[29] Privacy Act 1985, section 3, (h) the views or opinions of another individual about a proposal for a grant, an award or a prize to be made to the individual by an institution or a part of an institution referred to in paragraph (e), but excluding the name of the other individual where it appears with the views or opinions of the other individual, and (i) the name of the individual where it appears with other personal information relating to the individual or where the disclosure of the name itself would reveal information about the individual, but, for the purposes of sections 7, 8 and 26 and section 19 of the *Access to Information Act*, does not include (j) information about an individual who is or was an officer or employee of a government institution that relates to the position or functions of the individual including, (i) the fact that the individual is or was an officer or employee of the government institution, (ii) the title, business address and telephone number of the individual, (iii) the classification, salary range and responsibilities of the position held by the individual, (iv) the name of the individual on a document pre- pared by the individual in the course of employment, and (v) the personal opinions or views of the individual given in the course of employment, (j.1) the fact that an individual is or was a *ministerial adviser* or a member of a *ministerial staff*, as those terms are defined in subsection 2(1) of the *Conflict of Interest Act*, as well as the individual's name and title.

[30] Ibid.

In Dagg v Canada (Minister of Finance)[31] a leading decision in Canada regarding the proper approach to interpreting the *Privacy Act* and the *Access to Information Act*. In particularly, the case provided the basis for the interpretation of "personal information" according to the PA. This case concerned a request under the *Access to Information Act* for copies of logs signed by employees entering and leaving the Department of Finance workplace on weekends during the month of September, 1990.[32] The Minister of Finance disclosed the logs, but deleted the employees' names, identification numbers and signatures on the grounds that this was "personal information" and therefore did not need to be disclosed. The Information Commissioner agreed with the Minister's approach.[33] The requester applied to the Federal Court. The Federal Court concluded that the names were not personal information and should be released.[34] On appeal by the Minister, the Federal Court of Appeal reversed that decision and ordered that the names not be released. The Court then discussed the interpretation of the term "personal information" as defined in the *Privacy Act*. It noted that:

> Section 3 of the *Privacy Act* states that "personal information" means "information about an identifiable individual that is recorded in any form including, without restricting the generality of the foregoing…", and then goes on to list several examples.[35]

The Court also stated that this:

> phraseology indicates that the general opening words are the primary source of interpretation, and that the subsequent enumeration merely identifies examples of the type of subject matter encompassed by the general definition. Consequently, if the record is captured by those opening words, it does not matter that it does not fall within any specific examples. The interpretation of "personal information" is therefore very broad, and "captures any information about a specific person.[36]

On the facts, the information requested revealed the times during which employees attended their workplace on weekends. Even the names alone would disclose information about those individuals. This is "information about an identifiable individual" and therefore falls within the definition of "personal information" in the *Privacy Act*.

Later in 2008, the case of *Gordon v. Canada (Health)*,[37] again in reference to the Privacy Act and the definition of personal information, the Federal Court decided that information will be about an identifiable individual where there is a serious possibility that an individual could be identified through the use of that information, alone or in combination with other available information.[38] The case highlighted

---

[31] [1997] 2 S.C.R. 403.

[32] Ibid.

[33] Ibid.

[34] Ibid.

[35] Ibid.

[36] Ibid.

[37] *Gordon v. Canada (Health)*, 2008 FC 258.

[38] Ibid.

how a reporter from the CBC made an *Access to Information Act* request for the Canadian Adverse Drug Reactions Information System ("CADRIS") database maintained by Health Canada.[39] Health Canada disclosed most of the fields in CADRIS to the CBC. It refused to disclose certain fields that directly identified individuals or for other reasons that were not contested. However, Health Canada also refused to disclose the "province" field, which referred to the province from which the report in question was received (not necessarily the province of residence of the individual who suffered the adverse health product reaction). Health Canada refused to disclose that field on the grounds that it could be used to identify the individual who suffered the adverse health product reaction. The Information Commissioner agreed with Health Canada, but the reporter applied to Federal Court to resolve the matter. The Federal Court ruled that the:

> 'province' field in combination with other publicly available information was personal information under the *Privacy Act* and should not be disclosed.[40]

This case turned largely on the interpretation of the term "personal information" and what constitutes information "about" an identifiable individual. The Federal Court concluded that:

> information is "about" an identifiable individual if it "permits" or "leads" to the possible identification of the individual, whether alone or combined with sources otherwise available – including sources publicly available.[41]

The Court went on to conclude that:

> Information will be about an identifiable individual where there is a serious possibility that an individual could be identified through the use of that information, alone or in combination with other available information.[42]

The Court highlighted that the definition of personal information provided by the PA is to be interpreted broadly, and can include personal information that has been recorded in a data base. Importantly, and while health data has not been provided a separate and distinct definition similar to sensitive data under other data protection laws such as Australia and the EU GDPR.

More recently in 2011, Canada again had to consider the definition of personal data under the PA. The Federal Court of Appeal in *Nault v Canada (Public Works and Government Services)*,[43] had to decide on whether the information about the work experience and educational activities of individuals before they join the public

---

[39] Ibid, CADRIS is a database containing information collected by Health Canada relating to suspected adverse reactions to health products marketed in Canada. Information regarding these reactions is collected on a voluntary basis through reports by health professionals and consumers, and on a mandatory basis from drug manufacturers. CADRIS contains approximately 125 data fields, with information about approximately 180,000 adverse reactions between 1965 and 2006.

[40] Ibid.

[41] Ibid.

[42] Ibid.

[43] *Nault v. Canada (Public Works and Government Services)*, 2011 FCA 263.

service is personal information and does not need to be disclosed to the public. An unsuccessful candidate for certain positions in the federal public service filed a request under the *Access to Information Act* for documents submitted by each of the 61 successful candidates in the recruitment opportunities in which he participated. The head of Public Works and Government Services Canada ("PWGSC") refused to disclose those documents on the grounds that they were personal information of the successful candidates. The Information Commissioner agreed with PWGSC, as did the Federal Court.[44] The Court ruled that:

> information about work and educational experience before becoming a public servant is personal information and does not need to be disclosed to the public.[45]

The Federal Court of Appeal identified that:

> the requested information is clearly "information relating to the education… or employment history of the individual" and therefore clearly within the definition of personal information in the *Privacy Act* – specifically, paragraph (b) of that definition. The only issue was whether this information was excluded by paragraph (j) of the definition as being related to "the position or functions" of an employee of a government institution.[46]

The Court of Appeal further rules that information concerning achievements at an educational institution or a previous employer do not relate to the "position of functions" with a government institution, but rather concern a position or functions with the educational institution or previous employer.[47] The Court of Appeal went onto consider the candidate's argument that this information was necessary so that the Canadian public can satisfy itself that the incumbents of positions in the federal public service satisfied the requirements of their position. However, the Court of Appeal noted that courts have already decided that evaluations of government employees are "personal information" and cannot be disclosed. If information about competency is excluded, then information about personal qualifications should be excluded too.[48] What these cases demonstrate is the extent to what and how personal information will be defined and viewed more broadly by the courts. While the cases do involve the public sector under the PA, they nevertheless, also highlight the need for individuals and entities even in the private sector to be vigilant of what constitutes personal information, because the PIPEDA has a much broader definition.

Today more than ever, personal data can more easily be re-identified from the combination of data elements which, on their own, say little or nothing of about any one particular person.[49] Our online tracks are tied to smartphones or personal computers through Unique Devise Identifiers (udids), ip addresses, 'fingerprinting' and

[44] Ibid.

[45] Ibid.

[46] Ibid.

[47] Ibid.

[48] Ibid.

[49] Bennett, C., Bailey, R, (015) *Privacy Protection in the Era of Big Data: Regulatory Challenges and Social Assessments,* in Bart vander Sloot, Dennis Broeders, Erik Schrijvers, Exploring the Boundaries of big Data, Amsterdam University Press, (2015) 205–227.

other means. Bennett and Bailey assert that “given how closely these personal communication devices are associated with the individuals who use them, information linked to these devices is, to all intents and purposes, linked to individuals”.[50] They go onto say that the “sophistication of contemporary re-identification science gives a false sense that data can ever be stripped of identifying markers”.[51] Therefore, Big Data can increase the risk of re-identification, and in some cases, inadvertently re-identify large swaths of de-identified data all at once. Thus, the issue for children is arguably that the very definition of personal data in the Canadian context being different for the public and private sector will pose problems in AI.

13.3 Rights [Access]

The PA provides for the right of data subjects to access personal data. That is, section 12 provides that every Canadian citizen or a permanent resident has a right to request and be given access to their personal information about the individual contained in a personal information bank.[52] Citizens can also gain access to their personal information that is under the control of a government institution. Furthermore, every data subject has the right to request correction of their personal information where the individual believes there is an error or omission. A data subject is also able to require that a notation to be attached to the information reflecting any correction request. Further, the data subject can require that any person or body to whom that information has been disclosed for use for an administrative purpose within 2 years prior to the time a correction is requested or a notation is required under this subsection in respect of that information. They must be notified of the correction or notation. Finally, the government institution must make the correction or notation on any copy of the information under its control.

In order for a data subject to access their personal data in accordance with section 12, they need to follow the procedural process in accordance with section 13. That is the request must be made in writing to the government institution. Any request made to a government institution must be conducted within 30 days. That is, unless there has been a request for an extension to the time limit in accordance with section 15. Within the 30 day time period, the government institution must respond to the

[50] Ibid.

[51] Ibid.

[52] Personal Information Protection and Electronic Documents Act, S.C. 2000, section 12. Personal information to be included in personal information banks 10 (1) The head of a government institution shall cause to be included in personal information banks all personal information under the control of the government institution that (a) has been used, is being used or is available for use for an administrative purpose; or (b) is organized or intended to be retrieved by the name of an individual or by an identifying number, symbol or other particular assigned to an individual. Exception for Library and Archives of Canada (2) Subsection (1) does not apply in respect of personal information under the custody or control of the Library and Archives of Canada that has been transferred there by a government institution for historical or archival purposes.

individual in writing, informing them of whether access will be granted or otherwise, and where access is granted outline what personal information will be provided. A section 15 extension can only be granted for a further 30 days. However, and while an individual may be granted access to their personal data, they can also be refused access. Even when a government institution has not met the required time lines set out above, it is deemed that the institution has refused access to that data. This is something to note, because under section 16 the government institution is effectively provided an exemption, when they do not meet the required timelines. This does not mean though that the institution has closed the matter, and they still have the discretion to provide the personal data, even after the timeframe has expired.

Notwithstanding the above, the process or form in which access can be obtained to the personal information, the government institution can allow the individual to examine that personal information upon providing a copy of the that information.[53] Any access to personal information granted to a data subject is to be provided in one of the official languages of Canada, such as English or French.[54] In the event the personal data is only recorded in the English language and the request has been made that it be in the French language, the government institution is obliged to translate the personal data into the French language. Additionally, in accordance with section 17(3), where the data subject has a disability, and that individual requests the information to be provided in a particular format, the government institution must undertake to do so. However, the institution must consider that it is reasonable in the circumstances to convert the data to the format requested by the data subject.

In *Oleinik v Canada (Privacy Commissioner)*[55] the Court had to consider whether the data subject was afforded access to their personal data in accordance with the law. *Oleinik #1* involved an individual who applied unsuccessfully for a Social Sciences and Humanities Research Council (SSHRC) grant in 2007. In 2008, the individual submitted an access to personal information request to SSHRC in connection with his failed application. SSHRC complied with this request. However, the Applicant was dissatisfied with SSHRC's response, and subsequently filed a complaint with the Privacy Commissioner. The Privacy Commissioner concluded the complaint was not well founded. Instead of applying to the Federal Court in accordance with section 41 of the *Privacy Act* for an order against SSHRC, the Applicant applied for judicial review against the Privacy Commissioner's report. The Applicant alleged that the Privacy Commissioner erred in not upholding his complaint that SSHRC had withheld personal information, and also alleged that the

[53] Privacy Act 1985, section 17.

[54] Official Languages Act R.S.C 1985.

[55] *Oleinik v Canada (Privacy Commissioner)* 2011, affirmed by 2012 FCA and 2013 FC 44 (Oleinik #1 and #2).

Privacy Commissioner breached the rules of procedural fairness in the manner of the investigation into his complaint.[56] The Federal Court concluded:

> the Applicant could not challenge the substance of the Privacy Commissioner's actions by way of an application for judicial review. The Privacy Commissioner does not make decisions; he or she only makes recommendations. The Applicant's only recourse is to bring an application pursuant to section 41 of the *Privacy Act* against SSHRC. The Applicant could bring an application for judicial review against the Privacy Commissioner in respect of alleged breaches of procedural fairness. The process of the investigation itself was amenable to review, even though Privacy Commissioner's final recommendation was not.[57]

The Applicant also alleged that the Privacy Commissioner's investigator erred by failing to consider all available and material evidence. The Court rejected that argument:

> finding that the report was "balanced and thorough." Second, the Applicant alleged that the investigator should have sent him a draft report and given him the opportunity to comment.[58]

The Court also concluded that there was no obligation to share a draft of the report and, in any event, the investigator had a "continuous dialogue" with the applicant throughout the investigation. The applicant also alleged that the Privacy Commissioner had an institutional bias in favour of government institutions generally, and specifically against him because of his ethnicity. The Court:

> rejected both claims out of hand because there was no evidence in support of either argument.[59]

Thus, based on the above, the Federal Court dismissed the application. Nevertheless, the case would continue, which would form part of *Oleink #2*. While *Oleink #1* was continuing, the application filed a second complaint against SSHRC. The OPC, however, concluded as *Oleink #1* decision. In summary, *Oleink #2* was based on the two access requests that had been lodged to the OPC. The access request was for all the documents held by the OPC. Even though the OPC disclosed some documents, they decided to withhold others, and subsequently the individual applied for judicial review in the Federal Court. The Court noted that:

> 'the application was, in part, an attempt to re-litigate the finding in *Oleinik #1* that the Applicant could not challenge the substance of the Privacy Commissioner's report by way of judicial review'.[60]

The Court therefore struck that portion of the application on the basis that it was an abuse of the Court's process. The Court further argued that the proper processes were not implemented, and while the Privacy Commissioner is not a legislated position, an individual must still file a complaint with that official before proceeding to Federal Court. Thus, the cautionary tale from *Oleink #2* is that individuals making

---

[56] Ibid.

[57] Ibid.

[58] Ibid.

[59] Ibid.

[60] Ibid.

a complaint must do so in accordance with the process established by the law (Privacy Act). In conclusion, both the Federal Court and Federal Court of Appeal upheld the Federal Court's decision without expanding upon the Federal Court's reasons.

Jonathan Obar[61] makes the point that the principle of access is certainly an important first step toward data privacy self-management. He is of the view there is a problematic presumption that users can control the vast consent and data-management responsibilities associated with big data, and access to that data. He points out that it protects individuals by requiring that they:

(1) initiate review processes with data managers working at potentially thousands of entities, both seen (e.g., an internet service provider, social network, or bank) and hidden (e.g., data brokers), all over the world, likely in different languages, through interfaces and processes that have yet to be standardized and made user-friendly;
(2) deal with the threat mosaic associated with these entities, defined by endless and evolving consent materials and datasets, each one of which is unique to the myriad data managers that deal with individual dossiers; and
(3) address the uncertainty associated with the possibility that different entities "may have disclosed information".[62]

What remains is a question of delivery. He notes that in 2018, the Office of the Privacy Commissioner of Canada (OPC, 2018) recently conducted a consent consultation, and has proposed a variety of "guidelines for obtaining meaningful consent" (para. 1). Among them is the need for clearer and less complex consent materials. Interactive, customizable, and dynamic consent processes are encouraged, as they move individuals away from static PDFs placed at the margins of sites or apps, which are rarely accessed and less often read.[63] While these ideas suggest improvements, none of them address the challenge of the evolving mosaic of materials, or the tangential nature of consent processes to online behaviours. He argues that along with other scholars that a fiduciary duty should be established to rectify this issue. However, Obar cautions on relying exclusively on a fiduciary model because it ignores the individual stories and threatens the realization of data justice. Canada needs to do more as the country moves towards a digital strategy, 'we should not discard the individual access principle, in light of access to big data via consent materials and data management'.[64] Obar goes onto say that, without the opportunity of access, individuals would have no method for even beginning the oversight process. Similarly, access to detailed and useful consent materials is also an essential

[61] Obar, J, *Canadian Journal of Communication,* Canadian Journal of Communication Policy Portal Vol. 44 Issue 2, (2019) 35–41.

[62] Ibid.

[63] Ibid.

[64] Ibid.

first step; without the opportunity to review and learn from these materials, the truth would certainly be hidden.[65]

13.4 Personal Information – Index

Section 11 enables the relevant Minister to publish an index that outlines the personal information bank. The publication of the information bank describes the bank, the registration number and class of individuals, the name of the government institution which is in control of the bank, along with the title and address of the officer who is responsible for receiving the personal information.[66] The Information Bank is a register that records and stores personal data. This is an administrative process afforded to government institutions.

13.5 Consent

The application of the concept of consent under the PIPEDA and the PA vary. Consent under the PIPEDA is similar to other data protection laws around the world. Section 6.1 states that 'consent of an individual is only valid if it is reasonable to expect that an individual to whom the organization's activities are directed would understand the nature, purpose and consequences of the collection, use or disclosure of the personal information to which they are consenting'.

The OPCC have highlighted the importance of consent as a requirement for the collection, use and disclosure of personal information.[67] Organizations are required to inform individuals about what personal information they will collect, how they plan to use or disclose that information, and for what purposes, to enable individual to

---

[65] Ibid.

[66] Privacy Act 1985, section 11. (iv) a statement of the purposes for which personal information in the bank was obtained or compiled and a statement of the uses consistent with those purposes for which the information is used or dis- closed, (v) a statement of the retention and disposal standards applied to personal information in the bank, and (vi) an indication, where applicable, that the bank was designated as an exempt bank by an order un- der section 18 and the provision of section 21 or 22 on the basis of which the order was made; and (b) all classes of personal information under the control of a government institution that are not contained in personal information banks, setting forth in respect of each class (i) a description of the class in sufficient detail to facilitate the right of access under this Act, and (ii) the title and address of the appropriate officer for each government institution to whom requests relating to personal information within the class should be sent.

[67] Office of the Privacy Commissioner Canada, Consent and Privacy: A discussion paper exploring potential enhancements to consent under the *Personal Information Protection and Electronic Documents Act*, https://www.priv.gc.ca/en/opc-actions-and-decisions/research/explore-privacy-research/2016/consent_201605/#fn1-rf

decide whether or not to provide consent. This aims to provide individuals with control over how their information will be collected, used and disclosed.

> In order for consent to be considered meaningful, individuals should have a clear understanding of what will be collected, how their personal information will be used, and with whom it will be shared.[68]

Consent is only valid if it is reasonable to expect that an individual to whom the organization's activities are directed would understand the nature, purpose and consequences of the collection, use or disclosure of the personal information to which they are consenting.[69] Therefore, section 7 largely deals with the knowledge a data subject provides for the collection and disclosure of their personal information. Section 7 allows an organization to collect the personal information of data subjects without their consent (4.3 schedule 1 Principle 3- Consent). Thus, the PIPEDA places a considerable level of importance on the concept of consent. The knowledge and consent of the individual are required for the collection, use, or disclosure of personal information, except where inappropriate. In certain circumstances personal information can be collected, used, or disclosed without the knowledge and consent of the individual.[70] For instance, legal, medical, or security reasons may make it impossible or impractical to seek consent. When information is being collected for the detection and prevention of fraud or for law enforcement, seeking the consent of the individual might defeat the purpose of collecting the information. Seeking consent may be impossible or inappropriate when the individual is a minor, seriously ill, or mentally incapacitated. In addition, organizations that do not have a direct relationship with the individual may not always be able to seek consent. A further example is when an individual or entity is seeking consent and it may be impractical for a charity or a direct-marketing firm that wishes to acquire a mailing list from another organization. In such cases, the organization providing the list would be expected to obtain consent before disclosing personal information.[71]

However, this only applies when, the collection is clearly in the interests of the individual and consent cannot be obtained in a timely way, or, it is reasonable to expect that the collection with the knowledge or consent of the individual would compromise the availability or accuracy of the personal information collected. Yet, it has to be for the purpose(s) related to investigating a breach of an agreement or a contravention of the laws of Canada or a province within Canada. The knowledge of consent also applies where the personal information was produced by the individual in the course of their employment, business or profession and the collection is consistent with the purposes for which the information was produced. This also

---

[68] Ibid.

[69] Ibid.

[70] Personal Information Protection and Electronic Documents Act, S.C. 2000, 4.3 schedule 1 Principle 3- Consent.

[71] Ibid.

includes when the personal data is collected solely for journalistic, artistic or literary purposes and is publicly available and is specified by the regulations.[72]

Moreover, consent is somewhat limited when compared to other data protection laws. Section 7(2) allows the use of personal information without consent, when an organization becomes aware that the personal information can be used in an investigation under any Canadian law. Further, no consent is required when the personal data will be used in respect of an emergency that threatens the life, health or security of an individual, or, contained in a witness statement and the use is necessary to assess, process or settle an insurance claim. Consent is also not required when the personal information was produced by the individual in the course of their employment, business or profession and the use is consistent with the purposes for which the personal information was produced.[73] This also extends when the personal information is used for statistical, or scholarly study or re- search, or is publicly available. Finally, the disclosure of personal information without the knowledge or consent of the person can be undertaken by an entity, where that disclosure is made to, in the Province of Quebec, an advocate or notary or, in any other province, a barrister or solicitor who is representing the organization. This also extends to for the purposes of collecting a debt owed by the individual to an organization, or where the data subject is required to comply with a subpoena or warrant that has been used or an order made by a court, person or body with jurisdiction to compel the production of information, or to comply with rules of court relating to the production of records.

Unsurprisingly, the PA has expressed the concept of consent to form an integral part of a public entity using, disclosing and obtaining personal information from a data subject. Beginning with section 7, whereby, personal information that is under the control of a government institution cannot without the consent from the data subject to be used by that institution, unless, the personal information was obtained or compiled exclusively by that institution. The personal information can only be used for the purpose to which has been collected. Secondly, section 8 requires that consent from the data subject must be obtained where their personal information will be disclosed. However, consent is not required when there is a sufficiently direct connection between the purpose for which personal data was collected and its proposed use. Nonetheless, there are specific conditions around the disclosure of certain personal information such as home contact details to a union. For instance, an employee's home contact information to a union who represents that employee is permitted. However, before the home contact information can be provided to a union, an employer is to ensure:

- the union can use the home contact information only to permit it to fulfil its representational obligations;

[72] Ibid, section 7 (e) the collection is made for the purpose of making a disclosure (i) under subparagraph (3)(c.1)(i) or (d)(ii), or (ii) that is required by law.

[73] Ibid, section 7, purposes that cannot be achieved without using the information, the information is used in a manner that will ensure its confidentiality, it is impracticable to obtain consent and the organization in- forms the Commissioner of the use before the information is used.

- the union cannot disclose the information to anyone other than those officials responsible for fulfilling its obligations;
- the union should undertake to be bound by the principles of the *Privacy Act* and an employer's internal privacy policies;
- the home contact information must be password-protected or encrypted;
- the employer has to advise employees on their initial appointment that their home contact information will be shared with their union; and
- the union must dispose of home contact information when it receives updated information from the employer.[74]

In addition to the above, consent will also be required for personal information that has been obtained in confidence and where the disclosure is authorized. For instance, according to section 19, the head of a government institution can refuse to disclose any personal information requested under subsection 12(1) concerning the organization or institution described in subsection (1) if the government, organization or institution from which the information was obtained consents to the disclosure; or makes the information public. Under the PA, the only other obligation where consent is required is where the Privacy Commissioner applies to the court for a review of any refusal to disclose personal information requested under subsection 12(1) in respect of which an investigation has been carried out by the Privacy Commissioner.[75] However, the Commissioner needs the consent of the individual who requested access to the information.

On the other side, consent in the Canadian context has not come without its criticism.[76] The Officer of Privacy Commissioner Canada (OPCC) highlighted as a part of a review in 2016 that, in order for the privacy laws to be effective organizations are required to obtain individuals' consent to lawfully collect, use and disclose personal information in the course of commercial activity. The OPCC go onto say that without consent, the circumstances under which organizations are allowed to process personal information are limited.[77] Nevertheless, the OPCC are concerned that technology and business models have changed significantly that they question the feasibility of the current day concept of consent. This was emphasized in 2015, whereby during the Office of the Privacy Commissioner's Privacy Priority Setting, some stakeholders questioned the continued viability of the consent model in an ecosystem of vast, complex information flows and ubiquitous computing.[78]

It was noted that the PIPEDA predates technologies such as smart phones and cloud computing, as well as business models predicated on unlimited access to

---

[74] Privacy Act 1985, section 8.

[75] Privacy Act 1985, section 42.

[76] Officer of Privacy Commissioner Canada: A discussion paper exploring potential enhancements to consent under the *Personal Information Protection and Electronic Documents Act* Prepared by the Policy and Research Group of the 2016, https://www.priv.gc.ca/en/opc-actions-and-decisions/research/explore-privacy-research/2016/consent_201605/#fn1-rf

[77] Ibid.

[78] Ibid.

personal information and automated processes. Stakeholders echoed a larger global debate about the role of consent in privacy protection regimes that has gained momentum as advances in big data analytics and the increasing prominence of data collection through the Internet of Things start to pervade our everyday activities. There have been calls for relaxing requirements for consent. Rather one proposal is to take a greater focus on the accountability and ethical use of personal information (risk-based approach). More importantly, the concept of consent, the legal framework that supports it, and the practical technology that enables to consent, has become so complex that people choose to ignore it, and consent anyway. Therefore, it is increasingly becoming even more complex and difficult to expect individuals to take an active role in deciding how their personal information is used in all instances is increasingly unrealistic.[79] Based on the above, the concept of consent has become problematic. There have been calls for the concept to be strengthened. In the Canadian context, it is believed that consent should be strengthened to increase transparency so as the data subject has more control over their data. However, the discussion in this section, and the criticisms afforded to consent, is in the context of the PIPEDA. Nonetheless, Canada needs to do more work on reconciling the differences in application of consent between the public and private sectors. Why hold one sector to a higher level of account than the other? They are of the view, which we support that, by removing the concept of consent would significantly undermine fundamental individual rights, protections and freedoms.[80] It is our view that unless there is a more appropriate option or concept to enhance a data subjects control over personal data online, consent is here to stay. At issue is whether consent under the Canadian framework is adequate to take into account the implementation of future technology such as AI (robotics). This is an area for further research.

Moreover, in *Canadian Association of Elizabeth Fry Societies v Canada (Public Safety and Emergency Preparedness)*[81] the question arose as to whether consent continued or survived an individual's death. In 2007, Ashley Smith, a youth offender had been imprisoned since she was 15 years of age, and committed suicide in her cell on October 19. However, prior to her death, she requested access to her personal records under the *Privacy Act*. She sought the assistance of the Elizabeth Fry Society. Subsequently, she signed a Consent for Disclosure of Personal Information Form to permit Correctional Services of Canada ("CSC") to disclose this information to the Elizabeth Fry Society and her lawyer. CSC received her request on June 18, 2007. On July 18, 2007 CSC advised Ms. Smith's lawyer that a 30-day extension beyond the statutory 30-day limit in s. 14 of the *Privacy Act* would be required to process the request. CSC did not disclose the records at the conclusion of the 30-day extension. When the Elizabeth Fry Society followed up with the request on May 23, 2008, CSC responded that all files were exempted because of Ms. Smith's

---

[79] Ibid.

[80] Ibid.

[81] *Canadian Association of Elizabeth Fry Societies v Canada (Public Safety and Emergency Preparedness)*, 2010 FC 470.

death. The Elizabeth Fry Society complained to the Privacy Commissioner, who concluded the records should be disclosed. CSC still refused, as such the Elizabeth Fry Society commenced an application in Federal Court.

The Federal Court ordered that the records be disclosed, and ruled that:

> her consent was not vitiated by her death, and that the consent was not intended to lapse or be of no force and effect because she died. In other words, an individual's right to grant access to their personal information survives their death. Section 10 of the *Privacy Regulations* sets out who may exercise rights under the *Privacy Act*. It states that those rights may be exercised on behalf of a deceased person by the estate administrator, or on behalf of any other individual by a person authorized in writing to do so.[82]

During the case, CSC argued to the court that the provision dealing with estate administrators was the only way that personal information could be obtained on behalf of a deceased person. However, the Court disagreed and stated that:

> as long as the consent is in writing, the requesting party can rely upon that consent regardless of the individual's living status. Ms. Smith was alive when she signed the consent and also alive when CSC was deemed to refuse to provide the records (30 days after their last request for an extension, or August 17, 2007) and therefore the refusal crystallized on that date.[83]

The Court criticized CSC for breaching sections. 14 and 15 of the *Privacy Act* by failing to provide the information within 30 days or within the 30-day extension of time. The CSC submitted that these delays "happen all the time", but the Court stated that "the fact that the delay is normal does not excuse the respondent from being in breach of the law by not fulfilling the request within the prescribed time period under the *Privacy Act*."[84] CSC attempted to rely upon section 22(1)(b) of the *Privacy Act* because there was, at one point, a criminal investigation into four CSC officers about Ms. Smith's suicide. However, there was no such investigation at the time the documents should have been released, and the investigation was over by the time the Court heard this case. The Court concluded that:

> CSC did not present any tangible evidence of harm to an investigation: CSC simply asserted that the disclosure would harm an investigation. Further, the records requested all pre-dated Ms. Smith's suicide (which was the subject of the investigation), so the investigation could not have related to the information in the requested records.[85]

The importance of consent cannot be underestimated. The concept is arguably supported by many other elements of the law, but, neither the PIPEDA or the PA define the concept. Apart from being prescribed by the law, it is also largely left to the judiciary to determine whether consent is required, and has it been achieved or not. What has emerged, whether it is Canadian, US, Australian South Korean or one of the other state's laws discussed in this book, the application and prescribed form for the use of consent varies from state to state.

---

[82] Ibid.

[83] Ibid.

[84] Ibid.

[85] Ibid.

13.5.1 Disclosure

The PA largely deals with disclosure of personal information differently to that of the PIPEDA. Under the PA, disclosure has largely been dealt with above under the concept of consent. They go hand in hand, and in order for personal information to be provided to an individual or entity, it is to be disclosed, which can be in different forms. This section will examine what the courts have said in relation to disclosure.

Nevertheless, in *Attaran v Canada (National Defence)*[86] the Court was required to determine the level of personal information not to be disclosed. The case involved photographs of the faces of individuals could not be redacted (by using a black line through the eyes, or otherwise) to ensure that the individuals could not be identified; therefore, the government institution was right to black out the entire face. The facts are that Professor Attaran made an access to information request to the Department of National Defence ("DND") seeking information concerning detainees who had been transferred by the Canadian Forces to the Afghan Ministry of Defence. DND withheld some of the requested information, including photographs of the faces of the detainees — in particular, three detainees whose medical records suggested they suffered facial injuries while being captured. Professor Attaran had made a similar request to the Correctional Service of Canada ("CSC") who provided him with photographs with the faces partially blacked out.

Professor Attaran complained to the Information Commissioner, who concurred with DND's decision not to release the photographs. He then applied to the Federal Court. The Federal Court upheld DND's decision to refuse to release the photographs. All parties agreed that the photographs constituted "personal information" under the *Privacy Act*. The main issues were whether the photographs could be released in a redacted form and whether they should be released because the public interest in disclosure outweighed any privacy rights.[87] However, in terms of redacting, the Federal Court disagreed with Professor Attaran's argument that redaction should be tested against the probability of disclosure. The Court concluded that:

> redaction is an exercise that requires "a high degree of certainty", "no room for error or risk of disclosure of one's identity", and that "extreme caution" is justified — particularly in the circumstances in this case, where identifying the detainees would place their families at risk of reprisals within Afghanistan. Redaction is not a balancing exercise between the interests of privacy and disclosure.[88]

The Court criticized CSC for releasing the redacted photographs. Professor Attaran further argued that the public interest in disclosure outweighed the privacy interests in that case and therefore the information should be disclosed under s. 8(2)(*m*) of the *Privacy Act*. The Court concluded that:

> there was a real risk that the disclosure of the identity of these detainees could put them or their families in harm's way because of a suspicion of collaborat ion. Further, there was no public interest in disclosure because DND released medical reports that described the

[86] *Attaran v Canada (National Defence)*, 2011 FC 664.

[87] Ibid.

[88] Ibid.

> extent of the injuries that could have been seen on their faces. The photographs themselves would not have been useful in the assessment of the conduct of Canadian Forces or officials. Further, the photographs did not depict a pattern of "systemic and depraved abuse of prisoners.[89]

The decision by the Court highlighted the complex balancing act that is required between the privacy interests of the data subject and those of the broad concept of the public interest. In this case, it was demonstrated that, at times, there will be situations where the privacy interests of the individual(s) outweigh the public interest in disclosure.

More recently in *Bernard v Canada (Attorney General)*[90] the Court had to determine whether the PA did not prohibit the disclosure of an employee's home addresses and telephone numbers to that employee's bargaining agent, provided that certain safeguards are put in place to protect the security of that information. The appellant was an employee of the Canada Revenue Agency ("CRA"). She is represented by the Professional Institute of the Public Service of Canada ("PIPSC"), but she is not a member of PIPSC. She is a so-called "Rand" employee: she pays union dues and is represented by a union, but she is not a member of that union. In 2007, PIPSC filed a complaint with the Public Service Labour Relations Board (the "Board") that the CRA's refusal to provide it with home contact information for members of the bargaining unit breached the *Public Service Labour Relations Act*. The Board agreed, and ordered PIPSC and the CRA to reach an agreement on how much contact information needed to be disclosed to PIPSC. They eventually agreed that CRA would disclose, on a quarterly basis, the home addresses and telephone number of members. PIPSC agreed to three privacy-enhancing features: (1) it could use the home contact information only for legitimate purposes under the *Public Service Labour Relations Act* i.e. to permit it to fulfil its representational obligations; (2) it could not disclose the information to anyone other than those officials responsible for fulfilling its obligations; and (3) it undertook to be bound by the principles of the *Privacy Act* and the Government Security Policy. The Board turned this agreement into an order.[91] The applicant learned about this order and challenged the order by way of judicial review. The Federal Court of Appeal concluded that the:

> Board erred by simply adopting the agreement without examining the privacy implications, and ordered that the Board reconsider its decision – this time, with the participation of the applicant and the Privacy Commissioner. The Board reconsidered its decision and confirmed its original decision, but with three additional privacy safeguards: (1) the home contact information must be password-protected or encrypted; (2) the CRA has to advise employees on their initial appointment that their home contact information will be shared with PIPSC; and (3) PIPSC must dispose of home contact information when it receives updated information from the CRA. The applicant unsuccessfully challenged the Board's second decision in the Federal Court of Appeal.[92]

---

[89] Ibid.

[90] *Bernard v Canada (Attorney General)*, 2014 SCC 13.

[91] Ibid.

[92] Ibid.

The Supreme Court of Canada upheld the Board's decision. The issue raised in accordance with the PA was the Board's conclusion that disclosure of an employee's personal information to their union was permitted under section 8(2)(a). The Supreme Court of Canada decided that:

> section 8(2)(a) there must be a sufficiently direct connection between the original purpose and the proposed use, such that a person would reasonably expect that the information could be used in the manner proposed.[93]

The Court concluded that an employer who collects home contact information, in part, for the purpose of contacting employees about terms and conditions of employment, and that the union's proposed use is consistent with this purpose. It also concluded that a union needs home contact information to carry out its representational obligations. The Court demonstrated that there will be a number of varied issues that can arise from disclosure, and this will change from organization to organisation.

13.6 Commissioner

This section has been divided into two parts. Part one deals with the Commissioner roles and responsibilities under the PIPEDA. Part two identifies how the equivalent position of the Commissioner has been dealt with under the PA.

13.6.1 PIPEDA

The Canadian Commission has been afforded an extensive role and obligations under the PIPEDA. Apart from the confidentiality requirements related to the disclosure of information.[94] The Commissioner or any person acting on behalf or under the direction of the Commissioner shall not disclose any information contained in a report made under subsection 10.1(1) or in a record obtained under subsection 10.3(2). However, this is subject to sections (2) to (7),[95] 12(3), 12.2(3),[96] 13(3),[97] 19(1),[98] 23(3) and 23.1(1)[99] and section 25[100] of the PIPEDA. Disclosure of personal information can be undertaken by the Commissioner in accordance with section

[93] Ibid.

[94] Personal Information Protection and Electronic Documents Act, S.C. 2000, section 20.

[95] Ibid, section 2–7, Definitions Purpose, Purpose Application, Application, Business contact information, Certificate under Canada Evidence Act, Compliance with obligations, Effect of designation of individual, Valid consent, Collection without knowledge or consent.

[96] Ibid, section 12, Examination of Complaint by Commissioner.

[97] Ibid, section 13, Commissioner's Report.

[98] Ibid, section 19, Report of findings and recommendations from Audits.

[99] Ibid, section 23, Consultations with provinces, Disclosure of information to foreign state.

[100] Ibid, section 25, Annual report.

20(7). This is based on where the Commissioner has had to intervene under paragraph 50(c) of An Act, which is based on promoting the Canadian economy, and to amend the Canadian Radio-television and Telecommunications Commission Act, the Competition Act, the Personal Information Protection and Electronic Documents Act and the Telecommunications Act or in accordance with subsection 58(3) or 60(1) of that Act. On the other side, the Commissioner will not be a witness in relation to personal information, unless the personal information forms part of a prosecution under section 28[101] of the PIPEDA, or under 132 of the Criminal Code (perjury).

13.6.1.1 Breaches of Security Safeguards

An organization is able to report a breach of the laws to the Commissioner where the breach creates a real risk of significant harm to an individual.[102] In order to report is to provide personal information that can identify the individual. Furthermore, a further safeguard requires that an organization is to notify an individual of any breach of security that, could have resulted in their personal data being breached. Apart from informing the data subject of the safety breach, they must also be informed of how the risk of harm is being addressed. Any notification is to be provided directly to the individual data subject. Furthermore, the timing of notification, while not specifically prescribed, it is to be undertaken as soon as practicably.

Despite the requirement for managing safety breaches, and important feature of the PIPEDA is the definition of 'significant harm.[103] That is, significant harm includes bodily harm, humiliation, damage to reputation or relationships, loss of employment, business or professional opportunities, financial loss, identity theft, negative effects on the credit record and damage to or loss of property. Furthermore, factors that need to be considered in relation to a breach and the impact being a significant harm to data subjects, include, the sensitivity of the personal information involved in the breach; the probability that the personal information has been, is being or will be misused; and any other prescribed factor. The broad approach taken under this provision cannot be underestimated. It arguably provides a level of tort, whereby, a data subject can take action for the breach of their personal data that, has resulted in a level of harm, identity theft or personal and financial loss. More pervasively, the theft of a data subjects' identity can also pose cyber security and criminal issues. Of the data protection or privacy laws examined in this book, or the first

---

[101] Ibid, section 28, Offence and punishment 28 Every organization that knowingly contravenes sub- section 8(8), section 10.1 or subsection 10.3(1) or 27.1(1) or that obstructs the Commissioner or the Commission- er's delegate in the investigation of a complaint or in con- ducting an audit is guilty of (a) an offence punishable on summary conviction and liable to a fine not exceeding $10,000; or (b) an indictable offence and liable to a fine not exceeding $100,000.

[102] Ibid, section 10(1).

[103] Ibid, section 10.1 (7).

book do not go to any detail to provide a definition of harm. This is something that, particularly, common law countries need to consider further.

In addition to the above, the management of a breach of security safeguards requires the organization, in accordance with section 10.2 to not only inform the data subject, but also, any other organization, including a government institution of the breach. The further notification requirement while placing a further obligation of the organization where the security breach occurred, it also provides a further layer of control over the data because, it may affect other entities. Notifying other government institutions and entities is to be undertaken within a timeframe that is reasonable to do so. This is not an onerous requirement, however, organizations where the security breach has occurred must keep in mind that not being able to show that notification was not undertaken within a practicable timeframe, that organization may come under criticism of the commissioner. However, it must be noted that any disclosure in accordance with the security safeguards does not require the organization to obtain the consent of the data subject. This is provided that the organization was initially informed of the security breach, along with ensuring that the disclosure is made for managing and reducing the harm to data subjects. Under the requirements of a security safeguard breach in accordance with section 10.3(1), the organization should keep and maintain a record of every breach of personal data that is under its control.

Apart from the obligations surrounding the requirements related to the disclosure of personal information, the Commissioner is responsible for managing complaints that have been received from individuals across the community. It allows individuals to file a complaint with the Commissioner, and for the Commissioner to initiate a file of complaint against an entity. However, according to section 11(3), any complaint made in relation to section 8 (Retention of information), must be filed within 6 months, or a period allowed by the Commissioner.

13.6.1.2 Filing and Investigating Complaints

While procedural the filing of a complaint against another organization, according to section 11(1),[104] requires that it is to be in written form. Although where the complaint has been made by a written request in accordance with section 8, PIPIEDA, it must be filed within a 6-month period, following the refusal or expiry of the request. The Commissioner is to give notice of a complaint to the organization against which the complaint was made.

The Commissioner is responsible for investigating complaints in accordance section 12(1) of the PIPEDA. However, the complaint may not be investigated where the Commissioner is of the opinion that the complainant ought first to exhaust all review procedures available. Nevertheless, there are exemptions to this requirement. In other words, the Commissioner does not have to conduct an investigation of a

---

[104] Ibid, section 11(1), Division 1 or 1.1 or for not following a recommendation set out in Schedule 1.

complaint, if the Commissioner is of the opinion that the act, if proved,[105] would constitute a contravention of any of sections 6 to 9 – which covers issues related to the management of personal information. Thus, at all material times, the potential impact to personal information is considered. Nevertheless, regardless of whether the complaint is undertaken or otherwise, the Commissioner needs to notify the complainant or organization that, the investigation will not proceed, and, where the investigation is discontinued[106] or there is compelling reasons not to investigate.[107] However, there is no guidance of to what extent compelling reasons apply. Having a complaints mechanism available provides a further layer of accountability and transparency in the law. In so doing, it builds a further layer of trust in the framework of data protection.

13.6.1.3 Powers of Commission [PIPEDA – PA]

The Commissioner has specific powers under the PIPEDA, to conduct an investigation of a complaint.[108] This power extends to allowing the Commissioner to summon and enforce the appearance of an individual before the Commissioner. The Commissioner can compel the individual to give oral or written evidence on oath and to produce any records and things the Commissioner considers necessary to investigate the complaint. An important feature of the PIPEDA is the ability for the Commissioner to resolve any dispute by mediation and conciliation. Moreover, 1 year after the day the complaint is filed or is initiated by the Commissioner, they are to prepare a report that outlines the findings and recommendations and any information that has contributed to the settlement of the matter. Thus, where a mediation has been undertaken, the Commissioner must outline in the report those specific details that were raised in the mediation. However, the data subject upon receiving the Commissioner's report can in accordance with section 14(1) apply to the court for a hearing of the matter. This further demonstrates that data subjects are able to demand a higher level of accountability of the processes governing personal data, by appealing to the courts for review of any decisions made by the Commissioner.

To assist in facilitating and improving practices for the management of personal data, the Commissioner has the power to establish compliance agreements[109] with an organization. The Commissioner has been afforded quite some discretion as to

[105] Ibid, section 12(1)(2), Exemption - of An Act to promote the efficiency and adaptability of the Canadian economy by regulating certain activities that discourage reliance on electronic means of carrying out commercial activities, and to amend the Canadian Radio-television and Telecommunications Commission Act, the Competition Act, the Personal Information Protection and Electronic Documents Act and the Telecommunications Act or section 52.01 of the Competition Act or would constitute conduct that is reviewable under section 74.011 of that Act.

[106] Ibid, section 12.2(1).

[107] Ibid, section 12(1)(3)(4).

[108] Ibid, section 12(1).1.

[109] Ibid, section 17.1.

what they consider necessary to raise the level of compliance of an organization in the government of personal data. However, any compliance agreement does not preclude the individual data subject from applying to a court for a hearing to resolve the matter. In addition to the compliance agreement the Commissioner can undertake an audit in accordance with section 18(1) to ensure compliance with the PIPEDA.

13.6.1.4 Whistleblowing

Whistleblowing has become an important feature of transparency and accountability. The PIPEDA allows anyone who believe that a person has contravened or intends to contravene any provision of Division 1 or 1.1 (Protection of Personal Information, Breaches of Security Safeguards) may notify the Commissioner,[110] so as the matter is investigated. Once the Commissioner has received information under the whistle-blower provision the Commissioner is obliged to keep that information confidential. More importantly, there are safeguards for employees who provide information to the Commissioner, whereby they should not be dismissed, suspended, demoted, disciplined, harassed.[111] This is an important feature of the Canadian model. While the other states examined do not have similar provisions within their data protection laws, there are other laws that deal with whistleblowing, which can be invoked.

13.6.2 PA

A notable different between the PA and the PIPEDA is the ability for a Commissioner and an Assistant Commissioner to be appointed in accordance with section 56(1) of the PA. The collective duties also differ. That is, the Commissioner has the ability to undergo studies to better understand the privacy of individuals over the Internet across the Canadian society. Such a study can also examine whether the rights afforded to data subjects should be extended, particularly in relation to the

[110] Ibid, section 27.

[111] Ibid, section 27(1) 1. (a) the employee, acting in good faith and on the basis of reasonable belief, has disclosed to the Commissioner that the employer or any other person has contravened or intends to contravene a provision of Division 1 or 1.1; (b) the employee, acting in good faith and on the basis of reasonable belief, has refused or stated an intention of refusing to do anything that is a contravention of a provision of Division 1 or 1.1; (c) the employee, acting in good faith and on the basis of reasonable belief, has done or stated an intention of doing anything that is required to be done in order that a provision of Division 1 or 1.1 not be contravened; or (d) the employer believes that the employee will do anything referred to in paragraph (a), (b) or (c). (2) Nothing in this section impairs any right of an employee either at law or under an employment contract or collective agreement.

collection, retention, disposal, use or disclosure of personal information. Any study (report), can be tabled in Parliament.[112]

The Commissioner appointed under the PA is held to a similar standard of confidentiality to that of the Commissioner appointed under the PIPEDA. This is largely because they are one in the same person. That is, the Commissioner appointed under the PIPEDA, is the Privacy Commissioner appointed under section 53 of the PA. They are also subject to the confidentiality and disclosure requirements pertaining to personal information governments.[113] It is out of scope of this book to deal with the other administrative functions of the Commissioner appointed under the PA.

13.7 Electronic Documents

The PIPEDA can be distinguished from the PA for specifically dealing with electronic documents. Section 31 defines electronic documents to be data that is recorded or stored on any medium in or by a computer system or other similar device and that can be read or perceived by a person or a computer system or other similar device. It includes a display, print-out or other output of that data.[114] Its purpose is to provide for the use of electronic alternatives in the manner provided for in this Part where federal laws contemplate the use of paper to record or communicate information or transactions.[115] Yet, this part of the PIPEDA is largely procedural whereby all government agencies, are accountable to the Canadian Parliament, which may use electronic means to create, collect, receive, store, transfer, distribute, publish or otherwise deal with documents or information whenever a federal law[116] does not specify the manner of doing so. Section 34 provides for a payment that is required to be made to the Government of Canada that, may be made in electronic form in any manner specified by the Receiver General.

Nevertheless, section 35 sets out the obligations required for the use of the appropriate form.[117] Furthermore, section 36 allows for the use of a certificate or other

[112] Privacy Act 1985, section 60.

[113] Privacy Act 1985, section 63–64. 64 (1) The Privacy Commissioner may disclose or may authorize any person acting on behalf or under the direction of the Commissioner to disclose information (a) that, in the opinion of the Commissioner, is necessary to (i) carry out an investigation under this Act, or (ii) establish the grounds for findings and recommendations contained in any report under this Act; or (b) in the course of a prosecution for an offence under this Act, a prosecution for an offence under section 131 of the *Criminal Code* (perjury) in respect of a statement made under this Act or a review before the Court under this Act or Part 1 of the *Access to Information Act* or an appeal from a review of that Court.

[114] Personal Information Protection and Electronic Documents Act, S.C. 2000, section 31.

[115] Ibid, section 32.

[116] Ibid, section 33.

[117] Ibid, section 35, filing includes all manner of submitting, regardless of how it is designated.

documents can be signed electronically.[118] Therefore, with the filing of any document or record there is the storage of that document and its retention. Section 37, provides that where a federal law requires a [electronic] document to be retained for a specific period, in a particular format, and that it must be readable, and any information identifying the documents origin, destination including date or time is to also be retained.

Moreover, the Commissioner can make any personal information available to the broader community, where it has been determined that it is in the public interest to do so. The public interest is a broad term that includes, but not limited to national security, community health and welfare amongst others. The disclosure of personal information by the Commissioner can be undertaken where there is an investigation or an audit. Section 20 (4)[119] allows the Commissioner to disclose personal information in the course of a prosecution, a hearing before a court or a judicial review. That disclosure in accordance with section 20(5) is broad and relates to any offence committed against any law of Canada. Viewed this way, the Commissioner may also disclose personal information contained in a report made under subsection 10.1(1) or in a record obtained under subsection 10.3(2) where there are reasonable grounds to believe that the information could be useful in the investigation of a contravention of the laws of Canada.

13.8 Offences of an Organisation

Any organization that does not meet the requirements of Written request,[120] Report to Commissioner,[121] Records,[122] or Prohibition[123] are liable to a fine up to $10,000, for only summary offences. Such a fine can be increased to $100,000 where there has been a breach of an indictable offence. In addition, there is Parliamentary oversight[124] of all of Part 1 of the PIPEDA, whereby every five years there is to be a review by the committee of the House of Commons, or of both Houses of Parliament, to examine its operational effect. Having such oversight provides the government to

[118] Ibid, section 36.

[119] Ibid, section 20(4), (4) The Commissioner may disclose, or may authorize any person acting on behalf or under the direction of the Commissioner to disclose, information in the course of (a) a prosecution for an offence under section 28; (b) a prosecution for an offence under section 132 of the *Criminal Code* (perjury) in respect of a statement made under this Part; (c) a hearing before the Court under this Part; (d) an appeal from a decision of the Court; or (e) a judicial review in relation to the performance or exercise of any of the Commissioner's duties or powers under this Part.

[120] Ibid, section 8.

[121] Ibid, section 10.1.

[122] Ibid, section 10.3(1).

[123] Ibid, section 27(1).

[124] Ibid, section 29(1).

better examine the issues related to the full life cycle of data protection, to improve the legal framework.

13.8.1 Tort

Canadian courts have shifted to a tort for the misuse of personal information. The 2012 Canadian case of *Jones v Tseige*[125] was concerned with an individual's privacy interest in confidential banking information. There, the Claimant asserted that her privacy interest in her confidential banking information had been "irreversibly destroyed". She claimed damages of CAD$70,000 for invasion of privacy and breach of fiduciary duty, and exemplary and punitive damages of CAD$20,000. The Court considered whether the tort of invasion of privacy was "binding and dispositive" in the common law of Ontario.[126] The Court held that the motion judge's reliance on *Euteneier v Lee*,[127] for the proposition Ontario law excludes any and all claims for breach of privacy interests was misplaced. The plaintiff in Euteneier had been arrested and detained on criminal charges. She complained of her treatment while in police custody and sought damages for negligence, assault, civil conspiracy and breach of her ss. 7, 9, 12 and 15 rights under the Canadian Charter of Rights and Freedoms. The trial judge found that, based on the appellant's own behaviour while in custody, which included an apparent suicide attempt, the defendant police officers had conducted themselves in a reasonable and prudent manner. They had breached no duty nor exhibited any bad faith or malice to ground any of the claims she had asserted and the claim was dismissed.[128] Furthermore, in considering whether the trial judge had accurately described the plaintiff's privacy and dignity interests, Cronk J.A. observed "[the plaintiff] properly conceded in oral argument before this court that there is no 'free-standing' right to dignity or privacy under the *Charter* or at common law."[129] In distinguishing the facts in *Jones v Tseige* from those in *Euteneier*, the Ontario Court of Appeal stated that the Respondent:

> Tseige committed the tort of intrusion upon seclusion when she repeatedly examined the private bank records of Jones. These acts satisfy the elements [that] the intrusion was inten-

[125] *Jones v Tseige* 2012 ONCA 32.

[126] Ibid, at 10–13. *Euteneier v Lee* [2005] O.J. No. 3896 concerned a lawsuit brought by a woman whose clothes were forcibly removed by police following her suicide attempt while she was detained in a holding cell.

[127] *Euteneier v Lee* (2005), 77 O.R. (3d) 621, [2005] O.J. No. 3896, 260 D.L.R. (4th) 123, 202 O.A.C. 278, 133 C.R.R. (2d) 292, 142 A.C.W.S. (3d) 340 (C.A.), revg [2003] O.J. No. 4239, 113 C.R.R. (2d) 44 (Div. Ct.) [Leave to appeal to S.C.C. refused [2005] S.C.C.A. No. 516].

[128] Ibid.

[129] Ibid, [63].

> tional, it amounted to an unlawful invasion of Jones' private affairs, it would be viewed as highly offensive to the reasonable person and caused distress, humiliation or anguish.[130]

Two years later in 2014, the Ontario Superior Court of Justice in *Evans v Bank of Nova Scotia*,[131] reinforced the position taken in *Jones v Tseige* that the tort of "intrusion upon seclusion" was the test applied in relation to personal information. In *Evans*, customers of the Bank sued the bank as a result of an employee of the bank disclosing their personal information to his girlfriend. She allegedly disseminated that information for fraudulent and improper purposes, causing several bank customers to become victims of identity theft or fraud. The Ontario Court of Appeal recognized a tort for the intentional or reckless invasion of the privacy of another individual without lawful justification.[132] The harm from such an invasion of privacy, it held, must be such that "[a] reasonable person would regard the invasion highly offensive, causing distress, humiliation or anguish."[133] It maintained that damages should be "a modest conventional sum", in the range of CAD$20,000.[134] The Court of Appeal awarded the Claimant CAD$10,000.

Nevertheless, in 2016 the Ontario Superior Court of Justice in *Jane Doe 464,533 v D*[135] applied a tort to the breach of privacy to the public disclosure of a private information in a "revenge porn" case. The Court examined the law governing the breach of confidence and intentional infliction of mental distress, in recognizing a tort of public disclosure of a private fact. The Court awarded the Claimant CAD$141,000 including costs. Based on the above, it is argued that an element of a tort related to personal data has emerged in Canada. Other states could consider adopting a similar approach. For example, section 4(2) of the Canadian Manitoba (a state of Canada) *Privacy Act 2008*[136] provides considerations in awarding damages. These include:

(i) the nature, incidence and occasion of the defendant's wrongful act;
(ii) the effect of the wrong on the plaintiff's health, welfare, social, business or financial position;
(iii) any relationship, whether domestic or otherwise, between the parties;
(iv) any distress, annoyance or embarrassment suffered by the plaintiff arising from the wrong; and
(v) the conduct of the parties, both before and after the wrong, including any apology or offer of amends made by the defendat.

The Canada wide *Personal Information Protection and Electronic Documents Act*, S.C. 2000 goes further by defining "significant harm" as to include bodily harm,

---

[130] Ibid, 89.

[131] 2014 ONSC 2135.

[132] 2012 ONCA 32.

[133] Ibid.

[134] Ibid.

[135] 2016 ONSC 541.

[136] Canadian Manitoba *Privacy Act 2008*, https://web2.gov.mb.ca/laws/statutes/ccsm/p125e.php

humiliation, damage to reputation or relationships, loss of employment, business or professional opportunities, financial loss, identity theft, negative effects on the credit record and damage to or loss of property.[137] However, it is not fully settled how far a tort will apply to data protection over the Internet in Canada. Along with other common law countries that recognize a tort in privacy, this is, in our view, another area of vigilance to see how the courts will react in the future.

13.9 Conclusion

Rights have been a core part of Canadian history that date back to the 1700s. In other words, the Royal Proclamation of 1763 is a key document in Canadian history. More importantly, this became the basis of Canadian treaty law. In the same year, the Proclamation was also mentioned in the *Canadian Charter of Rights and Freedoms*. The Charter saw the beginning of the guarantee and protection of many rights or freedoms. This, also went some way to the establishment of Canada as an independent state. It was not until 1867 that the *British North America Act 1867* was established. The significance of this legislation, created what is now understood to be the current day Canada. More importantly, it was also the country's first Constitution, laying out many of the rules and traditions that still govern Canada today. It provided for property and civil rights, amongst others. The legislative instrument never went further than this, and does not make any reference to the right to privacy.

The data protection and online privacy framework of Canada is separated between the public and private sectors. The PIPEDA and PA have to be read and implemented separately. More pervasively they have specific roles and obligations that are unique to Canada and not found in similar legislation of other states. Despite the current day legal framework in Canada they are fully aware of the challenge's society faces in regards to personal data being effectively governed and protected over the Internet. While writing this book, the PA was under review. What the future holds for what recommendations will come from this review and whether they are implemented is a matter for Canada.

The definition of personal information differs markedly between the PIPEDA and PA. The PIPEDA defines personal information means information about an identifiable individual. Artificial intelligence such as biometric information such as facial and body mapping would come within this definition, along with the traditional identifying information such as name, address and date of birth. The PIPEDA

[137] *Personal Information Protection and Electronic Documents Act*, S.C. 2000, Canada, Part 1, Division 1, Marginal note: Real risk of significant harm — factors (8) The factors that are relevant to determining whether a breach of security safeguards creates a real risk of significant harm to the individual include (a) the sensitivity of the personal information involved in the breach; (b) the probability that the personal information has been, is being or will be misused; and (c) any other prescribed factor.

goes onto identify personal health information. As highlighted earlier in the chapter, it states that personal health information constitutes whether the individual is living or deceased, and includes information concerning the physical or mental health of the individual; any health service provided to the individual; and the donation by the individual of any body part or any bodily substance of the individual or information derived from the testing or examination of a body part or bodily substance of the individual. Additionally, personal health information also constitutes information that is collected in the course of providing health services to the individual; or is collected incidentally to the provision of health services to the individual. On the other hand, the PA, has what can be regarded as one of the most comprehensive definitions of personal information. Personal information means information about an identifiable individual that is recorded in any form including race, national or ethnic origin, colour, religion, age or marital status of the individual. It also includes any information relating to the education or the medical, criminal or employment history of the individual, financial transactions, identifying number, symbol or other particular assigned to the individual, address, fingerprints or blood type of the individual.

The PA has included health data and information into this definition. Personal information also constitutes, personal opinions or views of the individual except where they are about another individual or about a proposal for a grant, an award or a prize to be made to another individual by a government institution or a part of a government institution specified in the regulations. It also includes correspondence sent to a government institution by the individual that is implicitly or explicitly of a private or confidential nature, and replies to such correspondence that would reveal the contents of the original correspondence. At issue is whether this definition in the PA will be effective enough when AI becomes mainstream. The PA goes onto include, the views or opinions of another individual about the individual. Furthermore, personal information constitutes that information about an individual who is or was performing services under contract for a government institution, including the terms of the contract, the name of the individual and the opinions or views of the individual given in the course of the performance of those services. It also includes that personal information relating to any discretionary benefit of a financial nature, including the granting of a licence or permit, conferred on an individual, including the name of the individual and the exact nature of the benefit, and information about an individual who has been dead for more than twenty years. The challenge from these definitions is apart from applying to different sectors, more work is needed to better understand whether either would address the concerns that will arise from AI. This will be particularly important for the most vulnerable groups in society.

On the other side, the concept of consent in Canada, under the above-mentioned legislation also vary. That is, consent under the PIPEDA provides that consent of an individual is only valid if it is reasonable to expect that an individual to whom the organization's activities are directed would understand the nature, purpose and consequences of the collection, use or disclosure of the personal information to which they are consenting.

Consent is only valid if it is reasonable to expect that an individual to whom the organization's activities are directed would understand the nature, purpose and consequences of the collection, use or disclosure of the personal information to which they are consenting. It places a high level obligation on the knowledge of the data subject to what they are consenting too.

The PA on the other hand has expressed the concept of consent to form an integral part of a public entity using, disclosing and obtaining personal information from a data subject. However, consent is not required when there is a sufficiently direct connection between the purpose for which personal data was collected and its proposed use. Nonetheless, there are specific conditions around the disclosure of certain personal information such as home contact details to a union. For instance, an employee's home contact information to a union who represents that employee is permitted. Consent will also be required for personal information that has been obtained in confidence and where the disclosure is authorized. What can be demonstrated how the notion of consent when applied through different laws will create confusion and a regulatory environment that is inconsistent. Furthermore, in the new digital economy the ability for the general public, let alone business to reconcile the differences in approach will further complicate the regulatory framework when AI needs to be considered. AI will not be discriminatory, and not necessarily neatly separated so as the laws, as is the case in Canada can deal adequately with data protection by the public and private sectors. Therefore, further work is needed by Canada to better understand how AI will impact their data protection laws and cybersecurity framework. More importantly, will having a higher level of accountability for consent placed on the public sector be relevant to the private sector going forward? This, in our view needs to be addressed. In the modern day world, it is arguable whether having a lower threshold test for the private sector is good enough. It has the potential to send the wrong message to the community. Even where the economic impact might be significant, other states have placed consent on an even level playing field for both the public and private sectors.

References

Beck, S. (1968). Canadian bar review. In A. Flinn & H. Jones (Eds.), *Freedom of information: Open access, Empty archives?* (Vol. 2009). London: Routledge.

Bennett, C., & Bailey, R. (2015). Privacy protection in the era of big data: Regulatory challenges and social assessments. In B. v. Sloot, D. Broeders, & E. Schrijvers (Eds.), *Exploring the boundaries of big data* (pp. 205–227). Amsterdam University Press.

Hayward, R. (1984). Federal access and privacy legislation and the public archives of Canada. *Archivaria, 18*(1), 47–58.

Hazell, R., & Worthy, B. (2011). Assessing the performance of freedom of information. *Government Information Quarterly, 27*(4), 352–359.

Larsen, M., & Walby, K. (Eds.). (2012). *Brokering access: Power, politics and freedom of information process in Canada*. Vancouer: UBC Press.

Chapter 14
The United States

Abstract The right to privacy in the United States (US) can be traced to the late 1800s. However, and while the right to privacy has a long history in the US, it would not have been conceived that today the right has become one of the most important and contested rights. This is because it competes with many other policy areas of government such as national security and the economy. Nonetheless, the US is home to some of the largest Internet companies in the world. The data protection laws in the US can be vest described as being sectorial based. To date this has served the state well, however as there are increasing concerns in relation to the misuse and abuse of personal data, governments and regulators have sat up and taken note of the many anomalies.

Due to the breadth and depth of the sectorial approach to data protection, this Chapter while generally focuses solely on the laws of the Federal Trade Commission and Health. The Chapter briefly highlights the other laws that consider personal data such as the Children's Online Privacy Protection Act, amongst others. The Chapter further outlines how some states such as California have developed specific data protection laws.

In considering the wider cybersecurity and AI risks posed by new technology, this Chapter, consistent with the other chapters will discuss the definition of personal data and the concept of consent. Despite the sectorial approach taken by the US, they have thought about the implications to children from smart home appliances, toys and other AI devices that will come onto the market. This Chapter briefly highlights some of the work that has been undertaken by the US in this area of policy and the law.

Moreover, further work is needed by the US to also consider what and how smart home technology such as fridges, televisions, to toys and robots will have an impact more generally to Americans. This work is urgently needed to better understand the potential impacts to the disabled and elderly members of society. On the other side, one of the most vulnerable group, in our view are children, and the sectorial regulatory approach may no longer be viable to protect this cohort. Arguably, of all the laws discussed and compared in this book, the US is the most complex to understand what and where a data subjects right to data protection lies. With the implementation of the new state-based privacy laws of California, it remains to be seen whether this will result in major changes at the federal level. There have been calls for more specific data protection laws at the federal level.

R. Walters, M. Novak, *Cyber Security, Artificial Intelligence, Data Protection & the Law*, https://doi.org/10.1007/978-981-16-1665-5_14

14.1 Introduction

The United States (US) is yet another state/territory that had been colonised. Dating back to the 1600s, and in 1697, British colonists settled permanently on the American continent.[1] Both the Declaration of Rights of Virginia and its constitution would be the first declaration of rights in the US. The importance of these legal instruments cannot be underestimated. That is, Virginia's constitution has been one of the most influential across America. The first paragraph states that:

> all men are by nature equally free and independent, and have certain inherent rights, of which, when they enter into a state of society, they cannot, by any compact, deprive or divest their posterity, namely, the enjoyment of life and liberty, with the means of acquiring and possessing property, and pursuing and obtaining happiness and safety.[2]

Moreover, and coupled with the above, Virginia's constitution was the first to proclaim the sovereignty of the People: "all power is vested in, and consequently derived from, the people".[3] Apart from the now well understood doctrine of separation of powers, it also provided a definition of the place occupied by the government in the new constitutional order. Luis Grau believes, the importance of the Declaration and constitution went further by providing and being the first state to establish a written list of inherent rights of the individual that should act as the basis and foundation of Government. Those rights included the free exercise of religion; the freedom of the press; the right of suffrage and of free elections; and that individuals could not be deprived of their property for public uses without adequate compensation. Its citizens were entitled to a speedy trial by an impartial jury with all due process, and they were protected from cruel and unusual punishments.[4] Throughout this period saw many other states follow Virginia and establish state-based constitutions. What followed was the introduction of the 1787 Bill of Rights, which resulted in up to ten amendments into the constitution. While out of scope of this chapter to examine the bill of Rights, it came into effect in 1791 and has been instrumental in setting the platform for human rights to be protected across the country.

On the backdrop of the above, Samuel Warren and Louis Brandeis espoused the notion of the right to privacy in 1890[5] however, it took until 1965 for the Supreme Court to find a right to privacy in the *"penumbras"* and *"emanations"* of other

---

[1] Grau, l, (2012) *An American Constitutional History Course for Non-American Students* Carlos III University of Madrid https://core.ac.uk/download/pdf/29403732.pdf

[2] Ibid.

[3] Ibid.

[4] Ibid. Other rights that appear for the first time in the Pennsylvania Constitution are "[t]hat the people have a right to bear arms for the defence of themselves, and the state," which years later was to be included almost literally in the federal Bill of Rights as the second Amendment; "[t]hat all men have a natural inherent right to emigrate from one state to another that will receive them, or to form a new state in vacant countries, or in such countries as they can purchase, whenever they think that thereby they may promote their own happiness," rights which, in this case, were to be expressly forbidden in the federal Constitution.

[5] Warren, S., Brandeis, L, *"The Right to Privacy."* Harvard Law Review 4:5, (1890), 192–196.

constitutional protections.[6] On the other hand, the right to privacy in the US has faced similar challenges, obstacles and debates, as it has, in other nation states. In the American context, the evolution of privacy has been summarized by Dorothy Glancy[7] in referring to Warren and Brandies that:

> Indeed, much of the force of their argument for legal recognition and enforcement of the right to privacy derives from their ingenious evocation of a broad historical sweep in which such legal recognition and enforcement appear as natural and inevitable developments.[8]

Glancy believes that Warren and Brandeis were also participants in what Roscoe Pound called the organizing, systematizing era after the Civil War. Accordingly, they carefully located the right to privacy within the context of the highly schematic jurisprudence of the late nineteenth century American law. They placed the right to privacy within the more general category of the individual's right to be let alone.[9] The right to be let alone was itself part of an even more general right being the right to enjoy life.[10] Glancy goes onto say that the right to life was part of the familiar triad of fundamental, inherent, individual rights reflected in the fifth amendment to the United States Constitution: "No person shall . . . be deprived of life, liberty, or property, without due process of law . . . .".[11] Thus, Glancy views the position taken by Warren and Brandeis as disassociating the right to privacy, from the right to liberty and right to property. Nevertheless, for Warren and Brandeis, the right to liberty secures extensive civil privileges, but not privacy. They also contrasted the right to life with that of the right to be let alone and privacy.[12]

The US would evolve into a world super power by WWII, and Grau in referring to Robert Cushman noted that in the 1946 of Leading Constitutional Decisions, Cushman stated that the:

> most relevant civil and political rights of citizenship were; double jeopardy; privacy of personal communications; certain aspects of blacks' voting right; freedom of the press; freedom of expression; freedom from coercion "to be a witness against himself;" "to have the Assistance of Counsel for his defence;" equal services for blacks and whites; and freedom of contract.[13]

This would be one of the first explicate expressions of the right to privacy. More importantly, it was in a period when WWII was concluding, and 2 years out from the 1948 Declaration on Human Rights being established. Interestingly, the right to protect personal communication at this time would have largely been oral and written, through letter correspondence, newspapers amongst others. However, in 1946

---

[6] *Griswold v. Connecticut*, 381 US 479 (1965).

[7] Glancy, D, *The Invention of the Right to Privacy*, Arizona Law Review Vol. 21 (1979).

[8] Ibid.

[9] Ibid.

[10] Ibid.

[11] Ibid.

[12] Ibid.

[13] Grau, L, (2012) *An American Constitutional History Course for Non-American Students* Carlos III University of Madrid https://core.ac.uk/download/pdf/29403732.pdf

there was little technology available, the mobile phone or computer were not part of mainstream society. Some 30 years later privacy would again become an important consideration of the judiciary.

Following the 1948 Declaration of Human Rights, William Prosser began writing about privacy in the American context. Scholarly discussion about privacy had been asleep for a number of decades. Neil Richards and Daniel Solove when referring William Prosser, highlight how any discussion of often referred back to Warren and Brandeis's famous 1890 *Harvard-Law Review article, The Right to Privacy.*[14] They go onto say that the Anglo-American common law had protected a variety of interests that modem lawyers would consider as involving privacy. Legal doctrines protecting these interests included blackmail law, evidentiary privileges, and duties of confidentiality imposed on a variety of special relationships.[15] On the other hand, they are quite critical of Prosser, because, in their view, for the failure of the privacy tort to evolve in response to the technological and cultural developments. Prosser shaped the tort into their current form, and their strengths and weaknesses flow directly from his vision of privacy. In other words, any discussion of a tort of privacy took a narrow view.

According to Richards and Solove, Prosser was not the architect of a tort of privacy, but rather, through careful attention he gave it, the order and visibility that only a scholar of his influence could have done. Prosser's engagement with the privacy tort over four decades allowed him to reduce a mess of hundreds of conflicting cases to a scheme of four related but distinct tort actions.[16] He accomplished this feat through careful reading and scholarly pruning in the twentieth-century doctrinal tradition. Thus, by 1960 he could confidently assert that Warren and Brandeis's "right to privacy" consisted of not just one tort but "four different interests of the plaintiff, which are tied together by the common name, but otherwise have almost nothing in common except that each represents an interference with the right of the plaintiff."[17] Richards and Solove believe that Prosser organized the torts as follows (1), intrusion upon the plaintiffs seclusion or solitude, or into his private affairs, (2), public disclosure of embarrassing private facts about the plaintiff, (3), publicity which places the plaintiff in a false light in the public eye, (4), appropriation, for the defendant's advantage, of the plaintiff's name or likeness.[18]

In *Roe v Wade*[19] the case centred around developing a precedent granting a woman the right to terminate a pregnancy in certain circumstances. This issue has divided society over a long period from religion to politics. The topic of abortion raises extreme public reaction and, in this case, the Supreme Court was confronting

[14] Richards, N., Solove, D, (2010) Prosser's Privacy Law: A Mixed Legacy, California Law Review Vol. 98:1887,1888–1920.

[15] Ibid.

[16] Ibid.

[17] Ibid.

[18] Ibid.

[19] *Roe v. Wade*, 410 US 113 (1973)

the right to privacy of women with the reserved powers of the states. The particular issue was to determine whether the state laws prohibiting or regulating abortion procedures violated the constitutional right of a woman to her privacy or her freedom to decide a particular outcome in family or marriage matters.[20] The 7-to-2 decision of the Supreme Court ruled that the:

> legitimate right to privacy under the due process clause of the Fourteenth Amendment extended to a woman's decision to have an abortion. But her right to privacy had to be balanced against the state's legitimate interests to protect the life of the unborn or, in the words of the Court's opinion, the "potentiality of human life.[21]

Nonetheless, as Gau points out, the Constitution does not explicitly mention any right to privacy. In a line of decisions going back to 1891, the Court had recognized that a right to personal privacy, or a guarantee of certain areas or zones of privacy, does exist under the Constitution. He goes onto say the Supreme Court found the roots of the right in the First, Fourth, Fifth, and Ninth Amendments, and in the penumbras (rights guaranteed by implication) of the Bill of Rights, or in the concept of liberty guaranteed by the first section of the Fourteenth Amendment. He believes the only personal rights that can be deemed "fundamental," or "implicit in the concept of ordered liberty," are included in this guarantee of personal privacy. The right to privacy has some extension to activities relating to marriage, procreation, contraception, family relationships, childrearing, and education.[22] Since then, the right to privacy across the US has evolved and today, taken into consideration the right to a level of privacy over the Internet.

Dieter Dörr and Russell Weaver, highlight how privacy in the US now pervades the criminal arena.[23] Privacy doctrines have advanced more slowly than, perhaps, any other area of the law. When the Fourth Amendment to the United States Constitution was adopted in the eighteenth century, modern technologies were not in existence or even imagined.[24] The new Americans were concerned about the fact that British colonial authorities had used Writs of Assistance that allowed them to do no more than specify the object of a search, and thereby obtain a warrant allowing them to physically search any place where the goods might be found, without limit as to place or duration. They were also concerned about the use of "general warrants" that required colonial officials only to specify an offense, and then left it to the discretion of executing officials to decide which persons should be arrested and which places should be searched. They note that these searches involved actual physical searches of places or people by conventional means rather than by the use

---

[20] Ibid.

[21] Ibid, 164.

[22] Luis Grau, L, (1973) *An American Constitutional History Course for Non-American Students* Carlos III University of Madrid https://core.ac.uk/download/pdf/29403732.pdf. *Rowe v Wade* 410 US 113, 152–153.

[23] Dörr, D., Weaver, R, (2014) *Perspectives on Privacy: Increasing Regulation in the USA, Canada, Australia and European Countries – Privacy and the Fourth Amendment*, De Gruyter, 3–6.

[24] Ibid.

of advanced technologies. The threats to privacy today are strikingly different than the abuses that the colonists suffered. In the eighteenth century, limited technologies were available for prying into people's lives. Eavesdropping was commonplace.

Today, governmental surveillance practices have gone high tech. Governmental officials have listening devices that allow them to overhear conversations from distant locations, even through walls, and they have super-sensitive microphones that allow them to overhear conversations through remotely placed technology. More pervasively, this equipment and the data it gathers, is in large part, personal information/data. More recent technology that has emerged is also posing complex challenges with privacy over the Internet, not only in the US, but most, if not all other states that take a human right approach to protecting personal information/data. These include, using closed circuit television systems, to detect and ticket speeding motorists with automated technology, to monitor the location of individuals and things using the Global Positioning System (GPS) and to overhear cell and cordless telephone conversations using special listening devices. Governmental officials also have X-ray technology that allows the police to peer through the walls of homes using drive-by X-ray vans. Dörr and Weaver, go into say that as PCs and the Internet have come into common usage, new threats to privacy have emerged. For example, devices have been created that permit individuals to monitor the keystrokes and other computer. They argue, which the story is no different around the world that, 'the US Supreme Court's Fourth Amendment jurisprudence has failed to keep pace with advancing technology or to provide much protection to individuals against governmental use of new technologies. Individual justices have pushed for changes in the Court's jurisprudence, and the US Supreme Court has rendered protective decisions, but the balance of decisions have not provided much protection for the citizenry'.[25] They further argue that there is a lack of protection, which has become not only a challenge but is quite worrying as new forms of technology continue to come online. Importantly, the authors note that when it comes to government action, the Fourth Amendment is problematic. For Dörr and Weaver argue, who argue that under the US Constitution, the principal protection against invasive governmental use of technology comes from the Fourth Amendment, which protects individuals against "unreasonable searches and seizures."[26] However, like many provisions of the Bill of Rights, the Fourth Amendment limits only governmental action and not private action. As a result, the Fourth Amendment cannot come close to dealing with modern threats to individual privacy, many of which come from private sources.

Neil Richards reinforces the above, however he refers to the First and not the Fourth Amendment. Thus, in the American context he is of the view that, laws regulating the collection, use, and disclosure of personal data are (mostly) constitutional, and critics who suggest otherwise are wrong.[27] For Richards, American law

[25] Ibid.

[26] Ibid.

[27] Richards, N, (2015) Why Data Privacy Law Is (Mostly) Constitutional, *56 Wm. & Mary L. Rev. 1501.*

has rested on the wise judgment that, by and large, commercial regulation should be made on the basis of economic and social policy, rather than blunt constitutional rules. This has become one of the basic principles of American constitutional law.[28] He highlights how the United States Supreme Court's decision in *Sorrell v IMS Health Inc*. changes the state of affairs, arguing such readings are incorrect. Sorrell involved a challenge to a poorly drafted Vermont law that discriminated on the basis of both content and viewpoint.[29] Richards argues that, such a law would have been unconstitutional if it had regulated even unprotected speech. As the Sorrell Court made clear, the real problem with the Vermont law at issue was that it did not regulate enough, unlike the "more coherent policy" of the undoubtedly constitutional federal Health Insurance Portability and Accountability Act of 1996. Therefore, Richards takes the position that, data privacy law should rarely be thought of as implicating serious constitutional difficulties, and this is a good thing. As we move into the digital age, more and more of our society will be impacted by data flows, we face a similar threat. If "data" were somehow "speech," virtually every economic law would become clouded by constitutional doubt.[30] He further points out that economic or commercial policy affecting data flows—which is to say all economic or social policy—would become almost impossible. This might be a valid policy choice, but it is not one that the First Amendment commands. Any radical suggestion to the contrary are unsupported by our constitutional law.[31] In a democratic society, the basic contours of information policy must ultimately be up to the people and their policy-making representatives, and not to unelected judges.[32] Richards concludes that, we should decide policy on that basis, rather than on odd readings of the First Amendment.

Notwithstanding the above, in the case of *Carpenter v United States*,[33] the Supreme Court in 2018 concluded that the Fourth Amendment's protection of privacy extended to protecting some information from government intrusion even where that information was shared with a third party. In this case, the Court concluded that:

> individuals maintain an expectation of privacy, protected by the Fourth Amendment, in the record of their movements as recorded by their cellular provider.[34]

The case distinguished earlier cases which had relied upon the principle that information shared with third parties was generally not subject to Fourth Amendment scrutiny, concluding that "an individual maintains a legitimate expectation of

---

[28] Ibid.

[29] *Sorrell v. IMS Health Inc* 131 S. Ct. 2653, 2672 (2011), in Neil Richards, *Why Data Privacy Law Is (Mostly) Constitutional*, 56 Wm. & Mary L. Rev. 1501 (2015)

[30] Ibid.

[31] Richards, N, (2015) Why Data Privacy Law Is (Mostly) Constitutional, *56 Wm. & Mary L. Rev. 1501.*

[32] Ibid.

[33] *Carpenter v. United States* 138 S. Ct. 2206 (2018)

[34] Ibid.

privacy in the record of his physical movements as captured through [his cellular phone]".[35] The Court's holding means that, in the future, the government must obtain a warrant supported by probable cause to obtain this information. The Fourth Amendment thus provides a limited bulwark against government intrusion into digital privacy.[36] There appears to be a subtle disconnect between the courts and scholars on where data privacy might sit within the constitution. Scholars, to date, have taken a cautious approach to the application of the First and fourth Amendments. However, the courts, have, at least, begun to consider the constitutional implication that, need to be reconciled between individual's personal data and information, and its protection.

Notwithstanding this position, privacy over the Internet in the US has thrown up the similar challenges to other states around the world. Since the implementation of the EU GDPR, the US has drifted even further apart from the EU rights-based model.[37] Arguably, it takes a greater focus on consumer rights. Without exploring all the elements that differ between the two, one is the extra territorial reach of the EU law.[38] Stephanie Schiedermair noted that, another important change for the European-American relationship is the more detailed regulation of the transfer of personal data to third countries in Articles 40–43. As a general rule Article 40 provides that any transfer of personal data which are undergoing processing or are intended for processing after transfer to a third country may only take place if the conditions laid down in Chapter V and the other regulations of the GDPR are complied with by the controller and processor, including onward transfers of personal data from the third country to another third country. The GDPR provides three basic possibilities for the transfer of data to third countries (Articles 41–43).

Even though the EU framework has been hailed by many across the world as being the benchmark for the protection of rights over the Internet, the US has not been as complementary. It is argued that many comprehensive data privacy models have resulted in "long, legal, regulator-focused privacy policies and check boxes, which only help a very small number of users[.]"[39] Rather than pursuing a

---

[35] Ibid.

[36] Ibid.

[37] Schiedermair, S, *The New General Data Protection Regulation of the European Union – Will it Widen the* Gap between Europe and the US? 72–78, in Dieter Dörr, Russell L. Weaver, (2014) *Perspectives on Privacy: Increasing Regulation in the USA, Canada, Australia and European Countries - Privacy and the Fourth Amendment*, De Gruyter, 3–6.

[38] Article 3 (1) GDPR regulates that the GDPR applies to the processing of personal data in the context of the activities of an establishment of a controller or a processor in the European Union. According to Recital 19 it is irrelevant whether the processing of personal data takes places within the European Union or without. It is also insignificant in which legal form the arrangement takes place, whether through a branch or a subsidiary with a legal personality. The GDPR applies to controllers in third countries insofar as personal data of individuals that reside in the European Union are involved and the processing is carried out to offer goods or services to such data subjects in the European Union or to monitor their behaviour (Article 3 (2)).

[39] Ross, W, US Secretary of Commerce, *EU Data Privacy Laws are Likely to Create Barriers to Trade*, FIN. TIMES (May 30, 2018), https://www.ft.com/content/9d261f44-6255-11e8-bdd1-

prescriptive model in which the government defines (or prescribes) data protection rules, and advocates for what it describes as an *outcome-based* approach whereby the government focuses on the "outcomes of organizational practices, rather than on dictating what those practices should be."[40] However, this view may change with change over time.

Even on the backdrop of the current position taken by the US, there have been calls by the business community that the current legal framework needs reviewing. In September 2019, the Chief Executive Officers from Amazon, IBM, Salesforce called on the US Congress to pass a consumer-based data privacy law.[41] If realized, this may not necessarily depart further from the current EU legal framework, on the contrary, it may include more of the EU legal regime. The letter summarized below states:

> Dear Leader McConnell, Speaker Pelosi, Leader Schumer, Leader McCarthy, Chairman Wicker, Chairman Pallone, Ranking Member Cantwell and Ranking Member Walden. We write to urge you to pass, as soon as possible, a comprehensive consumer data privacy law that strengthens protections for consumers and establishes a national privacy framework to enable continued innovation and growth in the digital economy. There is now widespread agreement among companies across all sectors of the economy, policymakers and consumer groups about the need for a comprehensive federal consumer data privacy law that provides strong, consistent protections for American consumers. A federal consumer privacy law should also ensure that American companies continue to lead a globally competitive market. Consumer trust and confidence are essential to our businesses. We are committed to protecting consumer privacy and want consumers to have confidence that companies treat their personal information responsibly. Consumers should not and cannot be expected to understand rules that may change depending upon the state in which they reside, the state in which they are accessing the internet, and the state in which the company's operation is providing those resources or services. Now is the time for Congress to act and ensure that consumers are not faced with confusion about their rights and protections based on a patchwork of inconsistent state laws. Further, as the regulatory landscape becomes increasingly fragmented and more complex, US innovation and global competitiveness in the digital economy are threatened. We urgently need a comprehensive federal consumer data privacy law to strengthen consumer trust and establish a stable policy

cc0534df682c. ("GDPR's implementation could significantly interrupt transatlantic co-operation and create unnecessary barriers to trade, not only for the US, but for everyone outside the EU."). Walter Copan, Director, Nat'l Inst. Standards. & Tech, Dep't of Commerce, Developing the NIST Privacy Framework: How Can a Collaborate Process Help Manage Privacy Risks (Sept. 24, 2018), https://www.nist.gov/ speech-testimony/developing-nist-privacy-framework-how-can-collaborative-process-help-manage-privacy. [hereinafter Copan Keynote] ("It is too soon to tell how large an impact these regulations will ultimately have on products and services that rely on access to users' data, and whether there will be a substantial measurable improvement in desired privacy outcomes."). Developing the Administration's Approach to Consumer Privacy, 83 Fed. Reg. 48,600, 48,601 (Sept. 26, 2018). In Data Protection Law: An Overview Congressional Research Service March 25, 2019 https://fas.org/sgp/crs/misc/R45631.pdf

[40] Ibid.

[41] 51 CEOs from companies such as Amazon, IBM, Salesforce, Target and more, https://www.cnbc.com/2019/09/10/business-roundtable-urges-congress-to-pass-consumer-data-privacy-law.html

> environment in which new services and technologies can flourish within a well-understood legal and regulatory framework. We stand ready to work with you.[42]

More importantly, the US have recognized that American citizens now transmit their personal data over the internet at an exponentially higher rate than in the past, and their data is collected, cultivated, and maintained by a growing number of both consumers facing and data brokers. As a consequence, the privacy, cybersecurity and protection of personal data has emerged as a major issue of consideration.[43] The report highlights the interconnectedness of data protection and cyber security, and that having to govern both areas is complex and technical, and lacks uniformity at the federal level. Nevertheless, the current day data protection and privacy laws of the US have been summarized by Daniel Solove and Woodrow Hartzog as being diffuse and discordant.[44] Unlike the privacy laws of many industrialized nations, which protect all personal data in an omnibus fashion, privacy law in the United States is sectorial, with different laws regulating different industries and economic sectors. This sectorial approach also leaves large areas unregulated.[45] This position by Solove and Woodrow has been reinforced by Heck who argues that the United States has a patchwork of laws at both the federal and state levels relating to data protection and information sharing.[46]

Yet, the constitutional right to privacy developed over the course of the twentieth century, but this right generally only guards against government intrusions and does little to shield the average internet user from private actors. The report highlights that there are a number of federal statutes where personal data overlaps with cyber security. These include but not limited to the Gramm-Leach-Bliley Act, Health Insurance Portability and Accountability Act, Children's Online Privacy Protection Act, and others. And a number of different agencies, including the Federal Trade Commission (FTC), the Consumer Finance Protection Bureau (CFPB), and the Department of Health and Human Services (HHS), enforce these laws.[47] However, at issue for the US, is that their legal framework has taken largely a sectorial approach, regulating specific area of the economy and industry.

Beginning with the Gramm-Leach-Bliley Act[48] (GLBA), it imposes several data protection obligations on financial institutions. These obligations are centred on a category of data called "consumer "nonpublic personal information"(NPI), and comprise of: (1) sharing NPI with third parties, (2) providing privacy notices to

---

[42] Ibid.

[43] Data Protection Law: An Overview Congressional Research Service March 25, 2019, https://fas.org/sgp/crs/misc/R45631.pdf

[44] Solove, D., Hartzog, W, (2014) *The FTC and the New Common Law of Privacy*, 114 Colum. L. Rev. 583–587.

[45] Ibid.

[46] Heck, Z, (2018) *A Litigator's Primer on European Union and American Privacy Laws and Regulations*, 44 LITIG. 59–59.

[47] Ibid.

[48] 15 U.S.C. §§ 6801–6809. In Data Protection Law: An Overview Congressional Research Service March 25, 2019, https://fas.org/sgp/crs/misc/R45631.pdf

consumers, and (3) securing NPI from unauthorized access.[49] The GLBA prohibits financial institutions from sharing NPI with non-affiliated third parties unless they first provide the consumers with notice and an opportunity to opt-out. Furthermore, financial institutions are prohibited altogether from sharing account numbers or credit card numbers to third parties for use in direct marketing. It also requires financial institutions to maintain administrative, technical, and physical safeguards to ensure the security and confidentiality of customer (as opposed to consumer) NPI, and to protect against any anticipated threats. Financial institutions regulated by federal banking agencies are further required to implement a program for responding to the unauthorized access of customer NPI.[50] Secondly, the Consumer Financial Protection Bureau (CFPB), FTC, and federal banking agencies share civil enforcement authority for GLBA's privacy provisions. However, the CFPB has no enforcement authority over GLBA's data security provisions. This banking sector generates huge quantities of data daily.

Secondly, the Fair Credit Reporting Act[51] (FCRA) covers the collection and use of information bearing on a consumer's creditworthiness. FCRA and its implementing regulations govern the activities of three categories of entities: (1) credit reporting agencies (CRAs), (2) entities furnishing information to CRAs (furnishers), and (3) individuals who use credit reports issued by CRAs (users). In contrast to the GLBA, there are no privacy provisions in FCRA requiring entities to provide notice to a consumer or to obtain his opt-in or opt-out consent before collecting or disclosing the consumer's data to third parties.[52]

Third, the Telecommunications Act of 1996[53] amended the Communications Act to impose data privacy and data security requirements on entities acting as common carriers. Generally, common carrier activities include telephone and telegraph services but exclude radio broadcasting, television broadcasting, provision of cable television, and provision of broadband internet. The privacy and security requirements imposed on entities acting as common carriers are primarily centred on a category of information referred to as "customer proprietary network information (CPNI)."[54] In addition to common carriers, the Communications Act 1934 imposes a number of data privacy and security requirements on how cable operators and satellite carriers.[55] On the other hand, the Communications Act of 1934[56], as

---

[49] Ibid.

[50] Ibid.

[51] Ibid, 15 U.S.C. §§ 1681–1681x.

[52] Ibid.

[53] Ibid, Pub. L. No. 104-104, 110 Stat. 56 (1996) (codified throughout 47 U.S.C.).

[54] Ibid.

[55] Ibid, Cable operators are defined to include anyone who uses the cable system to provide any video or other programming service. §§ 522(5)–(6). Satellite carriers are defined as any entity that uses the facilities of a satellite or satellite service to establish and operate a channel of communications for point-to-multipoint distribution of television station signals. § 338(k)(7); 17 U.S.C. § 119(d)(6).

[56] Ibid, 47 U.S.C. ch. 5.

amended, established the Federal Communications Commission (FCC) and provides a comprehensive scheme for regulation of interstate communication. Most relevant, the Communications Act includes data protection provisions applicable to common carriers, cable operators, and satellite carriers.

Fourth, the Video Privacy Protection Act (VPPA) was enacted in 1988 in order to preserve personal privacy with respect to the rental, purchase, or delivery of video tapes or similar audio-visual materials.[57] The VPPA does not have any data security provisions requiring entities to maintain safeguards to protect consumer information from unauthorized access. However, it does have privacy provisions restricting when covered entities can share certain consumer information. The VPPA prohibits video tape service providers a term that includes both digital video streaming services and brick-and-mortar video rental stores from knowingly disclosing PII concerning any consumer without that consumer's opt-in consent.[58]

Fifth, the Family Educational Rights and Privacy Act of 1974 (FERPA) creates privacy protections for student education records. Education records are defined broadly to generally include any "materials which contain information directly related to a student and are maintained by an educational agency or institution.[59]

On the other hand, the federal securities statutes and regulations do not address data protection. However, under Section 13(b)(2)(B) of the Securities and Exchange Act of 1934 (Exchange Act), public companies and certain other companies are required to devise and maintain a system of internal accounting controls sufficient to provide reasonable assurances that transactions are executed in accordance with management's general or specific authorization, and that access to assets is permitted only in accordance with management's general or specific authorization.[60] Additionally, the federal securities laws may require companies to discuss data breaches when making required disclosures under securities laws.

Seventh, the Children's Online Privacy Protection Act[61] (COPPA) and the FTC's implementing regulations regulate the online collection and use of children's information. Specifically, the COPPA applies to: (1) any operator of a website or online service that is directed to children, or (2) any operator that has any actual knowledge that it is collecting personal information from a child (covered operators).[62] Covered operators must comply with various requirements regarding data collection and use, privacy policy notifications, and data security. Arguably, in the modern world, it is this group that are, in our view, the most venerable in the community.

[57] Ibid.

[58] Ibid.

[59] Ibid.

[60] Ibid.

[61] Ibid, §§ 6501–6506.

[62] Ibid.

Eighth, the Electronic Communications Privacy Act[63] (ECPA) was enacted in 1986, and is composed of three acts: the Wiretap Act, the Stored Communications Act (SCA), and the Pen Register Act. The ECPA is directed at law enforcement, providing Fourth Amendment like privacy protections to electronic communications. The Computer Fraud and Abuse Act[64] (CFAA) addresses data protection issues such as the collection or use of data. Specifically, the CFAA imposes liability when a person intentionally accesses a computer without authorization or exceeds authorized access, and thereby obtains information from any protected computer.[65]

Nineth, the Consumer Financial Protection Act[66] (CFPA) prohibits covered entities from engaging in certain unfair, deceptive, or abusive acts. Enacted in 2010 as Title X of the Dodd-Frank Wall Street Reform and Consumer Protection Act, the CFPA created the Consumer Financial Protection Bureau (CFPB) as an independent agency within the Federal Reserve System.[67] The Act gives the CFPB certain organic authorities, including the authority to take any action to prevent any covered person from committing or engaging in an unfair, deceptive, or abusive act or practice (UDAAP) in connection with offering or providing a consumer financial product or service.[68]

The federal sectorial approach taken to date by the US has largely focused on regulating specific industries and professions such as health, education, finance and credit, consumer protection, communications, trade and most important protection of children online. This group are arguably considered the most venerable cohort in the community. This Chapter will only discuss the Federal Trade Commission Act and Health Insurance Portability and Accountability Act. The next section introduces these laws, and then moves onto identifying and discussing the relevant principles of consent, definition of personal data/information, data security, enforcement, amongst others. This Chapter does not discuss any of the state-based privacy or data protection laws. However, with the California privacy laws being implemented in 2020, this Chapter concludes by highlighting its key provisions.

14.2 The Federal Trade Commission Act

The data protection-privacy laws of the US demonstrate that their current framework is ad hoc and fragmented approach of both federal and state law. However, this approach appears to be serving them well. Due to the structure of the Federal Trade

---

63 Ibid, Electronic Communications Privacy Act of 1986, Pub. L. No. 99-508, 100 Stat. 1848 (1986) (codified at 18 U.S.C. §§ 2510–3127).

64 Ibid, § 1030.

65 Ibid.

66 Ibid, Consumer Financial Protection Act of 2010, Pub. L. No. 111-203, tit. X, 124 Stat. 1376, 1955–2113 (2010) (codified at 12 U.S.C. §§ 5491–5603).

67 Ibid.

68 Ibid.

Commission Act (15 U.S.C. §§41–58)[69] (FTC Act), this Chapter and section will not be structured in the same way as other Chapters. It is largely considered the central federal consumer protection law that prohibits unfair or deceptive practices and has been applied to offline and online privacy and data security policies. The FTCA came into effect in 1914. The Act gives the FTC jurisdiction over most individuals and entities, although there are several exemptions. The FTC gives effect to the Fair Information Practice Principles in Operation (FIPPS).[70] Fred Cate argues that following their inception in the 1970s and early 1980s, FIPPS were broad, aspirational, and included a blend of substantive (data quality, use limitation) and procedural (consent, access) principles. They reflected a wide consensus about the need for broad standards to facilitate both individual privacy and the promise of information flows in an increasingly technology-dependent, global society.

Cate in referring to Professor Paul Schwartz, notes that as a leading scholar of data protection law in the United States and Europe, is of the view that "[f]air information practices are the building blocks of modern information privacy law".[71] Cate notes that Schwartz describes FIPPS as being "centered around four key principles: (1) defined obligations that limit the use of personal data; (2) transparent processing systems; (3) limited procedural and substantive rights; and (4) external oversight".[72] However, Cate is of the view that as translated into national law in the United States, Europe, and elsewhere during the 1990s and 2000s, FIPPS have increasingly been reduced to narrow, legalistic principles (notice, choice, access, security, and enforcement). Thus, for the US, one of the challenges, should they choose to fully embrace the internationally accepted data protection principles is to reconcile whether one initial problem of basing a data protection regime on FIPPS is determining which set of FIPPS to apply. The OECD Guidelines provide eight, the EU data protection directive eleven, and the FTC principles only five (or four).[73]

Cate goes onto highlight how the Federal Trade Commission and states attorney's general encouraged US operators of commercial websites to adopt and publish online privacy policies. However, the adoption of such policies was voluntary, yet, compliance with them was not. The Commission interprets section five of the Federal Trade Commission Act, which empowers the FTC to prosecute unfair and deceptive trade practices, to include violations of posted privacy policies. Thus, the, to date, five core principles of privacy protection include Notice-Awareness,

---

[69] Federal Trade Commission Act (15 U.S.C. §§41–58) https://uscode.house.gov/view.xhtml?req=granuleid%3AUSC-prelim-title15-chapter2-subchapter1&edition=prelim

[70] Cate, F, Consumer Protection in the Age of the Information Economy The Failure of Fair Information Practice Principles, (2018) https://www.ftc.gov/system/files/documents/public_comments/2018/12/ftc-2018-0098-d-0036-163372.pdf. Schwartz, P, *"Privacy and Democracy in Cyberspace,"* 52 Vanderbilt Law Review 1607, 1614 (1999).

[71] Ibid.

[72] Ibid.

[73] Ibid.

Choice-Consent, Access-Participation and Integrity-Security.[74] Thus, the US in asserting their sovereign right have stepped away from the EU model, which many other states have embraced. However, it must be highlighted that it has generally become the norm to analyze data protection and privacy law through the lens of the EU, and not the US, China or Singapore.

Woodrow Hartzog and Daniel Solove argue that the FTC used the predominantly self-regulatory approach to privacy and data security as its foundation to build a foothold in the area of data protection.[75] They go onto say that today, the FTC has evolved into the broadest and most powerful data protection agency in the United States. No other agency has such a broad scope of power over so many different industries. In their view, the Department of Health and Human Services ("HHS") is limited to regulating entities subject to the Health Insurance Portability and Accountability Act ("HIPAA"), and countless industries do not fall under HIPAA.[76] Similarly, they point out how the Federal Communications Commission has jurisdiction over telecommunications, satellite, broadcast, and cable companies, but its range does not extend much further. In contrast, the FTC's scope covers nearly any for-profit entity that handles personal data. Except for a few small industry carve-outs, nearly every industry is subject to FTC enforcement power, including industries such as automotive, financial, health, retail, online services, hospitality, entertainment, manufacturing, data processing, food and beverage, transportation, and many more.[77] Thus, what has evolved, is where any industry where consumers are involved is typically within the scope of FTC enforcement power. The FTC Act exempts common carriers, non-profits, and financial institutions such as banks, savings and loan institutions, and federal credit unions.[78]

---

[74] Ibid.The most fundamental principle is notice. Consumers should be given notice of an entity's information practices before any personal information is collected from them. Without notice, a consumer cannot make an informed decision as to whether and to what extent to disclose personal information. Moreover, three of the other principles discussed below—choice/consent, access/participation, and enforcement/ redress—are only meaningful when a consumer has notice of an entity's policies, and his or her rights with respect thereto. The second widely-accepted core principle of fair information practice is consumer choice or consent. At its simplest, choice means giving consumers options as to how any personal information collected from them may be used. Specifically, choice relates to secondary uses of information—i.e., uses beyond those necessary to complete the contemplated transaction. Refers to an individual's ability both to access data about him or herself—i.e., to view the data in an entity's files—and to contest that data's accuracy and completeness. Both are essential to ensuring that data are accurate and complete. Data must be accurate and secure. To assure data integrity, collectors must take reasonable steps, such as using only reputable sources of data and cross-referencing data against multiple sources, providing consumer access to data, and destroying untimely data or converting it to anonymous form.

[75] Hartzog, W., Solove, D, (2015) *The Scope and Potential of FTC Data Protection,* 015 Vol. 83 No. 6, 2231–2248.

[76] Ibid.

[77] Ibid.

[78] 15 U.S.C. § 45(a)(2).

Woodrow and Solove highlight the importance of the matter of *FTC v Wyndham Worldwide Corp*,[79] whereby, there was first and one of the most significant challenges to the FTC's data protection power to date.[80] In this case, the FTC alleged that Wyndham, a company that manages hotels and sells timeshares, suffered a series of three breaches, where the breaching parties used similar techniques in all three instances to access personal information stored on the Wyndham-branded hotels property management system servers, including customers payment card account numbers, expiration dates, and security codes. FTC claimed that "[a]fter discovering each of the first two breaches, defendants failed to take appropriate steps in a reasonable time frame to prevent the further compromise of" its network".[81] According to the FTC, more than 619,000 consumers' payment card account numbers were compromised, and consumers and businesses suffered financial injury, including, but not limited to, unreimbursed fraudulent charges, increased costs, and lost access to funds or credit. Consumers and businesses also expended time and money resolving fraudulent charges and mitigating subsequent harm.[82] The resulting effect was more than $10.6 million in fraud loss. Consumers and businesses suffered financial injury, including, but not limited to, unreimbursed fraudulent charges, increased costs, and lost access to funds or credit. Consumers and businesses also expended time and money resolving fraudulent charges and mitigating subsequent harm. Thus, FTC brought this action, seeking a permanent injunction to prevent future violations of the FTC Act, as well as certain other relief.

In addition to the above, the FTC went onto claim that Wyndham deceptively stated in its privacy policy that it protected its customers' personal information by using "industry standard practices" and "a variety of different security measures designed to protect personally identifiable information from unauthorized access by users both inside and outside of our company."[83] Other allegedly deceptive statements included a promise that Wyndham takes "commercially reasonable efforts to create and maintain 'fire walls' and other appropriate safeguards to ensure that to the ex-tent [Wyndham] control[s] the Information, the Information is used only as authorized by [Wyndham] and consistent with [its] Policy, and that the Information is not improperly altered or destroyed."[84] The FTC alleged that Wyndham actually provided deficient data security practices contrary to their representations of following industry standard practices.[85] The FTC identified practices that "unreasonably and unnecessarily ex- posed consumers' personal data to unauthorized access and

[79] *FTC v. Wyndham Worldwide Corp.*, 10 F. Supp. 3d 602 (D.N.J. 2014), in Woodrow Hartzog, Daniel J. Solove *The Scope and Potential of FTC Data Protection*, 015 Vol. 83 No. 6 (2015), 2231–2248.

[80] Ibid.

[81] Ibid.

[82] Ibid.

[83] Ibid.

[84] Ibid.

[85] Ibid.

theft."[86] Among other things, the FTC alleged that Wyndham failed to use readily available access guards (firewalls), allowed misconfiguration, resulting in storage of credit card information in clear text, failed to ensure implementation of adequate security policies before connecting to main network.[87]

In conclusion, it was ordered that Wyndham Hotels and Resorts, LLC's motion, (D.E. No. 188), certifying the Court's April 7, 2014 Order, (D.E. No. 182), for interlocutory review that was confirmed that the Federal Trade Commission can bring an unfairness claim involving data security under Section 5 of the Federal Trade Commission Act, 15 U.S.C. § 45(a); and must formally promulgate regulations before bringing its unfairness claim under Section 5 of the Federal Trade Commission Act, 15 U.S.C. § 45(a). It was also ordered Wyndham Hotels and Resorts, LLC shall file a Petition for Permission to Appeal with the United States Court of Appeals for the Third Circuit in accordance with Federal Rule of Appellate Procedure 5(a)(2); and it is further motions requesting leave for certain individuals or entities to file brief amici curiae in support of Defendant Wyndham Hotels. In conclusion the Court held that FTC authority over data security could coexist with the existing data security regulatory scheme.[88] The Court further held FTC did not need to formally promulgate rules because the proscriptions in § 45 are purposefully flexible, that the agency had adequately alleged substantial consumer injury that was not reasonably avoidable by the consumers themselves.

Four years after Wyndham, the FTC was back in court over personal data again. However, it must be noted that when initially established the FTC was largely responsible for enforcing anti-trust law. This was reinforced in *Inc. v Fed. Trade Comm'n*[89] where the Court stated:

> [A]t the time of the FTC Act's inception, the FTC's primary mission was understood to be the enforcement of antitrust law. In 1938, the Act was amended to provide that the FTC had authority to prohibit 'unfair . . . acts or practices.' This amendment sought to clarify that the FTC's authority applied not only to competitors but, importantly, also to consumers.[90]

The FTC Act is a critical law that is relevant to data privacy and security across the US. As some commentators have noted, the FTC has used its authority under the Act to become the go-to agency for privacy, effectively filling in gaps left by the aforementioned federal statutes. Daniel Solove and Woodrow Hartzog, are of the view that the statutory law is diffuse and discordant.[91] They go onto say, unlike the privacy laws of many industrialized nations, which protect all personal data in an omnibus fashion, privacy law in the United States is sectorial, with different laws regulating different industries and economic sectors. The resulting effect has seen a

86 Ibid.

87 Ibid.

88 Ibid.

89 894 F.3d 1221, 1228 (11th Cir. 2018).

90 Ibid.

91 Solove, D., Hartzog, W, *The FTC and the New Common Law of Privacy*, 114 Colum. L. Rev. (2014) 583–587.

number of areas unregulated. This will become problematic as data is increasingly used in cross border transfers.

Beginning at §41, the Federal Trade Commission is established, which determines its membership, vacancies and seal. While largely an administrative process, it provides that the original Commission was to be composed of five Commissioners that, were appointed by the President. Their appointment was on the advice from the Senate. By 1950 there were changes that saw some of the functions of the Federal Trade Commission, were transferred to Chairman of such Commission by Reorg. Plan No. 8 of 1950. However, it is out of scope of this Chapter to discuss the functions that were transferred in any depth. The essential elements transferred to the Flammable Fabrics Act, and the Consumer Product Safety Commission. [92] Further reform was undertaken in 1999, whereby it clarified the jurisdiction of the Federal Trade Commission.[93]

One of the most important provisions of the FTC is section 5 that, declares unfair or deceptive acts or practices (UDAP) in or affecting commerce. That is, an unfair act or practice occurs when there has been a cause substantial injury to consumers which is not reasonably avoidable by consumers themselves and not outweighed by countervailing benefits to consumers or to competition.[94] While the statute does not define deceptive, the FTC has clarified in guidance that an act or practice is to be considered deceptive if it involves a material representation, omission, or practice that is likely to mislead [a] consumer who is acting reasonably in the circumstances. Under the FTC Act, the agency may enact rules defining specific acts or practices as UDAPs, often referred to as trade regulation rules or Magnuson-Moss[95] rulemaking.

[92] Federal Trade Commission Act (15 U.S.C. §§41-58), [section 1191 et seq. of this title] and under this subchapter to extent that such functions relate to administration of Flammable Fabrics Act, and (2) under Act of August 2, 1956. [section 1211 et seq. of this title], transferred to Consumer Product Safety Commission by section 30 of Act Oct. 27, 1972, Pub. L. 92–573 [section 2079 of this title]. By section 3 of act Sept. 26, 1914, Bureau of Corporations abolished and all employees and functions of said Bureau transferred to Federal Trade Commission.

[93] Ibid. (a) Clarification of Federal Trade Commission Jurisdiction. Any person that directly or indirectly controls, is controlled directly or indirectly by, or is directly or indirectly under common control with, any bank or savings association (as such terms are defined in section 3 of the Federal Deposit Insurance Act [12 U.S.C. 1813]) and is not itself a bank or savings association shall not be deemed to be a bank or savings association for purposes of any provisions applied by the Federal Trade Commission under the Federal Trade Commission Act [15 U.S.C. 41 et seq.]. (b) Savings Provision. No provision of this section [amending section 18a of this title] shall be construed as restricting the authority of any Federal banking agency (as defined in section 3 of the Federal Deposit Insurance Act [12 U.S.C. 1813]) under any Federal banking law, including section 8 of the Federal Deposit Insurance Act [12 U.S.C. 1818].

[94] Ibid, section 5.

[95] Ibid. However, to enact TRRs the FTC must comply with several procedures that are not required under the notice-and-comment rulemaking procedures set forth in Section 553 of the Administrative Procedure Act, which are the default rulemaking procedures for federal agencies. These additional procedures require the FTC to publish an advance notice of proposed rulemaking, give interested persons an opportunity for an informal hearing, and issue a statement accompanying the rule regarding the prevalence of the acts or practices treated by the rule.

The most settled principle of the FTC's common law of privacy is that companies are bound by their data privacy and data security promises.[96] However, in more recent times, this has been significantly tested. The FTC has taken the position that companies act deceptively when they gather, use, or disclose personal information in a way that contradicts their posted privacy policy or other statements, or when they fail to adequately protect personal information from unauthorized access despite promises that that they would do so. In addition to broken promises, the FTC has alleged that companies act deceptively when they make false representations in order to induce disclosure of personal information. For example, in *FTC v. Sun Spectrum Commc'ns Org., Inc.*,[97] the FTC alleged that several telemarketers acted "deceptively" by misrepresenting themselves as a credit card company and requesting personal information from individuals, ostensibly for the purpose of providing non- existent credit cards to the individuals. The FTC has further maintained that companies act deceptively when their privacy policies or other statements provide insufficient notice of their privacy practices. The complaint involved group of US and Canadian telemarketers will pay $415,000 to settle Federal Trade Commission charges they were selling nonexistent credit cards to US consumers, the agency announced today.[98] The defendants are banned from selling credit-related products through telemarketing and must stop their attempts to deceive consumers into giving out their personal financial information.

According to the Commission, the defendants targeted consumers with poor credit, offering major credit cards with a $2500 limit for an advance fee of $197 to $300. The telemarketers claimed to have information showing that the consumers recently had been denied credit, and pitched the credit card offer as a means of improving their credit rating. Implying that they were merely verifying data, the defendants requested information about the consumer's bank accounts, such as account numbers, routing numbers, and the account holder's name, as well as personal identifying information, such as date of birth, mother's maiden name, and Social Security number. They also allegedly misrepresented that they had the ability and authority to issue major credit cards. The important point from this matter was the use of personal identifying information, so as to enhance the business of credit.

More recently in *Lenovo*[99] Lenovo acted deceptively by installing third-party software on consumers' computers that collected extensive personal data and simply telling consumers that the software would let them "discover visually similar products and best prices while [they] shop". The matter involved an electronic

---

[96] In Data Protection Law: An Overview Congressional Research Service March 25, 2019, https://fas.org/sgp/crs/misc/R45631.pdf

Ibid.

[97] *FTC v. Sun Spectrum Commc'ns Org., Inc.*, No. 03-CV-8110 (S.D. Fla. Oct. 3, 2005)

[98] Ibid, and see also Federal Trade Commission, US and Canadian Telemarketers Pay $415,000 to Settle FTC Charges, Defendants Charged with Selling Nonexistent Credit Cards, https://www.ftc.gov/news-events/press-releases/2005/10/us-and-canadian-telemarketers-pay-415000-settle-ftc-charges

[99] No. C- 4636 (F.T.C. Dec. 20, 2017).

manufacturer of toys VTech Electronics Limited and its US subsidiary. The company had breached the Children's Online Privacy Protection Act (COPPA),[100] which resulted in VTech being forced to pay $650,000 as part of the settlement with the FTC.[101] In addition, VTech is permanently prohibited from violating COPPA in the future and from misrepresenting its security and privacy practices. They were also forced to establish a comprehensive data security program, which is subject to independent audits for 20 years. The FTC highlighted that some of VTech's electronic toys collected the personal information of hundreds of thousands of children, and that the company failed to provide direct notice to parents or obtain verifiable consent from parents concerning its information collection practices, as required under the Children's Online Privacy Protection Act (COPPA).[102] They alleged that: "VTech failed to use reasonable and appropriate data security measures to protect personal information it collected."[103]

The COPPA requires that entities collecting personal information from children under 13 online follow steps to ensure that children's information is protected, including clearly disclosing to parents the information it collects, how the information will be used, and seeking verifiable parental consent. They must also take reasonable measures to protect the confidentiality, security and integrity of the personal information they collect about children. As of November 2015, about 2.25 million parents had registered and created accounts with Learning Lodge for nearly 3 million children. This included about 638,000 Kid Connect accounts for children. In addition, about 134,000 parents in the United States created Planet VTech accounts for 130,000 children by November 2015.[104] The FTC concluded that:

> it failed to provide direct notice of its information collection and use practices to parents and did not link to its privacy policy in each area where personal information was collected from children, in relation to Kid Connect product.[105]

More pervasively, the FTC alleged VTech falsely stated in its privacy policy that personal information submitted by users through the Learning Lodge and Planet VTech would be encrypted. However, it was later proved that this was not the case, and encryption of this information never took place. In settling this matter, the FTC collaborated with the Office of the Privacy Commissioner of Canada. Moreover, the ongoing enforcement process of requiring ongoing audits for the next 20 years is, in our view, an important feature of the US model. It will ensure there is ongoing continuous improvement processes and systems in place that, will to varying degrees provide further trust in the protection of personal data and information, particularly for children. On the backdrop of the above, the Federal Trade Commission has hosted a public workshop on 7 October, 2019 to explore whether to update the

---

[100] Ibid, *Children's Online Privacy Act 1998*, 15 U.S.C 6501–6505.

[101] Ibid.

[102] Ibid.

[103] Ibid.

[104] Ibid.

[105] Ibid.

Children's Online Privacy Protection Rule.[106] At the time of writing this book, the findings from this meeting and the proposed way forward had not been finalized or made public. Importantly, the workshop and review will examine whether there is a need to update the COPPA Rule in light of evolving business practices in the online children's marketplace, including the increased use of Internet of Things devices, social media, educational technology, and general audience platforms hosting third-party child-directed content. The COPPA Rule came into effect in 2000 and was revised in 2013. This, in our view, is going to be an ongoing process because the technology changes will result in not only Rules having to be revisited, but also, there may be a need as AI begins to pervade those areas where children have access, new Rules may be required.

Later in 2018, the FTC found themselves being challenged in the court over its decision in relation to requiring a medical laboratory to revise its data security program. This challenged did not end up all that well for the FTC. However, they continue to be active in the area of privacy and data protection. In *LabMD, Inc. v Fed. Trade Comm'n*,[107] it was highlighted how LabMD operated a medical testing laboratory that collected sensitive medical and financial information of more than 750,000 patients. Despite holding this amount of personal data, it was argued that the company failed to take even basic steps to protect the information. Subsequently, FTC concluded that LabMD's had established data security practices, which were substandard and breached the Act. It would not clear sailing for the FTC. Back in 2013, the agency issued a complaint alleging that the company's lack of data security was an unfair practice that violated the FTC Act (§ 45(a)). However, a Judge initially held that the:

> FTC's complaint counsel failed to prove that LabMD's data-security failures caused or were likely to cause substantial consumer injury, as required by Section 5(n) of the FTC Act,[108]

What followed saw the Commission take a different pathway, and its opinion focused on whether LabMD's data security was an unfair practice under the FTC

[106] Federal Trade Commission, The Future of the COPPA Rule: An FTC Workshop https://www.ftc.gov/news-events/events-calendar/future-coppa-rule-ftc-workshop

[107] 894 F.3d 1221, 1237 (11th Cir. 2018). See Federal Trade Commission, https://www.ftc.gov/system/files/documents/cases/labmd_ca11_ftc_opposition_to_fee_request_2018-1119.pdf. How the development of new technologies or business models, the evolving nature of privacy harms, and changes in the way parents and children use websites and online services, affect children's privacy today. How the Rule should address parental consent for education technology vendors that collect personal information consented to by schools, Whether the Rule should include a specific exception to parental consent for audio files containing a child's voice that website operators collect and then promptly delete. Whether the Rule should permit general audience platforms to rebut the presumption that all users of child-directed content are children, and if so, under what circumstances. Whether the revisions to the Rule made in 2013 have worked as intended or require modification; and Whether the Rule should be amended to better address websites and online services that do not include traditionally child-oriented activities, but that have large numbers of child users.

[108] Ibid.

Act. The Commission in adopting this approach looked as whether LabMD had cause[d] or [was] likely to cause substantial injury to consumers which is not reasonably avoidable by consumers themselves and not outweighed by countervailing benefits to consumers or to competition (§ 45(n)). The Commission held that LabMD's:

> data security practices were unfair. First, the disclosure of deeply personal medical data to an unauthorized recipient by itself is a "substantial injury" within the meaning of Section 5(n), even without economic loss. Second, unauthorized exposure of the file to millions of potential viewers created a high likelihood of a large harm, which satisfied the "likely to cause."[109]

Subsequently, the Commission entered into a remedial order. The order had three main provisions. First, it required LabMD to implement a comprehensive information security program[110] to protect the security, confidentiality, and integrity of personal information collected from or about consumers. Second, the order required LabMD to obtain a third-party professional's assessment of its data security plan every other year and report the assessment to the Commission. Third, it required LabMD to notify consumers whose information had been exposed. However, LabMD did not accept the validity of this order and subsequently the matter was heard by the court. At Court, largely the argument from LabMD claimed that the commission was relying on section 5 of the FTC Act and that they lacked fair notice of the Commission's data security requirements.[111] The resulting effect saw the Court ruling to vacate the order, because it was insufficiently specific because it does not instruct LabMD to stop committing a specific act or practice.[112] The Court went further finding the order devoid of any meaningful standard informing the Court of what constitutes a reasonably designed data- security program. It must be noted that the Court only addressed the issue of enforceability of an order issued by the commission. Interestingly, the personal data in this case was medical data. However, this medical data, while sensitive, did not fall with the health laws. More pervasively, it will be interesting to see whether future rulings will apply to the order issued by the Commission, to improve the data protection practices of entities. The ongoing implication of the use and enforcement of these orders is not settled for privacy and data protection. Further work is required to better understand what, if any, and how they can be improved. The question arises do similar orders or otherwise exist under the Health Insurance Portability and Accountability Act.

---

[109] Ibid.

[110] Ibid. The program was required to be "fully documented in writing" and to "contain administrative, technical, and physical safeguards appropriate to respondent's size and complexity, the nature and scope of respondent's activities, and the sensitivity of the personal information collected about consumers." It set out specific safeguards that the program must include, such as: (1) an employee designated to oversee information security, (2) the identification of security risks, (3) the design and implementation of safeguards to control those risks, (4) requirements that service providers also maintain appropriate safeguards, and (5) that the program be regularly evaluated and adjusted.

[111] Ibid.

[112] Ibid, *LabMD, Inc. v. FTC*, 891 F.3d 1286, 1300 (11th Cir. 2018)

14.3 Health Insurance Portability and Accountability Act

The Health Insurance Portability and Accountability Act[113] (HIPAA), protects a category of medical information called protected health information (PHI). In addition, the HIPAA is supported by the *Standards for Privacy of Individually Identifiable Health Information* (Privacy Rule). The Rules establish a set of national standards for the protection of certain health information,[114] such as standards to address the use and disclosure of individuals' health information. The Rule strikes a balance that permits important uses of information, while protecting the privacy of people who seek care and healing. Given that the health care marketplace is diverse, the Rule is designed to be flexible and comprehensive to cover the variety of uses and disclosures that need to be addressed.

HIPAA regulations define protected health information as individually identifiable health information transmitted or maintained in electronic media or any other form or medium. Individually identifiable health information is defined as health information that: (1) identifies or can reasonably be used to identify an individual; (2) is created or received by a health care provider, health plan, employer, or health care clearinghouse; and (3) relates to an individual's physical or mental health, health care provision, or payment for provision of health care.[115] Generally, HIPAA's privacy rules prohibit covered entities from using PHI or sharing it with third parties without patient consent, unless such information is being used or shared for treatment, payment, or health care operations purposes, or unless another exception applies.[116] Covered entities generally may not make treatment or services conditional on an individual providing consent. Second, with respect to consumer disclosures, covered entities must provide individuals with adequate notice of the uses and disclosures of [PHI] that may be made by the covered entity, and of the individual's rights and the covered entity's legal duties with respect to [PHI]. These notices must be provided upon consumer request, and covered entities maintaining websites discussing their services or benefits must prominently post the notices on their websites.[117]

Importantly, the Department of Health and Human Services, in 2018, imposed a US$16 million fine to Anthem, Inc. This matter highlighted the interconnectedness of data protection/privacy and cyber security law. The matter began in 2015, whereby in March, Anthem filed a breach report with the HHS Office for Civil Rights detailing that, on January 29, 2015, they discovered cyber-attackers had gained access to their IT system via an undetected continuous and targeted

---

[113] §160.103. In Data Protection Law: An Overview Congressional Research Service March 25, 2019, https://fas.org/sgp/crs/misc/R45631.pdf.

[114] Health Information Privacy, HIPAA Privacy Rule, Department of Health and Human Services, https://www.hhs.gov/hipaa/for-professionals/privacy/laws-regulations/index.html

[115] Ibid.

[116] Ibid.

[117] Ibid.

cyberattack for the apparent purpose of extracting data, otherwise known as an advanced persistent threat attack.[118] After filing their breach report, Anthem discovered cyber-attackers had infiltrated their system through spear phishing emails sent to an Anthem subsidiary after at least one employee responded to the malicious email and opened the door to further attacks. Office of Civil Rights (OCR's) investigation revealed that between December 2, 2014 and January 27, 2015, the cyber-attackers stole an estimated 79 million individuals, including names, social security numbers, medical identification numbers, addresses, dates of birth, email addresses, and employment information.[119] The OCR also required the entity to undertake a robust corrective action plan to comply with the HIPAA Rules. Such a corrective action plan, is arguably a plan that forces the entity to improve its cyber security and data protection measures. While out of scope of this Chapter, further research is needed to better understand what the difference, legally is, between a corrective action plan and the order issued under the FTC, to confirm whether their establishment and enforcement can be reconciled. In other words, would the corrective action plan have similar enforcement issues to that of the order issued under the FTC.

14.4 Definition Personal Data

The FTC Act does not define personal data or sensitive personal data. On the other hand rather than define personal (general or sensitive) data or information, the HIPPA Privacy Rules define 'health information', 'protected health information', 'individual identifiable health information' and 'genetic information'.[120] Firstly, 'health information' means any information, including genetic information, whether oral or recorded in any form or medium, that is created or received by a health care provider, health plan, public health authority, employer, life insurer, school or university, or health care clearinghouse. In addition, it means relating to the past, present, or future physical or mental health or condition of an individual; the provision of health care to an individual; or the past, present, or future payment for the provision of health care to an individual.[121] Secondly, protected health information means individually identifiable health information that is transmitted by electronic media, maintained in electronic media; or transmitted or maintained in any other form or medium. However, protected health information excludes individually identifiable health information. Thirdly, individually identifiable health information is

[118] Anthem Pays OCR $16 Million in Record HIPAA Settlement Following Largest US Health Data Breach in History, Department of Health and Human Services https://www.hhs.gov/about/news/2018/10/15/anthem-pays-ocr-16-million-record-hipaa-settlement-following-largest-health-data-breach-history.html

[119] Ibid.

[120] HIPPA Privacy Rules, § 160.103, Definitions, https://www.hhs.gov/hipaa/for-professionals/privacy/laws-regulations/combined-regulation-text/index.html

[121] Ibid.

information that is a subset of health information, including demographic information collected from an individual, and is created or received by a health care provider, health plan, employer, or health care clearinghouse. This information can relate to the past, present or future physical or mental health or condition of an individual.

Furthermore, the provision of health care to an individual; or the past, present, or future payment for the provision of health care to an individual; and identifies the individual; or believes the information can be used to identify the individual.[122] Fourth, genetic information means information with respect to an individual, information about genetic tests, the genetic tests of family members of the individual and the manifestation of a disease or disorder in family members of such individual. In addition, genetic information also constitutes any request for, or receipt of, genetic services, or participation in clinical research which includes genetic services, by the individual or any family member of the individual.[123]

14.5 Consent

It must be noted that the FTC Act does not specifically address consent. Under section 57 b2, consent only applies to a person who produces the material, thing or transcript. The application of consent under this section is fluid at best. It provides that while in the possession of the custodian, no documentary material, tangible things, reports or answers to questions, and transcripts of oral testimony shall be available for examination by any individual other than a duly authorized officer or employee of the Commission without the consent of the person who produced the material, things, or transcripts.[124] Nothing in this section is intended to prevent disclosure to either House of the Congress or to any committee or subcommittee of the Congress, except that the Commission immediately shall notify the owner or provider of any such information of a request for information designated as confidential by the owner or provider.[125] The FTC's Behavioural Advertising Principles suggest website operators should obtain affirmative express consent before using sensitive consumer data. However, it stops short of providing any further information or guidance as to its functionality and application.

The HIPAA[126] generally requires covered entities to obtain consent in writing from a data subject before disclosing that data (with certain exceptions, for example, to provide medical treatment). Consent must generally be in writing and contain

[122] Ibid.

[123] Ibid.

[124] Federal Trade Commission Act (15 U.S.C. §§41–58).

[125] Ibid.

[126] United States Health Information Privacy, https://www.hhs.gov/hipaa/for-professionals/privacy/laws-regulations/combined-regulation-text/index.html

the signature of the data subject and the date. The HIPAA Privacy Rule provides specific statements that must be included in the consent. These include, the Implementation specification, un-emancipated towards minors.[127] The Rules go onto say that the minor consents to such health care service; no other consent to such health care service is required by law, regardless of whether the consent of another person has also been obtained; and the minor has not requested that such person be treated as the personal representative. Furthermore, the minor may lawfully obtain such health care service without the consent of a parent, guardian, or other person acting in loco parentis, and the minor, a court, or another person authorized by law consents to such health care service; or a parent, guardian, or other person acting in loco parentis assents to an agreement of confidentiality between a covered health care provider and the minor with respect to such health care service.[128]

Moreover, §164.506 provides for the uses and disclosures to carry out treatment, payment, or health care operations, and the standard permitted uses and disclosures. Except with respect to uses or disclosures that require an authorization under §164.508(a)(2) through (4) or that are prohibited under §164.502(a)(5)(i), a covered entity may use or disclose protected health information for treatment, payment, or health care operations as set forth in paragraph (c) of this section, provided that such use or disclosure is consistent with other applicable requirements of this subpart. Moreover, the standard of consent for uses and disclosure are permitted, when 1) a covered entity may obtain consent of the individual to use or disclose protected health information to carry out treatment, payment, or health care operations. Additionally, consent shall not be effective to permit a use or disclosure of protected health information when an authorization, under §164.508, is authorization for the use or disclosure of protected health information for a research study.[129] Finally, informed consent of the individual is to be obtained for the individual to participate in the research. On the other side, there is no clear direction as to what informed consent constitutes.

Due to the sectorial approach taken by the US, there appears to be no clear direction of how and when consent will apply. The stand-alone approach, differs significantly to the other jurisdictions examined throughout this book. There is no express terms or provisions of express or implied consent, or whether and how an express consent is to be obtained. The varied approach taken by the various jurisdiction towards consent will challenge the protection of personal data. However, the question has to be asked what are data subject consenting too? The next section of this book highlights the varied approach taken in defining personal data.

[127] Ibid, section 3

[128] Ibid.

[129] This also extends to another authorization for the same research study, with an authorization for the creation or maintenance of a research database or repository, or with a consent to participate in research

14.6 Collection, Correction, Disclosure, Access and Deletion

Under the HIPAA, the collection of health data is protected from fraud and abuse in accordance with section 221. The healthcare fraud and abuse of data collection program, enables the reporting of adverse actions that, against health care providers, suppliers, or practitioners as required by subsection (b), with access as set forth in subsection (c), and shall maintain a database of the information collected under this section.[130]

The further management of information from an adverse action that, is to be reported to the Secretary in relation to a health care provider, supplier, or practitioner, the Secretary can require the disclosure of the information, upon request, to the health care provider, supplier, or licensed practitioner, and any procedures in the case of disputed accuracy of the information.[131]

The correction of personal data and information is important allowing the data subject and entity to have accurate information. Moreover, each government agency and their respective health plans are to report any corrections of information that, has already be reported as having an adverse action.[132] This is to be in the form prescribed by the Secretary, however it is out of scope to explore this. Furthermore, this does not avail a data subject the ability to have their data or information deleted. Thus, the right to be forgotten in the US does not exist.[133] The access to reported information and its availability requires that any information stored within a database, can be made available to Federal and State government agencies and health plans pursuant to procedures that the Secretary shall provide by regulation.[134] This is a very broad provision, clearly related to government agencies managing information and data of individuals.

14.7 Controller and Processors

There is no requirement under either the FTC or the HIPAA to appoint specific controllers or processors. However, under the HIPAA there is a requirement for an individual within an organization to be responsible for data security. Additionally,

---

130 Health Insurance Portability and Accountability Act 1996, section 1128E, referring to section 221, https://www.congress.gov/104/plaws/publ191/PLAW-104publ191.pdf

131 Ibid.

132 Ibid.

133 Siegel, R, *Tech Policy, Google scores major victory in E.U. 'right to be forgotten' case* https://www.washingtonpost.com/technology/2019/09/24/google-scores-major-victory-eu-right-be-forgotten-case/

134 Ibid.

the HIPAA also requires that Business Associate Agreements[135] be established in relation to the transfer of health information.[136] The HIPAA Privacy Rule applies only to covered entities' health plans, health care clearinghouses, and certain health care providers. However, most health care providers and health plans do not carry out all of their health care activities and functions by themselves. Instead, they often use the services of a variety of other persons or businesses.[137] The Privacy Rule allows covered providers and health plans to disclose protected health information to these business associates if the providers or plans obtain satisfactory assurances that the business associate will use the information only for the purposes for which it was engaged by the covered entity, will safeguard the information from misuse, and will help the covered entity comply with some of the covered entity's duties under the Privacy Rule.[138] The process establishes and strengthens the broad risk management approach that, has been applied across the sectorial legal framework. In other words, the fragmented approach has resulted in different processes to assess risk.

14.8 Commission

In accordance with § 41. The Federal Trade Commission is established, which outlines its membership, vacancies and relevant seal. The FTC is to be composed of five Commissioners, who shall be appointed by the President, by and with the advice and consent of the Senate. However, there may be no more than three of the Commissioners members of the same political party. Importantly, the first Commissioners appointed shall continue in office for terms of 3, 4, 5, 6, and 7 years, respectively, from 26 September 1914, the term of each to be designated by the President, but their successors shall be appointed for terms of 7 years, except that any person chosen to fill a vacancy shall be appointed only for the unexpired term of the Commissioner whom he shall succeed. Yet, this is on the basis that, upon the expiration of his term of office a Commissioner shall continue to serve until his successor shall have been appointed and shall have qualified. The President shall choose a chairman from the Commission's membership. No Commissioner shall engage in any other business, vocation, or employment. Any Commissioner may be removed by the President for inefficiency, neglect of duty, or malfeasance in office. A vacancy in the Commission shall not impair the right of the remaining Commissioners to exercise all the powers of the Commission.

[135] A covered entity's contract or other written arrangement with its business associate must contain the elements specified at 45 CFR 164.504(e).

[136] Business Associates, 45 CFR 164.502(e), 164.504(e), 164.532(d) and (e), https://www.hhs.gov/hipaa/for-professionals/privacy/guidance/business-associates/index.html

[137] Ibid.

[138] Ibid.

On the other side, and in accordance with the HIPAA there is no specific requirement for a Commission to be established. The FTC by establishing a Commission is principally responsible for the appointment of a Commissioner, who has the authority to conduct and be a hearing examiner, or an employee or employee board, including functions with respect to hearing, determining, ordering, certifying, reporting or otherwise acting as to any work, business, or matter. Yet, this is subject to the section 7(a) of the Administrative Procedure Act (60 Stat. 241), as amended [5 U.S.C. 556].[139]

14.8.1 International Effect

The FTC enforces key international privacy frameworks, including the EU and US. It also enforces the Swiss and US Privacy Shield Framework.[140] The EU and US Privacy Shield Framework provide a legal mechanism for companies to transfer personal data from the European Union to the United States. This Framework, administered by the Department of Commerce, protects consumers' privacy and security through an agreed set of Privacy Shield Principles. The FTC also serves as a privacy enforcement authority in the APEC CPBR system. The APEC CBPR system is a voluntary, enforceable code of conduct designed to enhance the privacy and security of consumers' personal information transferred among the United States and other APEC members. Under the system, participating companies can be certified as compliant with APEC CBPR program requirements that implement APEC's nine data privacy principles.[141]

[139] Section 7(a), In hearings which section 4 or 5 requires to be conducted pursuant to this section—(a) Presiding Officers.—There shall preside at the taking of evidence (1) the agency, (2) one or more members of the body which comprises the agency, or (3) one or more examiners appointed as provided in this Act; but nothing in this Act shall be deemed to supersede the conduct of specified classes of proceedings in whole or part by or before boards or other officers specially provided for by or designated pursuant to statute. The functions of all presiding officers and of officers participating in decisions in conformity with section 8 shall be conducted in an impartial manner. Any such officer may at any time withdraw if he deems himself disqualified; and, upon the filing in good faith of a timely and sufficient affidavit of personal bias or disqualification of any such officer, the agency shall determine the matter as a part of the record and decision in the case.

[140] Privacy and Data Security Update, 2018, Federal Trade Commission https://www.ftc.gov/system/files/documents/reports/privacy-data-security-update-2018/2018-privacy-data-security-report-508.pdf

[141] Ibid. In 2018, FTC had brought 51 actions, 39 under an older US EU Safe Harbor program, 4 under APEC CBPR, and 8 under Privacy Shield.

14.8.2 Enforcement

Unlike the other state's studies throughout this book, the enforcement approach taken by the FTC is very different. In accordance with section 45 of the FTC Act, breaching of the law is limited to the punishment of deceptive trade practices. That is, the Act states that, the Commission can prevent persons, partnerships, or corporations, from using unfair methods of competition in or affecting commerce and unfair or deceptive acts or practices in or affecting commerce. However, this does not apply to banks, savings and loan institutions,[142] Federal credit unions,[143] common carriers subject to the Acts to regulate commerce, air carriers and foreign air carriers,[144] and persons, partnerships, or corporations.[145]

Recently in 2017, one of the largest fines was issues by the FTC to Equifax to Pay $575 Million as Part of Settlement with FTC, CFPB, and States Related to a data breach.[146] The original complaint arose from the alleged failure by Euifax to secure a large quantity of personal information that had been stored on its network. Thus, the resulting effect from the breach exposed an estimated 147 million consumers (names and dates of birth, Social Security numbers, physical addresses, amongst other personal information). The FTC noted that:

> As part of the proposed settlement, Equifax will pay $300 million to a fund that will provide affected consumers with credit monitoring services. The fund will also compensate consumers who bought credit or identity monitoring services from Equifax and paid other out-of-pocket expenses as a result of the 2017 data breach. Equifax will add up to $125 million to the fund if the initial payment is not enough to compensate consumers for their losses. In addition, beginning in January 2020, Equifax will provide all US consumers with six free credit reports each year for seven years—in addition to the one free annual credit report that Equifax and the two other nationwide credit reporting agencies currently provide. The company also has agreed to pay $175 million to 48 states, the District of Columbia and Puerto Rico, as well as $100 million to the CFPB in civil penalties.[147]

[142] Ibid, described in section 57a(f)(3) of this title.

[143] Ibid, described in section 57a(f)(4) of this title.

[144] Ibid, subject to part A of subtitle VII of title 49.

[145] Ibid, insofar as they are subject to the Packers and Stockyards Act, 1921, as amended [7 U.S.C. 181 et seq.], except as provided in section 406(b) of said Act [7 U.S.C. 227(b)].(3) This subsection shall not apply to unfair methods of competition involving commerce with foreign nations (other than import commerce) unless, (A) such methods of competition have a direct, substantial, and reasonably foreseeable effect (i) on commerce which is not commerce with foreign nations, or on import commerce with foreign nations; or (ii) on export commerce with foreign nations, of a person engaged in such commerce in the United States.

[146] Equifax to Pay $575 Million as Part of Settlement with FTC, CFPB, and States Related to 2017 Data Breach.

Settlement includes fund to help consumers recover from data breach, Federal Trade Commission, https://www.ftc.gov/news-events/press-releases/2019/07/equifax-pay-575-million-part-settlement-ftc-cfpb-states-related

[147] Ibid.

Moreover, the FTC highlighted how companies that profit from personal information have an extra responsibility to protect and secure that data. Equifax failed to take basic steps that may have prevented the breach. For the FTC, the settlement requires the company take steps to improve its data security going forward, and will ensure that consumers harmed by this breach can receive help protecting themselves from identity theft and fraud.[148] Apart from the breach to personal information, the matter also highlighted how in the US breaches of personal information have ventured past simple data violations, but also to cybersecurity breaches.

14.8.3 *Do Not Call Registry*

The Do-Not-Call Implementation Act authorizes the FTC to collect fees for the implementation and enforcement of a Do-Not-Call Registry,[149] expressly authorizes the FTC under Section 3(a)(3)(A) of the Telemarketing and Consumer Fraud and Abuse Prevention Act to implement and enforce a Do-Not-Call Registry, and ratified the Registry provision of the FTC's Telemarketing Sales Rule, 16 C.F.R. § 310.4(b)(1)(iii).[150] The Implementation Act has been amended by the Do-Not-Call Registry Fee Extension Act of 2007, specifying the Registry fees for telemarketers and revising reporting requirements in the Telemarketing and Consumer Fraud and Abuse Prevention Act; and by the Do-Not-Call Improvement Act of 2007, prohibiting automatic expiration of registry listings.[151] While out of scope of this book, it is worth noting that many US states have established their own specific communications regulations, which overlap with federal responsibilities. Many of the state-based operations pre-date the federal operations, explaining this overlap. The resulting effect has seen the both federal and state Do Not Call registers.[152] The Do Not Call Registry has many similarities to that of the Singapore and Australian equivalents. However, this Chapter does not go into any further discussion, to highlight any differences.

---

[148] Ibid.

[149] Do-Not-Call Registry. Public Law No. 108–82.

[150] 15 USC Ch. 87A NATIONAL DO-NOT-CALL REGISTRY, https://uscode.house.gov/view.xhtml?req=granuleid%3AUSC-prelim-title15-chapter87A&edition=prelim

[151] Ibid.

[152] Andrews Group, Australian Communications and Media Authority – Unsolicited Communications Research Findings Report – May 2018, https://www.rand.org/content/dam/rand/pubs/technical_reports/2012/RAND_TR1218.pdf

14.9 States of California and New York

While out of scope of this book to address the ongoing issues federally and at a state level from the fragmented approach towards privacy online and data protection, this section will provide a brief overview of the more recent additions to the state based regulatory framework. This section will discuss the new California Consumer Privacy Act of 2018 and the New York Privacy Act. The question is whether from the progress being made at a state level will there be the political will for a national privacy/data protection law to be established?

14.9.1 California's New Privacy Laws—2020

The California Consumer Privacy Act of 2018 (CCPA),[153] has arguably emerged as possibly the new direction of privacy and data protection law in the US. While it is state based law, and focuses largely on consumer protection, the new controls would see these laws come closer to the EU framework. Coming into effect on 1 January 2020, the CCPA grants a consumer a right to request a business to disclose the categories and specific pieces of personal information that it collects about the consumer, the categories of sources from which that information is collected, the business purposes for collecting or selling the information, and the categories of 3rd parties with which the information is shared.[154] The CCPA requires a business to make disclosures about the information and the purposes for which it is used. More importantly, the CCPA grants a consumer the right to request deletion of personal information, and allow a consumer the right to request that a business that sells the consumer's personal information, or discloses it for a business purpose, to disclose the categories of information that it collects and categories of information and the identity of 3rd parties to which the information is to be sold or disclosed.

One the one side, the new laws apply broadly to the community, particularly the business sector. On the other side, there is a number of exemptions for the small business sector. That is, those small business that buy, sell or share personal information of 50,000 consumers or devices, have a gross revenue of 25 million+, or derive 50% of their annual revenue sharing personal information. In addition, further exemptions apply to where non-profits that do not operate for profit or financial benefit, financial institutions that are regulated under the Gramm-Leach-Bliley Act. On the other side, consumer reporting agencies that are regulated under the Fair Credit Reporting Act are exempted along with health care providers that are regulated by the Health Insurance Portability and Accountability Act.

---

[153] AB375, Title 1.81.5, The California Consumer Privacy Act of 2018, and see, California Legislative Information, https://leginfo.legislature.ca.gov/faces/billTextClient.xhtml?bill_id=201720180AB375

[154] Ibid.

The definition of personal data, has been revised to include, a broad list of characteristics and behaviours, personal and commercial, as well as inferences drawn from this information. "Personal information means information that identifies, relates to, describes, is capable of being associated with, or could reasonably be linked, directly or indirectly, with a particular consumer or household. It includes, but is not limited to, the following: (A) Identifiers such as a real name, alias, postal address, unique personal identifier, online identifier Internet Protocol address, email address, account name, social security number, driver's license number, passport number, or other similar identifiers. (B) Any categories of personal information described in subdivision (e) of Section 1798.80. (C) Characteristics of protected classifications under California or federal law. (D) Commercial information, including records of personal property, products or services purchased, obtained, or considered, or other purchasing or consuming histories or tendencies. (E) Biometric information. (F) Internet or other electronic network activity information, including, but not limited to, browsing history, search history, and information regarding a consumer's interaction with an Internet Web site, application, or advertisement. (G) Geolocation data. (H) Audio, electronic, visual, thermal, olfactory, or similar information. (I) Professional or employment-related information. (J) Education information, defined as information that is not publicly available personally identifiable information as defined in the Family Educational Rights and Privacy Act (20 U.S.C. section 1232g, 34 C.F.R. Part 99). (K) Inferences drawn from any of the information identified in this subdivision to create a profile about a consumer reflecting the consumer's preferences, characteristics, psychological trends, preferences, predispositions, behaviour, attitudes, intelligence, abilities, and aptitudes".[155]

However, the law excludes certain elements of what constitutes personal information. In other words, personal information does not include publicly available information. Publicly available means information that is lawfully made available from federal, state, or local government records, if any conditions associated with such information. What it does not mean or include biometric information collected by a business about a consumer without the consumer's knowledge. Information is considered not publicly available if that data is used for a purpose. In addition, publicly available does not include consumer information that is de-identified or aggregate consumer information.[156] The right to privacy has been expanded through this new law that, provides consumers with an effective way to control their personal information by:

- knowing what personal information is being collected about them.
- knowing whether their personal information is sold or disclosed and to whom.
- say no to the sale of personal information.
- access their personal information.

[155] Personal information means information that identifies, relates to, describes, is capable of being associated with, or could reasonably be linked, directly or indirectly, with a particular consumer or household.

[156] Ibid.

- equal service and price, even if they exercise their privacy rights.[157]

This very broad and descriptive definition of personal information covers a lot of different policy areas from security, technology, biometrics, amongst others. The question will be with the AI, Quantum and other new technologies being mainstream over the coming decade, will this definition withstand the future challenges facing data protection, privacy and more broadly cyber security.

14.9.1.1 Collection, Disclosure, Deletion

A consumer has the right to request that a business that collects a consumer's personal information disclose to that consumer the categories and specific pieces of personal information the business has collected. Nonetheless, apart from the application of the collection of personal information, another important introduction to the Californian laws is the use and application of privacy notices. Thus, a privacy notice can be provided by a company to a data subject that describe the types of personal data the company collects. The notice also outlines how the entity uses that data, where the data is being shared and what protections have been afforded to the data. Furthermore, the CCPA also requires that a business provide all Californians a privacy notice, on what personal data and information has been collected. The privacy notice is to be given to the individual at or before the point of collection of the information.

Notwithstanding the above a business that collects personal information is to inform the individual of the various categories of personal information to be collected. They must also be informed of the purpose for which that personal information will be used. However, an entity is not to collect any further information, unless the data subject is provided a notice outlining the purpose of that collection. The entity is to also provide information to the data subject only upon receipt of a verifiable consumer request. An entity that receives a verifiable consumer request from a consumer to access personal information is to take steps to disclose and deliver, free of charge to the data subject that personal information.[158]

---

[157] Ibid.

[158] Ibid. 1798.100–110. The information may be delivered by mail or electronically, and if provided electronically, the information shall be in a portable and, to the extent technically feasible, in a readily useable format that allows the consumer to transmit this information to another entity without hindrance. A business may provide personal information to a consumer at any time, but shall not be required to provide personal information to a consumer more than twice in a 12-month period. (e) This section shall not require a business to retain any personal information collected for a single, one-time transaction, if such information is not sold or retained by the business or to reidentify or otherwise link information that is not maintained in a manner that would be considered personal information. (1) Retain any personal information collected for a single, one-time transaction, if the information is not sold or retained by the business. (2) Reidentify or otherwise link any data that, in the ordinary course of business, is not maintained in a manner that would be considered personal information.

Arguably, one of the most important introductions is the right for a consumer to request that their personal information be deleted.[159] Thus, a business that collects personal information about consumers has an obligation to disclose to the consumer of the right that the individual consumer can requests their personal information be deleted. Any request received by an entity for the deletion of personal information is to also direct any service provider(s) to also undertake the same task. In other words, the entity that has received the request of personal information is to inform the third-party service provider to also delete that personal information.

14.9.1.2 Deletion [Right to Be Forgotten]

The service provider does not have to comply with the request of deleting the personal information, if it is a business requirement, so as to complete the transaction, provide a good or service, or fulfil the performance of a contract between the business and the consumer. Deletion of personal information will not have to be undertaken when there is a security incident or a need to protect against malicious, deceptive, fraudulent, illegal activity, or, to prosecute those responsible for that activity. This will also apply where there is a need to debug in order to identify and repair errors that impair existing intended functionality. Nevertheless, there are additional exemption that apply to the deletion of personal information, which extend to the exercise of free speech, so as to ensure the right of another consumer to exercise his or her right of free speech or another right provided by the law. It will also apply to those individuals that are engaged in public or peer-reviewed scientific, historical, or statistical research in the public interest that adheres to all other applicable ethics and privacy laws, when the businesses' deletion of the information is likely to render impossible or seriously impair the achievement of such research, if the consumer has provided informed consent.[160]

Even though there are number of clear exemptions[161] to the exercise of the right for an individual to have their personal information deleted, this addition has, in

[159] 1798.105.

[160] Ibid. (5) Comply with the California Electronic Communications Privacy Act pursuant to Chapter 3.6 (commencing with Section 1546) of Title 12 of Part 2 of the Penal Code. (7) To enable solely internal uses that are reasonably aligned with the expectations of the consumer based on the consumer's relationship with the business. (8) Comply with a legal obligation. (9) Otherwise use the consumer's personal information, internally, in a lawful manner that is compatible with the context in which the consumer provided the information.

[161] Ibid, Information is used internally in a manner that is compatible with the context of the collection. Information is necessary to comply with a legal obligation. Information is necessary for internal uses of a company, if those uses are reasonably expected by consumers. Information is necessary for scientific, historical or statistical research in the public interest. Information is necessary to promote free speech. Information is necessary to identify and repair errors. Information is necessary to protect against deceptive, fraudulent or illegal activity. Information is necessary to detect security incidents. Information is necessary to complete a transaction requested by the data subject or to perform a contract.

part, bought the US or a state (California) within the US closer to the EU version of the right to be forgotten. However, as noted by Neil Richards, as the law stands at the federal level the right to be forgotten runs into First Amendment problems when it starts to resemble the old disclosure tort.[162] In fact, the proposal has generated so much free-speech concern because the versions of the right proposed for the revisions to the European Union Directive have taken the tort form. Richards argues that, it is one thing to give an Internet user the ability to restrict or retract information he or she provides in the context of a commercial relationship, and quite another to allow a person the right to edit any and all information about them on the Internet. Thus, when fully implemented, further research is needed to reconcile where the right has evolved differently across the Atlantic.

14.9.1.3 Disclosure at the Request of the Consumer

A consumer has the right to request that a business disclose[163] personal information, the sources, purpose and any third parties that the personal information has been provided too. They are to also reidentify or otherwise link any data that, in the ordinary course of business, is not maintained in a manner that would be considered personal information. In accordance with 1798.120. a consumer shall have the right, at any time, to direct a business that sells personal information about the consumer to third parties not to sell the consumer's personal information. This right may be referred to as the right to opt out. It enables the data subject to be informed of when a business sells their personal information to a third party. As part of this step in the process, it provides the data subject with an opt out, whereby they can restrict their personal data being sold to a third party. Nonetheless, where a business that has received direction from a consumer not to sell the consumer's personal information that, information cannot be sold. Interestingly the law uses the term direction instead of consent. On the other hand, where the sale involves a minor, that minor is to provide their consent, pursuant to paragraph (4) of subdivision (a) of Section 1798.135. The restrictions to minors, who are, as it has been stated on a number of occasions throughout this book being the most venerable in society. Thus, an entity is not to sell personal information of data subjects, if that entity, has knowledge that the individual is less than 16 years of age, unless the consumer, in the case of consumers between 13 and 16 years of age, or the consumer's parent or guardian. In the case of the person is less than 13 years of age, clear and affirmative authorization will be

---

[162] Richards, N, (2015) *Why Data Privacy Law Is (Mostly) Constitutional*, 56 Wm. & Mary L. Rev. 1501–1503.

[163] 1798.110. (a) and (b) A business that collects personal information about a consumer shall disclose to the consumer, pursuant to paragraph (3) of subdivision (a) of Section 1798.130, the information specified in subdivision (a) upon receipt of a verifiable request from the consumer. (c) A business that collects personal information about consumers shall disclose, pursuant to subparagraph (B) of paragraph (5) of subdivision (a) of Section 1798.130

required. Moreover, an entity that disregards the individuals age is deemed to have had actual knowledge of that person's age. This right may be referred to as the right to opt in.

14.9.1.4 Discrimination

Another important feature of the CA law is the position it takes in relation to discrimination against data subjects.[164] Thus, as a further protection for data subject more generally, they cannot be discriminated against in denying them goods and services. Discrimination further extends to where different or suggesting a price or prices or rates, along with discounts or a different quality of goods or service will incur a penalty to data subjects. Arguably, this position extends beyond human rights, but also, anti-competitive behaviour. A further element of discrimination can be providing a different level or quality of goods or services to the consumer, if the consumer exercises the consumer's rights under this title. However, it must be noted that provided there is a reasonably related value to the data subject, then a penalty will not be provided. As part of this process the business entity can offer financial incentives, including payments to the data subject (s) as compensation, for the collection of personal information, the sale of personal information, or the deletion of personal information. A business may also offer a different price, rate, level, or quality of goods or services to the consumer if that price or difference is directly related to the value provided to the consumer by the consumer's data. The process to offer a financial incentive must be carried out to 1798.135. which requires:

- "Provide a clear and conspicuous link on the business' Internet homepage, titled "Do Not Sell My Personal Information," to an Internet Web page that enables a consumer, or a person authorized by the consumer, to opt out of the sale of the consumer's personal information. A business shall not require a consumer to create an account in order to direct the business not to sell the consumer's personal information.
- Include a description of a consumer's rights pursuant to Section 1798.120, along with a separate link to the "Do Not Sell My Personal Information" Internet Web page along with:
  - Its online privacy policy or policies if the business has an online privacy policy or policies.
  - Any California-specific description of consumers' privacy rights.
- Ensure that all individuals responsible for handling consumer inquiries about the business's privacy practices or the business's compliance with this title are

[164] Ibid, 1798.125.

informed of all requirements in Section 1798.120 and this section and how to direct consumers to exercise their rights under those sections."[165]

Moreover, an entity that offers a financial incentive or enters into a financial incentive program, also need to notify the individual according to the above. In applying the above, no entity can use a financial incentive that is unjust, unreasonable, coercive, or usurious in nature.

14.9.1.5 Reasonably Access

The right to know requires a business to make "reasonably accessible" general disclosures. Therefore, a business is required to disclose, through its website privacy policy or elsewhere on its website:

- *at or before collection of personal information*, the categories of personal information collected and how the business will use the information;
- how a consumer can exercise his or her right to know about the collection and sale or other disclosure of his or her personal information;
- the categories of personal information collected during the preceding 12 months; and
- separate lists of the categories of personal information sold and disclosed during the preceding 12 months *or* a statement that no sale or disclosure was made.[166]

However, it must be noted that, neither right to know requirement mandates a business to retain information collected for a single transaction or to link de-identified information to personal information unless, in either case, the business' usual practice is to do so.

14.9.1.6 Obligations

Apart from the general requirements of a business to conform, with the above, they are also, in accordance with 1798.145 that they comply with federal, state, or local laws. Additionally, they are required to comply with a civil, criminal, or regulatory inquiry, investigation, subpoena, or summons by federal, state, or local authorities.

---

[165] Ibid, 1798.135 (4) In addition, data subjects that exercise their right to opt out of the sale of their personal information, refrain from selling personal information collected by the business about the consumer. (5) For a consumer who has opted out of the sale of the consumer's personal information, respect the consumer's decision to opt out for at least 12 months before requesting that the consumer authorize the sale of the consumer's personal information. (6) Use any personal information collected from the consumer in connection with the submission of the consumer's opt-out request solely for the purposes of complying with the opt-out request.

[166] Ibid, 1798.130. and Civil Code § 1798.130(a)(5). 1798.100(c). § 1798.130(a)(5)(A). § 1798.130(a)(5)(B). § 1798.130(a)(5)(C). Also see, Jeffrey King, Alidad Vakili, Julia B. Jacobson, with assistance from Brian Philips (Counsel, Raleigh) and Jenny Sneed (Associate, Raleigh), K&L Gates Frequently Asked Questions About the California Consumer Privacy Act of 2018 (CCPA), http://www.klgates.com/frequently-asked-questions-about-the-california-consumer-privacy-act-of-2018-ccpa-07-31-2018/

Any business will need to also cooperate with law enforcement agencies concerning conduct or activity that the business, service provider, or third party reasonably and in good faith believes may violate federal, state, or local law.

While this Chapter has limited its focus to the sectorial approach of the FTC and HIPAA at the federal level, states are going it alone. California and a number of other states are also looking to establish stronger regulatory regimes for data protection. Interestingly, the US model takes a different approach to that of the EU, Singapore and China. In our view, the US model forms (does not matter what order they are placed) the 4th model in the data protection regime that, is consumer based. Another state of the US that has a proposal is New York, however, it appears to be more problematic in that state.

14.9.2 New York

In May 2019, the State of New York had also introduced new privacy laws. Issie Lapowsky believes that following the giants and lobbying groups race to defang California's landmark consumer privacy before it takes effect in 2020, lawmakers on the other side of the country, in New York are considering a bill that in her view is even more drastic.[167] Lapowsky goes onto say that in May 2019, the proposed New York Privacy Act was put forward by state senator Kevin Thomas. It is based on similar consumer protections as California's model, and would give residents there more control over their data than in any other state. Furthermore, it would also require businesses to put their customers' privacy before their own profits. At the time of writing this book, the bill is still seeking a cosponsor in the state assembly, Lapowsky in referring to comment made by Kevin Thomas who stated that he is confident that he has majority support in the senate and hopes to pass the bill this summer.[168]

With it, the Empire State is poised to become the next battleground in the fight for state privacy laws. California became the first state to pass such a law last year with the California Consumer Protection Act; industry groups and consumer advocates have been sparring over its language ever since. Lapowsky states that the business community believe the Californian law is overly broad and that complying with different laws in every state is unworkable, preferring instead a lighter touch regulation at the federal level. If realized the proposal would take a significant step forward for the protection of personal data over the Internet across the state of New York. Even though it is out of scope of this look to compare the proposed New York law with California's, there are some important features to not. That is, the definition of personal information or personal data has been defined as identified

[167] Lapowsky, I, (2019) *New York is poised to become the next battleground in the fight for consumers' rights over their personal data,* https://www.wired.com/story/new-york-privacy-act-bolder/

[168] Ibid.

or identifiable natural persons, who can be identified through specific information such as name, identification number, specific geolocation data or an online identifier. In addition, the proposal describes in detail what personal data constitutes. Apart from ones' name, alias, signature, date of birth, gender, sexual orientation, marital status, physical characteristics, postal address, telephone, unique person identifier, military number, online identifier, internet protocol address, email address, telephone number, employment, commercial information or biometric information amongst others.

Moreover, the proposal aims, as Lapowsky identifies a data fiduciary in addition to consumer rights, and incorporates internationally agreed principles and concepts of transparency, consent, responsibility (controller) and de-identification. It further provides that, privacy risk would result from when there is a potential adverse consequence to consumers and society more broadly.[169] However, this would be restricted to processing where it can be proved that there is a direct or indirect financial loss or an economic harm. It would also apply where there is a physical, psychological and significant inconvenience or expenditure of time. The proposal would also provide data subjects with the opportunity to have their personal data deleted.[170]

However, while writing this book, it was noted that by 19 July 2019, the National Law Review noted that the proposed privacy law of New York's failed to materialize in the latest legislative session and is now presumed dead.[171] The proposed New York law, in fact, was broader than the CCPA in many ways. The law would have applied to non-profits as well as for profits, and included a private right of action for data breaches of $10,000 per consumer. The proposed law also would have designated businesses that collect personal information of New York consumers as "information fiduciaries" and imposed on such companies a "duty to exercise loyalty and care" in how the business uses personal information.[172] The resulting effect from these state based laws arguable see the US internally heading in different directions. On the one side they have, to date, imposed fewer restrictions at a national level, on what and how personal data is collected and used. On the other side, some US states are moving closer to the EU framework. Michael Rustand and Thomas Koenig reinforce this point that, under the US framework, privacy law is less restrictive firstly on how much personal data may be collected, and secondly how such data may be used, and how long that data may be kept.[173]

---

[169] The New York State Senate, New York Privacy Act Bull Number: S5642 https://www.nysenate.gov/legislation/bills/2019/s5642

[170] Ibid.

[171] Ballard Spahr LLP, The National Law Review, New York State Data Privacy Law Fails, https://www.natlawreview.com/article/new-york-state-data-privacy-law-fails

[172] Ibid.

[173] Rustad, M., Koenig, T, *Towards A Global Data Privacy Standard*, Florida Law Review Vol, 71, (2019).

14.10 Bilateral—Multilateral Approach

A more recent development has arisen out of the US and the United Kingdom, is the first Clarifying Lawful Overseas Use of Data Act (CLOUD Act) agreement,[174] whereby, Australia has also agreed to join this agreement. In further highlighting the interconnectedness between data protection, cyber security and to a lesser extent AI, this new law provides the platform for the timely access to electronic data held by communications-service providers as being an essential component of government efforts to protect public safety and combat serious crime, including terrorism. Moreover, section 6 recognizes that international agreements provide a mechanism for resolving the potential conflicting legal obligations where the United States and the relevant foreign government share a common commitment to the rule of law and the protection of privacy along with the general protection of civil liberties. Section 105 goes onto provide that Executive Agreement on the Access to data by foreign government that, an executive agreement governing access by a foreign government to data subject shall be considered to satisfy the requirements of this section if the Attorney General, with the concurrence of the Secretary of State, determines, and submits a written certification of such determination to Congress, including a written certification and explanation that the domestic law of the foreign government, including the implementation of that law, affords robust substantive and procedural protections for privacy and civil liberties in light of the data collection and activities of the foreign government that will be subject to the agreement, amongst other things. While not specifically mentioning data protection, it appears to consider the impacts that this law may have towards privacy over the Internet.

Daskal and Swire argue this new approach will enable law enforcement agencies, with appropriate authorization, to demand electronic data regarding serious crime, including terrorism, child sexual abuse, and cybercrime, directly from tech companies based in the other country, without legal barriers. Daskal and Swire in referring to the William Barr, the Attorney General, note that this:

> agreement will enhance the ability of the United States and the United Kingdom to fight serious crime – including terrorism, transnational organized crime, and child exploitation – by allowing more efficient and effective access to data needed for quick-moving investigations. Only by addressing the problem of timely access to electronic evidence of crime committed in one country that is stored in another, can we hope to keep pace with twenty-first century threats. This agreement will make the citizens of both countries safer, while at the same time assuring robust protections for privacy and civil liberties.[175]

---

[174] Daskal, J., Swire, P, *The U.K.-US CLOUD Act Agreement Is Finally Here*, Containing New Safeguards, October 2019, https://www.lawfareblog.com/uk-us-cloud-act-agreement-finally-here-containing-new-safeguards, CLOUD Act text, https://www.justice.gov/dag/page/file/1152896/download

[175] Ibid.

While the proposal appears to have far reaching consequences that, could have an adverse impact to data protection generally, Daskal and Swire believe there are enough safeguards in place to ensure compatibility with data protection laws. As part of the general procedure for acquiring data, the proposal requires that, permission is obtained before using data gained through the agreement in prosecutions relating to a Party's essential interest—specifically, death penalty prosecutions cases implicating freedom of speech.

Nevertheless, and on the backdrop of the above, there have been some concerned about the operation of the CLOUD Act and its potential to data protection law. Some have viewed the CLOUD Act as being soft in the area of privacy protection.[176] The authors go onto to highlight how European Regulators found that the CLOUD Act could cause service providers to face a conflict between complying with US law and complying with the personal data protections required by the General Data Protection Regulation (GDPR) and other EU laws. However, it is outside of scope analyse the challenges between the CLOUD Act and other national laws. More importantly, the sharing of personal data, from online activity, between countries now transcends both data protection and cybersecurity/crime law. The interconnectedness is likely to grow, as criminal activity over the Internet increasingly become apparent.

14.11 Smart Appliances

As highlighted in Chap. 1, the development and use of smart home appliances, toys, clothes, personal robots and personal drones. These products are increasingly becoming a concern for governments and regulators not for the products themselves, but because of the cybersecurity and data protection concerns, particularly to the most vulnerable in the community. While it is out of scope of this book to compare and examine all the laws of other states in this area, the US is an example of how a state in having sectorial laws that, do provide a level of protection and convergence of these problematic products.

The US federal Children's Online Privacy Protection Act of 1998 (COPPA), applies to directed to children, or any operator that has actual knowledge that it is collecting or maintaining personal information from a child.[177] The definition of "personal information" under COPPA is quite broad and includes: names; addresses; online contact information; screen or user names; telephone numbers; social

---

[176] Evans, M., (UK), Kessler, D., (US), Lennon, J., (AU) Ross, S, (US) US, *CLOUD Act and International Privacy*, Norton Rose Fulbright August 1, (2019), https://www.dataprotectionreport.com/2019/08/u-s-cloud-act-and-international-privacy/

[177] Federal Trade Commission, FTC Strengthens Kids' Privacy, Gives Parents Greater Control Over Their Information By Amending Children's Online Privacy Protection Rule https://www.ftc.gov/news-events/press-releases/2012/12/ftc-strengthens-kids-privacy-gives-parents-greater-control-over

security numbers; persistent identifiers that can be used to recognize a user over time across different websites or online services; geo-location; and photographs, video, or audio containing the child's image or voice.[178] However, it is restricted to children under the age of 13.

Notice of Data Practices - this requires operators give direct notice to parents of its data collection practices. Certain statements are also required, including how consent is to be given, and that no personal information of a child will be collected, used or disclosed without parental consent. The operator also has to reveal the personal information that will be collected and link their privacy policy.[179]

Parental Consent - verifiable parental consent must be given before an operator can collect personal information from a child. The consent has to take into account available technology and can include: (a) asking parents to sign and mail a hard-copy consent form; (b) allowing parents to use an online payment system to provide notification of each transaction to the primary account holder; (c) having parents provide consent via phone or video; or (d) checking government-issued identification.[180]

Required Reasonable Security - operators are also required to have and maintain reasonable security procedures to "protect the confidentiality, security, and integrity of the personal information collected from children." If any of the information is transferred to a third party, the operator must ensure the third party has taken similar steps to protect the protected data.[181]

Data Collection - operators can only keep personal information collected online from a child as long as reasonably necessary to fulfil the purpose for which it was collected for. When the personal information is no longer needed, the data must be deleted through reasonable measures.[182]

The legislative measures while being in place since 2012, it highlights how the US has identified this as a broader issue for the community. It further highlights and reinforces the concerns facing children in the future and what states, private entities and individuals that the Internet and the many different products coming onto the market, which could be so intrusive that, children's futures could be compromised through bias. The issues as to how toy manufacturers technically comply with COPPA given the functionality of the toys are complicated.[183] Dickson Wright highlights an example how some smart toys will not need parental permission if there is no collection of personal information. Non-personal data that would *not* trigger COPPA would include achievement levels in games, a user's keypress

---

178 Ibid.

179 Jodka, S, (2017), The Internet of Toys: Legal and Privacy Issues with Connected Toys https://www.dickinson-wright.com/news-alerts/legal-and-privacy-issues-with-connected-toys

180 Ibid.

181 Ibid.

182 Ibid.v

183 Ibid.

responses, such as parental consent would also not be required for connected toys that collect and use a persistent identifier, which would include information such as an IP address or toy/device ID.[184]

14.12 A New Decade and Cyber Security

A new decade and in January 2020, the US were quick to begin by rolling out national guidelines for federal agencies to develop regulation for AI. While there was no specific reference to cyber security and data protection, the Trump Administration through Executive Order 13609, "Promoting International Regulatory Cooperation," calls on the Regulatory Working Group, which was established by Executive Order 12866, to consider "appropriate strategies for engaging in the development of regulatory approaches through international regulatory cooperation, particularly in emerging technology areas."[185] Accordingly, agencies should engage in dialogues to promote consistent regulatory approaches to AI that promote American AI innovation while protecting privacy, civil rights, civil liberties, and American values. Importantly the Memorandum makes particularly reference to the rights of citizens and their right of privacy. The Principles of Stewardship for AI have detailed the following key areas that need to be considered during the regulatory development process, these include:

- Public Trust;
- Public Participation;
- Scientific Integrity and Information Quality;
- Risk Assessment and Management;
- Benefits and Costs;
- Flexibility;
- Fairness and Non-Discrimination;
- Disclosure and Transparency;
- Safety and Security; and
- Interagency Coordination.[186]

Apart from setting a balance between innovation and economic development, the Stewardship Principles do incorporate many elements of the principles that can be found in data protection. These include, but not limited to trust, risk management, transparency, security, disclosure and quality of information. The Stewardship Principles require that adequate measures are established to manage and address cybersecurity threats and risks. The Stewardship Principles further require

[184] Ibid.

[185] Memorandum For the Heads of Executive Departments and Agencies, Guidance for Regulation of Artificial Intelligence Applications, https://www.whitehouse.gov/wp-content/uploads/2020/01/Draft-OMB-Memo-on-Regulation-of-AI-1-7-19.pdf

[186] Ibid.

flexibility in the regulatory approach to ensure they conform with assessment schemes, protect health and safety, but more importantly privacy, and other values, will be essential to a successful, and flexible, performance- based approach. The point about fairness and non-discrimination while not fully explored in this Chapter, it can, arguably go some way to accommodating and creating a regulatory environment that requires children in particular and other vulnerable groups to be considered as part of the regulatory response and development of AI technology.

While the regulatory framework is in its infancy, these principles once fully implemented, establish the roadmap for future regulation in this area. Importantly, they pick up the need for protecting privacy. However, what and how this will look like in any future regulatory response will need careful consideration. More importantly, what can be seen from these Principles is the convergence of cyber security in AI along with privacy (data protection should be part of the future regulatory landscape).

In summary, the US has established a regulatory framework for addressing cyber security matters. However, it is out scope of this Chapter to compare these laws with data protection law, or the laws of the other states discussed in this book.

Federal Law: 18 U.S.C. §1029, §1030, §1362, §2511, §2701, §2702, §2703	Restricting activity in connection with access devices, computers, communication lines, stations, or systems. Prohibiting interception and disclosure of wire, oral, or electronic communications, unlawful access to stored communications, and disclosure of contents.
National Infrastructure Protection Act of 1996	Providing for the protection of all US government computers, covering computer use in electronic commerce, and punishing as a felony any recklessness that causes damage to critical infrastructure.
Cyberspace Electronic Security Act of 1999	Enabling law enforcement agencies and officers to obtain criminal evidence legally from encrypted data.
Patriot Act of 2001Q	Expanding surveillance powers of the FBI by allowing it to monitor lines of electronic communication, including phone conversations, email and voice mail.

14.13 Conclusion

The US have a long history of privacy and more recently have embraced the idea and need to protect personal data over the Internet. However, there is not specific single laws at the federal level that protect personal data. It is rather fragmented, and in our view, the current framework has taken a consumer approach. The fragmented approach taken across the US, has in our view resulted in the data protection debate becoming very political.

The fragmented approach could pose significant challenges in the future particularly to the definition of personal data and the concept of consent. This Chapter neither confirmed or otherwise, or compared the definition of personal data in each of the sectorial laws of the US. Thus, in focusing on what is considered general and more sensitive personal data, this Chapter compared the FTC and HIPPA definitions. The FTC Act does not define personal data or sensitive personal data. The HIPPA Privacy Rules define 'health information', 'protected health information', 'individual identifiable health information' and 'genetic information'. It further means any information, including genetic information, whether oral or recorded in any form or medium, that is created or received by a health care provider, health plan, public health authority, employer, life insurer, school or university, or health care clearinghouse. In addition, it means relating to the past, present, or future physical or mental health or condition of an individual; the provision of health care to an individual; or the past, present, or future payment for the provision of health care to an individual.

As highlighted above, protected health information means individually identifiable health information that is transmitted by electronic media, maintained in electronic media; or transmitted or maintained in any other form or medium. However, protected health information excludes individually identifiable health information. Thirdly, it can include information collated from or by a health care provider, health plan, employer, or health care clearinghouse. Fourth, genetic information means information with respect to an individual, information about genetic tests, the genetic tests of family members of the individual and the manifestation of a disease or disorder in family members of such individual. There has been concerted effort under the HIPPA to protected health data that is quite extensive. Problematic though is how the FTC does not define personal data at any level. While it was out of scope to determine whether the definition in other laws would apply, this needs to be considered, but, this alone, appears to be a significant gap. It remains to be seen whether this definition or the definition in any of the laws will be adequate to deal with AI products in the home or used generally in business.

In addition to the above, the FTC Act does not specifically address consent. Consent only applies to a person who produces the material, thing or transcript. The application of consent under this section is fluid at best. However, when coupled with the FTC's Behavioural Advertising Principles suggest website operators should obtain affirmative express consent before using sensitive consumer data. The FTC's Behavioural Advertising Principles suggest website operators should obtain affirmative express consent (which can be provided online) before using sensitive consumer data. Nevertheless, it stops short of providing any further information or guidance as to its functionality and application. This will no doubt pose challenges in AI products used by general consumers.

The HIPAA generally requires covered entities to obtain consent in writing from a data subject before disclosing that data (with certain exceptions, for example, to provide medical treatment). Consent must generally be in writing and contain the signature of the data subject and the date. The HIPAA Privacy Rule provides specific statements that must be included in the consent. These include, the Implementation specification, un-emancipated towards minors. The Rules go onto say that the minor consents to such health care service; no other consent to such health care service is required by law, regardless of whether the consent of another person has also been obtained; and the minor has not requested that such person be treated as the personal representative. There are also specific rules for minors as discussed above. Thus, due to the sectorial approach taken by the US, there appears to be no clear direction of how and when consent will apply. The stand-alone approach, differs significantly to the other jurisdictions examined. There is no express terms or provisions of express or implied consent, or whether and how an express consent is to be obtained. The challenge again, will be similar to the definition of personal data, further work is needed where individuals and entities depending on the laws that apply will need to be aware of what level of consent is needed to be obtained for the use of personal data. Moreover, further work is needed to how the US will reconcile the differences in consent when AI is used across and within different sectors.

However, there is a transition occurring, with the need to afford greater protection of children has recently emerged. Arguably, this move, highlights how the US is also taking the rights of its citizens in this area more seriously. They have also recently issued an Executive Order that call upon government agencies that are developing regulation in the area of AI to consider privacy, data and cybersecurity matters as a collective. This whole of regulatory approach is a significant step forward and can only place the US is a strong position to govern and regulate the impact of smart home devices, toys, personal robots and drones, amongst others and their impact to personal data going forward. Therefore, AI, privacy and cybersecurity are beginning to converge in the US. However, their current sectorial approach may be a benefit when dealing with smart home, clothes, toys and personal robots. These pose some of the most formidable risks and challenges facing regulators and the community. They could become so pervasive that when used, the personal data and the ease of security breaches could see children and other vulnerable people in the community being subversively segregated.

References

Dörr, D., & Weaver, R. (2014). *Perspectives on privacy: Increasing regulation in the USA, Canada, Australia and European Countries – Privacy and the Fourth Amendment* (pp. 3–6). De Gruyter.

Glancy, D. (1979). The invention of the right to privacy. *Arizona Law Review, 21*, 2–28.

Hartzog, W., & Solove, D. (2015). The Scope and Potential of FTC Data Protection, 015. *George Washington Law Review, 83*(6), 2231–2248.

Richards, N., & Solove, D. (2010). Prosser's privacy law: A mixed legacy. *California Law Review, 98*, 1887.

Schiedermair, S. (2014). *The new general data protection regulation of the European Union – Will it widen the* gap between Europe and the US? In D. Dörr & R. L. Weaver (Eds.), *Perspectives*

on privacy : Increasing regulation in the USA, Canada, Australia and European countries – Privacy and the fourth amendment (pp. 72–78). De Gruyter, 3–6.
Schwartz, P. (1999). Privacy and democracy in cyberspace. *Vanderbilt Law Review, 52*, 1607–1614.
Solove, D., & Hartzog, W. (2014). The FTC and the new common law of privacy. *Columbia Law Review, 114*, 583–587.
Warren, S., & Brandeis, L. (1890). The right to privacy. *Harvard Law Review, 4*(5), 192–196.

Chapter 15
Comparison, Challenges and a Way Forward

Abstract This Chapter compares the data protection laws of the Canada, China, Hong Kong, Lao, Macao, Taiwan, The Philippines, South Korea, United States and Vietnam. It does not provide a comprehensive discussion of the policy or legal gaps between the respective jurisdictions. However, it will focus on comparing the key principles and concepts outlined in each of the jurisdictions. Due to the breadth and depth of the privacy law, it will address the following concepts and principles:

- Privacy and Data Protection Laws;
- Application to Public and Private Sectors;
- Definition of Personal Data;
- Consent.
- Data Localization;
- Rights-Right to be Forgotten, Correction and Deletion; and
- Data Transfers.

This Chapter has limited the comparative analysis to the above concepts and principles because they are considered the most important at this early stage of AI technology being developed. These principles and concepts are considered to be the most vulnerable to cyber security intrusions. This Chapter argues that a further and more comprehensive study is required to determine what other provisions of data protection law will need to be reviewed to ensure adequate protection is retained over personal data. It calls for a review of the current day data protection laws to determine whether the current definition of personal data and the concept of consent are adequate, in the context of AI devices in the home. It must be noted that this Chapter will duplicate some of the law that has been discussed in the country specific chapters.

Chapter 15 is one of the most important chapters of this book because it identifies a limited pathway forward. One of the most pressing challenges is the lack of understanding and impact that AI have on children and the most vulnerable in the community. It will identify not only the challenges that lie ahead, but touch of some of

R. Walters, M. Novak, *Cyber Security, Artificial Intelligence, Data Protection & the Law*, https://doi.org/10.1007/978-981-16-1665-5_15

the issues that need to be reconciled to ensure personal data is protected when that data is captured and used by AI devices.

15.1 Introduction

The data protection laws discussed in this book differ greatly. They vary in approach, structure and achieve very different things. This Chapter will repeat some of the material outlined in country chapters, so as to highlight the comparative differences. The predominant reason for the varied approach is acceptance and treatment of privacy as a fundamental right, while on the other side, differences in the manner in which that right is construed and protected. Yet, one of the main drivers is that different states have different social, economic and cultural traditions and needs. Moreover, what has emerged from this book, and the previous book mentioned, is the lack of consensus of what privacy constitutes over the Internet. This is further compounded when having to consider AI and cyber security within data protection law. In other words, when examining the potential issues and gaps in the law pertaining to personal data that will be captured by AI devices, becomes problematic when the laws themselves have not yet fully realised and addressed the problem.

The influence of past rulers, legal families, culture, international and regional law cannot be underestimated. A very good example is the territory of China and its respective Administrative regions. Hong Kong and Macau have both been ruled by European states and this is reflected in their current day data protection laws, and their legal framework more generally. Macau's legal framework has retained elements of Portuguese civil law. While Hong Kong has retained its common law heritage of the UK. While this poses challenges in understanding the respective laws, it should not be viewed as a significant obstacle to protecting personal data. Nonetheless, the data protection laws of Hong Kong do differ in structure, composition and content, from the other laws examined in this book. On the other hand, it is argued that Hong Kong's data protection framework is relatively mature, when compared to other countries in the region. The laws have been established to deal with different issues such as direct marketing, matching procedures, access amongst others. It is asserted that the laws of Hong Kong have been heavily influenced by the European legal framework, dating back to 1995. Moreover, on the one side, Macau's data protection laws are the most succinct, comprising of only 45 Articles. Article 1, highlights how the act establishes the legal regime on the processing and protection of personal data. On the other side, the processing of personal data shall be carried out transparently and in strict respect for privacy and for other fundamental rights, freedoms and guarantees set out in the Basic Law of the Macao Special Administrative Region, the instruments of international law and the legislation in force.[1] The data

[1] Act 8/2005 Personal Data Protection Act, Article 2 General principle.

protection laws apply to the processing of personal data whether manually or by an automated system or platform.[2] The laws also apply to video surveillance and other forms of capture, processing and dissemination of sound and images allowing persons to be identified. However, this is on the basis that the controller is domiciled or based in the Macao Special Administrative Region.

The respective laws of Hong Kong and Macau do take a stronger focus than mainland China in protecting personal data. Mainland China, on the other side, has, rather focused on regulating the systems, networks and platform that support the collection and use of personal data. For China, there have been four stages of development of privacy, (1), protection by analogy,[3] (2), personality interest protection,[4] (3), protection by tort law,[5] and (4), a separate human right, whereby privacy is protected under Article 110 of the General Provisions of the Civil Law that was enacted in 2017. Arguably, of the states examined in this book, China have, to date taken a focus on a greater focus on protecting the infrastructure that is used to collect personal data. Even so, they have recently strengthened the protections for children. However, they are yet to release specific data protection laws. Taiwan being governed democratically has adopted a data protection regime that can be best described as being similar to the EU.

Notwithstanding the above, the approach taken by South Korea has largely implemented a similar approach to the EU, and they have been considered by leading legal experts and scholars in the field as having some of the strictest data protection laws in Asia. A distinctive feature of South Korea's data protection laws is the way data subjects have specific rights that have been established by the law. Article 4 provides that a data subject shall, in relation to the processing of his or her own personal information, have certain rights. These include the right to: be informed of the processing of such personal information; consent or not, and to elect the scope of consent, to the processing of such personal information; confirm the processing of such personal information, and to demand access (including the issuance of certificate, hereinafter the same applies) to such personal information; suspend processing of, and to make correction, deletion and destruction of such personal

[2] Ibid, Article 3. This Act shall apply to the processing of personal data regarding public safety without prejudice to special rules in instruments of international law and inter-regional agreements to which the MSAR is bound and specific laws pertinent to public safety and other related regulations.

[3] Ibid, in the 1980s, privacy was protected under the General Principles of the Civil Law by deeming it as part of the right to protection of a person's reputation.

[4] Ibid, starting from the early 1990s, privacy was recognised as a personality interest. An individual whose privacy has been infringed was granted a right to seek compensation for psychological damages under Article 1 of the Interpretation of the Supreme People's Court on Issues Regarding the Ascertainment of Liability for Compensation for Psychological Damages in Civil Torts. However, privacy was not yet recognised as a separate human right.

[5] Ibid, privacy right was expressly recognised as one of the protected interests under the Law of Tort enacted in 2009. An individual may take civil action for infringement of privacy right under the Law of Tort. For the first time, the concept of privacy right has been acknowledged under the civil law in the mainland of China.

information; and appropriate redress for any damage arising out of the processing of such personal information in a prompt and fair procedure.[6] While not specifically stated, the right to be erased/forgotten (RTBF) does exist within Korea. Apart from providing that a data subject can request that their personal data be deleted and destroyed, in 2016 guidance was issued by the government on the RTBF.

Bennett and Raab in 2006 developed the idea of dividing data protection and privacy laws into regions.[7] Their idea of policy blocs can be best described as the OECD and European Union - Council being one entity in regard to the data protection and privacy policy they have adopted. They believe, the Asia-Pacific Region constitutes the United States, Australia and Southeast Asian countries of Japan, China, and Korea, as a new bloc.[8] Their idea of grouping the Asia-Pacific countries this way, is somewhat different to the way we conceive this Region. However, Bennet and Raab wrote during a period in which most of South East Asian countries, within ASEAN, had no specific data protection laws.[9] Today, this has changed significantly, with Singapore and Malaysia having introduced specific data protection laws, although Indonesia's data protections laws remain in development. Nonetheless, grouping data protection and privacy law into blocks is a viable option because these blocks of countries have very different economic and social policy needs. Furthermore, grouping data protection with cyber security and AI law, in our view will become increasingly viable.

North America taking in Canada have also adopted a different approach to their counter-parts in Asia and amongst themselves. Beginning with Canada they have, arguably taken a sectorial approach separating out the application of data protection law from public and private sector. They have developed a statutory tort for privacy generally that can arguably be applied to privacy over the Internet. This approach has made a clear distinction between the two areas and consequently the laws differ. On the other side of the border the US while also taking a sectorial approach, have not divided the public and private sectors in the same way as Canada. As highlighted in (see Chap. 14) the US have established a body of law that include the Gramm-Leach-Bliley Act, Health Insurance Portability and Accountability Act, Children's Online Privacy Protection Act, and others.

Of the countries compared in this book, the Philippines, Lao and Vietnam are all members of ASEAN. It could be assumed that the data protection laws of these countries would have many similarities. However, this is far from the case. The Philippines laws do consider the rights of individuals by providing for the right to delete one's personal data. They have, over a long period of time embraced the right to privacy, more generally. The Philippine legal system can be best described as a blend of customary usage, and Roman (civil law) and Anglo-American (common

[6] Greenleaf, G., Park, W, *Korea's new Act: Asia's toughest data privacy law* Privacy Laws & Business International Report, Issue 117, 1–6, June 2012, Article 4.

[7] Bennett, C., Raab, C *The Governance of Privacy*. Cambridge, MA: MIT Press (2006).

[8] Ibid.

[9] Ibid.

law) systems. Nonetheless, in some Southern parts of the islands, Islamic law is observed. Lao, on the other hand, is landlocked and one of the smallest countries in South East Asia. Lao can be best described as adopting a similar data protection framework to its neighbour China, which may explain why they have not followed other ASEAN countries. Being part of ASEAN, they have to date, largely gone their own way in this area of law. They have, at least on paper, embraced the concept of privacy, which has been reaffirmed in the 1991 constitution. For an ASEAN member, Vietnam and Lao's's laws distinguish themselves from the other members. They have taken a cyber security approach similar to its neighbour China. Vietnam have taken a sectorial approach, and are yet to establish specific data protection laws. Of the law compared there are varying levels of interconnectedness between AI, cybersecurity and data protection. Some states such as China who have no specific data protection laws appear to be moving in that direction. However, other states have a fragmented and confusing approach to protecting personal data. This, in our view is problematic because, AI is likely to be everywhere in our daily lives, and without adequate protection people's personal data will be easily accessible. Thus, this Chapter calls for more research to be undertaken so as to better understand whether the current definition of personal data and the concept of consent are adequate to protect children's data that can be collected from AI devices.

15.2 Application to Public and Private Sectors

It is important to understand whether the respective data protection laws apply to both the public and private sectors. Why? Because as AI is adopted by both sectors knowing where and how the laws apply could have an impact to personal data collected by Smart Home devices. Firstly, these types of devices once purchased and used by the public sector could be used by the private sector to make significant intrusions to government activity. It is unlikely that government are going to develop Smart Home devices, and make them available on the open market. However, it cannot be ruled out. Thus, the application of the laws is central to where personal data should be protected as part of AI products, used personally in the home and elsewhere.

China through their Cyber Law imposes obligations on specific agencies to ensure measures are established to protect individuals, business and the state from cyberattacks. Thus, the laws apply to both the public and private sectors, with an emphasis to, and of, protecting the state. Interestingly, the laws of South Korea are silent on whether the laws apply to both the public and private sectors. However, Article 14 requires that the government is to establish policy measures so as to enhance the data protection standard in the international environment. The government shall work out relevant policy measures so that the rights of data subjects may not be infringed upon owing to cross border transfer of personal information.[10]

The laws of Hong Kong apply to both the public and private sectors.[11] However, there are exemption for complying with the Ordinance for domestic and recreational purposes, along with certain employment related personal related personal data and relevant process. National security is now an important part of the policy discourse in relation to data protection. Therefore, further exemptions apply from access and use limitation requirements for data which are likely to prejudice security, defence and international relations; crime prevention or detection; assessment or collection of any tax or duty; news activities; health; legal proceeding; due diligence exercise; archiving; handling life-threatening emergency situation.[12] Similarly, Macau also applies to both the public and private sectors. The data protection laws apply to the processing of personal data whether manually or by an automated system or platform.[13] The laws also apply to video surveillance and other forms of capture, processing and dissemination of sound and images allowing persons to be identified.

The Philippines data protection laws apply to both the public and private sector. However, for Lao, their laws are largely silent on where and how they apply. Nevertheless, they do apply to the private sector, however, it is unclear whether they also apply to the public sector. Taiwan on the other hand, not only regulate private entities but also imposes rules for data collection, use, and disclosure by the public sector. Vietnam's laws, when examined as a collective apply to both sectors. However, due to the extent of the laws in Vietnam, depending on the laws that apply, an individual would need to confirm whether those laws apply across the private and public sectors. For instance, and without examining the Law on Postage No. 49/2010/QH12 as part of this book, confirmation would need to be undertake to confirm what sector the law applied to, if any, outside Postage.

Canada, while not taking a sectorial approach, have, established separate laws for the public and private sectors. Even though the public sector laws are currently under review, they are specific to government organisations. On the other hand, the private sector laws apply to all of the private sector. This is contrast to its southern neighbour, who has taken a sectorial approach to data protection. The US, have made a clear distinction between sectors and in some cases, such as the Health sector who implemented specific laws. More broadly, the US take a consumer approach to data protection in the private sector, which has been reflected in their current legal framework. Even so, some states in the US have been reviewing the current status or data protection law, and begun to develop similar laws that resemble those of the

[10] Ibid, Article 14.

[11] Data Protection Principles in the Personal Data (Privacy) Ordinance – *from the Privacy Commissioner's perspective (2 Edition)* (2010) section 3.

[12] The Personal Data (Privacy) Ordinance (PDPO) Cap 486, Part 8.

[13] Ibid, Article 3. This Act shall apply to the processing of personal data regarding public safety without prejudice to special rules in instruments of international law and inter-regional agreements to which the MSAR is bound and specific laws pertinent to public safety and other related regulations.

EU. It will be interesting to monitor whether the calls for similar laws be enacted federally come to life.

As highlighted in Chap. 1, there are concerns that AI can result in unintended consequences and harm - to individuals. The quality of data used by AI will be crucial because they will be able to collect, aggregate, de-anonymise, and repurpose data (with a loss of the original context for its collection) from an increasing array of data from different objects in the home and on the body (such as personal home assistants and fitness trackers), from which inferences can be drawn. It is argued that states should review their laws to determine whether they are adequate in providing for a consistent approach to AI used in the home and in the office (private and public sectors). When data protection When data protection laws began to be implemented, it was understandable that states looked to regulating the public and private sectors separately. However, as AI becomes more mainstream it will collect similar or exactly the same data whether use in the home of office. Therefore, making the delineation between the private and the public will be complex. Thus, it is argued that the laws should be revised to ensure there will be adequate protections across all sectors. Therefore, the starting point has to be the definition of personal data, as provided for by data protection laws. The definition of personal data helps to identify what data is protected and what is not. It will be demonstrated that the current laws compared in this book vary greatly. This is problematic because, AI devices will not be limited to a single state. They could be produced anywhere in the world, and it would be difficult for a manufacturer to comply with the different laws in place.

15.3 Definition Personal Data – Information

Data protection has also been characterized as a tool of 'privacy'. There needs to be a continued need for a balance in the trade and protection of personal data. Data protection underpins privacy and been characterised as the personal data used to identify a person. Unlike the privacy laws of many industrialized nations, which protect all personal data in an omnibus fashion, privacy law in the United States is sectorial, with different laws regulating different industries and economic sectors. This sectorial approach has left areas unregulated. This also applies to defining personal data. The Federal Trade Commission Act, largely considered the central federal consumer protection law that prohibits unfair or deceptive practices and has been applied to offline and online privacy and data security policies, does not define personal data or sensitive personal data. On the other hand rather than define personal (general or sensitive) data or information, the Health Insurance Portability and Accountability Act Privacy Rules define 'health information', 'protected health information', 'individual identifiable health information' and 'genetic information'.[14] It further means any information, including genetic information, whether oral or recorded in any form or medium, that is created or received by a health care provider, health plan, public health authority, employer, life insurer, school or university, or health care clearinghouse. In addition, it relates to the past, present, or future physical or mental health or condition of an individual; the provision of health care to an individual; or the past, present, or future payment for the provision of health care to an individual. This confirms the centrality of the consumer protection approach to data protection and privacy in the US, which is to a certain extent extended by a concern to protect data on health issues. There has been concerted effort under the HIPPA to protected health data that is quite extensive. Problematic though is how the FTC does not define personal data at any level.

In focusing on what is considered general and more sensitive personal data, the FTC and HIPPA definitions need to be compared. The FTC Act does not define personal data or sensitive personal data. The HIPPA Privacy Rules define 'health information', 'protected health information', 'individual identifiable health information' and 'genetic information'. It further means any information, including genetic information, whether oral or recorded in any form or medium, that is created or received by a health care provider, health plan, public health authority, employer, life insurer, school or university, or health care clearinghouse. In addition, it relates to the past, present, or future physical or mental health or condition of an individual; the provision of health care to an individual; or the past, present, or future payment for the provision of health care to an individual.

Problematic though is how the FTC does not define personal data at any level. While it was out of scope to determine whether the definition in other laws would apply, this needs to be considered, but, this alone, appears to be a significant gap. It remains to be seen whether this definition or the definition in any of the laws will be adequate to deal with AI products in the home or used generally in business. However, there is a transition occurring, with the need to afford greater protection of children has recently emerged. Arguably, this move, highlights how the US is also taking the rights of its citizens in this area more seriously. They have also recently issues an Executive Order that call upon government agencies that are developing regulation in the area of AI to consider privacy, data and cybersecurity matters as a collective. This whole of regulatory approach is a significant step forward and can only place the US in a strong position to govern and regulate the impact of smart home devices, toys, personal robots and drones, amongst others and their impact to personal data going forward. Therefore, AI, privacy and cybersecurity are beginning to converge in the US. However, their current sectorial approach may be a benefit when dealing with smart home, clothes, toys and personal robots. These pose some of the most formidable risks and challenges facing regulators and the community. They could become so pervasive that when used, the personal data

[14] HIPPA Privacy Rules, § 160.103, Definitions, https://www.hhs.gov/hipaa/for-professionals/privacy/laws-regulations/combined-regulation-text/index.html

and the ease of security breaches could see children and other vulnerable people in the community being subversively segregated.

In Canada the definition of personal information differs markedly between the *Personal Information Protection and Electronic Documents Act*, S.C. 2000 (PIPEDA), and *Privacy Act 1985* (PA). The PIPEDA regulates the private sector, while the PA is only applicable to the public sector. The definition of personal information differs greatly between the PIPEDA and PA. The PIPEDA defines personal information means information about an identifiable individual. This all-encompassing definition arguably means what it states that all and any information that can identify a data subject, is considered personal information.[15] Based on this definition elements of artificial intelligence such as biometric information such as facial and body mapping would come within this definition, along with the traditional identifying information such as name, address and date of birth. In support of the definition of personal information, the PIPEDA goes onto identify personal health information. The PIPEDA defines personal information means information about an identifiable individual. Artificial intelligence such as biometric information such as facial and body mapping would come within this definition, along with the traditional identifying information such as name, address and date of birth. The PIPEDA goes onto identify personal health information. On the other hand, the *PA has what can be regarded as one of the most comprehensive definition of personal information. Personal* information means information about an identifiable individual that is recorded in any form including race, national or ethnic origin, colour, religion, age or marital status of the individual. It also includes any information relating to the education or the medical, criminal or employment history of the individual, financial transactions, identifying number, symbol or other particular assigned to the individual, address, fingerprints or blood type of the individual.

China's Cybersecurity Law of the People's Republic of China do not define personal data or personal information or sensitive personal data. The only reference to personal information can be found in Article 22. It states that where network products and services have the function of collecting users' information, their providers shall explicitly notify their users and obtain their consent. If any user's personal information is involved, the provider shall also comply with this law and the provisions of relevant laws and administrative regulations on the protection of personal information.[16] However, such a definition can be found in the Information Security Technology-Personal Information Security Specification (ISTPISS),[17] for both personal informant and sensitive personal information. Firstly, personal information constitutes all information whether recorded by electronic or other means. It also means that that information can be used alone or combined with other information

[15] Personal Information Protection and Electronic Documents Act, S.C. 2000, section 2.

[16] Ibid, Article 22.

[17] TC260 Chinese, (English version) Information Security Technology-Personal Information Security Specification, https://www.newamerica.org/cybersecurity-initiative/digichina/blog/translation-chinas-personal-information-security-specification/ Chinese Version, https://www.tc260.org.cn/upload/2018-01-24/1516799764389090333.pdf

and can identify a natural person. Personal information also extends to that information that reflects the activities of the natural person. A person being able to be identified from their activities is a unique feature of the framework, and is something that in not explicitly stated in third countries laws. Personal information generally is consistent with other states, including the EU, names, date of birth, identity card numbers, biometrics, addresses, telecommunication contact methods, communication records and content, account passwords, property, credit, location data, accommodation, health, physiological and transaction information. Arguably, China have taken a slightly different approach to other states in regards to defining sensitive personal data. Sensitive personal information includes that once leaked, illegally provides or abused can threaten the personal property and property security of the individual. It also extends to that information that can cause personal reputational, physical or mental health damage, or, discriminate against the individual. Similar to general personal information, sensitive information includes identity card numbers, biometrics, addresses, telecommunication contact methods, communication records and content, account passwords, property, credit, location data, accommodation, health, physiological and transaction information. It also includes all personal information pertaining to children under the age of 14,[18] which, as stated above has been afforded extra protection in 2019.

Taiwan has embraced a broad definition that constitutes a person's name, date of birth, ID Card number, passport number, features, fingerprints, marital status, family information, education background, occupation, medical records, healthcare data, genetic data, data concerning a person's sex life, records of physical examination, criminal records, contact information, financial conditions, data concerning a person's social activities and any other information that may be used to directly or indirectly identify a natural person. Rather healthcare personal data, is any other data pertaining to check-ups or treatments implemented by physicians or other medical professionals for the purpose of treating, correcting or preventing diseases, harms or disabilities of human body or for other legitimate medical reasons, or shall mean other data produced from the prescription, medication, operation or disposition based on the findings of the above-mentioned check-ups. Moreover, personal data that would include genetics, means the information on a heredity unit, consisting of one segment of DNA of human body, for controlling the specific functions thereof. The sex life of an individual is considered sacrament, and personal data that discloses this information and data constitutes the personal data on sexual orientation or sexual habits.

---

[18] Ibid, section 3.1, 3.2. Sara Xia, *China's New Child Privacy Protection Rules*, (2019), https://www.chinalawblog.com/2019/09/chinas-new-child-privacy-protection-rules.html Huton Andrews Kurth LLP, China Issues Provisions on Cyber Protection of Children's Personal Information, https://www.lexology.com/library/detail.aspx?g=625d3bb3-ec70-4626-b37d-ae0b9092c307&utm_source=lexology+daily+newsfeed&utm_medium=html+email+-+body+-+general+section&utm_campaign=australian+ihl+subscriber+daily+feed&utm_content=lexology+daily+newsfeed+2019-10-09&utm_term

The Philippines definition of personal data (information), constitutes any information whether recorded in a material form or not, from which the identity of an individual is apparent or can be reasonably and directly ascertained by the entity holding the information, or when put together with other information would directly and certainly identify an individual. Furthermore, sensitive personal information includes, a data subjects race, ethnic origin, marital status, age, colour, and religious, philosophical or political affiliations. Sensitive data also includes health, education, genetic or the sexual life of a person, along with any proceeding for any offense committed or alleged, or, the sentence of any court. Sensitive information has been extended to also include other identifiable information that, has been issued by government, such as, social security numbers, previous or current health records, licenses or its denials, suspension or revocation, and tax returns. The definition is limited. While a more comprehensive definition can be problematic because it is difficult to account or describe every piece of personal information, it is our view that the current definition should be reviewed.

Macau have largely based the definition of personal data on both the EU and Hong Kong legal frameworks. The data protection laws apply to the processing of personal data whether manually or by an automated system or platform. However, the laws also apply to video surveillance and other forms of capture, processing and dissemination of sound and images allowing persons to be identified. Yet, this is on the basis that the controller is domiciled or based in the Macao. The definition of personal data while consistent with other states, in that, it is a broad definition, its most important elements are identifying individuals directly or indirectly. However, and while the definition addresses the more sensitive elements of personal data, such as philosophical or political beliefs, political association or trade-union membership, religion, privacy and racial or ethnic origin, health or sex life, genetic data, it is questionable whether it will capture all data that can be captured by AI.

For Hong Kong the current definition of personal data is similar to other states whereby it is a catch all meaning of personal data. It picks up the point that people can be identified by what is termed as a personal identifier. Arguably, this would also mean the identifying information that can be obtained through, and by AI systems. However, it is unclear whether the definition would be flexible enough to protect personal data in AI. Thus, it is recommended that Hong Kong review this definition, test it, or amend it to ensure AI will be included. Furthermore, more needs to be done to protect the youth of Hong Kong, and thus, a review of the current definition would also confirm or otherwise whether they are going to be protected from smart home appliance, toys and personal robots.

The strict nature of the South Korean laws is also reflected in a recent decision by the European Commission[19] to open dialogue and discussions about meeting the adequacy requirements under the EU GDPR. The relevant law defines personal data to mean any information which relates to a living natural person who can be

[19] European Commission, Adequacy Decisions, https://ec.europa.eu/info/law/law-topic/data-protection/international-dimension-data-protection/adequacy-decisions_en

identified or identifiable from those data including name, resident registration number and image, etc. (including the information that does not, on its own, permit direct identification of a specific individual, but that does identify specific individual when it is easily combined with other information). This broad definition could mean anything and everything that can identify a person. It provides a strong basis for Korean's to argue that anywhere, or, anything that captures any personal data would fall within this meaning. However, and while the courts are yet to determine what personal data actually constitutes within the above meaning, the current definition could pose challenges to individuals because of the lack of clarity. On the other hand, having such a broad definition does provide South Korea with room to move when new technology enters the market and also captures personal data, such as AI. Despite this definition, South Korea has not defined sensitive personal data. However, they have described sensitive data to constitute a person's ideology, belief, admission/exit to and from trade unions or political parties, political mindset, health, sexual life, and other personal information which is likely doing harm to privacy of data subjects. The flexibility in this approach is twofold. Firstly, the Presidential Decree which prescribes other elements of data that would be considered sensitive, and allows sensitive data outside of the relevant article to be prescribed quite narrowly. Secondly, it does allow South Korea to prescribe other areas of personal data to be sensitive, when it is required to do so.

Lao has defined personal data as 'data related to or referred directly to the character or activity of individuals, legal entities or organisations in a direct or indirect way'.[20] In addition, they have defined the term "User Data", to mean any data sending to the user, such as postal address, electronic address, geographical address, Internet code number, telephone number or others that being used in the computerized system. This is important because, it expand on the definition of personal data by providing the general personal identifiers that general identify a person. Thus, it is argued that both terms would likely need to be read concurrently to understand how personal data is defined across the Lao state. As highlighted in Chap. 9 viruses, malicious code and phishing have also been defined.[21] In other words, a virus has been defined to mean a special program being created which can be expanded, cause damages and destroy the computerized system, computer network and computer data. Additionally, malicious code refers to a set of computer command created in order to destroy the computerized system or to steal the computer data. Nonetheless, phishing refers to any newly created website that is similar to the former one in order to deceive data from the users. However, and while there is no specific reference to personal data or data that can identify a person, the respective definition does mention data generally. It is argued that data (generally) would include personal data, although further clarification is needed from the regulator or the courts to confirm this position.

[20] Ibid Part 1 General Provisions, Article 3 Definition of Terms.

[21] Ibid. Article 3 Definition of Terms (11) Virus, (12) Malicious Code and (13) Phishing.

Finally, Vietnam, similar to the US is a little more complex to discuss and compare the definition of personal data. This is because of the sectorial approach taken by the state that, has resulted in multiple laws regulating various elements of personal data. Thus, the comparison in this section will be limited to the LNIS. Article 3 defines personal information as information associated with the identification of a specific person. Again, it is another example of a state providing a broad definition. It is argued that this could mean any information that has been, and can be, collected and used over the Internet. It does not specifically refer to children, although it can be argued that the definition would embrace children's personal data. The definition, in its current form, could include personal information/data that is collected and used by AI.

The definition of personal data from the states examined in this book vary greatly. The respective definitions do however contain many similarities such as the basic personal data that has been collected for more than a century. As highlighted above, and within the country specific chapters, some states take the position of providing an all-encompassing definition that, is broad and can be interpreted as covering everything. On the other side, states have adopted a more specific approach and describing those high priority elements that can identify a person such as race, religion, health information, amongst others. Some states do separate general data from sensitive data. Arguably sensitive data is the data that is afforded a higher level of protection. A three staged approach needs to be considered to revising the definition of personal data. What is not evident, and this book calls for a re-think that, children's data, at a minimum should be defined differently from the general population. It could be a distinct definition, or, it could fall under sensitive personal data. This would provide a greater level of control and protection over that data, particularly with the onset of AI devices in the home that will capture their data, and be subject to illegal misuse. Secondly, health information/data needs to be reviewed within the respective laws.

Based on the above, more work needs to be undertaken of defined health personal data. It is our view that the challenges facing the health sector from AI are enormous, and therefore, it is argued that health data should also have a separate and clear definition of its own. They are likely to transform the health sector and resolve medical issues a lot quicker than any time in the past. Additionally, they will store more personal data that could not only be vulnerable to misuse and illegal access from cyber-attacks. Health data could be obtained from some Smart Home devices. Moreover, the World Health Organization (WHO) has released a Guideline[22] on the management of health data. The WHO make an important point that there have been increasing concern of health authorities regarding data reliability are undoubtedly multifactorial and include increased regulatory awareness and concern regarding gaps between industry choices and appropriate and modern control strategies. Furthermore, the WHO is of the view that contributing factors include failures by organizations to apply robust systems that inhibit data risks, to improve the detection of situations where data reliability may be compromised, and/or to investigate

[22] World Health Organization, Guidance on good data and record management practices https://www.who.int/medicines/publications/pharmprep/WHO_TRS_996_annex05.pdf?ua=1

and address root causes when failures do arise. For example, organizations subject to medical product good practice requirements have been using validated computerized systems for many decades but many fail to adequately review and manage original electronic records.[23]

Arguably the concerns from these practices is likely to continue to increase as AI becomes mainstream. Furthermore, as states centralize the availability of health data, allowing a doctor, with the consent of the data subject to access their health data from another doctor, the vulnerability of this data will be heightened. The WHO Guidelines while encouraging and promoting good risk management of personal data through having the right systems and processes in place to manage and protect personal data, it stops short of discussing cyber security and AI. In our view, and while it is out of scope of this Chapter to comprehensively discuss the WHO Guidelines, as AI is introduced into the health sector, these guidelines will need to be reviewed to ensure they are up to date. More pervasively, most nation states have not mentioned these Guidelines within their national policy or legislative frameworks for data protection. States could also consider making reference to these guidelines within enforceable codes of practice, for those that require codes to be established. While this Chapter and book has not examined whether the respective legislation provides provision for enforceable codes of practice to be established, it is another area where further study is required.

To date some states have provided a higher level of protection and control over health data. Some states have a catch all definition of personal data, while others have separated certain data to be categorized as sensitive personal data. The challenges facing the health sector from AI are enormous. They are likely to transform the health sector and resolve medical issues a lot quicker than any time in the past.

In summary, this book proposes that states reconsider the definition of personal data-information in their data protection legal frameworks. In reinforcing the above, it is time to consider a specific definition of personal data for children. Secondly, health data needs to be considered as having a separate and clear definition, particularly as smart home AI devices are likely to capture some if not all health data. This is already the case with people having apps on their iPhones and watches that capture some health information. Thirdly, and in keeping with the WHO's position, guidelines should be mandatory for the governance of health data, however, they must be enforceable.

15.4 Consent

The concept of consent has arguably emerged as a fundamental concept that underpins the definition of personal data. Consent by a data subject for the use of their personal data, can only constitute that has been defined by the law. Thus, it is important to understand that the concept of consent also varies significantly between the states compared throughout this book.

[23] Ibid.

Beginning with the US, the FTC Act does not specifically address consent. Consent only applies to a person who produces the material, thing or transcript. The application of consent under this section is fluid at best. Nonetheless, coupled with the FTC's Behavioural Advertising Principles operators should obtain affirmative express consent before using sensitive consumer data. Yet, it stops short of providing any further information or guidance as to its application. On the other side, the HIPAA generally requires entities to obtain consent in writing from a data subject before disclosing that data (with certain exceptions, for example, to provide medical treatment). Consent must generally be in writing and contain the signature of the data subject and the date. The HIPAA Privacy Rule provides specific statements that must be included in the consent. These include, the implementation specification, un-emancipated towards minors. The Rules go onto say that the minor consents to such health care service; no other consent to such health care service is required by law, regardless of whether the consent of another person has also been obtained; and the minor has not requested that such person be treated as the personal representative. The current approach, differs significantly to the other jurisdictions examined. There is no express terms or provisions of express or implied consent, or whether and how an express consent is to be obtained. The challenge again, will be the need to be aware of what level of consent is needed to be obtained for the use of personal data.

The concept of consent in Canada varies between the public and private sectors. In other words, consent under the PIPEDA provides that consent of an individual is only valid if it is reasonable to expect that an individual to whom the organization's activities are directed would understand the nature, purpose and consequences of the collection, use or disclosure of the personal information to which they are consenting. On the other hand, the PA has expressed the concept of consent to form an integral part of a public entity using, disclosing and obtaining personal information from a data subject. However, consent is not required when there is a sufficiently direct connection between the purpose for which personal data was collected and its proposed use. In addition, there are specific conditions around the disclosure of certain personal information such as home contact details to a union. Thus, consent is required for personal information that has been obtained in confidence and where the disclosure is authorized. Consent under the Canadian framework, arguably when applied through different laws creates a level of confusion as the regulatory environment is inconsistent.

China, to date, have taken a minimalist role in relation to consent. This is due to the structure of their respective laws. Currently they are largely focused on protecting the infrastructure that support the collection and use of data. Therefore, it is understandable that the concept of consent is hardly required. Nonetheless, with the implementation of the Cyber Protection of Personal Information of Children (CPCPCI), the concept of consent has emerged. This is an important step for China as they have implemented specific protections for children. Thus, the CPCPCI obliges network operators to establish personal information protection rules, designate a person responsible for protecting children's personal information, and obtain parental consent for collecting using, transferring or disclosing children's personal information. The personal information of children can only be collected and used by a network operator, for the specific purpose of that operator. The obligations imposed on network operators also extend to limiting their employees access to the personal information of children under 14 years of age. However, and where a network operator engages a third party to process children's personal information that, network operator must conduct a security assessment of the third party and sign an agreement with the third party in addition to obtaining parental consent to utilize the third part. In addition, consent appears to be at the forefront of the ISTPISS, to ensure that data subjects provide a level of express consent for the purpose, method, scope and rules pertaining to the processing of personal information.

Of the jurisdictions compared in this book, it is asserted that Taiwan has the most expansive application of consent. In other words, consent comes in the form of actual, express or presumed-implied consent. There are specific requirements for consent for government and non-government agencies when collecting, processing and using personal data. Article 7 effectively describes how consent can be and will apply according to other provisions with the PDPA. Consent comes in the form of actual, express or presumed-implied. In other words, consent, referred to in subparagraph 2, paragraph 1 of Article 15 and subparagraph 5, paragraph 1 of Article 19, means a declaration of agreement given by a data subject after he/she has been informed by the data collector of the information required under the PDPA. Arguably the declaration of consent is a form of express consent. Furthermore, consent in subparagraph 7, paragraph 1, Article 16 and subparagraph 6, paragraph 1, Article 20, means a separate declaration of agreement given by a data subject after he/she has been informed by the data collector of any of the purposes other than that originally specified, the scope of other use, and the impact of giving or not giving consent on the rights and interests of the data subject. Moreover, an implied level of consent has been presumed to have been provided by the data subject in accordance with subparagraph 2, paragraph 1, Article 15 and subparagraph 5, paragraph 1, Article 19 if the data subject does not indicate his/her objection and affirmatively provides his/her personal data after the government or non-government agency has informed the data subject of the relevant information specified in Paragraph 1, Article 8 of the PDPA. Note that this applies to both government and non-government agencies. Finally, the collector of the personal data within these agencies has the burden of proof that the data subject has provided consent.[24] The challenge is how would express consent work within AI devices?

Across the Philippines consent has largely been limited to the processing of personal data. For the processing of sensitive data, specific consent if required prior to any processing and goes further to require that all parties consent. Consent is not required in certain circumstance where the processing is provided by an existing law such as protecting health, amongst other national security and commercial matters. However, any transfer of sensitive personal information to third parties can only be undertaken with the consent form the data subject. On the other hand, the

[24] Personal Data Protection Act 1995, Article 7.

concept of consent in Macao is limited to the extent that is has not been described in detail as to how it would be applied. At best Macao has in accordance with Article 4 (9) defined the concept to mean any freely given specific and informed indication of the data subject's wishes by which he or she signifies his agreement to personal data relating to him being processed.[25] This reinforces the problematic issue emerging by the inconsistent approach to data protection law and how data subjects personal data can be protected adequately by AI devices. Macao's neighbour Hong Kong has adopted a distinctively different approach again. Section 30 of the laws, state that a data user shall not carry out, whether in whole or in part, a matching procedure unless and until each individual who is a data subject of the personal data the subject of that procedure has given his prescribed consent to the procedure being carried out. In addition to the above, data matching cannot be undertaken unless and until the Commissioner has consented under the procedure[26] being carried out unless the procedure belongs to a class of matching procedures specified in a notice and is carried out in accordance with the conditions, if any, specified in the notice. However, the requirement may be subject to the Provisions of Ordinance under which Matching Procedures are Required or Permitted.[27] This is something individuals and entities will need to confirm. On the other hand, the transfer of personal data outside of Hong Kong can be undertaken provided the data subject has provided consent for doing so. However, this is limited where it is practicable to do so. Thus, there is an implied level exception to this consent. Consent is not required where it is not practicable to obtain that consent. This broad approach to consent for the transfer of data outside the territory obviously meets the sovereign needs of the one state two systems across the territory. Furthermore, and as highlighted in Chap. 5, consent for such a transfer of data can be undertaken if it was practicable to obtain such consent, and the data subject would provide it. Thus, if, and when the data subject failed, or, refused to provide consent any such transfer of data could not be achieved. The level of consent is largely controlled through procedure, rather than providing the power to the data subject.

South Korea have adopted a strict approach to consent for the use of personal data of minors. That is, the controller is required to obtain consent for the processing of personal information of minors of age below 14, however, this is to be undertaken through their legal representatives. In this case, the minimum personal information necessary to obtain the consent from legal representatives may be collected directly from such minors without the consent of their legal representatives. However, companies obtaining personal data (e.g. location) are now required to ask the children aged under 14 whether their parents or legal guardian give consent. Parental consent can be given via payment information, authentication through

[25] Act 8/2005 Personal Data Protection Act, Article 4.

[26] The Personal Data (Privacy) Ordinance (PDPO) Cap 486. Section 32.

[27] Ibid.

smartphones or through text.[28] More broadly, when the personal information controller obtains the consent from the data subjects with respect to personal information processing under this Act, the personal information controller shall notify the data subjects of the fact by separating the matters requiring consent and helping the data subjects to recognize it explicitly, and obtain their consent thereof, respectively. Upon obtaining consent,[29] the controller is to segregate the personal information which needs the data subjects' consent to processing, from the personal information which needs no consent in executing a contract with data subjects. The burden of proof that no consent is required in processing the personal information shall be borne by the personal information controller.

On the other hand, Lao and Vietnam have taken different approaches to the above countries examined in this chapter. Lao, for instance has not adopted the concept. In Vietnam, from the laws examined, consent has been limited to the LIT and LNIS (see Chap. 10). However, the LIT is limited and does not provide for a data subject to consent for the collection and use of their personal data. As highlighted in Chap. 10, an individual and organisation has the right to distribute contact addresses available in the network environment after obtaining the *consent* of owners of such addresses. On the one hand, the address of individuals would constitute personal data that in other states has a level of protection. Yet, on the other hand, Article 21, obliges an organization and individual(s) may collect, process and use personal information of other people without their consent only when signing, modifying or performing contracts on the use of information, products or services in the network environment. Consent is not required when calculating charges for use of information, products or services in the network environment. The storage and supply of personal information in a network can be undertaken provided that the data subject requests of the organisations to store their personal information in the network environment to inspect, correct or cancel such information. However, the personal information stored cannot be forwarded to a third party without the consent of the data subject.[30]

The LNIS provides for a limited form of consent. Article 17 becomes important because the collection and use of personal information can only be undertaken after obtaining the consent of its owners regarding the scope and purpose of collection and use of such information.[31] This article has incorporated some of the OECD principles to effectively govern the use of personal data. Article 17 goes onto state that the use of personal information is to be undertaken for the purpose for which it was obtained.[32] The dissemination of personal information to a third party cannot be undertaken without the consent of the owner (data subject). In addition to the above

[28] South Korea revises child data protection laws, https://gdpr.report/news/2019/06/24/south-korea-revises-child-data-protection-laws/

[29] Ibid, Article 22,

[30] Ibid, Article 22.

[31] Article 17, Law on Network Information Security No 86/2015/QH13.

[32] Ibid.

requirements, any data that has been collected by state agencies must ensure that its storage is secure, and a data subject can request an outline of what data has been collected and stored.[33]

What has been demonstrated above, is that states have adopted significantly different approaches to the concept of consent. This will, in our view, be problematic for AI devices. The current laws make little to no distinction between adults and children in the application of consent. It requires a broader and in-depth analysis of how not only will the law respond, but also, how technology developers will respond to consenting of personal information being collected and stored by AI devices in the home and office. Doing so, will place the protection of personal data within AI technology of an even footing.

15.5 Data Localisation

Data localization is increasingly being established within national laws. As highlighted above, data localization refers to domestic laws or regulations that force localization of data, limiting the storage, movement and processing of data to specific jurisdictions, or limiting companies that can operate with countries' data.[34] However not all states have established this control mechanism. In practice it restricts the transfer of data to a third country. Article 15(1) of the Act on the Protection of Location Information states that, no one shall collect, use, or provide the location information regarding an individual or mobile object without the consent of the individual or the owner of the mobile object. It regulates the collection of location information without consent from the owner of that location. No other country has the same legal strictness around on location information nor have separate law regulating the collection of such information.[35] Article 17(3) of PIPA states that, when a personal information manager provides a third person at any overseas location with personal information, he/she shall notify a subject of information of the matters referred to in each subparagraph of paragraph (2) and obtain the consent thereto, and shall not enter into a contract concerning the transborder transfer of personal information stipulating any details contravening this Act.

While Hong Kong do not have specific data localisation requirements, unlike the US and China, according to, section 33 prohibits the transfer of personal information outside of Hong Kong unless the data subject has provided for consent in writing, and transfer to countries with adequate protection (where adequacy has been achieved such as with the EU) However, section 33 has not yet been adopted. Arguably, this is an area where most states are likely to review their respective laws

[33] Ibid.

[34] Hill, JF. (2014) The Growth of Data Localization Post-Snowden: Analysis and Recommendations for US Policymakers and Business Leaders, *Cyber Governance,*3.

[35] Yoon, J. (2018) *South Korean Data Localization: Shaped by Conflict, Data Localization Laws & the International Movement of Information* University of Washington.

in coming years. In the context of this book, it may be a further pressing issues that need to be reconciled sooner rather than later because of the vulnerabilities faced by children and other vulnerable citizens.

On the other hand, China under its Cyber Security Laws, provides for a level of data localization, However, and as highlighted in Chap. 12, they use a very broad definition of "critical information infrastructure." Thus, it rests in the regulation and controls of the infrastructure supporting localization of data storage. Additionally, in later wording this phrase was changed to "important data," further broadening the regulating scope. The law provides detailed explanations of data localization regulation, but broad terminology leaves room for unrestricted government intervention in any industry. Thus, China can never be singled out for this practice.

15.6 Right to be Forgotten, Correction and Deletion

South Korea arguably have some of the most robust and strictest data protection laws in the modern period. A unique feature of their data protection laws is the extensive layer of rights afforded to data subjects. South Korea, above most other countries outside the EU, have afforded further specific rights to data subjects such as access to the data held by an organisation.[36] Importantly, the additional layer of oversight for a personal to obtain access to their personal data, is the ability for Ministerial intervention. That is, a data subject can apply to the relevant Minister to get their data.

Central to the rights of data subjects to control their personal data, is the ability to have it corrected or deleted. Therefore, South Korea provide for a level of the right to be forgotten.[37] Article 36 provides that a data subject, who have access to his/her own personal information in accordance with Article 35, may seek correction or deletion of their personal data to the personal information controller. However, this can only be achieved provided that deletion is not allowed where the personal data shall be collected under other laws and regulations.[38] In fulfilling this requirement, the controller must undertake to allow for the correction or deletion

[36]Article 35, Personal Information Protection Act, Amended by Act No. 14839, Jul. 26, 2017.

[37]The Korea Communications Commission "Guidelines on the Right to Request Access Restrictions on Personal Internet Postings, 2016.

[38]Article 36 (3) Personal Information Protection Act, Amended by Act No. 14839, Jul. 26, 2017. The personal information controller shall take measures not to recover or revive the personal information in case of deletion pursuant to paragraph (2). (4) When the demand of data subjects is applicable to the proviso of paragraph (1), the personal information controller shall, without delay, notify the relevant data subjects of its content. (5) While investigating the personal information in question pursuant to paragraph (2), the personal information controller may, if necessary, demand to the relevant data subjects the evidence necessary to confirm the correction and deletion of the personal information. (6) Necessary matters in relation to the demand of correction and deletion, notification method and procedure, etc. pursuant to paragraphs (1, 2, 4) shall be provided by the Presidential Decree.

without any delay and take the necessary action to correct or delete the data. In addition to the above, South Korea has gone one step further by allowing a data subject to demand that their personal data, on being processed by a controller, be suspended. Article 37 goes onto specifically provide that the suspension of any processing of personal data can only be undertaken of and to that data, which is contained within the personal files pertaining to the data subject.[39] On the other hand, any suspension will not apply where it is specified by the law, or there is the potential of danger or damage to a person.[40] Suspension of personal data is a further control mechanism that, places the data subject in a position of greater control over the use of their data. The exercise of the above-mentioned rights can be delegated to attorney or legal representative for minor under the age 14.

Hong Kong, while having no formal right to be forgotten, data subjects do have the ability for their personal data to be erased. Hong Kong deals with the ability for a data subject to erase their personal data, differently from the other states compared in this book. In other words, section 26, provides that a data subject can request that their personal data be erased when and where that data is no longer required. Yet, the requirement of erasure of personal data, in our view is not settled. This is because section 26 allows the data user to only take all practicable steps to erase personal data held by the data user where the data is no longer required. However, this does not apply where the personal data is prohibited under any law or it is in the public interest (including historical interest) for the data not to be erased. This, in itself provides a high level of flexibility for when and where the personal data might be erased.[41] Thus, this is subtly different to the concept of the right to be forgotten in the EU and the other states compared in this book. As the Privacy Commissioner has issued the *Guidance on Personal Data Erasure and Anonymisation* to provide practical advice to data users as to when personal data should be erased, as well as how personal data may be permanently erased by means of digital deletion and/or physical destruction. In addition to the above, Data Protection Principle (DPP) 2(2) in Schedule 1 supports section 26 in the administration of erasing personal information. Thus, DPP 2 provides that to the Ordinance requires data users to take all practicable steps to ensure that personal data is not kept longer than is necessary for the fulfilment of the purpose (including any directly related purpose) for which the data is or is to be used.[42] Furthermore, DPP2(3) provides that if a data user engages a data processor, whether within or outside Hong Kong, to process personal data on the data user's behalf, the data user must adopt

[39] Article 37 Personal Information Protection Act, Amended by Act No. 14839, Jul. 26, 2017.

[40] Article 37, 3. Personal Information Protection Act, Amended by Act No. 14839, Jul. 26, 2017.

[41] For the avoidance of doubt, it is hereby declared that a data user must take all practicable steps to erase personal data in accordance with subsection (1) notwithstanding that any other data user controls (whether in whole or in part) the processing of the data; the first-mentioned data user shall not be liable in an action for damages at the suit of the second-mentioned data user in respect of any such erasure.

[42] Office of the Privacy Commissioner for Personal Data, Hong Kong, *Guidance on Personal Data Erasure and Anonymisation*, https://www.pcpd.org.hk/english/publications/files/erasure_e.pdfv.

contractual or other means to prevent any personal data transferred to the data processor from being kept longer than is necessary for processing of the data.[43] DPP4(1) requires a data user to take all practicable steps to ensure that personal data held by it is protected against unauthorised or accidental access, processing, erasure, loss or use, including the consideration of: (a) the kind of data and the harm that could result if any of those incidents should occur; (b) the physical location where the data is stored; (c) any security measures incorporated (whether by automated means or otherwise) into any equipment in which the data is stored; (d) any measures taken for ensuring the integrity, prudence and competence of persons having access to the data; and (e) any measures taken for ensuring the secure transmission of the data. There is work being undertaken across China to establish Hong Kong as a potential data storage hub. If realized, this will radically transform the legal framework for China and its Administrative Regions.

Similar to South Korea and some of the other states, under Hong Kong a data subject has the ability to gain access to their personal data have it corrected.[44] Section 18 enables individuals to obtain access to their personal data. An individual, or, a personal who has the authority to do so, such as a legal practitioner, can on behalf of the data subject make a request for access to that personal data. On the other hand, section 18 (1)(b) ensures that where a data user holds personal data that, data is to be supplied by the data user with a copy of the data.[45] Importantly, the above must be understood in accordance with section 55. Section 55 provides for the process of a relevant process, and DPP6 along with section 18 (1)(b) is exempted (for example, no need to comply with a data access request) until completion of a relevant process in determining suitability, eligibility or qualification of the data subject for employment or appointment to office. Nonetheless, this only applies to a process where an appeal may be made against a determination. As highlighted earlier in this book (Chap. 6). The correction of personal data ensures that the principle of accuracy is maintained. Section 22 provides that where a copy of personal data has been supplied by a data user in compliance with a data access request; and the individual, or a relevant person on behalf of the individual, who is the data subject considers that the data is inaccurate, then that individual or relevant person, as the case may be, may make a request that the data user make the necessary correction to the data.[46] However, if a data user, subsequent to the receipt of a data

---

[43] Ibid.

[44] Data Protection Principles in the Personal Data (Privacy) Ordinance *–from the Privacy Commissioner's perspective (2 Edition)* (2010) https://www.elegislation.gov.hk/hk/cap486!en-zh-Hant-HK.pdf?FROMCAPINDEX=Y.

[45] Ibid, (2) A data access request under both paragraphs of subsection (1) shall be treated as being a single request, and the provisions of this Ordinance shall be construed accordingly.

[46] Section 22, 23, 24 and 25, The Personal Data (Privacy) Ordinance (PDPO) Cap 486. A data user who does not hold the personal data but controls the processing of that data in such a way as to prohibit the data user who does hold the data from complying (whether in whole or in part) with section 23(1) in relation to a data correction request which relates to the data, shall be deemed to be a data user to whom such a request may be made, and the provisions of this Ordinance (including subsection (1)) shall be construed accordingly.

correction request but before complying with the request[47] or refusing to comply with the request,[48] discloses to a third party the personal data to which the request relates, then the user shall take all practicable steps to advise the third party that the data is the subject of a data correction request still under consideration by the user (or words to the like effect). A person who, in a data correction request, supplies any information which is false or misleading in a material particular for the purpose of having the personal data corrected as indicated in the request, commits an offence and is liable on conviction to a fine at level 3 and to imprisonment for 6 months. DDP 6 underpins the access to personal data, whereby data subjects have the right of access to and correction of their personal data held by data users.[49] Data users are required to comply with such request within 40 days after receiving the request. For instance where a customer may make a request to an insurance institution to be informed whether it holds his personal data contained in, for example, an insurance application form, medical report, risk assessment questionnaire or claim form, and be supplied with a copy of such data within 40 days or 12 month period.[50] Where the correction cannot be made within the expiration period the data subject requesting the correction must be informed that the correction will not meet this requirement. This time limitation is something that is specific to Hong Kong, and is in our view an area that requires harmonization amongst states.

Macau, another Administrative Region of China, has adopted a form of the right to the be forgotten. They have provided for a broader set of rights. The Personal Data Protection Act provides a number of rights to data subjects including the right to information, right to access personal information and the right to object. Article 10 and the right to information. The controller is responsible for providing a data subject with the following information when requested; 'the identity of the controller and of his representative; the purposes of the processing; the recipients or categories of recipients; whether replies to the questions are obligatory or voluntary, as well as the possible consequences of failure to reply; the existence and conditions of the right of access and the right to rectify, provided they are necessary, taking account of the specific circumstances of collection of the data in order to guarantee the data subject that they will be processed fairly'.[51] As highlighted in Chap. 7, the

---

[47] Ibid, in accordance with section 23.

[48] Ibid, in accordance with section 25.

[49] Ibid, section 23, Guidance on the Proper Handling of Customers' Personal Data for the Insurance Industry, Office of the Privacy Commissioner for Personal Data, https://www.pcpd.org.hk/english/publications/files/GN_insurance_e.pdf.

[50] Ibid. (3) A data user is not required to comply with subsection (1)(c) in any case where the disclosure concerned of the personal data to the third party consists of the third party's inspection of a register or other like document— (a) in which the data is entered or otherwise recorded; and (b) which is available for inspection by the public, but this subsection shall not apply if the third party has been supplied with a copy, certified by or under the authority of the data user to be correct, of the data.

[51] Act 8/2005 Personal Data Protection Act, Article 10.2. The documents supporting the collection of personal data shall contain the information set down in the preceding paragraph. 3. If the data are not collected from the data subject and except where he already has it, the controller or his

obligation to provide information may be waived by (1). a legal provision; (2). on the grounds of security and criminal prevention or investigation; or (3). in particular for processing for statistical purposes or for the purposes of historical or scientific research, when the provision of such information proves impossible or would involve a disproportionate effort or if recording or disclosure is expressly laid down by law or administrative regulations, in which case notification to the public authority is required.[52] On the other side, and even though there does not appear to be a comprehensive right to erasure, Article 11(4) provides for their personal data to be rectified, deleted or blocked, including any incomplete or inaccurate data. Specifically, the rectification, erasure or blocking of data can be undertaken where the processing does not comply with the provisions of the Act. It applies to data that is incomplete or inaccurate. However, where it can be proved that to undertake the rectification, erasure or blocking of personal data that, it is impossible to achieve or disproportionately cumbersome, the entity would not be required to undertake this step. A further exemption that applies is where the processing of personal data relates to security and criminal prevention or investigation, the right of access shall be exercised through the competent authority in that case. Apart from the right to access one's personal data and information, the right to object provides another layer of control to data subject over their personal data. Thus, Article 12 enables a data subject to object to the processing of their personal data.[53] A data subject has the right to object to the processing of their personal data at any time. Although, once objected to that processing, the entity in control of the processing of that data, must cease any further data processing.

Moreover, and on the backdrop of the above rights, the right of access to information relating to health data, including genetic data. This builds in a higher level of control, and another procedural step over personal health data. It appears to relate to any health data, no matter the age of that data. If the data are not used for taking measures or decisions regarding any particular individual, the law may restrict the right of access where there is clearly no risk of breaching the fundamental rights, freedoms and guarantees of the data subject, particularly the right to privacy, and when the data are used solely for purposes of scientific research or are kept in personal form for a period which does not exceed the period necessary for the sole purpose of creating statistics.[54] On the other side, Article 13 provides a data subject

representative must provide the data subject with the information set down in paragraph 1 at the time of undertaking the recording of data or, if a disclosure to third parties is envisaged, no later than the time the data are first disclosed.

[52] Ibid, subject to paragraph 3 of Article 11, the obligation to provide information under this Article shall not apply to the processing of data carried out solely for journalistic purposes or the purpose of artistic or literary expression.

[53] Ibid. Article 12 Right to object. Save where otherwise provided by law, the data subject has the right to object at any time on compelling legitimate grounds relating to his particular situation to the processing of data relating to him, and where there is a justified objection the processing instigated by the controller may no longer involve those data.

[54] Act 8/2005 Personal Data Protection Act, Article 11(6).

with the right not to be subject to automated individual decisions. This is an important feature of their laws. That is, every person shall have the right not to be subject to a decision which produces legal effects concerning him or significantly affects him and which is based solely on automated processing of data intended to evaluate certain personal aspects relating to him, in particular his performance at work, creditworthiness, reliability or conduct. Article 13 goes onto say that without prejudice to compliance with the other provisions of this Act, a person may be subject to automation decision where that decision is taken in the course of the entering into or performance of a contract. However, this is provided that, the request for the entering into or the performance of the contract has been satisfied, or that there are suitable measures to safeguard his legitimate interests, such as allowing the individual to put his point of view.

As discussed in Chap. 8, the Philippines has also established rights for data subjects outside of, and in addition to the right to be forgotten. The *Data Privacy Act of 2012* (DPA)[55] provides a number of rights to ensure that the data subject is fully informed of the what personal information is to be processed, and the entry of that information into a processing system by the relevant controller.[56] In addition, the data subject is to be informed of the purpose for processing the personal data, along with the scope and method of the processing. While there is a requirement for the data subject to be notified of the above, there are exemptions to this rule. Thus, a notification would not apply where there is a subpoena or when the collection and processing generally including for the performance of a contract or a service is to be met. Further, personal information has been corrected, the controller is to ensure the data subject has access to the new and retracted personal information. This is based on whether the[57] third parties who have previously received the personal information be informed of its inaccuracy and its rectification upon reasonable request of the data subject. In addition, this is also based on the suspension, withdrawal or order the blocking, removal or destruction of personal information from the controller's filing system upon discovering that the personal information is incomplete, outdated, false, unlawfully obtained, used for unauthorized purposes or is no longer necessary for the purposes for which they were collected. On the other hand, the right to be forgotten is still being developed. It is far from settled. At issue is that under the DPA there is no provision that specifically enable for the erasure or deletion of personal information. Rather, section 3 defines processing to include any operation or any set of operations performed upon personal information including,

[55] Republic Act No. 10173 An Act Protecting Individual Personal Information in Information and Communications Systems in The Government and The Private Sector, Creating For this Purpose a National Privacy Commission, and for Other Purposes.

[56] Ibid, section 16. (5) Methods utilized for automated access, if the same is allowed by the data subject, and the extent to which such access is authorized; (6) The identity and contact details of the personal information controller or its representative; (7) The period for which the information will be stored; and (8) The existence of their rights, i.e., to access, correction, as well as the right to lodge a complaint before the Commission.

[57] Ibid, section 16.

but not limited to, the collection, recording, organization, storage, updating or modification, retrieval, consultation, use, consolidation, blocking, erasure or destruction of data. Sections 16 and 20 are the only sections that refer to the destruction of personal information.

Taiwan have arguably adopted similar data rights to that of its regional neighbours such as South Korea and Japan. Article 3 of the PDPA provides data subjects with rights that may be exercisable and cannot be waived or limited unless by contractual arrangements. Data a subject's rights include the right to'make an inquiry of and to review their personal data; request a copy of their personal data; supplement or correct their personal data; demand the cessation of the collection, processing or use of their personal data; and erase their personal data.'[58] While unique to Taiwan, they have become important to the citizenry of the territory, to ensure they maintain a level of liberal thought. One of the most important rights provided to data subject is the right to erase their personal data. Arguably, this reinforces the proposition below that the right to be forgotten exists in Taiwan. As highlighted in Chap. 9, the PDPA in accordance with Article 3 provides individuals with the right to request that an entity, store or organisation delete his or her personal information from its database or system.[59] Furthermore, Article 20 also provides that an individual who requests their unwillingness to receive any marketing material, the entity must cease to send that individual any marketing material using their personal information.[60] Failure to follow the requirements of these two articles in particular the entity will be liable, and it arguably highlights how the right to deletion underpins the notion of the right to be forgotten. In October 2014, the Court awarded civil damages of NT$26,000 in accordance with the Taiwan civil Code and the PDPA, because an entity failed to delete the personal information of an individual, who had requested it be deleted.[61] As stated earlier, the right to be forgotten has been embraced by some states and not others. Will there be global harmonization on the right to be forgotten? This is unlikely, however, forms of it will exist by providing a data subject with the ability to delete their persona data.

Laos, does not provide for the right to be forgotten. It does however, allow a data subject to to delete their data and the obligation to ensure the data is correct.[62] Arguably they are considered to be equivalent to data controllers and processors that are established by law in other states. The Data Administrative Authority also has rights with respect to interception, inspection and suspension of services where data

---

[58] Personal Data Protection Act 1995, Article 3.

[59] Ibid.

[60] Ibid, Article 20.

[61] Chang, H., Tsai, C., *Taiwan-first court case based on the right to be forgotten*, Baker McKenzie, https://www.lexology.com/library/detail.aspx?g=644356dc-6da9-4fc8-ad3e-1deb18f48848

[62] Ibid, Article 5 Rights and Obligations of the Data Owner, Articles 27-28.

adversely affects society.[63] However, Vietnam do not provide for an extensive list of rights for its citizens, and there is no specific right to be forgotten.

China have taken a very different approach to regulating and protecting personal data. As highlighted in Chap. 12, individuals and entities are required to comply with not only the general law, but also, the constitution, to observe public order, and respect social morality. There is no right to be forgotten, and the ISTPISS[64] extends the rights of citizens to seek that their personal information is managed to rectify and correct an error or that information is incomplete, the controller is to modify the information.[65] Moreover, Article 7.6 allows a data subject to request of a controller that their personal information be deleted. Although, the ability for personal information to be deleted can only be achieved when a controller has violated the laws in relation to the collection of that information, or the agreement for the collection of that information has been violated. This also extends to any agreement for the transfer of the personal information to third parties and disclosure of that information. Any transfer to a third party is to cease as soon as possible upon a request by a data subject is received for the deletion of their personal data. The disclosure of personal information is to also cease as soon as the data subject has requested that it be deleted.[66] While not specifically clear, and further clarification would need to be sought as to the operation of this deletion provision, it provides a layer of protection to data subjects that, goes beyond the regulation of the systems and infrastructure, which China's laws largely do.

Canada has separated out their respective data laws to regulate the private sector from the public sector. The *Personal Information Protection and Electronic Documents Act*, S.C. 2000 (PIPEDA), and *Privacy Act 1985* (PA). At the time of writing this book the Canadian government were undertaking a review of the Privacy Act 1985. The PIPEDA regulates the private sector, while the PA is only applicable to the public sector. Broadly the rights according to the PA, provides for the right of data subjects to access personal data. That is, section 12 provides that every Canadian citizen or a permanent resident has a right to request and be given access to their personal information about the individual contained in a personal information bank.[67] Citizens can also gain access to their personal information that is under

[63] Ibid, Chapter 6 Rights and Obligations of the Data Administration Authority, Article 29 rights of the Data Administration Authority.

[64] Chinese, (English version) Information Security Technology-Personal Information Security Specification, https://www.newamerica.org/cybersecurity-initiative/digichina/blog/translation-chinas-personal-information-security-specification/ Chinese Version, https://www.tc260.org.cn/upload/2018-01-24/1516799764389090333.pdf

[65] Chinese, (English version) Information Security Technology-Personal Information Security Specification, https://www.newamerica.org/cybersecurity-initiative/digichina/blog/translation-chinas-personal-information-security-specification/ Chinese Version, https://www.tc260.org.cn/upload/2018-01-24/1516799764389090333.pdf, Article 7.5.

[66] Ibid.

[67] Personal Information Protection and Electronic Documents Act, S.C. 2000, section 10. Personal information to be included in personal information banks 10 (1) The head of a government institution shall cause to be included in personal information banks all personal information under the

the control of a government institution. Furthermore, every data subject has the right to request correction of their personal information where the individual believes there is an error or omission. A data subject is also able to require that a notation to be attached to the information reflecting any correction request. A notable difference between the states compared is how there is a time limit imposed by Canada, That is, in order for a data subject to access their personal data in accordance with section 12, they need to follow the procedural process in accordance with section 13. The request must be made in writing to the government institution. Any request made to a government institution must be conducted within 30 days. That is, unless there has been a request for an extension to the time limit in accordance with section 15. Within the 30 day time period, the government institution must respond to the individual in writing, informing them of whether access will be granted or otherwise, and where access is granted outline what personal information will be provided. A section 15 extension can only be granted for a further 30 days. Canada has not yet formally recognized the right to be forgotten.

Finally, the US, does not specifically provide for the right to be forgotten. However, according to the HIPAA[68], the collection of health data is protected from fraud and abuse in accordance with section 221. The healthcare fraud and abuse of data collection program, enables the reporting of adverse actions that, against health care providers, suppliers, or practitioners as required by subsection (b), with access as set forth in subsection (c), and shall maintain a database of the information collected under this section.[69] The further management of information from an adverse action that, is to be reported to the Secretary in relation to a health care provider, supplier, or practitioner, the Secretary can require the disclosure of the information, upon request, to the health care provider, supplier, or licensed practitioner, and any procedures in the case of disputed accuracy of the information.[70] The correction of personal data and information is important allowing the data subject and entity to have accurate information. Moreover, each government agency and their respective health plans are to report any corrections of information that, has already be reported as having an adverse action.[71] This is to be in the form prescribed by the Secretary, however it is out of scope to explore this. Furthermore, this does not avail a data subject the ability to have their data or information deleted. Thus, the right to be

control of the government institution that (a) has been used, is being used or is available for use for an administrative purpose; or (b) is organized or intended to be retrieved by the name of an individual or by an identifying number, symbol or other particular assigned to an individual. Exception for Library and Archives of Canada (2) Subsection (1) does not apply in respect of personal information under the custody or control of the Library and Archives of Canada that has been transferred there by a government institution for historical or archival purposes.

[68] Health Insurance Portability and Accountability Act 1996, section 1128E, referring to section 221, https://www.congress.gov/104/plaws/publ191/PLAW-104publ191.pdf

[69] Health Insurance Portability and Accountability Act 1996, section 1128E, referring to section 221, https://www.congress.gov/104/plaws/publ191/PLAW-104publ191.pdf

[70] Ibid.

[71] Ibid.

forgotten in the US does not exist.[72] The access to reported information and its availability requires that any information stored within a database, can be made available to Federal and State government agencies and health plans pursuant to procedures that the Secretary shall provide by regulation.[73] This is a very broad provision, clearly related to government agencies managing information and data of individuals.

15.7 Data Transfers

In South Korea, have placed limitations on the processing, use and consignment of personal data.[74] In other words, they have strong controls, whereby, a data subject must be informed that their data will be transferred and to which company or entity. They are to be provided the address, telephone number and other contact points of the recipient of the data. The method and procedure to withdraw the consent is where the data subject would not want the transfer of his/her personal information.[75] Upon receiving the personal information, the transferee shall without delay notify data subjects of the fact of such transfer. The transferee may, in case of receiving personal information owing to business transfer, merger use, or provide to a third party, the personal information only for the initial purpose prior to transfer. It must be noted that this form of obligation on an organisation is different to that of data portability, where a data subject can request an organisation that their data be transferred to another entity.

As highlighted in Chap. 6, on a daily basis the personal data of its citizens is transferred regionally and internationally. Section 33 prohibits the transfer of personal data outside the territory under specific circumstances. Section 33 does not apply to personal data other than personal data collected, held, processed or used within Hong Kong. The transfer of personal data by a data use cannot be undertaken to a place (country) outside of Hong Kong unless (a). the place is specified for the purposes of this section in a notice under subsection (3); (b). the user has reasonable grounds for believing that there is in force in that place any law which is substantially similar to, or serves the same purposes as, this Ordinance; (c). the data subject has consented in writing to the transfer. Furthermore, the transfer outside of Hong Kong can only take place where the user has reasonable grounds for believing that the transfer is for the avoidance or mitigation of adverse action against the data subject; or it is not practicable to obtain the consent in writing of the data subject to that transfer; and if it was practicable to obtain such consent, the data subject would

[72] Siegel, R, *Tech Policy, Google scores major victory in E.U. 'right to be forgotten' case* https://www.washingtonpost.com/technology/2019/09/24/google-scores-major-victory-eu-right-be-forgotten-case/

[73] Ibid.

[74] Article 27, Personal Information Protection Act, Amended by Act No. 14839, Jul. 26, 2017

[75] Ibid.

give it.[76] Moreover, as outlined in Chap. 6, section 33 is further underpinned by DPP3. Therefore, the transfer of personal data to a place outside Hong Kong would require the data subject's prescribed consent. However, at the time of writing this book section 33 has not yet been implemented.

For Macau, Article 19 establishes a number of principles that require any personal data being transferred to a third country must have an adequate level of protection. Similar to Hong Kong, citizens personal data is transferred outside of the territory daily. Consideration needs to be undertaken in relation to the purpose and duration of the proposed processing operation or operations, the place of origin and place of final destination, the rules of law, both general and sectorial, in force in the destination in question, and the professional rules and security measures which are complied with in the destination state. In addition to these considerations, it is up to the public authority to decide whether a legal system ensures an adequate level of protection referred to in the preceding paragraph.[77] This provides a lot of flexibility for a public authority, and there appears little oversight from the regulator to ensure similar levels of controls are in place at the destination state. Nonetheless, in the context of Macau, a lot of data would be entering China and other regional states, which, in part, would not have similar level of controls over personal data. Thus, a level of discretion is required, which is expanded upon by Article 20. any transfer of personal data to a destination state where the legal system does not ensure there is an adequate level of protection of the data. In order to achieve this transfer, it can be done on the condition that the public authority is notified, and that the data subject has given his consent unambiguously. Furthermore, a transfer can take place where that transfer of data is in the 'vital' interest of the data subject, and if it is made from a register which according to laws or administrative regulations is intended to provide information to the public and which is open to consultation either by the public in general or by any person who can demonstrate legitimate interest, provided the conditions laid down in law for consultation are fulfilled in the case.[78] The OPDP noted that "According to Article 4(1)(1) and 3(1) of the PDPA, collection of the applicants' personal data by Organization A, through its website, was an automatic processing of personal data that is subject to the regulations of the same Law."[79] The OPDP went onto to say that any transfer of personal data to a location out of the Macao SAR, Article 19 and 20 must be complied with. Consequently, it would be revealed that the server of the said online application system was in fact located in Hong Kong SAR. Therefore, its transfer would only be legitimate as long as Article 20 was fulfilled.[80] In 2018, the OPDP was required to determine whether Article 20

[76] Ibid, section 33. Office of the Privacy Commissioner for Personal Data, Guidance on Personal Data Protection in Cross-border Data Transfer, https://www.pcpd.org.hk/english/resources_centre/publications/files/GN_crossborder_e.pdf

[77] Ibid, Article 19.

[78] Ibid, Article 20 (1).

[79] Ibid.

[80] Ibid.

had been complied with, in relation to the transfer of employee personal data to the parent company in Hong Kong.[81]

Similar to the other states compared throughout this book, the transfer of personal data is controlled considerably. The Philippines, is no exception. However, for the Philippines, it is somewhat limited and in applying section 21 requires that the controller has sole responsibility for the transfer of personal information nationally and transnationally.[82] The level of responsibility can be delegated to another individual or group of individuals within the organisation. They are also held to the same level of accountability to that of the controller, when in the control of personal information being transferred to a third country or another location within the state. The transfer of personal information outside of the country of origin to where it was first collected is increasingly becoming more common. As a result, and unlike the other states compared, the Philippines laws have extraterritorial reach.

For Taiwan, the transfer of personal data is regulated by, Article 21, which requires that where personal data will be transferred outside of Taiwan, and is carried out by a non-government agency, the central government authority in charge of the industry concerned may impose restrictions on such a transfer. Any limitation of cross border transfer only applies to where that data is a major national interest or where an international treaty or agreement applies. Importantly, where the country receiving the personal data lacks proper regulations on protection of personal data and the data subjects' rights and interests may consequently be harmed any transfer of data may be limited or not proceed. Indirectly, Taiwan is ensuring there is a level of protection equivalence in data protection when data is being transfer to third countries. Many other states have established the same procedure. However, it is out of scope of this chapter to provide that comparative analysis. This limitation also extends to where the cross-border transfer of the personal data to a third country (territory) is carried out to circumvent the PDPA.[83] Furthermore, Article 22 requires that the central government authorities in charge of the industries or the municipality/city/county governments concerned may, when they deem necessary or suspect any possible violation of the PDPA, inspect compliance with the security control measures, the guidelines on disposing personal data upon business termination, and the restrictions on cross-border transfers, or conduct any other routine inspections by having their staff enter non-government agencies' premises upon presentation of their official identification documents and order relevant personnel at the non-government agencies to provide necessary explanations, cooperate on adopting relevant measures, or provide supporting documents.[84] This extension to municipality-city -county governments is a unique requirement specific to Taiwan. No other state compared has this specific requirement.

---

[81] Complaints Case Note No: 0035/2018/IP, Transfer of employee personal data to the parent company in Hong Kong, Office of Personal Data Protection.

[82] Ibid, section 21.

[83] Ibid, section 21.

[84] Ibid, Article 22.

On the other hand, the Republic of Laos, Vietnam, China, Canada do not provide for specific rules around data transfers either within or outside the state. Finally, The FTC enforces key international privacy frameworks, including the EU and US. It also enforces the Swiss and US Privacy Shield Framework.[85] The EU and US Privacy Shield Framework provide a legal mechanism for companies to transfer personal data from the European Union to the United States. This Framework, administered by the Department of Commerce, protects consumers' privacy and security through an agreed set of Privacy Shield Principles. The FTC also serves as a privacy enforcement authority in the APEC CPBR system. The APEC CBPR system is a voluntary, enforceable code of conduct designed to enhance the privacy and security of consumers' personal information transferred among the United States and other APEC members. Under the system, participating companies can be certified as compliant with APEC CBPR program requirements that implement APEC's nine data privacy principles.[86] It remains to be seen how far the Safe Habour framework will be extended to other third countries. Yet, a more pressing issue has recently arisen, whereby, the European Court of Justice delivered a ruling in the Schrems II case, that the EU-US Privacy Shield to be invalid.[87] The ruling in this case, demonstrates the vulnerability of the current regulatory systems that has been established to facilitate the flow of data, but also, attempting to provide a high level of security.

15.8 Challenges and a Way Forward

It has been demonstrated that AI will pervade society in ways that most in the community today, are unlikely to realise or even contemplate. The rise of Smart Home technology and even the rise of children's toys that will have AI technology, pose some of the most pervasive intrusions in personal data. That is, Smart Home appliances have the ability to capture all forms of personal data that, can be used for the wrong reasons. Additionally, children's toys are also being made available on the market that has AI systems within them that could capture personal data and be used at a later time by insinuating a bias. This can also occur for people that have disabilities. Should this be realised the policy and regulatory settings are far from adequate

[85] Privacy and Data Security Update, 2018, Federal Trade Commission https://www.ftc.gov/system/files/documents/reports/privacy-data-security-update-2018/2018-privacy-data-security-report-508.pdf

[86] Ibid. In 2018, FTC had brought 51 actions, 39 under an older US EU Safe Harbor program, 4 under APEC CBPR, and 8 under Privacy Shield.

[87] Joshua P. Meltzer, *The Court of Justice of the European Union in Schrems II: The impact of GDPR on data flows and national security 2020*, https://voxeu.org/article/impact-gdpr-data-flows-and-national-security Senior Fellow, Brookings Institution and lead of the Digital Economy and Trade Project. Schrems and Facebook Ireland v Data Protection Commissioner ("Schrems II") (2020) CJEU Case C-311/18.

to protect the most vulnerable in society. Equally concerning is the onset of smart clothes, personal robots, drones and other products that will be mainstream that, come with their own security and data protection issues. These products have complex AI systems, and it is far from conclusive whether the systems and infrastructure that supports them are secure enough to stop cybersecurity incursions and illegal use of personal data. Moreover, these products are connected to the Internet. They are vulnerable to attacks. Other products and platforms which have also emerged such as Google Assistant, Apple's Siri, Facebook's M, and Amazon's Alexa–powered Echo also pose security and privacy concerns.[88] However, for all the benefits they are bringing to individuals and entities that will use these in the home and business, there are harms that have not been fully resolved. For instance, the potential anticompetitive consequences from a dominant assistant will likely take a toll on privacy and broader elements of society.[89] Again, what can be demonstrated is the need to take a wider legislative approach that will reconcile the gaps and converge the law. A further and more problematic issue is the lack of international coordination and the need for internationally agreed policy direction, legal norms and principles to regulate these areas.

As highlighted in Chap. 1, the OECD Principles have been pivotal in providing a platform for the development of data protection law. However, there has been some debate as to their applicable or otherwise in the new world of AI and data protection. Fred Cate and Rachel Dockery,[90] argue that it is time for data protection law to be improved if it is to be effective in protecting privacy, and address the challenges presented by AI. The authors call for five key areas of reform that is needed to data protection laws, to bring them in line with the new digital economy and AI over the next decade. They are of the view that there is a need to shift from individual consent to data stewardship, enhance current risk management framework to a systemic approach, a greater focus on data users and their impacts, develop a comprehensive framework of harm, and building greater transparency and redress into the framework.[91]

Chapter 1 also confirmed that the definition of AI is far from settled, it is only beginning to emerge as a statutory definition, which has come out of the US. The courts have not yet intervened and provided a settled definition of the concept. It is rather conceived broadly because the systems, infrastructure and platforms that suit behind this technology vary, depending on the uses. For instance, it can be applied to motor vehicles, televisions, light switched, vacuum cleaners, machine learning whereby the technology is able to predict mood and patterns of behaviour. Thus, the international community should come together and develop and agree definition of AI. While this could be problematic where AI is used in military products and

---

[88] Stucke, M., Ezrachi, A, *How Digital Assistants Can Harm Our economy, Privacy, and Democracy*, CY, 32 Berkeley Tech. L.J. 1239 (2018).

[89] Ibid.

[90] Cate, F., Dockery, R, Artificial Intelligence and Data Protection: Observations on a Growing Conflict, https://ostromworkshop.indiana.edu/pdf/seriespapers/2019spr-colloq/cate-paper.pdf

[91] Ibid.

appliances. Legislators could exclude anything military and other national security AI devices from this definition.

One of the most significant challenges that has arguably emerged if how personal data has been defined. Cate and Dockery reinforce this point, whereby, they assert that the line between what is "personal" and what is not has been substantially blurred by the correlations and inferences that can be made from aggregated data sets. Information that once seemed to be non-personal now has the potential to be personal data, and data users and regulators alike are faced with the difficult task of determining which data should be the subject of regulation.[92] At issue, is how the countries discussed in this book have adopted very different approaches to the definition of personal data. South Korea defines personal information to mean "information pertaining to any living person that makes it possible to identify such individual by their name and resident registration number, image, etc.," and specifically includes "information which, if not by itself, makes it possible to identify any specific individual if combined with other information." On the other hand, Macau has defined personal data through Article 4 to mean, any information of any type, irrespective of the type of medium involved, including sound and image, relating to an identified or identifiable natural person ("data subject"); an identifiable person is one who can be identified, directly or indirectly, in particular by reference to an indication number or to one or more factors specific to his physical, physiological, mental, economic, cultural or social identity.

Despite the lack of a definition of sensitive personal data, Article 7 provides some guidance of what constitutes this type of data. Sensitive personal data includes data that discloses the philosophical or political beliefs, political association or trade-union membership, religion, privacy and racial or ethnic origin, health or sex life, including genetic data. To reconcile the gaps and disconnect between data protection, AI and cyber security, one of the steps must be to ensure that there is harmonization in the definition. Furthermore, and to be specific within data protection law, the word Artificial Intelligence should be inserted into the definition of personal data. Doing so, provides clarity to all. As highlighted in the book by Walters et al. that a Model Law and International Treaty would provide a clear definition of AI and assist in providing a level of convergence of AI, cybersecurity and data protection law.

Nonetheless, for the definition of personal data to fit neatly into AI is complex and not fully understood. Cate and Dockery argue that AI, and the variety of data sets on which it depends, only exacerbates the challenge of determining when data protection laws apply by expanding the capability for linking data or recognizing patterns of data that may render non-personal data identifiable. In referring to Professor Latanya Sweeney they highlight how it has been 'demonstrated that 87% of the US population is uniquely identified with just three data elements: date of

[92] Ibid.

birth, gender, and 5-digit ZIP Code'.[93] More pervasively, there are well-publicized examples of Google, Netflix, AOL, and others releasing deidentified data sets only to have the data reidentified within days by researchers correlating them with other data sets.

Cate and Dockery further make three important observations. Firstly, even wholly non-identifiable data may act to identify unique users or machines. For example, browser choice and font size can provide an accurate, unique online identifier. Simply stated, the more data are available, the harder it is to de-identify them effectively. AI only makes deidentification harder, in two ways.[94] It facilitates the demand for more data, for example, from the sensors in cell phones, cars, and other devices. Secondly, it provides increasingly advanced computational capabilities to work with collected data. Facial features, gate, fingerprint, and other forms of biometric recognition technologies provide an apt example: they collect thousands of discrete, nearly meaningless data points and then combine them in a way to provide reliable identification of individuals.[95] Further complicating the role of personal data, identification may not be necessary for AI to take action and make a decision. For example, the sensors in vehicles might be capable of collecting enough data about pedestrians to identify them, but identification would not be necessary to avoid hitting them. AI only needs to determine that the object is a pedestrian; any personal data collected is not meant to identify a specific individual.[96] Thirdly, for AI to predict the probability of heart attacks occurring in women over 50, personal data is needed, but identification of individuals is not. While data protection laws and regulations attempt to protect sensitive data and similar variables, AI algorithms need to include such data in the analysis to ensure accurate and fair results. For example, when predicting the likelihood of death in pneumonia patients, researchers at Microsoft discovered that a history of asthma resulted in a lower risk of death, likely because these individuals are likely to seek earlier treatment.[97] Thus, the application of personal data is going to vary depending on the AI technology that is being used, its purpose and by whom. Furthermore, and what is not so apparent is the concept of consent. Again, its definition and application vary greatly from country to country. How does an entity that constructs AI technology allow the consumer to consent to the gathering and use of personal data, when the laws are so different? This may be overcome by AI technology itself, and be provided part of the instructions when a consumer purchases the item and proceeds to use it. It may be an automatic consent. However, is the current technology adequate for children, the disabled and elderly? It could automatically result in discrimination on age, race, ethnicity, and disability grounds. In part, through facial recognition technology, this can already be achieved. Thus, a level of regulatory response is required that, needs to see government and regulators play a more active role. In our view they need to

[93] Ibid.

[94] Ibid.

[95] Ibid.

[96] Ibid.

[97] Ibid.

set a minimum standard that ensure the protection of those principles which have been espoused by the US (Public Trust; Public Participation; Scientific Integrity and Information Quality; Risk Assessment and Management; Benefits and Costs; Flexibility; Fairness and Non-Discrimination; Disclosure and Transparency; Safety and Security; and Interagency Coordination).

While it is understood that these may not be accepted or agreed upon by the international community, they go a long way to providing a starting point for the development of minimum standards. Additionally, they underpin any future international or national regulatory response, in the same way as the OECD Principles.

However, the current OECD Principles according to Cate and Dockery are far from adequate in addressing the dichotomy and challenges faced by data protection in AI systems. In their view, they are of the view that, Collection Limitation, Purpose Specification, and Use Limitation, Data Minimization, Transparency, Data Quality, Access, Correction, Retention Limitation will increasingly be challenged. Cate and Dockery argue, The challenge, of course, is how to comply with these requirements in the context of AI when data is being used for unforeseen and often unpredictable purposes, by advanced algorithms that are not always understood by their programmers and will increasingly be created only by computers.[98]

In referring to Georgetown Professor Paul Ohm, who makes the point that, when a program "thrives on surprising correlations and produces inferences and predictions that defy human understanding.... [h]ow can you provide notice about the unpredictable and unexplainable?"[99] More importantly, the volume and variety of data typically involved in the development and deployment of AI is going to be enormous. AI technology can use vast amounts of diverse data to improve itself and its interaction with humans.[100] Thus, how do these principles stack up within the current frameworks being implemented to protect personal data.?

In their view, because of the heavy burdens placed on individuals and entities to conform with data protection, would, in the world of AI increase the transactional costs of compliance. In other words, the transactional burden imposed by many modern data protection regulations (for example, returning to the individual to obtain new consent for an originally unanticipated use) may slow or block beneficial uses of AI.[101] Governments, regulators, practitioners and scholars in trying to catch up are continuing pushing the notion of transparency and trust in the legal framework along with the technology. Transparency creates certainty and trust in the products and the law. Doing so provides consumers with a level of comfort that the use of AI would have adequate protections built in to the systems to manage personal data. However, another concern raised by Cate and Dockery is the difficulty is addressing and meeting the principle of transparency. This is, because decisions made by AI applications have complex algorithms that cannot be fully

[98] Ibid.

[99] Ibid.

[100] Ibid.

[101] Ibid.

understood or explained. Therefore, they believe these applications can be in tension with the transparency principle of data protection.[102] For retention limitations, the underlying tension is that setting short retention periods and deleting data after its original purpose has been fulfilled would deny individuals, organizations, and society of the potential benefits of using that data for AI training and deployment. Furthermore, data localization laws have been increasingly used by states to protect and control their citizens' personal data, would challenge AI. That is, AI systems that are connected will transcend national boundaries, and that data could be stored in a third country by default.

Cate and Dockery further highlight how Data Quality, Access, and Correction challenge AI and transparency and suggest, another concern with AI is data quality and the need for individuals to be able to identify and correct their data. AI technology, can be hindered by inaccurate, incomplete, or non-representative data sets that, result in making decisions in a non-transparent (within a "black box" environment), compromising its accuracy. Therefore, ultimately fairness become a substantial concern.[103] In noting what Singapore has concluded, their Singapore's Personal Data Protection Commission recently explained in a discussion paper on AI, data accountability and accuracy are impacted by the completeness of the data required, how recently the data was collected and updated, whether the data is structured in a machine-understandable form, and the source of the data.[104] They argue that the volume and variety of data used in developing and operating most AI applications make compliance with the data quality, access, and correction principles more difficult.

This alone is quite a challenge to overcome. The response will need to be multi-layered. It cannot be left to government to implement legislation to address these issues. It will take, in our view, legislation to set the minimum standards and provide for the development of codes of practices and other mechanisms so as individuals and entities alike can manage the risk of the misuse of personal data by these systems. As highlighted above, Cate and Dockery believe their five area of reform will go some way to addressing the tension between AI and data protection. Apart from shifting from individual consent to data stewardship, enhance current risk management framework to a systemic approach, a greater focus on data users and their impacts, develop a comprehensive framework of harm, and building greater transparency and redress into the current framework, needs to occur where other areas that can assist. The consent model has been criticized because of its binary character: a "user" finding herself in a controlled online environment, being offered a restricted, mostly binary choice of options and expecting gains from a rewarding

[102] Ibid.

[103] Ibid.

[104] Ibid, Singapore Personal Data Protection Commission, "Discussion Paper on Artificial Intelligence (AI) and Personal Data—Fostering Responsible Development and Adoption of AI," (5 June 2018), at 9, available at https://www.pdpc.gov.sg/-/media/Files/PDPC/PDF-Files/Resource-for-Organisation/AI/Discussion-Paper-on-AIand-PD%2D%2D-050618.pdf

online activity is keen and encouraged to provide consent.[105] Lilian Mitrou asserts that new approaches to consent have been proposed to overcome the shortcomings of this binary model: the Information Commissioner has proposed "a process of graduated consent, in which people can give consent or not to different uses of their data throughout their relationship with a service provider, rather than having a simple binary choice at the start", which could or should be related to "just in time notifications". Mayer-Schönberger and Padova propose shifting from collection-based mechanism to use-based mechanism. However, it remains questionable if the so called "notice and consent" model is suitable or practical in a "big data-AI context".[106]

Applying a stewardship model to the concept of consent may go someway to overcoming the above mentioned tensions. This approach is nothing new and has been successfully used in regulating risk and harm to consumers in other sectors. Trakman, Walters and Zeller[107] highlight that the use of agricultural and veterinary chemicals is a good example.

The internationally agreed framework for the management of agricultural and veterinary (agvet) chemicals has many similarities to data protection law.[108] Both frameworks have elements drawn from cognitive and self-management models. Agvet chemicals are regulated under a comprehensive risk management framework that involves government, the industry regulator and chemical manufacturers and producers.[109] That regulatory framework requires both industry regulators and chemical manufacturer to undertake a risk analysis/assessment (economic, human health and environmental). The purpose is to enable chemical products to be made available on the open market to users who are properly informed about the attributes and risks involved in using those chemicals.[110] As part of that regulatory framework, government requires the manufacture of chemical products to provide adequate regulatory information to the end user. That information includes a product label (which is a legal document) that outlines the risks in using the chemical products.[111] The label is intended to provide users with adequate information to protect themselves, livestock and the environment. Thereafter, it is the choice of the user to

[105] Mitrou, L, *Data Protection, Artificial Intelligence and Cognitive Services is The General Data Protection Regulation (GDPR) Artificial Intelligence-Proof.*? University of the Aegean 2018.

[106] Ibid.

[107] Trakman, L., Walters, R., Zeller, B, (2020) *Digital Consent and Data Protection Law – Europe and Asia –Pacific Experience- forthcoming.* Information and Communications Technology Law, 218–209.

[108] Ibid, Risk Management and Food Safety, Report of a Joint FAO/WHO Consultation Rome, Italy, 27 to 31 January (1997). Working Principles for Risk Analysis, Risk Analysis Principles Applied by the Codex Committee on Food Additives and Contaminants, CCFAC Policy for Exposure Assessment of Contaminants and Toxins in Foods or Food Groups.

[109] Ibid, Australian Government, Australian Pesticide and Veterinary Medicines Authority, Risk Management, https://apvma.gov.au/node/987

[110] Ibid.

[111] Ibid, this is in the form of a chemical product label.

decide whether or not to follow the product label. They note that the same principles apply when a consumer purchases pharmaceutical products.[112] These products have instructions of use, it is the individual consuming the product that, either chooses to follow these instructions or not. In both of these sectors users of the products are informed by the seller of the product to follow the label directions and how the product is to be used. The problem with online Internet access and consent, is that people largely are in a hurry to access the information and not give due consideration to what they are consenting too. They go onto say that given these regulatory aims relating to contamination through the use of chemical products, we believe that a similar regulatory approach could be adapted to the collection and use of personal data. Specifically, regulation is needed to ensure that manufacturers and providers of technology and apps that collect personal data provide adequate information to data subjects to enable the latter to make informed decisions about the use of their data.[113]

The authors go onto say that the attendant purpose is for manufactures and developers of data systems and apps to enable digital consumers to make informed decisions about impending risks in the use of their personal data – before those consumers provide consent to that use.[114] Once this information is provided to data subjects, they could then decide whether to evaluate prospective infringements of their data privacy before consenting to that usage. It is our view that this approach will provide data subjects with sufficient information to make informed decisions about the use of their data.[115] More broadly, they will gain a better understanding of the potential economic and social risks from the use of that data. It will also establish a balance between the self-management of personal data and the cognition required for digital subjects to operate effectively within a regulated, but not over-regulated, legal framework.[116]

Even though, the regulation of personal data is different from regulating agvet chemicals in that the misuse of agvet chemical can be easily measured through scientific analysis of the contamination to humans, livestock and the environment. Personal data is not subject to such tangible scientific measurement in determining its impact on data subjects. However, it is important not to overstate the difference between scientifically measuring the impact of chemical risks and not being able to do so in relation to personal data. Trakman et al. highlight that there are emerging sources of law that measure harm from the misuse of personal data to the data subject.[117] Pertinent, too, chemical product labels generally provide warning statements – for instance – keep out of reach of children. Translate this into regulating

[112] Note, Dr. Robert Walters was employed for a decade in agriculture and veterinary chemicals regulation and risk management within a government agency, in Australia.

[113] Ibid.

[114] Ibid.

[115] Ibid.

[116] Ibid.

[117] Ibid, see also Trakman, L., Walters, R., Zeller, B, (2019) *Tort and Breach of Data Protection Law – are there any lessons to be learnt?* European Data Protection Law Review, 500–519.

the Internet, by providing additional information about the data systems that impact minors, can strengthen the protection of minors before they consent to access and use of their data and on a continuing basis. The misuse of personal data is capable of a quantitative measurable, such as through market assessments of personal data use and abuse, and in measuring the effectiveness of remedial action through sample studies.[118] Regulators can require that data collectors use comparable algorithms to those used to filter personal data, in order to assess whether data users have provided data subjects with adequate data to provide an informed consent.

It is however acknowledged that technology may evolve to address the concerns in relation to consent in AI and particularly children. It could also be addressed through consumer protection law, whereby, upon purchase of the smart home appliance, personal robot or toy, the parents automatically consent to a level of use of personal data, of their children. This, is also problematic unless there is adequate information available to the consumer to make that choice. However, this will not overcome the cybersecurity concerns, from the illegal gathering and use of personal data by these devices. It will be even more problematic where some states have identified specific personal data as sensitive, thus, raising the level of consent required for its collection and use. Another problem area that has not been fully explored that will warrant further study, is the storage and retention of personal data gathered by AI. Again, while technology could be developed to manage this, the legal frameworks, to date fall far short of setting adequate minimum standard for the storage of this data. In other words, the question arises what is an adequate time for a toy, robot or other AI system to store the personal data of anybody (parent, adult or child)? Is 1 day, 1 week, 1 month, 1 year or even 1 decade sufficient? This needs to be addressed. Governments and regulators should minimise the extent to which personal data can be stored by these devices, it would be for a set period, and then once that period expires, the technology should automatically reset itself? Nonetheless, this needs to be answered and a minimum standard established within the law.

What they have not highlighted is how to deal with accountability more broadly. In other words, currently under most data protection laws organisations are required to establish a controller or processor. The title can vary from country to country, but nonetheless, they are responsible of collecting, storing and using the data. In AI systems positions or people of responsibility are so much harder to appoint and detect. Thus, take for example a smart home appliance, once in use is it the owner that has responsibility for the data it collects? This would be difficult to achieve, when it is organizations and individuals accessing the technology or the entity that developed the appliance that can access the data. It is not clear as to how this can be overcome?

In our view, more than in any other time in history the challenge will be for governments and regulatory to develop laws that are more adaptable. This will require innovation and possibly a rethink of the current way primary and subordinate

[118] Ibid.

legislation is developed. It will require a faster response from regulators and governments to establish laws that overcome the challenges faced by AI and data protection. It will also require greater alignment of these laws with cyber security law to ensure personal data retains a high level of protection, and enables consumers to control their data. Under the current risk-based model, which can be seen in many other industries from food and agriculture production to environmental protection, the use and application of risk assessment will become even more critical. However, any risk assessment should not be imposed on the end consumer, it needs to lie with the manufacturer. This raises another issue of, how can the risk assessments be undertaken to secure data in home appliances? It would require individuals to provide access to the manufacturer at some point. What point this is needs to be substantiated by a standard with the law. The further problem is the speed with which this technology can become outdated resulting in intrusions being carried out with ease. Lilian Mitrou further points out how AI may affect privacy in various aspects: with regard to informational privacy, including surveillance privacy, interests but also to autonomy of a person. She takes that position that informational privacy responds to the requirement that everyone should be in control of the information concerning her so as to formulate conceptions of self, values, preferences, goals and to protect her life choices from public control, social disgrace or objectification. Intimidation effects which could have a negative impact on the exercise of fundamental rights.[119] Even the current technology that is available does not appear to be sophisticated enough to ensure the security of personal data in AI, let alone addressing privacy. Moreover, Egress notes that while there have been significant inroads to developing this technology, it still has its challenges and risks. They are of the view that:

> AI can make testing and vulnerability-scanning stronger using algorithms to close the gap between thinking something that is in production is unsafe and knowing it's unsafe. AI can play a very important role in the prevention of data breaches in the near future. As cyber attacks increase in variety and volume, security vendors will need to meet fire with fire. Artificial intelligence can act as a powerful tool in helping make businesses more secure and stopping malware before it executes. The main challenge in using machine learning to prevent data breaches is about perception and understanding hype from reality. Businesses should be aware that deployed an AI-based or machine learning-based solution will not 100% mitigate the cyber security threat, but rather help reduce the impact of an attack by identifying a breach sooner than an unaided security team. AI, for example, can make data connections more efficient. They can use machine learning techniques to audit every connection and pinpoint when data travelling is deviating from its predetermined path we can now leverage predictive analytics to understand the patterns of past behaviours of data and use them to prevent repeat data breaches. However, the main problem is understanding the complex configurations because there is no inter- and intra-company set of metrics. With AI monitoring and analysing all of this data, you can see how you stack up against industry threats. This allows you to mark your security solution, because no one can prevent attacks 100% of the time, how can you hold security officers accountable in a fair way? AI could have great promise for intrusion detection and endpoint security software, but there are

[119] Mitrou, L, (2018) *Data Protection, Artificial Intelligence and Cognitive Services is The General Data Protection Regulation (GDPR) Artificial Intelligence-Proof.*? University of the Aegean.

> some huge challenges – the fact that most machine learning architectures require customers to hand huge amounts of sensitive data to a vendor in order to train classifiers; the difficulty of telling which products provide really accurate recognition of malware or exfiltration; and the lack of standardized datasets and benchmarks for comparing products. If anyone figures out how to solve all these problems together, it could be a huge advance for computer security.[120]

What can be demonstrated is that there will be no silver bullet that address these issues. Even the experts in the field from a technical perspective view the role of technology in AI as having varying levels of success in protecting personal data. It is a formidable challenge for both the public and private sector to resolve in the short term. This is on the backdrop that there is little appetite for countries to fully harmonise their respective data protection or cyber security laws. On the other hand, the legal framework for AI is only starting to emerge, with little to no enactment of laws by governments.

Aaron McIntosh makes the point that today more than ever we are in a period where the dangers of cybersecurity are increasingly becoming more complicated.[121] McIntosh argues that, as a result of rise of the AI, each individual will generate 1.7 megabytes of data per second. As new applied sciences evolve, cyber criminals adapt and uncover new hacking strategies to apprehend delicate knowledge. AI has the potential to revolutionise society, however what occurs when these new applied sciences are weaponized by cyber criminals?[122] He notes that cellular units, fee playing cards and fee data are all being made accessible to platforms (corresponding to Google) and automatic units (like Amazon's Alexa) that can be utilized to purchase your groceries within the age of sensible houses.[123] The attraction of getting this data saved on these platforms and units is the comfort it brings to on a regular basis life; nevertheless, the fact is that lots of people do probably not know what is occurring to their knowledge. How can we actually think about these units? For producers, the principle focus with these units is buyer expertise and value, and in consequence, it is not clear how a lot expertise is being centred on securing these units to guard the folks which are utilizing them and their knowledge.[124] In relation to healthcare, McIntosh is of the view the dangers lie at the person stage. Central this stage is how there are a number of units embedded-type units that may be present in or on the human physique, corresponding to pace-makers or transfusion units.[125] Regardless, of the clever healthcare expertise that these units present, they are liable to malware on account of the low-level cybersecurity that is put in on

[120] The Future of AI in Data Protection, *What do the experts say?: Experts Predict the Future of Artificial Intelligence in Data Protection*, EGRESS 2018, https://www.egress.com/artificial-intelligence-for-data-protection

[121] McIntosh, A, *The dangers of IoT and AI: The risks of cybersecurity are more complex than ever*, https://www.techradar.com/sg/author/aaron-mcintosh

[122] Ibid.

[123] Ibid.

[124] Ibid.

[125] Ibid.

them. For McIntosh, the information that is save, and weak, being vulnerable to incursions. It allows a 3rd party to get together and data being extracted from the units. To address this problem, he believes units must have a stage of belief constructed into them so that people can stop any unauthorized entry. Not doing so, may lead to the place a hacker may entry a pacemaker and deactivate it or intentionally trigger it to malfunction. Thus, McIntosh believes that where a single gadget does not present ample safety to stop cyber-attacks, all the community of that gadget is instantly uncovered. Even at this extreme end, it is not outside the realm of possibility and must be considered as part of the legal framework.

To reinforce the substantial point raised in this book, it is our view that the current data protection laws need to be reviewed in light of AI devices, which will be purchased by consumers and used in the home and office. This, position is on the backdrop of the excellent work undertaken by Singapore, who have proposed to address the potential cyber risks through the implementation of a Cybersecurity Labelling Scheme (CLS). At the time of writing this book, the CLS was in its infancy and there was not a lot of detailed information available as to the extent of protections that will be provided from cyber intrusions through AI devices. Nonetheless, the CLS scheme will comprise different levels of cybersecurity ratings to help consumers make informed choices about the security features of the smart devices they purchase. To begin with, the Cyber Security Agency will introduce the CLS to two product types – Wi-Fi routers and smart home hubs.[126] They propose that the cybersecurity labels will provide an indication of the security provisions in the registered products, based on a series of assessments and tests to meet a basic security requirements such as ensuring unique default passwords; adherence to the principles of Security-by-Design; absence of common software vulnerabilities, and resistance to basic penetration testing.[127] It aims to incentivise manufacturers and product vendors to develop products with recognised and improved security features. If realised and becomes the industry standard there will be many benefits and the CLS will provide another level of trust is securing personal data over, and through, AI devices. Currently, consumer smart devices are often designed to optimise functionality and cost. These products are also characterised by a short time-to-market cycle, where there is less scope for cybersecurity design to be incorporated at the beginning.[128] While in its infancy and more details are to be provided, what is not clear is how the CLS would protect personal data, particularly children's and vulnerable groups data. It will however, go some way to providing a level of trust in the market, whereby consumers will have confidence that there will be an element of security. It will also place the responsibility on the developers of these AI devices to ensure that these products are secure before they reach the market. There are many questions that will arise from the CLS scheme, and it will be important that

[126] Cybersecurity Labelling Scheme, the Cyber Security agency of Singapore, https://www.csa.gov.sg

[127] Ibid.

[128] Ibid.

this or any similar scheme addresses the personal data question. That is, to what extent will personal data be protected through AI devices used in the home or office? How would such as scheme keep up with and maintain a level of security when these devices are upgraded with more sophisticated AI technology? How do governments, corporations, small and medium sized businesses protect themselves and their employees when adopting this technology? Therefore, a further and more comprehensive study is needed to ensure the current data protection laws, along with cyber security and AI law establishing a standard that will ensure and force developers to provide a high level of protection.

Based on the above, the principles of data protection law have been limited to data localization, storage limitation, right to be forgotten, extraterritorial reach, data portability. In addition, we begin to see the interconnectedness between data and cyber security along with AI. This is achieved by the platforms, systems and technology that underpin and support the adoption, implementation and operation of most, if not all data protection collection points, use and storage now and into the future. In addition, the principles and concepts highlighted below highlight how they have found their way into national and supranational legal frameworks. While this book has not compared whether the current data protection laws require industry or public sector organisations to establish codes of practice, this, in our view is another area of research that needs to be undertaken. In other words, some states do require for codes of practice to be established by the law. These codes are then enforceable. This is another area of the law that could go some way to strengthening the links between personal data, AI and cyber security. Codes could be, and are, viewed as an extension to legislation, and it could be mandatory that a code is to clarify concepts and principles of data protection such as the definition of personal data and the concept of consent as they relate to AI.

Table highlights five selected models that have been discussed in this book and the previous book

Jurisdiction	Direction-Focus	Legislative instrument
European Union	Delivers on human Rights and single market policy objectives.	General Data Protection Regulation 2018
Singapore	Business friendly- assists in delivering Singapore's smart nation policy.	Personal Data Protection Act 2012
United States (Federal)	Consumer protection – Sectorial approach. This does not consider state laws.	Federal Trade 1914 Privacy Act 1974
China	Own characteristics, moving closer to the EU. Focus on the state having control over the systems, networks, platforms and infrastructure that support the collection and use of data.	Cybersecurity laws 2018–9
Australia (Federal)	Combination of the above - excluding China.	Privacy Act 1988

The above table highlights the different models that have emerged that are distinctly different in their approach to regulating the protection of personal data. Arguably the regulatory landscape today has been developed within a framework whereby jurisdictions have opted to protect their own sovereign needs. In our view, the table above demonstrates this sovereign approach. Countries like China is a stand out, not for the wrong reasons, but for the way in which they have taken a very different approach to that of other jurisdictions. China, largely have adopted a state based approach, which serves to identify and look at the infrastructure, systems and platforms that underpin the collection and use of personal data. This is the strongest regulatory approach that closely aligns with cybersecurity. Yet, when coupled with the release of the TC260 national standard for the personal Information Security Specification, increasingly they are many similarities between China's and the EU legal frameworks. The cybersecurity laws of China have largely set the minimum whereby they also hold individuals such as network operators to high account, in the same way as controllers and operators in other states and the EU. The TC260 Specification largely underpins the minimum standards and reinforced those broader principles for the collection and use of personal data. To date, the US has largely adopted a sectorial approach whereby they have separated out their laws for health and consumer protections. While Canada is not featured in this table, they have largely adopted a national approach, with different laws for the Quebec region. However, it is out of scope of this book to compare those laws. The EU, which it is well understood have adopted a framework that underpins and supports their Single Market policy objective, while ensure that privacy over the Internet is a fundamental right to be protected. It is our view that the EU approach signifies the strongest level of protection and control afforded to data subjects. Thus, what we see from these models is the ability for data subjects to opt-in or opt-out. For instance, the EU South Korea, Canada and others largely provide for data subjects to opt in. Whereas, the US model focuses on the ability for data subjects to opt-out. This is particularly the case whereby, the respective laws provide for consent, because it enables the data subject to agree to their data being used or otherwise. The variables, as highlighted above is the fact that consent differs greatly from state to state and it can come in the form of express, actual or implied consent.

Nonetheless, as these and other models around the world continue to develop and evolve, the consumer model could evolve as providing the strongest set of controls. Some see state intervention as being more applicable than others. While Singapore have adopted, what we conceive as a framework to promote their economic needs ahead of their social needs. On the other hand, Australia has largely adopted elements of these models and it is argued that over time Australia is appearing to adopt a more consumer lead model. The models will require vigilance as the landscape and priorities change for states to respond to AI and cyber security incursions and threats. This, along with the way other states have adopted these laws, in part, is due to how they approach the right to privacy and human rights more generally. Despite the differences there are a lot of similarities emerging and legal convergence is occurring. The question arises what model will best suit the way forward?

Despite the above, there and various regulatory models that exist that include but not limited to government regulation, co-regulation between government and industry, sectorial regulation whereby industry sectors have dedicated and specific laws, to self-regulation. Arguably, in the contemporary world it cannot be left for government to regulate every aspect of data protection, that includes its collection and use, the networks and systems used to capture this data and the entities that trade in the data. Food and agriculture production[129] for many years have had to deal with a multilayered response to regulate these activities from the farm to processing, manufacture, supply chain, delivery and consumption. They have had to resolve multiple issues such as human and animal health, market access, environmental standards, and the use of chemicals. The world community has been largely successful in minimizing the risk, establishing agreed norms and standards to ensure consumers, the environment and animals have a strong level of protection. To achieve this government could not have taken sole responsibility for regulating the entire production cycle of food from the farm to the plate. It has been successful through government setting the minimum standards for industry to achieve, then left it largely to industry to resolve practical (what is otherwise termed as on the ground) risks through self-regulation. Therefore, in our view, data protection, AI and cyber security have many similarities.

No single model, to date, is more superior than the other. It will take a concerted effort for government to reconcile the differences between the areas as they continue to evolve and come even more aligned in practical terms. The other area lacking is international law. While there has been a concerted effort to establish principles and concepts, at least in the area of data protection at the international level, to date this is lacking in the area of AI and cyber security. The international law across the three areas is far from being established. In 2018 the United Nations General Assembly voted to establish two separate groups to study international law and norms in relation to cyberspace.[130] Resolution 73/27 proposed by a number of countries, including Russia—created an open-ended working group on the subject. Another group of countries—including Australia, France, Germany, the United Kingdom and the United States—supported a resolution advocating continuing the debate within the framework of a group of governmental experts (GGE) reporting to the secretary-general.[131] However, it is far from settled by member countries of

[129] Note the author Dr. Robert Walters has more than a decade experience in regulation and risk management of government and industry regulation in Australia in the areas of agriculture, food production, human health and environmental management.

[130] Acchten, N, *New U.N. Debate on Cybersecurity in the Context of International Security*, Cyber & Technology September 30, 2019, https://www.lawfareblog.com/new-un-debate-cybersecurity-context-international-security

[131] Ibid. Both U.N. dialogues are based on the substantive U.N. GGE reports from 2009 TO 2015. Most importantly, the 2012/2013 report confirmed that international law—in particular the U.N. Charter—is applicable to the ICT environment. The applicability of international law to the ICT environment was also confirmed by a number of delegations in oral statements during the substantive meeting of the OEWG last week (for example, by China, Czech Republic, Egypt, Japan, Mexico, Russia, Singapore and Switzerland). And some states confirmed the general applicability of international law to the ICT environment in their working papers submitted to the chair of the OEWG (Australia, Canada, China, Iran, UK. The 2014/2015 the OEWG, the majority of state representatives confirmed that the 2014/2015 report should be the starting point for further discussions of cyber norms. Overall, state representatives agreed that the applicability of existing

the UN as to what any future international law in this area would look like. Some believes that there is a need for such law, while others are, at this stage not fully supportive of the idea. One of the most influential conventions that exists in relation to cybersecurity is the Budapest Cybercrime Convention (Council of Europe).[132] The Convention is the first international treaty on crimes committed via the Internet and other computer networks, dealing particularly with infringements of copyright, computer-related fraud, child pornography and violations of network security. It also contains a series of powers and procedures such as the search of computer networks and interception. Its main objective, set out in the preamble, is to pursue a common criminal policy aimed at the protection of society against cybercrime, especially by adopting appropriate legislation and fostering international co-operation.[133] The importance of this convention cannot be underestimated. It is yet again another reminder of the influence the EU legal framework is having in regards to the Internet. In other words, as of 1 January 2020, there were a total of 64 states that had ratified the convention. Notably, Australia, the United States (have acceded with reservations) and the UK (while still a member state of the Union). Neither Singapore nor China are signatories or have ratified the convention. Of the ASEAN countries only, the Philippines has ratified the convention. Canada has signed the convention however they do have reservations. It is arguably one of the first international steps to gain convergence and harmonization. There is however a lot of work to do in the international sphere to reconcile these challenges. The problem they face is similar to that of the national level whereby, technology advancements are outpacing policy and legislative development.

Notwithstanding the above, how can these challenges and risks be overcome through regulation. It is our view that to address the challenges and risks to governments and society, at large, the approach must be multifaceted. It requires international law, legal norms, concepts and principles to converge and account for data protection, cyber security and AI. At the 2019 Japanese G20 meeting leaders declared states needed to recognize the sovereignty of each state's laws in these area (see Chap. 1), yet, there is a need for the G20, United Nations, EU and other international and regional organizations to better coordinate an agreed response and not look at these issues in silos. There needs to be a whole of technology and legal-policy approach. Only then will the community fully understand what the threats and risk are, and how to address them through the law. Furthermore, a multilayered approach to co and self-regulatory models need to be promoted by governments, and ensure their enforceability through legislation or codes of practice. This will force greater accountability and promote trust in the legal framework and Internet sector. This position has been reinforced by Ugo Pagallo, Pompeu Casanovas and

international law to cyberspace and the implementation of the cyber norms agreed upon in 2015 are essential to sustaining international peace and security in cyberspace.

[132] Budapest Cybercrime Convention, ETS No.185. https://www.coe.int/en/web/conventions/full-list/-/conventions/treaty/185/signatures?p_auth=CrOlxEo9

[133] Ibid.

Robert Madelin[134] who argue that a combination of a comprehensive, sectorial and self-regulatory model will be needed to address the risks between AI and data protection law. They have called for a hybrid model to be established. The authors also point out that the success or otherwise of this hybrid model will only work if there is the political will of governments to make it happen. In doing so, they have identified the need for a strong co-regulatory model to embrace. Arguably, this model of regulation represents, what has been stated earlier, as having similarities to the food and agriculture production. However, more work is needed at the international level for this to work. Only when there is international agreement will there be an agreed framework that can then drive reform at the national level. This is a long way off, and, it begs the question, whether it can be achieved, given the current divergent views of states. Yet, if there is a silver lining, at least in the area of data protection, there is a level of convergence and harmonization, even though the EU are having the most significant influence.

Finally, this book has not been able to reconcile the major challenge facing government, regulators and the community as to how to find the balance between the digital economy, and developing a strong robust legal framework for cyber security, AI and data protection that would be accepted universally by all nation states. AI has been pervasive in military, but, it is a long way off for this technology to be fully used in the home and office. When it comes into our mainstream lives, it will capture large amounts of personal data. More problematic is balancing the economic benefits of the new digital economy with that of protecting personal data. It is our view that as a minimum, more work is needed to protect the most vulnerable in the community (children, elderly and those with a disability). However, it is acknowledged that our personal data may be lost, unless a combination of both technology and regulation is reformed to address these issues. It is also acknowledged that as nation states continue to develop the law to suit their own sovereign needs, any level of harmonization is a long way off, even though many of the data protection laws that exist today have converged at a high level.

15.9 Conclusion

This book has demonstrated the interrelationship between AI, cybersecurity and data protection is real and growing. By drawing on the data protection laws discussed in each of the country chapters has identified many potential problems that will need to be reconciled as AI technology increasingly is made available on the market. It is asserted, and can be demonstrated throughout this book that, these three areas need to converge a lot more. There is a lot of work for the international community to reconcile the gaps in the law and address the technological, policy and legal risks to government, individuals and the broader community, along with

[134] Pagallo, U., Casanova, P., Madelin, R, (2019) *The middle-out approach: assessing models of legal governance in data protection, artificial intelligence, and the Web of Data,* The Theory and Practice of Legislation, 7:1, 1–25.

business. As the world community becomes even more integrated through technology, it is likely that there will be even more calls for legal harmonisation and convergence.

To date, most states have opted to take the sovereign approach to regulating these areas, however, it is time to re-think that model and for the international community to come together to resolve an international issue. The exception to this, will be where states consider that their framework is far more superior to any other country, and use AI, cyber security and personal data to control individuals, whereby privacy over the Internet becomes obsolete.

The book proposes that states, within the confines of their sovereign needs reconsider specific areas of the law to ensure there is a continued balance between economic activity, innovation, but also the protection of personal data through AI devices. It proposes more work needs to be undertaken to reconcile the gaps and fragmentation in the laws to protect children the vulnerable groups who will be exposed to AI technology. More importantly, the book calls for reconsideration of the definition of personal data-information in their data protection legal frameworks, and the application of consent. It also asserts that the current sectorial approach and in some cases the distinction between the public and private sectors has been warranted in the area of data protection, although it is time to rethink this model. This is because, AI, like the internet will not be confined to a particular sector and AI devices that are used in the home will find their way into the public and private sector (offices). Finally, the book encourages states to collaborate more in this area of the law, because it will be difficult for technology developers to bring their devices to market where the laws lack consistency in their application.

To embrace the internationalisation of data protection, cyber security and the emerging area of AI law, has to be considered. It is our view that international organizations such as UNCITRAL, UNIDROIT, OECD and others have a responsibility in promoting and obtaining a higher level of transnational harmonization. More needs to be done to coordinate these international organisations to ensure there is a coherent and consistent response. There is no better time now to begin with AI, to develop high level principles similar to those of the OECD in relation to data protection. Doing so will reinforce the rules-based system and rule of law. The rule of law is the epitome of anthropocentrism: humans are the primary subject and object of norms that are created, interpreted, and enforced by humans.[135] In the case of automated processing, decision-making by machine is tolerated provided that the legitimacy of such decisions can be ensured through the protection of rights and interests, in certain cases explicitly including the right to bring your concerns before another human being.[136]

Moreover, though legal constructs such as corporations may have rights and obligations, these are in turn traceable back to human agency in their acts of creation,

---

[135] Simon Chesterman, *Artificial Intelligence and the Problem of Autonomy*, Notre Dame Journal on Emerging Technologies (2019), 211–248.

[136] Ibid.

even as their daily conduct is overseen to varying degrees by human agents. True autonomy of AI systems challenges that paradigm. As we have seen, however, the challenge occurs in different ways. The emergence of autonomous vehicles is exposing gaps in the liability and criminal law regimes governing the roads, but these are ultimately practical problems to be addressed by amending those rules.[137] Therefore, when comparing this proposition to AI in smart home devices along with other personalized used AI appliances, further and additional work is required to better understand its impact to personal data.

In response to the ensuing regulatory gaps and divergent approach, the EU appear, at this stage, to be maintaining their consistent approach towards placing Convention 108 and the rights-based approach as the forefront. The EU, consistently argue that data protection and AI are by necessity correlated. Therefore, a similar convention could be prepared for AI. This would set the benchmark for global AI regulation. Leaving aside science fiction scenarios, the rapid evolution of AI applications over recent years has its roots in the progressive process of datafication, with the result that personal data has become both the source and the target of AI applications. Against this background, different approaches are emerging in AI development, use and regulation.

In reality, AI is largely unregulated and often not grounded on fundamental rights, relying instead mainly on data processing. Regarding data processing, the global framework offers a range of ways to safeguard fundamental rights and, in particular, the right to the protection of personal data. Nevertheless, a way forward is the need for greater legal convergence and hamonisation of national laws. There needs to be consideration of what international law can be developed to ensure a coherent approach, because, AI and the security issues surrounding personal data is not confined to a single state. The legal and regulatory issues are transnational.

References

Chesterman, S. (2019). Artificial intelligence and the problem of autonomy. *Notre Dame Journal on Emerging Technologies 83*, 211–248.

Mitrou, L. (2018). *Data protection, artificial intelligence and cognitive services is the General Data Protection Regulation (GDPR) artificial intelligence-proof?* Mytilene: University of the Aegean.

Pagallo, U., Casanova, P., & Madelin, R. (2019). The middle-out approach: Assessing models of legal governance in data protection, artificial intelligence, and the web of data. *The Theory and Practice of Legislation, 7*(1), 1–25.

Trakman, L., Walters, R., & Zeller, B. (2019). Tort and breach of data protection law – Are there any lessons to be learnt? *European data Protection Law Review, 5*, 500–519.

Trakman, L., Walters, R., & Zeller, B. (2020). Digital consent and data protection law – Europe and Asia –Pacific experience- forthcoming. *Information and Communications Technology Law 55*, 218–209.

[137] Ibid.

Index

R. Walters, M. Novak, *Cyber Security, Artificial Intelligence, Data Protection & the Law*, https://doi.org/10.1007/978-981-16-1665-5